ISBN 978-1-331-46438-9
PIBN 10193744

1 MONTH OF
FREE
READING

at

www.ForgottenBooks.com

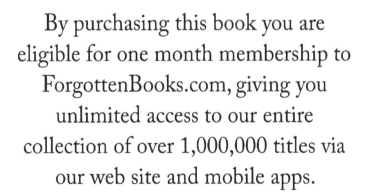

By purchasing this book you are eligible for one month membership to ForgottenBooks.com, giving you unlimited access to our entire collection of over 1,000,000 titles via our web site and mobile apps.

To claim your free month visit:

www.forgottenbooks.com/free193744

English
Français
Deutsche
Italiano
Español
Português

www.forgottenbooks.com

Mythology Photography **Fiction**
Fishing Christianity **Art** Cooking
Essays Buddhism Freemasonry
Medicine **Biology** Music **Ancient**
Egypt Evolution Carpentry Physics
Dance Geology **Mathematics** Fitness
Shakespeare **Folklore** Yoga Marketing
Confidence Immortality Biographies
Poetry **Psychology** Witchcraft
Electronics Chemistry History **Law**
Accounting **Philosophy** Anthropology
Alchemy Drama Quantum Mechanics
Atheism Sexual Health **Ancient History**
Entrepreneurship Languages Sport
Paleontology Needlework Islam
Metaphysics Investment Archaeology
Parenting Statistics Criminology
Motivational

SEAFIELD
CORRESPONDENCE

FROM 1685 TO 1708

Edited, with Introduction and Annotations, by

JAMES GRANT, LL.B.

COUNTY CLERK OF BANFFSHIRE

EDINBURGH

Printed at the University Press by T. and A. CONSTABLE

for the Scottish History Society

1912

INTRODUCTION

THE Chancellor Earl of Seafield, James Ogilvie, second son of James, third Earl of Findlater, and of Lady Anna Montgomery, eldest daughter of Hugh, seventh Earl of Eglintoun, was born on 11th July 1663. Apart from his own undoubted ability, he was able to command that influence which, in the age of autocratic and aristocratic government two centuries ago, was a necessary aid to a successful public career in Scotland. Assistance came from both sides of his house, for the relatives of his father and of his mother were numerous and influential.

The Ogilvies, Earls of Findlater, were descended from Sir Walter Ogilvy of Auchlevyn and of Deskford, a cadet of the Ogilvies of Airlie, who about 1436 acquired the estates of Deskford and Findlater in Banffshire, through his marriage with Margaret, heiress of Sir John Sinclair. Sir Walter's grandson James married Agnes, daughter of George, second Earl of Huntly, head of the powerful house of Gordon. James's son Alexander married, before 21st June 1509, Janet Abernethy, second daughter of James, third Lord Saltoun, and, secondly, Elizabeth, natural daughter of Adam Gordon, Dean of Caithness, founder of the Earldom of Sutherland, and son of Alexander, first Earl of Huntly. Sir Walter Ogilvie, great-grandson of Alexander, married, in 1582, as his second wife, Marie Douglas, third daughter of William, fifth Earl of Morton, and of Agnes, daughter of George, fourth Earl of Rothes. He was created on 4th October 1616 a

Peer of Scotland under the title of Lord Ogilvie of Desk-ford. Their eldest son James was created on 20th February 1638 Earl of Findlater, thus obtaining, though a cadet, precedence over Lord Ogilvie of Airlie. He married as his first wife, Elizabeth Leslie, second daughter of Andrew, fifth Earl of Rothes, and had two daughters. His second wife was Marion, fourth daughter of William, eighth Earl of Glencairn.

Having no male issue he procured a second patent from the crown carrying the honours of his earldom to his distant blood relation, Sir Patrick Ogilvie of Inchmartine, Perthshire, who had married his eldest daughter, Elizabeth, with precedence as if Sir Patrick had been his eldest son. This condition was strongly challenged by the Earls of Airlie ; and by reason of an explanatory letter granted by the King, Airlie succeeded in getting his name enrolled before Findlater's in the rolls of Parliament, an act which gave rise for long to systematic protests on behalf of the Earls of Findlater. The following letter from the Earl of Eglintoun to his daughter, the Countess of Find-later, refers to this question of precedence.

Edr., ii *Dbr.* '65·

HONORED DOGHTER,—Having hard yt the Lord Ogelvie is to give ane neu warrant to the Comissioner from his Matie to pas his fathers patent of presedensie to your Lords prejudis, I have acquentted him yt he may cum hire, and I shall be als cairfull as I can in the tyme I am hire yt your Lord sustine no wrong. Bot ye toune is so prejudiall to my helth, being becum werie bressie, yt I cannot stay long, so wishing to hire of your welbeing and your children, I am, Your most affectionat father and servant,   EGLINTOUN.

The first Earl's second daughter Anne married, *c.* 5th April 1637, William, ninth Earl of Glencairn, Lord High Chancellor of Scotland. Sir Patrick, whose mother was Anne, third daughter of Sir Duncan Campbell of Glenurquhy, ancestor of the Earls of Breadalbane, succeeded as second Earl in 1652. He died between the 2nd and the 31st days of May 1659, his son, the third Earl, on that latter date writing to his grand-uncle, Alexander Ogilvie, laird of Keith, with the tidings of his father's death. James, third earl, had married, probably towards the close of 1658, Anna, daughter of the seventh Earl of Eglintoun, and widow of Robert Seton, younger of Hailes, who died in 1655 leaving a son by her called Robert. On 7th May 1659, Anne, Duchess of Hamilton, writing from Beill to her cousin, the Countess of Findlater, congratulates her on her 'safftie and being with chyld and heartellie wishes' her a 'hapy deleverie.' She sends her '2 rouls of the salve for sore breasts,' and adds, 'what I humblie conceaved usfull to be tacken for your selff or chyld you will fynd in the recepts.'

Two Ogilvies of Findlater had contracted marriages with Marion, daughter of William, sixth Lord Livingston, c. 30th October 1558, and with Agnes, daughter of Robert, third Lord Elphinstone. Daughters of the house of Findlater had, before 1660, married into the families of the Earl of Buchan, the Lord Forbes of Pitsligo, the Lord Gray, the laird of Grant, Urquhart of Cromarty, Dunbar of Westfield, and Munro of Fowlis, etc. The Ogilvies of Findlater were also chiefs of the Ogilvies of Boyne, and of the Ogilvies of Banff, who became, on 31st August 1642, Lords Banff.

If James Ogilvie had powerful relatives and connections on his father's side, he had, if possible, more powerful ones on his mother's side of the house. Anna Montgomerie his mother was the only child of Hugh, Lord Montgomerie, afterwards seventh Earl of Eglintoun, by his first wife, Lady Anna Hamilton, daughter of James, second Marquess of Hamilton. In this way he inherited the strong influence of the powerful house of Hamilton. As Lady Anna Hamilton's contract of marriage was dated 7th and 13th April 1631, and as she died at Struthers in Fife on 16th October 1632, his mother, Lady Anna Montgomerie, must have been born sometime that latter year. Lady Anna Hamilton's two eldest brothers were the first and second Dukes of Hamilton. James, the first duke, fought as a Royalist in the Civil War, and was beheaded in Palace Yard in 1649. Her brother William, the second duke, fought for King Charles at Worcester, and died on 12th September 1651, nine days after that battle. Her sister Margaret married John, seventeenth Earl of Crawford and Lindsay, and had daughters, Anna, who married John, Earl, afterwards Duke of Rothes, Christian, who married John, Earl of Haddington, and Elizabeth, who married David, Earl of Northesk. These three ladies, influentially married, were therefore first cousins of Lady Anna Montgomerie. They frequently corresponded with her, especially Anna Lindsay, wife of the Duke of Rothes, who during the reign of Charles the Second was a powerful Scots politician.

Writing on the 9th of November 1664 from ' Halirud hous ' to the Countess of Findlater, A. Lindsay, as she signs herself, says :—

Sinc ye are pleased to inquyr if my Lord be Chanseler, I shall tell you it hath plased his Magestie to apoint my Lord to keep the seill till such time as on be nominat ; and for sume time hath ordened him his Comitionar, ther being ane Asemblie to sit in sume munthes. Such a weghtie charg his frindes could have wished he had not layne onder ; bot he hath submited to the King's comands. The Lord derect him, for he never stoud in more neid of help from God.

Anne, eldest daughter of the first duke, and cousin of

Lady Anna Montgomerie, succeeded William, the second duke, as Duchess of Hamilton in her own right. On 29th of April 1656 she married William Douglas, Earl of Selkirk, who was at the Restoration created third Duke of Hamilton. The duchess's letters to her cousin, the Countess of Findlater, show that both she and her husband the duke were tinged with the strict religious views of the West of Scotland, and that he, though anxious for place, had little influence in the councils of Charles, and James. At the Revolution he supported William, and his influence then became supreme in the government of Scotland. Her letters also show that she and the duke fully recognised the claims of kinship, and that they were ready to use, and did on occasion use their influence on behalf of James Ogilvie.

Duke William's eldest daughter Anne, who was one of the beauties at the Court of Charles Second, married in 1664 Lord Carnegie, afterwards third Earl of Southesk. The interest attaching to one who figures in Pepys's *Diary* and in Count Grammont's *Memoirs* may excuse the inclusion of the following family letter from the duchess to her cousin at Findlater.

Hamilton, 25 Septr. 1665.

DEAR COUSEN,—The concerne you express for our uncles daughter[1] is verie acceptable to me, as also I take verie kindlie y^r Lords carrage in itt. But allas as to her she is rueined on so menie accounts, that I cannot tell you on which most; for that of y^r brother in law itt is long since itt hes bene talked, but with y^r owne brother she has sufered more in her honner. She is at present at Keperington with her sister Killmars;[2] but what her carrage now is since she went to that place, which is about a month agoe, I know not. Itt is long since she past my power; but the perticulars of this is to teadeous

---

[1] Anne Hamilton, Lady Carnegie.
[2] Elizabeth, wife of Lord Kilmaurs, eldest son of the Earl of Glencairn.

to writt, and besides a verie unplesent subject, so I shall leave itt, and lett you know that my sister was verie wel in France the last time I heard from her. She is with Queen mother, and I blese God in verie much reputation ; and tho we ar all so farr distant on from another, yet I doe not dispare of all our metting heire againe, which that itt may be sone I doubt not but that you will joyne in the wishing with, deare cousen, Your most affect. cousen and servant, HAMILTON.

Duke William's third daughter Mary was three times married : first to the Earl of Callander, then to Sir James Livingston of Westquarter, and third to James, third Earl of Findlater.

The Eglintoun connections were also large and powerful. Lady Anna Montgomerie's grandfather, Alexander Montgomerie, son of Robert Seton, first Earl of Winton, married, on 22nd June 1612, Anna, eldest daughter of Alexander, first Earl of Linlithgow. Her father, Hugh, was a learned nobleman. Both grandfather and father were zealous Royalists and suffered in that cause.

Writing to Ladie Anne Montgomerie from ' Bredicke ' on '11th Apriell 1651,' in answer, the Duchess of Hamilton says :—

DEARE COUSEN,—I have receved both yours, and must tell you that I have a part of your grefe, you shoulde not be senceablie of what has befallen your granfather. I can not wishe but to be so afflected as I finde you are, may ofende the Lord, who even in this dispentation has showed great mercie to you. Your father tho takein yet itt plessed the Lord to delivere out of thare hands, and your granfather is alife ; and if the Lord thinke fett he will allso deliver him. And, my deare cousen, submite to the Lord who doth all thinges for the best to them that love him ; and in so doien you shall finde comfort in your greatest troble, etc. . . .

Her uncles, Colonel James Montgomerie of Coilsfield and Major-General Robert Montgomerie, also fought on the Royalist side in the Civil War. Her aunt Margaret married, as his second wife, William, eighth Earl of Glencairn. By his second wife, Marie Leslie, eldest daughter of John, sixth Earl of Rothes, Hugh, seventh Earl of Eglintoun, had a numerous family : two sons, Alexander, who became eighth earl in March 1689, and Francis of Giffen; and five daughters, who all made influential marriages. Mary married, on 4th September 1662, George, fourth Earl of Winton. Margaret married, on 30th April 1667, James, third Earl of Loudoun. Christian married, on 16th February 1672, John, fourth Lord Balmerino. Helenor married David Dunbar, younger of Baldoon. Anne married first, *c.* 30th December 1675, Sir Andrew Ramsay of Waughton; and second, in the last week of December 1682, Sir Patrick Ogilvie of Boyne, Lord Boyne.

In his rising these manifold family relationships, with their intricate intercrossings, were of great advantage to James Ogilvie ; and when he had attained political greatness they were much urged in return as reasons why favours should be granted by him. It will be seen in course, that those relationships mentioned do not nearly exhaust the tale of his relatives. They may be taken, however, as James Ogilvie's own estimate of what he considered most influential in his own family connections. Years afterwards, in 1704, when he had reached the proud position of Lord High Chancellor of Scotland, round his portrait he had engraved the names of the following noble families with whom he was connected, the Duke of Hamilton and the Earls of Morton, Glencairn, Rothes, Linlithgow, Broadalbin, Eglinton, and Findlater.

James, third Earl of Findlater, figures largely in the following correspondence, and abundant light is thrown upon his character and pursuits. He was a nobleman of genuinely religious instincts and of scholarly tastes, his book bill forming a considerable item of his yearly expenditure. He was a keen sportsman and a kindly neighbour. Like most Scots nobleman of his time, he was in deep chronic money difficulties. He and his countess were devoted parents to their large family.

A few notes on the family culled from the Seafield Correspondence prior to 1685 may be of interest as amplifying the account in the latest Peerage of Scotland. Their first-born seems to have died at birth in 1659. Writing to the countess on 14th July 1660, her cousin, Anna Lindsay, wife of the Earl of Rothes, says how pleased she is to hear of her ' safe delivre of a liveing chyld.' This was Walter, Lord Deskford. The inscription on the monument in Cullen Church, placed by his son, the fifth Earl of Findlater, gives James's birth as 11th July 1663. Two years later Patrick, their third son, was born. On 31st May 1665, the Duchess of Hamilton writing from Hamilton to the Countess of Findlater, says :—

DEARE COUSEN,—I was verie glad to heire of yr beien safe delivered, none of yr friends beien more concerned in you then I am. When you did me the kindness to send heire I was then lyin in, which I beleve my La. Margret Kennedie accquainted you with. I will now say but lettell to you, knowing that itt is best for you to faver yr eyes much for a while after yr bearing a child, etc. . . .
HAMILTON.

A daughter was born before July 1666, but did not live long. Writing from Lesly on the 2nd December 1666 to the Countess of Findlater, Anna Lindsay says :—

I ame sorie for the bad news that yr leter broght me of the remowall of yr suit litell lady. The Lord santifie that trayell to you, for to part with a beloved chyld is no small deficoltie.

In the summer of 1667 the children came safely through

the hazard of smallpox; and somewhat later that year another daughter, named Marie after the Countess of Eglintoun, was born. In July 1668 a son was born, and was named Hew after the Earl of Eglintoun. In 1669 the countess writes of having four sons and one daughter. Later that year, about July or August, she had another child; and in December she writes of the death of some of the children. Who these were can only be surmised. They were not Lord Deskford, James, Patrick, nor Marie. About June 1670 she had a daughter, probably Anna. Before 19th April 1672 she had another son; and in February 1673 she had a son, named Robert after her uncle, Robert Montgomerie. Lady Findlater was a careful mother of great good sense, whose time was much taken up with the care and upbringing of her numerous children.

In 1673, while the earl and she were in the south visiting their relations at Loudoun and Cassillis, the children were left to the care and teaching of Mr. Patrick Innes, a clergyman who continued for some years to act as tutor to them, and who afterwards was presented by the earl to the charge of Banff. In May 1675, Walter, Lord Deskford, and James Ogilvie were sent to the University in Aberdeen. They were accompanied by their tutor, Mr. Innes, under whose care they remained. Over all three a general oversight was entrusted to the Rev. Mr. George Meldrum, a clergyman of Aberdeen, a lifelong friend of the family, whose voluminous and sanctified letters to the countess, with their many quotations from Scripture and crabbed writing, give every information except what one wishes. We find from the registers of Marischal College, Aberdeen, that Lord Deskford and James Ogilvie, his brother, entered that University in 1675. Lord Deskford distinguished himself in sport, winning in 1676, the Archery Prize, a silver arrow.

Mr. Patrick Innes, their tutor, thus speaks of them and their entering College in 1676 :—

To LO. FINDLATER

MY LORD,—. . . Your Lo^{ps} children, blessed be God, are in health, and diligent at their books. My Lord Deskfoord is desirous that the peace for the silver arrow be made ; and I cannot imploy anie in it, till I receive that fancie and motto your Lo^p would have on it. I intreit your Lo^p will send it with the first occasion. William Thomson tells me there are some of your Lo^{ps} books come to Leith, and he expects them shortlie in this town. . . . I have entered the children to the Colledge, where they were entertained with much respect and great protestations of kindnesse from all the masters. The Councill of Abd., upon Baillie Molisones desire, hes appointed the marriage desk in the old church for their seat. I am satisfied to see how respectfull the carriage of all in this place is toward them, and on the other hand how obleidging they are. . . . MR. PAT INNES.

Abd., May 12, '76·

Next month Mr. Meldrum reports thus favourably on them.

To LA. FINDLATER

MADAM,—. . . Your noble and hopefull children are in good health and very carefull to improve all meanes of their education, as much as the meanest in the place. . . . MR. G. MELDRUM.

Abd., June 3*d,* 1676.

They returned presumably for their second session in December 1676.

To LO. FINDLATER

MY LORD,—. . . They are in health, and have sustained no prejudice by their journey ; they are diligent at their book, and have allreadie neer come up to the rest of their classe in the logicks. MR. PAT INNES.

Abd., Decr. 14, 1676.

The following letter from Mr. James gives a glimpse of life at the University of Dugald Dalgetty :—

To LA. FINDLATER

Abd., Januarie 3, 1677.

MADAM,—. . . I intreat that your La. may send in the horses for us the nixt week. I asure your La. I shal give no les pans to my book when I am in Cullen then I doe now, but rather more. Thier has been a pley in the Marischal Colledge leatly ; and, when the masters were going to punish them that were fighting, the old town colledginers came over to the new town with swirds and pistols, and did take the lads that should have been punisched over to the old town with them. I shal leave off to truble you any more, but that I am, Your La. most deutiful and obedient sone. JAMES OGILVIE.

The following letters show that they attended Marischal College at least a third session, and that they did not neglect dancing.

To LA. FINDLATER

Abd., March 1, 1677.

MADAM,—. . . I think I have not forgot my dance as yet, for I am sure al the dances I danced before Hacknie [?] I danced them as weal as ever I did in my life. . . .

JAMES OGILVIE.

To LA. FINDLATER

MADAM,—Your noble and hopefull children arrived here yesternight about 5 aclock at night, when we were not expecting them ; and though their coming was very refreshfull to me, yet the joy was somewhat diminished with the fear they might be prejudged with the rayn they gott. Bot I found, blessed be God, they valued it not ; and were no whit worse, and are this morning in good health. . . .

I find . . . your Ladyship hath been very fordward to send them in seasonably to the colledge, which was very comendable, and doth shew your affectionat desire of their company, and your satisfaction therin, to be ruled

by reason, and that you preferre their good education therto. . . . MR. G. MELDRUM.
Abd., Janry. ii., 1678.

These were the days of Regents in the Scots universities, encyclopædic teachers who usually in turn carried their students through their whole curriculum from start to graduation. A Regent's prelections, included logic, physics, arithmetic, geometry, moral philosophy, and economics. The University registers do not show whether Lord Deskford and James Ogilvie graduated or not.

In June 1680, James Ogilvie was in Edinburgh. The following letters to his mother and father, if they do not disclose what he was following after, show the everlasting dependence of youth.

To LA. FINDLATER

Edenbrugh, June ii., 1680.

MADAM,— . . . I intreat your La. would speak to my Lord to send me some mony, as soon as he can ; for the expense I was on the rod, and the buying of my cloths has spent the litle money and gold I had of my own when I came from Cullen ; and, if I get not money sent me shortly, I will be forced to cheang some of your La. gold. . . . JA. OGILVIE.

To LO. FINDLATER

Edr., July the 1, 1680.

MY LORD,— . . . I have litle or no money at a, and I have no expectatione of geting money from Boin ; for although he promised once to give me some money, yet since that time he has gone to the west, and has left no word to me from whome I might expect the money. And I know I wil get none from him, for he has very many seeking money from him hier that has goten none. I hope your Lo. wil take some speedy course for geting me money, for I have none. Their is no neus in this toune ; and we expect none til the Duke of Rothes come. I shal leave to your Lo. any furter bot that I am, Your Lo. most obedient sone, JA. OGILVIE.

Whether James Ogilvie was then studying law or not the correspondence does not disclose, though very favourable accounts of him were sent north by his relatives in the south. On the 20th of December 1681, A. Lindsay, Duchess of Rothes, announcing to her cousin the death of the duke after thirty-three years of wedded life, speaks of Mr. James as 'your son a youth so hopefull in my opinion as I sie few so well qualified of any condision.' His parents' ambition for him and for Lord Deskford was the army. The two following letters of 30th March, 1682, from the Duchess of Hamilton and her son, Lord Aran, show this :—

To LA. FINDLATER

Hamilton, 30 March '82.

DEARE MADAME,—Yrs of the 20 instant was verie wellcome, and the more that y^r son did me the kindnes to come heere with itt. And I am verie glad to see him so hopefull a young man. . . . My son Jeames is heere, who professes all the inclinations posseable to serve y^r sons my Lord Deskfourd and his brother in what you propose ; but that regement whereof the Prince of Orang has given him the comand is an old on, and att present all full of officeers, but if you think fitt to lett them come thare, when James is in Holland att which time you shall be advertised, he will doe all he can for there serves, in which if he failed none should blame him more then I. But, what fault soever he has, he is not guilty of unconcernednes in his friends, when any way in his power to serve them ; and heere-after men for the levies may come in better session then att this time, where they have almost gott up what they wanted. . . . I doubt not but you have heard of the death of my deare son Will. . . . My Lord is not yet come home. He has ben most of this session att Ed. . . . Adieu.

For THE COUNTESSE OF FINDLATER

Hamilton, March 30, 1682.

MADAME,—I can't but think I ame oblidged to give

yow manie thankes for the kind offer your Lord and yow meakes me, in suffering your sone my Lord Deskford to taike a shaire of my fortune in the worlde; and ther is nothing I regrait more then not beieng able to serve him as he deserves and as I incline. The regiment that is to be under my comand in Holland is of ane old standing, and the recrutes that I ame now meaking are onlie to adde to the companies that are alridie ther; soe I have it not in my pour to disposse of anie companies, but ther being manie Dutch in my regiment will meak me indeavour, when I ame upon the place, to gett them some otherwayes provided, and by that means I may be able in some measure to serve my freindes. But that will be the worke of some tyme, tho you may be suir nothing will meak me soe sollicitous in effectuating this designe then the serving thos I love so weel as your childirine. I ame not to be thanked for this, since it is so naturall to me love what is come of a Hamilton soe well beloved by my grandfather. If, when I ame in Holland (of which yow shall not faill to be aqwanted), yow will send your sones ther, they may assure them selves of all the service I ame capable of shoieing them and yow that I ame, Madam, Your La. most affectionat cusing and humble servant,

ARAN.

I can't but again returne your Lord thankes with assuring him of my constant service.

Whether Lord Deskford went to Holland is not specifically stated. Writing on 26th June 1683 to his niece, Lady Findlater, Robert Montgomerie says : ' I wes most glade to hear that yor sonne had gotten a company in the States service and everie on commends him as a fyne gentleman.' It is certain that Mr. James was in Holland at that time, and he may be referred to. The following letter shows that he did not remain long abroad.

To LA. FINDLATER

Edr., Septr. 2, 1683.

MADAM,—I doubt not bot befor this time your La. hes heard of my being come home. I would have writtne

to your La. immediatly after my landing, bot that I
thougt to have been in the north sooner then any letter
could come to your La. hands. Bot having the occasione
of Mr. George Meldrume goeing north, I having resolved
to delay my jorney until my Lord Boyn goe, . . . I
thoght it my dutie to let your La. know that, blissed be
God, I am come safe this lenth, and nothing the worse
of my woage. I would have come by London, bot that
since the conspiracie ther are none comes from Holand
bot are immedially sent to prisone, and when they are att
London they most have ther pass under the Great Seale
othewayes they will be stopt att evrie willage. . . .

JA. OGILVIE.

After his return from Holland he pursued his legal studies
in Edinburgh. His aunt, Lady Loudoun, writing to his
mother on 2nd April 1684, speaks of him as a ' credit to
al his relasions, and a confort to you in your ould eage,
for I never hirde a yong person so generallie estimed.'
In January 1685 he was admitted an advocate.

The following Correspondence, which commences in 1685
and ends in 1708, is published for the first time. It is
only a contribution to the numerous published letters
written by, to, or concerning the Chancellor Earl of Seafield. In the *Carstares State Papers and Letters* more
letters from Mr. James Ogilvie are printed than from any
other single correspondent. Many Seafield letters are
published in the *Marchmont Papers*, and in other publications dealing with contemporary statesmen. The Historical MSS. Commission has twice made drafts on the
correspondence at Cullen House, and the letters published, especially in the *Fourteenth Report*, Appendix,
Part III., are of special value. The present collection has
been divided into chapters synchronising with the various
important periods of Mr. James Ogilvie's career. The
letters touch on many varied interests, and are written
by many persons. In editing them the thinnest narrative

setting, and annotations on the less known correspondents and persons and events referred to have been introduced to illustrate the varied subject-matter. Only the briefest summary, therefore, of the principal incidents treated is necessary here.

During the comparatively obscure reign of James the Second, where fresh material is always interesting, Mr. James Ogilvie was in Edinburgh building up, with the assistance of his relatives, the Hamiltons, Eglintouns, and Sir Patrick Ogilvie, Lord Boyne, his practice as an advocate. Apart from the current family news about the Findlater family and their relatives and acquaintances, including suchlike matters as the negotiations for Lord Deskford's marriage with the Archbishop of St. Andrews' daughter, the rupture between Lord Boyne and his lady, referred to by Lord Fountainhall, and Mr. James Ogilvie's own marriage and his mother's death, the political incidents of Argyll's rebellion, the opposition of Parliament and the country to the Romanising policy of the King, and the landing of William of Orange are illustrated in the Correspondence, mainly from a Banffshire point of view. In William's reign similar northern views are given of incidents in the rising of Dundee, and in the subsequent pacification of Scotland by General Mackay. The same local colouring characterises many of the letters throughout the collection, and, apart from its general Scottish interest, gives it an interest specially peculiar to the north of Scotland.

On 1st March 1689, Mr. James Ogilvie was returned to the Convention Parliament as Commissioner for Cullen. Later that year he was knighted. In March 1693, aided by his relative the Duke of Hamilton, William's chief minister in Scotland, he entered the Government of Scotland as Solicitor-General. In that position, and in various higher ones, he held office continuously down to the union of the Parliaments in 1707 and later. His career thus became identified with the political history of his time,

and the Seafield Correspondence, besides illustrating contemporary political history, affords material for a revised
and higher estimate than the common one borrowed from
Lockhart and other contemporary political annalists, of
his worth and integrity as a patriotic statesman.

In the letters of the period when he held office as Solicitor-
General interesting references are made to the last romantic
episode of Dundee's rising, the siege of the Bass, to the
struggle for sea power between England and France, to
depredations on Scots sea-borne commerce by French
privateers, to threatened invasion of Scotland from France,
and to Jacobite intrigue in England and in Scotland.
Much information is given of the slow abandonment of
Episcopacy, and of the consequent slow establishment of
Presbytery in the north of Scotland, a settlement which
was not completed when Queen Anne came to the throne.
Many matters of ordinary administration are mentioned,
and an old world reference to trial for witchcraft may be
noted.   References during this and subsequent periods to
the use of influence or 'moyen,' with judges to bias their
decisions, are notable, as showing that our law-courts have
now reached a more detached and impartial position.

The great continental struggle with Louis XIV. was still
in progress when Sir James Ogilvie, who as Solicitor-
General had visited London more than once, and who had
favourably impressed King William, was promoted in 1696
to the important office of Joint Secretary of State for
Scotland.   With his advancement to that office commenced
his long, voluminous, and important correspondence with
Carstares, King William's chaplain and confidential adviser
in Scots affairs.   With that same year came the outburst
in colonising and trading activity in Scotland associated
with the incorporation of the African Company.   The
expedition to Darien followed, with its subsequent political complications and ill-fated ending.   Fresh light is
thrown on various phases of this tragic episode in Scots

history, whose most redeeming feature was its compelling effect on a corporate union of England and Scotland ; and Seafield's intervention in the matter of Darien was all through probably more patriotic than his contemporaries allowed. A necessary outcome of the wars of William and Anne was the development, for the defence of the growing sea-borne commerce of Scotland, of the Scots navy, one of the least-known subjects of the history of the period, and several important notes on the small Scots navy of these reigns are scattered through the Correspondence.

The policy of an incorporating union, so urgent on account of the complications arising out of the Darien episode, was handed on to his successor by William, whose sudden death in the spring of 1702 is graphically described by the Countess of Seafield. In Queen Anne's reign Seafield, unlike most of William's ministers, maintained his position, and amid the many changes necessary in the troubled negotiations that preceded the union, he was continuously in office, occupying as circumstances dictated the positions of Secretary of State or Lord High Chancellor. The tragic incident of Captain Green and his crew in 1705, which is voluminously discussed, finally impressed on Scots and English statesmen alike the absolute necessity of an incorporating union, and Seafield, with his suave and diplomatic methods, contributed as Lord High Chancellor more than his share towards that great consummation. Various jarring incidents of administration which followed the union are mentioned ; and this Correspondence ends with an original contemporary and partly official account of the French invasion of Scotland in 1708.

During his public career Seafield had at his command the faithful services of several assistants, for whom in turn he secured promotion. Nicolas Dunbar, Sheriff-Depute of Banffshire ; John Anderson, Depute-Clerk to the Privy Council of Scotland ; James Baird, Writer to the Signet ; Alexander Ogilvie, Deputy Keeper of the Signet, after-

wards Lord Forglen; and John Philp, his private secretary, were amongst these, and their numerous letters on the
public and private affairs of the time enhance the interest
of the collection.

Amid all his public work Seafield did not neglect the
interests of his family, or his own interests as a landlord.
His courteous and considerate treatment of his father,
who had early handed over to him the burdened family
estates, is notable, as was also the care and attention he
and his countess bestowed on the education of their son
Lord Deskford. At the same time, his moderation in
pressing the advancement of the material interests of his
relations was remarkable in such an age. In the management of his estates he had the able and wise assistance
of his wife and of William Lorimer his chamberlain, and
many of the letters illustrate a bygone phase of land-
ownership, when rents were mostly paid in kind, and the
proprietor had to engage in the pursuit of a grain merchant, exporting bere, oats, and meal to Leith. Scotland
was then miserably poor. Many of the letters contain
little more than requests for loans, and for the repayment
of money lent. Land, the chief wealth of the country,
seems generally to have been mortgaged to the hilt, and
many landowners, with no adventitious means of increasing
their wealth, were falling into decay and were being sold
out. Sir Patrick Ogilvie of Boyne, on whose park at
Boyne Portsoy, Seafield, his brother Patrick, and young
Boyne had played long gauff in 1690, was one of many
such proprietors. On Boyne's fallen fortunes Seafield,
who had out of his handsome official salaries redeemed his
own family estates, extended his holding in land, and with
other purchases, such as Kempcairn in Keith, refounded
the extensive domain of Seafield. Similarly Braco, ancestor of the Duke of Fife, was then building up the
extensive Fife domain, and we have a glimpse of the
process in his purchase of the Airlie estate in Banff, which

the Earl of Airlie, whose sportsmanlike letters, with their references to his falcons and airie, have an old-time note, was forced to relinquish in 1700. The Correspondence throws light on many other phases of the domestic history of Scotland in those days not touched on here, and illustrates in many ways the condition of the country and the manners and customs of the time.

In editing the letters no alteration has been made on their text except the use of modern punctuation, and the substitution of capital letters for small ones, according to modern usage, and *vice versa*. A very few conjectures filling small gaps in the letters are enclosed in square brackets. The annotations are in smaller type.

A very few of the papers and letters published are, where stated in the notes, taken from State Papers of Scotland in the Record Office, London.

I desire to convey my best thanks to the Countess-Dowager of Seafield for the unrestricted use of the original letters, and gratefully to acknowledge the valuable assistance in transcription and advice I have received from Miss Norah Kerr, London. I desire also cordially to thank Dr. Maitland Thomson, Honorary Secretary of the Society, for his ever ready advice and help.

JAMES GRANT.

BANFF, *September* 1911.

The above note of thanks was written before the lamented death of the Countess-Dowager of Seafield at Cullen House on 6th October 1911, a lady of innate modesty and singleness of purpose and very charitable, who for twenty-seven years managed the extensive Seafield estates with great wisdom. J. G.

BANFF, 11*th October* 1911.

SEAFIELD CORRESPONDENCE

CHAPTER I

LETTERS DURING THE REIGN OF JAMES,
FROM 1685 TO 1688

ON the 6th of February 1685 Charles II. died at Whitehall. On the 11th the Duchess of Hamilton, writing to her cousin, refers to the King's death, and to her children's prospects in the following letter :—

For THE COUNTES OF FENDLATOR

Holyrud House, 11 *Feb.* 1685.

DEARE MADAM,—I have receved y^{rs} and has seen y^r letter to y^r brother; as also y^r sister since I came heire has tould me y^r condition, which I am veric senceable of, and the more that I know so littell how to helpe efectually those presing defeculties you ar lying under. I beleive my Lord Boyne may doe more then others to prevail with y^r Lord; but in any way you judge fettest I shall be most willing to use my indevores for y^r serves, and therefore while I am in toune that I may heire from you, which itts like may not be so long as was thought, for the sad news of the Kings death has put a close to that Part that was to have satt in March. My Lord has not ben well of laitt, and on the account of his health will stay as short while heere as he can. He presents his humble serves to y^r La. My son Aran has ben so unhappy as to be in France at this time, and so not waiting on the King in his sicknes and death, which will be a verie great grife to him. I have three sons besides him in France. My too youngest ar att the colledge at Glasgow. My daughter Susan is maryed to my Lord Cochran; and I have only my youngest daughter Meg with me. I heire y^r daughters ar verie handsume wemen. I should be verie glad to see you and them; and hopes we may yet have a happy metting, notwithstanding all the defeculties that lyes in the way.—So, deare cusen, adieu.

The Scots Parliament was called sooner than the Duchess of Hamilton had anticipated, and the 23rd of April saw its down-sitting in Edinburgh. Five days later George Leslye of Burdsbank, representative of the Royal Burgh of Cullen, gives his impressions of the session in the following letter to his friend and neighbour the Earl of Findlater.

ffor THE EARLE OFF FFINDLATER thes

Edr. Ap. 28, 85.

MY LORD,—I acknowledge my owersight and neglect off my duty, that till now I have newer giwen you the trouble off ane lyne since my heircomeing; ffor till now I had little qrwith to trouble your Lo^p. Your sone my Lo. Deskfoord is weill; and I assure your Lo^p, ffor any thing I can find or see, caries wery weill, liwes handsomelie yet saweinglie, and hes abundance off ffawour from his noble relationes and ffrinds heir, and sall not want all the encurradgement ffrindship and serwice in my power. The first day ther wes little done in Parliat, the rolls called, the Commissioners commissione read, the Registers patent as Wiscount of Tarbett read and published, the Articles settled, ther being non benorth Tay on them, and all members took the test. Yesterday the Parlatt satt qn many off the contrawerted elecns wer cleired. Some shyres, to witt Air and Merse, are ordered to elect off new. Pitmedden[1] and Pittrichie[2] caries for Abd. The Protestant religione is secured by ane act off fywe or six lynes, all fformer acts made theranent being ratified and approwen. The excyse setled till the first of Aug. enseweing as it wes institute in Midletouns Parliatt; and therefter it is ffor ewer annexed to the croun, to this

---

[1] Sir Alexander Seton, Lord Pitmedden.   [2] Sir Charles Maitland.

King, and to his lañoll airs and sūrs qtsoewer, with this
qualitie that its collected according to the act in the last
Parliatt, only to be lewied from off the breawers, the
commissioners and land rent being to be free. This is
all that is done as yett. The Parliament sitts on ffryday
againe att ten acloack. Ther is ane anssr drawen to the
Kings letter to be sent to his Majtie. The present taxmen
are endeawouring to farm the excyse off the whole natione;
and it is only continowed till Aug., till they settle upon
it. Ther wes ane great traitt that night, efter the Parliatt
wes ridden, giwen by the Commissioner to the members
off Parliatt who wer invited, to qch I wes ane witnes and
partaker, and did see particularlie how things wer ordered ;
bot most tell your Lop this Parliatt hes not that splendour,
as your Lop and I both hawe seen, and ther way now is
farr unlyk to the deportment off thes who are now away
and gone. I presume on your Los ffawour in respect I will
by this tyme be scant off strae att Banff, that qn James
Cock sends my hors to your Lop ye will doe me that kyndnes to permitt him runn in your park till I come home.
My Lo. Airly looks not so weill upon it, and says he will
be north this summer. Its thought the Parliatt will sitt
all May. The fforfaulters are to be in shortly. I offer
my humble duty and service to your Lop and to my Ladye,
and by conveniencie att some tymes qn sure occasiones
offers your Lop sall have account off the transactiones
heir from, My Lord, Your Los very affec⁀nat and oblidged
servant,   GEO. LESLYE.

I fforgot to tell your Lop how ffor honour off our good
toun off Cullen I did ryde the Parliatt. I wes prest to it
by severall frinds. I did it on little expenss, and wes weill
mounted on ane hors off Sr Wm Sharps.[1]

This day the Lo. Gosfoord [2] is gone ffor London, wt ane
return to his Majties letter ; and the Burrows this day
haveing mett are to putt in to be reponed to ther old
priviledges . . .

---

[1] Of Stonyhill, brother of Archbishop Sharp.
[2] Sir Peter Wedderburne, Commissioner for Haddington.

A reference to the Acts of the Parliaments of Scotland shows that some of the Lords of Articles chosen had interests benorth the Tay, and that the reference to Merse is inaccurate.

On the 2nd of May Argyll sailed from Holland on his ill-fated expedition. On the 6th he anchored near Kirkwall. Meantime the King, exercising his dispensing power, had appointed the Earl of Dumbarton Lieutenant-General of Scotland, and the Duke of Gordon to the command of the heritors of Aberdeen and Banffshire, though both were Roman Catholics and were legally incapable of holding office. The following letters to the Earl of Findlater from Bailie John Gordon of Banff, Captain of the Burgh militia, from the Duke of Gordon, from James Cock, Town Clerk of Banff, and from Sir Patrick Ogilvie, Lord Boyne, who was as ready to serve in the field as on the bench, throw light on the preparations made in the north to suppress this rebellion, and on the proceedings of the Parliament which sat through the rising.

ffor THE RIGHT HONNOBLL THE EARLE OFF FFINDLATER

My Lord,—I am to have a rendevouz of my companie of millitia foott att Banff upon Monday nixt be ten acklock, confor to orders receaved yester night from the Earle of Erroll and my Lord Boyne, which cam from Edñbrh by Major Hay. I judged it theirfore my dutie to aquaint yor Lo. of the day and place, houping yor Lo. will be a good example to the rest of the shyre in sending yor men weill mounted in new hats reid coats shoes and stockings wt lininges conform, but above all weill fixed armes. Yor Lo. knowes the nesessitie, the King and cuntries interest being at the stake, which wt my most humble service presented to yor Lo. my Lady and all yor children is all att present, but that I abyd, My Lord, yor Lo^s most humble servitor,   Jo. GORDON.

Banff, 9 May 1685.

I must beg yor Lo. to doe me the favor to caus ane of yor millitia men intimat this to the magistrats of Cullen, and any others concerned neir yor Lo's bounds.

Auchmeden being heir att mciting intreats yor Lo^s

prescence att Banff on Monday nixt to concur with the rest of the comissioneres of the shire, who are to meett heir on Monday nixt be ten acklock, off which meetting the Shireff[1] hes given Duke Gordon advertisment pr expres, and is to send over all their names yt does not meett to the Counsell.

For THE EARLL OFF FINDLATERR

MY LORD,—Yesterday I receavd the favor off a letter from y^r Lo. I designd befor that, as now I doe, to give y^r Lo. acount that the Cuncell has been plesd to ordder that I shuld assemble the heretors off Banffshyr, and command them when itt shuld bee orderd to march. I have apointed a randevus at Huntly Tuesday nixt, wher Ill expect the honnor off y^r Lo. company. Y^r Lo. would dooe weell to thinck agan that tim, off whom y^r Lo. will mack use for commanding a trupp off w^h y^r Lo. is to bee capptan. I humbley kiss my Laddy Findlaterrs hands, and I am, Yo. Lo. humble servant,   GORDON.

20 *May* 85.

Y^r Lo. will dooe me a pleseur to lett me have the use off the prospeck I gave y^r Lo. to trey an experiment.

ffor THE EARLE OFF FFINDLATTER these

Banff, 20 *May* 85.

MY LORD,—Being hurried with tyme I cannot so ffullie wreit to yow as I wold ; but ffinding youer Lo. bearer hear, I could not omitt to let yow know, that just now I received ane lēr ffrom Burdsbank, who desyres me to tell youer Lo. that my Lord Deskffoord is werie weill in health, and Burdsbank desyres to be excused that he has not written to youer Lo. He wreits there past 5 acts in Parliament the oyr day, 1, that all Protestants are obldged to take the test ; 2, is ane act ffor eight moneth cess yearlie dureing the Kings lyffe tyme, qch is 3 moneth yearlie by what is alradie imposed ; 3, act anent perscriptiones ; 4, anent

---

. [1] Sir James Baird of Auchmedden.

cetationes and interuptiones ; 5, ane act ratifieing the justices off pace priviledges. There also past three fforfaltures the said day, wiz. the fforfaltur off Hamiltoune off Monkland, Jereswood, and Argyll. This is the greatest off the newes I have ffrom him. Youer Lo. may be pleased to rei[d] the inclosed proclamatione, qch is to be intimat at all the paroches church nixt Sabath preceislye, as also this inclosed ffrom Ballzie Gordone. Being in haist, I am, My Lo., Youer Lo. most humble servant,

JA. COCK.

ffor THE EARLE OFF FFINDLATER

MY LORD,—I am just now, being about 3 in the morning, com to Banff, and shall, God willing, sie yor Lo. att ffordyce tomorrow. Meanetyme I beseech yor Lo. cause intimat to ffordyce, Cullen, and Deskford tomorow att the churche, that our reidgment is to march upon Monday the first of June ; and theirfore all the leaders are to send out good bodies of men, weell furnished with sufficient armes red coates hates stockings etc., and tuentie dayes pey in money, and iff any faill they will be seveirlie punished.—So till meeting I abyd, My Lord, Yor Lo. most humble servantt,   PATRICK OGILVIE.

Banff, 23 *May* 1685.

My Lord, yor son will be home this night.

Lord Findlater was not long in choosing his lieutenant in Alexander Gordon of Laquochie, now Dufftown, in the Lordship of Balvenie, Banffshire.

For THE EARLE OF FINDLATER

Laquochie, the 26 May 85.

MY LORD,—I was informed by my cousine, Mr. Gordon, my Lord Duk's maister husald, that your Lo. disired him to speake to me to be your Lo. leivtenant, and that your Lo. would give me pay ; and if so be your Lo. be still of y^t oppinion, their shall non be mor ready to serve your Lo. then my selfe ; and if not, I disir your Lo. to advertis me by the bearer, y^t I may dispose of my selfe otherways.

If yor Lo. has gott the list of the troupe, I hope you will have the goodnes as to let me knowe, if his Grace has continued the Balvenie gentelmen in y^r Lo. troupe as they listed themselves, that I may cause them order their bagage ackordingly.—Wth my dutyfull respects, I am, My Lord, Y^r Lo. most humble and most obedient servant,

A. GORDON.

The three following letters recount the plight of Mr. William Joass of Colleonard, sometime minister of Alvah, a Banffshire heritor, who was unable to take the field, and was therefore compelled to employ an approved substitute.

ffor THE VERY NOBLE EARLE MY LORD FINDLATER
these

Colleonard, May 30, 1685,
from my bedsyde.

MY LORD,—I have just now seen a lyne from yor Lo: to the minister of Bamff, proporting some things anent my out going at this tyme, and insinuating that you would suffer to imploy a man to list in my Lord Bamff his troup, so y^t I would give yor Lo. so much money, though it would not be well taken if I should list yr in persone. In trueth my Lord Bamff never spok to me on that head ; nether resolve I ever by myself or myne to turne back to yor Lo^s interests nor willingly stand under anothers banner, nor will I give mony that I may be sufferred to doe so. For I resolve not both to give my money and turn my back on such a noble freind, but truelie so that yor Lo. will be-freind in this bussines I wil be very willing to be very thankfull ; and if James Ogilvy be shye I will come, if I can, provyded w^t another man who hes given ample prooff of his dexteritie in such exercises. And if he be rejected, I shall follow, though I should be carried in a cart or on a litter, as at this tyme I can not otherwyse be transported considering my present conditione. And I am confident my Lord Duke himself will pitie me on sight. I did not indeed speak to my Lord Bamff on that head, though yr was some litle indirect encouragment given,

but I did not much believe it. Now, dear my Lord, if
you can befreind a distrest servant for the tyme, I
beg it of yor Lo., and let me have some significatione
of it, for I can not come the lenth unless I would
resolve to ly at Cullen till the day of the rendevouz
come, for I can nether ryd stand nor walk. Yet I am
resolving to ingadge, though I should never returne;
and truelie I am expecting to ingadge in a warefaire of
which yr is no discharge, befor wee need fear any feild
fighting.—This beeing all my present resolution and
request, I rest, My Lord, Yor very humble and very much
obleidged servant,   W. JOASS.

For THE EARLE OF FINDLATER

MY LORD,—My brother in law continues sick, and is
not able to get out of bed, far more unfitt to travail with
the forces; and I am sure it is not the will of Councill
in their proclamation that sick men go to the fields, nor
can they reasonably be given up as deficient, if they send
any in their room. My Lord, he would get severals to goe
for him for a peece of money, and seeing himself was
unable to travail and necessitated to give money to another to appear for him, I intended that the money given
that way should, as much of it as could, come to your
Lops use; and if I could have got the designe effectuated
I thought it was no disservice to your Lop, and Walter
Ogilvie being to goe however, I conjectured the pitching
on him might promote that designe. If Walter be not
engaged for another, Colleonard will allow him besides
the five peeces I formerly wrote of, wch your Lop may
imploy as you will, twentie pounds scots; and if he be
engaged, my brother in law will employ another whom
my Lord Duke and your Lop shall approve as qualified;
but I shall not wish this, for indeed, my Lord, as I have
said, I would wish the money come your way. My Lord
Boynd thinks this proposal reasonable and for your Lops
interest, else I should not have offered it again. If
Colleonard be able, he will yet come in person and attend

your Lo^p; neither had he any designe to list himself or any that should serve for him under any other then your Lo^p. I beg your Lo^{ps} answer by the bearer, that my brother may know what resolutions to take.—I am, My Lord, Your Lo^{ps} most humbly devoted servant,

MR. PAT INNES.

My Lord, your Lo^p will assure Colleonard that he shall not be delated as deficient, otherwise he cannot to no purpose bestow charges and expence; and that being given, no more can be expected but the horse during that service.

Banff, June 1, 1685.

For THE EARLE OF FINDLATER

MY Lord,—Being very credibly informed that Mr. Wm Joasse of Colleonard is tied to a sick bed, and altogether unable to take out with the present forces, and yet, I hear, very willing to bestow what can be rationally expected for the outing of another in his place, it is my opinion that you imploy your own man Walter Ogilvie for that use; and as for a little money more then has been offered already (wch is known to yourself and the minister of Banff), a single peace or thereabout, it will be also given. And this being done I persuade myself, on the ministers testimony of his condition, you will get him off at Duke Gordon his hands, and can give him assurance thereof. Master William is an obleidging man though little made for fighting; and if Walter Ogilvie be otherwise engaged any other whom he shall offer, if qualified, cannot be refused considering his circumstances; and though he were able, it were fitt for your Lo^p to have rather a pretty man to back you, than a man only bred a schollar. This overture I hope you will not the more unwillinglie consent unto, that it is the desire of, My Lord, Your Lo^p humble servant,

PATRICK OGILVIE.[1]

Banff, June 1, 1685.

---

[1] Lord Boyne.

On the 3rd of June the Duke of Gordon had not begun his march south.

For THE EARLL OFF FINDLATER

MY LORD,—I sent sum days agon to know the Cuncells orders as to the gard off the cuntrey in the ab. off the heretorrs. I expect the return verry shortly, off w^h y^r Lo. shall bee informmd at metting. I know nothing off the cavallrie marching south. Doun[1] has particular commission from his Majesty to command the Murray heretors in plac off Duffus. I know nothing considderable off newes. I kis my Laddy Findlaterrs hands, and, I am, Y^r Lo. most humble servant,   GORDON.

Jun. 3, '85·

On the 9th of June the Duchess of Hamilton, writing to her cousin from Edinburgh, describes the movements of her family; and indicates the troubles and difficulties of the time.

For THE COUNTES OF FINDLETOR

Ed., 9 June 85.

DEARE MADAM,—I would have wreten to you with y^r son my Lord Desford, but his goeing away was so suden as did not alowe me time to doe it ; and now I am also stratened being, if itt please God, to goe aborde this day in a yaught with my Lord for London. We thought to have gone by land, but our sons Aran and Charles came sudenly, to whom my Lord gave his horses, and takes this occasion, which I hope by the blesing of God shall be more easie then if we had gone by land. Thes is a time of great trobles, but God is alsofeshint ; and truly amongst meny perplexing defeculties I am under I doe not forgett to beare a share with you in y^rs. And thus in meny disorders, deare cousen, my Lord is y^r humble servant, and I am with much kindnes so to all y^rs, and hopes we may yet have a happy metting. Adieu.

The northern levies under the Duke of Gordon, having moved south, were concentrated mainly on Stirling, the strategic key to the situation in Scotland, should Argyll gain headway and

---

[1] Lord Doun, eldest son of the Earl of Moray Secretary of State for Scotland.

advance on Edinburgh. On the 18th of June Lord Boyne dictated the following letter from Stirling to the Earl of Findlater, who was operating under the Duke of Gordon against the rebels in Dumbartonshire. The day before, Argyll and the royalists were within musket-shot at Killearn. In the night the rebels, distracted by contending factions and bad leadership, melted away on the moor of Killearn without striking a blow; and when Lord Boyne wrote, Argyll was a prisoner on his last journey to Edinburgh.

For THE EARLE OF FFINLATER thes

Sterling, Jun 18, 85.

My Lord,—I have not had occasion to wreat much to you sinc we pairted, but wold not neglect this occasion. I can give no news from this pleace save we wer expecting the rebells hear this two days bygon; but its lyk befor this reach your hands yow will know better then we wher they ar. I intreat to hear how all freinds are with yow, and that yow will present my service to Duck Gordon.— I am, My Lo., Your most humble servant,

Patrick Ogilvie.

I wrot to my son last day.

On the 30th of June Argyll was beheaded. Next day news came to Edinburgh that his lieutenant, Sir John Cochran, second son of the Earl of Dundonald, had been captured, and was on his way to the tolbooth of Edinburgh. On the 6th of July Monmouth was defeated at Sedgemoor, and the rebellion in England stamped out. He and Lord Grey were taken prisoners; and with short shrift on the 15th of July Monmouth was beheaded on Tower Hill. This news had in part filtered through to the north of Scotland, when ' Eliza Gordon,' who may have been Elizabeth Howard, Duchess of Gordon, second daughter of the Duke of Norfolk, wrote on 24th July the following letter to her neighbour Lord Findlater.

ffor THE RIGHT HONBLE THE EARLE OF
FINDLATERE these

Gordon Castle, the 24 *Jully* 85.

My Lord,—Upon Fryday last my Lord begun his jorney for London, and intended to be theire upon Munday. He has noe designe of making any long stay, but when peeple goe soe far off, they can hardly be sairtaine of their diett. It is true that Sr John Cocharan on hopes of his life plays the good bairne as well as posibly he can, but it is not yet known what will become of him, or what discovereys hee has made. The Duke of Monmouth and Lord Gray are both in the Tower. I expect by the next to heare what will become of them. It is said our states men goe up in August, soe after that its like newes may be expected, but as yet theire is noe other, then what I have told y^r Lo^{pp}. If I can doe you any further service, I shall be glad to show y^r Lo^{pp} how much I am your Lo^{ps} humble servant,   ELIZA: GORDON.

Sir John Cochran and Lord Grey 'played the good bairne' to such purpose that, after giving evidence against their accomplices and paying heavy fines, they received full pardon.

Mr. James Ogilvie was early engaged in unravelling his father's pecuniary entanglements. These alone seem to have given him extensive legal practice. Writing home on the 13th and 21st of November 1685, after referring to those debts and to his father's taking the test in accordance with the act of Parliament, he details the current political and family news. The revocation of the Edict of Nantes in November 1685, though the Pope on political grounds opposed it, drove the Huguenots from France, and greatly stiffened English opposition to the Romanising policy of King James. The Parliament of England, which met on the 9th of November, took a strong stand against the King's breach of the last test act in employing Roman Catholic officers. The Commons addressed the King on the subject, and Parliament was prorogued in consequence.

For THE EARLE OF FINDLATER

Edr., Nov. 13, 1685.

MY LORD,—Having the occasion of James Ogilvies servant going north, I have presumed to give your Lo. ye trouble of this letter. Mr. Ramsay hes assinged my bond to one Mr. Hamiltoune, who threatnes to use diligence both against me and ye cationers ; and unless I get him ane thousand merks immediatly he will not att all delay. It is nou time that we knew what are your Lo. resolutions concerning the test; so I intreat your Lo. will be pleased to wreat to me anent it, that, if your Lo. resolve to take it, their may be time to apply for ane commissione. I am this evening to wait upon my Lord Carse [1] to speak annent your affair with Brigtoun, so with the nixt post you may expect some accompt of it. I find old Pourie hes not as yet given that claim which he hes against your Lo. to his sone, so I am not so free for submitting it as I was formerly; bot I have condescended to meet with him once the nixt weeke, and he is to choise one advocat and I another, and we are to have ane commoning befor my Lord Boyne. I hope your Lo. will be deligent in seeking of money against the nixt terme, for we have verie mutch to doe with it.

As for neus their are non save that the Duke and Dutches of Hamiltoune are safe come doun, and that the Duke is made one of the Secret Comity, and hes got ane regement of horse in England secured for his sone the Earle of Arran. It is not as yet known what is the Kings pleasur concerning our stats men, only it is surmised that the Chanclour [2] is lyke to carie it. The Parlament of England sate doune upon Moonday last. The Protestants persecution in France still increses, and it is heer reported that the Pope hes caused harbour a great many of them in his territories. My aunt, my Lady Baldoun, is dead and was buried this last Thursday. I hope your Lo. will not surprise your Lady with the neus of it. I know it will be ane great trouble to her. The bearer scearsly aloues me so mutch time as to wreat this letter; so I hope your Lo. will make my excuse att my Lady my mothers hands, that I have not writne to her, your doing of which will be ane verie great obligation upon, My Lord, your Lo. most obedient sone and most humble servant,

JA. OGILVIE.

---

[1] Sir Patrick Lyon of Carse.   [2] The Earl of Perth.

For THE EARLE OF FINDLATER ATT CULLEN IN
BANFFSHEIR with cair

Edr., Nov. 21, 1685.

MY LORD,—. . . As for neues, it is certain that my
Lord Chancelour is turned Popish, and that the King hes
turned off the Councel the Duke of Ormund, the Earles
of Halifax and Bridgwater, and the Bishops of London
and Eli. His Majesty in his speatch to the Parlament
does verie freely declair that he will make use of souldiers
not qualified according to the tests in England, and lykwayes declaires that he finds it absolutly needful that he
have more forces, and theirfor desirs ane subsidie. The
Popish lords gave in ane bil that they might have liberty
to sit in Parlament, which was refused them. The Parlament hes made ane adres to his Majesty to remove all the
Popish officers out of the army, it being against ther
lawes they should be in itt, and have as is reported refused
the subsidy, and have desired the King in ye first place
to secure ther religion. The Marquis of Athol hes got
three thousand pounds out of Hardens fyne, and the
Earles of Strathmor and Kintor have got ane considerable
soume out of the Muray fynes. The Earle of Dumbarton
hes goten the Laird of Saltons esteate. Sir William
Bruce is made General of the Mint, and it is to be opned
when ever he comes to Scotland. Your Lo. hes now both
ane ful accompt of your affairs and of the neus. I shal
not therfor give you any further trouble att present, bot
that I am, My Lord, Your Lo. most obedient son and most
humble servant,   JA. OGILVIE.

The Rev. Mr. Patrick Innes, minister of Banff, in the following
letter refers to the same events in England.

For THE EARLE OF FINDLATER

MY LORD,—The inclosed came to my hands yesternight late; and I finding no occasion of a bearer for
Cullen, and not knowing of what importance these may be,

have sent my boy with them. I doubt not but, if they be of a later date, your Lo^p hes an account of any current news, particularly that the Parliament of England is prorogued to the tenth of February. I cannot tell if your Lo^p hes seen the addresse of the House of Comons to the King wch hes occasioned, as is said, the prorogation of the Parliament. I gott it yesterday from Glassaugh,[1] and have sent it here inclosed. I according to my bound dutie wish your Lo^p your Lady and children all happinesse, and am, My Lord, your Lo^{ps} most humblie devoted and obleidged servant,   MR. PAT. INNES.

Banff, Decr. 4, 1685.

The ' peaper,' referred to in the following letter, ' got as ane great present from one of the Papists,' was probably a print of two papers found in a strong box of Charles Second in the handwriting of that monarch, detailing arguments in favour of Roman Catholicism. These papers King James had published.

For THE EARLE OF FINDLATER

Edr., Januarie 5, 1686.

MY LORD,—I did admier, when I sau my brother Deskfoord in toune compleaning, that by my negligence I had put him to a great dale of trouble in travling in so bad weather, wheras it was in my pouer to have hendred it by geting him ane commission for taking the test in the north. Your Lo. knowes that I wrot to your Lo., that he could have been in no hazard, since none that are in his circumstances have as yet taken it. Houever since he is hier it is fit he take it. My Lord, I am much concerned that your Lo. will not be att so much pains, as to search for thes peapers that concern Pouries proces, for he is immediatly to insist, becaus he believes not you can instruct your grounds of compensation ; and if he once obtain decriet it will be harder redusing it then nou stoping it. I have done litle in your affairs since my last letter, bot that I have keept up Balizie Scrumsiers proces for mails and diuties thes tuenty dayes, and hes litel or

---

[1] Mr. John Abercromby of Glassaugh, Banffshire.

nothing to say against it nou when I most return it.   Bot
houever I will use my endeavours to get it cassen over
for this session, that so we may have this summers respyt
for doing what we can for geting money to satisfy your
creditors.   I doubt bot, if your Lo. consider your condition,
you will be diligent in endeavouring to provid money
against the nixt term.   If your Lo. could assure us of money
att the terme, I would immediatly goe treat with all your
creditors, for I find them worse to setle with then they
wer the last year ;   and I am affraid they grou alwayes
the longer the worse.   We have no neues in this place
bot that this day the Laird of Saltoun was forfalted, and
that thes that are laitly come from court say that the King
certainly comes to Scotland the nixt spring.   Sir William
Sharp is dead ;   and my Lord Pitsligo is werie ill.   Their
is a verie great mortality hier by reason of the open
winter.   I pray God may prepair us for what is His will.
Receive this inclosed peaper which I got as ane great
present from one of the Papists.   You most not contradict it, for you see the King ouning it and his subscription
att it.   I was sorie to read in your Lo. letter that you was
ill of the cold.   I pray the Lord may recover and preserv
you in your health, which is all att present from, My Lord,
Your Lo. most obedient son and most humble servant,

JA. OGILVIE.

On the 24th of December 1685 the Chancellor Perth returned
from London a convert to Roman Catholicism, and at once established and attended the public celebration of Mass in Edinburgh.
On the 31st of January and on the 1st of February 1686 the
Puritan populace rose in riot, threatened to pull down the Mass-
house, and threw mud on the Chancellor coming therefrom.   The
following copy of the King's letter to the Council dealing with
the incident was sent north by James Ogilvie to his father the
Earl of Findlater on the 22nd February 1686.

Suprascribitur.

JAMES REX

RIGHT TRUSTY and RIGHT WEEL BELOVED CUSSING and
COUNSELOR, Right trusty and inteirly beloved Cussings

and Counselors, Right trusty and Right weil beloved Cousins and Counsellors, Right trusty and weel
beloved Cousings and Conselors, Right trusty and
weill beloved Counselors and trusty and weil beloved
Counselors,—

Wee greet yow weil : Having bein extreamly sur[pry]sed
to hear of the insolencies comitted by a tumultuous rable
in o^r city of Edinburgh, whilst yow and our uther judi-
cators wer in ye place, and y^t ther insolency should have
gon the lenth of affronting o^r cheif minister, and yet so
much lenity showin in punishing a cryme so imediatly
touching o^r Royall Person and authority, wee have now
thought fitt to let yow know that wee have not only ye
character but lykwayes the person of o^r Chanclour so much
in o^r particular care, as wee will suport him in despyt of
all ye attemps or insolencies of his enimies, and therfor
doe require you to take y^t care of his persone and have
y^t respect for his character, as may convince us of your
affectione to us and obedience to o^r comands.   In the
nixt place wee heirby requir you to go about the punishing of all y^t wer guilty of this tumult w^t ye outmost rigour
of our lawes.   Nor can wee imagin any either remiss hes
bein or will be in ys, except those who have bein favorers
of yr re[bellious] designe.   But above all is o^r express
pleasur y^t yee try into ye bottom of this matter, to try out
those who have eyr by worde insinuatione or utherwayes
sett on ys rable to ys villanus attemp, or incouradged
ym in it, and y^t ffor ye finding of ys out ye spare no legall
tryell by tortur or uyrwayes, this being of so great im-
portanc y^t nothing more displeasing to us or mor dangerous to our Government cd posibly have bein contryved,
and wee shall spar no expence to know ye rise of it.   Wee
again comand yow again to be diligent in ffinding out
ye whole matter and punishing the guilty, as lykwayes
to use your utmost endeavours for preventing ye lyk
vilanies for ye futur.   Efter wee shall hear what ye nixt
post shall bring, yow shall know o^r ffurther pleasure in ys
matter.   In ye meantym wee bidd yow heartily fare weil.
Givin att our Court at Whythall ye 9th day of ffebry 1686

and of oᵣ reing the 2ᵈ year.   By his Maties comand,
Subscribitur,   MORRAY.

Sir George MacKenzie, Lord Advocate, was at this time suspected by the King and Chancellor of being opposed to the repeal
of the penal statutes, and was dismissed next May.   His successor
was then temporarily found in Sir George Lockhart Lord President of the Court of Session.

The negotiations regarding Deskford's proposed marriage with
Anne, eldest daughter of Arthur Ross, the last Archbishop of St.
Andrews, are characteristic of this and of later periods.

Edr., February the 22, 1686.

MY LORD,—That I did not wreat to your Lo. with William
Innes was, becaus I did not know of his going until he was
gone.   I had sent Morisone sooner north, bot that Pourie
prest me verie hard to have ane mee[ting] with him
annent your business.   Bot after I had consulted the
Kings Advocat Sir John Dalrympel and Sir David
Thors, and had caused them draw ane information, and
was ready to have informed my Lord Harcars[1] and my
Lord Kemny,[2] who wer to have given their opinion of your
affair, he t[he]n did not proceed any further in it ; bot gave
it over until the first of November, becaus we did found
one of our grounds of compensation upon the contract
past betuixt your Lo. and your uncle Murie[3] att Edr.
Bot in the mean time he is to rais and cause excecut
his sumonds against you this session, and he hes promised
the nixt year to offer your Lo. peace providing you will
submit your affair.   I am hopful this delay may prove
very advantagius to your Lo., becaus, if my brother
Deskfoord mary, it will be easie for us to get all the diligences against your Lo. estate bought in, and will be able
to exclud all personal creditors, and so we may the less
valou what be the event of Pouries process against your
Lo.   I could have wished that my brother had advertised
me of his sending his man north, for I had not only
writne to your Lo. of my brothers intentions to mary the
Primate of Saint Andues daughter, bot lykwayes had

---

[1] Sir Roger Hog of Harcarse.   [2] Sir George Nicolson of Kemnay.
[3] William Ogilvie of Murie, brother of the second Earl of Findlater.

given your Lo. ane accompt of what wee may rationly
expect he may get with her in portion, which both my
Lord Boyn and I conjecturs may be about fourtie thousand
merks. And the reason wee have for thinking this is
because the Bishop did give to Major Balfour who maried
his second daughter thirty thousand merks; and the
Bishop did promise to my Lord Boyn to extend him selfe
as far as he could. The Bishop is nou gone to London,
and so I am afraied that befor his return their can be no
thing done in my brothers mariage. As for Scrumsier
he hes nou called his sumonds for mails and duties. I
compeared my selfe, and denyed his lybel, and craved he
might condeshend upon his *modus probationis*, which he
did, viz. by the tennents oths which I found relev^t, and
got commission for taking their oths in the north, and hes
gotne the first of Nōr for reporting the comission; so I
think wee will have this sumer f[or] setling of your Lo.
affairs. In the mean time your Lo. would doe weel to be
providing money against the nixt term, that, in cais my
brothers mariag doe not succeed, your Lo. may houever
be able to doe your oun affairs. As for John Innes his
bargan with your Lo., I intreat your Lo. may neither give
it over nor perfite it until my Lord Boyn and I com north,
and then your Lo. perhaps may make ane better bargan
then nou you can. I am informed that the book your Lo.
desired me to get for you is forbiden to be sold. You
may easily conjectur the reason. I have bought the
garden seeds your Lo. wrot for confor[m] be the inclosed
not. A[s] for the other things your Lo. wrot for, I shall
endeavour to get them for your Lo. befor my north going.
As for neus it is certain that the Chanclour hes got from his
Majesty 8000 punds sterling. My Lord Athol hes got
2000 pound. It is talked that the Duke of Gordon hes
got Locheil his estate, bot this yet needs confirmation.
Your Lo. hes no doubt heard of the foolish tumult we had
in this place, so shal not trouble your Lo. with ane accompt
of it; bot by this inclosed letter of the Kings you will find,
hou it hes been represented to him, and what is his
Majestys opinion annent it. Duke Gordon my Lord

Register [1] and the Laird of Grant part from London once this week ; and what neues after ther aryval is reported your Lo. shal have ane accompt.   It is thought that the Parlment will not meet the day appointed, bot will certainly meet within ane very short time ther after.   It is not yet knowen who will be commioner ; bot many are in the opinion that Duke Hamiltoun is fair for to cary it. I have nou given your Lo. the trouble of ane long letter ; and therfor shal add no more att present, bot that I am, My Lord, Your Lo. most obedient son and most humble servant,   JA. OGILVIE.

Writing on the same date to his sister the Countess of Findlater, Francis Montgomerie mentions the death of their ' two dear sisters Loudon and Baldune.'   Lady Loudon therefore died before the 22nd of February 1686.

Further details of Lord Deskford's proposed marriage are given in the following five letters.   In the end it came to nothing.   On the 7th of June 1687 the Archbishop's daughter married, as his second wife, Lord Balmerino.

For THE EARELE OFF FINDLATER thes are

Edenburge, 13 [*Feby.*] 1686.

MY LORD,—Your Lordship will perhaps thinke strainge that I send my sarvant to you in such heast ; but when yee read my letter I hope it will satisfie you.   My Lord, the reasone that makes me send this expresse is of some importance, blissed be God for his goodness to me att this occaisione in this affair.   This day I was seeking the Duke of Hamiltons advice concerning a match betwixt my Lord Sant Andarous his daughter and me, which did satisfie his Grace very much ;   and he did desire me to send my sarvant to you in all heast, because the Primat hath got a call from the Kinge, and is to goe this inshouinge week too the court.   He will give a considrable porsione which, as I am informed, is about 40 or 50 thousand markes.   I desire your blissing and concent, which will incourage me very much.   It is my judgment yee will neither be so unjust to me and so pregiudiciall as to deny

---

[1] Viscount Tarbat.

this petitione, that is for your advantage and also mine.—
Being in heast, I rest, Your obedient sone,   DESKFOORD.

For THE COUNTES OF FFINLATER thes
Edb., March 9, 86.

MADAM,—Your son Desford being gon north to have
your La. and my Lords advyce and assistanc in this desyn
of his, which I am hopfull (if it tak effect) will tend to his
satisfaction and the preservation of your familie, your
son will be fuller in the particulars; only I shall presum
to say that, if your La. doe not at this tym show your
kyndnes to your son in renūncing som considerable pairt
of thes lands yow ar infeft in, it will not be possible to
give any joyntur to yowr sons ladie, without which its
not to be imagined the desyn can tak effect. And, if it
feall on that syd, I know it will be werie trowblsom to yowr
son, who I hop shall deserve the extraordinarie cares your
La. hath had of him, and will be found to have greater
capacities for many things then many did apprehend. I
hop yowr La. will not mistak my offering my oppinion in
yowr concerns; sinc, if this occasion be neglected, I am
affraied ther will be hardly ane other so convenient for
the interest of yowr familie found.—I am, Ma., Yowr
most humble servant,   PATRICK OGILVIE.[1]

For THE COUNTES OF FINDLATER
Edr., March 9, 1686.

MADAM,—I could not be so far wanting of my dutie as
not to wreat to your La. having so sure ane occasion as my
brother Deskfoord, who by the advise of most of his friends
is att this time gone north. He hes nou very near secured
himselfe of ane match, by which the family may be put
in ane beter condition then it hes been nou of a long time.
He hes very good reason to expect ane good portion with
her; and I knou nothing that can nou hender his mariage,
unless it be that wee be not able to make her ane suitable
lifrent. Yet I am confident both my Lord and your La.
will doe all that lyes in your pours for effectuating this,

---

[1] Lord Boyne.   .

reserving alwayes to your selfs ane competency both to your selfs and childeren to live upon. I need not nou trouble your La. with ane accompt of your relations, seing my brother Deskfoord can sufficienly inform your La. of them. I nou put my selfe in the hops of having the honor to see your La. very shortly, the session being nou very near ane end. I shall nou add no mor; bot that all hapiness may attend your La. shal be the continual prayer of, Madam, Your La. most obedient son and most humble servant,   JA. OGILVIE.

I give my humble service to my brothers and sisters.

Edr., Merch 9, 1686.

DEAR SISTER,[1]—Thogh I have not had the good fortune to hear from yow of a long tyme, yet to convince yow that nothing shall alter me from that affectione to which I ame obleidged both by nature and inclination, I have given yow this trouble with my Lord Desford, who will give yow ane accompt of his desinge of a match with the Archbishop of St. Andrews doughter, for which I feind ane inclinatione from himselve and from severall of his relationes hier, which they thinke will be a mienes of frieing your family of many incumberances to which it is at present lyable. And it is expected yow will grant the same favore to him yow formerly consented to for the good of your family, and especialy to him for whom I know yow have so much keindnes, which otherwayse I ame affrayed maye put a stop to his mariadge. My wyfe giveth her humble service to yow, as we doe both to your Lord and children.—I rest, Dear Sister, Your affectionat brother and most humble servant,

F. MONTGOMERIE.

For THE EARLE OF FINDLATER

Edr., March the 10, 1686.

MY LORD,—Having the occasion of my brother Deskfoord going north I thought it my dutie to wreat to your Lo. this letter, by which you may be pleased to know that

---

[1] The Countess of Findlater.

seing he hes gained the Primats daughter her affection, and lykwayes hes goten the Bishops Ladys consent, and that nothing does hender my brothers mariage bot that the Primat is not yet returned from London, it is thought fit by all his relations hier that he should goe north, and indeavour against the Bishops coming to Scotland to be in some capacity to give ane jointur and lifrent sutable to what portion the Primat shal be pleased to give with his daughter. I doe not in the least doubt bot that your Lo. will doe all that lyes in your pouer for the standing of your family; and I doubt not bot my brother by this mariage may put it in ane very good condition. I doe not question bot my Lady my mother will goe ane great lenth for furthering of my brothers mariage, it being evident that it is the interest of the family, and will be very much for my brothers advantage, the Lady being both witie and discreit. As for the portion may be expected, and what lifrent may be desired by the Primat for his daughter, I shal leave that to my brother himselfe to give your Lo. ane accompt of. I have nothing more to wreat to you anent your affairs then what I wrot in the letter I sent with Morison, which I doubt not bot befor this time is come to your hands. The session will nou very shortly be over; and I resolve, God willing, immediatly after to be north. I shal not trouble your Lo. any further att present, bot that I am and shal alwayes continou to be, My Lord, Your Lo. most obedient son and most humble servant,   JA. OGILVIE.

I doe not question bot, as at this time your Lo. will look to the standing of your family, so you will be mindful of the interest of the rest of your childeren, and will see us som way secured att the puting my brother in the fee of your estate.

The following manuscript newsletter from London is given as a sample of these anticipations of the modern newspaper, almost the only printed paper of this period being the *London Gazette*. In this newsletter and in others of this reign accounts are given of the progress of European and domestic affairs.

London, 18th and 20th of May 1686.

OUR French letters say that the Kings ulcer is broke up again.

Yesterday Doctor Turner B^p of Elie took the oaths and test.

Yesterday the Queen Dowager went to Windsor, and after that goes to reside at Hampton Court this summer.

The camp begins on Saturday in Whitsun-week. The difference between the French and Spaniard is concluded for 250,000 crouns to be paid this summer and the like summe the next year.

The French have at sea 39 men of warre from 40 to 70 guns, 8 gallies, 9 fireships, and five small friggots. They are fitting out 20 sail more at Rocthfoord, and it is said are designed northward, wch putt the Dutch in some fear of their East India fleet.

The Duke of Lorrain having leave of the Emperour is gone to the army, and its said will open the campaigne with the siedge of Buda.

We have letters from Algiers wch say that Sir Thomas Soams his late Majesties ambassadour to the Grand Segniour was arrived there and kindly received by these corsiers, who declared to him that they would inviolably keep the peace concluded w^t England.

Our Venetian letters say that the Grand Vizier was parted from Adrianople with 16,000 Spachies and 6000 Janizaries to joyn the army, wch its said will be very numerous agt the Christians this summer ; that the Venetian fleet appearing before Constantinople made such a terrour among the people that the Grand Segniour had sent for him with his forces to keep his people in quietnesse. His Majesty hath ordered 47,000 libs to be sent unto Mr. Grossiers hands towards the paying the late Kings debts to his servants.

Cope of a private letter from E^{dr}, May 26, 1686. Being Weddensday the Pārlt sat this day, and therein were 3 acts past, one for dissolving some forfeited lands from the crown ; another appointing the magistrats of Ed^r to lay down such methods as the streets and turnpiks may be keept clean, and driving out of beggars, vagabonds, etc., and impowering the Lords of the Session to impose such a stent on all the inhabitants as may defray the charges yrof, and they are to see the same duly applied; another act declaring all recognitions to be burdened with the ground of an prior inhibition duly executed. The acts anent the summer session, and for ingathering of supplies, and anent the subscriving of all the executions and interloquitors were this day by an particular letter from the King touched with the scepter, and the Parliat adjourned till Friday. There was a comittee of 12 appointed for drawing the act anent moderation, etc. They mett several times but concluded nothing till yesterday; and there was a scroll drawn by the Arch Bp of St Andrews and the Bp of Edr allowing them private exercise of yr religion in families. It was expected to have come in Parliat but came not, but its beleeved the same will be sent up, and receive the Kings pleasure yranent.

I doubt not but you have heard Dr. Sibbald is returned Protestant to the satisfaction of some and displeasure of others.

London, May 22, 1686.

THE incampment in Holmsley heath will be opened on the 9th of June.

They write from Geneva that the magistrats of that city out of fear of being attacqued by the French and Savoyards keep gairds a leg round the citie, that the Switzers in their general assembly have resolved all the 13 cantons to defend Geneva in caice it be attacqued. They have made a reveiw of 16000 men, wch they have dispersed in several encampments in the countrey of Vaux.

The Queen and Princesse being indisposed hindered his Majesties coming hither yesterday. Her Majestie not being well stayes at Windsor.

From Holland they write that on the 27th their fleet sailed from the Texel consisting of 8 men of warre and 3 fire ships. They adde that great fire and lightening falling on the church and steeple in Tarvar in Holland destroyed it to the ground.

It is written from Ed^r, May 29, 1686, that the double of the act anent the penal statutes, as it is prepared by an Comittee of the Articles for the Articles and Parliat, is as followes :—

That Papists shall be under the protection of his Majesties government and laws, and shall not for the exercise of their worship and religion in private houses (all publick worship excepted) be under the hazard of any sanguinary or other punishments contained in the acts of Parliat. It is alwayes hearby expresly declared that this immunity and forbearance to Papists shall not import allowance or approbation of the Popish religion, nor evacuate nor take away the laws agt them, but that they shall remain in full force excepting in so farre as they are heirby innovated and restricted.

Several estates being forfeited and dissolved from the crown, the estate of Torwoodlie is gifted to the General,[1] and the estate of Kennedy of Grainge to the Provost of Ed^r. That yesterday a letter from his Majesty was read ordering Sir Geo. Lockart to be president and advocate both, whereby he may attend his Majesties concernment and interest in all places, that his prerogative suffer no detriment.

The three following letters from Mr. George Leslye, commissioner for Cullen, give account of the proceedings in the Scots Parliament. The feeling soon became so strong against the remission of the penal statutes against Roman Catholics, that a measure to remove these disabilities, though supported by the King, was not even tabled by the court party ; and Mr. Leslye expressed the prevailing opinion when he declared in his letter of June 12 that ' this Parliatt is the most renowned Parliatt hes bein heir thir many yeirs, ffor ther resolutiones in standing fixt to ther religione.'

The date of Lady Balcarres's death referred to in Mr. Leslye's letter of May 29, 1686, does not seem to be otherwise noted.

---

[1] General Drummond.

ffor THE EARLE OFF FFINDLATER thes

Edr., May 27, 1686.

MY LORD,—My sone going north, with him I have
givine your Lordship this trouble, and to give yow ane
accompt of our yesterdays acts of Parliament, which ware
four. The 1 act is wherin all forfeted lands holding of
uther superiores then the King are disjoyned from the
croune and patremoney thereof. The 2 act is ane
gift of Earlstones forfeter with some other lands in
fawores of ane Sir Theophelus Ogillthorpt and Maine,[1]
Inglesh men, for ther servece done att Boduellbridge. The
3 act is wherin all inhebitiones dulie execute in tyme
coming doeth afect lands for proper debt therin contained
against ward and taxward wasels lands, althogh the
samen bee disponed in wholl or for the most pairt without
the superiors consent, notwithstanding of anie regog-
nitione may folowe therupone. The 4 act is ane act
maide appoynting the magistrats of Edr. by the consent
and owersight of the Lords of Sesione to uphold and
rectefie the streets and laines of the citie, and to cause
cleinge the samen, and allso to purge the samen of wago-
bonds and beigers, anent which act ther was great debeat.
They are obleidged yeirly to doe this under the failzie
of ane thousand pund, and they are to impose upon
the toune and inhabitents for what may defray this
nesesary expens. Dewk Hamiltoune and maney with
him wold have had it comitted to the owersight of the
Lords of the Secret Counsell, and not to the Lords of
Sesione. It was first woted, and the Lords of the Sesione
caried it by tuo wots only. It was woted againe by Dewk
Hamiltons intersesione, aledging the wotts not to have
beine right marked by Sir Alexander Gibsone, and wold
have had Sir William Patersone to have owerseine the
marking of the wots; and being againe receited they fell
to be equall, and so sisted at the Chanclers woll, who
disyded it in fawores of the Lords of Sesione. Ther was
5 acts yesterday tucht by the sheptore, the act anent

---

[1] *The Acts of the Parliaments of Scotland*, vol. viii. pp. 323 and 586.

the summer sesione, the act anent the yooll wacuence, the act anent the subscryving wittness, the act anent the subscryving of all interloquiters pronunced be all judges, and the act anent his Majesties supplie. This with the former account givne to your Lordship is the sum of all as yet done. The Parliament againe sits the morow. Ther is [no]thing as yet come in anent the penull statuts. I am informed that Deuk Hamiltone and the Chancler does not agree so weill upon that poynt, which with my servece to your Lordship, to my Lady, and all your famelie at present is all from, My Lord, Your Lordships werie affectionet and obleidged servantt,

GEO. LESLYE.

Turn over.

MY LORD,—In my letter sent yow last week by Arnbaths [1] man I gave your Lo^p some account off your son my Lo. Deskfoords mariadge, qch stands in the same terms I then wreit off to your Lo^p, and I apprehend it will nott goe forward. It is fitt your Lo^p both wreit to your sone and to my Lord Boynd theranent. I am not wanting (as in duty I am oblidged) to give my Lo. Deskfoord my weak adwyse swa farr as I am capable; and will not, so farr as I can, consent to any thing that may reflect upon him, or baffle him; and desyres him to be encurradged not to have any mor thoughts that way, since I find obstructions. Iff your Lo^p be weill stored wt grass this yeir in your park, I intreit the ffawour that my hors may have libertie in it a whyle, till I come home and prowyd for him; and this will be additione to former obliga^{o}ns your Lo^p hes been pleased to shew me. My Lo. Boynd and Mr. Oswald [2] now understanes other pretty weill; and er long I hop wee all may come to ane full cleiring. This morning I am told the King is acquanted wt all our precedours, and who are his ffrinds and who nott. I sall labour by the Saterdays post to give your Lo^p ane account off our acts and newes qch passes to morrow. I had allmost fforgott to tell your Lo^p how — Mill, Provest off Linlith-

---

[1] Alexander Hay of Arnbath, Fordyce, Banffshire.
[2] James Oswald of Fingaltoun.

gow, last night now hes declaired himself in oppositione to the passing off the penall statuts, or to any thing that looks lyke ane tolleratione to the Papists, both to the Commissioner and Chancellour; and ffreely told them he wold divest himself off all his publict imployments befor he consented that way. And I doubt not bot your Lo^p hes heard off Doctor Sibbald conversione, who this last Sabbath wes in church, and is willing to subject himself to any pennance our clergie will putt upon him for his apostatiseing.

George Leslye's 'sone' was Patrick Leslye of Melross, Banff-shire. On 10th September 1703 he was appointed conjunct Sheriff Clerk with his father. From 1705 to 1714 he was County Collector. He died between 13th August and 1st September 1714.

ffor THE EARLE OFF FFINDLATER thes

Egr., May 29, —86.

MY LORD,—Bot the other day I gawe your Lo^p the trouble off ane letter by my sone, q^ch with thes I suppose all may come to your hands about on and the same tyme, and sall referr your Lo^p much to that letter as to our news. Yesterday ther past only tuo acts in Parliatt, the first ane gift off Torwoodlies ffortune and forfaulter in ffawours off Generall Drummond, the second ane gift off Grange Kennedies estait in the present Prowest of Egr his ffawours Sir Thomas Kennedie. Its said to be bot ane small thing. The Parliatt is adjourned till Wedensday nixt, my Lady Ballcarras [1] corps being to be interred on Tuesday. Ther is nothing as yet come in as to the penall statuts; bot yesternight I did see from ane wery noble lord off good intelligence, ane relatione off your Lo^p, the draught of that bitt actie so termed now heir, who told me he thought it wold come in not by the Articles, bot rather by the Commissioner [2] by wertew off the Kings prerogatiwe power. By the nixt your Lo^p sall hear further; and iff I can sall send yow the double off that act. Your sone

---

[1] Jean Carnegie, eldest daughter of David, second Earl of Northesk.
[2] The Earl of Moray.

my Lo. Deskfoord is in good health. His first designs are now altogither giwen over; and some off his noble ffrinds are thinking to engadge him some other way, qr he may hawe ane ffarr greater competencie to his qualitie, in qch I think he should be encurradged, and off qch mor efterwards iff any such thing be proposed. Mr Oswald hes been so taken up wt his wyff this tuo or three days being in childbirth, that he cannot be spoken too; bot I think the nixt week may putt ane close to that effeir. Ther are great solemnities heir this day, and the Provest off Egr is to giwe the Commissioner ane great treat.—So being in hast this is all save that I am truly, My Lord, Your Los wery affec°nat and oblidged serwant, Geo. Leslye.

For THE EARLE OFF FFINDLATER thes

Egr., June 12, —86.

My Lord,—I hawe the honour off both your letters, the on off the 24 May last, the other off the dait the 4 current by this bearer, and am glade to hear that your Lop and familie are weill; and I doubt not bot befor this tyme your Lop hes my former letters sent yow both by my sone and post. I can say little further as to John Innes effeir, till it pleas God wee all be north, and I hop all things sall terminat then to your Los. and all our satisfactions, who may be concerned in that matter. I hawe not as yet cleired fully wt Mr. Oswald. I have fully completed him in mōy, except that qch concerns my Lo. Boynd his exemptions with some militia receipts, all qch will certeinly allow. Bot the truth is dureing this sessione off Parliātt all have been so hurried and tist, that I cannot gett all things so instantly exped till this heat be ower, qch I hope will now be wery shortlie. And I think since maters are so Lyfftennant Sharp needs not exspect from our shyre, except it be ane complement; ffor I am necessitate to supplicat the Lords off Theasourrie to gett allowance off thes things, considering all things and some little differences and mistaks being betuixt the receiwers, so that I cannot gett them to meett to cleir wt me; but if the

Parliatt wer ower I hop wee sall soon cleir all thes things. The Parliatt sitts on Moonday, and its thought then will adjourn or rather dissolwe. The Commissioner is to goe up once the nixt week. I sall referr your Lo^p to the inclosed ane account of the acts of Parliatt past since I wrote last and prior to this daite. Muretoun wes knighted att Dinnibisle last day, and now called in rolls of Parliatt Sir James Callder. My Lord, pardon the trouble to caus deliwer the inclosed to the Baylies off Cullen. This Parliatt is the most renouned Parliatt hes been heir thir many yeirs, ffor ther resolutiones in standing fixt to ther religione, qch I hear is much approwen by our nighbour natione England. I giwe my humble duty to your Lo^p to my Lady, and to all your ffamilie.—So being hasted att the tyme, this is all from, My Lord, Your Lo. wery affec°natt and most humble serwant,   GEO. LESLYE.

My Lord, just as I wes to seall this letter I had yours by fforskans [1] sone.

Henceforth James, in England as well as in Scotland, ruled without a Parliament, freely using his prerogative in carrying out his policy.

The key to the disagreement between Lord Boyne and his Lady disclosed in the following letters of 1st, 2nd and 26th October 1686, and more incidentally referred to in the letters of the 27th of November and 21st of December 1686, is found in Fountainhall's note of 11th March 1686: 'Campbell of Calder, younger, invades and affronts Ogilvie of Boyne at 12 o'clock, after he had come of the bench (being Lord of the Session) and spat in his face in the High street of Edinburgh. The cause was, he was said to have lyen with Boyne's lady, daughter of Earle of Eglintoun.' On the 27th April following, Lady Boyne's brother, Francis Montgomerie, in a letter to his sister, writes: 'Sinc the sad breach betuixt my Ladie Ann and her Lord is too notour, I only express myself trulie afflicted therwith and wishes heartilie an reparation.' .

---

[1] William Gordon of Farskane, Rathven, Banffshire.

For THE COUNTES OF FFENLATER

Boyne, 1 *day October* 1686.

DEIR SISTER,—The suden surpryse of ye death of my neise Lady Margrat Montgomerie hes exceidinglie troubled me, who dyed of a fever fyve weiks agoe. I trusted to my Lord Boyns promese in seinding to Abd. to bring a meidwyfe to bring me to bed, in a chaire ; and now when I expect he should doe it will not condiscend, so I send [thr]ie dollers and intraits ye will send a fott man with this inclosed to my Lady Abd., who will send ye meidwyfe, as she wrets in her letter qch I have sent to you. My Lady Abd. is at Abd. and not att Colley.[1] I regrat ye conditione of my Lady Mary ; bot I hope it will [not] be ane stop to my satisfactione in seing yow, qch I long for, for ye gellding ye use to ryde on is redy to wait on yow when ye please ; and I have sēall simptoms that I cannot be long befor I be brought to bed. Ye thrie dollers are to hyre a horse to ye medwyfe, and ane other for ye chair. Hopeing yt I shall hear good neuse of my deir neises being better and ye confort of sieing yew, I shall not give farder troublee at present ; onlie if ye have any love for me ye will obey this desyre, for I am her who is Your most affectionat sister and humble servant,

ANNA OGELVIE.

Octob. 2, 86.

MY LORD,—I cannot expres the trowble my wyfs deport-ment hath occasoned me sinc I saw yow ; but I most endevor to bear all the best I can. I cannot rationally mentin to be in a hows with her, sinc burning is the least she threattins ; and banish myself from my owen hows I cannot ; but she most resolve to goe somwher and be brought to bed. I shall not spair monie on her expenc, but in my hows she shall never com. I wish som of her freinds deall with her to goe to som convenient pleac, and not expos herself mor then she hath done, to be the talk of all who hear of her. Sinc yowr Lo. wes pleased to call for me this day I judged it my dewtie to let yow

---

[1] Kelly, now Haddo House, Methlic, Aberdeenshire.

know my thoughts in this affair.—I am, My Lo., Yowr most humble servant,   PATRICK OGILVIE.

ffor THE EARLE OFF FFINDLATER thes

Banff, Oct. 26, —86.

MY LORD,—I hawe presumed to giwe your Lo^p this trouble, tho perhaps it come unseasoneablie to your hands, and thought ffitt to tell that my Lady Ann, Boynds Lady, is now heir att my hous.   I am sory I hawe not accomodatione for hir, that is suitable to on off hir qualitie ; but as it is shee is wery wellcome to it.   It wer tedious to giwe your Lo^p account of all the passadges off this day, and I sall only modestly say shee meetts with a little seweritie and hardship.   Shee is heir on hir road ffor Abd.; and this same night I hawe taken the ffreedome to wreit to my Lord Boynd, to qch letter I caused Achmedden [1] (who is att this place as yet) subjoyne ane post script.   And both off us are pressing with Boynd to come in heir to morrow, and speak wt hir, and bot consent that ane midwyff ffrom Abd. be sent for by some discreet person to be brought hither.   Its lyk maters may be composed, and off all ewills the best is to be chosen ; and on thir terms probablie shee may be perswaded to stay in this toun, and rather in the ministers hous heir then in any place els.   Wher ffor since shee cannott be att the Boynd, she will stay in no place qrin he is interested ; so iff my Lord Boynd come in and consent to hir propositione its lyk maters may be settled.   And iff not I find hir positiwe shee will goe forward to Abd. tho shee trawell bot ane myle in the day on ffoott.   So since your Lo^p is to be att the Boynd to morrow morning, my weak opinion is, that ye wold be a little the mor tymelie, and truly tho Boynd wold dissent to come in, I wold adwyse your Lo^p to perswad him to come in, and to come alongst wt him, and I doubt not bot Achmedden being heir this effeir may be taken up by adwyse and the mediatione off ffrinds.   I sall leawe thes to your Lo^ps consideratione ; bot I think it necessarie ye

---

[1] Sir James Baird, Sheriff-Principal of Banffshire.

come in and bring my Lord Boynd alongst wt your Lo^p, for both prudence, and I may ewen say charitie is to be obserwed in such caices. I think it not ffitt my Lord Boynd see this letter, or know that your Lo^p hes hard from me, but let all flow simply as from yourself.—And I am in all duty, My Lord, Your Los. very affec°nat and oblidged servant,   GEO. LESLYE.

In the following letter Mr. James Ogilvie, writing to his mother, gives her the current social gossip of Edinburgh.

For THE COUNTES OF FINDLATER

Edr., Nor. the 27th, 1686.

MADAM,—I received the honor of your La. letter with very great satisfaction ; because it gave me the assurance of your being in good health, and I was exceedingly affrayed it had been otherwayes, considering the pains and trouble your La. was att about us when wee were unweal. The Dutches of Hamiltoun is in the toun, and I did neaver see her look better. Your sister [1] is come to the toune, bot her child is not as yet christned, neither is there any appeerence of of ane reconciliation betuix her Lord and her. Your uncle [2] the Major General's lady [3] is maried [4] to one liftennan Douglas,[5] ane brother of Kilheads, which will certainly be much to the prejudice of her children. There hath been ane report here that my Lady Mountrose was to be maried with John Bruce, Sir William Bruce his son, bot I hear this day that she hes discharged him her lodgings. Since the Dutches of Hamiltoun and several others of your freinds are in toune, if your La. wreat to them, I shal deliver your letters. Your brother, Mr. Francis, does frequently ask kindly for you. I have nou nothing more that is worthy of your notice to

---

[1] Lady Boyne.
[2] Robert Montgomerie, fifth son of the sixth Earl of Eglintoun.
[3] Elizabeth, daughter of James Livingstone, first Viscount Kilsyth.
[4] The *Scots Peerage*, vol. iii. p. 450, places this marriage 'before 24 January 1688.'   [5] George Douglas.

give your La. ane accompt of.—So shal only add that I am, Madam, Your La. most obedient son and most humble servant,   JA. OGILVIE.

I give my humble service to all my brothers and sisters.

In the following letter we get a glimpse of the ways and means of upholding the post in Scotland.

ffor THE EARLE OFF FFIND[LATER]

Banff, Nor. 27, 86.

MY LORD,—I had the honour off yours this morning. My wyff and I are weill, and att your Lo^s serwice; and both off us are oblidged to wish all health to your Lo^p and prosperitie to your ffamilie. Immediatlie efter receipt off yours I sent to inhibite James Gordon from goeing to Cullen till Tuesday nixt as your Lo^p desyres. Ther are nott any news come to this place by our last post, the postmaster Mr. Mill being gone to Edr., bot I suppose by the nixt wee may have some. James Baird wreits to me that Lady Ann is not yet com ower ffrom the North Queens, and that hir child is not as yet christened. Our post is now lyk to decay and will not goe to Abd. againe bot once, till he againe be reestablished. I wold be glad to hawe your Lo^s opinione in this, or iff you be content to contribute ffor another yeir. Boynd befor he went away told me he wold contribute, and wold hawe it to continow. Iff ther be any difficultie it will be by this toun, who scruples a little, yet I apprehend they will be perswaded to continow as formerly. Sir George Mackenzie hes putt on the goun againe as ane ordinary adwocat. I will wait on your Lo^p once the nixt week. Till then and allways I am bound to be, My Lord, Your Lo^s wery faithfull and oblidged servant,

                                    GEO. LESLYE.

In 1685 London, notwithstanding the King's wish, had cele- brated the anniversary of the Gunpowder Plot on the 5th of

November in the old style. This year bonfires had been reluctantly omitted.

ffor THE EARLE OFF FFINDLATER

My Lord,—I receaved yor Lo^s leter to yor son Mr. James, and shall be carefull to delliver it to him out of my oune hand. I tak jorney from hence on Tuesday morning be day is light (God willing). Kindlie saluting yor Lo., my Lady, and all yor noble familie, I am, My Lord, Yo^r Lo^s most affectionat and humble servant,

Jo. Gordoun.[1]

Banff, 31 Nor. 1686.

Last newes leters beare that the 5 of Nor. was punctualie observed at London, but no bondfyres. The princes was at sermon in the chapell royall.

With his relative Sir Patrick Ogilvie, Lord Boyne, on the bench in those days of influence and 'moyen' Mr. James Oglivie's practice at the bar grew rapidly. We had besides the backing of other powerful relatives in the Hamiltons and Eglintouns ; and the following letter to his mother shows that these and other influences were being worked.

For THE COUNTES OF FINDLATER

Edr., Decr. the 21st, 1686.

Madam,—I received the honour of your La. letter, and did deliver the inclosed to Mr. Francis Mountgomerie, who promised to wreat to your La. I had the honour to see the Dutches of Hamiltoun this day. She did ask very kindly for your La., and desired me to tel you she wondered that you did not wreat to her. And when your La. does it, I intreat you may be pleased to desir her Grace may speak to the Duke to countenance me, for his countenance would be of great use to me. I am this affternoon to see the Archbishop of Santandrus who is to give me his imployment. I am to be this vacance with Tillibody,[2] for he hes very kindly invited me to the

---

[1] Bailie of Banff, and captain of the burgh militia.

[2] George Abercromby, cadet of the Abercrombies of Birkenbog, and ancestor of Sir Ralph Abercromby.

countrey.   I have presumed to send your La. two duzen
of limons.   They are not worthy of your La. acceptance,
bot I sent them because I know you can make good use
of them.   My Lord Boyn and his Lady are not yet recon-
ciled.   All the rest of your La. relations are weal; and
having nothing more worthy of your La. notice to give
you ane accompt of, I shal only add that I am, Madam,
Your La. most obedient sone and most humble servant,

JA. OGILVIE.

In pursuance of his religious policy, James, on 25th December
1686, had, with unusual finesse summoned Sir John Dalrymple,
though a whig, to London.   That supple politician returned to
Edinburgh King's Advocate on 11th February 1687.   With
strange perversity the King, on 7th January 1687, accentuated
the opposition to himself in England by depriving his Protestant
brother-in-law Lawrence Hyde, Earl of Rochester, of his office as
Treasurer of England.   These and other matters are referred to
in the following letter.

For THE EARLE OF FINDLATER, ABD. TO BANFFE

Edr., January 13th, 1687.

MY LORD,—Since I wrote last to your Lo. I have had the
honour to receive tuo letters from you ; and in obedience
to the first I shal deliver your Lo. letter to the Earle of
Strathmor, and shal end business with him whenever
he comes to the toune.   I shal lykwayes obey your Lo.
commands in the second in advanceing the money due by
the toune of Cullen to ye Exchequer.   I have nothing
to wreat to your Lo. concerning your affairs more then
I have writne formerly ; bot probably by the nixt occasion
your Lo. will get ane accompt hou your money in Mour-
tons [1] hand will be disposed of.

Wee have no neues in this place, bot that Sir John
Dalrympel is called to court ; and it's expected both his
father and he will be in favour with the King.   The
Tresurary in England is put out of his place, and it is

---

[1] Sir James Calder of Muirton, Inverness-shire.

turned in ane commission. Liftennan Colonel Windrom is Lifennant of the Castel in Major White's place. The Chancelour hes been dangerously ill of the colick, and is not as yet fuly recovered. It is nou talked by thos, who understand the affairs of the court, that Pitmedens [1] place will be bestoued upon Mr. Malkom [2] ane advocat. Wee have no more neues hier att present, bot when they occur your Lo. shal have ane accompt of them; so att present shal give your Lo. no further trouble, bot shal close when I have wished your Lo., my Lady and my brothers and sisters ane happy neu year, which is all frome, My Lord, Your Lo. most obedient sone and most humble servant,   JA. OGILVIE.

The recall of the commissions of the Privy Councillors and of the Judges of the Court of Session concentrated more power in the hands of the King, making the members more amenable to court influence. This policy was characteristic of Charles II. and of James.

For THE EARLE OF FINDLATER

Inshmartin, May 3d, 1687.

MY LORD,—I could not let this bearer goe without performing my duty to your Lo. in wreating to you and giving you ane accompt of our jorney. My Lord Boyn and I came both together to Pourie, and I blees God none of us the worse of our jorney; and he then went for Edr., and I came here. I shal not trouble your Lo. with business til I be att Edr., and then you may expect ane ful accompt of your affairs by the first sure occasion. I have heard no neues bot that the King hes recaled al the comissions to the Prive Counsel and Session, and is to send down neu comissions to such of them as he hes

---

[1] Sir Alexander Seton of Pitmedden, Aberdeenshire, Lord Pitmedden.
[2] Alexander Malcolm of Lochore, afterwards Lord Lochore.

service for.   I beg pardon for this trouble and I am,
Your Lo. most obedient son and faithful servant,

JA. OGILVIE.

In August 1687 the Countess of Findlater died.

For THE EARLE OF FFINDLATERRE

MY LORD,—I ame verie sorie of your Lordships loss of
my dear sister, and I ame sure nixt to you and your
children non cane be more sensible of our misfortune
then my-selve, haveing loosed so keind and ane affectionat sister.   I intreat your Lo. wold be pleased to give
my humble service to all your children, and belive I shall
alwayes continou to wish you and them all happines and
shall ever remaine, My Lord, Your Lo. affectionat brother,
and most humble servant,   F. MONTGOMERIE.

Inshlesly, Agust 15, 1687.

For THE EARLE OF FINDLATER

Hamilton, 18 *August* 1687.

MY LORD,—I received yours with the notice of your
Ladys death which my wife and I does heartely regrate,
and are very sory for the great lose yʳ Lo. and your famely
has by the want of so fine a lady.   If it be in our pouer
to controbute any thing to you or you famelys interrest,
yʳ Lo. may friely comand us.   My wife remembers her
humble service to yow, and I am, My Lord, your Lo. most
affecᵗ humble servant,   HAMILTON.

For THE EARLE OF FINDLATER

Edr., January 14, 1688.

MY LORD,—Since I wrote to your Lo. with Mr. David
Cuming, ther hes nothing occured concerning your Lo.
affairs worthy of your notice.   I have according to your
Lo. command sent you north some books.   I have sent
you one that was not in your commission to Mr. Ogstoun.
It is the Amours of the Duke of Munmouth and my Lord

Gray.   Wee have no neues bot that it is thought that if
Collentoun [1] die, my Lord Advocat will get his place, and
Sir George Mackenzie will be reponed to his oune pleace.
My Lord Milfort's daughter is maried to the Master of
Strathalan ; and yong Boyn within ane week or tuo
is to be maried with Mistres Anna Arnot.   I have sent
you your stafe.   I doe not know if it will pleas your Lo.,
bot it hes been trice meade.—This is all the trouble att
present from, My Lord, Your Lo. most obedient son and
most humble servant,   JA. OGILVIE.

The anticipations regarding Sir George Mackenzie in course
materialised, as will be seen from Mr. James Ogilvie's letter of
the 20th February 1688.

John Drummond, second son of James, third Earl of Perth,
created on the 14th April 1685 Viscount, and on the 12th August
1686 Earl of Melfort, was Secretary of State for Scotland
during the reign of James.   He was a zealous convert to Roman
Catholicism, and afterwards followed his King into exile.   His
daughter Elizabeth married William, who became second Viscount
of Strathallan.

James Ogilvie younger of Boyne, eldest son of Lord Boyne,
duly married Mrs. Anna Arnot before 20th February 1688.
Returned as one of the Members of Parliament for Banffshire in
1702, he strongly opposed the Union.   He was active in the
Jacobite movements of 1707-8, and was in consequence outlawed.   He was also out in the '15·   We shall hear more of him
hereafter.

For THE EARLE OF FINDLATER thes

Edr., January 30, 1688.

MY LORD,—The accompt I had from the chamerlan of
the continuence of your Lo. wealbeing was ane very great
satisfaction to me.   He gave me lykwayes ane accompt
of your Lo. frugality in manadging your family, which does
clearly shou hou much your Lo. has been formerly abused
by your servants.   I have been seeking for ane cook to
your Lo., bot as yet I can find none that can both serve
in the kitching and beakhouse ; houever I shal doe what

---

[1] Sir James Foulis of Colinton, Justice-Clerk.

lyes in my pouer to get one befor my northcoming. My Lord Northesk is desirus wee transact with him ; and if I kneu of any money in the north that might be raised att Whitsonday nixt I would end with him, for I am informed that his phisitians does not rekon that he can live above ane year, and if he wer dead ther would be no possibility of transacting with his sone, he being a minor. I expect to hear from your Lo. anent this. For all that I know yet, ther is nothing will hender me from coming north just affter the session ; so I desir your Lo. may send over Anderson against the beginning of the first week of March with my oune horse, bot I resolve to buy one for my servant to ryd uppon. Ther is great talking hier that the Duke of Hamiltoun is to come doun Tresierer, and that Sir John Harper is to be one of the Lords of the Session. The King of France and Parlament att Paris have declared that the Pope is only first Bishop, and hes no pouer to excomunicat bot for maters mierly ecclesiastik, and that his excommunicating of Leuarden is most redicolus and unjust. Ther is no other neues att present, bot what the bearer will give you ane accompt of ; and therfor I shal give your Lo. no further trouble att present, bot add that I am, My Lord, Your Lo. most obedient son and most humble servant, JA. OGILVIE.

The struggle for place with an autocratic King was incessant. The letter of the 20th February shows that Hamilton was at this time unsuccessful in this pursuit.

Edr., Februar 20, 1688.

MY LORD,—I beg pardon for detaining your footman so long ; bot the true reason of it was that I was att Boyns mariage for five dayes altogether, and it being the throngest time of our session I had no time for providing what was writtne for til nou. Your Lo. will receive from the bearer ane periwig and ane pair of blak gloves conform to your order. I have caused help your Lo. suord. I would have givne it ane neu handle, bot I could see none better then whatt it had befor. I have lykwayes sent you the garden seeds conform to the not your Lo. sent me. I have not as yet setled with Northesk, for his Lady's death did hender his coming to the toune. As for neus wee have none bot that the Countes of Weems is dead and the Earle of Southesk and my Lady Semple did both die this last week. Sir John Dalrympel is made Justice Clerk, and Sir George Mackenzie is made Advocat ; and it is reported that the Earle of Marr is to be reponed to his place in the Castel of Stirling. The Duke of Hamiltoun is come doun, but it is not thought that he hes great court. I am nou hopful shortly to see your Lo., for I expect my horse against the third of March ; and if your Lo. have any further commands for me, I expect them with Anderson, and they shal punctualy be obeyed by, My Lord, Your Lo. most obedient son and most humble servant,

JA. OGILVIE.

Mr. James Ogilvie, probably early in June 1688, married Anne, daughter of William Dunbar of Durn, a neighbour of his father in Banffshire. The following letter refers to this event and to the Earl's purpose, afterwards carried out, of conveying his estate past Lord Deskford, who had become a Roman Catholic, to Mr. James his second son.

ffor OUR LOVING SON MASTER JAMES OGILVIE

The 18th of Junie '688.

LOVING SON,—I heave received ane letter from your Lady in ansuer of one I sent hir, to see hou she was. I will troulie say I did not expect to had seen one of hir breeding wreat such sence in such well connected tearmes. I did see three other letters of hirs all of different subjects to verie good purpose. God Almightie bliss her to you, and grant that ye and she may be to my familie as Jacob and Rachell wear to the Isralitts. I heave at this time little to wreat to you, butt heaving so sure ane occasion I cannot butt desier you to remember to consult your bussines of the convayence of my esteat in your person ; for although Walter be nou in my house, yett be his still frequenting the Popish chappell and continouing in odd and most unacountable actions, ther can be no good expected of him, so ye need to be the mor circumspect in garding your selfe against his evell. I am verie sorie the victuall sent south with the chamberland came to so litle effect. I pray you take course with the rest of it. I intreat you gett monie from my Lord Boind, and putt my doughters outt of murning, for poore things I will not discourage them. Any letters ye wreat to your Lady, if they come to my hands, I shall transmitt them to hir ; for I intend frequentlie to send to see hou she does. I pray you present my service to my Lord Boind and to his son and his Lady, and lett me knoue when they are expected north. I thinke verie long to hear from you. So wishing the Lord to bliss you in all your just under-takings, I shall add no more butt that I am Your loving father,   FFINDLATER.

I reffer severall things to the bearer.

Rumours of a descent on England and Scotland by the Prince of Orange reached the north before the expedition finally sailed on the 1st of November 1688. On the 5th of October Sir George Gordon of Edinglassie and Carnousie, conjunct Sheriff-Principal of Banffshire, writing to the Earl of Findlater gives him an account of a false but prevalent report, that William had landed on the coast of Yorkshire; and recounts other news of the day regarding the situation in England, and the measures taken in Scotland to cope with the threatened invasion.

My Lord,—I receaved your Lops this morning, and you may bee sure wherin I can I will serve you. I had advertisment from my Lord Aberdein this morning, which maks mee delay taking journey while Wednsdays morning. For news I have account that the Dutch are landed at Brilington Bay and are on ther march for York. Ther number is said to bee fourtie five thousand fighting men—Prince Orange generall, cald genrall of the Protestant League, and Marishall Shomberg livetenant generall. The Lord Dartsmouth was ordered by the King to put the fleet to sea and to feght them, tho ther number wer double ; but he told the King that he neither found oficier souldier or sea man willing to doe ther dutie. Nether was the navie in conditione for it, though ther number had bein equall, which account troubled the King verie much ; and it is talked that the fleet is nou come in again. By a leter from Melfort to the Councell it is enformed that the Dutch intends 15 of ther fleet for Scotland, fiftie other ships with 10 or 15 thousand men, so that he advised the Counsell and Session to remove to Stirling. Ther is on Captan Wallace appoynted with tuo companies of foot to guard Drumond Castle. The King efter christning of the Prince declared solemnly in Councell that he was the Queens chyld, requyring the Queen douager with many Protestant witnes to depon upon ther having sein him born, which accordingly they did. The King is to bee at the head of his armie himself and to keep them neir London. Queensberie and Castles are called to sit in Councell. I am, My Lord, your Lōps most faithfull and obedient servant, G. GORDONE.

Carnoussie, 5 Octor. 1688.

William landed at Torbay on Monday the 5th of November. The following letter of the 22nd November from the Minister of Banff gives an account of the news that had then reached the north regarding the invasion, and the measures taken earlier that month in England and Scotland to meet the crisis. The reference to Balfour of Burleigh, one of the assassins of Archbishop Sharp, and to William's relations with him, is of interest.

Forr THE EARLE OF FINDLATER

MY LORD,—I would have according to your Lo^{ps} direction by our post have sent an expresse, if we had received any news of import. The black box was said to have been taken out Dumbar, and so we had no news with the last post. I saw a private letter, wch gave account that though the Prince of Orange was certainly landed, yet the place where and the number of his forces is not given account of. I am jealous, if matters were going with the court partie as they desire, we should not be keept in the mist as we are. It is said the King hes displayed his standard ; and on the 9th of November, when at night he gott the news of the Dutch landing, he sent of a battalion of Irish to the west of England, comanded the forces that had gone to the north to countermarch to the west, and called for the Mair and Aldermen of London and desired them, if he should happen to fall in battell, that they should proclaim the Prince of Wales King; but we heard nothing of their answer.   It is reported Philipsburg is retaken by the Germans.   The French lost many of their nobilitie in the taking, and in the Germans recovery of it; and the Dauphine is sore wounded.   This is said to have been reported by a Leith skipper, who very lately came ther from Holland or France, I know nott whiche.   There is a proclamation issued out by the Councill of Scotland inhibiting the reading of the Prince of Orange manifesto and the declaration of the States of Holland, and prohibiting the telling any news to the disheartening of the Kings subjects, so that *vera dicere est periculosum*, if it be against the court interest.   We had an account that one of the murderers of the Primate of St. Andrews, Balfour, being fordbid the company of the Prince of Orang, who told he would have no known murderer in his service, is arrived in Scotland, and hes gott together in the south wast about a thousand men, on what designe is not known.   What truth is in this we expect to know by this nights post.   If he bring any considerable news, I shall send an expresse to your Lop. with them. We have a sad breach in this place this morning by the death of William Fife one of our ballies, who was worth many in this place.   I heartilie commend your Lop. and all your noble familie to the divine grace, and am, My Lord, Your Lo^{ps} most humble devoted and faithfull servant,

MR. PAT. INNES.

Banff, Novr. 22, 1688.

By the 22nd of November the north and west of England had risen in William's favour.   Rapidly the bulk of James's officers and army deserted, and he was forced to return to London.   After fruitless negotiations with William, on the 11th December 1688, he left the capital for France; and his reign came to an end, William becoming King *de facto* in his stead. England forthwith allied herself with the European combination against King Louis of France.

CHAPTER II

LETTERS DURING THE REIGN OF WILLIAM AND MARY
FROM 1689 TO 1693

ON the 7th of January 1689 the Scots noblemen and gentlemen in London met at Whitehall under the presidency of the Duke of Hamilton, and two days later requested William to call a Convention of the Estates of Scotland, and meantime to undertake the military and civil administration. The Duke of Hamilton, now in political power for the first time, drew his relative the Earl of Findlater to the side of the revolution settlement, and got him commission to embody and command the fencible men of Banffshire. The following letter to the Earl from Patrick Steuart of Tannachy, Banffshire, an ancestor of the Steuarts of Auchlunkart, shows the commission in course of execution.

For THE EARLE OFF FFINDLATER

MY LORD,—Not being at home when yōr Lōp's letter cam to my house, I hav sent this to let yōr Lōp know that I can not conveniently get the cuntrie rendevowed this week by reason of the Elgin fair, which drawes most of them away ; bot God willing on Munday next I shall conveen the western parte of Rathven paroch, and on Tuysday therafter Bamffshire parte of the paroch of Bellie, and therafter yōr Lōp shall hav ane acompt. I now daylie expect our Duk home, and if I by this post get aney assurance of his dyet yōr Lōp shall hav ane accompt from Yōr Lōp most obedient srvand, P: STEUART.

Tanachy, ij feb. (89)

The Duke of Gordon did not come north, but remained in Edinburgh in command of the Castle, which he held for James until 13th June 1689.

There was surcease of justice in the Court of Session from

November 1688 to November 1689; and Mr. James Ogilvie advocate and his wife during part of that time were in residence at Pittulie, a small estate west of Fraserburgh, belonging to the Cumines of Lochterlandich Mortlach, now represented by the Cumines of Auchry, Aberdeenshire. Mr. James Chalmers,[1] recommended in the following letter for the vacant charge of Cullen parish, was chaplain to the Earl of Erroll. He was the son of Mr. William Chalmers minister of Fettercairn. He was admitted minister of Cullen on 8th May 1689, and was deprived in 1695.

For THE EARLE OF FINDLATER thes

Pittulie, febru. 16, 1689.

My Lord,—I just nou received tuo letters in favours of Mr. Chamers, one from the Countes of Marischal and ane other from my Lord Boyn. I find, if your Lo. pleases to place Mr. Chamer in your church of Cullen, it will be taken kindly by ane great many of your relations ; bot since he has such recommendations att least your Lo. should hear him preach, and if he pleas you, I think you cannot bestou your church onn any so generaly commended. I have inclosed my Lady Marshal's letter to me, by which your Lo. will see so eanrest as my Lady is, that you grant the presentation presently. I am resolved shortly to wait onn your Lo. att Cullen, and therfor att present I shal not trouble your Lo. any further, bot shal only add that I am, My Lord, Your Lo. most obedient son and most humble servant,   Ja. Ogilvie.

My wife gives your Lo. and my sisters her most humble service.

Through his father's influence James Ogilvie was on the 1st of March returned commissioner for the Royal Burgh of Cullen to the Convention of Estates, which met in Edinburgh on 14th March. This was his first election to the Scots Parliament. He was not a member of the 1681 Parliament as stated by some authorities.

---

[1] Dr. Cramond, *The Church and Churchyard of Cullen*, p. 78.

For MASTER JAMES OGILVIE son to the EARL OF FINDLATUR   att   Edr.

to be delivered with car

March the 29, 1689.

My Dearist,—Your leatter did give very much satisfaction to me, and your resolution of coming hom ; for as I still beliued my self unhappy when you was from me, so nou I think I haue mor reason then ever to think so, when you are in a pleas wher ther is so much confousion and danger. I wish the Lord may preserve and protat you ; for I beliue ther was never a tym wher in popel had mor reason to diseyr that ernastly then nou. I shall not trubl you longer, but to intreat that you may not chines your resolution, but com hom hou sun you can, and that I am till dath, Dear heart, Your most affectionat and fathful   Anna Ogilvie.

On the 4th of April James Ogilvie is said to have voted against the resolution of the Convention declaring the throne vacant and settling it on William and Mary.[1]

On the 18th of April, in view of Dundee's activity, an act was passed for a levy of five hundred horsemen out of the several shires of Scotland, of which forty-four were apportioned to Banffshire and to Erroll's part of Aberdeenshire. These were put under the command of the Master of Forbes on 22nd April. The following letter from the Sheriff-Clerk of Banffshire details the procedure taken in that county. Major Hugh Buntein of Kilbryde, Ayrshire, was muster-master of the whole levy.

ffor THE EARLE OFF FINDLATER

thes

My Lord,—I have received ane act from the Conventione of Estates, wheirby I am ordoured to give advertisment to all the comssrs. of militia and outputters of horse theirto within this shyre to meete att Banff upon Thursday nixt the 2^d of May for outreicking the ffourth horse of the ordinar militia, and that they be ready to be presented heir agt the 9th of the sd month with ten dayes provision

---

[1] Anderson's *Scottish Nation*, vol. ii. p. 215.

to Major Bountin or any whom he shall appoint, the horse being att the raite of ten pounds sterling and the armes and equipage att ffive pounds.   This, as is appointed me, is intimate to your Lo. by, My Lord, Your Lo. most humble servant,   GEO. LESLYE.

Banff, 26 *Aprile* 89.

If James Ogilvie did vote against the resolution regarding the settlement of the crown, he soon afterwards fell into line with the government.   On the 23rd of April he was appointed one of twenty-four Commissioners to treat concerning the union of the two kingdoms.[1]

Meanwhile Dundee was in the north levying war for James. The Estates adjourned on 29th April, and next day the Committee appointed by the Convention issued a commission to the Earl of Findlater and to Sir George Gordon of Edinglassie, joint Sheriff Principal of Banffshire, to call together the fencible men in that county, and to take orders from Major-General Mackay.[2] The following letter of F. Ogilvie from Innes, Morayshire, to the Earl of Findlater gives account of Dundee's second ride to the north in his last great campaign, and of the current rumours of the time.

ffor MY LORD OFF FINDLATER
heast

Innes, 2 *Maij* 1689.

MY LORD,—Your Lo. shall know that my Lord Dundie went by Elgin yeisternight to Forroes after sevin houres at night.   He had about 60 hors.   My Lord Dumfarling was halff our behend him.   He had about 16 hors and sex bagedg hors.   Ther is on Makay folling them w[t] two redgments off hors and foot.   He was yeisternight at Wheytloumes or therby.   My Lord Dundie did intersept ane packet off lētrs that was comg over the Carne to the Master off Forbes with ane comission to reas men and severall other letrs and newes, which gave my Lord Dundie so heastie newes to remove for his auin saftie. They talk ya[t] the newes thay got in the packet caries ya[t] my Lord the Dewck off Barrick is landed in our eyls neir

---

[1] *The Acts of the Parliaments of Scotland*, vol. ix. p. 60.
[2] *Ibid.*, Appendix, p. 2.

Mackincleans lands, which holds treu or not I know not. This is all at present from, My Lord, Your humbell servant,   F. OGILVYE.

Whitelums is in the parish of Gartly, Aberdeenshire. On the 8th of May the Committee of Estates sent out a new commission to the Master of Forbes 'for raising his Troop, in place of the former which was intercepted.'

When the Convention met again on the 5th of June, James Ogilvie is entered in the rolls as Sir James Ogilvie. There is a subsequent entry in the rolls of Parliament for the new session beginning 15th April 1690, where he is designed 'Mr.'; but he had received the honour of knighthood before that date. In the sederunt of the Convention of Royal Burghs, which he attended on 2nd July 1689 as the representative of Cullen, he is entered as Mr. At a particular Convention held on 14th August he was designed Sir James, and was appointed one of three commissioners to proceed to London, to present an address to the King to have the grievances of the Royal Burghs especially as to trade redressed. Sir James Ogilvie proceeded to London, and met the King. In the written reply of his Majesty, dated 27th September, he is called Sir James.[1] His territorial designation of Churchhill the editor has been unable to identify.

Killiecrankie was fought on the 27th of July. On the 1st of August Parliament authorised the Privy Council to call out all the heritors and fencible men within the kingdom, with their best horses and arms and forty days' provisions. On the 3rd of August James Ogilvie, who was then heartily in sympathy with the government, sent his father the following account of the state of affairs and of the defensive measures taken after Mackay's defeat. The letter dated 7th August from John Innes, laird of Edingight, refers to the levy ordered on 1st August.

Edr., August 3d, 1689.

MY LORD,—I received your Lo: leter with one inclosed for General Major McKay, bot he being with the army, I could not get his letter delivered to him. I therfor went to the Commissioner,[2] and did read to him both the Generals letter and mine, and did hold out to him the steat and

---

[1] *Records of the Convention of Royal Burghs*, 1689, pp. 99-104.
[2] William, Duke of Hamilton.

condition of the shire; bot in respect that Edenglassie hes shouen himselfe so forward from the begining of this revolution, it is the Duks opinion that your Lo: doe not trouble your selfe with the command of any pairt of the shir, bot you may doe it or not as you find convenient for your selfe and your freinds; bot as for what you have done the Duke hes promised that neither you nor the gentrie you had under your Lo: command shal sustain any prajudice. I am confident you have all been much alarumed with the accompt of the feight att Gillechranke; bot bleessed be God it was not so as was att first reported, for although more of the common souldiers wer killed onn our side then onn Dundees, yet all our officiers are safe returned except Collonel Balfour and Liftenant Colonel McKay, who they say are taken prisoners. Dundee and Pitcur and several others of qualitie are killed onn the other side; and since ther hes been ane ingadgement att St. Jonstoun att the place wher Hendrie Wen fought, wher the Hylanders wer totaly defeat and the toun retakne from them. The Earle of Argyl is nou att Stirlen, and ther will be of horse and foot in it and about it of English and Scots horse foot and dragoons near twelve thousand, and most of them are marching towards the enimy. The Parlament is adjorned til the eight of October; and ther is ane order come doun from the King discharging all to goe out of the kingdom, bot thes that are trafecting merchants. Its thought houever shortly the Duke of Hamilton will be aloued to goe to court. I have many more neus to wreat, bot since I resolve, God willing, to be north verie shortly, I shal only add that I am, My Lord, Your Lo. most obedient son and humble servant,   JA. OGILVIE.

I give my humble service to all freinds with your Lo.

ffor THE EARLL OFF FFINDLATER
thes ar in heast

Graing, 7 Agust 1689.

MY LORD,—I have sent your Lo. the inclosed intimatione which is sent be the shereif and was intimat at the church this day, to let your Lo. consider it, and yt wee within this paries may knou your Lo. mynd what way wee shal behave. Wee being within your Lo. division, all of us resolvs to wait upon your Lo. command. The heritor[s] desyrd me to send this expres to your Lo.; so what com- mand you put upon us shal be obeyed.—Waiting your Lo. ansuer, I still remain, My Lord, Your Lo. reall freind and houmble servant,   Jo. INNES.

By the 15th of August General Mackay was in Strathbogie opposing the Jacobites under Cannon at Auchendoun in Banff- shire. The two next letters from Alexander Ogilvie of Kemp- cairn Keith to his relative the Earl of Findlater, throw light on that part of the campaign. The Kempcairn Ogilvies were cadets of the Findlater family. The first of them, Alexander, was second son of the first Lord Ogilvie of Deskford and brother of the first Earl of Findlater. He died before 1669. The writer of these letters was probably his son. The reference in the letters to his 'wife' and the 'litle bell' seems a kind of Jacobite cypher. In February of next year the Town Council minutes of Banff bear that four indwellers were fined for ' con- celling and abstracteing there horses efter they were ordained to have them in radienes ffor convoyeing the persones of Charles Lord Oliphant and his Ladie, the Laird of Kempcairne, and uyrs presoners.' They were arrested as Jacobites by a party of Colonel Livingstone's dragoons on 18th February 1690.

These are

For THE EARLE OF FINDLATER

15 August 1689.

MY LORD,—The laudable desire your Lop. hade to in- formation prevented my dutifull inclination; and hade not humane reason moved a guardian against the present surprise (altho uncertain), omission of dutie hade appeared. Information from the camp at Straithboggie informes of no foot or horss auxiliaries; and the forces too consist of 1500 horss. My information from Dundies armie hes been impeded; only they lye inteir at Achindown and Glenfiddigh. Edinglassie hes two dayes bypast been maggotishly stout in scouting; but the 3d tym is feared, in respect the last escape was so narrow. Till too morrow

I ask your Lops. pardon to subscrive that I am ever, My Lord, Youres as becometh ALEX[R] OGILVIE.

Turn over.

MY LORD,—James Hamiltoun in Keith was taken be Edinglassie at Lochpark, and one Tho. Duncan tayler at Upper Achannassie. Thomas Duncan is liberat. The samen day being Wednesday last, Dundies armie took a page of the Inglish officiers. No forces were or past any way at Fochabers, neither hath Leslies regiment removed from Inverness ; no joyning of Grants or Straithneavers forces. The Master of Forbess troup being well horssed and all accordingly joyn'd on Tuesdays night.

My Lord, my wife is so confusedly affrighted that I have resolved the use of her to your Lop., as I will be ansuerable to the smallest toull of the ringing the litle bell any part of Straithilla.[1]

These are
For THE EARLE OFF FINDLATER
Haughes, 17th August 1689.

MY LORD,—'Twas not want of dutie, but rather want of certain information, which occasioned such delay ; neither could my information engaged me to these hade not dutie oblidged. Pardon then this truble with the comon report, which is that the Hyland armie is now in and about Lumffanan ; and if wee shall credit those that pretends to be hearers, Mackay sent a desire be sound of trumpet invitinge a 2[d] ingagement, whose return was in like manner answered, that they waited their motion and bid their cause give him and all concerned a defyance. 'Tis expected this night, a removeall of the horsss armie from Straithbogie to the Enzie. Keithmore Duff hes dealt very treacherously, which he is like to suffer for by the Hylanders. Edinglassie hes been foollhardie adventerous in scouting and hes escaped, but the nixt essay is much feared. The consternation of the Straithboggie forces is much talked of by overseers. My last imported the designe of recomending the use of my wife to your Lop., but now

---

[1] *The Acts of the Parliaments of Scotland*, vol. ix. Appendix, p. 7.

'tis resolved that by the influencing charme of the harmonius litle bell necessity will be supplyed by your Lops. recomendation to, My Lord, Your oblidged faithfull servant, while   ALEX^R OGILVIE.

My L.   *Turn over.*

My LORD,—Altho I have been loath to write of what the good expectation is, viz. that your Lop. will furnish a regiment of well armed goodly foot, and a troup of your Lops. freends horsmen, which is like from Straithboggie may be required and is publickly talked off ; yet if a simple presumable thought may be ushered in (as formerly so now should be) untill greater luminaries appear without eclipse, recomend these to your Lops. reading and then burning.

Sir George Gordon of Edinglassie [1] was second son of Sir John Gordon of Park, Banffshire.   In 1665 he married Marie, daughter of Sir Alexander Abercrombie of Birkenbog.   In 1669 he first appears in the suite roll of the barons and freeholders of the county for Edinglassie in Mortlach.   In 1681 he was knighted, and on the 24th of August that year he was appointed joint Sheriff-Principal of the county with Sir James Baird of Auchmedden.   In 1681, and again in 1685, he and Sir Patrick Ogilvie of Boyne were elected commissioners to the Scots Parliament for Banffshire.   At the revolution he early acquiesced in the new régime, and vigorously supported it in the field, practically superseding his more peaceful coadjutor in Banffshire, the Earl of Findlater.   Early in June, before Killiecrankie, Dundee regarding him as a renegade, Gordon burnt his house of Edinglassie, and naturally in August Edinglassie was eager to retaliate.   General Mackay, in a letter to Secretary Melville on 31st October 1689, strongly recommended him to the King for the command of a troop of Dragoons, vacant through the death of the laird of Blair,[2] and he received the commission accordingly on 18th December.

Alexander Duff of Keithmore,[3] Mortlach, ancestor of the Duke

---

[1] 'Banffshire at the Revolution of 1689,' by the editor, in *Banffshire Field Club Transactions*, 1906, p. 78, etc.

[2] Mackay's *Memoirs*, Appendix, p. 293.

[3] 'Banffshire at the Revolution of 1689,' by the editor, pp. 85, 86, 87, etc.

of Fife, held Keithmore in wadset of the Duke of Gordon. During the Commonwealth he began to acquire land in Banffshire, thus laying the foundation of the extensive Fife estates. In 1650 he bought Succoth, in 1657 Lettoch and Alldachlaggan, and in 1660 Pittyvaich and Fittie, all in Banffshire. Later he acquired part of the lordship of Balvenie and the estate of Braco. For long he was Baron Bailie to the Duke of Gordon in Auchindoun. His wife Helen Grant was daughter of Alexander Grant of Allachie of the Ballintomb Grants, cadets of the Chiefs of Grant. He first appears in the suite roll of the barons and freeholders of Banffshire at the Michaelmas court of 1675, where he is entered for the lands of 'Lettach and Auldachlagane.' At the Pasch court of 1678 he appears also as superior of Buchrom and Millne-towne of Balvenie, which had formerly been held by his father-in-law. Additional light is thrown on Cannon's treatment of Keithmore in the records of the Scots Parliament of 1695, where it is related that in August 1689, old Keithmore then seventy years of age was taken by the rebels out of his house of Keith-more, which was plundered and destroyed, and was kept in a starving condition until he was 'necessitat to pay a ransome for his relief.' [1]

For THE RIGHT HONOURABL THE EARL OF FINDLTUR

Pittuly, Siptem. 2, 1689.

MY LORD,—It is a very great trubl to me that you are in so great a fere in the Boyn. I wish the Lord may disconfit all them which is the occation of it, that we all may injoy our formar peace agan. I belive my father will wat on your Lo. the end of this week, but as for me, my parans will not let me stir from Pittuly till Mr. James return, which I wish may be very shortly. I shall add no mor but that I am, My Lord, Your most obedant dag[ht] and devoted servant to dath,

ANNA OGILVIE.

In November, with the re-opening of the Court of Session, Sir James Ogilvie resumed his practice at the bar.

---

[1] *The Acts of the Parliaments of Scotland*, vol. ix. p. 447.

The laird of Grant's regiment was concentrated at Elgin in November, owing to a rumour from Inverness, where Sir James Leslie commanded for William, that the Jacobite Highlanders were again rising. The writer of the following letter was probably Sir William Hope of Kirklistoune,[1] who on 25th April received from the Convention a commission as captain of a troop of horse. A troop of dragoons was then stationed at Elgin.[2] The Earl's daughters were the Ladies Mary and Anna.

ffor THE EARLE OF FINDLATER ATT CULLEN
these

Elgin; Nov. 20, 1689.

My LORD,—When I received yours last night we were all dancing very mirrilie in my Lord Duffases, and wanted nothing to make our mirth alltogather compleat but the pleasant companie of your two fair daughters, for whom I assure you I have a very great respect, and wisheth them all imadginable hapines, which I hope your Lo. will doe me the favour to lett them know as from me. I confess I am so much beholding to your Lo. kindness, that I am affraid it shall not be in my pour to repay it; but wheir opportunity offers you nead not in the least doubt of my inclinations. I thank your Lo. most kindly for the trouble you have given your selfe in sending to see how I was. I thank God for it, we are all heere in very good health, and if our allarums prove noe truer then the last shall I hope likwise be but in very little hazard. I doubt not but you have heard, that the rise of it was from the contention of some Healanders who desired to steall; but it seems Sir James Leslie took the allarum to hottly, and expected that they were drawing all togather in a body, and desined to fall doun upon him, which was the occasion of his giveing the forces thes false allarume. When we shall have another, or whither it shall be as false as the last, that I cannot tell, but for my oun part I wish it may. I confess altho we meet with discreet people heer and that our quarters are not very bad, yeet I shoud

---

[1] *The Acts of the Parliaments of Scotland*, vol. ix. pp. 63, 64.
[2] Mackay's *Memoirs*, Appendix, pp. 299-304.

be satisfied to be ordered to my old quarters again at
Bamf, which when it shall please the commanding officer
to doe I shall not faill to pay my respects, as is my duty,
to your Lo.   I need not write you ane acount of the last
posts news knowing that you have gotten them already;
and therefore untill I have the honour to waite upon you
again, I remain, My Lord, Your Lo. most humble servant,

WILL. HOPE.

By 18th December James Ogilvie had rejoined his wife at
Pittulie.   His neighbour in Buchan, William Earl of Buchan,
referred to in next letter, had come from Ireland to Lochaber
in July with Colonel Cannon, and was present under Dundee at
Killiecrankie.   He was included in the process of forfeiture[1] instituted by Parliament in May 1690 against the heads of the
rebellion, and on 13th June the libel was found proved against
him.   On 14th July the Lord Advocate intimated that as the Earl
had lately been taken prisoner, he did not then insist on his
forfeiture.   He was confined in Stirling Castle, and died in 1695.
Charles, fourth Lord Fraser, brother-in-law of Lord Buchan, also
had Jacobite leanings.   He was in arms in 1690, and surrendered
in October of that year.   Alexander, third Lord Forbes of Pitsligo,
died in December 1690.   His wife, Sophia Erskine, daughter of
John Earl of Mar, whom he married in 1676, was a close friend
of the Countess of Findlater, to whom she frequently wrote.

For THE EARLE OF FINDLATER thes

Pittulie, Decr. the 18, 1689.

MY LORD,—I shal, God willing, wait onn your Lo. att
Cullen onn Tuesdays night, and shal come provided for
what you need for the cess.   I shal have all things readie
pact upp for the horses against Moondays morning.   I
find the Jacobins in this countrey in very good humor,
and my Lord Buchan appears openly both in my Lord
Frasers house and in Pitsligo, bot I have not seen his Lo.
I find I most stil be troubelsom to your Lo., for my wife
just nou tels me that her woman hes no syde sadle to ryd
onn, and ther is none to be boroued in this countrey.   If
their be none in the house, I intreat James Walker may

---

[1] *The Acts of the Parliaments of Scotland*, vol. ix. Appendix, pp. 52-59.

endeavour to borou one.   It shal not be the worse, and
after this I shal be better provided.   It most be sent
with the bagadge horses.   I shal not trouble your Lo.
any further att present, bot shal only add that I am,
My Lord, Your Lo. most obedient son and most humble
servant,   JA. OGILVIE.

My wife gives her most humble service to your Lo. and
my sisters.

The manning of William's navy was occupying attention in
Scotland.   The Burgh records of Cullen show that early in
February 1690 the Earl of Crawford, President of the Privy
Council, acting on a Royal proclamation, wrote to the town
council requiring them to levy seamen for the English navy.   The
writers of the following letter, who were Bailies of Cullen, refer
to this matter.

THE RIGHT HONOURABLE SIR JAMES OGILVIE OF
CHURCHHILL, ADVOCATE AT EGR
in all haste thes

ffor ther Majties speciall service.

Cullen, ffebry ii, 1690.

RIGHT HONBLE,—The many proofes wee have already
hade of your Ho. kyndnes to us, hes made us presume to
give your Ho. this trouble, to delyver the inclosed report
to the Counsell, which yee may read and seall.   Wee
intreat, in caice ther come any press, since yor Ho.
knowes qt kynd of persones wee have to doe wt, yee
may indeavour to gett the petitione in the close of or
letter granted.   As lykwayes, since the place is not able
to advance money for the transporta ne of these men to
be pressed to any port qr they are to be shiped, wee are
hopefull yee will advert to it, and endeavour to gett us
ane order for als much of the excyse of any place nixt
adjacent, as wee shall use upon the forsaid accompt more
yn or oun will amount to.   So your Honours care in this
will add ane furder obligatione upon, Right Honourable,
Your Ho. most obdient and most obligded servants,

JA. SANDERS.
JOHN OGILVIE.

The writer of next letter was probably an officer in the laird of Grant's regiment, part of which may then have been holding Gordon Castle. Sir Thomas Livingstone, who commanded for William in the north, had on 1st May gained the battle of Cromdale over the Jacobite Highlanders under General Buchan. Bellachastill, near the Haughs of Cromdale, was later called Castle Grant; and Ballindalloch, ten miles further down the Spey, was in the possession of John Grant, who was one of Dundee's most active lieutenants, and who was forfaulted the same year.

ffor THE EARLE OFF FFINLATER

Gordone Castle, 9 *May* 1690.

MY LORD,—I hade one from Leivistoune yesternight. He left him at Bellachastill one Wedinsday last. He told me yt it was reported in the camp befor he came away, that yr were some Hyghlanders lying at Bellnadalloch, and that Sr Thomas Leivistone desyned to goe ther yesterday; and I asure your Lōp ther wes noe ingadgment in Badenoch, onlie Sr Thomas went yr and seased Clunnie and severall other gentlmen. Soe except the Highlanders have been at Bellnadalloch, when they came ther, which wes yesternight, ther hes been noe laite rancounter since Cromdell. As for what hes been at Breamarr, I hear nothing of it neither *pro* nor *contra*. I expect notice from the camp this night; and if I can get occasione, if ther be anie laite bussines yt is worth the writeing to yor Lop., I shall give yor Lop. ane accompt.—Being in hest, I ame, My Lo., Your Lops. most humble servt,

GEORGE GRANT.

We have seen that Sir George Gordon of Edinglassie had practically superseded the Earl of Findlater as joint commander of the Banffshire levies.

For THE RIGHT HONBL THE EARLL OF FINDLATER

MY LORD,—I wonder much to sie you at such trouble, for what is not worth your pains to put pen to paper. I am so ill stated for wreating that, wer not the respect I ow you, I wold not have wretn so much for all the bussines in hand. I can not goe and come upon my orders efter once agreed on. If any prove refractorie they may be made comptable for it.—I am, My Lord, your Lōps˙ most humble and obedient servant, G. ˙GORDONE.

Ednglassie, 6 *Jun.* 1690.

On the 14th of June the Burgh records of Cullen bear that an order was produced from Sir Thomas Livingstone on some of the Banffshire heritors to have fourscore horses and sacks at Gordon Castle on the 17th to carry provisions for their Majesties' army. Next letter deals with the provisioning of the troops.

For THE EARLE OF FINDLATER

MY LORD,—I beleeue most of the baggage is already gon, and the sacks ar ordered to be at Gordon Castle to-morrow morning, and the horses on Tuysday's morning; nor knowe I any that will give a recept unles thes of the forces give it, who ar to be their guard. As for this Lōp, the lists being called, the horses of the deficients wer doubled, and the owners poynded besids by the dragoons ; bot I heard of no recept, only that nottes wer taken. Ferguson's landing has been rumor'd of a long tym, bot as little assurance as yet, for what can be learned by, My Lord, Your Lōp's obedient seruat, H. GORDON.

15 *Juny.* 90.

Ferguson was probably not the Plotter, but Major Ferguson, who was then carrying out an expedition from the Clyde to occupy Inverlochy in order to overawe the western Highlands. The *Dartmouth* of the Royal English navy, under Captain Pottinger, ' with the rest of the squade under his commands,' acted as his convoy.[1]

This month of June the town council of Cullen allowed Sir James Ogilvie, advocate, as their commissioner for attending the Convention of Estates, and for attending Parliament and the Convention of Burghs, £100 Sc. in satisfaction of his expenses.

The eighth Earl of Eglintoun in 1676-7 entailed his estates on

---

[1] Mackay's *Memoirs*, Appendix, pp. 322-324.

his eldest son, Lord Montgomerie, with remainders, but under the reservation of an annuity to himself of 6000 merks.

For MY LORD MONTGOMERIE these

Edr., July 14, 1690.

MY LORD,—I find your father hes consulted in order to bring in ane proces against you befor the Parlament. I know in lau he can get nothing from you; yet in this Parlament wee find ourselfs not strictly limited by lau, and therfor the event of this process might be dubius. Its the opinion of all your freinds hier that you advance my Lord ane thousund merks, and give your consent to the filling of ane clerks place, which is vacant in one of your jurisdictions. This will cost you no money, and its what you cannot refuse to grant, seing my Lord during his life hes the administration of the jurisdictions. Its verie fit in my opinion that your Lo. shun hearing with your father, seeing you can have your peace att so easie ane rait. I aknouledge this to much prasumtion in me to priescrive ruels to your Lo., bot its the respect I have for you and your familie hes made me wreat so freely, and I hope youl pardon me for it, seing I am, My Lord, Your Lo. most affectionatt cousing and most humble servant,

JA. OGILVIE.

Since wreating my letter, I find the clerkships of both your jurisdictions are vacant, and the Commissioner, Advocat, and all your relations thinks it proper your Lo. subscrive consenter to both commissions. If this be refused, I know your father will immediatly goe onn in his process; and you can have no honor to be heard with him since you may agree so easilie.

The nominations to the vacant clerkships were of value, because these and many other judicial appointments were in those days bought and sold.

The story of Montgomery's plot is detailed in all Scots histories. The abbreviations in the following letter may be thus filled up: An. the Earl of Annandale; R. the Lord Ross; Sk.

Sir James Montgomery of Skelmorlie; D. Q. the Duke of Queens-berry; M. A. the Marquis of Athole; M. the Earl of Melville; L. G. D. Lieut.-General Douglas; and D. H. the Duke of Hamilton. The handwriting is that of Sir William Hamilton, Under-Secretary of State for Scotland, and one of the commissioners sent by the Convention of Royal Burghs on 14th August 1689 to interview the King in London. He was subsequently appointed a Judge of the Court of Session, and took the title of Lord Whitelaw. In 1697 was made Lord Justice-Clerk.

ffor SIR JAMES OGILVIE OF CHURCHHILL

SIR,—I caused severall tymes speak to Buchan about that money. He sayes he shall get it as soon as he can, and pay ārent therfor till that tyme; for the toune of Edr. was oweing him money. I caused tell him wee wold not let that money ly on ārent, and I have spoken to the provest and George Sterling, that the toune may advance alse much of what they owe to Buchan as will pay us. If I had not been concerned myselfe I could have craved harder for you. I spoke lykewayes to the provest and George about the tounes gratificaᵒne which was pro-mised. They said they had taken course with that, and the thesaurer wold shortlie give me ane accompt therof; and you may assure yourselfe you shall soon therafter be acquainted therof by me.

ffor newes it is alse confidentlie said as ever that An., R., and Sk. were upon the plott for bringing back the late King. Sk. is still on his keeping. An. mist narrowlie been taken at the Baith by a messinger. R. was closs prisoner in the Tower, but now he hes gotten more libertie therin. The Ladyes R. and Sk. take journey for court the nixt week to see what they can doe there for their husbands. The breach betuixt the tuo Dalrimples and M. is greater then ever. Young D. they say hes joyned with D. Q. and M. A. for beating doune of M. and presbytrie together; and yisterday eight dayes they sent away Douglas of Gogar to the King to negotiat with Leivetennent Generall D. in their behalfe with the King. The morrow after W. Carstairs was sent by M. to counter them. Wee hear since, none of them went to Ireland, but that they went from Portpatrick to Chester to meet the King, who was to returne from Ireland upon Sunday last, for Watterfoord is surrendered to him and L. G. D. hes taken Athlon by storme. Blair the postmaster who came here yisterday from Ireland sayes the accompt he got as he returned of the slaine at the watter of Boyne was ten thousand at the least, for their were many discovered dead in the boigs since the break. It is expected that both the Dutch and English fleets will at sea before this, and that the ffrench, who have lyen upon the coast of Sussex this whyle bygone, dar not now land their men, when the fleets are out, and the King comeing home. Your freind D. H. is come to toune, but continues very ill of the gravell. I wish that he and M. were in a good understanding. You have a good lyfe, who hes your ease in the countrey whill your old collegue is troubled with the comissiones. But whether he be at leasure or not, he is constantlie, Sir, Your most humble servant. Adieu.

Edr., August 2, 1690.

Two days earlier the English and Dutch fleets had engaged the French off Beachy Head. Owing to the cowardice of the English Admiral Torrington, the allies were driven into the Thames. This naval defeat opened England to a French invasion; and General Mackay was ordered from Inverlochy to the Lowlands of Scotland to be in readiness to march into England. In August the Jacobites under Cannon and Buchan were therefore able to make headway in the north, and to drive the Master of Forbes and Colonel Jackson into Aberdeen. Mackay, reassured from England, soon took measures for the defence of Aberdeen by marching north again. Sir James Abercromby, laird of Birkenbog, in next letter deals with the situation thus created in Aberdeenshire.

For THE RIGHT HONORABLE THE EARLE
OF- FINDLATER these ar

Abdn., August 22, 1690.

MY LORD,—I received your letter, and renders your Lo. many thanks for ye truble ye haue ben at, in sending in

your man heir to see houe we are. As for neues, we dare
not wreat them for fear of being intercepted, becaues y^r
are no lèrs that pases without breaking up. The Tuesdays
lèr brought in no neues that was remarkable. Ther cam
in neues to the toune this morning that Inverei was taken,
and twelf more with him. They report that Dumferling
is about a thousand horse and eight hunder foot besids
the clans, and that McKaie is four thousand foot and
one thousand horse ; but your Lo. cane haue a suerer
accompt of that then we, becaues as we heer they are
but a litle aboue Strathbogie yet. If your man could
have stayed till Saturday ye might have had ane fuller
account. We are expecting in two thousand of McKaies
foot this night, and we hav Kenmures regment alreadie
heire. My Lord Banf is prisoner heire, although he hath
the Counsels pass. So wishing your Lo. good health, I
still remaine in all sincerity, My Lord, Your most affectionat
godsone and most humble servant,

JA. ABERCROMBY.

My wife and I gives our good wishes to your Lo. and the
young ladies. Likways offer my service to Sir James, and
I will chaleng him one his promise when we meet.

John Farquharson of Inverey, Deeside, known as the Black
Colonel, was not so easily taken.

James Ogilvie, younger of Boyne, with a Latin quotation from
Ovid's *Heroides,* invites his cousins from Cullen House to play
long gauff on the sea braes, near Boyne Castle in Banffshire.

Boyne, the ij of September 1690.

SIR,—I have sent order for the trees my Lord has
written for, and have sent the news. My father is gone
towards Carnustie this day ; and ife Mr. Patrick and you
have a mind for a touch at long gauff tomorrow lett
me know this night wher I shall waitt on you with a
second, or if yee would doe me the honour to come this
lenth, because the links ar better, and we shall see ife ye
cannot make better use of a club in this countrey then ye

did at Eden.   This is not that I doubt but ye made good
use of your short putting club ther.   So hoping ye will
give my humble service to all the Ladies and Lords with
you, I remain Yours,   JAMES OGILVIE.

Nihil mihi rescribas attamen ipse veni with Mr Patricke.

Carnoustie or Carnousie in Forglen, Banffshire, was the property
of George Gordon of Edinglassie.

Of the few north of the Grampians, who from the outset actively
supported the revolution, no one was more convinced of its
justice or more influential than Ludovick, eighth laird of Grant.
Elected commissioner for Inverness-shire to the Convention, he
supported the settling of the crown on William, and was one of
the select committee nominated to settle the government.   When
Dundee broke north, General Mackay at once concerted measures
with him.   In consequence the laird of Grant hurried north to
raise his clan, embodying it in a regiment under his own command.
It did excellent work for William in the north during the whole
rising.   The following letter is to his brother-in-law Lord Boyne.

ffor MY LORD BOYNE thes

Ballachastell, the 22 September 1690.

MY LORD,—I have returned the mear ye wreat off, and
if any more off your servants horses can be gott tryel off
in this country they shall not want them ; but for what
is off them in Badinoch I canot serve you in that, for
I want a hundered horse went from this with Collonell
Livistoune, and I supose the greatest pairt off them ar
with my nighbours off Badinoch.   But wherin I can be
off use comand me as being, Your affectionat brother and
humble servantt,   LUDOUICK GRANTT.

The act abolishing patronage on condition that patrons were
compensated was passed on 19th July 1690.   On 7th June
1690, Parliament established Presbyterian church government,
but the actual settling of the church on its new basis in the
north took several years.

E

The 6th of Octobr -690.

VERIE LOVING FRIEND,—I intreat you doe me the favour to send me north with this bearer the leat act of Parliement taking away the patronages, with the act of retention passed in the last session of Parliement, and what they cost you my son James shall pay you. I intreat you likways doe me the favour to heave all my peapers that are by you readie to deliver to my son, which will verie much oblidge Your verie reall friend,   FFINDLATER.

The following is one of several letters from Edinburgh booksellers showing the Earl of Findlater's taste in reading.

MY LORD,—According to yor Lo. orders I have sent Beaumonts and Fletchers plays, w^t ii[1] of the best taileduces I have ; and w^t the first occasione shall send to London for Don Quixot and ye 2^d p^t of Chardins Travells, if ther be such a book, for yor Lōps use; and when Sir James comes to toune, to receive yor Lōps further comands shall be the honor of, My Lord, Yo^r Lo. most humble servant,

WM. JOHNSTON.

Edr. 7 Octor (90).

Turn over.

Beaumont and Fletcher's plays	.	.	.	18	00	00
3 largest taileduces—viz.:						
1 Kings statue	.	.	.	.	.	01 10 00
1 Seige of Buda	.	.	.	.	.	00 18 00
1 Discors concordia	.	.	.	.	.	00 18 00
1 Ld Maitland	.	.	.	.	.	00 14 00
1 Q. Mary	.	.	.	.	.	00 14 00
1 Dauphin of France	.	.	.	.	00 14 00
1 Dutches of Cleveland	.	.	.	00 14 00
1 Ld Russell	.	.	.	.	.	00 08 0
1 7 Bishops	.	.	.	.	.	00 08 0
1 K. W^m	.	.	.	.	.	00 08 0
1 Honslow heath camp	.	.	.	00 08 0
					25 14 00

---

[1] Meaning 11, as the list shows.

The handwriting of the following letter regarding the upholding of the post in Banffshire is that of Mr. Patrick Innes minister of Banff. It is no doubt written to his patron the Earl of Findlater.

MY LORD,—I knew not till yesternight that there were any letters brought by the last post, directed to your Lo^p. Our magistrats have been at the expense of keeping up the post this long time, and they have no help from the shire, whereupon besides the postage to Abd. they have resolved to take 2s. sc. for every single letter from Abd. to Banff; and this I am informed is the reason they keep up any letters directed to any in the shire. But I shall endeavour yt in after time none of your Lo^{ps} letters shall be stopped, for I shall call for them how soon ever the post comes on, and send them with the first bearer to Cullen, and if I cannot have one, shall send an expresse with them. There came no considerable news with the last post to this place : They write of great preparat[ions on all] hands for the next campaigne. The Gene[ral Assemb]ly of the Presbyterians is adjourned till Novem [ber next]. I am grieved to hear that my Lady Anna's [dist]emper continues. The good Lord recov[er her].

Banff, Novr. 29, 1690.

With the assistance of his brother, Robert Ogilvie, born *c.* February 1673, was about to begin his career as a cavalry officer. Later in this year, on 30th July, he applied to Sir James for a charger.

For MASTER ROBERT OGILVIE SON TO THE EARLE OF FINDLATER

ROBEN,—I nou think it time for you to come south. You shal be recomended to thes who have the disposal of anie of the vacant places. If my Lord Boyn pleases to advance you five pound uppon my Lord my fathers recept, I shal compt with my Lord Boyn att meeting. You may come by your majors house att Fyfe, and he will inform you wher your troup lyes. This is all att present from Your affectionatt brother, JA. OGILVIE.

Edr., Februarie 2d, 169i.

Wee James Earel of Findlater, Lord Ogilvie of Deskfoord and Inshmartien grants us to heav receaved the within mentioned fyve pound sterling from my Lord Boind, which soume forsaid we be these oblidge us to hold count for to Sir James Ogilvie of Church-hill.   Given under our hand at Cullen the ijth of feby -69i   FFINDLATER.

The letters concerning Charles, seventh Lord Oliphant, of 10th February and 25th April 1691, show that he had fallen into strait-ened circumstances.   He married, c. 17th October 1678, Mary, daughter of John Ogilvie of Milton Keith.   Newmilne is in the parish of Keith, Banffshire.

These are
ffor THE EARLE OFF. FFINDLATER

Newmilne, ffebr. 10th, 9i.

MY LORD,—The Lord Oliphant is removed from this countrea with his Ladie and familie, so y^t I cannot give your Lo. anie ansuer from him unlesse I could hav spoken with him myselff; bot I fear he is not provyded to give your Lo. monie at this tyme, and I may say I know so much by exsperience in ane affair of my own.   It is lyk I may sie your Lo. som day this weick, and I shal use mor freidome in this affair then now I can doe; n^r think I y^t your Lo. may mowe much in this session.   And I know he does realie desing your Lo. satisfaction, though he be not prepared for the tyme; yet I judge it is meit your Lo. and he should meit and cleir things, y^t he may endeavor to doe busines at the nixt tearme.   And this is all I can say for the tyme, bot y^t I am, My Lord, Your Lo. humbel servant,   JHONE OGILVYE.

The following extract from a London newsletter shows the danger of foreign invasion following on the loss of sea power by the defeat at Beachy Head.

ffor THE RIGHT HON^{LL} THE EARLE OF
FFINDLATOR thes

London, 7 *Apryl* 1691.

LETTERS from Brest of the 3^d say, the day before the

7 men of warr with 28 transport ships sailled hence for Ireland, yr being Monsr St. Ruth and diverse other French officers with 1500 souldiers on board, and are charged with some important designe, its whispered to retake Kingsaill or Cork, ther being instructions sent to Tyroniell to bring down ane bodie of Irish. Before the letter Monsr Torveill is come down with his last ordors to hasten the grand fleet to sea.

Plymouth 5th tell us, a day before a Dutch shipp arryved here from Bilboa. She says she came thence 8 dayes agoe in companie with 16 English and 14 Dutch capers, but yt 4 French men of warr, 3 of which were of 60 guns each, fell in with them, upon which the merchants were making yr escape and the men of warr were preparing to feight. This day two French ships, having French goods on board, were sent in there by the abovesaid capers, and say when they cam away the said capers and the Hanniball were hotlie engaged with the 4 French men of warr; that before they cam away the ffr. hade taken 7 English merċts, and yt when they were out of sight they continowed to heir smart shooting. Ther was a report that the Hanniball was taken by the sd men of warr, as also 6 or 7 more of Bilboa fleet, and were in chase of the rest. The Lord Colchesters regment of hors now quartered at Worcester is ordored furthwith to march in ordor to imbarq for Flanders.

Wee hear yt hir Mātie hes sent ordors to the Deputtie Levīs of the sēall counties boarding on the sea coasts to have the millitia in readieness to march upon some houres warning. One of the last weeks packett boats from Holland is still wanting, and thought to have been taken by the ffr., with diverse passengers on board, among whom are thought to be Doctor Scott and Doctor Grote.

Wee have just now ane accompt att io acloak that a fyre broke up suddenlie at Whythall, which made the Queen walk on foot to St. Jameses with a guard. Some say it began in Dutches of Portsmouths lodginges, but being so late we cannot give yow more confirmaᵒne till the next.

ffor THE EARELL OFF FFINDELATORE
thesse

Aprill the 25, 69i

MY LORD,—I receved your Lo. immedeatlie, as leak-wais anie line from Park[1] the outher day conserning that affaire, and I hope your Lop. knowes I was alwaies willing to doe what was just and incumbent for me; and accordinglie I am resolved to send anie espress, God willing, the begining of this inshuing week for my peapers to Edbr. from my Lord Pittmeden, whereby I may be in a condishione to treat w^t Sr John, q^{ch} w^t my wyfe hir service and myne presented to your Lo. and famellie is all from, My Lord, Your Lo. humbell servant,

OLIPHANT.

For MISTRES ANNA MURAY DAUGHTER TO LIFTENNANT COLLONEL JAMES MURAY, GOVERNOUR OF THE CASTEL OF EDR.

Cullen, April 30, i69i.

MADAM,—The former experience I have of your La. fav-ours hes incuraged me to praesume to give you this trouble, and to desire ane favour from you for my sister Anna, which is to choise for her ane gase head dress with ridans [2] conform, and to cause some of your servants putt it upp cairfuly. My faithers chamerlan will wait onn your La., and give out the money for it att your direction. I hope youl pardon this trouble givne you by, Madam, Your La. most faithful servant,   JA. OGILVIE.

My sister gives you her humble service.

James, second Earl of Airlie, writer of next letter, had at this time his chief seat at Banff, where part of the ' Hoose of Airlie ' still stands in the gardens of Duff House. In common with many Scots noblemen of that period, he was in straitened circumstances, and in 1700 Alexander Duff of Braco, son of Alexander Duff of Keithmore, bought his Banffshire estates.

Banff, 19 *May,* 1691.

MY LORD,—I hear your Lodps airie holds this year, which I am glade of, seeing your Lodp. once was pleased

---

[1] Sir John Gordon.   [2] Probably miswritten for *ribans.*

to promise me some; and if ye could allowe me ane falcon or tuo at this tyme, I shall cause haulk one of y̅m̅ for your owen use, yᵗ ye may knowe the goodnes of your airie; and when they are fitt to be herried, upon your Lod̄ps advertisement I shall send my man for y̅m̅. This favor I hop ye will not refuse to him who is, My Lord, Your Lodps most affect°nt cousine and humble servant,

AIRLIE.

Alexander Ogilvie,[1] younger brother of George, third Lord Banff, in next letter writes from Allardes in Kincardineshire, the home of his first wife, Mary, eldest daughter of Sir John Allardes of that Ilk. Related to the family of Findlater he was a frequent correspondent of theirs, and several of his letters are included in this collection. Apart from the facts disclosed in these letters, it may be noted that he was probably born in 1660. Through the influence of his cousin, Seafield, he was appointed in 1699 Deputy Keeper of His Majesty's Signet. On 13th March 1700 he got sasine of the family lands of Forglen and part of Inchdrewer. In 1701 he was created a Baronet. He represented the royal burgh of Banff in the Scots Parliament from 1702 until the Union in 1707.. On the 29th of March 1706 he was made a Judge of the Court of Session, and took the title of Lord Forglen. He actively supported the union of the Parliaments, and was appointed one of the commissioners for the treaty. In the troubled times after the death of Queen Anne and down to 1723 he took an active part in the county government of Banffshire. His grandson Sir Alexander Ogilvie became seventh Lord Banff.

For SIR JAMES OGILVIE OF CHURCHHILL,
ADWOCAT, EDR.

Allardes, 15 *July* '91·

RIGHT HONŌBLL SIR,—The Earle of Craufoord having stoped resignation to be made upon ane disposition be my Lord Bamff to me, upon the pretence that my Lord Bamff was in the rebellion, qtch is a mistacke, for my

---

[1] 'Banffshire Roads,' by the editor, in *Banffshire Field Club Transactions*, 1905, pp. 81, 82; and *The Scottish Peerage*, vol. ii. p. 23.

Lord being in his north goeing at Forvie was by ane partie of the Hilanders caried to there camp, qhare he stayed hardlie halfe one day, and thereafter at Aberdein by Jacksone was detained upon inconciderat expressiones, as Jacksone alleadged and my Lord Bamff still deneyed; and I belive all proceed from my Lord Bamff his being in drink as I uas credablie informed, I have wreaton to the Veicecount of Arbuthnot to represent the caise to the Earle of Crauford, and deall with his Lo. that I may be aloued the comon course of justice, and I intreat, Sir, ye may be pleased to goe withe the Veicecountt to the Earle of Crauford and speack with him, and if that faill then by ane bill represent the mater to the Lordse of the Exchequer. I am hopefull the Veicecount will prevaill with the Earle of Crauford; for q^{tt}ever expenses or deficulties I am putt to, all will returne upon the Master of Bamff for reliefe out of the fie; and concidering Arbuthnot his relation to the Master, I believ he will doe all he can to prevent his harme, concidering the estate is brought werie lou; and if there be ane stop upon the disposition, it being butt a corroborative right of the adjudecationes, I shall infeeft myselfe upon them, butt I desyre not to accumulat expenses, and I am still, Sir, Your humble servant, ALEX^R OGILVIE.

Colonel Jackson was driven into Aberdeen in July 1690 by Colonels Cannon and Buchan. Robert second Viscount of Arbuthnott married, c. March 1658, Lady Elizabeth Keith second daughter of William seventh Earl Marischal. Their grandson Robert was the Viscount Arbuthnott of the letter. The Master of Banff's mother was Jean third daughter of the seventh Earl Marischal.

ffor SIR JAMES OGILVY OF CHURCH HILL
SON TO THE EARLE OF FINDLATER

The 28th of Jully, -69i.

DEAR SON,—Heaveing the occasion of Master Baird I wold not butt acquent you that your Lady and son are verie weall. Your sister Anna is at Pitterhead . . . well, for against my will, I admier ye heave given me no advyse about the plantation of the Kirke of Deskfoord, for its said it must be planted against the 10th of August nixt. I intreat your advyse with the first post. I shall add no mor, but that I am Your loving father,

FFINDLATER.

Master Baird was James Baird,[1] Cullen, afterwards secretary to Sir James Ogilvie, and founder of the family of the Bairds of Chesterhall, Midlothian. He is the writer of several letters in this collection.

SIR JEAMES OGILVIE OF CHURCH HILL
thes

Duns, july th 30, 169i.

LOVING BROTHER,—I having the occation of this berer thoght it fit to acquant you that I stand in very great nid of ane horse, and Captan Johnstoun is in toun. If you place to give him muny he wille affourd me ane horse, that he wille oblidg himself for ; therfor I humbly intreat you may dou me this great kyndness amongst the rest of the favors you have dun me. No more at present but that I rest still, Your most humbel and obedient brother and servant till death,   ROBERT OGILVIE.

James Brodie, laird of Brodie, commissioner for Morayshire in the Convention of 1689, favoured the revolution settlement and the establishment of Presbytery. The following letter to Sir James Ogilvie deals with the settlement of the parish of Dyke, Morayshire.

MUCH HOND. AND DEAR COOSING,—You gave us your concurrance at . . . in that call, qch this parish of Dyke gave to Mr. Allex[r] Forbes, and y[r hav]ing still an interest amongst us, [and] being fulie persuaded of your goo[d] affection to vhat is the real good and interest of this parish, ve have sent this express to you entreating you may concurr

---

[1] *Genealogical Collections concerning the Sirname of Baird,* 1870, pp. 95, 96.

yet furder vith us, and subscrive this prō^dne and varrant
to yor frind Whitereath or Mr John Campbel or both of
them to appear befor the Sinod of Glascow, for discussing
an appail that lyes befor them anent Mr. Alex^r Forbes
his transplantation to Dyke.   Ther has bein a great deal
of difficultie to effectuat this mater, and nou al depends.
vpon the right managing of this appail, and I am hopful
that all vil goe veil anuffe.   I shal say no more, bot my
service to your Ladie, and good vishes to both of you,
and I am stil, Yo^r affectionat freind and coosing and
serv^t,   J. BRODIE.

Brodie, 25 7br. '91·

Sir,—you may be pleased to brake open my letter to·
Whitvreath or Mr. Campbel, in caice it com sealed to·
from Elgin and seal it again.

Frasor, the writer of next letter, was Charles, fourth Lord Fraser.
Inverallochy, who was either Simon Fraser or his son William, was
unsuccessful in his suit.

ffor THE RIGHT HONARABELL SIR JAMS OGILVIE OF CHURCHIL

Carnbulg, 12 Oct. 91.

RIGHT HONARABELL,—I hawe just now reseived ane
sumons of laborrus from Docktor Gordon, who heath
reased a most fals and envidius laybell as ever was, but
I hoop we shall put him to trubell and expens wirth his
pains.   Invralachie is much dejected he heath not the
happines of a lien from my Lady Anna, but all he can
meet with will not make him desist.   I hoop ye will
resolev upon allowing me the fawor of mor then on night,
when ye cum to this cuntray, which is much longed for.—
Right Honorabell, Your most affectionat humbell serwant,
                                            FRASOR.

My wif and I giwes our serwice to my Lord Findlatur
and all your good cumpanie.

John, second Earl of Dundonald, died on the 17th of May 1690,
leaving three young children and a widow, Susannah, sister of

the Duke of Hamilton.   This relationship accounts for the Duke's writing to Sir James Ogilvie in the interests of the Earl's heirs.

Hamilton, 26 *Octo*ʳ 91.

Sʀ,—My Lord Duke Hamilton is informed that there is a process depending at yᵉ instance of my Lady Cochran agaᵗ Sʳ John Cochran of Ochiltry, which will tend to the prejudice of the Earle of Dundonalds heirs. Therfor his Gr. desires you as their agent to adwert to it, and take it up to be seen by their adwocats, so that what may be to their prejudice may be prevented.   Which is by his Gr. command from Yoʳ most humble servᵗ,

Da. Cʀᴀᴜꜰᴏʀᴅ.

Mᴜᴄʜ Hᴏɴᴏʀᴇᴅ,—The particular Conventione of Borroues qch satt at Edr in October last haveing receaved informatione that ther wer indeavours used at court by seall p̃sons both Inglish and Scotts joyntlie in obtaining a patent for erecting a manufactorie of linnen cloath uithin this kingdome, and that the double of the sd patent was produced to the sd Conventione, which in respect of the infrequencie of ther meetting, and that the sd project was of ane gratt concernment to the wholl Royal Borroues, it was ther opinion that the said affair should be remitted to the consideratione of a mor gñall meetting of the Borroues, qch they appointed to conveen at Edr̄ the first Wednesday of ffebr̄y next: These are therfor requyring your Burgh to send ane comissioner to the sd gñall meetting at the day and place forsd sufficientlie instructed in the premisis.   And to the effect yōr Burgh may be fullie informed as to the nature of the said project, receave the inclosed double of the said patent certifeing yōr Burgh that, if it send not a comissioner to the sd meetting, to be look upon as Burgh not regairding the interest of the Royall Burghs, and be lyable to such fynes as the said meeting shall impose conforme to the act of the sd parlar Conventione daited the 22 day of October last.   This is signified to you by Your most humble servant,

—Jᴀ: Rᴏᴄʜᴇɪᴅ.

Edr., the 8*lk day of Jar̄ij.* 1692.

The circular letter of Sir James Rocheid, Clerk to the Convention of Royal Burghs, had the desired effect. The patent was
stopped, and the two Secretaries of State for Scotland with the
Under Secretary, Sir William Hamilton, received gratuities[1] from
the Burghs for their services.

George Leslye, besides being Sheriff-Clerk of Banffshire, was
Collector of Excise for the county. In the following letter he
threatens to exact tax from brewers whether they brew or
not.

ffor JAMES LAWTIE OF TOCHIENEILL TO BE COMUNICATE
          TO BAILLIE ORD IN CULLEN
                    thes

                              Banff, 2d ffebry. 92.

SR,—I received your letter yesternight and Baillie
Ords this day, and am not satisfied with either of your
lers, though I cannot but confess both of your selfs are
fair as to your owen pairts, and thinks yee have done verie
fairlie in offering to others what yee did ; and since they
are so obstinate and ignorant as not to compley with
favours offered to them, lett them be att there hazard,
and for there contumacie and contempt for lying drey,
doe me the favour to shew ane and all of them that they
may be assured I shall be even with them, and upon there
expenss. Continue on your selfs. Yee shall find all the favour
my power. And for these who have proven contumacious,
they may be perswaded they shall pay drey excyse att
the highest rate, whither they brew or not. This tell them
from me, and that they shall never find me where they
left me ; and if the pairty which I have here from Bellen-
dallach were not allreadie ingadged and imployed otherwayes and upon some other persons, they should have
imediatlie have bein sent to Cullen, ffor I see that poeple
are so daft that I must give them some divertisment. All
these I leave to your owen caire, and desyres that with my
ffathers man who comes to Boyndie to me on Thursday
nixt ye lett me have your return of this from him, and ane

---

[1] *Records of the Convention of Royal Burghs*, 1692, pp. 146-151.

list of these who intends to ley drey.—And this is all from, S^r, Your humble servant,   GEO. LESLYE.

John Grant of Ballindalloch was in arrear with his land tax, and a party of soldiers had in consequence been quartered on his lands.

ffor THE LAIRD OF DURN, ELDER

the 18th of february –692.

MUCH HONORED SIR,—The greatest pairt of the northern forces being to march southward the close of this weeke and the nixt occasions me to trouble yu with this line, intreating you to favour me with the lean of fyftie merkes scots, which shall be faithlie restored agaien with the interest from this deat. I hope er long not onlie to pay you, butt likways manifest the sinceritie of my respect to you.—I am, Your oblidged servant,   FFINDLATER.

The fyftie merks delivered bee Mr. Patrik.

Sir John Dalrymple, Master of Stair, one of the Secretaries of State for Scotland, in the following letter refers to Sir James Ogilvie's appointment as Sheriff of Banffshire, his first step in political preferment.

For S$_R$ JAMES OGILVY, ADVOCAT

London, March 8, 1692.

S$_R$,—Sinc my last, I hav taken occasion to intertain his Maj^{ty} upon that subject you wer pleased to propose to me of the sherifship of Buchan, and now I hav incouragment to desir you to transmitt to me a signater of that office, such as yow desir it. The King givs no offices bot during pleasur (excep to the Lords of Session), so yow will not desir it in other tearmes ; bot his Maj^{ty} hath retained many that did not deserv it at his hands, yett he hav givin us no example that he threw out any man that did not deliberatly oppose him, so I conclud as to yow, it will be the sam thing as for yr life, for I persuad myself yow will never do anything unworthy of yr honor nor his Maj^{tys} favor.—And I assur yow I am sincerly, S^r, Yr very humble serv^t,   JO. DALRYMPLE.

The County Records of Banffshire bear that ' in July JMVJC and ninety ane yeirs Sir James Baird of Auchmedden Shirreff Priñll of Banffshyre dyed, and there was a vaccancie of the Shirreff Court and Surcease of Justice in the Shyre till ffebrii ɪᴍᴠɪᴄ and nyntie thrie yeirs, At qch tym Sir James Ogilvie of Churchhill obteined a Comissione to be Shirreff Priñll of Banffshyre, and on the second of ffebry 1693 the Earle of ffindlater, his father, presented his Comissione, with a Comissione by Sir James to Nicolas Dunbar of Castelfield of Shirreff Depute of Banff, and opened the Court.'

For SIR JAMES OGILVIE

Ballachastell, the : 15 Aprile 1692.

Rɪɢʜᴛ Hᴏɴōʟʟ,—I was werie unueil at Edinbrugh, uhich keeped me a longe tyme so that I cam not home till Saterday last. I am useing my indevore in what you advysed me as to Gordonstouns affair, and when your conveniencie can alloue you to keep a meiting I shall wait one you ; but my affairs in Wrquhart ar in such a condition, and my land altogither weast, that it oblidges me to goe ther imediatly, wher I take my wyffe with me to stay for some tyme ; but I will be home against the terme, so that how sone I returne I shall acquant you, and I hope ye will alloue us two ore three days er ye goe south to see if it can be taken avay. I shall not descend one anie affair till I have the good fortoune to see you. My wyffe and I give our humble deuty to the Earle off Findlater, your Ladie and all with you.—I am, in much realitie, Sir, Your most affectionat cousine and humble servantt,   Lᴜᴅᴏᴜɪᴄᴋ Gʀᴀɴᴛᴛ.

Castle Urquhart, on Loch Ness, was held by a garrison for William during the revolution, but Glenurquhart, which belonged to the laird of Grant, was otherwise open to the raids of the Jacobite Highlanders. Sir Robert Gordon was laird of Gordonstoun in Morayshire.

The following is one of many letters characteristic of times when landowners' rents were paid mostly in kind, and when most Scots noblemen were wholesale grain merchants. Other letters the same year bearing on this subject include those from Alexander Fella, dated 3rd, 9th, 12th, and 17th May. Alexander Leslie, Provost of Banff, 1690-91 and 1695-99, was laird of Kininvie, Mortlach.

For SIR JAMES OGILVY OFF CHURCHHILL
thes

Bamff, 22 off Apryll 1692.

RT HONLL,—Provest Leslie hes bein telling me, that yee have vse for ane bark about fyftein chalder to com to Portsoy within this fourtnight. I have my bark heir wch is just fyfteine chalder, and shall bee reidie (God-willing) against Satterday com eight dayes to come to Portsoy to serve you, wind and wether serveing. Thee fraught is ten punds scotts per chalder, with ane boll of meill and ane boll of malt. So y^{or} Honor may caus Andrew Craik draw tuo charter pairttyes, and I shall caus the skipper whos nam is Allex^r Norry subscryve yor doub^{ll} and returne it to you. I wish it wer in my power to serve you to any better purpose, and I only add that I am, Rtt Hon^{bl}, Your Honores most humb^{ll} ser^{tt},

GEORGE OGILVY.

Next letter throws light on the methods of the two Aberdeen Universities, Marischal College (New toun) and King's College (Old toun), in beating up for students. The writer, William Black, was probably an Aberdeen lawyer, who afterwards practised in Edinburgh.

For THE RIGHT HONORABLE S$_R$ JAMES OGILVIE
OFF CHURCH HILL thes

RIGHT HONO$^{\overline{LL}}$,—

. . . .

Among v$\bar{y}$r troubles I give yow, I prosume to wreit something in ffavovr of your Alma Mater. Mr. Allex̄r Moir on of the regents of the Newtoun Colledge, haveing the Bejane class this yeir, is lyk the important sturdie beggars useing all methods to gett schollers. Among the rest, he hes hops of some ffrom your toun of Cullen, viz., the sone of on Bailzie Ord ; and, if ye have any influence that way (q^{ch} I doubt not ye have), it will doe him a singular kyndness if yow recomend him ; or at least, if your affair w^t the Old toun Colledge hinder, that ye wold not concern yourself (if ye should be importuned by any of the masters of the Old toun Colledge) ags^t him. I hop ye will pardone my useing this ffreedome, ffor I am, Right Hono[ll], Your most oblidged and humble serv[t],

WM. BLACK.

Abd., 25 Aprill 1692.

The following letter endorsed, 'The Chancellour Tueedell's letter to Grant to stay in his own cuntrey for keepeing it in ordor,' arose out of the then threatened French invasion, which was frustrated by the naval engagement of La Hogue fought from the 19th to the 24th May. The subsequent letters of 9th, 12th, 17th, 21st, and 28th May all refer to the apprehended invasion.

For THE RIGHT HONOURABLE THE LAIRD OF GRANT
ONE OF THEIR MAJESTIES MOST HONOURABLE PRIVIE COUNCILL

SIR,—By ane express wpon the apprehensiones of a descent ffrom ffrance the Councill wes ordored to be called, and frequentlie to meet and consider the meanes for putting the countrey in a postoure of defence neccessary on such ane exigent; for which end it wes thought needfull all the Privie Councellors should be present heir upon Thursday the fyfth of May att ten in the fforenoon, to take such resolutiones as that affair may require, whereby your presence would also have bein required, if the Councill had not considered your continwance and stay att home within your ouen countrey to be of neccessary use for their Majesties service : Therefore yow are desyred to give all dilligence for keeping the countrey in peace, and for observeing and causeing execute such commands as the Councill shall send yow, and that yow make report of the state of the countrey to the Councill from tyme to tyme, and yow shall be accquainted what farder occures in this matter. This by ordor of Councill is signified to yow, By, Sir, Your humble servant,

TWEEDDALE CANCEL.

Edr., 27 Apryle 1692.

Sir John Dalrymple's recommendation of Sir James Ogilvie to the King bore fruit in the following warrant issued from the Hague on 30th April 1692. This gift, however, does not seem to have been acted on.

WART.[1] for a gift of the office of Shirefship of BAMFF in favo^r.
of SIR JAMES OGILVY of   Advocate

WILLIAM R.

OUR Soveraign Lord and Lady Considering that the
office of Sheriff of the shire of Bamff is now vacant in their
Ma^{ts} hands and at their gift and disposall by and through
the decease of   , and being
sufficiently informed of the loyalty abilities and other
good qualifications of Sir James Ogilvie of
advocate, Therefore ordain a letter of gift to be
made and past under their Ma^{ts} great seale of their
ancient kingdom of Scotland giving and granting, likeas
their Ma^{ts} by these presents give and grant unto the said
Sir James Ogilvy of   advocate,
the office of Shirefship of the said shire of Bamff during
their Ma^{ts} pleasures only : With power unto him to exerce
possess and enjoy the said office, as fully and freely in all
respects and conditions, as the same was formerly exerced
possessed and enjoyed by the said deceased
          or any of his predecessors Sheriffs of the sd
sherifdom of Bamff, or may be exerced possessed and enjoyed in any time coming, and to uplift the haill profits
emoluments priviledges and casualities whatsoever belonging thereunto : And particularly with power to the said
          to nominate and appoint
deputs and substitutes in the said office (for whom he
shall be answerable) and all other members of court needfull, excepting the clerk of that court : Provided always,
likeas by the acceptation of this comission, the said
          is to be answerable for the
uplifting, compting for, and making payment unto the
Lords Com^{rs} of their Ma^{ts} Treasury and Lords of Ex-
cheq^r of the ffew duties, retoures and blench duties, and
other duties and casualities belonging to their Ma^{ts} formerly and now used and accustomed to be uplifted,
compted for and paid in manner foresaid, and for per-

---

[1] *State Papers* (*Scotland*), *Warrant Books*, vol. xv. p. 121, in Record Office,
London.

forming the other duties and services that the Shireffs of shires are obliged to by lawes of the said kingdom, and the nature and duty of their office : Promising to hold firme and stable all and whatsoever things that the said or his deputs or substitutes shall lawfully do in the exercise of the said office. And their Ma^{ts} ordain the said letter of gift to be further extended in the most ample and best forme with all clauses needfull, and to pass their Ma^{ts} great seale aforesaid *per saltum* without passing any other seale or register : In order whereunto these presents shall be to the Directors of their Ma^{ts} Chancellary and their deputs for writing the same, and to the Lord High Chancellor or Lords Comissioners appointed for keeping the great seale for the time being, for causing the same to be appended thereunto, a sufficient warrant. Given at the Court at the Hague the last day of Aprile 1692 and of their Ma^{ts} reign the 4th year.

MAY IT PLEASE YOUR MATS,

These contain your Ma^{ts} war^t for a letter to pass (*per saltum*) under the great seale of your ancient kdom of Scotland giving and granting unto Sir James Ogilvie of advocate, the office of Sherifship of the shire of Bamff during your Ma^{ts} pleasure only, with power to him (*ut antea*).   Jo. DALRYMPLE.

The two next letters fix the date of the birth of Elizabeth, daughter of Sir James Ogilvie, between the 4th and 6th of May 1692. She afterwards became Countess of Lauderdale.

For ALLEX^R DUMBAR, MER̅T̅ IN ELGINE,
AND IN HIS ABSENCE TO HIS WYFFE these
Cullen, 4th May 1692.

S_R,—Being affrayed that my wyffe surpryse me in being brought to bed befor I gett such things as are necessarie for hir, have sent the bearer to yow to desyre that yow and your bedfellowe may doe me the favore to buy such wyne and the uyr particulars, as are contained in the [note] heir incloased, and that with all possible dispatch. I would hade sent yow money, bot know not whatt they may amount to; bot send me the accompt with the particulars, and I shall give the money to your good sister Elspett: Which is all from, Sir, Your assured freind,

JA. OGILVIE.

I intreat yow dispatch the bearer.

For THE MUTH HONLL SR JAMES OGILVIE,
SREFF PRINLL OFF BANFF

Banff, Maij 6 : 92.

MUTH HONLL,—Acording to you comands I delyvered the inclosed to her G., qroff receave the anssr. On Monday her G. is going to Gordoncastl, and will see you all in her bygoing about four aclok. In the afternoon her G. will dyn heir, and will stay somtym at Cragaboynd. My humble service to my Lord ffindlater and all the hon[ll] familie.—I am, Muth Hon[ll], Your most obedient and humble servant qll,   Jo. STEWART.

I wish you muth joy off your yong Eliza.

Cragaboynd, where the Duchess of Gordon was to stay, was the older name of Boyne Castle, Sir Patrick Ogilvie's residence.

Alex[r] Fella, the writer of the three following letters, in 1687 was tenant of the farm of Lichiestoune, in Deskford. He was Sir James Ogilvie's agent in Leith for the disposal of his grain. Besides giving prices, he gives the current political news about the threatened French invasion, and the measures taken to cope with the situation in Scotland and with the bogus Jacobite conspiracy in London called Young's plot.

For SIR JAMES OGILWIE OFF CHURCHHILL
TO BE FOUND AT CULLEN these

Leith, 9th May 1692.

HONORED SIR,—Haveing the occasione of this bearer George Watsone, I thought fitt to acquant yow about your wictuel, espeatlie the weshell that is not come vp as yet. I am meassring ower to the merchants the meall, and am affraid that it shall goe in, but the bearer shall give yow ane accompt of it. As for master Gairdner and Charles Robertsone, they are not lyk to tak noe mor of your beir nor fyve hunder bolls. I am asking for merchants

for the rest of it, and will not ingadge with me till it come
vpon the place, that they may sie the sufficiencie of it.
The best beir that is come from our countray is sold at
four pound the boll, and noe readie money.   The Orknay
and Cathnes beir is sold for four merks the boll heir, and
is daily falling and espeaHie the meall.   As for the money
that I have gotten for thes meall, I have it in readines ;
and noe thing hinders me now but onlie waiting for that
weshell, and the longer she is comeing vp I fear the mercat
for her loadning will be the worse.   I offered it to your
merchants till Mertimes for fyve pounds, and will not
accept of it, and hes taken it to advyse.   They alleadge
that ye have gotten a wery great pryce for that fyve
hunder bolls beir, and are repenting wery sore.   As for
your meall, I wish it stayed home, although it hade lyen
these four years to come in the girnels.   What ye will
ordour me to doe with your moēy I have gotten, I shall
obey your Honors comands.   As for newes, ther are soe
maney goeing heir that some of them are uncertan ; but
yeasterday at Edr and heir all betwixt sixtie and sixtein
were mustered ane myle distant from Edr, and what
the event yrof may prove I can not tell.   Ther is a great
talking amongst the Gillichrankies that King James is
landed in England, but noe certantie for it ; but yeasterday, after the English fleett sayled from this with the
souldiers, ther went ane express to them, after they were
the length of the mouth of the firth, to land them in the
first English ground they touched at ; and if the wind did
not srve them, to come vp and land them heir ; and
what the meining yrof is I can not tell.   The meall is
compleatlie meassred, and is intaked six firlots and two
pecks less nor the bill of loadning ; and whither it be the
metsters fault or imbazlement in the ship I know not.
I never took such paines in attending said wictuel my
liftyme as I have done this ; and the ingaing and badnes
of the mercat is ane anger and greiff to me ; this being
all at presentt save onlie that I rest, Honored Sir, Your
humble and obedient srvant whill I am

                                    ALEXR. FELLA.

My Lord Syforth is escaped out of Edr and gone for the north, at which escape thir is ane great vproar heir, and makes the mercat for wictuel worse nor it wold be.

Att closing heirof I receaved ane lyne of the fourth of this moneth dated from yow, wherin ye desyre me to wreat to yow, and accordinglie since I cam heir I have written four letters to yow, and marvels that they are not come to your hands by reason I sent them with sure bearers, that they might not be miscaryed.

The Earl of Seaforth as a 'profest papist' was on 18th May 1689 superseded as Sheriff-principal of Ross-shire.[1]　His uncle Mr. Colin M'Kenzie was on 14th July 1690 forfaulted as having been in the rebellion with Dundee.[2]　In 1693 Seaforth himself was charged with high treason.[3]

For SIR JAMES OGILWYE OFF CHURCH HILL
AT CULLEN these

Leith, 12th May 1692.

HONORED SIR,—Haveing the occasione of this bearer, James Mackye in Newmilne of Keith, since I wrot to yow last, I have been treying for merchants to buy the super-plus of your beir. I expect to gett fyve pounds for every boll of it till ane day, and seven merks in hand mo͞ey, if it were heir vpon the place ; and it is ane great hinderance to me to stay vpon that weshel, seeing I have noething to doe heir more. I desyre your Honor most earnestlie to let me know what I shall doe. They are mightilie affrighted heir with the drought. That is that makes the beir give more nor it hes bein formerlie. As for newes, wee hear them daily, but can not give trust to them. And ther is ane plot latlie discovered at London, that soe maney Earles Lords Squaires etc. were vpon ane conspiracie to tak the Queens lyff and to burn the Citie, and ane considerable number of them apprehended and are in the Tower, as this dayes newes letter mentions. As also the newes letter gives ane accompt that King James forces in France comeing for

---

[1] *The Acts of the Parliaments of Scotland*, vol. ix. Appendix, p. 33.
[2] *Ibid.*, p. 61.　　　　　　　　　[3] *Ibid.*, p. 74.

England were all shipped at Brest, and are stopped ther by the English and Dutch fleets; and it is just now presentlie reported heir, that ane considerable number of the fleett are called in to England, to witt the comanders of them who were suspected to be partakers of plott, and are in the Tower. Haveing noe more at present to trouble, but requests your Honor to send the weshel heir, and sooner she comes it may furder your advantage, for pryces of wictuel are vp the one day and doun the vyr, is all at present from, Right Hono[ll], Your Ho. most humble and obedient srvant till death,   ALEXR. FELLA.

The moēy of the meall I have gotten, and knowes not what to doe with it, as I told yow in my last sent with George Watsone, this being four or five tymes I have wrīne to your Honor, but hes never gotten ane lyne from yow but one.

Remember my lowe and kyndnes to my Lord and master.

Though several of the officers of the fleet were strongly suspected of Jacobitism, the Queen, who was acting in the absence of her husband, did not send them to the Tower, but successfully appealed to their patriotism.

For THE MUCH HŌRED SIR JAMES OGELVIE OFF
        CHURCHHILL ATT CULLON OFF BOYND
                these wt care   3d

Leith, ye i7 *May* i692.

MUCH HŌRED,—I ame very anctiouss to be relleivd, but sees no apearance off that weshall as yett, and the pryces falls evry day, and troubles and confusion incresses heer and lyk to be over all. Its thought the fleets have mett by this tyme; but litle neues can be hade in regaird some pacquets are taken, and some lērs qn they come are keept ore burnt. Ther is sēall great men and officers in Ingland secured. Most off nobillety and gentrie heer hes ther horsses and armes all seazed, and the wholl forces is to be incamped this week in Gladsmoor. My Lord Seaforth haveing absented from Edr is aprihended

att Pancatland, and brought in yesterday. As for y^e
orders concerning the forces off ye north, it will be att yōr
hand beffor this.   Its still expect the sumer session will
not be much, iff att all.   Iff ye bear wer heer I expect 5^lb
to a day, ore 7 merks raidy mony; but non will barguen
till they see it.   John Strachen advysed me rather to
ye 7 merks rady mony.   Merchd̄s are very affrayed to
medle at this tyme.   Those that hes meall is expecting
it be seccured for ye publicqe.   As for yōr Hōrs mony,
I have about therteen hundreth merks, but knows not
what to doe with it.   The tymes are so troublsom, that
I ame affrayd to carie it north utout yōr Hōrs spetiall
comand.   I offered it to sēalls coming north, but they
wold not medle ūt it,   So lett me have comands in this
and q̃t elss concerns yōr Hōr heer, and they shall be
observed by Yōr Hōrs most obedient servant,

ALEXR FELLA.

For THE RIGHT HONOURABLE SIR JAMES OGILVIE
OF CHURCH[HILL]

RIGHT HONOURABLE,—I have sent inclosed all the news
that are come with this dayes post.   There came only one
print proclamation for secureing the peace in the northerne
shires ; and the clerk depute is to cause proclaim it at
the crosse, and tells he must keap it for his warrand ;
but I have sent inclosed an exact double of it.   I had from
Abd account that the whole English and Dutch fleets
were on the coast of France, and it is thought by many
that they and the French fleet have ingaged by this time,
that Doctor Sprat, Bishop of Rochester, is seized as
being on the plott, that the execution of the designe of
the plot should have been the 12th of May, if God had
not prevented it by a timous discovery.   The Earle of
Seafoorth, who lately upon the news of the invasion
escaped from Edr̄, is again apprehended.   What further
account of news comes to this place I shall send them to
Durne, and the Laird of Durne hes promised imediatly to
dispatch ym to the Earle of Findlater and your Honour.

I am to My Lord, to your Honour, your most worthy
Lady, and all the noble familie a most obleidged and
most humble devoted servant,   MR. PAT. INNES.
   Banff, May 21, 1692.

Two days before the minister of Banff wrote the sea-fight of
La Hogue which lasted until the 24th began.   It was fought and
won before Francis Montgomerie uncle to Sir James wrote.

For SIR JAMES OGILVIE

DEAR SIR,—I have giwen my Lord your father the trouble
of a letter, intreating he wold help me with haukes this
summer.   All I had are dead, so I intreat your help and
assistans to prucure some from him, or from any of your
friends and relationes.   I doubt not bot yow hawe heard
the newes of ane intended inwasion on Britane by French
and Irish; and had not the weind prowed long cross to
them, it had bien in all probabilitie before much preparation had bien made at sea or land to oppose them.   Both
fleets are now at sea, and a feight is dayly expected.   Ther
hath bien a great discovery made of a plott in Ingland,
wher severall noblemen and others are apprehended and
many fled, amongst whom are the Earles of Midletone
Newbrugh and Dinmore my Lord Forbes and Sir Andrea
fforrester.   Begging your pardon for this trouble, and
intreating yow wold give my humble serwice to your Lady
and brothers and sisters, I rest, Dear Sir, Your affectionat
uncle and most humble servant,

FFR MONTGOMERIE.

Winton, Maye 28, 1692.
   Charles, second Earl of Middleton, a staunch Jacobite was
imprisoned for a short time in 1692.   After his liberation he went
to St. Germains.   He was tried in absence for treason, and was
outlawed by the High Court of Justiciary on 23rd July 1694.   In
exile he was principal Secretary of State for James.   Charles
Livingstone, second Earl of Newburgh, was a state prisoner in the
Tower from 16th July to 15th August 1690.   He died in 1694.
Lord Charles Murray, second son of John, first Marquess of Atholl,
was created Earl of Dunmure on 16th August 1686.   He was
Jacobite in sympathy, and on the 16th May 1692 was committed

to the Tower on a charge of high treason.   He was admitted to bail of £13,000.

ffor SR JAMES OGILVIE, Advocatt thes

Ballachastell, the 9 : *July* 1692, *Munday.*

Right Honoll,—I had the inclosed from Gordonstoune Saterday last, wherby I perceave he desyns south.   I am to-morow goeing for Urquhart and from that to hold courts att Killichumen, so that it is not possible for me to goe to Edinbrugh at this tyme.   Therfor I have sent yow inclosed the Chancellors letter to me, which I judge warant sufficient to stay at home till called ; and at least I think the Councel will doe nothing against me till they alloue me a day to apear.   I have sent yow a blank letter, uhich yow will be pleased to fill up for the Chancellor, for I refer the wording off it to yow.   If ther be a necessitie for my comeing, I will one your call come ; but if it be possible I wold wish it might be delayed till November.   My confidence is in yow, and I hope ye will excuse this truble, since from Your affectionat cousine and humble servantt,   Ludouick Grantt.

Ye may wryt to me by the post, and lett it be directed to Invernes.

Ludovick laird of Grant was Sheriff-principal of Inverness-shire. Killichumen after 1746 was known as Fort Augustus.   The Chancellor's letter, dated 27th April 1692, has already been given.

Sir Patrick Ogilvie of Boyne in next letter refers to the intended marriage between Lady Anna, sister of Sir James Ogilvie, and George Allardes of Allardes, Arbuthnot, Kincardineshire, which took place in the autumn of this year, the marriage contract being dated 20th October 1692.

For [SIR] JAMES OGILVIE OF CHURCHHILL, Advocat
at Edb

Boyn, July 20, 1692.

Sr,—I have wreat the inclosed to Brigtown[1] as yow desyred me.   I will endevor to perform, tho yow know I

---

[1] John Lyon.

have much busnes on my hand.   All yowr freinds ar weill.
I am told ther is propositions from Ardes to yowr sister
L. Anna.   If his circumstances be as they ar represented,
I dout not it pleas all freinds.   Yowr northcoming is
longed by all yowr freinds, and particularly by, S^r, Yowr
affectionat cusing and humble servant,

PATRICK OGILVIE.

I have wrott to Mr. Jams Elfingstown,[1] if he have any of
my monie undisposed off, that he send it north with yow,
which I hop yow will caus your servant cary.

For SIR JAMES OGILVIE OF CHURCHILL
Banff   heast heast   3d

Edr., the i5th of Sptr. 92.

RIGHT HONORABLE,—. . . I expected befor this tyme to
haue had commission from you for taking of Ladie Annas
nesesaries, but in that you may dou a[s] you thinke fitt.—
I trou[b]lie you no farder, but that I still ame, Sir, Your
most affectionat and humble srt,   JA. DUNBAR.

Turn over.

For neues ane Ostende ship cam to Lith last day, who was
but four dayes betuixt Holand and this.   He gives ane
accoumpt that befor he cam off the wholl Confedirat armie
had invested Dunkirk be land, whell a great manie of the
Inglish and Duch flitts wer bombarding it by sea.   This
is both the greatest and leatest neues we haue heir.
Adeu.

James Dunbar, Younger of Durn, was brother-in-law of Sir
James Ogilvie.   Late in July William and the Confederates were
defeated by the French at Steinkirk, and Dunbar's news about the
bombardment of Dunkirk points to the date of the letter being
1694.

Martha Stevensone, bookseller, Edinburgh, continued to supply
the Earle of Findlater with books.

Eden., Sept. 22d, 1692.

MY LORD,—According to yowr Lordship's order I have

---

[1] Of Logie, commissioner for Aberdeenshire.

deliverd the books yow writt for to Mr. Creake. I have no new books that I can give yowr Lordship an account of att present, only the Duke of Lorrains life, and a discours on natruall and reveled religon by C. Nursy. I have ane deffence of Episcopasy by D. Maurice. I have given a commission for some book, and I expect the fift volum of the Turkish spy. I have sent as your Lordship desired ane account of the whole.—Your Lord[ships] humble servant,

MARTHA STEVENSONE.

1692   The names and prices are these :—

		lib.	s.	d.
ffeb 10th	15 Mercury's bd in calf leather .	05	08	00
Aprile 18th	Charins travells folio, voll 1th .	16	16	00
	Gentelmans recreations, 8vo .	04	16	00
June 11th	Bohun's geographicall dictionary, 8vo	05	08	00
	Temple's memoirs, 8vo . . .	03	02	00
	Don Quixot folio . . .	10	04	00
	Dr. King's state of the Protestants in Ireland, 8vo	04	04	00
	Turkish spy in 4 voll. . .	09	12	00
	Suma	60	00	00

Sir William Hamilton, Advocate, Under-Secretary of State for Scotland, in next letter discusses the political situation in Scotland, and the race among Scots politicians for place.

ffor SIR JAMES OGILVIE OF CHURCHHILL

SIR,—I was much refreshed by your letter, and with the good account your servant gave me of your health, for I longe much for November, when I hope to have the happyness to see yow. ffor newes about courte affaires, noe wonder yow have many uncertaine reports therof with yow, for ewen here the different factiones vent different newes very confidentlie. These that are in court think never to be out of it ; and these that are out are

still hopeing to be in. It is thought by some that their
will be some alterationes when the King returnes. This is
hoped and feared by different pairties. On Munday last
Breadalbin and Tarbet went for London. The reason of
their so sudden departure was that their came a letter
to the Chancelour that post, which he was to intimate to
the councellours, commanding them not to leave Scotland
without the Kings particular warrand. Cullodin went to
courte with Secretarie Johnstoune. Polwart is to take
journey presentlie for courte. The behawiour of some
folks here, when the invasione was feared, is thought
will be the subject of informatione against them at courte.
What the ewent therof will be, I can not prognosticate by
this letter, but I hope againe wee meet some things will
be plaine, which are now mysteries to us. Give my humble
service to your Lady and to my Lord your father (tho I
have not the honour of their acquaintance) ; and doe me
the justice as to reckon me, Sir, Your obleidged and
obedient servant,   WILL. HAMILTON.

Edr., Septer 23, 1692.

James Cock, Town Clerk of Banff and County Collector, gives
Sir James Ogilvie an account of the results of the first essay in
Jacobite intrigue of James Ogilvie Younger of Boyn.

ffor THE RIGHT HONLL SR JAMES OGILWIE OFF
CHURCH HILL these

Banff, 3 October 92.

RIGHT HONLL,—There is ane great pairtie come heir
yeasternight off Collonell Buchans regiement, consisteing
of ane captaine lyvetenent ensigne sēall subalterns
cadies and 60 sentinells, who have something in hand
besyde the cess, there being noe more resteing but
this last Lambas terme, being 2875 ℔s. 10s ; and
it wes never heard in this shyre that· ane pairtie wes
soe soone emitted, there being noe preceidings resteing.
The captaine off the pairtie went out this night, by wirtue
of ane warrand ffrom the Councill, with 24 men to apprehend youer ffrend young Boyne ; but I presume unles he

be werie vnffortunat, he is out of the way, being ffor-
warned. This youer Ho. may keep to youer selfe. And
now I have sent youer account of resteing cess to you,
qch must be here this night preceislye, vyrwayes I
cannot exeem the lands ffrom ane pairtie. Your Ho. will
send the wholle sume required; ffor youer Ho. will
ffind the 100 ℔s. peyt by the daills sent, and 29 ℔s. dew
by my Lord youer ffaither. This is peremptor, so that
youer Ho. will excuse this ffreedome ffrom, Right Honℏ,
Your Ho. humble srvant,   JA. COCK.

Colonel John Buchan of Auchmacoy, Aberdeenshire, was brother
of Major-General Thomas Buchan the Jacobite leader.

Next day James Cock writes: 'The pairtie that went out last
night as I told your Ho. in my last hes missed yr mark and are
returned. I wish God that bussines were done away, and that
youer Ho. were at Edr.'

For SIR JAMES OGILVIE

DEAR SIR,—Im sory to hear yr bussines should make it
uneasy for you to doe my cussine the favour to be att
hir mariage. I hope you'll gett it so ordered as to come
one Tusday. All of us intreats it; and I particularly beg
it, for Im pleased wt all occasions wher I can have the
good fortune to waite one you, and mey convinc you hou
intyrly I am, Drst Sir, Yr most affectionatt humble servant,
                                                 KEITH.

Inverugie, Octr. 23, 1692.

Lord Keith was William, afterwards (1694) ninth Earl
Marischal.

ffor THE RIGHT HONBLE THE EARLE OF FINDLATIRE

MY LORD,—I shall be glad of any thing I can doe to
serve yr Lop and famely, and have sent yr Lop the drinke
for the head ack, which is to be warmed a litle, and half an
English pint drunke at night iust going into bed, and as
much the next night in the same maner. I am sory to
heare Sr James's Lady is soe indisposed. I send her some
histerick water as desired. She is to take but the one

half at once, when she finds the fit come one her ; the other half may be laid by till the next day or next occation therafter.   If I can doe yr Lo^p or her any furder seruice none shall be more willing ; and the next weeke I hope to receave yr comands and tell you how much I am, My Lord, Yr Lo^{ps} humble serv^t,   ELIZA: GORDON.[1]

last De^r. 92.

A second royal warrant[2] for a gift of the office of Sheriff of Banff in favour of Sir James Ogilvie was signed at Kensington on the 23rd of December 1692.   Drawn in similar terms to the one given at the Hague on the 30th of April 1692 it ends as follows :—

MAY it please your Ma^{ts},—These contain your Ma^{ts} warrant (upon the considerations above mentioned), for a gift to be past (*per saltum*) under the great seale of your ancient kingdom of Scotland nominating and appointing Sir James Ogilvie above designed Sheriff Principall of the sherifdome of Bamff and bounds thereof, during your pleasures allenarly, giving and disponing to him the said office of Sheriff Principall, with all fees casualities emoluments and profits belonging thereunto, with full power to nominate deputs one or more, sergeants officers procurator fiscalls and all other members of court needfull (except clerks) for which he shall be answerable, and to performe all other things belonging to the said office and jurisdiction, with equall right liberty and priviledge as the deceased Sir James Baird of Auchmedden and Sr George Gordon of Edinglassie, conjunct Sheriffs thereof, or any other Sheriff Principall within your said kingdom exerced, or might have exerced the same in any time bygone.

Given at the Court at Kensingtoun the 23d day of December 1692 and of their Ma^{ts} reign the 4th year,

JO. DALRYMPLE.

The County Records of Banff bear that the new Sheriff's

---

[1] See letter at pp. 11, 12.

[2] *State Papers (Scotland), Warrant Books,* vol. xv., in Record Office, London.

commission was presented by his father, the Earl of Findlater, at Banff on the 2nd of February 1693. It would thus seem that the earlier commission of 30th April 1692 had not been acted on.

Sir James Baird fifth of Auchmedden was appointed Sheriff-principal of Banffshire on 4th February 1664. In October 1668 he was elected along with Sir Patrick Ogilvie of Boyne commissioner to Parliament for Banffshire. In 1672 his son James, who predeceased him, was appointed conjunct Sheriff-principal with him. Sir James died in July 1691.

The letters of Martha Stevensone, bookseller, Edinburgh, dated 12th January and 28th March 1693, throw further light on the literary taste of the Earl of Findlater.

For THE EARLE OF FFINLADER

MY LORD,—I have sent yor Lop with the bearer the Duke of Lorrains lyfe, Norris practical discours, Sir Will Temples essayes, which is all the new bookes I have at this tyme, which I think fitt to send to yor Lop. I have sent a commission for London for others viz., L'Estranges paraphrase of Esops fables, Drydens translation of Perseus, Burnetts pastoral care, Temple's observations vpon the Netherlands, Sherlock on death, idem on judgement, idem on Haven and Hell, and some others which if yor Lop. have a mynd for shall be sent when they come. And as for the Mercuries, the November and December Mercuries are not yit come out, and vntill they come furth wee doe not bind the whole tuelvemoneth vp, bot after they come furth the whole shall be sent. As for the order yow have given Sir James for my payment I thank yor Lop. I have not yit called for it at Sir James, because he is so thronged with bussines. Besydes the three bookes above, I have lykewayes sent with the bearer at this tyme Eachards description of Ireland, Christian prudence by Bishop Santcroft, Eachards geography, which vpon second thoughts I did lykewayes think fitt to send. These are all at present from, My Lord, Yor Lop. most humble and most oblieged srv^t,

MARTHA STEVENSONE.

Edinbur̄., Jary. 12, 1693.

Pryces of the books sent :—

	lib.	sh.	d.
Duke of Lorrains lyfe	3	06	0
Norris practical discours	2	08	0
Temples essayes	4	16	0
Eachards descript. Irel.	1	16	0
Christian prudence	2	08	0
Eachards geography	1	10	0
	16	04	0

There is lykewayes sent at this tyme to yor
   L^{op} 5th vol. Turkish spye   .   .   .   02   08   0

                            Sum. tot.   18   12   0

I expect shortly down the sext vol.

The Master of Stair in next letter refers to the two commissions granted to Sir James Ogilvie appointing him Sheriff-principal of Banffshire.

             For S^R JAMES OGILVY, ADVOCAT

                    London, Janry. 19, 1693.

S^R,—I hav yrs, and am glad any thing I can serv yow in is acceptable to yow. The thing itself is not valuable, bot it imports that by the Kings givin yow that mark of his favor formerly and renewing it now, that he retains no displeasur nor suspition against yow, which is all yow can wish for. Bein of yr capacitys and quality in a good lucrativ imployment in this age, wher ther ar so few eminent men for the publick, yow may be sur yow will be brought in befor it may be advantageous for yow ; for in a privat imployment a man becoms better founded, and as weill reworded as oftims he can expect in the publick. I do asur yow, that good fortun and prefeerment may attend yow shall be allwys the wish of, S^r, Yr very humble servant,   JO. DALRYMPLE.

CHAPTER III

LETTERS DURING THE REIGN OF WILLIAM AND MARY FROM 1693 TO 1696

SIR JOHN DALRYMPLE's anticipation on 19th January 1693, that Sir James Ogilvie would soon be brought into the government, was immediately realised, when on 31st January he was appointed Solicitor to their Majesties. The two next letters refer to this important advance in his political career.

For THE EARLE OF FINDLATER   thes

Edr., Febry 28, 1693.

MY LORD,—I doubt not bot your Lo. hes ane accompt of my being made Sollicitor, and I have five hundreth pound of pension. It will keep me some time longer in this place then I intended. It's thought our Parlament will sitt. Wee have no other neus. I intreat that the magistrats of Banffe be leatne understand that I will look to the Kings interest so long as I am Shirife, and will not alou them to incrotch; and if it wer not that I have kindness for them I would inquier affter what is done alreadie. It will also be fitt Alex̄r Grant know that all who have acted in any publict station may be chalenged, if they have not qualified them selfs ackording to lau; bot if once it pleas God I come home, I will inquier further in this matter.—I am, My Lord, Your Lo. most obedient son and humble servant,   JA. OGILVIE.

For THE EARLE OF FINDLATER thes

Edr., March 8, 1693.

MY LORD,—I cannot promise as yet for some time to come home. My imployment keeps me hier, bot as soon as possiblie I can, I resolve to be with your Lo. I know not bot I may be necessitat to goe to London, bot if I doe I will stey bot veric short, while I shal wreat to your Lo. from time to time. I have not yet sold my victual, and I will endeavour to doe it to the greatest advantage.

Wee have no neus, bot what the bearer will give you ane accompt of ; and I am, My Lord, Your Lo. most obedient son and humble servant,   JA. OGILVIE.

Sir James, as he anticipated, was in London soon afterwards, as appears from his half-brother Robert Seton's letter to him of 6th July 1693.

For THE EARLE OF FFINLADER

MY LORD,—I have sent with this bearer Norris essayes, Nurcyes essayes, Sherlock on death, Sherl. on judgement, Bp. Burnetts pastoral care, Norris Christian blessednes, descript. of Savoe. As for L'Estranges Esopes fables, Dryden's Juvenal, there was but one of a sort sent to me, they being dear, and I could not get them keept, since I was uncertain of ane occasion wherby to send them to yor Lop. I am to have them and some other new bookes shortly, and I thowght fitt to acquant yor Lop. of these tuo bookes. The pryce of L'Estranges Esope is 14 lib, and Drydens Juvenal is 13 lib. 4 sh.; so that if yor Lop. be satisfied with the pryces, let me have a lyne that I may keep them for yor Lop. As for the 6th vol. of the Turkish spye, it is not yit come heir, bot it is out at London, and I will have it shortly. As for the volume of Mercuries I have not them bound vp at this tyme, bot with the first occasion they shall be sent. According as yor Lop. told me that yow had ordered Sir James to pay me, so I sent to him ; bot he told that he behooved to send the dowble of the accompt to yor Lop. first, that yow might see it. I have sent the dowble of it heirwith, that if yor Lop. think fitt yee may appoynt Sir James to pay it. It comes to nyntie eight pound tuo shill. scotts, and I doe not exact one farthing more from yor Lop. then what I sell to others for reddic money. These are all at present from, My Lord, Yo^r Lop. most humble servant,

                                        MARTHA STEVENSONE.

Edinburgh, march 28, 1693.

The Earl of Findlater had not up to March 1693 attended any of the sessions of the Parliament of 1689. In common with most north of the Tay he supported the Episcopal form of church government, which was displaced in 1690 for the Presbyterian. In the following letter his son, now a minister of the Crown, gives him advice as to his attitude on public affairs, if he is to attend the coming session of Parliament.

For THE EARLE OF FINDLATER
thes

MY LORD,—I find nou the Parlament will sitt.   If you have inclinations to come over you may doe it, and I will as mutch as I can assist you with money ; bot it will be needless unless you resolve to comply with the Presbiterian interest, and to concurr with the circumstances of the times in evry point.   If you can think of this, Secritarie Johnston will be hier, and I will doe whats my diutie to your Lo.   Lett me quicklie hear annent this, and I will order bussiness ackordinglie. . . . My Lord, Your Lo. most obedient son and humble servant,

JA. OGILVIE.

Edr., March 29, 1693.

Parliament sat on the 18th of April 1693, with the Duke of Hamilton as Commissioner, though Alexander Duff of Braco, one of the representatives of Banffshire, did not know of its downsitting.

ffor THE EARLE OFF FFINDLATOUR
thes

MY LORD,—I have been extrordinarlie unweill, and now, praised be God, I am som way recovered ; and I am anxious to know from your Lo. if you have laitlie heird from your sonne Sr James, and if your have certaine intelligence that the Parliat is sitteing ; and if it be sitteing, if your Lo. have anie commands for him, they shall be delyverd within thir few dayes by Your Lo. most obedient and humble servant,

A. DUFF.

Neithermilne, 24 *Apryll* 1693.

On the 25th of April Parliament enacted that several members including Sir Patrick Ogilvie of Boyne and Alexander Duff of Braco, the commissioners for Banffshire, who had not signed the assurance, should do so before the 5th of May, failing which their places would be declared vacant.[1] On the 28th of April Sir Patrick Ogilvie was fined[2] for his absence. On the 2nd of May Duff of Braco took the oath of allegiance and assurance;[3] but the laird of Boyne, who did not do so, was deprived. On the 15th of May his fine was remitted on the ground that he was absent by reason of his private affairs.[4] Coubin, referred to in next letter, was Alexander Kinnaird, whose estate of Culbin, in Morayshire, was devastated by sand in 1695.[5]

For THE EARLE OFF FINDLATER
thes

Edr., May 6t, 1693.

MY LORD,—It is with great difficultie I have got your absence excused ; bot houever it is fit that you wreat to the Commissioner and give him ane accompt of your indisposition. I will send with the post ane commission to you, that you may depon in that affair of Coubins. I have some discharges which I will cause double, and if more be peyed you may give your oth theranent. You may drau ane bill on me for fifteen pieces peyable affter the term, and I shal ansuer it ; and then my brother Deskfoord should be provid of what he needs. We want nou ane comissioner for our shire. My Lord Boyn and you would advert that some fitt person be elected. If Sir James Abercrombie would accept, I think him fitter then any I know. It is fitt that the accompts diu to the shire be sent over, that they may be staated by the Parlament. I know Durn hes some of them, and if James Cok or Burdsbnk have any of them, let them be sent.—I am, My Lord, Your Lo. most obedient sone and humble servant,   JA. OGILVIE.

Mr. Francis Mountgomerie desirs to have some of the haulks, if they hold.

The freeholders of Banffshire followed Sir James Ogilvie's advice and elected Sir James Abercrombie of Birkenbog commissioner

---

[1] The Acts of the Parliaments of Scotland, vol. ix. p. 249.   [2] Ibid., p. 250.
[3] Ibid., p. 251.   [4] Ibid., p. 261.   [5] Ibid., pp. 452, 453, 479.

in room of Sir Patrick Ogilvie, on the 23rd of May 1693. Durn was Sir James's father-in-law, William Dunbar.

The Presbyterian settlement of the church north of the Tay was so far advanced in April 1689, when the Convention appointed all parish ministers under pain of deprivation to pray by name publicly for William and Mary. Many Episcopal clergymen, who were extreme Jacobites, disobeyed; and the ensuing deprivations and placing of Presbyterian ministers in the vacancies paved the way for the Presbyterian settlement. On 22nd July 1689 Parliament abolished prelacy. Early in the session of 1690 the surviving Presbyterian ministers who were 'outed' after 1st January 1661 were restored; and later in the session Presbytery was formally established. Many moderate Episcopalian clergymen conformed; but the progress of Presbytery in the north, where the people were attached to Episcopacy, was very slow. Its ultimate establishment was only accomplished by Parliament on 16th July 1695 allowing the nonconforming Episcopal clergymen, who took the oaths of allegiance, to remain in their charges, and by settling Presbyterian ministers as these died out. Many of the Seafield letters, besides the following one and those of 26th June, 17th and 19th July, and 2nd August 1693, throw light on the settlement of the Scots church.

For THE RIGHT HONOURABLE SIR JAMES OGILVIE
OF CHURCHHILL their Majesties Solicitor
these

RIGHT HONOURABLE,—Though it may be thought rude- nesse at such a time, when you are imployed in weightie matters to give you any diversion by a trifling line, yet having myself been allowed accesse to you, when you have been much busied, I presume this will not be rejected. I am refreshed with the account I have of the pains you take in behalf of the ministerie in the north, and the great civilities you have shewed to some of their representatives. I hope your Hor. will never repent your endeavours to make a good understanding betwixt the differing parties; and seeing God hath raised you to a station wherein you can be instrumental in this, I persuade myself your pains heerin, as it doth not passe unobserved by men, so neither will it be unrewarded by God. The procuring union in the

Church is an honouring God, and them that honour him he will honour.

I am informed Robert Stewart the mēssr hath an unjust action against the Lady Abergaildie, and in this place he hath boasted of your Hors. owning him, wch having come to the ears of one of her neer relatione heer, hath occasioned her grief ; but I have assured that I so well know your just temper, that that man hes spoken only at random. The cause of a widow is the work of a King to hear and redresse ; and I am sure such a solicitor as now their Majesties have will never have occassion to do any thing oppressive against such. I heartily wish you successe in all your under-takings and affairs, and a greater increase of honour temporal and eternal ; and pleading you will pardon this unseasonable addresse, I subscrive myself, Right Ho^ll, Your Hors. most obleidged and faithfull servant,

MR. PAT. INNES.

Banff, May 30, 1693.

The Lady Abergaildie was probably Euphemia Graham, daughter of Robert Graham, the laird of Morphie, widow of Alexander Gordon, eighth laird of Abergeldie.[1] Mr. Patrick Innes, minister of Banff, was the first in Banffshire to conform to Presbytery. He and five ministers of Aberdeenshire were the clerical nucleus of the Presbyterian Church government of these counties, which met in Aberdeen on 11th July 1694.

Patrick Ogilvie, the writer of next letter, third son of the Earl of Findlater, was born in 1665. In 1690 he was appointed a Commissioner of Supply of Banffshire under the designation of 'Pittenbringand' a part of the Findlater estate near Cullen House. In July 1692 he was resident at Cairnbulg, near Fraserburgh, an ʃestate which he acquired in 1695 from the Frasers. William Baird, in his *Genealogical Collections concerning the Sirname of Baird,* says that he married Elizabeth Baird, daughter of Sir James Baird of Auchmedden, and widow of Sir Alexander Abercrombie of Birkenbog, to whom she was married on 22nd August 1666, and by whom she had Sir James Abercrombie, Mr. Alexander Abercrombie of Tullibody, and several other children. By her second husband, he says, she had one daughter, Lady

---

[1] *The House of Gordon*, New Spalding Club, by J. M. Bulloch, vol. i. p. 92.

Tyrie (Fraser), who was probably the 'chyld' mentioned in next letter. Patrick Ogilvie married a second time, probably in 1708, his first cousin, Elizabeth, daughter of the Hon. Francis Montgomerie of Giffen. He died at Inchmartine, on 20th September 1737, in his seventy-second year. Considerable detail about him will be found in the Seafield letters.

For THE RIGHT HONORABLE THE EARL OF
FINDLATER
these ar

My Lord,—I haue giuen your Lo. the trouble of this letter, to let you knou that my wife and chyld and my self is saf com hear. I long to knou hou your Lo. and al the rest of the famlie is. We giue your Lo. our houmble douty, our seruice to my sisters.—So wising you all good halth, I continou, My Lord, Your Lo. affectionat son and houmble seruant,   PAT. OGILVIE.

Jun 8, 1693.

William, Lord Inverurie, eldest son of Sir John Keith, first Earl of Kintore, was out with the Jacobites in 1690; but having received a remission on 27th November that year, he seems thereafter to have lived at peace.

For THE RIGH HONBL THE EARLE OF FINDLATERRE
thes

My Lord,—In obedience to my fathers commands I am forced to give yor Lo. this trowbel, that yow may be pleased to doe him the favowr to help with the cariage of some lyme to Keithhall. Yor sone the laird of Pattenbringand will tell yor Lo. the pleas from whence the lyme is to be caried, and the time. I beg yor Lo. pardone for this trowbel, and yow shall alwayes find me, My Lord, Yor Lo. most obedient and humble servant,

INVERURIE.

Kendall house, 9 *June* 1693.

My Lord, anie retwrn you are pleasd to give this, let it be sent to yor sone Mr. Patrick.

The sea victory of La Hogue of 19th to 24th May 1692, which reduced the power of France in battleships and made invasion impossible, encouraged French naval efforts in fitting out privateers. These preyed on the commerce of England and Scotland, and the remote waters of the Moray Firth even were not immune from their attacks, as the following letter from three Bailies of Banff, another, dated 25th June, from Patrick Ogilvie, and several other letters show. These privateers were popularly known as capers or keapers, kaper being the Dutch term for privateer.

ffor SIR JAMES OGILWIE OFF CHURCHHILL THERE
MATTYS SOLICITOR
these

RIGHT HONO^{LL},—Wee have presumed to trouble your Ho. in giving yow this following accompt, that ther ten or twelve dayes bygone ther hes been priviteirs on this coast under French cullors, who took last week ane ship off off the back off ffindhorne belonging to one Turnebull in Borrowstonness loaded with goods to Muirtone, who wes forced to ransome her ; and one Saturday last in Gamry Bay in wiew off this place took one Wm. Hay in Abdn goeing to Spey ffor wictuell, and caryed the ship with them, the men having run ashoaer ; and what is become of the pryze wee knowe not, butt the ffriggett wes seen of this place yesterday about four acloak in the afternoon. This ffirth is soe pested with priviteirs, that noe ship can goe alongs the coast. Wee judged it therfor fitt to acquant your Ho. heirwith, being that you are not onlie connected with the countrey, but also that ye have your owen victuell goeing south, which may alse soon incurr the hazard of taking as vthers, that yow may be pleased, if ye think it fitt, to procure som frigott or vȳr to cruize one this coast and the Buchan heads, vy^rwise it will be impossible to ships to travaile. But this wee leave to your owen consideratione, and subscryves, Right Hono^{ll}, Your wery humble srvants,   JO. GORDONN.
ALEX. WALLACE. R. SANDERS.

Banff, 12 Junij 1693.

On 19th June the Earl of Findlater qualified himself to government, in accordance with the act of Parliament of 19th May 1693. That same day, writing to his son Sir James, he says, ' I am glead to hear of the well-being of your Lady and daughter.'

There seems at that time to have been a recrudescence of Jacobitism in the north-east of Scotland, though Sir James Ogilvie treats it lightly in his letter of 26th June.

ffor OUR LOVING SON SIR JAMES OGILVY OF CHURCH HILL

Boind, the 20th of Junie 93.

My DEAR SON,—I was yesterday in Bamffe taking the oath of aleagence and singing the insurance, and administrating them to others. I can not at this time give you ane acōnt of the condition of this shier, many are so puffed up wth the aprehension of King James landing, and they conclued King William gon, that troulie King Williams friends are a litle discouraged. God that created the wordle, and is the Lord of hosts secour and protect the Protestant interest, and bring order out of our confusions. I long exidinglie to sie yu; and that the Lord wold be propitious to you and preserve you from all inconveniencie whatsoever, is the daylie prayer of Your loving father,

FFINDLATER.

For THE RIGHT HONORABLE THE EARL OF FINDLATER thes ar

My LORD,—This is to let you knou that we ar all will hear, and longs to hear the lyk of you and my sisters. I was at the Slans on Fryday, and my La. Erll told me that ther was a wessel that belonged to Sir Jeames Ogilive was chesed in to the Buller of Buchon with a caper, and was werey nir taken, but blised be God he wan frei. Ther is just nou wrey maney keapers on this cost. Your Lo. will excuse this trouble, and beliue me to be, My Lord, Your Lo. affectionat son and houmble seruant,

PATRICK OGILVIE.

My wife and I giues my sisters our houmble seruice

Carnbulge, Jun 25 1[6]93.

For THE EARLE OFF FINDLATER

Edr., June 26, 1693.

My LORD,—I received your Lo., and I am glaid your

Lo. hes qualified your selfe in the terms of the act of Par. I wish all our ministers may give obedience, and if they doe they will be protected.   I am nou keept hier till the Councel rise, which will be once this week ; and I wait for my meal bark, and am ordering my bear, bot the nixt week, God willing, I will be home.   Wee have no neus, bot expects dailie to hear of action ; and for your Jacobin intelligence its not worth noticeing.—I am, My Lord, Your Lo. obedient son and humble servant,

JA. OGILVIE.

The act referred to was passed on 12th June 1693 'for setling the quiet and peace of the church.'

The English merchantmen trading to the Mediterranean, called the Turkey or Smyrna fleet, left England in June 1693, to the number of nearly four hundred, under a strong English and Dutch naval convoy.   Thinking they had left behind them in Brest the French Atlantic squadron, the two English senior admirals returned on 6th June to the Channel, leaving Rooke with a small squadron to continue the convoy.   Meantime the French Atlantic and Mediterranean squadrons had joined forces, and before Robert Seaton wrote on 6th July, had encountered Rooke near the Straits of Gibraltar, destroying many of the merchant-men and driving him back by way of Madeira to Cork.   The two letters dated 11th August also refer to this disaster.

For SR JAMES OGILVIE his Majesties Sollicitor
to be left att the Post Masters house in Edinburgh
these
London, July the 6th, 1693.

DEAR BROTHER,—Thogh yow soe absolutly forgett me yet I can not yow.   I have writt severall times to yow, but can not have the favour of a return, which trubles me more then I will express in this.   I am sorrie my wyfe should take notice that my freinds never wryte to me, nor inquire efter me.   Noe body hes a trewer love and esteem for their relations then I have, but to be soe verry absolutly neglected is verry hard.   When yow parted from this place, yow promissed me a correspondence, which would be verry acceptable to me.   Lett me beg of yow to give me ane accompt of my Lord Findlater and all my brothers and sisters and other relations. I heare Capt Mountgomerie,[1] Lord Eglintons son, is dead, and that my Lord Mountgomerie was verry ill. I long to heer a litle news. I live as thogh I had not a ffreind in the world but one, who I thank God I yet have, but was verry neer loasing of her within this forthnight. She hes a great esteem for yow makes me concerned to see yow show soe litle respect. Both she and I hes been in great hopes of seeing yow heer. Pray give both our humble services to all relations. I have a verry trew honour for Mr. Francis Mountgomerie and his Lady. Accept of all kyndnes and freindship from, Dr. Brother, Y^r aff^{tt} humble servant,   RO. SETON.

′ I shall know by the return of this if acceptable. Direct to me, for Robert Seton in St. Jameses Street, neer St. Jameses Gate, Pall Mall, London.

Turn over.

We heare noe news of our Turckey fleett allarums our marchants and the whole exchange. Taxes heer are verry hie. King W^m is expected heer speedily, and it is reported he will goe on w^t the desent. Noe fight yet in fflanders. We have had a great deall of raine and thundr, but not neer soe much heer as in fflanders. If yr Lady be w^t yow, give both our humble services. If this place affords any thing I can serve yow in, pray command me. The picture I told yow of before, would be verry acceptable. It would be easily sent by the black box. I never see my father makes me more curious to have his picture. Concludes hastily yours in all things.   R. S.

The following letter to Sir James Ogilvie from his old friend in Aberdeen, the Rev. George Meldrum, refers to the settlement of the parish of Deskford.

MUCH HONORED,—I did expect to have seen you in this country, and wish to you a comfortable meeting with your Lady, and other relationes, who long for you. I left them all well on Saturday, and parted with them, especially

---

[1] John, third son of Alexander, eighth Earl of Eglintoun.

with your worthy Lady and sister, with much reluctancy
on my part as well as theirs; bot I was so circumstantiated,
that I could not well stay. Now I presume by this lyne
againe to commend unto your favour Mr. David Meldrum,
my nephew. He hath been with me in Murray, and hath
the kindnesse of the Presbyterian ministers there. If
you be pleased to continue your favour to him, and design
his setlement at Deskfuird, on a lyne anent it and your
desire for his return to him and me, he will come and wayt
on you. I hear ȳ is one Mr. John Murray preacheth
there, and as a prelaticall deacon baptizeth and marryeth,
which office we doe not allow; and I find the Presbyterian
ministers in Murray not well pleased with him, and some
of thes with whom he adwysed desired him to forbear
anent this and some other things. My cusing[1] will discourse with your Lo. at more lenth then I can writ.
Only I expect your favour to me and mine, and I hope it
shall not be to the ingratle. I give my service to my
Lord Findlater and the Lord Deskfoord and your sister
Lady Mary and your own worthy Lady, for whom on so
little accquaintance I have a great honer. I comend you
and all yours to the favour of God, and subscrywe that
I am, Sir, Your Honors much oblieged servant in the Lord
Jesus,   MR. GEO. MELDRUM
. *Banff, July* 17, 1693.

The many letters to Sir James Ogilvie, their Majesties'
Solicitor, from John Anderson, depute-clerk to the Privy Council
of Scotland, throw light on the proceedings of that body as well
as on the current political events of the time. These letters
were chiefly written when Sir James was absent from Edinburgh.

For SIR JAMES OGILVIE OF CHURCH HILL, ADVOCAT,
    THER MAJESTIES SOLICITOR   BANFF   6d

Edr. i7 *July* 1693.

RIGHT HONBLL,—Ther hes bein no Councill nor meitings
of statesmen here since ye went off; only on Thursdays

---

[1] The Rev. Patrick Innes, Banff.

morning Mr. John Guthrie slter wes secured till he wes examined anent some things contained in a ler wreitten to him by Sir Aineas M^cpherson,[1] and his papers wer searched, and having cleared himself wes dismist upon bale. The Secretary is this morning gone for Carmichaell, wher he stayes till the nixt post lers come to hands, which will determine him anent his goeing off or returning here. Ere he went off he receaved such papers anent Mr. Peyne and Duke Gordon [2] as he called for, which wer in my custodie. Receave the inclosed for newes from, Right Honll, Your most humble servant,

Jo. ANDERSON.

Next letter on the settlement of the Church of Scotland in the north-east of Scotland is most probably to Mr. James Steuart younger of Coltness, Lord Advocate.

Cullen, Julie 19, 1693.

MY LORD,—Nou when I am deprived of your Lo. companie, I most intreat when you have leasure that you will alou me the satisfaction of hearing from you. I find this countrey verie peaceable ; bot almost the whol Episcopel clergie have refuised the oths, bot most of them continou to preatch in ther churchis. They are desirus to know if they can doe this safely. I told them I thought they could not, seing the certification is depriva-tion ; and likwayes by the act all preatchers are ordained to take the oths. I desire your Lo. may let me know what measurs the Councel will probablie take with them. Ther are some would yet comply, if they wer sure to keep ther churches. If your Lo. have any service for me in this place, putt your commands onn me, and they shal be punctualie obeyed by, My Lord, Your Lo. most obleidged and most humble servant,   JA. OGILVIE.

I long to hear if ther be returns from the King from Flanders.

---

[1] *Sheriff Court Records of Aberdeen*, New Spalding Club, vol. iii. pp. 104, 105.
[2] *The Acts of the Parliaments of Scotland*, vol. ix. p. 323, and App., pp. 92 and 93.

The oaths were those of allegiance and assurance enacted on 19th May 1693.

On the 25th of July 1693 Sir James Ogilvie's sister, Lady Allardes, had a son.

For SIR JEAMS OGILVIE thes

DEAREST BROTHER,—It having pleased God to send uss ane good acompt of ye fruts of our labors, therfor I have mead you bothe ane unckle and godfather ; and I wissh we may see the same effects of your present works, for ye have got a long berething time, so that I hope all things will work togither for yt effect. I shall be wery glead to heare of your safe aryvel, and how ye have kiped your health since ye camme home ; and I ever am, Deare Brother, Your most effectionat and obedient servant,   GEO. ALLARDES.

I beg ye will give my humble duty to your Lady.

Allardes 25 *July* 93.

David Ross[1] of Balnagowne, Ross-shire, favoured the revolution, and co-operated with the laird of Grant in supporting General Mackay in the north. His letter to the Sheriff of Banffshire and those of 18th and 26th August 1693 are typical of judicial methods, when 'moyen' counted for much.

For SIR JAMES OGILVIE

RIGHT HOÑOBLE,—Ther is a flieeing report com to this cuntrie [that] on Donald Ross whos parents ar my tenents, and who him[self] hes srved honestly in Bamff-shyre thes 13 yeires, is nou in prison in Bamff, in order to underly ane seize, for alleidged stealling of horses out of my Lord Lovats lands.

Sir, I am a stranger to the affaire, and so will not medle to propon thos legall defenses which in law ar proper ; bot because I am in certane knowledge of his innocence as to the stealling of thes horses (as I am credibilly informed), therfor I intreat you to doe me the favor not

---

[1] Mackay's *Memoirs, passim* ; *Old Ross-shire,* by W. MacGill, *passim* ; *The Acts of the Parliaments of Scotland,* vol. ix. App. pp. 13, 33.

to asysze him, bot giue him any arbitrarry punishment ye please, onlye saue his lyff and credit by not pannalling him. Sir, I confess my confidence in this demand borders with indiscretion, bot the poor man being my kinsman, and being to be tryed wher I haue n^t the benefit of acquantances saue yorsf, that forces me to giue you this trouble; and iff you favor me in this request it sall oblidge many to srve you, and in speciall, Right Hono^{ll}, Your most humble sertt,　DAUID ROSS OFF BALNAGOUNE.

Balnagoune, 1 *Augst* 1693.

For SIR JAMES OGILVIE OF CHURCH-HILL, ADVOCAT, THER MAJESTIES SOLICITOR　BANFF　6d

Edr., 2d *August* 1693.

RIGHT HONLL,—Receave the inclosed newes. I ame sorie they are so ill, but ther is great talking here that by ane efter engadgment the ffrench wer routed. Yours for the Lord Secretary wes delivered to Henry Douglas, to be saifflie convoyed (wth the other lers for him) under his covert. My Lord Advocat receaved your line, and gives you his respects, but delays wreitting till the Councill day be over. I will putt it in my Lord Advocats memoriall, to cause extend the warrand for the Aberdein ministers taking the oath the wholl bounds of the diocese, in case ther be any motion of Councill anent it. I have spock Sir Thomas Moncreiff,[1] who gives you his respects, but protests he cannot, nor knowes not howe to gett you payed, for he cannot gett money to pay the charitie precepts, nor cane he propose a fond, unlesse ye could find out some good Sreff Æqs to be made. James Moncreiff sayes he will be lyable in a ballance which he will endeavour to bring your way, but Moncreiff fears it will not prove effectuall. Duncan Ronald hes bein out of toun, but is noue returned, and promises to exped my Lord your fathers newe precept as soon as cane be, and I shall send it north. I have gott in a report of most of the valuāns of those fyned to be presented to Councill. The lers agt

---

[1] Clerk to the Treasury.

Lovat Mr. of Tarbat Bedindalach and others in the shyre of Rosse Innevernes and Murray will be call'd to morrowe, and the lers agt Inverey and Doors being in Rot Stewarts hands will be continued. Ye shall have all newes I cane gather for you, and shall ever have the humble duty and affection of, Right Honll, Your most humble st,

Jo. ANDERSON.

Landen, the engagement referred to, was fought in Belgium on the 19th of July 1693, when William and the allies were heavily defeated by the French. The letters of 4th, 7th, and 11th August all refer to this engagement.

For THE RIGHT HONORABLE SR JAMES OGILVIE, OFF CHURCH-HILL THER MATIES SOLICITOR ATT FINDLATER 3d

TO THE CARE OF THE BAMFF POST

RIGHT HONORABLE SR,—I understand by John Andersone that he sends yow the publict letters; so I judge it is rather a trouble and expence to yow then any thing els to send them, so shall only tak occasione (as I promised) to give yow aco^t of any thing I heir of import. No doubt the actione in fflanders hes been considerable, but persons talk of it here as they affect. Some say that the Confederat army are irrecoveably routed, and that the Kings wound is mortall, and that the ffrench have taken Brussells, that most of the Inglish and Scots officiars and redgm̄ts are lost, parṫie Lo. Geo. Douglass. Uȳrs who are better affectit to ther Māties governm^t say that the ffrench loss is double ours, and that the King is perfectly weell, that his army is incamped near Brussells, and that he needs no reinforcem^t haveing only lost 4000 men, q^{r}of only 1300 of his oun subjects, that Lo. Geo. Douglas is alyve, and many uȳrs, who wer said to be killed, have comm to the camp haveing gott off saffly. Its further added that his Mātie had the knott of his scarff shot away by a cannon ball on the on syd, and the lock of his periwig by the shott of a cannon on the uȳr, and yet preserv'd;

and its thought ther will be a second boutt, ffor the Confederats are resolv'd to keep closser as ever. Ther wes
litle don yesterday in Counsell. John Andersone told me
he wold send yow the minuts, so shall not repeat them.
I give yow my most humble service, and shall only trouble
yow with a letter, when I hear any privat accōts that are
not in the publict; ffor I am, Right Hono^ll S^r, Your
most oblidged and devouted serv^tt,   WM. BLACK.

Edr., 4th August 1693.

The reference in next letter by the Lord Advocate to the old
Scots navy is interesting. On the 3rd of March 1692 the Duke
of Hamilton received from the King a warrant for the gift of the
office of Lord High Admiral of Scotland,[1] hence the Duke's objection to the Lord Chancellor's proposals. In 1689, in face of the
troubles with Ireland,[2] two frigates had been placed on the
western coast by the Scots Parliament; but since the commence-
ment of the war with France nothing had yet been done on the
east coast to ward off French privateers. Scots seaborne commerce on the North Sea had depended entirely on the protection
of the English navy.

To SR JAMES OGILVIE OF CHURCHILL TO THE
CARE OF THE BAMPH POŚT

3d   *Edr., 7 Aug.* 1693.

SR,—I have tuo of yours. The Lady Achlunckart was
not called. I was passive in the mater at your desire,
but she had freinds that urged it as much as I could,
but there was no place for it. We had three diets of
Councel, but did litle bussiness. All petitions from the
late prisonners were barred by what was told them before-
hand, that at this season and untill the Kings minde were
knoun, there was nothing to be done. There were also
feu petitions; but the bussiness took us up was in the
verie entrie a proposal was made by the L. Chancoll^r for
a ship to defend the cost, but D. Hamilton moving that
its comission must be from the Admirality, and the Chan-

---

[1] See *State Papers* (*Scotland*) *Warrant Books*, vol. xv. p. 118.
[2] *The Acts of the Parliaments of Scotland*, vol. ix. pp. 17, 24, 25, 43, 44, 53,
58, 67, 79, 85.

H

coll^r not naming the D. on the committie, occasioned a mistake that spent time and frustrat the mater, the D. contending that it was a mater of charges and belonged to the Treasurie. Then the Register moved a complaint āgt Mr. Anderson for publishing the acts of Parliat without his leave, but this was only *se defendendo*, for the woman had printed nothing save on the princ^{ll} warrants from himself, and he had a corrector of the press, and she gave him the first stitched copie on Tuysedayes night, and then on the Wednesday she gave me one; but I perceaved at the verie opening, that the act anent the Justice Court not touched was printed, and the act anent the fines and forfeitures touched was not printed, and several other errours, and finding 12 copies abroad told D. Hamilt. and then the Register. But E. Annandale, L. Justice Clerk, and L. Poluort getting also copies, the Register was greatly perplexed, and hath recalled the copies he could get, and is printing a neu impression; and you may easiely judge this would make noise eneugh. I thank you for y^r acc^t of the clergie. The Councel could not give a neu day. The neues from Flanders are still better. We have lost the point of honour, but the Frensh the strength of their armie at lest 2 for one. Portland is well, and the Sccretarie well arrived and receaved. More nixt, for I am interrupted. You knou I am, S^r, Y^r most humble and most affectionat servit^r, JA. STEUART.

The Councel adjurned till 5 Sept^r.

James Steuart was appointed their Majesties' Advocate on 20th December 1692.

The 'Minutes of the Privy Council,' the 'Siege of the Bass,' reprinted in *Miscellanea Scotica, The Memoirs of the Rev. John Blackadder*, by Dr. Crichton, *The Melville Papers*, and *State Trials* are authorities relied on by John Hill Burton in his account of the siege of the Bass between June 1691 and 18th April 1694, when this, the last Jacobite stronghold in Great Britain, was surrendered on terms to the Government of Scotland. The following letters give some account of the progress of the siege and the negotiations for surrender. The three men referred to in next letter were captured ashore, were convicted of high treason, but were included in the indemnity granted at the surrender. Four and not three names are given in the *Memoirs of Dundee,* viz. : Captain Alexander Haliburton, Captain William Fraser, Mr. William Witham, and Mr. William Nicolson.

For SIR JAMES OGILVIE

Edr., 9th August 1693.

RIGHT HONLL,—Receave the inclosed newes. I ame making readie the indytment agt the three men that came out of the Basse, who are to be tryed befor nixt Councill day. My Lord Advocat hes all the papers anent Seaforth [1] under his hands to be considered, in order to a proces agt him. Ther is no Scotts newes here. I ame, Your Lo. m[ost humble servant],   Jo. A[NDERSON].

ffor SR JAMES OGILVIE OF CHURCHHILL
To THE CARE OF THE POST MASTER IN BAMFF

Edr., 11 *Aug.* 1693.

SR,—I have yours of the i Aug. The Smirna fleet had certainly a bad rencontre ; and tho the worst of it fell on the Duch, yet the Inglish do complain much. Our last letters say that Admiral Rook and his men of war, and a great number of the Smirna fleet are come to Kingssale in Ireland. The engagement in Flanders was a verie severe one. By the Secretaries acct and a line from Mr. Carstaires out of the camp, I am assured that the King lost only the point of honour, that the Frensh have lost 2 or 3 to one, that our loss is not above 5000 men. Lord Geo. Hamilton is safe, but there are several prettie felloues of our captains killed, as Ava,[2] capt. Arch. Hamilton, capt James Denham and others. The Secretaries uill not agrie ; but Secretarie Jonstoun hath bloun off all the dust was cast on our actings in Parliat, and I am told that they are by all approven except Nottingham, who belives only what another sayes ; but in a word I conceave Secretarie Jonstoun to be verie well at court. The

---

[1] *The Acts of the Parliaments of Scotland,* vol. ix. p. 323.

[2] Sir James Erskine of Alva.

Kings armie is stronger then ever, and seeks to fight Luxenburg. The States dealt generously uith him, for upon the first ill report they wrot to the King not to be discouraged, and that they would stand by him while they had a farthing. They have also done another noble thing in declaring the loss of the Smirna fleet to be a publick loss, and that they uill repair these concerned. All things quiet here. We are to have a neu impression of the acts of Parliat, or the former amended. As for your three robbers, if you please to keep them till the nixt Councel, I shall move for a commission, and if it be refused they shall be ordered here. I am goeing on with the Bass men, and E Seaforth ; and there are other crimes also wherein you may be sure I want you, but I willingly dispense with it for your ease ; and y^r assistance was so great and steadable while here that I were unjust, if I did not nou allou you a part of that ease you then gave me. I doubt not but you will let me knou hou maters goe there, specially as to y^r clergie. They have a storie here, that the Mr. of Staires should have given passes [1] to 8 Inglish papists goeing abroad to scoles and monastries, that this should be challenged, and may be found an ill thing, but I only hear it ; and I shall be glad hou oft you give me the occasion to write to you, and to tell you hou much I am in sincerity, D. Sr, Y^r most humble and affectionat servit^r,

JA. STEUART.

For THE RIGHT HONORABLE SR JAMES OGILVIE OFF CHURCH-HILL ther Maties Solicitar ffor pnt Ffindlater

To the care of the Banff post. 3d.

RIGHT HONORABLE,—S^r, I receaved yours, and caused deliver the inclosed to my Lord Advocat and the vȳr to John Andersone. My Lord Advocats letter wes opin, but I scalled it before deliverie. Ther wes no fforraign maills last post, and so the news not considerable. Onlie the Jacobits alledge that the Dauphin and Prince Lewis have ffought on the Rhyne, and that Prince Lewis armie

---

[1] *Carstares State Papers and Letters*, p. 189.

hes mett w^t the same ffate that the Confederats have met w^t. They still look bigg, and talk much mor of the ffrench victorie then perhaps is true. They alledge that Luxenburgh suped in K. Williams tent, and wes served w^t his pleat w^tin two hours after the battell, that all the baggage ffell in the ffrench hands, and sixtie pcice of cannon. Ther is a noice of a descent ffrom ffrance, and that the redgm̄ts that wer goeing ffor fflanders ffrom Ingland are ordered to stay, and three redgm̄ts to com ffrom Ireland and two ffrom Scotland to help to defend the Inglish costs. The Jacobits pretend that ther is use for all thes redgm̄ts in fflanders, but that the Inglish will not suffer them to goe over. Its said that Ruck is in Kingsaill with ffiftie sail of the Smirnae ffleet. Thes are all that are passing. If thos newsletters I sent be not the same that Jo. Andersone sends, and if they bee not too expensive ffor postage lett me know, and if ye desyre them they shall be sent every post with what vȳr accōts passes. I give yow my humble service, and shall only ad that I am, Right Honorable, Your most oblidged and humble serv^t,   WM. BLACK.

Edr., 11 *August* 1693.

For SIR JAMES OGILVIE OF CHURCH-HILL, ADVOCAT, THER MAJESTIES SOLICITOR BANFF   6d

Sent from the lēr office of Abd 19 August 93 per Walter Merson in charge.

Edr., 16 *August* 1693.

RIGHT HONBL̄L,—Receave the inclosed. My Lord Justice Clerk promised to wreitt to you on Fryday. Sir Wm Hamiltoun [1] is in the west countrey. Your ler wes sent to him. The three prisoners that came from the Bass have receaved ther indytment to the 4th of September. I have imployed a messr to summond the witness in the countrey, ·and hope ther shall be no blame as to what relates to your office. The ler I sent expresse to the Chancelar on Mondays morning wes one that Henry

---

[1] Under Secretary of State for Scotland.

Douglas hade neglected to send by the Chancelars servant on Sabboth day, Henry being taken up at the comunion in the west kirk; so it appears to have contained no extraordinary thing, for ther hes bein neyr Councill no committies since.—I ame, Your Hōs most humble sr̄t,

Jo. ANDERSON.

The two following letters continue the story of Donald Ross. The writer of the second, Marie Huntlye, Marchioness-dowager of Huntly, daughter of Sir John Grant of Freuchie, and widow of Lewis, third Marquess of Huntly, married James, second Earl of Airlie, in 1668.

ffor THE RIGHT HONOLL SIR JAMES OGILVIE,
SHIRREFF OFF BAMFF thes

Baln: 18 Agust 1693.

RIGHT HONOB̄LE,—The kyndnes ye express and hes testified to me put a great difficultie on me, how to suittably recent it; bot I sall attend all occationes to repay the obligaᵒnes I owe yow.

Sir, by the longsonenes of the bearer of my last letter to yow, I find sentence of death is past on that poor fellow Donald Ross upon his confession off on dittay; so he is in yor mercies, and I hope and earnestly intreat that yᵒʳ mercie be not *sumum jus*. Blissed ar the mercifull for they sall find mercie, qch I pray may be yᵒʳ and my lott.

Sir, farr be it from me to plaide for any thing yᵗ is not consistant with justice mixt with mercie, without hazard or reflection on yor jurisdiction; bot in my humble oppinion, yow may saiflie keep the sentence in record and in force against the pannall, and superceid execution therof till ane uther dittay be found aḡst him, and in the meanne tyme giuc him voluntar banishment out of yʳ shyre. This will be a meane to saive both his soul and bodie, uheras his unnaturall death may ruine both. I haue found much peace in doeing the lyke, and it is much preferrable to presume on the law of natiōnes then on-Gods law as to the punishment of theft, especially ther being bot on single act.   Nixt his ingenuitie in confessing his guilt, and I hope his penitencie, with resolution never to comit the lyk, crys for mercie.   Wishing the merciefull God in whoes hand all our lives ar to direct yow, I continou, Right Hono[ll], yor most humble servant,

DAUID ROSS OFF BALNAGOUNE.

My wyff who joynes with me in this adress giues yow hir service.

For SIR JAMES OGILVIE

Banff, 26 Agoust 1693.

RIGHT HONORABILL,—Being informd that by yr pro-coorment and pouar a pour man callid Donalld Ross had gott his lyff effter he ves condemid, bot vith this cauiatt, that he sould remoue out off this kingdoom agenst the begining off Septembar, I most intret this faueor of yow, that you will be pleasid to recall his benishment, and suffer him to stey heir vithout hesart or dengar, he beheueing himselff honestlie and vithout blem all tyms heirefter— for vhich he will geat honest and responsell men vho is his frinds to be shourtie for him.   And sins yow haue bein so chiritabill and mersifull to him hitherto, I hopp you vill grant me this requyst that I mak to you be yilding to my diseyr, and allouing him the libertie that he mey stey vithin the kingdoom in anie place vhar he hes a mynd to be in.   And tho I beagg pardon for this trubill, yit I am confident that yr honor vill condishend to my diseyr, which vill much oblidge, Right Honorabill, Your Honors most sinserlie affectionet cusein and most humbill seruant,   MARIE HUNTLYE.

My Lord Airllie giuis you his humbill seruice, as I dou to yr Honor and all the nobill famellie, to vhum I am a most humbill servant and hartie veill visher.

The Lord Advocate, in his letter of 30th August, recounts the political news of the day.   No General Assembly of the Church of Scotland had been convened since 1690, and adjournments by royal warrant caused some conflict between the extreme covenanting section of the church and the royal prerogative. Mr. Robert Calder,[1] a deprived Episcopal minister, was tried on a charge of high treason.

ffor SR JAMES OGILVIE

Edr., 30 Aug. 1693.

SR,—I have yours of the 23. We had Councel yesterday and three letters from the King. Jon Anderson uill give you an accompt of what past there. We were just a quorum and no more. The King is expected over shortly; he uill leave Flanders in good case. The French on the Rhine are reteared to Philipsburg. St. Briget is takin and makes way to the taking of Pigneroll, which its hoped uill succeed. The whigs in London have lent money, an sheued such good affection as restores maters there. When the King comes he uill make changes in England. D. Hamilton hath got liberty to goe to court, but the Kings other letter shall, I hope, keep all others at home. It pleases well above that we put off the meeting of the Assembly the 16 instant. The King will call one this winter. Ill men make liis and say the brethren took instruments at the kirk door, and met and appointed another Assembly, but all is false. The Bass men are to be tried Munday, and Mr. Rob[t] Calder [1] on Wednesday the 6 7[r]. There are also a murder and a rapt to be tried. I shall be glad to see you in eit[r]. Commiss. Dalrimple is come. I have only sein him, becaus he went imediatly out of toun. I have not yet heared him on the politicks, but I perceave the Secretaries are quite brock. I wish you much satisfaction at home, and a happie return hither. Jon Anderson will write you about the robbers. You may think if it were not better to try them there by commission. My nixt shall give you Seaforths witnesss. I am, D. S[r], y[rs] entirely,   JA. STEUART.

---

[1] See *The Acts of the Parliaments of Scotland*, vol. ix. p. 250, and App., p. 74, and *Carstares State Papers and Letters*, p. 194.

For SIR JAMES OGILVIE OF CHURCH-HILL ther
Majesties Solicitor   Banff   6d
Edr., 30 August 1693.

Right Honbll,—Receave the inclosed for forraigne
and privat newes.   ffor Scots newes, ye have bein putt
to some expense in sending posts throwe the countrey
to bring in councelours to make a quorum, who when
they mett read the Kings ler adjourning the Parliat till
the 9th of January.   Another ler dischairging all persons
in public trust or office to goe off the kingdome without
the Kings leawe.   A newe proclamaᵒn is past anent the
beggars.   All these are this day proclaimed, and are to
be printed and dispersed with diligence.   The Kings ler
read signifeing his pleasure that the toun of Glasgowe shall
have the imposiᵒn granted them on aile by the Parliat [1]
for the space of 13 years, the Parliat having left that to
the Kings pleasure.   The Magistrats of Edr, Justices of
Peace and Sreffs are to meit with the committe of Councill
on Monday anent the highwayes.   Tarbat is appoynted
to revise the report anent takeing the oath of alleageance
and assurance, and to make report theranent agt̄ nixt
Councill day.   Irvine of Stank a man that hes bein long
a closse prisoner is liberat : James M'Gill your pensioner,
and Mr. Pat Smiths son are allowed oppin prison.
They speik anent transporting your Haked Stirk [2] and
his accomplices.   The Chancelar or Advocat will give a
warrand, when ther names are sent up.   This is all the
Councill did.   The Basse men are to be tryed on Monday,
and Mr. Robert Calder on Wedensday nixt.—I ame, Your
Hō̄s most humble servant   Jo. Anderson.

The Scots Parliament was adjourned from time to time, and
did not meet again until 9th May 1695.

For SIR JAMES OGILVIE OF CHURCH-HILL, Advocat
ther Majesties Solicitor   Banff   6d
Edr., 8t September 1693.

Right Honbll,—Receave the inclosed.   The court

---

[1] *The Acts of the Parliaments of Scotland*, vol. ix. pp. 328, 329.
[2] See *The Chiefs of Grant*, by Sir William Fraser, vol. i. pp. 281, 282 ; and
Historical Papers, New Spalding Club, vol. i. pp. 21, 22.

satt upon Mr. Robert Calder, and his affaire wes fullie debate by my Lord Advocat and Sir Pat Hume, and adwised with oppin doors ; and the Lords by ther interloquitor ffind that the manifesto mentd in the indytment does containe treasonable matters, but ffinds that the pannalls being the framer or wreitter yrof does not inferre the cryme of treason agt him, unlesse he hade showen or divulged it to some person befor it wes seazed on amongst his papers, yet ffind the same relevant to inferre ane arbitrary punishment. My Lord Advocat became highlie displeased with the interloquitor, and reclaimed agt it befor and efter pronunceing, and would not insist farder, and the pannall wes sent to prison and the matter continued till the 9th of Octor. Ther being some materiall witnesss agt the rebells from the Bass absent, and Sir Pat Hume being prepared for a long debate, that affaire is also continued till the sd 9th of Octor. The court is nowe sitting upon the sogor for killing a woman in Leith, and I think will condemne him ere they ryse. The Councill is adjourned till the third of Octor. I will send you by Mondays post a note of all that wes befor them, it being impossible nowe to doe it, I being in court. But this in generall, ther hes bein no great matters befor them.— I rest, Right Honll, Your most humble and obedient servant,   Jo. ANDERSON.

The following letter detailing the questionable methods resorted to by the Commissary-General to provide forage and provisions for the cavalry of the Scots army should be read along with the circular letter, dated 15th December 1693, to Sheriffs from the Commissioners of the Treasury, which aimed at correcting abuses.

For THE RIGHT HONORABLE SR JAMES OGILVIE OF CHURCH-HILL THER MATIES SOLICITAR

RIGHT HONORABLE,—Beeing this day in company wt Wm Livingstoune, who is comissary appoynted ffor furnishing the dragouns corn and strae ffor ther horses, I understand that some troups are lyk to ly in your shyre, and I beleive my brother as on of his deputs will be sent ther to order the magazins. Thos that have been ffurnishing vȳr magazins have great deficulty in getting them made up, some beeing unwilling to sell althoe vpon ready money, and vȳrs who will sell will not cary the corn and strae to the magazin, becaus ther is 32 ston of strae to be provyded ffor each boll of corn, q^{ch} hes occasioned some complaints (both on the souldiers part and the countries) to the Counsell, who have ordered letters to be direct to all the shyres recomending to the Shiriffs to nottice that the provisione to the fforces be sold at the current rates, and (if any refuise) to give acc̄o^t of the recusants to the Counsell. But its thought that this will be still uneasie, and therfor the comissarie is to use his indeavors in the severall shyres wher the troups lyes to gett the gentlemen to condiscend to a voluntar localetie. This is already done in Merns, and I beleiv will be thorowed in the shyre of Aberdeen; ffor they considering that troups will ly ther and that they must be ffurnished, they think it mor equall to consent that each should bear a part of the burden, then that thos nixt adjacent to thos places wher troups may be quartered should bear the wholl, ffor no doubt wher provision is it must be sold at adequat pryces. And as to the cariage, albeit they knew that they wer not oblidged to cary, yet they considered that, if the souldiers should cary y^r own fforrage ffrom the place it wes bought at, they might oppress ther tennts w^t great measure of oats and greater quanteties of straw then is allowed, and albeit the oats and strae wold be payed by the comissarie, yet they might fforce ther dyet gratis, and evin mak the tennts glad not to complien. So they rather thought convenient that ther tennts should cary eight or ten myles to each magazin, and receave ther pay^t ffrom the comissarie deput vpon delivery, then to have any thing to doe with the souldiers. As this will be a great ease and advantage to the comissarie, so it will be litle trouble to the countrie. And if this could be thorowed in your shyre of Bamff, Mr. Livingstoun wold use all his indeavors that your interest should be als ffree as posible. S^r, he is convinced this is in your

power, and your influence on the comissioners and
interest in the shyre will cary any thing that will not
wrong them. He tells me ther may be two troups only
ther ; but if the shyre consent to a localetie they must cast
on als much mor as serve transient quarters, q^{ch} superplus
may be applyed ffor releiff of your interest if the tennts
think it a trouble to cary. As ffor the pryce it will be
payed immediatly vpon recept at the rate the comissioners setts vpon it, q^{ch} in Merns is 4℔ ffor each boll of
corn and 32 ston of strae conform, q^{ch} is verie cheap. Hovever he will pay such reasonable rates as the comissioners
in your shyre will appoynt. And in respect yow will be
both at trouble and expence in calling and attending
thes meetings of the comissioners, that may meet ther
anent, Mr. Livingstoune is resolved (if the localetie be
thorowed) not only to ease your interest all he can (in
case they think it a trouble), but will give yow any gelding
yow ffancie to the value of twenty guineys, and tho yow
ffancie on worth ffyve mor he will not complean, but will
think all verie weell bestow'd. Mr. Livingstoune is a
ffreind of the Major Generalls, and a verie good ffreend of
myn ; and what ffavor and kyndness ye show him in this
affair will oblidg him to a suteable resentment. I humbly
beg pardone ffor useing this ffredome, but the many
obligations I still meet with on all occasions imboldens me
to mak addresses ffor my ffreends, q^{ch} I presum will not
be misconstructed, seeing it is ffrom on, who will be ever
bound to acknowledg himself, Right Hono^{ll}, Your most
oblidged and humble serv^{t},   WM. BLACK.

Edr., 8th Septer 1693.

SR,—If thes can be done, I intreat ane acco^{t} by the nixt,
becaus ther must be provisione laid in befor the troups
march ; and if ye could gett the shyre oblidged to cary
to any place (tho without the shyr) at ten myls distence,
it wold be som advantage, becaus perhaps half a troup may
ly at Turreff, q^{ch} I judg is in Abd shyre.

The three next letters give an account of the death funeral and
executry of Sir James Ogilvie's youngest brother, Robert Ogilvie,

cornet of dragoons. The writer of the second, Andrew Logie, was an Aberdeen lawyer. Lady Marie Graham, the writer of the third, was the mother of the laird of Allardes, Sir James's brother-in-law. She was the eldest daughter of John Graham, Lord Kinpont, and sister of William Graham, second Earl of Airth and Menteith, who died on 12th September 1694.

[FOR] THE EARLE OFF FFINDLATER
these

Edr., 19th Octobr 1693.

My Lord,—I knowe befor this tyme yow have hade ane accompt of the death of your sone, and which no doubt is ane great afflictione to yow. Bot, since the Lord who gave him to yow hes taken him from yow, it is yor Lops. deuty to submitt to providence. It may be your satisfactione that he died sencible and penetent, and was weill caired for the tyme of his sickness. I was fullie resolved to have wittnesed his interment, bot the multiplicity of my affaires, and being somewhat undisposed by reasone of the surpryseing account I hade of his death, necessitats me to stay heir. Hovever I have ordored money to be advanced to Allardyce, and hes lykewayes sent him his scutchion and brenches, and by ane letter have inveited the Provest and Baillies of Montrose to be present the day of the buiriall. I have ordored his horses north, till they can be conveniently and to advantadge disposed of, and I have allowed his srvant to stay with them for this insheweing halfe year. I have lykewayes wreitten to Aberdein to looke after what he hes ther in ane ordorly maner. I can wreit no more att present, bot I wish your Lo$\overline{p}$e comfort of your childrine that remaine, and I ame, My Lord, Yours Lops. most obedient sone and humble srvant,　　　Ja. Ogilvie.

ffor THE RIGHT HONO^{LL} SIR JAMES OGILVIE OF CHURCHHILL ther M$\overline{a}$ties Solicitor
these haist

Right Hono^{LL},—In pursewance of the desyre of your letter anent your deceist brothers ex$\overline{e}$rie (which I received onlie the tuentie-sevine instant late at night), receive the inclosed inventar subscrived by Comr Patersone off all those things which wer found in your brothers quarters. And Cairnbulg[1] tells me that ther wes ten guinies found in his pocket, and some litle money which, except the tuo guinies mentioned in the inventar, hes all spent on his funerall, to wit for ane shear cloath and to the doctors and other pettie debursements to beddalls, etc. And he gave in the inclosed accompts, which one John Allardes (now one of our baillies) haid furnished at your brother in lawes desyre, which extends to 133 ℔ i4 s. 4d. scotts ; and ther will be of small accompts (which John Gatt acknowledges to be true) resting to the dragoones and to his servant, who wes also a draggoon, besyde the i2℔ qch ye desyred I might give John Gatt, above eightein dollors. However I perceive ther will be no loss by medling, ffor it appears by all the informaⁿne I cane get, that your brother hes been rayr a comone lender yn borrower. His cloathes and furniture ar split new and fyne ; and it is Comr Patersones opinion als weill as myne (as it is also the comone practice in such caices), that the whole compleit sute (to wit, the coat vest clipe carabine belt padrontash baganet and belt), be all put to a roup among the officers, who will give more for them then any other ; and for that end it wer proper ye should writ to your brother Cairnbulg not to dispose of those things wherwith he medled, becaus they break the compleat sute. His haill linens it seemes were at Allardes, and many other things qrof ye will get acompt. And as ye desyred, I have sent the two truncks with ane fine broad sword to ffindlater locked and sealled, qrof receive the keyes inclosed. The cloathes may moth if not taken care of. I have not, neyr resolve I to pay a farthine to any, vntill I have your warrand. Neyr will what I have pay all that is owing, except the Dru . . .[2] money be got, and he alleadges most of it to be payed. The dragoones furnitur is detained in your brothers quarters, vntill Captain Johnstone come

---

[1] Patrick Ogilvie.

[2] Paper torn.

to towne, so ȳt I desyre to know how to carrie theranent.
It is not of much value except to the dragoon himself,
who (if he get it) may quite his wages, qranent ye may
writ to Captaine Johnstone; and whatever ye order
anent the premiss, prestable in toune or countrey, wt
me, God willing, as it is my duetie ther shall be nothing
neglected, and it will be ane hōr conferred vpon, Right
Honoll, Your most obedient and humble servant,

AND. LOGIE.

Abd., 30 *Octer* 1693.

Com̄r Patersone gives yow his humble service.

For SIR JAMES OGILLVIE, HIS MAGISTIS SOLISETER
EDEN   thees

Allardis, 8 *Novr*, 93.

RIGHT HONORABLE,—My son received yours on Fraday,
and sent a seruant northe as you ordored; and Forglen at
my entrety went to Mantithe wt him, which was a great
prowidenes, for he was going hom this day. That man on
all ocations is redy and his doun great thinges for this
family. And now, Sir, I am impatient to hear of my
poor brothers condition, that I presum to beg you will
lete me know ife he be dead, which ife I had not feared
I should agon myself tho I had never com back. And
it is so remot from this that, till ther return, I can have
no certinty, that I expect a line from you wt the first
post, what you hear of my brother. Your brother died
werie happily and his last words was to me, after som
eleadgiations, he had good neues to tell me, the great
God was comes for him. And he was cairfully atended
by his fititions. I crave pardon for this truble, and
subcrives my selfe, Right Honorable, Your most obledged
and humble serant,   MARIE GRAHAME.

Your sister is taking the sackrement, and not at hom.
Inbenoin this is wryten in my bed at 3 aclok in the
morning.

Endorsed — My Lady Marie Grahams lr̃e with ane
account of qt gold and money was in Cornet Ogilvies
pocket when he dyed.

For SIR JAMES OGILVIE, Advocat, Their maties
Solicitor and Shirreff Depute of Bamffe-shire
these

Edr., 15th Decemr: 1693.

Sir,—Whereas their Maties for the good and ease of their subjects have authorized us, and wee have agreed with a comissary generall, who is obleidged to provyde all their Maties horse and dragoones both in locall and transient quarters, with grass straw and oats upon the terms and allowances contained in that contract, yet his Matie being informed that in many places the comissary and his deputes had not made provisions accordingly, bot that the former abuses still continued, by the troopes being quartered upon the country and demanding localities and provisions to be caryed to them, which his Matie is firmly resolved to have redressed : Therefore he hath comanded us to enquyre into the matter, and to obleidge the comissary and his partners to the punctuall performance of their dueties by registrateing of their contract and exacting the penalty, and that wee see reparation made to the country, where they have suffered by being obleidged to furnish or cary, or where they have not received payment for what they furnished. Therefore wee desire that with all convenient diligence (after receipt of this) yow may conveen the comissioners of supply of yor shire, and comunicat this our letter to them, that wee may know from them and yow, how the troopes have been quartered in yor shire, since our contract with Sr Alex^r Bruce of Broomhall (which wes in May last) have been provyded, and in what manner it is done at present ; that in caice the comissaries have failed in their parts, or that punctuall payment hes not been made to any of yor shire, who have suffered by haveing souldiers quartered on them, or they obleidged to provyde or cary straw or oats, or who have not received payment therefore. This being of so universall good to the nation, and consequently to yor shire in particular, wee doubt not bot that both the comissioners of the supply and yow will take care to

return us a full and speedy account of this matter.—Wee
are, Yo^r affectionat ffreinds,   TWEEDDALE cancel
                                         LINLITHGOW,
                                         RAITH.

Endorsed—15 Dec. i693. Letter wretten by the Comssrs
of the Thesrie anent the Comssrs of the arme.

Now in office, Sir James Ogilvie began to acquire the wealth
that was in time sufficient to enable him to cut through the many
pecuniary entanglements of his father, redeem the paternal property, and build up the extensive Seafield estates in Banffshire.

For THE EARLE OF FINDLATER

Edr., Decr 25, 1693.

MY LORD,—I am sorie Park and Cokstoun[1] have disapointed your Lo., bot you need not be anxius, for I know
you will get that money att last, and it will doe you as
good service then as nou. I will this year be somwhat
straitned for money. All your debts comes onn me
together. I most pey John Ogilvies reprasentatives.
Baberton and I are near setled. Liteljohns executors
pratends you rest them fifteen hundreth pounds by bond.
Let me hear from you of this. Blakhils insists vigoruslie
and Lintush is most rigorus. If it wer not I gain money
and hes credit, I could not be able to pey so great soums
without woodsetting or selling. Lest ther be yet any defect
in my securitie, as I judge ther is none, yet it is thought
fit your Lo. grant me ane bond to be the foundation of
ane adjudication, and you most be charged to enter air
to your father mother grandfather or grandsher, and
I will take my infeftment on both. I know you will not
refuse this, and it shal be no further used, bot for securitie
of my lands disponed. I have sent the bond. Subscrive
it befor wittnesess and transmitt it by the post. I resolve
home immediatlie affter the session, and then I shal give
your Lo. all the assistance I can, and in the mean time
I am, My Lord, Your Lo. obedient son and most humble
servant,   JA. OGILVIE.

---

[1] Sir Alexander Innes.

Alexander, eighth Earl of Eglintoun, in next letter tells his success in getting a pension secured on the forfeited estate of Sir William Wallace of Craigie, Ayrshire, who espoused the cause of James at the revolution. Sir William came from Ireland with Cannon to Mull as a colonel of horse, and was present at the engagement of Dunkeld. On 14th June 1690 he was again in Ireland. He ultimately escaped to France, where he was in July 1695, when a remit was made by Parliament to the Justice Court to prosecute him and several other Scots rebels in France for treason.[1]

Thes

To SIR JAMS OGELVIE, ther Majistis. Solicetor

London, Mrch 6, 94.

DEAR NEPHEW,—I heve bean hear near thes four months soleseting the King for the performing of his promes; and nou it is conclouded by the great asistans of my great and good freand Secrator Jhonston, that the King wil give me a pension of tuo hainder pound a year, to be paied out of the first and rediest of Sir Wiliam Walas of Cragie his rents. Al my freands hear advaiseth me to take a comishon or a factore for the rents of that estat. They think it wil pot me in a probabil waie for the gift of forfatrie, when it is forfated. The Secrator hath disaiered Mr. Stevenston to draw several artikils, which he disayereth to be cleared of, which is to be derected to Mr. Heugh Cuningam; bot my whol troust is in your kear of this afear. If I get a comishon for upliftin thes rents, I know I most faind beal to be countabel to the Lords of the Thesorie for the superplus, which I wil doe by them I apoint factor; and al charges whatsomever is to be aloued to me in my acounts. The Secrator advaiseth me to goe to the King tomoro and give him thanks; and told him that I will leave the manashment of that afear to him, that he maie remember his Magistie to sain it the nixt month, when he is in wating. I most intrait you to asist Mr. Cuningam in dispatching an ansuar to the Secrator to thos things he disayereth to be informed of; for the King is sertanly to goe for Flanders in the

---

[1] *The Acts of the Parliaments of Scotland*, vol. ix., App. pp. 54, 56, 57, 115.

begining of Apraiel, and if it be not doon ther wil be an other years rent lost ; and if it be doon, I shal com doun to Scotland, and return you most hartie thankes and aknouladgments for thos manie singular favors and kaindneses you heve shain to, Dear Nephew, Your obledged wnkil and houmbel servant, EGLINTOUN.

Mr. Stevenson was an official under the Secretary of State for Scotland. He is several times referred to by Secretary Johnston in his letters to Carstares of 1693.

Towards the end of March Sir James Ogilvie went north to Cullen. During his stay of two months there he received accounts of the doings of the Privy Council, and of the General Assembly, with other political news of the day from James Steuart younger of Coltness, Lord Advocate, and from John Anderson, depute clerk of the Privy Council.

For THE RIGHT HONOURABLE SIR JAMES OGILVIE
OF THAT ILK, THER MAJESTIES SOLICITOR BANFF 3d.

Edr, 23d March i694.

RIGHT HONB^{LL},—Ther hes nothing occurred since ye went from this worthie of any notice. I have delivered ordors of Councill to Sir Thomas Livingstoun to cary John Trottér to Castletoun to be hanged ther on the 28 instant, and sent another to the Sreff to see the sentance putt to execution. Sir Thomas Livingstoun hes also receaved ane ordor of Councill for carying Capt James Midletoun to the Bass, and alloweing him to enter the rock upon sending out two hostages for him, and ther to treat for surrendering the Bass, and the lives of all condemned for it and of those in custodie ; and all those who are in the Bass are to be free upon surrender, and they are to be allowed to goe wher they please. They say the Generall Assembly will certainllie sitt the nixt week. The present lēr is worth nought. Ye are to have lēr and gazet by Mondays post. I hope ye have hade a saiff journey north. I pray for your health, and rest, R. Hħ, Your most humble and obedient servant, Jo. ANDERSON.

Serjant Park wes assolyed and sett free from the barr.

John Trotter [1] of Mortonhall, Midlothian, was condemned for assisting the defence of the Bass. His brother, Alexander,[2] was included amongst the Scots rebels in France who were proceeded against in July 1695 for treason. Sir Thomas Livingstone was Commander-in-Chief in Scotland.

For THE RIGHT HONOURABLE SIR JAMES OGILVIE OF THAT ILK, THER MAJESTIES SOLICITOR BANFF 6d.

Edr, 28 March 1694.

RIGHT HONB[LL],—This morning John Trotter hes bein taken to his sade journey to Castletoun, and will never make another. The Lord Carmichael ther Majesties Commissioner, and my Lord Justice Clerk,[3] and the heads of the ministers have bein closse with my Lord Advocat all this forenoon. The Assembly sitts doun to morrowe. Ther is [no] other newes here, nor any councill called.— I ame, Right Honb[ll], Your most humble and obedient servant,   JO. ANDERSON.

The General Assembly which met on 29th March was the second in William's reign—adjournments having been made through the years 1691, '92 and '93.

Edr, 30 March 1694.

RIGHT HONB[LL],—Yesterday the Generall Assembly satt doun. Mr. Crichtoun ther former Moderator preached. They mett in the efternoon, and the Commissioner made a speech to them relative to the Kings l[er], which wes read. The King promises them protection, and presrives to them modera°n, and will not have them midle with any of the Episcopall clergie who are in ther chairges, tho they have not complyed with the government; ffor he and his Councill will take course with them, and ease them of that trouble. Mr. John Lawe is choisen Moderator. Mr. Rule, Mr. Blair, and old man called Hamiltoun (not any of the Hamiltouns in Ed[r]), and Mr. Pat Sympson wer in the leit with him. They have appoynted a committie to drawe ane answer to the Kings l[er], and other committies for bills and overtures. The Councill hes sitten

---

[1] *Memoirs of Dundee*, etc., 1818, p. 76.
[2] *The Acts of the Parliaments of Scotland*, vol. ix. App. p. 115.
[3] Adam Cockburn of Ormistoun.

since ij aclock this day, and have appoynted another ship presentlie to be outricked, under the command of Capt Boswell in Kirkcaldie, for cruising with Capt Burd for stoping provisions for the Bass. Trotter was hanged at Castletoun on the 28 instant. A fyre ship is ordored to goe allonge with the convoyes and transport ships for the newe levies, for they fear hazard from Dunkirk men. Some reports wer made from the committie anent pressed men, both agt sojors and countrey men. Some sojors are remitted to Sir Thomas Livingstoun to be punished, and some countrey men appoynted to be cited. . . .

[Jo. ANDERSON.]

The feeble blockade of the Bass by the Scots navy, under the directions of the Privy Council of Scotland, came to an end on 23rd April 1694, when the rock was surrendered on terms honourable to the defenders.

The two next letters approximately fix the date of the death of George, eighth Earl Marischal.

For THE RIGHT HONORABLE SIR JAMES OGILVIE
OF CHURCHHIL   these ar

DEAR BROTHER,—I am glad to hear that ye ar com hom, and is in good halth. I hop to se you hear on Wadinday, if ye be to com to my Lord Marchels burial; fore I woll assoure you ye shall be hertly welcom to a dish of broth and somthing after it, and I woll promise ye shall be wated on by him who is, Dear Brother, Your affectionat brother and most humble seruant,   PAT. OGILVIE.

My wife and I giues our seruice to all our frinds.

Carnbulge, March 31, 1694.

For THE EARLE OF MARISCHAL   thes

Cullen, April 1*st,* 1694.

MY LORD,—When I received the honor of your Lo., I was fullie resolved to have waited upon you, and to have performed that diutie I oued to your Lo. father; bot I am called about pressing affairs to Elgin, which could admitt of no delay, and therfor I hope your Lo. will excuse my absence; and att all occasions I shal be readie to evince that I am, My Lord, Your Lo. most faithful and humble servant, JA. OGILVIE.

For SIR JAMES OGILVIE [OF THAT ILK, THER MAJESTIES SOLICITOR, BANFF]

Edr, 4th Apryll 1694.

RIGHT HONB^{LL},—Yesterday the Councill satt, and a ler from his Majestie in favours of my Lord Justice Clerk,[1] impowering him to nominat and subsitut clerks to the Justice Court, and investing him with all the priviledge belonging to his office weś read. The Bass rebells wer reprived till the first Fryday of May nixt by the Chancelars casting vote. M'Lauchlan, the teacher of ane Inglish schooll at Glasgowe, wes tryed, and appoynted to be scourged throwe Ed^r this day, and banished to the planta°ns; but the Councill have this day chainged the scourging to the standing on the pillorie here this day, and at Glasgowe this day eight dayes. His cryme wes the seduceing and persuading sojors to desert ther chairge. Troyilous Balyie ane ensigne recomendit to the Thesaurie for apprehending one Wm Gledstons, a Bass rebell, to receave 20 łib, st. A ler ordored to be wreitt to the King anent the tuo frigotts appoynted to cruise about the Bass and anent a fyre ship, and anent ther paymt. The ler wes this day read and approven. This day his Majesties lers adding the Lord Yester [2] and Sir John Hall [3] to the number of the Privie Councelours wes read, and they appoynted to be acquainted therwith. A proclama°n agt deserters and ther recepters, mostlie relative to the forces presentlie to be imbarqued, wes read voted and past; but the forces who craved it litle esteeme of it, as it is drawen and mendit. Ther wes much discourse upon complaints, both anent pressed men deserters and deficients, and these things are to be taken to generall consideräon befor the Councill ryse at this tyme. I have ordor to

---

[1] See p. 132, note 3.
[2] Lord Hay of Yester, Lord High Treasurer in the Parliament of 1695.
[3] Sir John Hall of Dunglass, commissioner for the Burgh of Edinburgh.

citt some of the forces to answer befor the Councill to morrowe, parlïe Leït Steuart for refuseing to give up pressed men notwithstanding of the committies ordor. The E. Hume, Oxfurd, Drumcarnie, Ednam, Gledstons, Gairltoun,[1] and other prisoners of the government are liberat upon caution to answer when called, and tuo myles confinement to ther houses, and the, Councill then adjourned till to morrowe at 3 aclock efternoon. The Generall Assembly also sitts. I hear not much they have yet done but answered the Kings ler, and appoynted committies, and that they are about retrinching the number of ther lay elders, so as ther may be four ministers for one elder, and that they are to take away the 'priviledge claimed by the toun of Ed^r of [calling] and getting any ministers they please from any par[ish in Scotland]. Culodin is working amongst them for ge[tting a number of] ministers to the Highland of Invernes, Ross . . . Prinll Patersons ler to James Baird will give mor [information than I] knowe. . . .—Right Honħ,)Your . . .

[Jo. ANDERSON.]

Hume, Oxfurd, and Drumcarnie were old Jacobites. Charlès, sixth Earl of Home, and Robert, second Viscount of Oxfuird, had been arrested in July 1689 on a charge of being implicated with Dundee in a plot against the Orange government.[2] Sir John Murray, Lord Drumcairne, Court of Session judge, had been cited on 13th and 17th May 1689 by the Committee of Estates to give an account of his correspondence with Dundee at Scone on 11th May 1689.[3]

James Baird[4] was the eldest son of John Baird, bailie of Cullen, a descendant of the Bairds of Ordinhivas. About this time he became associated with Sir James Ogilvie as his servitor and secretary. On 26th November 1696 he was appointed Clerk to his Majesty's Wardrobe in Scotland.[5] On 1st July 1697 he married Margaret, eldest daughter of John Anderson, depute clerk to the Privy Council. On the 19th day of the same month and

---

[1] Sir George Seaton.
[2] *The Acts of the Parliaments of Scotland*, vol. ix., App. p. 131.
[3] *Ibid.*, App. pp. 19, 30.
[4] See also *Genealogical Collections concerning the Sirname of Baird*, pp. 95, 96, 97. [5] *State Papers (Scotland) Warrant Books*, vol. xvi. p. 297.

year he was admitted a member of the society of Writers to the Signet. He was three times married. He died on 27th April 1746.

For SIR JAMES OGILVIE of that Ilk, ther Majesties Solicitor. Banff. 6d.

Edr, 6t Apryll 1694.

Right Honbll,—The Councill satt yesterday, and examined Leit. Coll Stewart for disobeying the committies commands for rendering up a countrey man taken up for a sojor ; and not being able to justifie himself he wes committed to prison, publictlie reproved, and is to lye in prison till the man be delivered, and longer during the Chancelars pleasure.

Sir Donald M'donald of Slait, the laird of M'Leod, and Countes of Seaforth, upon petitiones given in be them are allowed to send up their deficient men to Stirlin agt the 8^t May nixt.

The Commissioners of Justiciary for the Highlands are appoynted to meit at Invernes upon the 22d of May nixt.

Stewart of Alpin, a disaffected prisoner at ffortwilliam, is ordained to be transported prisoner to Ed^r.

Robert ffyff, prisoner for not taking the oaths liberat.

Belachans bill for libertie refused.

Andrew Brown watchmakers bill for his penaltie refused.

Seaforth vncle who wes at Stirlin, allowed confynmt to his owne house and tuo myle about.

The Skinners of Ed^r ordained to see and answer a bill offered for some, who crave a manufactory for dressing leather.

M'Lauchlan, the schoolmaster at Glasgowe, having uttered some unseemlie expressions when on the pilorie, is to be farder tryed.

Evan M'Grigors bill craveing liberty to use his name read, and allowed as to bygones preceeding the act 1693.

A Quaker being sent in by Quenisberry as one of his levie men, the Chancelar appoynted to wreitt to him to send another.

Old Belintolme excused from being a commissioner, and his son named in his place.

Leīt Aikenhead challenged anent pressing men, remitted to the committie.

The vaicand stipends of Prestonpans and Elie gifted to the resvē parroches.

The Countes of Errols papers, that wer at London and are sent doun to Mr. Hugh Dalrymple, appoynted to be putt in the Councill clerks hands.

Robert ffinnieson, late servant to Oswald and Dunlop Collectors, being a-dyeing, a committie appoynted to examine him anent some publict rests.

Lērs appoynted to be sent under the Advocats hand to all the shyres of the kingdome, to send in ther deficients— these on this syd Tay to Glasgowe the 28 Apryll, and those beyond it to Perth the 8t May. This with the proclamāon anent the deserters necessarlie calls for expresses to be sent throwe all the kingdome, for Shirriff deputs clerks and heritors are readie to load others with ther owne neglects.

The Assembly are upon appealls, and prepareing ther other matters. This is all at present from, Right Hon[ll], Your most humble and obedient servant,

Jo. ANDERSON.

I think the expresse I shall send with the circular lērs anent the deficients shall reach you as soon as this, for I hope my Lord Advocat shall this efternoon signe the lērs. Yet, least it should not, I putt you to the farder expense of this line.

Sir Donald M'Donald, younger of Sleat, Stewart of Appin, and Patrick Stewart of Ballachan, chamberlain of Athole, were active supporters of Dundee. They were included in the treason process instituted by government in 1690 against the principal rebells in Scotland.[1] On 15th June 1693 Parliament passed an act setting up a Justiciary for the Highlands to suppress depredations and robberies. That act revived the statute of 1633, which proscribed the clan M'Gregor. Hence Evan M'Gregor's bill.[2] Old Belintolme or Ballintomb was Archibald Grant, ancestor of the

---

[1] *The Acts of the Parliaments of Scotland*, vol. ix., App. pp. 54, 56, 58, 60, 61.   [2] *Ibid.*, vol. ix. pp. 355, 356.

Grants of Cullen of Gamrie, Banffshire, and later of Monymusk, Aberdeenshire. He had two sons, Sir Francis, who became Lord Cullen, and who acquired Cullen and Monymusk, and Alexander of Ballintomb. Archibald Grant died in 1717. The Countess of Errol, Anne Drummond, only daughter of James third Earl of Perth was Jacobite.[1]

ffor SR JAMES OGILVIE OF CHURCHHILL

Edr. 14 Apr. 1694.

SR,—I have yours of the 9. I see no more can be done to seaze these men. If young Boigs can be found, I doubt not but you uill secure him, and I shall put him in the sumonds of treason when raised, and like-uyse speak to Sr Thomas.[2] You need not any neu order, you may doe all that is to be done of yourself. The Assembly sits, and is drauing to a close. They have bein a litle uneasie, but I hope shall part fair. I am not like to be fond of another in the sam circumstances. We have no neues. The D. of H is coming doun not well pleased. The King goes nixt weak, or sone after.—I am, D. Sr, Yr most humble and affection. servitr,   JA. STEUART.

I have another daughter since you left us, and all mine salut you most heartiely.

Young Boigs may have been a son of John Dumbar of Boigs,[3] Morayshire, who was appointed a Commissioner of Supply in 1689 and 1690.

For THE RIGHT HONOURABLE SIR JAMES OGILVIE

OF THAT ILK, THER MAJESTIES SOLICITOR   BANFF   6d

Edr, 16 Apryll 1694.

RIGHT HONBLL,—The Generall Assembly ryses to-morrowe. The Councill hade a litle meiting explaning the proclamaon anent seazing the horse and armes of such as refuse the oathes, that the same does not extend to labouring horse, because some Shirryf deput in the west hes bein too severe that way. The sojors are daylie

---

[1] Browne's *History of the Highlands*, vol. ii. p. 149.
[2] Sir Thomas Livingstone, Commander-in-Chief in Scotland.
[3] *The Acts of the Parliaments of Scotland*, vol. ix. pp. 74, 145.

shiping here for abroad. Ane English regiment is also come here to be imbarqued. This is all the newes cane be learned by, Right Hon^ll, Your most humble and. obedient servant,   Jo. ANDERSON.

Duke Hamiltoun lers here this night.

On 19th May 1693 Parliament, to further secure the Protestant religion, enacted that the oaths of allegiance and assurance should be taken by all persons in offices and places of public trust—civil, ecclesiastical, and military—under penalty of not being allowed to keep any horses above one hundred merks price, or any arms beyond a walking sword.

For THE RIGHT HONBLL SIR JAMES OGILVIE
OF THAT ILK THER MAJESTIES SOLICITOR
BANFF   6d

haste   *Edr.*, 17 *Aprill* 1694.

SIR,—Receave some copies of the order of Councell to ye Shirriffs and oyrs Magistrats appointed to execute the proclamãone anent the horses and armes of such as refuise the oaths, which ye are to disperse to the Burghs and oyr jurisdictions w^tin your shyre ; and this charge I am ordored by the Lo/of their Majesties Councell to lay upon yow the Shirriff, that both Bailies of Royaltie and Regality and oyrs concerned may have due notice.—I am, Your humble serwant,   JA. STEUART.

The following letter is written on the same sheet as the preceding :—

Edr., 18 *Apryll* 1694.

RIGHT HONB^LL,—Yesternight the Generall Assembly arrose, and ane newe Assembly is indicted to sitt at Ed^r upon the first Thursday of Apyrll nixt. They have appoynted a commission of them to sitt and order all affaires in the mean tyme, and severall ministers to goe north. The Duke of Hamiltoun fell ill on his journey to Scotland, and wes four dayes ill on the road of a sore knee. Feverish and troubled with ane appoplexie he journeyed every day. The Dutches and doctors went from this to meit him, and with much adoe he wes brought yesterday efternoon to the Abbay, and dyed this morning at 5 aclock, to the great lamentāon and regrate of all who wish ther countrey well. The Bass have sett out a whytt flag, and thir tuo dayes are capitulating for a surrender. The Councell meits this day. Ye shall have ane accompt what they doe. The sojors and ther convoy is not yet gone off. Ther is much compleanings every day for pressing of men. I have sent off the inclosed prints to the other shyres.—I ame, R. H., Your Hos most humble servant,   Jo. ANDERSON.

For SIR JAMES OGILVIE

OF THAT ILK, THER MAJESTIES SOLICITOR   BANFF   3d

Edr., 20 *Apryll* 1694.

THER is not any thing of newes here, but that since the Assembly rose, the commission left and impowered by them are yet sitting ordoreing some matters, and that committie of them for the north will take journey shortlie.

The Councill mett this forenoon anent the overtures of capitulaᵒn proposed by the Bass, and I hear (the Councill being close) that the articles are so adjusted as its thought the Bass will presentlie surrender.   [Jo. ANDERSON.]

For SIR JAMES OGILVIE

OF THAT ILK, THER MAJESTIES SOLICITOR   BANFF   3d

Edr., 23d *Apryll* 1694.

RIGHT HONBᴸᴸ,—The sojors are all aboard, and sett sail yesterday; but the wind turned crosse, so as they are not yet out of the firth. The Councill is up till the first Tuseday of May, and the Chancelar gone to the countrey till then. The Bass is nowe surrenderd, and all that wer in it and those that hade come out and those condemned, and others who intercommoned with them, are all indemnified and free, and the condemned men are at libertie. The Justice Court mett and read the Kings ler in favours of my Lord Justice Clerk, restoring him to the priviledges of his office with power to name clerks, and did receave and admitt Lainshawe upon a newe gift from my Lord Justice Clerk, for which I hear he hes payed 150 lib sterline. —I ame, Right Honbl, Your Hoˢ most humble servant,

                    Jo. ANDERSON.

[For] SIR [JAMES OGILVIE] OF [THAT ILK] THER MAG[ESTIES SOLICITOR], CULEN.

Edr., 27 *Apryll* 1694.

RIGHT HONB^{LL},—I receaved both your lers yesterday.
. . . . Ther is non of your victuall come one as yet, and the pryces are lowe. Robert Dunbar[1] and tuo privateers with him came up to the Bass on Sabboth last to have putt in provisions for them, but finding it wes surrendered, and that four men of warr lay here in the road, and Burd[2] and Bosvell[3] hard by, they have gone off, but we fear skaith by them ere they returne. I pray it may be otherwayes. I hope ther shall be such quyetnes here as may allowe you to stay in the countrey all the vaicance. The poor sojors lye still in the road, be reason of the contrary winds, and some of them have dyed of vermine.—I ame, Right H[onbl. Your Ho^s most humble servant,]   JO ANDERSON.

The following letter by Principal Robert Paterson[4] of Marischal College, Aberdeen, is of a kind with the letter of 25th April 1692 from William Black.

For THE RIGHT HONORABLE SIR JAMES OGILVIE OF CHURCHHIL thes

RIGHT HONORABLE,—I presum so much on your goodnese, that since ye wes educat in Marshaill Colledge ye will continue a freind to ye sam, and now to evidence it, its exspected ye will speak to your Shiref deput Castelfeild to send his son to Mr. Pecock[5] to bee educat. Ye know he is ane good learned and painful maister, so yt he cannot bee better staited that way perhapes in Scotland. I know on word of your mouth will determin ye gen^{ll}man ; and since so easily ye may promot the interest of your

---

[1] *The Acts of the Parliaments of Scotland*, vol. ix., App., p. 115.
[2] *Ibid.*, pp. 41, 67, and App. pp. 9 and 30.   [3] *Ibid.*, p. 77.
[4] *Records of Marischal College and University*, New Spalding Club, vol. ii. pp. 28, 29, etc.
[5] *Ibid.*, vol. ii. p. 38.

Alma Mater, I houp it will not bee denyed to, Right Honorable, Your affectionat and humble servant,

RO. PATERSON.

Abd., 27 *Apprill* 1694.

Give my service to my Lord and your Lady. I am sorie for ye death of your great frend Hamilton.

It wer fit he com in onc in May to bee matriculat.

Nicolas Dunbar of Castlefield, Sheriff-depute of Banffshire, six years later attained fame as the judge who sentenced James Macpherson, the Highland reiver, to be hanged at Banff. Mr. George Pecock was one of the regents of Marischal College, encyclopædic teachers who each in turn carried their students through their whole curriculum from bajandom to graduation. The regent beginning his prelections on logic, went on to physics, and finished off with arithmetic, geometry, moral philosophy and economics.

ffor SR JAMES OGILVIE OF CHURCHHILL

Edr., 30 *Apr.* 1694.

SR,—I have yours, and see you ar bussie receaving converts. I heartiely wish all men may become wise to live and let live in peace. You have befor this time got the Councels regulation about horss and armes. They would not medle with what concerned heretors; but from above (as I think I told you), it is intimat that such only as are suspect, and have allreadie refused the othes should be dismounted and disarmed. We have no neues. Our Assembly went off easily eneugh; for the brethren willingly agried to take no advantage of the late act of Parliat for setling the church, and the commissions they have given are mostly for planting and assuming, and restricted eneugh in the mater of censure. Yet I see the northern ministers take the alarme at the commission for the north, and Aberdein mindes to be the metropolis of the Episcopal partie; but I belive the commission shall be veric moderat, and therefore I would have your countrie folks wise; for if they make any bussell agt such just and moderat things, it will only serve for a discoverie of their to much suspected disaffection. You will hear by this time that our great and good freind D. Hamiltoun died the mornine after he came home the 19 instant. I protest I regret his death from my heart. He was a rational and true man, true both to King and Kirk, without dissimulation, without resentment, and most usefull at this time, and I am sure his vertues will long long survive all his faults. You need make me no apologie for my want of your assistance. The surrender of the Bass hath eased of some truble, and there is litle els to be done. I have far greater missing of your good companie, but dare not grudge your honorable relations, to whom I wish all prosperity. Yesterdayes letters say the King was to part Wednesday last, and that E. Shreusberrie hath got D. H.^{s} [1] garter, and E. of Argile is to be Extraordinarie Lord of the Session. Its like E. Annandale or L. Carmichael may come into the Treasurie, but I apprehend the D^{s} place as Pres of Councel may vacke a while. The Admirality should be in commission.—I am, S^{r}, y^{r} most humble and affection^{t} servit^{r},   JA. STEUART.

The 'late act of Parliament for settling the church,' referred to by the Lord Advocate, was passed on 12th June 1693. It enacted that no person should be admitted or continued hereafter to be a minister or preacher within the church unless he took the oaths of allegiance and assurance, subscribed the Confession of Faith as his confession, and acknowledged Presbyterian church government.

For THE RIGHT HONOURABLE SIR JAMES OGILVIE
OF THAT ILK, THER MAJESTIES SOLICITOR BANFF 6d

Edr. Last Apryll 1694.

RIGHT HONB^{LL},—Receave the inclosed, which is all the newes at present from this place, except that severall of our Scots ships are come up from Holland, and that the winds keep crosse here for the fleits goeing off, and the poor sojors are in ill case. We fear skaith from ffrench privateers and those that wer with Dunbar. I wish your victuall well up for I hear nothing of it. Its hoped his Majestie is saiff in Holland ere this tyme, being determined

---

. [1] Duke of Hamilton.

to goe off on Wednesday last. The laird of Grant sayes he will answer your ler to him to your content with first conveniencie. The Councill sitts to morrowe according to adjournment, and what occurres ther ye shall be informed of it by, Right Honbl, your Hos most humble and obedient servant,   JO. ANDERSON.

For SIR JAMES OGILVIE

OF THAT ILK, THER MAJESTIES SOLICITOR   BANFF   6d

Edr., 2d May 1694.

RIGHT HONB^LL,—Both the barks with your victuall came to Leith harbour on Satterdays night in good condition, and yesterday and this day it is livering at. eight merk per boll. I hope the debitors and paymt will be good. I wes doun yesterday and aime to be doun in the efternoon. James Bairds brother and another young man wait on the vessells to keep compt, and see the tickets rune.

The Councill satt yesterday and my Lord Yester took his place as a councelor. Alex^r Tait, skipper, who hade bein in ffrance, petitioned for libertie, but wes refused ; and the other Alex^r Tait and his caur wer appoynted to be chairged. A shipe is engadged to cary over the Bass men to ffrance, who are appoynted to leave the kingdome betuixt and the 15 instant. Ther is a publict fast appoynted throwe the kingdome, for the causes ment^d in ane addresse from the ministers, which most be dispersed throwe paroch kirks. Thomas Weir gott certifica°n aḡt some persons anent Andersons piles. Osburne a skipper, who hade bein caryed to Dunkirk and wes sett ashoar by Robert Dunbar, wes appoynted to be examined by Lord Advocat, and to be at libertie or committed as he should see cause. The Earle of Marshall being refused a passe from my Lord Chancelar is gone off without one. The Secretarys are wreitt to anent it, and the E's of Erroll and Kintore his caūrs are lykwayes appoynted to be wreitt to.

The Lady Milnmark hade a proces aḡt her husband, which wes called, and a committie appoynted to aggree them or to take tryall. The Councill is nowe sitting.

Ye shall by the nixt knowe what they are doeing. I ame, Right Honb̄ll, Your most humble and obedient servant,

JO. ANDERSON.

Alexander Tait, skipper in Leith, and Captain Robert Dunbar, implicated in the affair of the Bass, were two of several Scots rebels in France against whom a process for treason was raised in 1695.[1] William, ninth Earl Marischal, succeeded in March 1694. He married c. 1690 Mary Drummond, eldest daughter of James, fourth Earl of Perth.

The two next letters deal with the difficulties experienced in raising the various quotas of the levy of 2979 foot soldiers sanctioned on 23rd May 1693 by Parliament, and the measures taken to overcome them.

For THE SHIRRIFF DEPUTS OF BANFF OR TO THE SHIRRIFF CLERK OR HIS DEPUTS, FOR THER MAJESTIES SPECIALL SERVICE   BANFF

Edr., 4 *May* 1694.

MUCH HONOURED,—There was sent to you befor by the Councils order a letter from me containing what they ordered anent the bringing up of deficients in the late levie to Stirlin upon ye eight instant, and to Glasgow on the tuentie-ffourth of Aprile last. What performance will be made at Stirlin cannot be knowen till ye day pass. But least it be not better then that at Glasgow, and to correct what was wanting there, these are to desyre you to send a particular list of the men delivered in your shyre, and to whom, as also a particular list of the deficients, I mean of the number of men and of the names of the heritors deficient, and that you doe your outmost to have the deficients sent up to the forsds places, and to the commanding officers there readie to receive them. And this account is demanded that it may be compared with the officers lists, and that such as are still wilfullie deficient may be duelie compelled, as they may expect to be with all rigor. And this being so necessary for the publict service your answer is expected without faill, for if ye failzie ȳrin, you and the heritors concerned may

---

[1] *The Acts of the Parliaments of Scotland*, vol. ix., App., p. 115.

receive a more peremptorie charge, which will not be so satisfieing either to you or to, S^r, Your most humble servant,   JA. STEUART.

This letter being sent to all the Shirriffs of Scotland, pray faill not to send a recept ȳrof by the bearer.

For SIR JAMES OGILVIE OF THAT ILK,
          THER MAJESTIES SOLICITOR   CULEN
                                        Edr., 4 May 1694.

RIGHT HONB^{LL},—I ame necesitat to send posts expresse throwe all the kingdome with the proclama°ns for the fast, and with my Lord Advocats letters to all the Shirriffs, for causeing send up the deficients of the levie, for they have bein in some places verie defective, and are readie to shift the blame off themselwes and to pretend short advertisement. The Councill is nowe adjourned till the 4th of June nixt ; and befor they rose (besids what I gave ane account of by the last post), they allowed Garletoun confinement to his house and tuo ₘyles about it, and Mr. Thomas Gordon libertie of the toun of Abdⁿ, and tuo myles about it. Lord John Hamiltouns commission as Generall of the Mint wes read, and my Lord Carmichael appoynted to tender him the oathes. The laird of Leys appoynted to tender the oaths to the Earle of Strathmore as Sreff of fforfar. Skiper Osburne, who hade bein at Dunkirk and wes sett a shoar by Dunbar, eftr being examined by my Lord Advocat wes committed to prison. Bill and answers read anent valua°n of fforfar shyre, and a stop putt to the valua°n. The laird of Kinnmond appoynted to be cited for some insolences committed be him relateing to the publict. A bill for a manufactory for dressing of laether read, and the skinners answers therto and parties heard, and the manufactorie approven of. The Lady Milnmark and her husband wer aggreed by the committie. Ane allowance of a thousand pound given to Sir Ja. Ramsay who is in great distresse. A bill anent the kirk session bookes of Stirlin appoynted to be sein and answered. The Thesaurie satt also, and called at me for ane account of diligence for the Councill fynes, which I gave them, and they commandit me to use the last diligence. Charles Robertson hes livered all his victuall, and payed the skipper, and given me his recept for the victuall. The other vessell is all livered by this tyme, and I shall pay the skipper, being to receave 20 shill of the boll from the buyers and ther bonds for the rest, which I told them wes to be payable the first of July. Non of your skippers will hazard north for fear of Dunbar and the capers; neyr think they should ye hazard any thing either to or from the north till the coasts be cleaner, for they are snatching up the poor men daylie, and they burne whom they doe not cary away. My Lord Advocat speaks of the strength of your vsquebea and gives you his service, as lykwayes doth my Lord-Justice Clerk. I shall indeavour for a particular account of the Assemblys proceedings.—I ame, Right Honbll, your most humble and obedient servant,　　Jo. ANDERSON.

Mr. Thomas Gordon[1] was in the reign of James ii. clerk to the Justice Court. He acted, along with Sir James Grant, as legal adviser to the Duke of Gordon in 1689, when terms were made for the surrender of Edinburgh Castle.

During Sir James Ogilvie's stay in the north, his father the Earl of Findlater conveyed to him the lands and barony of Ogilvie, and Sir James took infeftment on 17th May 1694.[2] He appeared thereafter in the County suite roll in place of the Earl, taking the designation of 'Ogilvie' instead of 'Churchhill' The embarrassments of the Earl, the verting of Lord Deskford to Roman Catholicism, and the rising power and wealth of Sir James, the second son, may account for the transaction.

By the end of May Sir James Ogilvie was on his way south to Edinburgh, and letters from the Lord Advocate and John Anderson cease for a time.

MY LORD,—After making many visets, I am att last come safe this lenth, and, God willing, I resolve to be att Edr. the morou. I hear no neus, and I missed my letters

---

[1] *The Acts of the Parliaments of Scotland*, vol. ix. pp. 14, 15, 18, 368.
[2] *Banffshire Sasines*.

att Abd. I wish your Lo. all happiness, and I am, My
Lord, Your Lo. obedient son and most humble servant,

JA. OGILVIE.

Ferrieportoun Craig, May 29, 1694.

On 25th August 1694 Sir James Ogilvie was again at Cullen.
The writer of next letter, Andrew Fraser of Kinmundie, was
Sheriff-depute of Aberdeenshire from 1682 to 1708.[1] The letter
illustrates the conflicts in jurisdiction then so common.

For THE MUCH HONORED SIR JAMES OGILVIE OF THAT
ILK, THEIR MATIES SOLICITOR GENERALL, FFOR THE PRESENT AT
CULLEN OF BOYN   BANFF   these

Aberdeen, 25th August 1694.

MUCH HONORED,—Yours of the 22[d] instant in favours
of Andrew Logie of Loanheid I received, and am glad to
see yow so much his freind, and I think he hath not reason
to doubt much of me, ffor in that mater I proceeded with
alse much moderation as possible, and wes not wanting
to doe him all the kyndness I could in justice. Only my
duty prompted me to doe what I did in citeing him for
that unhappy slaughter, off which it is alleidged he is guilty,
at least had accession thereto. And this I did to prevent
the citation of others, to wit the magistrates of Aberdeen,
who have always competition with me in every thing,
under the notion of being Sherriffs within themselves.
And I think he will be als well used in my hand as in theirs,
ffor albeit he dwells for the most part in the town, yet he is
ane heretor and often recidenter in the shyre, and so lyable
to the Sherriffs jurisdiction. But there is tuo arguments
yow use viz., that the slaughter wes not committed within
this shyre, and that so long tyme being elapsed I wes
incompetent without a commission. I humblie conceive
yow are not thereby in earnest, ffor albeit the slaughter
wes not committed within this shyre, yet the man killed
dwelt in the shyre, and the killer also as said is, and therefore *ratione domicilij* I conceive my self judge for citeing

---

[1] *Sheriff-Court Records of Aberdeen,* New Spalding Club, vol. iii. pp. 103,
104, 105, 106.

of the delinquent to compeır. And albeit some tyme be elapsed (as it wes not much when he wes cited), yet it is the duty of Sherriffs still to prosecute committers of slaughter, either by citation or attachment; and tho perhaps he cannot judge to a small sentence without a commission, yet he may declair fugitive in caice of not compeirance after citation, and he may imprison in caice of compeirance, and acquaint the Kˢ Advocat or Solicitor, as yow very well know. And if this power were taken from Sherriffs, their jurisdiction would signify nothing for subpressing of such crymes. And truelie I would not yeild my jurisdiction of this kynd willinglie, except I saw a positive authority against it. However, for the respect I have to your interposition, I shall proceed but leisurlie, untill I either meet or hear from yow, which I wish may be by the next post or occasion; and till then this is all from, Noble Sir, Your very much devoted and humble servant,   AN. FRASER.

That unhappy man that wes killed wes my debitor considerablie for many ryots, ffor he wes certainly a stuborn ill natured person.

Patrick Ogilvie lives in Scots history as the brother who re-torted on the Chancellor Earl of Seafield, when reproved for lowering the dignity of the family by taking to the trade of cattle dealing, ' Better sellin' nowte nor nations '—one of the mock pearls of Scots history, for Patrick was then a colonel in the army, and was soon to represent in the united Parliament the Elgin Burghs. The following letter, which seems to be in a humorous vein, represents him as in the cattle trade in 1694, but ready to take to preaching, and failing that, law.

For SIR JAMES OGILVIE OF CHURCHHILL
thes ar

. . . I admir what diuel ails the on half of the Presbi-terians to put ut the other, for I hir that Desfourd is nou wacant. I pray you send me a presentaio to it, and I shal com and preaich to you whither thy woul or not; [for] I loue the people of Deskfourd so will that I haue no woll thy want preaching. If this tred fell mi, I intend to tak yours nixt, for I think it is better then the drouen.

I shal say no mor till miting, and I hop, God woling, thàt shal be or long. Till then and euer I am, Dir Brother, Your affectionat brother and most humble seruant,

PAT. OGILVIE.

Carenbulge, Agoust 29, 1694.

Lord Findlater's bookseller in Edinburgh continued to supply him with the 'choysest new bookes.'

MY Lord,—I receaved formerly yor Lop. letter dated in August last ; bot, because I had then sent my commission, I could not give yor Lop. ane answer. Bot that since I have got them home, therfore I have sent yow the following bookes, being the choysest new bookes I have got, and which I thowght wold most fitt yor Lop.—I am, My Lord, Yo^r Lop. most humble servant,   MARTHA STEVENSONE.

Edinbur, October 2d 1694.

	lib.	ss.	d.
L'Estranges Esope fol.,	14	08	0
Medulla Historie Anglicane, 8°,	03	18	0
Monroes sermons, 8°,	03	06	0
Lock on goverment, 8°,	03	06	0
—— on education, 8°,	02	12	0
Conduct of a persone of quality, 8°,	01	10	0
Rapins comparison of Thucide and Livy, 8°,	01	10	0
Burthogs essayes, 8°,	02	08	0
Excellency of pen and pencil, 8°,	01	10	0
Account of Sweden, 8°,	02	02	0
Bp. Santcrofts sermons, 8°,	02	02	0
Dausons freindly conference, 12°,	00	18	0
Miscellanea of ingenious sayeings, 12°,	01	10	0
Rogers fall not out by the way, 12°,	00	18	0
Elliotts lyfe and death, 12°,	01	00	0
Poetical recreations, 8°,	03	06	0

Suma,	46	04	0

And there being owing by yor Lo. in August
last of ballance, ... 39 08 0

	lib.	ss.	d.
There is now resting in haill by yor Lop. this 2^d			
day of October 1694, ...	85	12	0

If yo[r] Lo. please, yow may have the author of ye whole duety of mans works in folio ; bot because the pryce is considerable, viz., 30 shillings, yrfore if yo[r] Lo. be enclyned for it let me know of it.

By 10th October Sir James Ogilvie had returned to Edinburgh. On his way south he advanced his arrangements with the professors of King's College, Aberdeen, for the redemption of part of his paternal estate, Redhythe, which had been wadset to Walter Ogilvie of Redhythe, who on 16th September 1678 and 1st November 1680 mortified it for educational purposes.

ffor THE EARLE OF FFINDLATER   these

Edr., 10th Octr. 1694.

MY LORD,—I have given over thoughts of goeing to London at this tyme, unless I be particularlie called, and which I doe not expect. I spoak to the maisters of the Old toune Collidge as I came south. They are verie faire, and I beleive would give me a verie good penniewourth of the houses, if they could carie my Lord Boyne alongs with them in it. They have promised within a short tyme to send some of ther noumber to the countrey, that the houses may be considdered, att which tyme your Lope and the others I have appoynted may be present. Bot this srves only for makeing us vnderstand hove to transact. I desyre that my name may be given in in the list with the rest of the parosh of Cullen, and that I may be steatted as one barron at tuentie-four pounds, and my sone being fyve yeares of adge at sixpence. Ther are no newes, only wee are impatient to hear ane accompt of the Imperiall airme in Hungarie. Your Lope will be pleased to cause Castelfeild[1] take up ane list of the names of the preists within the shyre of Banffe, ffor I find the Councell hes taken resolutions that non of them be allowed to stay within the kingedome, and the list most be sent over to me by the post. I shall give your Lope no furder trouble at present, bot remaines, My Lord, Your Lops most obedient sone and humble srvant,   JA. OGILVIE.

---

[1] Nicolas Dunbar, Sheriff-depute of Banffshire.

The poll money referred to above and in the following letter, and in those of 29th October and 6th November 1694, was imposed on the inhabitants of Scotland with certain exceptions by Parliament on 29th May 1693 to clear off arrears due to the country and to the army before 1st February 1691. It was farmed out, and was payable at Martinmas 1694.

ffor THE EARLE OF FFINDLATER   these

Edr., 10th Octobr 1694.

MY LORD,—I did detaine the bearer till the Councell day was over, that I might be able to retourne yow the more distinct anssre. I find that as yet the comissioners have incurred no penaltie by not sending up ther lists, ffor most of the shyres are defficient; bot no new day will be appoynted for that affect. And it is the desyre of the fermers of the pole that the countrey be neglegent; ffor in that caice they are posetiwe they will exact the quadruple, and therfor in this countrey everiewhair the lists are complaited, att laist they are goeing about the doeing of it with all dilligence. And therfor I doubt not the comssres of your shyre will loase no more tyme, bot prepaire ther lists and send exact doubles of them to the pole office in this place. I find lykewayes that, unless the accompts due to the countrey be sent over heir immediatlie, the shyre will loss the benefeit of retaineing, ffor the comssres can retaine nothing, bot conforme to staited precepts to be granted by the Lords of Theasurie. It is also fitt that the comissres attend the seall dyetts, which shall be appoynted by the fearmers, att laist so many of them as yow shall think fitt to appoynt for that affect; and they are unquystionablie judges to all quystiones that shall aryse betuixt the countrey people and the fermers. As to gentlemens sones vnder the adge of sixtein, in this countrey they class them at sixpence, and above that age at thrie pound; bot befor Mertimess this poynt will be determined by ane sentence of Councell, ffor I find the fermers pretends to thrie pound without distinctione of adge. As to srvants without fie, and who are not intertained for charitie, they may be recked at sixpence. I intreat yor Lope to cause these in whom yow are concerned be dilligent in prepaireing ther lists ; as also I expect the bookes of accompts and other documents in Durns[1] hand will be sent up, and if they come shortly I hope to procure ane precept. And if otherwayes, the comissres hes non to bleam bot ther selves, if the countrey   pay^t. What furder directions are neceissarie shall be sent from tyme to tyme, as the Councell comes to determine poynts debaitable.—Which is all at present from, My Lord, Your Lops. most obedient sone and humbl srvant,   JA. OGILVIE.

William Graham, eighth Earl of Menteith and second Earl of Airth, whose death is mentioned in next letter, was brother of Lady Mary Graham, who married on 8th October 1662 Sir John Allardes of Allardes, Kincardineshire. The Earl died on 12th September 1694. Before his death he had disponed to his nearest relative, his nephew George Allardes, the reversion of the barony of Kinpont.[2] Next letter fixes the date of the birth of a daughter to Allardes, probably Mary.

ffor THE EARLE OF FFINDLATER these

MY LORD,—I cannot express with what reluctancie I left the countrey without waiteing one your Lordship ; for that evining I gotte the express showeing me of the Earle of Monteithes death, I hade full resolutions to have waited one your Lordship the nixt morning, and to have spent five or six dayes wery mirryly with your Lordship. Hovever I hope, when I wreat to your Lordship at more lenth, ye will think my journey worth my paines. Blessed be God, this day your daughter is safely brought to bed of a daughter, and is one the way of recovery. Sr James was gone by befor I returned from Monteith, for which I was wery much troubled ; but I hope by the nixt occasione I may give your Lordship ane good accompt of my busieness, and at this tyme being on heast I ever continue, My Lord, Your Lordships most obedient son and humble serwant,   GEO. ALLARDES.

Allardes, 11th Octer. 94.

---

[1] William Dunbar.   [2] *Red Book of Menteith*, vol. i. p. 428.

For THE EARLE OF FFINDLATER these

Edr., 6th Novembr 1694.

MY LORD,—I have receaved from the bearer the pole lists, as also some of the accompts of the shyre. I shall taike caire to applay for ane precept hove soone the Theasurie sitts, which I beleive may be upon Wedensday nixt. I find those in our countrey hes neglected to returne lists of the hearths, which I beleive hes proceeded from ane mistake, they judgeing that they would have bein lyable, unless they could have produced dischairges. Bot ther own declara°nes that they hade payed was declaired sufficient, albeit ther dischairges hade fallen by ther hands. I beleive it shall coast me some money befor I obtaine the precept; bot I shall not stand on this, bot shall advance what is neidfull. As for what your Lope wrot to me anent Reidhyth, I can not be positive what I will doe, till I sie hove the sessione proves; bot if possible I will redeem it. I shall neglect no fitt oppertunitie of doeing what your Lope recomendit to me in your nott; bot I most waite till I vnderstand hove affaires goes after his Matyes returne. Wee have no newes, the airmies being decamped, and the fleits, att laist the great shipes belong-- ing therto, laid up, that of the Confederats at Cades, and the other at Tholune. The D. of fflorance and yᵉ Venetians have ouned and acknouledged the Kings title to the croune, and are lickly to joyne in the Confedracie; and the Dutch incresses ther airmie 15000 more then the last yeare, and it is thought the English will proceed with a great daile of frankness in the Parliāt. I shall be glaid to hear frequently from yow, which is all at present from, My Lord, Your Lops. most obedient sone and humble srvant,   JA. OGILVIE.

This day his Matjes birth day was solemnized with all the vsuall solemnaties, such as ringing of bells fyreing of gunes and shoutting of vollies by the train bands and elumena°nes.

In 1694 the tide began to turn for William and the allies in Flanders. The main force of his fleet had also been operating

in the Mediterránean with success against the French fleet, which
withdrew to Toulon. Admiral Russell wintered at Cadiz.

Next letter to the Earl of Findlater throws light on Lord
Deskford's condition at this time.

MY NOBLE LORD,—I ame most sensible off y^r Lo^s
afflictione anent the present condition off my Lord y^r
son, wherin I asseur y^r Lo. that I hav a sensible part
therin, and indevors in what I can to lessin both, as y^r
Lo. shall know, when I shall vait on y^r Lo. once this week
vith my Lord Huntly, who has his most dutifull respects
to y^r Lo. by these, vntill he vait on y^u, and bids me tell
y^r Lo. that though ther var no other impediment, it vould
be novays proper y^r Lo. should cum to this place in such
vather. And as for my Lord y^r sons designe off accom-
panying Huntly south, I know nothing off it; but if he
hawe any such resolutione I asseur y^r Lo. I vill divert it
on vay or other, it being novays proper at present. I
thinck y^r Lo. does very weell in keeping his hors from
him, w^h may oblidge him to returne home; and y^r Lo.
may be assured I shall tack all the cair in my power to
mowe Desford to returne home, and to live peaciblie and
calmlie, vithout going out to ye toune off Cullen, as he
promist me. Mor I shall not say till I hawe the honor
to vait on y^r Lo^p, but that I ame in all sinceritie, My D^r
Lord, Y^r Lo^s most humble and most faithfull servant,

A. DUMBAR.
Gordon Castle, 9 Novr. 94.

The commission of the General Assembly, appointed in April
1694 for the settlement of the church in the North of Scotland,
soon began to work. On 11th July 1694 a nucleus of six ministers
was formed into a joint presbytery for Aberdeenshire and Banffshire, and the Presbyterian settlement of these counties was
begun. The three next letters give account of the settlement of
a schoolmaster in Cullen, and of an attempt to settle a minister in
Deskford, Banffshire. The old schoolmaster, Mr. Robert Sharp,
was deprived on 10th November, because he had not taken the
oaths to government. On 2nd September Mr. James Henderson,
minister of Deskford, was 'inhibited in the exercise of his

pasturall office for his non-complyence with the civill government and disobedience to the lawes, and the kirk was declared vacant.' [1]

For THE EARLE OF FINDLATER   these

My Lord,—I being informed that the school of Cullen is declared vacant, have presumed by this to beg your Lo[ps] favour to Mr. Alexander Watt in order to his settlement there.   I know him to be an able humanist and very fitt for any imployment of that kind.   I am also persuaded y[t] he is a good man and I hope God, by giving him grace aright to improve his former circamstances and present straits, hes fitted him for doing him service in another station, and in his good time will open a door to him ;· but in the while he would wish not to be idle, but imploy any talent he hes to the best purpose.   My Lord, his wife is daughter to good Mr. Alexander Seton [2] who allwayes had a sincere deference for your Lo[p] and family ; and I am sure this will be motive to obtain your Lo[ps] countenance to him who, I am confident, will not prove unworthy of any kindnesse your Lo[p] honours him with. I will undertake for his pious and peaceable deportment and diligence and fidelitie in his imployment, and constant respect to your Lo[p] and yours.—I am, My Lord, Your Lo[ps] most obleidged and faithfull servant,

MR. PAT. INNES.

Banff, Novr. 20, 1694.

My Lord,—I adwenture on the freedom to giwe your Lop. the trouble to tell yow I hawe spoken to and prewailed wt Mr. Watt to preach att Cullen Thursday nixt, the minister of Cullen consenting, as I apprehend he will. This I hop will be satisfieing to your Lop., and to many in that parishin, and to all wnless it be to some disaffected persons, who may be prejudised wtout just ground ; and wt all thinks it necessary that the toun counsell be called on Fryday or Saterday therafter, qch God willing I sall attend, that Mr. Watt may hawe his presenta°ne, who

---

[1] Dr. Cramond's *Church of Deskford*, p. 17.
[2] Dr. Cramond's *Church and Churchyard of Cullen*, p. 76.

says, if he com ther, the schooll sall not waick on day
for him.   Mr. Robert Sharp being allowed to officiat bot
to the 15th of December nixt, Mr. Watt can hawe no less
then a weeks tyme to make rady to exerce as schoolmaster.
I think it not amiss your Lop. communicat thes to the
Baylies by your conveniencie, and I am in all duty, My
Lord, Your Los. affec°nat and most humble serwant,

GEO. LESLYE.

Banff, Nov. 30 : —94.

For THE EARLE OF FFINDLATER   these

Edr., 3d December 1694.

MY LORD,—The bearer Mr. Lesslie is recomendit to me
by severall persones weill affected to the governement.
He is desyrous to be settled att Daskfoord, and I inclyne
to it.   ffor my selfe I could have bein weill pleased with
Mr. Murray ; bot I have ane letter from the on halfe of
the parosh, wherin they testifie ther unwillingness to have
him ther minister.   And besydes I doe not find that the
Presbyterian ministers will as yet receave him for some
tyme ; therfor I expect that your Lope will incouradge
this young man, and, if he satisfie the rest of the parosh,
I ame willing to give him ane call.   We have no newes
heir bot that the Parliāt of England proceeds verie for-
wardlie in giveing the supplies that are necessar.   This is
all the present trouble from, My Lord, Your Lops. most
obedient sone and humble servant,   JA. OGILVIE.

Mr. Leslie was not appointed to Deskford.   Mr. Murray was
ordained on 26th June 1698 in succession to Mr. Henderson.

For THE EARLE OF FFINDLATER Abd to BANFFE
these   3d

Edr., 7th Jary. 1695.

MY LORD,—I was extreemly pleased with the newes of my
wyffes being saife brought to bed, especiallie seing she hes
given me a cautioner for James.   I wish God may inable
me to doe that deutie to them which is proper upon my
pairt.   I have wreitten to my Lord Boyne anent Reidhyth.
I have not as yet sold my wictuall, bot cause Allexr ffella

immediatlie send me over ane accompt what I can sell,
ffor I resolve verie shortly to dispose of it.   Cause him
also wreit to me how soone my wictuall may be readie,
att laist how soone I may send for the first loadning of
bear, ffor the soonner it is the better for me.   Excuise my
not wreitting with my oun hand, because of a deffluction
hes fallen doune in my face with the toothaick ;   naither
dare I wreit to my wyffe with one other hand, bot I hope
your Lope will remember me keindly to hir, and I will be
impatient till I hear of hir recoverie.   My present dis-
temper does not discouradge me, because I ame so frea-
quently accustomed with it.—I ame, My Lord, Your Lops.
most affectionat sone and humble srvant,

JA. OGILVIE.

I doubt not bot your Lope hes heard of the sade loss
wee have by the death of the Queen.

The ' cautioner' was probably his second son George.[1]

Later in January Sir James Ogilvie proceeded to London at
the King's command.   He was henceforward to take a more important part in the management of Scots public affairs.

For THE EARLE OF FFINDLATER   these

Qhytfeild, 28th Jary. 95.

My LORD,—I intended to have waited upon your Lordship, but the deepness of the snow necessitats me to bege
your Lordships excuse whill it be better traveling.   I
have given the bearer ane line to your Lordship from Sir
James, and one to his Lady, with ane gold watch to her
Ladyship.   Sr James hade ane great defluction in his
cheek, and it brock within three dayes befor he took journey, so that at his waygoeing he was wery well in health.
The Provest and Baillies of Eder did attend him at his
lodgeing that morneing he went from Eder, and hade ane
sak posset prepaired at the foot of the Caniegaite, qch
they gaive him befor he took his coatch.   The Laird and
Lady Allardyce have their humble service presented to

---

[1] Dr. Cramond's *Annals of Cullen*, p. 61.

your Lordship, and wold have wreaten to you, but becaues I wold not stay qûll ther constant kissing dayes vere over, they could not take tyme. So craveing your Lordships pardone for this trouble, I shall wish all prosperity to your family, and still continue to be, My Lord, Your Lordships most obedient servant,'

ALEXR. OGILVIE.[1]

For THE EARLE OF FFINDLATER

Edr. 7 Feb. 1695.

MY LORD,—I receaved two letters from your Lōp direct for my maister, on of which was in relatione to the shyres accompts, and immediatly went with the books and instructiones, and delyvered them to the Cownsell clerk. The other I sent to Londone to my maister who, praised be God, saiflie aryved at court Wednesday was eight dayes. I have sent your Lops. specticles, which I hope will please yow. Ther are no news heir, but that it is frequently talked heir of some changes about the court. The Parliament is said to be adjurned vntill the twentieth of March, about which tyme my maister will be down. Ther are no letters come from my maister as yet, but vnto my Lord Advocat. I give your Lōp no furder truble, but that I am, My Lord, Your Lōps most obedient and humble servant, AN CRAIK.

The bear and meall wold be in readines against the twentieth of this moneth, for I intend to have ships at Portsoy by that tym.

Andrew Craik, writer in Edinburgh, in the absence of James Baird in London, seems to have acted as agent or secretary for Sir James Ogilvie in Edinburgh.

For THE EARL OF FINDLATER

MY LORD,—I cannot expres hou much I long to see your Lo. I have ben ys eleven wiks bygon in Edn., and went out a part of ye way wt Sir Jeams, qñ he went for

---

[1] Afterwards Lord Forglen.

Loundon. I hope all his frinds shall be rejoysed w^t ye acompts of his preferment to ane higher station. I have ben singularly oblidged to his kyndness in my afairs. I have ane disposition to ye revertion of Killpont, and also ane legall right. They yt ar in posesion of it wold be conten to compond wt me, and I belive, if Sir Jeams had not gon for Loundone, it wold ben ended or now. Houever I will rether take ane soume of mōey then enter in ane law action ; and I hope from them and Mountros to get threty thousand merks qc̃h is ane very good unexpected casuality ; and if Killponts pepers be not clearer then I hear from themselves, I think to get much mor. If your Lo. met w^t Forglen,[1] he will give your Lo. a mor foull accompt y^n much wryting wold contin. I give your Lo. many thanks for ye many good vishes to my young family your Lo. is pleased to wryt, q̃n my wife or I hath ye onouer of ane lyne from your Lo. ; but I cane never think myselfe intirly hapey till I have ye long wished for honwr of seeing your Lo. in your daughtors hows,· who is a very honest woman and a herty god wiffe, and I ashur your Lo. wer men no trysters for our houmers simpathyses prety well. So giving your Lo. my blising, and recomending you to ye caire of ye Almighty, I ever am in all duty, My Lord, Your Lo. most obedient sone and devoted srt.,

                                        GEO. ALLARDES.

My mother gives hir humble duty to your Losp.
Allardes, 10 *Fbr.* '95·

Next letter contains the first reference to the long-continued quest of a pension by the Earl of Findlater.

        For THE EARLE OF FINDLATER SCOTLAND

                                London, Febrie 12, 1695.

MY LORD,—By your last I perceive you have not knowen of my going to court, when it was wrot. I was necessitat to alter my resolutions as to Ridhyth for on year, bot I

---

[1] Alexander Ogilvie.

hope ther will be time for it. I will speak of your Lo. to Sec. Jo., bot I know not what success I may have. The King is in good health, and both houses proceed with a great dale of frankness. I have no other neus to wreat. You can order my brother Deskfoord and his servants as you please. I will not medle with him, bot leave that to your Lo. He is your son.—I am, My Lord, Your Lo. most obedient son and humble servant,

JA. OGILVIE.

During his stay in London, which extended to the middle of April, Sir James Ogilvie obtained the following royal warrant on the Scots Treasury for payment of his expenses. It is taken from the *State Papers (Scotland) Warrant Books*, vol. xvi., in the Record Office, London.

WILLIAM R.

It is our will and pleasure, and we do hereby authorise and require you in consideration of the charges which our trusty and well beloved Sir James Ogilvie our Solicitor hath been at in coming hither by our order this winter upon publick bussiness, that you make paȳt to him without delay out of the first and readiest of our crown rents customes bishops rents or any other ffond whatsoever the sume of two hundred pounds sterline, ffor doing wherof these presents together with his receipt or the receipt of any having his order shall be to you and all others therein concerned a sufficient warrant.

Given at our Court at Kensington the 6th day of Aprile 1695 and of our reign the 6th year By his Mats command,

J. JOHNSTOUN.

To the LORDS COMMISSIONERS of our TREASURY of our ancient kingdom of SCOTLAND.

For
THE RIGHT HONBL THE EARLE OFF FFINDLATER

MY LORD,—I received ye honore of your Lops letter, wherin yee signe yt yee have been pleased to wreit to John Andersone to keep me from meeting wt truble from ye Admirall anent ye whale speck, qrin your Lop. hes don verie weill. I shall bring yow a snuff box such as yee desyr. I hade sent it w^t ye bearer, but I have not been at Edinbrugh since I came. I have bought ye herring and biskett qch Sir James Lady desyrs, and shall send ym w^t ye first weshell yt goes for Banff or Portsoie.—I am in all duty, My Lord, Your most ffaithfull and most humble servant,   ALEXR. LESLIE.[1]

Leith, Apryll 6th, 1695.

The Scots Court of Admiralty had *inter alia* jurisdiction in all questions of wreck. The Court of Session in 1739 decided, in the case of Hume against the Admiral-depute, that whales did not fall under the gift of wreck, but were *inter regalia.*[2]

For THE RIGHT HONOURABLE THE EARLE OF FFINDLATER   CULEN

MY VERIE NOBLE LORD,—I receaved your Lop̃s anent the whale fish. Andrew Craik spock to me anent it befor he went north, and I have spock with Kininvie anent it since; and it is certaine that no lawyer here, nor any other person of respect of your sons acquaintance would delay to doe ther outmost for what might be your Lōp or your sons interest; and the Judge of Admiralitie is ane advocat your sons freind, and the clerks are his servants, and all of them would forfault ther interest in so small a matter ere he wer disobleidged, at least would delay the affaire till he wer upon the place. It is my bound duty to give all the service I cane to your Lōp, or any of my masters freinds or servants, and I will not faill in it.

My Lord Advocat receaved yesternight a letter from your son Sir James, which gives account that he is in verie good health, but my Lord does not expect him to be upon the road (as I thought) for some dayes to come, since the Parliat is to be adjourned. James Baird wrott to me on the 28 of March, that Sir James wes goeing to recreat himself by visiting Windsore and Hamptoun Court, and

---

[1] Provost of Banff and laird of Kininvie.
[2] Lord Elchies's *Decisions* under 'Wreck.'

other considerable places not fare from court for some
dayes, and would then take journey home.   We hear
the King allowes him much care and free accesse, and
therfor think that he most wait on his Majestie till eyr
the King goe off, or the King's affaires bring him doun
here.   It is thought ther will be litle or no altera°n of our
statesmen here ; but we hope the King will consider
your sons session loss and services.   I wrott to Sir James
on Thursday last, and my Lord Advocat tells me that he
thinks if I wreitt to-morrowe it may overtake him, which
I will doe, and by that post will send my Ladys ler with
ordors to returne it, if he be come off.—I ame, My Lord,
Your Lops. most humble and most obedient servant,

JO. ANDERSON.

Edr. 8 Apryll 1695.

I could not wreitt by the man brought me your Lōps
ler sooner ; because I behooved to wait Sabbaths post
expecting lers.

Not only did Sir James Ogilvie receive a royal warrant for the
payment of his expenses and charges while in London, he also
got a King's letter,[1] on 27th April 1695, to the Lords Commissioners of the Treasury ordering them to pay him his disburse-
ments as his Majesty's Solicitor upon processes and for maintaining
witnesses.

For THE EARLE OF FINDLATER

Stamfort, April 20, 1695.

MY LORD,—I wrot to your Lo. from London that I
have promised to the King that you shal attend this
session of Parlament.   I therfor expect your Lo. att Eđr
about the ninth of the nixt moneth att furthest.   You
may get some money from my Lord Boyn or Burdsbank
for your expences onn the rod.   I wreat this least the
other hes not come to your hands.   I am, My Lord, Your
Lo. most obedient son and humble servant,

JA. OGILVIE.

---

[1] *State Papers* (*Scotland*) *Warrant Books,* vol. xvi. p. 29, in the Record
Office, London.

Parliament met on 9th May, and was adjourned on 17th July 1695. The Solicitor-General attended as member for the royal burgh of Cullen. His father, the Earl of Findlater, was also in attendance, as the rolls of Parliament and next letter from the Sheriff-depute of Banffshire show.

ffor THE RIGHT HONORABLE THE EARLE OFF
FFINDLATER att Edr. these

Castlfeild, 23 May 1695.

RIGHT HONORABLE AND MY DEAR LORD,—I could not omitt by this bearer to testifie to your Lo. that the comendations sent me by your Lo.'s letter to your daughter-in-law makes me know I am happier then I supposed, since I perceave yrby to have the honor to be somtymes in your memorie in a place wher your Lo. will be taken up in great affairs for the publict good ; for I had not the ambition to imagine ther could be any roum left for persons of so small importance as Schomberg and my selfe. I receaved the news of your Lo. saiffe arryvall at Edr. with much joy, and had the satisfaction to know that all things wer propitious to you in your jorney ; and to be diffident the conclusion will not correspond with so fair beggings wer to doubt the Almighties providence, or distrust his grace, for I am confident the divyne providence will at all tyms take a particular care of your Lo. and familie. My wyffe and I humblie kiss your Lo. hands and Sir James his. I recomend your Lo. and him to the protection of the all wyse and omnipotent God ; and takes leave of your Lo. with the protestation I heir make to live and die, My Lord, Your Lo. most humble, obedient and faithfull servant,   NICOLAS DUNBAR.

ffor THE RYTT HONOLL THE EARLL OFF FINDLATER
ar thes

Carnebulge, 3 June 1695.

MY LORD,—The manif[t] testimonies of yor kyndnes and freindshipe to me and my familie macks me to giue yow this trouble, intreating yow will give yor vtmost indeavores to excuse my absence from this Parliament, it being on no other heid I stay bott the circumstance of my fortune, and weack conditione of yor cusing my wyff, both qch I judg is sufficientlie knowin to yor Lop. I fformerlie wrot to yor sone Sr James, and am convinced yor Lop. and his sincere indevores with his Grace the Comissioner [1] will casilie obtayne my excuse, and be a most singular evidence of yor fawor and ffreindshipe done to, My Lord, Yor Lops. most affectionat humble srwant,   FRASOR.

Lord Fraser's wife was Marjory Erskine, daughter of James, seventh Earl of Buchan. Lord Fraser attended Parliament soon after, and on 2nd July 1695 took the oath of allegiance.[2]

At the close of this session of Parliament Sir James Ogilvie began his long correspondence with Carstares.[3] About this time he accompanied one of the Secretaries of State for Scotland, probably Mr. John Johnston, in a progress through the north with the view of advancing the Presbyterian settlement of the church.

ffor THE RῩT HONBLE SIR JAMES OGILVIE OFF THET ILK
HIS MAJESTES SOLICETOR

RῩT HṄBLE,—There goes such different reports heir off the Secretaries motion made me uncertain wher to wait on him, and occationed you this truble as the surest hand to know his dayet. If he come by the cost I hope ye will prevaile with him to honour me with a night ; and if he be determened ane other road acquant me, and wher ye judge most proper, he shall be waited on by, Sir, Your most affectionat humble servant,   FRASOR.

Give my humble deuty to my L. Secretary.
Castlefraser,[4] 15 *Agust* 95.

For THE RIGHT HONBLL SIR JAMES OGILVIE
OF THAT ILK HIS MAJESTIES SOLICITOR   BANFF   3d

RIGHT HONOURABLE,—The inclosed letter showes you that ther is little newes. Ther wants some mails. Murrays letter beares that ther wes a flieing report that the seidge

---

[1] John Marquess of Tweeddale.
[2] *The Acts of the Parliaments of Scotland*, vol. ix. p. 407.
[3] *Carstares State Papers and Letters*, passim.
[4] *The Acts of the Parliaments of Scotland*, vol. ix. pp. 436-437.

at Namuir wes raised, but it wes in no other letter, and its not beleived.

The Commissioners of Admirality have appoynted you Admirall deputt from ffindhorne exclusive to Buchan nesse inclusive.

The Earle of Kincardyns house of Culros is burnt to ashes by ane accidentall fyre.

The prolcama^on anent the excyse is not yet printed, but shall be sent you by the nixt.

I inclosed some of the acts explaining the proclama^on anent the pole, with severall other papers for James Baird in the box that brought my Ladys linings. It will refresh your freinds here to hear that ye are well efter your journey.—I ame, Right Honbll, Your most humble and obedient st., JO. ANDERSON.

Edr. 16 *August* 1695.

After the death of the Duke of Hamilton on 18th April 1694, the Admiralty was put in commission. The Earl of Kincardine was Alexander Bruce, third Earl.

Er., 19 *August* 1695.

RIGHT HONBL,—Receave the inclosed, which is the substance of all the forraigne newes by the last males. They report here that the Dauphin is coming to fflanders with the rake-hells of ffrance, whom God give ill success. Ther is nothing doeing here but a committie of Councill, who is to meit with the magistrats of Edr. anent adjusting the pole of this city.—I ame, Right Honbl, Your Hōs most humble and obedient servant, JO. ANDERSON.

On the 26th of August Marshal Boufflers surrendered Namur Castle to William; and the campaign of 1695 in Flanders ended for the first time in a decided success for the Confederates.

The act of 16th July 1695 for the settling of the quiet of the church allowed non-conforming Episcopal ministers, who were in charges at the revolution, to retain their places on taking the oaths of allegiance and assurance. This concession was not extended to clergymen who had been subsequently called. Next letter and several succeeding ones of 1695 deal with these matters.

For SIR JAMES OGILVIE

Philorth, 22 Agust 1695.

RIGHT HONORABLE,—I regreat it extreamly that my hous should be so farre out of the veay, uhen my Lord Secretare is making ane progrese thorrow our countray, for I vas in hops he would haue alloued me the honour to veat one his Lp. at this pleac ; and as it is but seldom we in this countray can haue the oppertunety to entertine a person of his charracter and meret, so it trubles me verie much I should be depraived of that honnour, when others in this sheir heas it, but non can vish him better then I dooe. As to what ye ar pleased to vrit anent our ministers ther qualefeing themselues, I haue beane taking pains with sume of them in it ; and for such old ministers as I am most conserned in (uho haue still geven unquestionable testimonies of ther loyalty), I dout not but in dew time they vill obay the law ;[1] and for the other ministers[2] letly called by the uholl heretors and popell of ther pareses, I imagen the greatest scrouple they haue is from ther being declared intreuders by the committe of the Generall Assemble, so if they head any asseurenc that ther taking the oathes would make ther kease equall to the old ministers, they would not be behynd them in dooing what in deuty they all aught to dooe on this occation. This letter being alredy tooe long, I ask your pardon for it, and humly intreats ye will dooe me the justis to believe I haue the greatest honnor and respeck imaginable for yow, which in deuty I am bound tooe, and shall ever be on all occations intyrly, Right Honorable, Your most humble servent,

SALTOUNE.[3]

My humble deuty to my Lord your father and your Lady.

ffor THE RIGHT HOLL THE EARLE OFF FFINLATER
thes

Durn, the 22 off August 1695.

MY LORD,—I head an ltr ffrom an ffreind off Brodies

---

[1] *The Acts of the Parliaments of Scotland*, vol. ix. pp. 449-450.

[2] *Ibid.*, pp. 420-421.

[3] William, eleventh Lord Saltoun, son-in-law of Archbishop Sharp.

sent exprese bee this bearrer desayring I might bee
infformed bee ȳr Lo. off the Secritaries dayett att ȳr
Lo⁸ house, and off his intentiones as to the staiges he
resolves to ryd ffrom ȳr Lo⁸, iff bee Elgin, and iff he
intends to stay an night ther, or bee Castell Grant or
Brodie, as he goes ffor Invernes. This I heave made bold
to truble ȳr Lo. wᵗ, and intreats ȳr Lo. may acquant mee
that I may returne an anͬr according to desayre, and is
all att p̄sent ffrom Yr Lo⁸ affectionat and humble servant,

                                                W. DUNBAR.

RIGHT HOͦBLE,—My Lord Secretary promised, when I
spoke to him in behalf of Mr. White my sone in law, whome
they reckon as ane intruder, that he should warrant him
if he took the oaths. I knew then he was clear to take
them, and now he is come willing to doe it. I have
thought fit to send him to see the Secretary, and I have
presumed to trouble you with this lyne desireing your Ho.
to introduce him to see the Secretary and befrind him,
both by your advice and assistance. So as I expect this
kyndness, I likewise beg pardon for this trouble, and I
still am, Right Hoͦble, your Ho. most oblidged and humble
servant,   ROBERT CRUIKSHANK.
    Agust 23, 1695.

For THE RIGHT HONOURABLE SIR JAMES OGILVIE
    OF THAT ILK HIS MAJESTIES SOLICITOR, BANFF   6d

                            Edr., 28th August i695.

RIGHT HONͦBLL,—Receave the inclosed. Ther is nothing
of newes here, only yesterday the committee of Parliat.
committed Sir John Cochran, Barntoun, and Sir Ja.
Oswald to prison, till they should give up ther bookes
and accompts anent the last pole.[1] It seemes they have
given satisfaction to the committie, for they are nowe at
libertie.—I ame, Right Honͦbll, Your Hoͦs most humble
and obedient servant,   JO. ANDERSON.

Sir John Cochran of Ochiltree and the others were the farmers
of the 1693 poll-tax.[1]

King William's bad years were now commencing.

---

[1] *The Acts of the Parliaments of Scotland*, vol. ix. pp. 453, 454.

For THE RIGHT HONOURABLE SIR JAMES OGILVIE
OF THAT ILK, HIS MAJESTIES SOLICITOR   BANFF   6d

Edr., 6t Septer 1695.

RIGHT HONB̄LL,—The letter for forraigne newes is
inclosed.   Ther is non here but the proclamaᵒn for a
publict thanksgiving throwe-out the kingdome, which is
to be keeped on the Sabboth dayes, because of the badnes
of the season, the dispatch wherof will coast you money;
but by that expresse I will indeavour to gett you all the
newes my Lord Advocat hes, who gives you his respects
and would have wreitten, but he is troubled with the gout
in both feit, and refuses any help but patience.   I will be
glad that all publict bussienes be so favourable as to afford
the kingdome good and you some libertie and repose for
your families concernes, till your imployment and money
bring you over.—I ame, Right Honłł, Your most humble
and obedient servant,   Jo. ANDERSON.

ffor SR JAMES OGILVIE OF THAT ILK

Edr., 9 7ʳ 1695.

SR,—It has bein a silent time since you parted.   It may
be, if we had heared soner of the taking of the Castle of
Namur, more of our dissenting clergie had come in.   Five
of nine in Hadingtoun presb. have qualified themselves,
and som feu in other parts, but allmost none in Perth
Angus and Fyffe that I hear of; and the truth is I was
never more indifferent, for, tho I was much for the act,[1]
yet I have often said that the best use of othes and subtions
in Scotland was to discover upon refusal.   For to my
certain knouledge they bind not any that take them uith
the lest aversion; and if the taking divide the partie it
offends bot the weakest, but the worst mistake nothing
and ar bettered by nothing.   I shall be glad to see the
Secretarie here.   The bringing in of some of the northern
clergie uill I hope be accounted better service in England
nor it is recknoned by some here.   We want three mails
from Flanders.   The old President is verie ill of his strang-

---

[1] *The Acts of the Parliaments of Scotland*, vol. ix. pp. 449-450.

urie. I have bein these eight dayes lame of both my feet by the gout, and am not yet able to walk. My L. Secretarie knoues he has many observers, and they talk of his entertainments and complements; but I hope his oun conduct and prudence uill disappoint all his ennimies. Cultness salutes my Lord y^r father and y^r self with all humility and kindness; and I protest I more and more regret that I had no more of my Lords converse while he was here; but I hope he doubts not but I am to him as most sincerely, S^r, Y^r most humble servit^r,

JA. STEUART.

James Dalrymple, Viscount Stair, President of the Court of Session, died on the 25th of November 1695.

For THE EARLE OF FINDLATER

MY LORD,—If the post had had any letters either to your Lo^p or the Solicitor, he would not have keept them till now. We had no account of the particulars of the surrender of the Castle of Namure with the last post, save that the whole garrison were made prisoners, so y^t it would seem they had surrendered on discretion. It was expected that we might shortlie hear of an ingagement in Flanders, some letters bearing that the two armies were within view of one another, and drawn up in battail array ready to fall on; but it is thought the French would have rather fought before the surrender of the castle. We had nothing more with the last post either in publick or private letters of any moment, as far as I can learne. Whatever letters come to your Lo^p or the Solicitor by our post, if he have not a present occasion of a bearer for Cullen, they shall be sent off per expresse by, My Lord, Your Lo^{ps} most obleidged and faithfull servant,

MR. PAT. INNES.

Banff, Septr 10, 1695.

ffor THE LAIRD OF COULL these

Cullen, i3th Septbr. 1695.

SIR,—Att pairting with my Lord Secritary he did recomend to me to get him ane accompt of the ministers

of the Episcopall preswasion, that have qualified themselves benorth Aberdein ; and lykewayes he is desyrous
to knowe of the number of the Presbyterian ministers
settled in churches since the revolution ; and I most
also informe him of the names of the other ministers in
possessione of churches that are unqualified.   I knowe
yow cane be helpfull to me in this matter within the bounds
of Ross and Inverness, ffor by calling for on or tuo of your
nighbouring ministers who have qualified themselves,
yow will gett full informa°ne.   I beg pardon for this
trouble, and expecting your ansre, I remaine, Sir, Your
most humble srvant,   JA. OGILVIE.

Sir Alexander M'Kenzie, laird of Coull, was one of the two
commissioners for Ross to Parliament in 1693 and 1695.

The Rev. James Chalmers, minister of Cullen, having failed to
qualify by the 1st of September, was deprived of office.   The Rev.
John Hay, minister of Rathven, was deprived by the Privy Council
on 7th November 1689, and was deposed in 1694.   The next
five letters deal with the filling up of these vacancies.   Cullen was
ultimately settled in 1697, and Rathven not until 1700, and even
then temporarily and only in form.

ffor THE EARLE OFF FFINDLATOUR

RIGHT HONOURABLE,—The Presbytry of Aberdein ffinding ye church of Cullin vacand in law, ye former minister
being deprived by act of Parliatt, have appointed our
reverend broȳr, Mr. John Sandielands minister of the
gospell to declare the sd vacansie Sabbath next the 29
instant ; and they have appointed me heirw̄t to signifie
soe much to your Lordship by this line, expecting your Lo.
concurrance in ‚yis affair according to law, and yt you
will be instrumentall as soon as possible to heave ye sd
church planted wt ane honest and weel qualified man, and
if your Lordship please and see it meett our broȳr Mr.
Sandilands may make the first step in order to ye choicing
of ane legall eldership, for ye more speedy settlement of
a minister ut you.—Beggs your Lordships pardon for yis
trouble, and tho I have not ye happieness of your Lordships acquaintance, yet I doe heirby subscribe my. self,

Right Honourable, Your Lo. verry humble and obedient servant,   W. TRAIL.

Aberdein, 26 *Septr.* 1695.

ffor
·THE RIGHT HONORABLE THE EARLE OF FINLATER

Achrie, 11 *Oct*. 95.

MY LORD,—Your favorable accepting of Mas^r Chambers at first, and the constant encouragment you have been pleasd to allou him doth call for sutable returne of grati- tude and service from him to your Lo^p and your familie, (q^{ch} I perceue him most uilling and foruard to give accord- ing to his pouer), and upon the certain notice I haue of your uninterrupted freindship to him under his present hard circumstances, q^{ch} he tells me uer equally surprising to you and your son, Sr James, the designe of declaring the church of Cullen vacant being caried on secretly, I am bound to acknuledge thankfully your Lo^p kindnes heirin, and uill· not faill to express the sam freindly regard to your Lo^p recomenda^{o}n uhen-ever ocasion offers, and I have only this requist on his behalf y^t, sinc he hath served till Michelmess, you uill let the stipend from Whitsunday com his way. My Lord, I had not used this freedom, if I uer not persuaded of your respect to all deseruing men in the church, and the antient gouerment of Episcopacie. Upon these grounds and your particular freindship to my self, I recomend the bearer and this affaire to your kindnes in this, q^{ch} vill be a good work in it self and a neu obliga^{o}n on, My Lord, Your Lo^p most faithfull and humble servant,   ERROLL.[1]

My Lord, be pleased to excuse the cursnes of this peaper.

For THE EARL OF FINDLATER

Abd., Novr. 1, —95.

RIGHT HONORABLE,—The presbytery of A𝑏d have ap-

---

[1] Sir John Hay, twelfth Earl of Erroll.

pointed me in their name to thank your L͠p for yo͏r countenancing of and concurrence with us in promoting the interests of the gospell in these corners, where you are specially and eminently concerned ; .and to entreat your L͠ps assistance in the speedy planting of Cullen [1] and Rathvan.[2] We hope your L͠p will interpose your influences with the heretors of Rathven (your near neighbours) to bring them to a concurrence with, or at least a consent unto our call to Mr. Tho. James, (which call your L͠p hes seen), that he may have the more easy peaceable comfortable and successfull access unto and labour and abode amongst them. This (with our serious desires after the welfare and prosperity spiritual and temporall of your L͠ps honorable family), is in the name of the presbytery humbly signifyed by Yo͏r L͠ps much obliged and humble serv͏t,   W. TRAILL.

For THE EARLE OF FINDLATER this

MY LORD,—I designed to have waited on your Lo͏p and been my self the bearer of the inclosed, but I am hindered from coming to Cullen so soon as I resolved. If your Lo͏p hath spoken with any of the heretors of Rathven anent our calling Mr. Thomas James to that place, the Presbytery who are [to] meet at Ab͏d this day eight dayes would desire to [k]now how they rellish it. But what ever be their sentiments it will be satisfying to the bretheren, and may be a means of prevailing with the General Assembly for transporting him, iff they had your Lo͏ps consent and concurrence in this businesse. We doubt not but the Solicitor will assist when the matter is brought in to the Assembly. The blessing of God be all wayes the portion of your Lo͏p and all yours.—I am, My Lord, Your Lo͏ps most obleidged and humble servant,

                MR. PAT INNES.

Banff, Novr. 5, 1695.

---

[1] Dr. Cramond's *Church and Churchyard of Cullen*, pp. 78, 79.
[2] Dr. Cramond's *Church and Churchyard of Rathven*, pp. 31-44.

For THE EARLE OFF FINDLATER

Edr., 8 Nov. 1695.

MY LORD,—Excuse me for not wreating with my own hand, for I ame a litle indisposed with the cold, and cannot hold down my head. The Secretarie mynds you kyndlie in his last letter to me, which was neir two sheit of peaper in lenth, and cam to my hands only yesterday. He is weill with the King for what we understand. He countersignes the letters for adjurneing the Parliament and Assemblie. The Maister of Stairs hes not as yet been in waiting, and its doubted if ever he will. Its written doun by my Lord Lauderdaill that it is not doubted he will lose his place. It is generallie thought that something will be done, but not neir so much as our pairtie wishes or expects for. This is all I know of our publict concernes. Keep them to your self, and make no noyse about them. This is all from, My Lord, Your Lo͠ps most obedent son and humble servant,

JA. OGILVIE.

Give my service to all freinds with you, particularlie minde me to my wife.

In the Parliamentary session of 1695 Glencoe had been freely used against the Master of Stair.

For THE EARL OF FINDLATER

Abd., Novr. 13, —95.

RIGHT HONORABLE,—Yours of the 8th instant I did comunicate unto the Presbytery, who are well satisfyed therewith, and thankfull to your L͠p. for your care of Cullen, and will not urge your L͠p. to any troublesome meddling with Rathven, so that what I now write is onely from myself, and not by any appointment of the Presbytery. Since I saw your Lp., I have heard of an able youth Mr. George Chalmers, son to Mr. Wᵐ Chalmers of Gartlay, who is coming north this winter to visit his father. I could wish your L͠p might see and hear him, and then do

as you finde cause and clearness. When I go back to
Edr, I shall endevour to speak with your son about his
progress in providing for Cullen, and give him all the little
assistance I can in that matter. As for Mr. Watt, the
Presbytery have appointed some to converse and confer
with him, that we may be better acquainted with him,
and may know how to represent his case to the Generall
Assembly or the comittee thereof; for the rules given
to this Presbytery of Abd do require them not to admitt
any person in Mr. Watts circumstances into ministeriall
comunion without advice from the Gen^{ll} Assembly or
comittee. Yet I have and will befriend Mr. Watt as far
as I can. But for a more full account of these things I
refer your Lp. to the relation of Mr. Innes. I do humbly
salute your Lps. family, and thank you and them for the
kinde reception I had at your house. Grace mercy peace
and wisdom be multiplyed upon your Lps. honorable
family, so prayes, My Lord, Your Lps. most obliged serv^t
in the gospell,   W. Trail.

Mr. George Chalmers was not settled in Rathven. Dr. Cramond
in his *Church and Churchyard of Rathven*, pp. 31-44, gives an account
of the long drawn-out fight in settling Presbytery in Rathven.

For THE RIGHT HONORABLE THE EARLE OF
FFINDLATER   6d

Edr., 26 Nov. 1695.

My Lord,—I hade the honor of your Lops lyne in
relatione to the comsirs rateing of what affaires passes
heir. I doubt not but your Lop. receaves the publict
news letters weiklie, which are transmitted at leist twyce
in everie weik. As for other affaires ther are few or of
litle import. The sederunts of the Councell receave.
President Stair dyed three dayes agoe, and this night
betuixt fyve and sex at night his corps was transported
from his loodges to the Abey of Holyruidhous under a
pale, the murners nobilitie and gentrie beng surroundit
on each syd of the strat with numerous torches. Who is

to succeid to his place is not as yet knowen, nether is
ther any accompt of our Scots affaires come as yet from
court. The Lord   dyed the last weik so that we
have now three vacancies in the Sessione. Receave a
proclamatione anent the poll; and when any bussines of
import occurres, your Lop. shall have an accompt therof
from, My Lord, Your Lops. most obedient and humble
servant,   AN CRAIK.

For THE EARLE OF FFINDLATER these

Edr., 31st Der. 1695.

My LORD,—

.   .   .   .

Wee have no newes. The heads of both pties are att
court, and the warr is caried on with great vigour, and
some of both sydes are lyke to fall. This is all from, My
Lord, Your Lops. most obedient sone and humble servant,

JA. OGILVIE.

Besides Glencoe, which was about to prove the downfall of the
Master of Stair, the 'act for a company trading to Affrica and the
Indies,' passed on 26th June 1695, was soon to cause trouble with
England, and to bring about the removal of Tweeddale, Secretary
Johnstone and other politicians who supported it. The next three
letters refer to these political changes.

For THE EARLE FINDLATER these

Edr., 2d Jarij. 1696.

My LORD,—

.   .   .   .

ffor newes, as Sr. James wreits to your Lope., ther is
non, bot that most pairt of the nobility on both sydes
are gone to court. The King hes appoynted ane audience
the tenth of this moneth, bot except our people that went
from this upon Munday last (wiz. Queensberrie, Broad-
albane, E. of Mortone, Lo. Montgomrie, Tarbat, Lo.
Murray, and the Advocat) take post horses they will not
be ther in tyme. I hope after that day ther will be newes

wourthie of your Lops. nottice. I wish they may be to
your satisfactione, and you shall have ane accompt of
them. Its thought that the Chancellour and both Secritaries will be turned offe. Sir James hes that advantage
that both sydes speekes honorably and weill of him, so
that, houever matters goe, he will be weill. I will not
faile to aquant your Lops. when any thing occurrs, seing
the laist of the deuty incumbant upon, My Lord, Your
Lops. most faithfull and obleidged humble servant,

JA. BAIRD.

Mrs. Ogstoune hes at me everie day to knowe if your
Lope. hes ordored hir payt. conforme to your lre qch I
delyvered to hir.

For THE EARLE OF FINDLATER ABERDEIN TO BANFF
haist these

Edr., 20th Jarij 1696.

MY LORD,—In my last I promised to wreit to your
Lope. when any thing of moment did occurr. I doubt not
bot befor this tyme your Lope. knowes of the Viscount of
Stairs his being off as Secritary, and the yisterdayes letters
both private and publict give accompt that my Lord
Murray is come in his place, and hes yrupon kissed the
Kings hand. The K. told him that he did owe his post
to no man for ther recomenaºne, bot that he was his oun
choise, so he hoped that he would be faithfull in his service.
To which he ansred that he was not wourthie of that post,
his Matye hade called him toe, bot since he hade bein
pleased to conferr that honour upon him he would lay out
himselfe to srve him and his interest faithfullie. So they
pairted, and the King told him they would speeke more
fully afterwards. My Lord Secritarie Johnstoune and he
are in verie good termes, and I hope shall continowe so.
My Lord Advocat was saifely arryved at London on
Fryday was eight dayes. Sir James hes gott tuo letters
from him. He was ille of the goute when he wroate last,
and hade not sein the King. The Secritarie wreits that
the East Indea act will fash him, as it will doe the S.
himselfe and Chancellour. The Advocat sayes when he

dreve the act, that he did not sie the Chancellours instructione for the same, and the Ch. sent the mērts to him, and desyred him to drave it in the termes of the English act for the Indean tread yr. Its thought some of the thrie will loase ther comissions upon that head. My Lord Chancellour is lykewayes loaded with alloweing the Parliāt to sitt without ane warrand, the tyme allowed by the King being runn out, and he not haveing applyed in tyme for a furder tyme, although the same came afterwards, and that the King's bussiness might have bein much sooner done. Whither his fault will requyre a remission or not I leave yor Lope. to judge. A litle tyme will determine severall things. Broadalbanes access I think will not be verie easie now betuixt the tuo secritaries. The Earle of Lauderdale is come of from court as is sayed disatisfied that he hes gott no post, and tho he hes taken the title of Earle upon him, since he hes gotten no better statione in the governement, resolves to take his seate in the session. This will be and is thought to be wrong in him by severalls. Sir James hes the good luck to be honourablie and weill spoake of by all, and my Lord Advocat wreits him so, and he hade ane verie kind łre from S. Johnstoune yisterday, although he was fearing a reproofe, haveing upon Mr. William Aickmans recomendaᵒne recomended the Earle of Strathmoore to him, shewing that if he were made Sreffe of Aungus, as his faȳr was, and gott incouradgement ůyr wayes, he would come in to the governement and take the oathes. Sir James hade lykewayes keind łres from my Lord himselfe, and did yrupon recomend him as aboue, wherupon the S. procured him ane comissione to be Sreffe of Aungus and ane letter to be ane Privie Councellour ; and when the Chancellour and Sr James wreit for him, he returned his añsre againe that he hade not friedome. The S. is verie angrie with Strathmoore upon his accompt, bot hes told Sir James that on whomsoever the blame lye it shall not be on him ; bot I ame affraid that this will bring all the Jacobits in Aungus to take the oathes or undergoe hardshipes. I hope your Lope. will keepe this łre to yourselfe. It is the summe of what is goeing at present. Wee have hade exterordinary windes these eight dayes past, by which on of the shipes with about 400 men in hir lyeing in the road to goe for Flanders broake hir cables, was driven from hir anchores, hade almost rune foule of the man of warr, went doune the firth. Ther is no accompt as yet heard of hir save that hir floatbote is cast in at Berwick and some mens hatts into it. The worst is feared of hir. I shewed your Lops. last lre to Mrs. Ougstoune, who intreated me to mynde your Lope. againe, for she sayes she hes much to doe with money. Sr. James expects your Lope. will ordore his wictuall als soone as possible, and does not doubt bot that the meall is aither gone or readie to goe by this tyme. I shall trouble your Lope. no furder at present, only wish yor Lope. and the family all health and happieness, for I ame, My Lord, Your Lops. most faithfull and obleidged servant,   JA. BAIRD.

Edinburgh, ffebruary ye 5th, 1696.

HONORED SIR,—Upon the 30th arived ffrom Holland 2 maills, 4 being due. The substance of what they bring are as ffolloweth. That the Grand Signior continues to dispose effaires to be early in Hungary on the head of 100,000 men. The Emperor of Germany hopes to bring into the feild against them 70,000, which he thinks will be sufficient number to obviat the designes of the Turk. On the 31 past the court of Spaine at Madrid sent orders by the introductor of ambassadors to Mr. Stanhop the English envoy to fforbear comeing to court. This is occasioned by ane affront put wpon Mo^r Sconenberg, the Duch envoy, who was by the King of Spains ordor put out of Madrid by 2 alcads or officers, wch difference is not yet accomodated, although it fell out in the beggining of winter. The envoy of Spaine at the Hague has declared at the congress held on the 26, that he had not yet recd any maner of order from the King touching the accomodation of that difference about the Sieur Sconenberg, wpon which he is preparing to go to Brussells to reside ther till the difference is accomodated. Its said that the K. of

Eng^d and States of Holland is to mantaine 6000 men wpon the Rhyn. The ffrench continue to make great prepara°ns in fflanders. The ffr. King has named the generall officers that are to command his army in Piedmont, which is to be augmented with 40 squadrons. The ffr. fleet at Toulon will be ready to saill by the 15 of the same month, which is composed of 50 vessells of line, the least of 56 peeces of cannon, a ffriggot 46, tuo bomb ketches, and 6 ffireships. All our leters this long time bygone has all agreed that, if the ffrench ffleet at Toulon Brest St. Malos Rochford and ffort Louis shall meet, that they will be 95 in line of batle 37 of them 3 decks ships, 30 ffriggots, 24 ffireships, 12 of them of ane new invention. Ther are on the other hand all diligence imaginable making to rigg out our ffleet to joyne Admirall Rook at Cadiz, whose fleet at pressent consists not of above 30 or 32 ships Duch and English. This is agreed on by all. Our English seamen are very scarce, by reason ther are so many gone aboard the merchand men to shun the Kings service, but orders are given for a press. Wpon the 30 past the *Royall Soveraigne*, one of the greatest and stoutest best ships that ever ploued the ocean, and who never failled to bafle her greatest ffoe that ever she mett with, and who so often contended with ye elements of fire and watter, was by the carelessness of a tarpalian about 5 in the morning set on ffire and burnt doune to the water, and in her some men consumed. All hands was at work, but not any releife, but to hinder her to comunciat her flames to the rest. Ther was non of her officers aboard, but they are all seized, and to be tryed for life for being absent, and the fellow that sett her on fire—

On the 27 his Maties ship the *Carlisle* of 60 guns ran a ground on the sand called the Ships wash, and was not gott off ye next day, and its feared she is lost. About the same time ther was a mert. ship of 200 tuns at Dover road burnt to ashes. We had very bad tideings of a ship bound for Jamaica in company of the Cannary ffleet, and was 200 leagues on their voyage, but by stress of weather lost her main mast and fore topmast, and forced to returne back to refitt. She sayes that most of them with one of their convoyes was in the same condition when he left them. We had advise by the way of Cadiz that tuo of the Touloun squadron in repassing the Streights met with some English cruizers and ingadged, qrin the *Lizard*, a 5th rate, was unfortunatly sunk, and most of her men drouned, the rest fforced to retire to Cadiz to refitt, being very much shattered.

We hear ther are great changes among our ministers of state at court. I doubt not but ye have allready heard that Staires was off from being Secretary, and its talked here among our grandees that Secretary Johnstoun is also off.

I have sent you this being the first at the desire of yo[r] brother Peter, and if it be acceptable I shall not miss any occasion to let yow know what passes here and at London. I shal add no more, but my wife gives her service to you, as also your godson does the same. So with my humble duty to your Honor and worthy ffamily, I am, Much Honored, Your most humble servant,   CHA. RICHIE.

CHAPTER IV

LETTERS DURING THE PERIOD SIR JAMES OGILVIE WAS SECRETARY OF STATE FOR SCOTLAND UNDER WILLIAM
FROM 1696 TO 1702

THE last writer's news that Secretary Johnston was 'off' proved correct; and on 5th February 1696 Sir James Ogilvie was appointed one of the two Secretaries of State for Scotland. The following warrant for his appointment is from volume xiv. pp. 140-142 of the *Warrant Books, State Papers (Scotland)*, in the Record Office, London.

WILLIAM R.

· OUR Soveraign Lord ordains a patent and commission[1] to be made and past under his Ma[ts] great seale of his ancient kingdom of Scotland, making mention that his

---

[1] *The Acts of the Parliaments of Scotland*, vol. x. pp. 7-8.

Ma^ty taking into his royall consideration that nothing is more conduceable to his service and the good of his kingdoms than that persons of known integrity loyalty and abilities be appointed by his Ma^ty to be chief ministers of his crown, and specially his Secretaries of State in whom his Ma^ty may repose speciall confidence, both in order to his oun authority and the good of his subjects, and his Ma^ty being well satisfied with the abilities upright-, nes and other good qualifications of his right trusty and well beloved counsellor, Sir James Ogilvie, son to the Earle of ffindlater, wherby he is exactly fitted for discharging the duty and office of one of his Ma^ts principall Secretaries of State for his said kingdom : Therfor and for severall other important causes and considerations his Ma^ty has made nominated constituted and ordained, likeas by these presents his Ma^ty makes nominats constituts and ordains the said Sir James Ogilvie to be one of the two Secretaries of State to his Ma^ty for his ancient kingdom during his Ma^ts pleasure only, and untill these presents shall be recalled and discharged in writing, co-principall and conjunct with his Ma^ts right trusty and well beloved cousin and councellor John Lord Murray, his Ma^ts other Secretary of State for his said kingdom, giving and granting likeas his Ma^ty hereby gives and grants during the space foresaid unto the said Sir James Ogilvie the place trust and office of one of the two principall conjunct Secretaries of State foresaid, with the just and equall half of all ffces profits benefits casualties liberties dignities and immunities which formerly did or might have belonged and appertained to the said trust office and place together with a yearly pension of one thousand pounds sterlin money conform to a gift of the same granted to him by his Ma^ty of the date of these presents : With full power to him to use exerce and enjoy the said place trust and office and specially to write docquet and present to his Ma^ty all gifts warrants and signatures of whatsoever nature passing his Ma^ts royall hand, and to intromet with and receive the just and equall half of all fees dues and casualties belonging to the same, and also to have equall power and privilege with the said John Lord Murray his Ma^{ts} other Secretary of State for his said kingdom in receiving intrometting with and keeping all the signets of the said kingdom, and to apply the equall half of the benefits and profits arising therby to his own propper use and commodity, as likewise in appointing deputs and keepers of his Ma^{ts} said signets, and in admitting and receiving all clerks and writers to the signet, with all the sheriff clerks and clerks to the peace within his said kingdom, and in giving them commissions therupon for brooking and enjoying the saids offices during all the days of the saids clerks their lives, and that as oft as the saids offices or any of them shall happen to vaik any manner of way, and in receiving the equall half of the compositions and benefits that shall arise by the admission of the saids clerks which he is to apply to his own use : Ordaining the said patent and commission to be further extended in the most ample and best form, with all clauses needfull and to pass his Ma^{ts} great seal aforesaid *per saltum* without passing any other seal or register, in order wherunto these presents shall be to the directors of his Ma^{ts} chancellary for writing the same, and to the Lord High Chancellor for causing the seal be appended thereto a sufficient warrant.

Given at his Mats Court at Kensington the 5th day of ffebruary 169$\frac{5}{6}$ *and of his Mats reign the* 7*th year.*

MAY IT PLEASE YOUR MATY,—These contain your Ma^{ts} warrant upon the considerations above mentioned for a patent and commission to be passed *per saltum* under your Ma^{ts} great seal of Scotland nominating . . . Sir James Ogilvie . . . to be one of your two Secretaries of State for your s^d kingdom of Scotland. . . .

For THE RIGHT HONOURABLE THE EARLE
OF FFINDLATER

Edr., 8 *Feb.* 1696.

MY LORD,—Their is apearance that I must change my residence for some tym. I beleeve the King designes that I shall succeid to Mr. Johnstoun as Secretarie. It was

sore against my ineclina°nes that he was turned out, or
that I should have any offer of his place. Your Lop.
shall heare more fullie efterwards from me, for I ame
huried with tym, and can wreit no more but that I ame,
My Lord, Your Lops. most obedient sone and humble
servant,   JA. OGILVIE.

For THE EARLE OF FINDLATER thes

London, Febrie. 20, 1696.

MY LORD,—I am nou setled for some time in this place.
It is more honorable then my last post, bot I belive of
mutch less profit; bot the King may make this upp, if
I deserve weal of him.   I will take some opportunitie of
doing for you.   Give my wife your advice in manadging
my affairs; and I am, My Lord, Your Lo. most obedient
son and humble servant,   JA. OGILVIE.

John Donaldson who writes next letter was a writer in Banff.
The Duchess of Gordon was then at variance with her husband.
The letters of 20th and 30th March and of 1st May all refer
to this.   It culminated in the Duke's suing her for adherence
on 8th June 1697.[1]

ffor THE RIGHT HONORABLE THE EARLE OF
FFINDLATER these

MY LORD,—On Wednesday last the Dutchese of Gordon
cam to this toune, and on ffryday Mr. Dunbar cam from
Gordone Castle to waite on hir.   She was uncertain of hir
dyet when she cam heir first; but since Mr. Dumbar cam
for heir, hir Gr. is to goe to Gordon Castle, how soone it is
furneished for hir receptance, and to stay there.   But my
Lord Airlie I am told will not let hir goe from his house
till Gordone Castle be furneished.   James Grant goes
south again to morrow from this place.   He telles me that
Grant and his Ladie are in good health.   My Ladie is not
yet brought to bed.   There cam no newes, for ought I
heired, to any persone in this place by the last post.   The

---

[1] Fountainhall's *Chronological Notes*, p. 276.

inclosed to your Lop. cam by the post yisterday. When I heir any thing of the Dutches motione from this place, I shall endeavour to give your Lop. account yrof.—I am in all sinceritie, My Lord, Your Lops. most obleidged humble servant, J. DONALDSONE.

Banff, 23d of Febry. 1696.

Next letter from James Baird, secretary to Sir James Ogilvie, gives some account of the assassination plot engineered by Sir George Barclay, and of the threatened invasion by France promoted by the Duke of Berwick. The letters of last February, 6th March, 1st and 29th April and 11th May all continue the account, and touch on the defensive measures taken by the Government.

For JOHN ANDERSONE ONE OF THE UNDER KEEPERS OF HIS MATJES SIGNET AT EDR., SCOTLAND

London, 24th ffebrij. 1696.

AFF. COMARADS,—These serves to lett you knowe that ther was discovered here on ffryday last the most horeid and wicked conspeiracie against his Matjes sacred persone to take away his lyffe, that perhaps hes bein heard of ; and the same was to have bein acted upon Satturday last as his Matje come home from Richmond from hunting, bot haveing gotten some informaⁿne of the designe, he was diswaded from goeing to hunting that day with much adoe. It is alwayes so leat when he comes from hunting, that he comes in with torch light ; and those who were to comitte the villany were mounted in the same fashone with the Kings gaird, that they might be the less notticed till they gott near the King's coach ; and then they designed all of them, consisting of near 40, to have fyred in upon his coach, and then being dark to gett of ; and tho the gaird should endeavore to attack them they were strong enough. If this first project failed (as blissed be God for it it did) then the same was to be acted the nixt day, being the Sabath, as he was comeing to St. Jameses chapell, bot being lykewayes informed of that did not goe to chapell that day. This hes bein ane verie deip and private contryvance al along caried on ; ffore King James is lykewayes at Kailes with fyftein thousand men readie to come over to invaide this dominion, but Vintenberge hes the lyke number readie to come over from Flanders to meitt him. Its thought many of our enemies are in our bosum. Ther is 29 of the traitors apprehended. The King hes ane list of 400 who are concerned in it. I hope, now that his sacred persone is saife, wee neid not so much fear the invasione; bot both wer designed to have bein about on and the same tyme; bot everie thing hes happened as God would have it, for the wind did not offer faire for them to come over, nor for 40 saile of our fleit was ordored to goe to Cades, and now they stay at home for our saifety. The Duke of Berwick and Earle of Midletoune are come to London upon this designe; and ther is ane procla°ne ishowed fourth for apprehending them, and ane soume of money puitt upon ther heads. Its sayed the Duke escaped only by halfe ane quarter of one houre. Both Houses of Parliat have bein with his Matje this night, and have declaired that they will mantain and assist his Matje and governement with ther lifes and fortunes. I shall trouble yow no furder at present, being in haist and the post goeing offe, bot give my srvice to all freinds.—I ame, Gentlemen, Your most aff. comorad to srve yow q^{ll} I ame,

J. B.

ffor Andrew Craick and John Andersone Wryrs in Edr. I shall ansre your tuo tres tomorowes post.

For THE RIGHT HONORABLE THE EARLE OF FFINDLATER

Last Feb. 96.

My Lord,—I hade a lyn from my maister the last post, wherby I vnderstand that he is fixed in his post as conjunct Secretarie, and enters to officiat on Monday next. He hes wreit severall instructiones to me, which at my north-comeing shall be impairted to your Lop. I wait for more, and then intends to be shortly north. What comands your Lop. hes for me at this place let me be honored with them.   In the mein tym, I ame and ever will be, My Lord, Your Lop.'s most obedient and humble servant.

AN. CRAIK.

Ther is no newes worth your Lops. notice.   Only our Affrican bank was opned on Wednesday last, and ther is more than two hundereth thowsand pund st. signed allreadie.   The nobilitie gentrie and others are verie fore-ward in it, and I beleive if they hold on they will make it swell to 1,200,000 lib. st.

Since the wreiting of this I ame informed that ther came ane express yesternight, which gives ane accompt of a designe of murdering the King; and sixtein of the plotters are taken into custodie, and this night Sir William Sharp [1] and Sir William Bruce [1] ware put in close prisone about three this mornning.   Ther is a great noyse heir of ane inuasione from ffrance, and that the late King James is lyeing at Calise, and shippeing severall battaliones in ordor to ane invasione.   Our King has sent for severall battaliones out of fflanders.   What this storme may pro-duce cannot be weill knouen as yet.   What furder occurres dureing my being at this place yor Lop. shall bee acquanted with.   I have sent your Lop. James Bairds lyn anent the plott, with all the jurnells of the Parliament and proclama-tiones.

The capital of the African company was originally fixed at £600,000 stg.; and one-half of it was subscribed in London, when in December 1695 the Parliament of England jealously intervened with the King against the scheme, and the English subscriptions were withdrawn.   Thereafter the capital was reduced to £400,000, which was all offered to and subscribed in Scotland between 26th February and 1st August 1696.   Subsequent letters will disclose some of the company's future colonising misfortunes in New Cale-donia or Darien.

For THE RIGHT HONORABLE THE EARLE OF
   FFINDLATER   Haist

Edr., 6 *March* 1696.

MY LORD,—I hade a lyn from my maister the last post,

---

[1] *Carstares State Papers and Letters*, p. 273.

which shews he is verie weill in health, but the court is much taken up with the intendit invasione. What certainty may be in this is not as yet knowen. This cuntrey is raising ther militia, and puteing themselfs in a posture of defense, and I wish the north were takeing the same measures. I have fraughted Thomas Gregorie and ane other ship for transporting of the victwall. They goe off within a few dayes. Thairfor cause the chamberlin have all in readiness. I wish it ware heir alreadie, for I have sold it. My Lord, be serious with the chamberlin anent the delyverie, for of the three hundereth and four bolls meall last sent ther was not on boll of outcum, which is wondered at heir ; but of this when I come north I shall speik more freilie. Caus the chamberlin have the bear weill dight. I intend to send home by Gregorie some of my maisters plenishing. The current news I have inclosed them in this. I crave pardone for this truble, but esteemed it the dewtie of, My Lord, Your Lops. most obledged and humble servant,   AN. CRAIK.

How soon I get my maisters affaires heir setled I intend north.

ffor THE RIGHT HONORABLE THE EARLE OFF
FFINDELATER   CULLEN

My LORD,—According to y^r Lo^s desyr I haw delyvred heirvith the Ladie Boyns book off tulliedouces from her Grace, which the bearer vill delyver to y^r Lo., with many thancks from her Grace and her dutifull service, who bids me show y^r Lo. that shee should be very much mortifyed, that y^r Lo. should in so storme vather as this is put y^r selff to the danger or trouble to giuc a visit, till it pleas God to send a mor seasonable season for taiking the air vithout danger. My Ladie Marie is in good health, and I ame vith all the sineritie off my hart, My Lord, Y^r Lo^s most humble and most faithfull servant,   A. DUMBAR.

Gordon Castle, 20 *March* 1696.

Lady Marie was the second daughter of the Earl of Findlater.

ffor THE RIGHT HONORABLE THE EARLE OFF
FFINDELATER these

MY LORD,—It vill be about Wednsday off the nixt week befor the Dutchesse off Gordon can part from this, who vill sie y^r Lo. as shee gois, and vith these has his dutifull respects to y^r Lo., Ladie Marie, and y^r Lo^s daughter in law. As for the news, I humblie thanck y^r Lo. Wee most taik them as they ar true or fals. A litle time vill maik the mater knowin, as it is. I sie Strechin at this place yesterday. The storme will be over by all probabilitie, or her Grace taik jurnay from this; and what may fall after belongs to Gods vill and providence. My Lord, I vill giue y^u no further trouble att the time, but the assurance that I ame inalterablie, My Lord, Y^r Lo^s most humble and most faithfull servant,   A. DUMBAR.

Go. Castle, 30 *March* 96.

To THE RIGHT HONOURABLE THE EARLE OF
FFINDLATER BANFF with haste 9d
Keepe the postage till the nixt occasion

MY LORD,—Your Lop^s letter with Durnes and my Lord Secretarys Ladys wer sent off yesternight to his Lop. Mr. Baird assures me that my Lord is in verie good health, and I knoue it most be so, for by the last post he sent doun a good many letters to the great men here all wreitten with his owne hand. The inclosed prints gives your Lop. ane account of the newes from England. At this place ther no great newes, but severalls of all qualities are entering in a voluntary association for the protection of the govern-ment, and distinguish themselves by a bleue ribband in ther hatt. It is hoped that non of our Scots men are ingadged in the unworthie assasina^{o}n or invasion; and we hope ther shall be no fear of ane invasion, for Rook with the squadroon he commands are expected home befor the Tholoun fleit. Ther are severall suspected persons under bail cited to appear, and the Councill are liberating some of those alreadie imprisoned upon getting bale. The Lord Drumond, who absconds, is ordered to be chairged to pay 1000 lib st., for which he is under bale. Horning is ordered

out agt all the colectors of the pole, for not paying in what
they have colected, and for not delivering in clear bookes
and lists. The heritors here are bussie proportioning and
putting out ther quotas of the 1000 men for the newe levie.

Your Lop. will be pleased to deliver my Lord Secretarys
letters to my Lady. Andrew Craik is with your Lop.,
and will informe you and my Lady of my Lords affaires
here, and what money lyes by me to be drawen north.
I have wreitten to Mr. Baird to send doun the English
newes for your Lops. use, which with what I cane learne
here shall be sent to your Lop. by, My Lord, Your Lops.
most humble and obedient servant,   Jo. ANDERSON.

Edr., 1*st Apyrll* 1696.

James Lord Drummond was the eldest son of James fourth
Earl of Perth.

For the EARL OF FINDLATER

London, 1*st Aprile* i696.

MY LORD,—I hade the honour of your Lops. some posts
agoe, and I most intreat your Lops. pardon that I have
not ansred the same sooner. Bot my Lord Murray being
in Scotland, the weight of the whole affaires lyes upon the
Secretary, and I in my station have lykewayes some share
of the trouble, and ame just now taken up in buyeing of
furnitur for the loadging ; bot I shall endeavore to make
up this breach by giveing your Lope. the trouble of ane
tre once or tuice everie weeke. I beleive ther hardly ever
was ane Secretary in Scotland hade more readie access to
his King, and dispatched more bussiness with pleasure
and satisfactione to both his King and his countrey then
my maister hes done since his entrie to that post. The
King hes bein pleased to give ane excelent charactar of
him to some of the best quality of England, and told them
that he was the only man in all Scotland he was seekeing,
and that he hade now gott ane man he could doe bussiness
with. If my Lord Murray were once come up, I hope ther
shall be some thing proposed and done for your Lope. ;
bot you knowe it would not relish weell from him. I did
give your Lops. srvice to Mr. Johnstoune, which was verie

acceptable to him.   Ther is no wourd of the Kings goeing
for Flanders as yet ; bot your Lope. knowes he makes no
great noise befor he goe.   The court was out of mourning
for the Queen, bot is gone in to it againe for the Prince of
Nassu.   All the ministers of steate here are continally
imployed in examina°ne of people suspected to be guilty
or accessory to the late hellish conspyracie agt. his Maties
sacred persone and governement, and ther are multitudes
of peopl seased everie day.   The E .of Ailsburrie, a man of
ane great estate, is comitted to the Toure, and its thought
will be found deip in the matter.   Thrie of the conspyrators,
wiz. Charnock King and Kees were hanged draven and
quartered last weeke at Tieburn.   Sir John ffreind and
Sr William Parkers have gotten the same sentence, and
is to be putt in execution to morrowe.   I hope all guilty
or accessorie to the villanie will be found out in due tyme,
and gett ther just reward ; and I hope the same will
perpetuate this goverement, and the King will knowe his
freinds.   The Secretary hade on from your Lope. yisterday, with one other from Durn in favors of on Mr. Gellie,
who delyvered them himselfe, and spoake with him.   The
young gentleman hes bein here all this winter attending
the cloathing of the regement, and is this day gone to
Flanders with them.   The S. desyred him to aquant him
when any vacancie happened, and he would sie to his
preferment, and I understand Mr. Gellie hes anough of
his collonalls favore.   Be pleased to receave one newes
letter and gazet.   I will endeavore to send you on everie
post, although I should have no tyme to wreit to your
Lope. yrwith, bot inclose them in halfe ane sheit of peper.
I shall never be unmyndefull of the obliga°nes I owe to
your Lops. family ; and that you may live ane long a
prosperous life to manadge the affairs therof, now when
my maister is so farr removed from your assistance, shall
be the hearty prayer and wish of, My Lord, Your Lops.
most faithfull and obleidged sr̄vant qll I ame,

JA. BAIRD.

Ther was ane ordore to apprehend Capt. Seatton upon some informaᵒne given agt. him, which did much trouble the S. ; bot it seemes the same hes bein false, for he went and surrendered himselfe the English S., and they allowed him freedome upon his and his brother in law Sr Henry Mearwoods parole, and wee have heard nothing of it these eight dayes. Please to show my Lady that the S. hade ane īre from hir yisterday, which I beleive he will not gett anśred this night haveing more then fyftie to anśre, which came yisterday by ane ordinary packatt and flyeing packatt.

Captain Robert Seaton was the half-brother of Sir James Ogilvie.

To THE RIGHT HONOURABLE THE EARLE OF FFINDLATER Banff 3d

My Lord,—The inclosed is all the newes I have since my last, except that here they are putting out the proportion of the newe levie of 1000 men, and that the Councill are to deall sharplie with all colectors of the pole, who have not sent up their bookes and money, and with those who have not listed and payed in.

James Baird wrott to me last post, that my Lord wes in veric good health, and he bids me have 100 ƚib st. of his victuall money readie for his draught, yet that needs not stop my Lady to drawe for all contained in my note, which Andrewe hes. My Lord is to take up his lodgings immediatly, and his plenishing from this will be at him befor these reatch your Lops. hand.—I ame, My Lord, Your Lops. most faithfull and obedient servant,

JO. ANDERSON.

Edr., 3d April 1696.

The bookes for the Affrican trade are closed, and 12,000 [ƚib] signed for more than the quota, and they are now listing ther manadgers.

Next letter is another example of seeking for 'moyen' with judges sitting on a case. Strachan of Glenkindie's suit is referred to at p. 364 of the *Acts of the Parliaments of Scotland,* vol. ix.

For THE RIGHT HONORABLE THE EARLE OF
FINDLATER these ar

Edr., 10th Apryll 1696.

My LORD,—I have sent your Lo. watch by Troup,[1] and
doe intreat pardon for that it did staye so longe, bot Mr.
Craike will tell the reason. I doe heerby returne thanks
for yor Lo. assistance to my brother Glenkindies affaire in
the Parliament. This cause is now verie farr advanced
before the session, bot the finall determinaᵒne is reserved
to the 1 of June. In respect I am not sure that I come
north this vacance, and that Glenkindie lyes at a great
distance from your Lo., I doe intreat that yoʳ Lo. wold
be pleased to recomend this just cause to tuo extraordinary
Lords off Session, to witt, the Earle of Annandale and
my Lo. Polworth, and if your Lo. please to recomend to
any others, I doe desir your Lo. maye send thes letters
and recomendaᵒnes with Mr. Craike to the begining of the
suɱer session ; and herein your Lo. will exceidingly favor
My Lord, Your Lo. most oblidged and most humble servant, AND. STRACHAN.

The next four letters deal with the assertion of Sir James
Ogilvie's rights as Admiral-depute from Findhorn to Buchanness
in respect of wreckage.

For THE EARL OF FINDLATER thes ar

My LORD,—The last week there was a feu stings cast
in about Rotrye. What els may com I knou not, but I
can not apear in any thing that conserns the Admirality
except your Lops. send me doun an wreaten comision,
altho my brother dsyred me to medl betuixt Banf and
Peterhead ; so I heave sent the bearer for an comision to
act in it. If nid be your Lo. may giue it in his absenc.
This woth my humble doutye to your Lops. and good
wishis to all the familey, I continou, My Lord, Your Lops.
most obdiant son and most humble seruant,
PAT. OGILVIE.

Carenbulge, Apryl 16, 1696.

---

[1] Alexander Garden of Troup, Banffshire.

N

For THE EARL OF FINDLATER

MY LORD,—Since I wrat to your Lops. last ther is the affects of an broken ship, for ther is a grit dell of fyn timber com in at Piterhid, Inuerugye, and at Rotrey, and sumthing about Inueralochy; and when I com to chalenges it wpon the account of the Admirallity I mit woth such language from our Gillicrankies that we ar euery on of us admirals within our selfs, which your Lops. woll se by the inclosed from Inueraloche his leter.   Ther is betuixt Piterhid and Ratrey com in alreadye the numbe of six or siuen score of dubel tris com in alreadye, so I desyre your Lops. to send doun Androu Crak immediatly and an factory to me subscrayed by your Lops.   Onely let it be James Ogilvie, that I may say it is from my brother, so that we may not be slighted by them.   I expect Androu Craik hir woth the bearer and the factrey or deputation, otheruays I cannot medel mor in it.   Bieng on hest I am, My Lord, Your Lops. obdiant son and humble seruant,

PAT. OGILVIE.

Carenbulge, Apryl 17, 1696.

Let me knou hou I shall carey woth my Lord Marciell and the gentel men about him, who hath the most of them. I would haue thee clark hir the morou.   It is not for the worth of thos things that I care.   I wol not haue my brothers afare and my self slightid, when we haue lau for it; and as your Lops. desyres I shall treat woth my Lord Marishall.   I am realey at an considerable expence alreadye.   I knou not what we may mak of it, but I shall kep my brothers right so far as lau woll alou.

For MR. PATRICK OGILVIE OF CAIRNBULGE thes

Inverallochie,

15 *Aprile* 1696.

RYT. HONOLL,—I showld be glaid to see your deputatione from the Admirall that I may be exonored of that litle triffles y^t are com in upon my land.   Ye know it is naither law nor practice to sett gairds to heritors shoars without intematione of a subscrived factorie aither from the King or the Admirall, which if ye have I oblidge myselfe by this to be lyable to the admirall law for what coms upon my bownds; therfor I hoop ye will excuse me to cawse my own tennants wait on my own shoar, which is all from Your most humble servant,   ALL. FRASER.

ffor THE RIGHT HONORABLE THE EARLE
OFF FINDLATER this is

MY DEAR LORD,—Your son went to Peterhead y^s morning and Andrew Craik with him. How soon I had the honour of y^r Lops. pacquet, I sent it immediatly affter him. The ffolly off thosse that questioned his right to medle will now appear. He hath been at very much paines on y^s account, and hath all his men-servants and severall others alongst ye coast till y^s day y^t he is gone him-selffe. Ane imployment y^t were worth his while were very weell bestowed on him, for he is very industrious in any thing q^rin he is concerned. I long to give y^r Lops. a legend off my liffe since we turned Buchanians. It were not ill company to givé a description off ye island we now live in, bot I will forbear till I doe by word. I wish y^r Lops. many happy dayes, and I intreat ye may estiem me, My Lo., Your Lop. most humble servant and obedient daughter,
ELIZA BAIRD.
Aprill 18, 96.

I give my humble duety to y^r Lo., my Lo. Deskford and both y^r Ladys. God bliss y^r grand-children.

I did not wreat so much y^s nyn month. My Lo., I will tak it as a curtesy, iff y^r Lo. will perswad Castelfeild to be so just as to give a pairt of Tochineills [1] rent to keep his poor wyffe Anna Forsyth from starving. I know her to be a good Christian, and I mak no doubt bot God will reward ye hard usage shee meets w^t. I beg pardon for troubling y^r Lo. w^t y^s. If it were not for a very great obiect of charity I would not be so rude.

Elizabeth Baird, who signs her maiden surname, was the wife of Patrick Ogilvie

---

[1] James Lawtie of Tochineal, near Cullen.

To THE RIGHT HONOURABLE THE EARLE OF FFIND-
LATER BANFF.   3d   Retein the postage.

MY LORD,—James Baird assures me that your son my
Lord Secretarie is well.   I troubled your Lop. last post
wi[th ane] long letter, but ther being no bussienes or newes
here [w]orthie of your Lops. notice, I transmitt to your
Lop. the inclosed print, and ame, My Lord, Your Lops.
most faithfull and humble servant,   Jo. ANDERSON.

   Edr., 24 *Apryll* 1696.

Your Lop. will be pleased to cause the Shirriff deput
send up ane account of his diligence in seazing the horss
and armes of disaffected persons, for the horss are to be
rouped and sold for the publict use, and the armes to be
disposed of to the nearest garison, and horning is coming
out agt Sreff deputs for that effect.

   [ffor THE RIGHT] HONORABLE [THE EA]RLE
       OFF FFINDELATER these

MY NOBLE LORD,—The bearer came inquyring yesternight for my Ladie yr daughter in laws hors, off whom yr
Lo. did my Ladie Dutchesse off Gordon the favour to
giue her the vse off, for wh her Grace vill give yr Lo. her
owin thancks shortly (being straitned vith time when the
horses var returned), and for the oblidging letter yr Lo.
vas pleased to send in her favours to my Lord Secrettarie
yr son.   The hors in good conditione vas returned to me
to this place on Fryday last, and I thought it my dutie
to giue him sume rest at this place, after so long a jurnay,
till I might present him my selff to yr Lop. my selff.   But
fearing yr Lo. might haue vse for him in the mine time,
the aproching terme not permitting me to vait on yr Lo.
so soone as I vould, I returne him to yr Lo. by the bearer,
vith the acknowledgment off the favour from her Grace,
and vith the most humble dutie and most sincer respects
off him, who most perfytly is, My noble Lord, Yr Lordships most humble and most faithfull servtt,

                                    A. DUMBAR.

   Gordon Castle, first May, 96.

For THE RIGHT HONOURABLE THE EARLE OF FFINDLATER Cullen, Banff   6d.

Edr., ii *May* 1696.

My Lord,—Whither what I wrott last to your Lop. hold true or not I cannot tell, for this tuo post ther came no letters anent it or other matters from the Secretarys, for they are attending the King at the port, who went aboard but came ashoar againe by reason of crosse wind. The ffrench King hes published a manifesto in his owne vindica°n anent any knowledge of or accession to the assasina°n agt King W^m, and offering as great a reward as our King hes done for apprehending these contained in our Kings proclama°ns. Ther is no word of the Tholoun fleit since they wer at Allicant. The armies are draweing to the feilds, and its said the Confederats will begine the campaigne with some considerable seidge. King James and the transport ships designed for the invasion are off the coasts. Our Privie Councill did litle expecteing chainges, ordored the citing in the heads of the Highland clans to find caution, the chairging colectors of pole to pay in ther money, Shirriffs to make reports anent seazing horse and armes, and did liberat allmost all states prisoners.

The laird of Lagg is to be indyted for clipping and coyning, but its thought will come off.

I expect my Lady draught for 1000 ſib. or 2000 mks which will be answered. I pray for the welfare of your Lop. and familie, and ame, My Lord, Your Lops. most humble and obedent servant,   Jo. Anderson.

For THE EARL OF FINDLATER

Whytehall, 2d *May* 1696.

My Lord,—I ame unwilling to trouble your Lope., bot when something occurrs wourthie of your nottice. The Secretary (blissed be God) keepes his health verie well. He hes gotten his Maties comands to goe into Scotland, and I think he will depart from this within a fourtnight or tuentie dayes, and be with your Lope. in 5 or 6 weekes yrafter. My Lord Murray goes to the Bath in a day or tuo, and intends to stay 5 or 6 weekes yr, and shortly after that goe to Scotland.   Its thought he will be Comissioner, and if this happen he owes it inteirly to my maister.   They live in perfect freindshipe togither, and I hope shall continoue to doe so, and they have so resolved betuixt themselves, q͞ch resolutions if they observe they neid not valoue who take up the gudgells agt. them.   If the Earle of Melvill will quite his place of Prive Scall and accept of being President of the Councell, the Duke of Queensberrie will be made Privie Seall.   The King hes signed both those comissiones in Flanders, and sent them over blank to be transacted in that maner ; bot if Melvill will not willingly chainge, then Queensberrie is President of the Councell. The Earle of Argyle is made captain of his Maties troup of gairds, so that by this settlement and the other alterations I gave your Lope. ane accompt of formerly, they have brocken the interest of both the divided pairties, and brought all into on united pairtie, who I hope will continoue in union and followe that which is for his Maties service with closeness.   Secretarie Johnstouns tuo sisters, wiz. Greden and Bogie, have gott ane pension of 200 l̈ib. ster. yearly.   The Duke of Queensberrie his letter goes doune this night, which makes him ane Exterordinary Lord of the Session.   Your Lope. will sie by the inclosed letter from Cornet Ogilvie what conditione affairs are in in fflanders. The Secretary is determined to doe for him, and will slip no opertunity that he thinks fitt for him.   Your Lope. will sie by the prints inclosed what furder newes pasess here at present.   I wish your Lope., my Lady, and all the family all happieness and prosperity, and I ame, My Lord, Your Lopes. ever obleidged and most humble srvant,

JA. BAIRD.

The Secretary hes furnished his loadging here verie nobly.

When Parliament met on 8th September 1696, Lord Murray, who was on 27th July created Earl of Tullibardine, was Commissioner, the Earl of Melville was Lord President of the Privy Council, and the Duke of Queensberry was Lord Privy Seal.

William Ogilvie, Cornet in the Royal Scots Dragoons, writer of the next letter, was son of William Ogilvie of Bachlaw near

Banff. In Flanders, during 1696, the campaign was one of stalemate.

For MR. JAMES BAIRD TO BE LEFT ATT SIR JAMES OGILVIE,
PRINCIPALL SECRETARIE OF STEATE FOR YE KINGDOME OF
SCOTLAND, HIS LOADGINGS ATT WHYTHALL LONDONE. per
Holand. 8d

D. CUSSEN,—I had wreten to you befor this, bott ther hes notheing fallen outt yett worth pains, onlie the King is daylie expected att Gent, and money is given outt to ye armie, qch wes 3 moneths in arair. The Frenshe armie of 60 thousand strong command by ye Marishall de Wilroy took ye feill ten days agoe, and came vithin 3 legs of Gentt. Att fust itt did alarme us extreamlie, we being all in quarters, and ye fust accompt we had of them wes by ye bouers careing ther goods to ye churches and driving ther catel to our syd of ye cuntrie. Our foott imediatlie besett ye passes one ye canaell betuixt Gent and Bruges, and one ye fourdable pleaces mounted canon and swans fethers to oppose ther horse. All ye dragoons are quartered vith ye bourrs neir ye foott vith orders to march bag and bagadge one a minutts advertisment, in caice ye enymie should attempt aney thing, qch they have nott yett doone. Our cavalrie continou yett in ther quarters. Peple speak differentlie of ye Frenshe disings heir. Some say they are to bombard Gent and Bruges, others that they onlie come to distroy ye cuntrie, and eat up ye foradge, by qch they secure ther lyns about Yipers, Knok, and Feirun, that we cannot after have aney camp or meat for horses, qch hinders our haveing aney campe one that syd. Since ye King is come we daylie expectt horse foott and dragoons to taik ye feild, qr things in a shortt tyme vill appair. We have good hops, and one for one belive we are able to doe ther bussines. The enymie vill in ye begining of campyne be stronger than we. They have receved considerable detashements from ye Ryne, bott most all returne qn ye Germans taik ye feild, who dra nott outt so earlie as we by six veiks.

The Marishall Bouflers comands ane other armie stronger

by some squadrons as Wilroys ; and the D. of Bavaria withe the Germans and Spainard, those of Mastuk, Huy, Brussells, and Namure are waiting his motione and to oppose his designs. Some think he designs to invest Namure, bott ye D. of Bavaria hes ye foott campt aboutt itt. Deserters from Wilroys armie come in daylie. They say that ye Frensh King wes expected in ther campe, bott this recevs litel creditt, and that great stors of amanitione and booms wer expected, and if they come befor we be strong for them they may als eaiselie bombard Gent as they did Bruzells. Yeasterday ther furadgers and outt gairds came vithin a mylle of Gent. In ye mein tyme ther wes never so much talk of peace, and burgers in Gent hold great oads that vithin six veiks ther shall be a cesatoine of arms, and that they are actuallie treating for peace. For my partt I doe not belive itt. This all we have heir, qch, if ye think worth ye pains, ye may lett my Lord hear, and how soon aney thing extraordinarie happens ye shall have itt.

I receved a letter from my father wherin he presses my comeing home, and that he hes vretten to my Lord to doe for me, and that my mother and he have vretten to you to putt my Lord in mynd. I ame afraid that nott onlie ye bott my Lord m[a]y be importuned. Haveing received my Lo. Findlaters letter to ye same effect I hope ye vill excusse your trouble. As for my Lord, I realie blusshe, and refer my appologie to your maiking. I ame in no haist except a good ocaisione offer, qch is farr better knowen to yuo then me. Itt is then tyme to putt my Lord in mynd, qch, uhen ocaisione offers, see it your selfe ; for itt is neidles to trouble him by leters or solistations for me. Ye know qt he said himselfe, bott, God villing, I vill keip peace to this campyne, bott that doeth nott hinder preferment. Ther is onlie one thing, if itt be waikant. We hear that Drumond is mead a captan in my Lord Bings redgment, by qch meins ye Generall Adjutant is waikant. If itt be, itt is a prittie post, and come peace or warr continues. If itt be waikant pray you mynd Sir James to wrett to Sir Thomas Livingstone in my favors, and ye letter uill neid to presse a litel in my favors the reasone why the Generall hes wreten to Major Hunter, that he hears that I ame putting in for a companie in Scotland, and designs to quyt his redgment. If itt be so, he says he did nott expect itt, and that my ambitione is lese as he thought itt, and he uill repent that he ever advanced me in his redgment. I disyred Major Hunter to wrett to him, and sho him that my Lord Secretarie wes pleast to look one me as his freind and neam, and wes resolved to advance me, and that I wes to be dispost as he pleast, bott in particular had nott propost aney thing. If ye mynd I told yuo that Sir Thomas wold nott villingly pairt vith me, bott that is notheing, and I ame youngest cornett bott one in this redgment, and itt is long or preferment can be had, qch is nott to be lacked qn itt can be had. Be pleast to acquant my Lord of this, and if ye G. Adjutant be waikant mynd my Lord to wrett to Sir Thomas a litel pressinglie be ye first post. Itt is said heir Capt. Stinsone hes gott itt, qch had I tymouslie knowen might have goott. Our Scotts freinds propost great things as troups of horse. I dont fly so highe. A companie of Inverloghie, or if ye captane levetent of Jedbrughe or Carmiglie wer to gaitt troups, in that caice I might pretend to be a capt. levetent first, and then a troupe coms in after. All I shall say, if aney such ocasione offer, or aney other convenient thing vithoutt ye armie offer, qch I may honestlie have bread by, propose ye same to my Lord, and I doe ashure yuo ye shall nott losse your labor for me more as for a stranger. I refer all to your selfe, onlie that Gen. Adjutant iff itt be waikant in particullar, and my best wishes and most humble dewtie to my Lord.—I rest, D. Cussen, Your affectionat cussen to serve you,   WILL OGILVIE.

Gehent, May 28, 96. *New style.*

I pray lett me hear from yuo, and direct for Cornett Ogilvie of ye Royall Scotts dragoons in ye campe Flanders. I expect to sie your brother how sein ye King coms from Holand. Lett me have your Scotts news, and qt is becom of Capt. Drumond and Capt. Ker of our redgment, uho wes to be exchanged vith him.

The two next letters and James Baird's of 24th November 1696 refer to the dearth in Scotland consequent on the failure of the crops of 1695 and 1696.

ffor THE RIGHT HONORABLE THE EARLE OFF
FFINDLATER these

MY LORD,—War it in my power to doe y^r Lop. greater service, y^r Lo. may be perswaded it should not be wanting. The pryce of this garnell is ten pund the boll, w^h I thinck to much, though I can not help it. The chamberlan is not hear at present, but I thinck the meall is giwin out by measur, being it pleasis the countrie people best. Y^r Lo. may send thos who ar to receave the meall aither on Saterday or Munday nixt, as y^u please, the sooner the better, for I never did sie or hear such outcryes for want of meall. God helpe the poor people. This being in heast, I shall ad no mor, but that I ame vith all dutifull respects, My Lord, Y^r Los. most humble and most faithfull servant,   A. DUMBAR.

Gordon Castle, **23** *July* 96.

For THE RYTT HONA^{LL} THE EARLE OF FINDLATR
thes are

Dolochie,[1] *the* 25 *of July* 96.

MY LORD,—I recaved your, and for ansr his Grace the Duks meall is all and evre pickell of it giuen out yesterdaye, and ther had bein lyk to be a mischeiffe abut the hinder end of it, stryving who should haue it amonsgt his ouen wassells. and servants in Achendoune, Glenliuet, Strathbogie, and Einze ; and I am greatle quarld be all, that your Lordshipe or anie ellse should haue anie, and anie of his Graces cuntry lyking to sterue. They tell me it is whigishe inclinations leids me to that prefference, so that Mr. Dunbare told me that he had consented that your Lordshipe should haue my chalder but none of his Graces ; and trulie, my Lord,

---

[1] In the parish of Bellie, Banffshire.

ther was sextein libs. for each boll prest upon me yester-night be John Hameltone for each boll, and he told me plainlie efter I had refust him that, if he had got it, he was assurd of 20 libs. for the boll within ten dayes.   Befor your Lo. letter came to my hand, I had wrat to Arnbathe and ane other letter to Castlfeild of the pryce, and what method was necessare to be taken about the convoying it out of this cuntraye, which I hope ye will get ane acompt of be Castelfeild and the bearer heirof.   Untill I get oper-tounitie to see your Lordshipe, I tak leave and continous as becomethe me in all sincear and dutifull respects, My Lord, Your Lordships ever obdent weill wishing and reade srvnt,   ALEX. GORDOUNE.

In the new Parliament Sir James Ogilvie, by the King's authority, sat and voted as Lord Secretary,[1] and the burgh of Cullen was authorised to elect another representative.[2]

For [THE RIGHT] HONOL THE EARLE OF FFINDLATER

Edr., 10 *Sepr.* 1696.

MY LORD,—My Lord Secretarie came saiflie heir on Saturday last, and on Twesday attendit the Comissioner to the Parliament, wher, efter calling the rolls and a short speech made by his Grace and ane other by Chancellar,[3] was adjurned to this day.   Its thought the Parliament will be soon over, nothing being designed by it but a subsidie for the maintinance of our forces.   Ther is no news heir but a great noyse of a generall peace.   The Parliament minister shall be sent your Lop. everie post. Receave the last flyeing post.   This is all the present truble from, My Lord, Your Lops. most obleidged and humble servant,   AN. CRAIK.

In the summer of 1696 Louis had opened negotiations with William for peace, but the early defection of Savoy from the Confederacy induced him to suspend these negotiations. .

---

[1] *The Acts of the Parliaments of Scotland*, vol. x. p. 8.   [2] *Ibid.*, p. 11.
[3] Lord Polwarth.

For THE EARLE OF FINDLATER

Edr., 10th Septbr. i696.

MY LORD,—I receaved the honour of your Lops. letter, and shall be veric myndefull of my promise to your Lope. at pairting. The Secretary hes wreitten to your Lope. by the bearer. The Parliament satt doune yisterday, being the tyme appoynted ; bot ther was little done, save only that the rolls were called, the Comissioners comission read, my Lord Secretaries as secretarie, and his letter from the King to sitt in Parliat. as on of the first four officers of state ; and then the Comissioner read his speech which was veric weell made ; and the Chancellour lykewayes made his speach. I would have sent them both to your Lope., bot they are not as yet come from the press. This being done, the Comissioner adjurned till tomorrowe, being Thursday at ten of the cloack. Ther hes bein straing clubs about the choiseing of the committies, and the nobility are in a great offence upon that head, the mobility, as they terme them here, endeavoring to carie all. I mean the borrowes, and a great many of the barrons. My Lord Secretary is verie weell with all sydes, bot it is verie fashous to him to gett all keepped, bot I hope he shall reconceall all. When I knoue more of occurrances here, your Lope. shall have ane accompt of them from, My Lord, Your Lops. most faithfull and obleidged srvant,

JA. BAIRD.

For THE EARLE OF FINDLATER this

MY LORD,—A general peace is the common talk, and yesternights letters bear that it is beleeved in France that it is concluded, upon wch some of the deputies from Languedock are said to have complemented the French King, telling him it is more glorious to be called the pacifick then the conquerour. The letters also bear that the late K. James is to have Christina of Swedlands lodgings in Rome for the place of his abode. I heard nothing of these disbanded souldiers ; but it is not doubted but that the French do own our K. as K. of Brittain ; for it is with him that the preliminaries to the peace have been concerted, and with him it cannot be supposed under any other chararter then King of Brittain. The Crankies themselves are drooping at the accounts wch. they have, and from that we may reckon the news are not favourable for their side. The French in their concertation stuck upon the act of the English Parliāt forbidding trade with France, and though some expedients were offered for their satisfaction, they said nothing could be concluded as to a free trade, till that act of the English Parliāt were rescinded. This is the substance of what we had the two last posts, except that the Fridays letters bere that the French K. had writte to acquaint the Grand Seigniour that his effairs obleidge him to make a peace, wch he was willing and desirous should be general, and that he should come into it. If any thing of moment come by post or otherwise, it shall as soon as possible be conveyed to your Loᵖ by, My Lord, Your obleidged and faithfull servant,

MR. PAT. INNES.

Banff, Septr. 14, 1696.

H. Munro, writer of the next letter, was the son of Sir John Munro of Foulis, one of the commissioners for Ross-shire to the Parliament sessions of 1693, 1695 and 1696.

To THE RIGHT HONĹL SIR JAMES OGILWIE On of his MATIES PRINCIPLL SECRETARIES OF STATE FOR THE KINGDOM OF SCOTELAND

MY LORD,—Tho I hawe not the honor of much of your Lo. accquentance, yet I presume to giwe your Lo. this trouble, finding that his Matie hath recomended to the Parliat. to put this kingdom in a posture of defence, qch. is most just and reasonable. And in regard that the castle and town of Invernes is a post werie necessarie to be secured for his Maties servyce, it being alwayes weil prowyded of corne and other necessaries, it lyeth in the mouth of the Highlands open and exposed to be seased and surprysed on a sudden, so that I entreat your Lo. will be pleased to procure to me from his Matie ane independant company of ane hundredth sentinelles with the nominaᵒne of my own officers and ane lieut. collonel or majors comissione and pay, and to comand the castle

and town of Invernes, and I would obleidge my selfe to
joyne tuo hundreth of my own men to the sd companie
on three dayes adwertishement in caice of necessitie, and
that the Kings servyce did requeir it, and I would by
the assistance of God doe what wer possible for such ane
number for preserwatione of the place. My Lo. Secretarie
Johnestone promished my father and me the last year to
gett me ane comission to this effect ; and I doubt not if
he had keept his feet he would hawe endeawoured to
effectuat it. My father intended to attend this session of
Parliat. and to hawe kissed your Lo. handes, but being
wisited with great seeknes thir ten weekes by past could
not effectuat his intentione, and if he had been now in
any health he would hawe written to your Lo. about some
affayres wherin our familie is concerned, in qch. your Lo.
was pleased to giwe your adwyse formerlie, so that I will
not trouble your Lo. at this tyme with them, till it please
God my father recower his health, and then he will accost
your Lo. with ane lyne. I depend on your Lo. kyndnes
and fawur ; and I doe assure your Lo. of my loyaltie and
faithfullnes to his Matie, and as I had the honor not long
agoe to wenture my lyf in his Maties serwyce and presence,
so I will newer declyne chearfullie to undergoe the sam
hazard when ewer I am called thertoo to assert his Maties
just right. And withall I hawe the honor to com of your
Los. familie wch. would be ane inducement to your Lo. to
act for me, and ane undeliable obliga°ne on all myne and
me in particullare to continow, My Lord, Your Lo. most
faithfull, most humble, and most obedient serawnt,

H. MUNRO.

Foulis, Septr. 28, 1696.

Parliament rose on 12th October 1696, and Sir James Ogilvie
shortly thereafter went south to London.

For THE RIGHT HONOURABLE THE EARLE OF FFINDLATER BANFF   6d

MY LORD,—I have heard nothing from my Lord Secretary or any in his company, since Sabboth wes eight dayes,
that he wes at Durhame in good health. The nixt will

bring account (I hope) of his being saiff at London. The Earle of Tillibardin is yet at Beford with his Lady, who continues ill. The Dutches[1] went yesterday to visit her. Her recoverie is hardlie expected. My Lord Jedburgh is also dangerouslie sick.

The English Parliat. promise fairly to the King for carying on the warr in order to ane honb[ll] peace. This is his Majesties birthday here, and we have no newes, for the Councill hes not yet mett, and the Session satt doun yesterday, but it is thought to be but a bad one.

Your Lop. will be pleased to cause Castlefeild execut the inclosed generall chairge agt. Tochoneal by a messr, and he may send it with the execution to John Donaldson to be execut at Banff agt. his tutors and curators, and then sent here for carying on the necessry diligences in dewe tyme. Mr. Robert Lauder is Clerk to the Sreff. Eqs. and hes not bein here since I wes at Cullen, else Castlefeild should have knowen what wes done by him as Sreff deput. He lives in East Lothian, and I see him ther, but he would not clear me till he wer at Edr. fforglen his brother in lawe is witnes to my speaking him on the subject. I hope Mr. Baird shall send doun the newes which I will transmitt.— I ame, My Lord, Your Lops. most humble and obedient servant,   Jo. ANDERSON.

Edr., 4th Nover. 1696.

For THE EARL OF FINDLATER

MY LORD,—Yesternight I receaved ane account from James Baird that my Lord your son was well at London on Thursday last, and hade kissed his Maties hands, and wes graciouslie receaved, and they wer all well on the road, only Rot Stakers horse gave over, and wes sold for 15 shillings at Stamford.

My Lord, I putt the inclosed for Balyie Baird under your Lops. covert, because his son wreitts me that it serves for a letter to my Lady, otherwayes I hade not been so ill manered, but I knowe it will come sooner and saiffer then if sent single.

---

[1] The Duchess of Hamilton, mother of Lady Tullibardine.

Ther is nothing of newes as yet.   I have wreitt againe
to James to send your Lop. the prints.

Ther is 500 lib. sterlin of my Lords money lyeing in Sir
Rot Dicksons hands here, which he offers to pay.   I have
wrott to my Lord to direct my Lady to take in the
equivalent in cess or excyse at home, and drawe upon him
or me to pay it here, and I expect my Lords directions.
Mean tyme my Lady may be speired out for money ther
to be answered here.   I hope your Lop. and my Lady and
the wholl familie are well, which I earnestlie wish and
pray for, and ame, my Lord, Your Lops. most humble and
obedient servant,   JO. ANDERSON.

   Edr., ij Nover. 1696.

As a result of the defection of the Duke of Savoy from the
Confederacy, Louis XIV. was in November seriously contemplating
an invasion of England, but it came to nothing.

For THE EARL OF FINDLATER

Whitehall, 24th Nov. i696.

MY LORD,—Nothing hes hapned here wourthie of your
Lops. notice, except what is contained in the publict newes,
which I send yow everie post; uyrwayes I would have
wreitten your Lope. ane accompt of them.   My Lord
Secretary keepes his health veric weell, which I think will
be as acceptable newes to your Lope. and his Lady as
any I can wreit;   and he is in veric good circumstances
with his maister.   The English Parliat. goes on frankly to
give the King the necessarie supplies.   Its talked here
that the ffrensh hes 3 or 4 regements of men readie to be
imbarked in ordore to ane invasion in some pairt of
Scotland;   and some say they designe upon Aberdein.
Ther is litle certainty for this ; so your Lope. may make
your own use of it, bot I think that number can doe litle
damnadge, if our people be unanimus for the Kings
interest.   I ame sorie to hear that wictuall is lyke to be
so scarce in Scotland this year, wherfor it will be advisable
to keepe what you have for some tyme, till it appear
whither ther will be a darth or not.   We have almost

constant raines here, and in the north of England deep snowe. I hope if my Lord Murray were come up something will be done for your Lope., and I shall be sure to keepe the Secretary in mynde. My Lady Tillebardine continoues still at Belford, and is in a way of recoverie. I beleive the ires to morrowe will bring ane accompt that his Lope. hes left her, for she is to returne to Scotland and stay at Hamiltoun all the winter. I wish your Lope. and the famely all happieness, and I ame, My Lord, Your Lopes. most faithfull and obleidged servant, JA. BAIRD.

For THE EARLE OF FINDATER

Whitehall, 2d ffebry. 1697.

MY LORD,—I hade the honour of your Lops. yisterday, and the Secretary hade tuo, and on for the Earle of Tullebardine. Ther will be applica°ne made for your pension a litle befor the King goes away abroad. The Secretary is in verie good termes with his maister. His moneth of waiting was out yisterday, and the King was pleased to say to him that he was veric well pleased with his choise of him to be his Secretary, and he did serve with pleasantnes and to his Maīts minde. He lykewayes told him that he would so privide for him as that he should be no loaser in his service, being sensible that he hade called him from a verie good and adventagous post. Meantyme hes given him a letter by way of precept upon his Theasierie for seven hundereth pounds ster in considera°ne of his exterordinary services and expenss of his jurnay into Scotland. I sent ane dozon and ane halfe of gloves to my Lady. I hope she hes receaved them befor this comes to your Lops. hands. I ame glaid your Lope. getts your newes punctually, for I never omitte on post sending them off from this. The Secretary receaves all your Lops. letters duely, altho he seldom makes ansres, and I doe not in the laist quystion bot Mr. Andersone is verie cairfull to forward all, both too and from your Lope. I ame with a profound respect, My Lord, Your Lops. most faithfull and obleidged servant q^{ll} I ame   JA. BAIRD.

Your Lops. pension would be proposed now, but that

the S. does not think fitt to mention it so soone after the Kings complement to himselfe, bot will doe it in tyme, and I will sie to mynde him of it.

On 8th February 1697 the King issued a letter[1] to the Commissioners of the Treasury ordering payment to Lord Secretary Ogilvie of £700 sterling, his expenses in attending the last session of Parliament, 'ffour hundred thereof out of the first and readiest of the profits and duties of the post-office . . ., and the other three hundred out of what money is arisen or shall arise by the composition of wards.'

For THE EARL OF FINDLATER

Edr., 15 *March* 1697.

MY LORD,—I hear my Lord Secretary is verie well. His tooth-ach is over without breaking eyr without or within, and he attends the King and his post this moneth. The print newes are inclosed. I wes necessitat to ommitt wreitting last post, being bussied at the signet, and lykwayes preparing matters for the tryall of severall witches in the west. The Parliament is to be adjourned till the 18 of August nixt. The Master of fforbes is to have my Lord Jedburghs regiment of dragoons here, and my Lord Jedburgh getts Cuninghames regment in fflanders. This is designed, but not yet past the Kings hand. Dalsellie having rouped the excyse for 30,000 lib. st., Barntoun and Livingstoun who are at court offered the King 32,000 lib. st. for it. The King wrott doun that they might have it, if at a roup non went beyond them. It wes againe rouped and non hes exceeded them, yet the Exchaquer think it dishonrable to break the first roup for 2000 lib., and have wreitten for adwise to the King anent it. The former tacksmen and Geo. M'Kenzie are at court pleading ease. The King hes promised them a hearing. It wes expected to be on Thursday last.

Skipper Grigorie is come over to aggree with your mert.

---

[1] *State Papers* (*Scotland*) *Warrant Books*, vol. xvi. p. 345, in Record Office, London.

Leishman by himself and another to cary about your victuall. He is to come about with his vessell from Dundie to Leith , and from that to you without delay. I fear it be the first of Apryll ere ye see him, for the longer the victuall is coming up the better for the merchand, if it escape sea hazard. Therfor I wish freinds wer spock to supplie you with the use of money, if ye need it at the terme ; for we shall want of our will, if ye gett not of your owne befor the terme. Yet we cannot be sure the victuall will be up, and the mert. most have some fewe dayes efter. When the victuall is shiped, I think your Lop. may drawe bills on the merct. for paymt. of a part, and may putt it in tuo or three bills that it may be taken off him by parcells, because his bargane is dear and he like to lose.

I fear I shall be at the west some dayes at the tryall of the witches, yet I shall order that your newes be deulie sent your Lop.—I ame, My Lord, Your Lops. most humble and most obedient servant,   Jo. ANDERSON.

Mr. Gellie, who writes presumably to the Earl of Findlater, was parish minister of Fordyce.

MY LORD,—I intreat you will be pleased to lend me Hammonds Practicall Catechism for a fourthnights tyme, and if your Lop have present use for it I shall return it to-morrow, for I would only see his sentiments of a text. I resolve (God willing) to preach upon Sunday next. No more, but comending your Lop and all your concerns to Gods grace and effectuall blessing, I rest, My Lord, Your Lop most humble and obliged servant,   A. GELLIE.

 Fordyce, March 30, 1697.

For THE EARL OF FINDLATER

Whitehall, 17th Aprile 1697.

MY LORD,—This serves only to aquant your Lope. with a sadd accident of fire that happned last night at Westminster upon the Theames syde, which burned doune above tuentie houses and was within tuo of ours. Ther was four blowen up to prevent furder incroachment, bot

all these opperations save the last proved unsuccessfull.
We had all our furnitur taken done, and readie to be caried
out in caice ther hade bein occasion for it. It was twice
quenched and begane againe. I never in my lifetime sie
any thing so terrible. The Secretary was out of bed all
night. It begane at nyne at night and continoued till 7
this morning, and hade its beginning in ane empty house,
and its said to have bein done of purpose by some Jacobite.
I thought it my deuty to give your Lope. and my Lady
this accompt to prevent uyrs that might not be reall. The
King goes away upon Thursday, and we will depairt from
this in fourteen dayes yrafter. I knoue not as yet whither
we will take the Bath in our way or not. The prints will
give your Lope. ane accompt of publict matters.—I ame,
My Lord, Your Lops. most faithfull and obleidged sert.,

JA. BAIRD.

Towards the end of April William crossed to Flanders. The
campaign was only languidly pressed, and negotiations for peace
were early opened by Louis.

For THE EARL OF FINDLATER

Edr., *25 May* 1697.

MY LORD,—Blissed be God, my Lord Secretary your
son and all his company came well here yesternight. The
second loadning of victuall is livered, and ther being a
part of it taken out at ffrasersburgh it came here in prettie
good condition. Only a steep or tuo wes like to heat,
and wes presentlie putt to malting. Ther is no money
hade yet for the victuall (it being all on the mans hand)
except fyve hundreth merks, neither cane any be hade
till he sell, and he waits a ryseing marcat, it being nowe
lowe. So your Lop. nor my Lady most drawe for no
money, till ye be acquainted by my Lord Secretary; and
I perceave his Lop. will need all cane be hade of the victuall
befor he goe off, for money is verie precious here, and it
will be a good tyme ere he cane gett his pension and
gratuities. I doubt not but my Lord wreitts to your
Lop. and my Lady by this post. However it is the duty

of, My Lord, Your Lops. most humble and obedient servant,   ⸜Jo. ANDERSON.

To THE RIGHT HONORABLE THE EARLE OF
FINLATER

MY LORD,—Your presence here upon Friday the eigh-
teinth day of June be ten aclock in the forenoon at the
funerall of my deceast father the Lord Forbess is humbly
intreated by, My Lord, Your most humble and most
obedient servant,   ARTH. FORBES.

Castle Forbess, June 8th, i697.

Arthur Forbes of Breda was the second son of the deceased
William, twelfth Lord Forbes.

For THE RIGHT HONA̅L̅L̅. THE EARLE OF
FINDLATER

Edr., 26th June 1697.

MY LORD,—I have the disposition of Reidhyth, bot it
is not right.   Houever it containes a clause of restteration,
and I will cause draue it over againe.   Castelfeild will tell
you my sentements as to the manadgement of my affairs.
You will receave inclosed a letter for Bracco, and Castelfeild will delyver yow Robertsons obligaᵒne.   I can not
be more sevear upon him.   What I have thought fitt to
exact I give it to your Lope.   I will lykewayes help you
in the payement of Blackhills debt; bot I most recomend
it to you to manadge as frugally as possibly you can, for
I have not so much as I hade befor consideering my
charges and expenss.   And you knoue even all the esteate
I have is bot verie small for supporting the dignety of
your famely.   My wyffe returns againe about the end of
the nixt moneth, and I shall wreit then fully.   Blackhills
decreit shall be extracted.   This is all from, My Lord,
Your Lops. most obedient sone and humble servant,
                                         JA. OGILVIE.

To THE RIGHT HONORABLE THE EARLE OF
FINDLATER

MY LORD,—Your leter wass very refreshing to me, sincs
by it I hav the acompt of your halth, which I -hartaly

wish the continounes of. Your son is weall, and is this
night at James Bards marag. I will be north in August,
and resolwes, God willing, to previd the houss with swit
metes and spices with the Sandend botes. I am lixwias to
bring north thre hundred marks for paying your Lord^s
part of Blakhiles muny. Your son hath given ordares to
Castllfild to communicat to your Lo. hou to walk with
Bracky in the mater of Robartson. I have likwayes told
Castellfild to secur timber for the kill baren. He will
advance the muny for it, if the muny be not com in for
the witell. Let the meall be sold at the reates of the
contry, for I kno the longer it is keept the less muny will
be got for it. This is all I shall trubell your Lo. with at
this tym, save only to intret you may look to James, and
keep your selff from melancoly is the erenest prayer of hir
who is, My Lord, Your most obedent daughtar and humbell
servant,   ANNA OGILVIE.

Edr., July the 1— 97.

For THE EARL OF FINDLATER

Edr., 22 *July* 1697.

MY LORD,—Receave your Lops. newes. I have sent
them off thir severall posts, and shall take care they come
to my hands that I may doe so allwayes. Ther is no
Scotts newes with ws here. If ther wer any thing of import,
I knowe my Lord Secretary your son would acquaint your
Lop. with them. Blissed be God, his Lop. and my Lady
are veric well. He is in much esteeme here amongst persons of all ranks, and befor the Councill or else wher, when
he is pleased to midle, he carys what he designes ; and ther
is reason for it, for his proposa[ls and] measures are just.
That your Lops. familie may prosper, and it may be still
well with my Lord Secretary is the heartie desyre of, My
Lord, Your Lops. most humble and most obedient servant,
                                JO. ANDERSONE.

After the failure of the English subscriptions, £200,000 of the
capital of the Darien company were offered to the merchants of

Hamburg for subscription.   The English resident at Hamburg and the English envoy to the court of Lunenburg opposed the project, and the King was appealed to by the directors of the company for redress.   The following letter will show that the appeal was so far effectual.   In the end, however, English opposition prevailed, and the foreign subscription fell through.

COPIE OF THE KING'S LETTER TO THE EARLE OF TULLI-BARDIN AND SR JAMES OGILVIE CONCERNING THE AFRICAN COMPANY WITH THEIR DECLARATION TO THE SD. COMPANY

2d Aug: 1697.
Superscribed WILLIAM R.

RIGHT TRUSTIE AND WELLBELOVED COUSIN AND COUN-CELLOR AND RIGHT TRUSTIE AND WELLBELOVED COUN-CELLOR,—Wee greet you well.   Wee do hereby impower you to signifie to the councel general of the African companie of that our kingdom that as soon as wee return to England, wee shall take into consideration what they have represented to us, and in the meantime wee shall give orders to our envoy att the courts of Lunenburgh, and our resident at Hamburgh not make use of our name and authoritie for obstructing the companie in the prosecution of their trade with the inhabitants of that citie.

And so wee bid you heartilie farewell.

Given at our camp att Cocklebergh the $\frac{15}{25}$ day of July 1697 and of our reign the 9th year.

By his Ma^{tles} command,

contresigned,   RO. PRINGLE.

Directed on the back thus :—

To our right trusty and well beloved cousin and coun-cellor, and our right trustie and well beloved councellor John Earle of Tullibardine and Sr James Ogilvy our prin-cipal Secretaries of State for our ancient kingdom of Scotland.

By the Right Honble John Earle of Tullibardine and Sr James Ogilvie Knight, Principal Secretaries of State.

MY LORDS AND GENTLEMEN,—Wee are impowered by the King to signify unto you that as soon as his Ma^{ty} shall return to England, he will take into consideration what you have represented to him, and that in the meantime his Ma^{ty} will give orders to his envoy at the courts of Lunenburgh and his resident at Hamburgh not to make use of his Maties name or authority for obstructing your company in the prosecution of your trade with the inhabitants of that city.

Signed at Edinburgh, the second day of August 1697.

Sic subt^r. TULLIBARDINE.

JA. OGILVIE.

To the Council-General of the Company of Scotland tradeing to Africa and the Indies.

Mr. Robert Pringle,[1] who countersigned the King's letter, was on 29th April 1695 appointed Treasurer-Clerk in Scotland and Keeper of the Register of all Infeftments and Confirmations. Later that year, on 26th October, he was appointed Under-Secretary for Scotland to attend the King in Flanders, and £500 was given him to meet his charges. On 25th May 1696 he was made Secretary-Depute for Scotland.

A new Commission of Justiciary for the security and peace of the Highlands was issued, with a list of persons who were to be commissioners, on 30th March 1697.[2] The letters of 3rd August, 15th and 21st September all refer to this Commission and its work.

For THE EARL OF FINDLATER

Durn, the 3d off August 1697.

MY LORD,—I intended to heave vaitted this day on ȳr Lo. and the rest off the Justitiars, bot my viff vas so vnveill yisterday and this last night, and I head my self this night such paines in my theese and knies, espetiallie in my left syd that I goit verie bad rest, and the ackings continue vt mee as yit, so that I daer not adventor from home ; qrfor I heave givein ȳr Lo. the truble off this l̄tr, intreating ȳr Lo. may heave my absense this day excuised, and yt ȳr Lo. may appologeise ffor mee to the vither commisrs ;

---

[1] *State Papers (Scotland) Warrant Books,* vol. xvi., in the Record Office, London.   [2] *Ibid.,* pp. 372-384.

and qr̄n I can bee off vise I shall not bee vanting according to my pouer to obey and serve as Ȳr Lo^s affectionat and huimble servant, W. DUNBAR.

For THE EARL OF FINDLATER

Huntly, 15th Septris 1697.

MY LORD,—I receawed your Lordships, and was truely sory, as was all ye Justitiars heir present y^t your Lo. conveniencie could not allow to com this lenth to this court, for yr was sev^{ll} processes befor ym as your clerk will inform. As your Lo. ordered, ye court is adjourned till ye first Thursday of October to meet at Cullen. I shall (God willing) wait on your Lo. at ye said tyme. I shall give your Lo. no further trouble att pnt., but yt I ame as becometh, My Lord, Your Lo. most obedient and humble servant, ARTH. FORBES.

By the Lord High Chancelour of Scotland.

THESE are requiring you to order parties of sogers under your command to seearch places and aprehend persons and to commit them to prison by the derection of and upon warrands given by the Earle of Finlatour, whom I have authorised upon a present occasion wherein the goverment is concerned. And this shall be your warrand.

Given under my hand at Polwart House, the 15 day of Septr 1697. MARCHMONT, *Cancellar.*

To the commanding officer of any of his Majesties garisons in the north of Scotland or of any part of the forces laying in that cuntrie.

The laird of Troup's letter of 1st October 1697 refers to Marchmont's letter, which was issued after the peace of Ryswick, but before the news of it reached Scotland.

For THE EARL OF FINDLATER

Edr., 2i *Septer.* 1697.

MY LORD,—I have inquyred at the councill chamber for any bill or act for additionall commissioners of Justiciary fr your countrey and ther is non ther, so it seemes needfull your Lop. should wreitt to my Lord Chanceler and Advocat anent it, and should send a list of the persons ye requyre to be added.

James Hay is not in toun that the old disposion of Reidhyth may be sent north.

The inclosed for your Lop, and my Lady I hope will give your Lop. satisfaction anent the peace. It is talked at London and here that the principallitie of Oraing is to be restored to our King, with all the estate his predicessors hade in Burgundie, that Luxenburgh, Mons, Dinant, Charleroy, Arth, and a great many other touns in fflanders are to be restored to Spaine, with all Catolonia, at least so much therof as wes in the possession of that croun at the treatie of Menungen,[1] and that the equivalent is offered to the Emperour for Strathsburgh and the Dutchie of Loraine. The peace is to passe the seals of England and ffrance, and to be therefter ratified with all diligence. I hope James Baird will lett your Lop. knowe what comes to his cares. Ther is no Scots newes here.—I ame, My Lord, Your Lops. most humble and most obedient servant,

JO. ANDERSONE.

Showe my Lord Secretary's Lady that Mr. Crauford continues yet to serve her Lord as Keeper of the Signet, that her Laps. letter shall be this night sent off, and nixt post I shall answer hers.

The treaty of Ryswick, which recognised William's title, was signed on the 10th and 11th of September 1697. The terms mentioned in John Anderson's letter were inaccurate. The news reached London on the 13th, and Edinburgh on the 17th September.

For THE EARL OF FINDLATER

MY LORD,—I pray your Lo. pardon my boldness in giving your Lo. this trouble, qh I doe being desyrous to see Hollyoaks dictionarie. If your Lo. hav it, and will be pleased to let me see it for a three weeks tym, your Lo. shall remain assurd I will tak mor car of it nor it war my oun, and return it saff. My Lord, a week or tuo agoe I

---

[1] Meaning probably Nimeguen.

recomended to, and I doubt but Castelfeld hath let your Lo. know of the desyn I hav to wait on your Lo., and hav your Lo^s thochts what farther is fitt to be returned in ansuer to my Lord Chancellor and Secretaris letters, qh I doubt not he hath comuni(cat) to your Lo., having lykways sent him the letters accordinglie ; and althoch that occasion did not call me, I will wait on your Lo. hou soon possible I can. Evrie bodie each is mor surprysed nor oyr at the news of the peac, but we hav had no accompt of the articles which is much longed for. I pray as I hop they be good and honorable. Begging pardon for this rudness, I am, My Lord, Your Lo^s Most ingadged and humble ser^{tt},

ALEXR. GAIRDNE.

Troup, Octr 1, 1697,

Alexander Garden of Troup, Banffshire, was the son of Major Alexander Garden of Banchory, who served under Gustavus Adolphus, and on his return from the wars purchased Troup in 1654. The sasine records of Banffshire show that Alexander succeeded his father by 28th August 1663. His name appears in the oldest extant suite-roll of the county in 1664. At the revolution in 1688 he was captain of one of the four Banffshire companies of the Earl of Erroll's regiment of militia. He married Bathia, daughter of Sir Alexander Forbes of Craigievar. His grandson was Lord Gardenstown.

The King's order to the Privy Council of Scotland, referred to in next letter, for the reduction of the Scots army and the laying up of the Scots ships of war is contained in *State Papers (Scotland) Warrant Books,* vol. xvi. p. 426.

For THE RIGHT HONOURABLE THE EARLE OF FINDLATER at CULLEN HOUSE IN BANFFE SHYRE

Whitehall, 19th *Octor.* 1697.

MY LORD,—The inclosed pepers in print containes all and much more then I can wreit in relation to the ratifica^one of peace, and the solemnities that hes bein this day used hier in the proclaming therof. Ther is a flyeing packett sent to the Privie Councell of Scotland with a letter from the King signefeing the same to them, and impouering them to emitte such proclamations for makeing the same knouen to the lidges, as hes bein knouen to have bein emitted upon the lyke occasions at any time befor, and lykewayes impouering ther Lops. of the Privie Councill to disband the regements comanded by the Earle of Tulli-bardin and Lords fforbes and Lindsay, and for reduceing of that regement in Fort-william consisting now of tuo battalions to on, and to lay up the thrie frigotts lately sett out for gairding of the coasts, and to pay of and dischairge the men in them.   The King is nou quickly expected over, and will be made verie welcome, and vast preparations of joy are makeing hier agt his comeing.   I knoue my Lord Secretary is as well with him as your Lope. could desire. The Secretarie is in paine till hier hou your Lope. is in your health, haveing heard that you was tender.   He will wreit to your Lope. nixt post, bot in the mean time I thought this short account due from, My Lord, Your Lops. most faithfull and humble servant,   JA. BAIRD.

For THE RIGHT HONORABLE THE EARLL OF
FINDLATER this ar

MY LORD,—I heaue giuen your Lop. the trouble of this letter to let you knou that I can get Bracos son to my daughtr, and he is to giuc hir tuanty thousand marks a year frie of any burden, and all the rest he hath affter his deth ; and he woll heaue from me woth my dauchtr all the land I heaue, but I am to get ten thousand marks and all the muabills, so I would heaue your Lops. opinion in it, for I think it a good bargon.   The bearer can inform your Lops. what pased amonst us.   So expting your ansuer woth the bearer, I continou, My Lord, Your Lops. most affectionat son and most humble servant,

PAT. OGILVIE.

Lesendrum, Oct. 29, 1697.

This match did not come off, Braco's son, William Duff, marrying Helen Taylor, while Mr. Patrick's only daughter by his first wife became Lady Tyrie.[1]

for THE EARLE OF FFINLATER thes

MY LORD,—I hartilie thank your Lo. for the frequent

---

[1] *Genealogical Collections concerning the Sirname of Baird*, p. 34.

expressions I have had of your kyndnes, and for mynding me to your son. It shall ever be my studie to serve your Lo. and familie, in all that falls in the powr of, My Lo., Your most humble servant, PATRICK OGILVIE

Boyn, De. i, 97.*

I have delayed my jurnay for som days, for I hear ther is no ryding betwixt this and Abd., untill the storm settell or goe off.

Patrick Ogilvie in 1660 had settled on him by his father, Walter Ogilvie of Boyne, the barony of the thanedom of Boyne in Banffshire. By 1662 he was knighted. In 1664 he married Mistress Anna Grant, daughter of James Grant laird of Grant. He succeeded on his father's death, *c.* 1666-7. In 1669 he was elected, along with Sir James Baird, to represent Banffshire in the Scots Parliament. Again in 1681 and in 1685 he was elected commissioner for the county, along with Sir George Gordon of Edinglassie. In 1681 he was created a judge of the Court of Session, under the title of Lord Boyne. He married as his second wife Anne, youngest daughter of Hugh, eighth earl of Eglintoun. There is considerable detail about him in this correspondence, in Dr. Cramond's *Annals of Banff*, and in the editor's *Banffshire during the Revolution of 1689*, etc.

For THE EARL OF FINDLATER

Edr., 16 *Decer.* 1697.

MY LORD,— . . . We knowe not well the pryce of victuall here, and brewers and victuallers are every day breaking, and we hear the pryce is high with you. This is the night of publict thankgiving, and I have nothing to enlairge on. . . . I wish all happienes to your Lop. and familie, and ame, My Lord, Your Lops. most humble and most obedient servant, Jo. ANDERSON.

After the peace the English Parliament completely reduced the King's Dutch guards, and challenged his alienations of crown lands to his Dutch courtiers.

For THE EARL OF FINDLATER

Whitehall, ffebry: 10*th*, 1698.

MY LORD,—I beleeve your Lo^p hes full accompts of all news forraign and domestick in the prints, except what concerns the English Parliament ; and I delayed to trouble your Lop. untill I might give you ane full accompt of there proceedings in the Kings business, but they ordinarly delay that untill the last, and the only things yet done are viz. : They have appointed all forces to be disbanded yt were raised since the death of K. Charles the 2ᵈ, and they allow 700,000 pound ster. for mantenance of the civil list, with 350,000 pound for guards and garrisones, without condescending on the number of fforces, and 10,000 men for the sea service and for yʳ pay 40,000 pound a moneth. They have also appointed six dayes full pay to each sentenell after disbanding to carry him home, and half pay to the officers untill they be provided otherwayes, only to those who are naturall born subjects of England ; and now they are upon the preparing bills for evacating all grants of estates and other interests in England and Ireland from the crowne since K. Charles the Second. There is ane act of Councill inhibiting any subject from goeing to engage in the service of any fforraign prince. Our Scotts forces qch are to stand are : the troope of guairds, Levingstone regiment, and my Lord Jedbrugh of dragouns, 4 ffoot regiments, Ramseye's Colliars, Rue's and Brigadeer Maitlands, who is made governour of ffort William, and will see yoʳ Loᵖ on his journey thither. This was my Lord Secretaryes doeings, who is in good health, blessed be God, and is very much in favour with his Maṫie. I pray your Loᵖ all health and happiness and to the noble family, and am, My Lord, Yʳ Lops. servant,

Jo. Philp.

John Philp, son of George Philp in Brunton, Cullen, and Elspet Lorimer, was born at Cullen in February 1673. At the date of the above letter he was acting as secretary to Sir James Ogilvie, and he continued as secretary for over twenty years. He was purse-bearer to Lord Seafield while Lord Chancellor. Several of his letters containing occasional autobiographical references appear in this collection. On 16th October 1705 he married Sophia, daughter of the Rev. Daniel Robertson, sometime minister of Hutton, Dumfriesshire, a cadet of the Robertsons of Struan, and ancestor of the Robertsons of Ladykirk, Berwickshire. After the Union he was appointed Deputy Auditor of Exchequer, and helped to manage the Scots estates forfeited after the rising of the 'Fifteen. On 7th October 1719 he bought the estate of Greenlaw, Midlothian, of which county he was a Justice of the Peace. In 1727 he was appointed an original director of the newly-founded Royal Bank of Scotland. He died on 29th December 1760, and was buried in Greyfriars Churchyard, Edinburgh. One of his grandsons was John Philp Wood the genealogist, and editor of *The Douglas Peerage*.

Edr., Febr: 15, 1698.

MY LORD,—Since my last I have had your Lops. of the 8th and 10th. That I have not writt fullie to your Lop. before this proceeded from the desire I had to be particular ; and after all the pains I have taken, I am still afraid I can give but litle satisfaction. Your Lop. would understand from others that the return sent to Sr Francis Scott was not receaved by the councell of the companie as on to there address, because it was not ordered to be communicat ; but its probable, if it had satisfied, that difficultie would easilie have been overcome. What the prevailing pairtie requires is what its like the King will not encline to grant, a declaration under his oun hand of there privileges and rights, and of there libertie to enter into contracts and termes for carying on of there trade with anie they shall pitch upon. All resolutions of further addressing seem to be waved at present, but not the rancour taken away, which hes been bred by the treatment they mett with at Hamburgh, which is heightned by the disappointment occasioned by the mismanagment of those who had gott credit amongst them ; and that this may break out to the prejudice of his Matys service, when anie occasion offers and particularlie in Parliament, I find the opinion of all the honest men amongst them, who are as zealous as anie for the interest of there countrey, but with a deu regard to his Matys service and these straits and difficulties under which he is brought by the opposition of our neighbours. I have discoursed some of them on the head, who doe think it may be much for his Matys service, by taking away as much as is possible all pretence from such as,

when the Parliament sits, will catch at anie handle for
obstructing the Kings affairs, and also for encouradging
honest men to appear, that the King should give the same
return under his oun hand to the late address, that he
ordered to be given in his name by his Secretaries, and
that this should be addressed to the councell of the companie. I lay this before your Lop. as the sentiment of such
in the companie of whose sincere affection to his Matys
service as well as there countreys interest there can be
no doubt; and I doe it the more freelie that I find just
grounds to apprehend that what hes hapned to the companie may be much made use of in the ensuing session of
Parliament, the generalitie of all ranks resenting highlie
what hes passed in Hamburgh, and the little care that is
taken to redress them. The directors are verie busie in
preparing all things in order to the setting out of the ships,
which its beleived will be within 6 weeks or two months
at furthest. I doe not hear that they have yet pitched
upon the place they goe to, but are upon it. There fleet
will consist of 3 large ships and two tenders, which may
carry in all about 900 persons with provisions for on year.
They are to be governed after landing by a councell which
is to consist of seven persons, of whom I hear onlie two
as yet condescended upon, a merchant of Glasgou whose
name does not at present occurr to me, and on Dr. Monro
who hes been some years in America. What these projects
may in consequence produce, and hou farr they may be
prejudicial to our neighbours is uncertain, but I think
there preparations are not such as need give anie umbrage
at present. As for the particular place to which they
design, as I have writt I beleive it is not yet resolved on,
but if the King continues in the mind that he should have
the design communicat to him before it is put in execution,
the Justice Clerk offers himself to that purpose, and
doubts not but to prevail with the directors or such of
them to whom the secret shall be entrusted, that he or
some other should be alloued to impart it to the King,
but would first knou this to be his Matys positive pleasure.
I knou not if he hes himself writt so to your Lop., but by

his allouance I doe it.   I have understood what passed in a comittee of the Assemblie in reference to an address to his Maty against immoralitie, of which I shall by the next give your Lop. account, as I shall endeavour to inform my self if in the Commission anie thing of that nature is still projected.   Brigadeer Maitland came here yesternight.   I have spoke of him to the Justice Clerk, who seems enclined to live in friendship with him.—I am, My Lord, Your Lops. most humble servt.

RO. PRINGLE.

Sir Francis Scott[1] of Thirlstane was agent for the African company.   Mr. Robert Pringle on 10th February 1698 had already given Mr. Carstares[2] an account of the excited state of feeling in Scotland, owing to the King's failure to fully support the colonising enterprise of the African company.   When the expedition at last set out on 17th July 1698, the governing council of seven were Major James Cunningham of Eickett, Mr. James Montgomery, Mr. Daniel Mackay, Captain Robert Jolly, Captain Robert Pennicuick, Captain William Veitch, and Captain Robert Pincarton.[3]

For THE EARL OF FINDLATER

MY LORD,—Receave your newes.   I ame sure to send them off altogither every Thursday, it being the post day that carys them from this to your Lop.   I back them for the post master of Banffs care ; and that the postage may be easie, I lett the newes be outmost.   I doe not think the post master will disclose or withhold any of them, since they are backed for your Lop.   My Lord ffraser is at liberty.   No bargane offers yet for victuall.   Your son my Lord Secretary is verie well, and in great favour. Ther are trees and basketts with hardie greins in good condition at Leith to be sent north with the first occasion offers.   I wish they come as well to you as they have come here.   I cause gardners and such as understand take notice of them.   My Lady will send me ane answer anent

---

[1] *The Acts of the Parliaments of Scotland*, vol. x. p. 135, and App., p. 18, etc., and *Carstares State Papers and Letters*, p. 370.

[2] *Carstares State Papers and Letters*, pp. 368-370.

[3] *The Darien Papers*, J. Hill Burton, p. 49.

the breweing lead.[1]—I ame, My Lord, Your Lops. most humble and most obedient servant,   Jo. ANDERSON.

Edr., 17 *ffebry* 1698,

Halgrien is dead in prison.

Kinaber is dead suddently crossing the Quiensferry for Edr.

Lord Fraser took part with Captain Fraser in preventing the marriage of the daughter of Hugh, tenth Lord Lovat, with the Master of Saltoun, and was in consequence imprisoned. He was liberated on 10th February 1698. John Fullarton of Kinaber was commissioner for Forfarshire in the Parliament of 1696.

For THE EARL OF FINDLATER

Whitehall, 22d ffebry. 1698.

MY LORD,—I have wreatten fully both to my Lord Boyne and Cockstoune concerning Kempcairns affairs. I wish the concluding posetively of any bargaine may be delayed till I come to Scotland, which I hope will be some time in Apprile, and I will goe to the north als soone as I arrive at Edinburgh. Yow will sie the letters, and so I neid not resume what is contained in them. I ame verie much concerned for that famely, and if I doe meadle it will be for ther advantage, bot I have come to no resolutione concerning what I will doe on it. It is a pairt of the barronrie of Ogilvie, and most of the lands lyes within the regality, which is the only reason that I have any inclination to it. I could easely gett through with it, if once I did turne my minde that way. I can not wreat to my wife this night, bot this upon the matter is ane answear to hirs, and I beleive she will be satisfied when she hears that I have thoughts to returne so soone. I wish my wictuall may be sold for readie money, ffor the merchants and brewers are veric uncertaine, and no body can buy and sell upon ther bonds. I ame [v]erie unwilling to meadle in the matter of your Lops. title, unless it were [with] my brothers consent. My esteate is tollerable for a gentleman, bot is [ver]ie unconsidderable for ane earle,

---

[1] Furnace vessel used in brewing.

bot at meitting we shall speak [fu]lly of this.—I ame,
My Lord, Your Lops. most obedient sone and most
humble s^{vt},   JA. OGILVIE.

The Kempcairne estate, in the parish of Keith, was ultimately
bought by Seafield.

ffor THE RIGHT HONOURABLE THE EARLL OFF FFINDLATER

RIGHT HONORABLE,—My brother, Mr. Francis Grant,
Advocat, tells me yōr Lorsp was pleased to condescend
to favour his father Bellintome wt the use and loan of some
books, parтly of Davilaes historie of the warrs of Franc,
qch my father (vho is now old and oblidged to and de-
lighted in a cedentarry life) intraits yōr Lorshp may send
him, and yt yor Lorshp will pardon and excuse this trouble,
and the book shall be specially cared for, and thankfully
restored be, My Lord, Yōr Lorsps most humble servant,
                                              ALEXR. GRANT.
Banff, Feb. the 25th, —98.

Alexander Grant was the younger son of Archibald Grant of
Ballintomb. His elder brother, Mr. Francis, was made a baronet [1]
on 7th December 1705, and was afterwards elevated to the bench
as Lord Cullen.

For THE EARL OF FINDLATER

MY LORD,—These give you the good newes that my
Lord Secretary your son has certaintlie much of the Kings
favour, and a great ascendant above his collegue, as is
demonstrated by procuring the Presidents chair of the
Session for Mr. Hugh Dalrymple without the knowledge
or consent of his collegue and against it. He hade bein
receaved this day, but wanted one to make a quorum ;
but the Lords are wrott to be present on Tuesday nixt
for that effer. Lord Whytlawe hes got 400 lib. st. of pension to please him, but that does not, for he and his freinds
are inraged, but the nation generallie pleased and approve
the choise. My Lord Justice Clerk hes gott 300 pound
sterline of pension, and is added to the Thesaurie, and

---

[1] *State Papers (Scotland) Warrant Books,* vol. xxi. p. 127.

retaines the office and fie of Justice Clerk. The present Earle of Crauford hes gott his fathers pension of 300 lib. out of the a-bprick of St. Andrewes continued on him. Tuo troups of Lord Jedburghs regiment of dragoons are brock. I have sold 400 bolls of your mail at 6 lib. half a merk free of all chairges except sea hazard, and 100 bolls of bear or more as will fill the vessell at 8 lib. 8s. It is to be receaved upon the 15 of Apryl. I hope to gett the rest sold about that pryce.—I ame, My Lord, Your Lops. most humble and most obedient servant,

Jo. ANDERSON.

Edr., 24 March 1698.

The Earl of Tullibardine strongly supported Sir William Hamilton, Lord Whitelaw,[1] for the President's chair vacant through the death of Viscount Stair on 23rd November 1695. Tullibardine was shortly after this turned out of the office of Joint Secretary of State, and went into opposition.[2]

In 1697 the Presbyterian settlement of the Church in the north-east was so far advanced that the single presbytery established in 1694 for Aberdeen, Kincardine and Banff was enlarged to three—viz. (1) Aberdeen and Kincardine, (2) Turriff, Alford and Fordyce, and (3) Ellon, Deer and Garioch.

For THE EARL OF FINDLATER

Aberdeen, Apr. 13th, 1698.

MY LORD,—I communicat your Los. letter to the synod, who accordinglie have left Mr. Murray[3] intirelie to the disposal of the presbytrie of Turreff. Neither did the former synod put any farther restraint then this, that in regard some informations had been given in against him, which were to be further inquired into, the presbytri of Turreff were inhibit to proceed to his ordination til first they had acquainted the other two united presbytrie of this province. And this was signified to your Lo. b

---

[1] *Historical MSS. Commission, Fourteenth Report*, App., Part. III., *Marchmont MSS.*, p. 146; *Marchmont Papers*, vol. iii. pp. 150-156; Fountainhall' *Chronological Notes of Scottish Affairs*, pp. 282-284; *Carstares State Paper and Letters*, pp. 338-340, etc.

[2] *Carstares State Papers and Letters*, pp. 391-393.

[3] Minister of Deskford, Banffshire.

a letter from that synod signed by the moderator and delivered to the clerk to be conveyed by your Lo. minister Mr. Tait,[1] so yt we know not how it hath miscarried. My Lord, as your Lo. hath been pleased to give countenance and incouragement hitherto to the Lords servants and work, so I nothing doubt but yow will do so to the end, which will be ground of peace and comfort in life and death. I pray the Lord multiplie his best blessings wpon your Lo. and your noble familie, and I am, My Lord, Yo[r] Lo. most humble servant, JA. OSBURN.

Mr. Tait was minister of Cullen from 1697 to 1700. He was brought north from Traquair.

James Osborne was professor of divinity in Marischal College from 1697 to his death in 1711.

Next letter from Brigadier Maitland, governor of Fort William, describes garrison life there, and the state of the fort and of the country, in 1698. Fort William, originally built by General Monk, was rebuilt and occupied by General Mackay in July 1690.[2]

ffort William, 17 *May* 98.

MY LORD,—I have received yours of the 21st Aprill. The Lords of the Treasurie have sent a masson and wright to viset this place, and I belive by this post my Lord Justice Clerk will be able to give you ane acount what it will cost to put both the fortificatione and houses in good condetione. I hope a lesser sume will doe it then what was proposd to your Lordsp. last. I wish there may no time be lost in faling about it, whilst the seasone will allow working here. The sumer is very short here, and it as yet scarcely well begun. I must confess I never saw so muth bad weather in so short a time, as since wee came to this place, yet the souldiers never kept thir health better. They were seasond befor they came here. There diet has been onley Scots pottage, ffor there was neither flesh fish butter or cheese to be had when wee came ; but I wonder not muth at that, for if some of our predecessors had got ther will, we would have found this place in ashes,

[1] Dr. Cramond's *Church and Churchyard of Cullen*, p. 85.
[2] General Mackay's *Memoirs*, pp. 79-99.

and it is said mony was given to preserve it.   At meeting
I shall be able to make this apeare, if my author hold out
till then.   He is still here.   The weather has hindred him
hithertoo, as he sayes, but there is still sume debts owing
him, that he would gladly have befor he part.   He gives
you his humble service, and desires that you would be
mindfull of what he wrot to you.   He pleads povertie,
and sayes all he has made since he came to this contrie
is a thousand pound st.   I kno seven hundred was bestowd
on the l^t collonels last voyage, and he gives a very just
acount how he deburst it.   I think it not strange that
some folks buys land.   I wrote to your Lord^p that he showd
me his comissione, which is to be second l^t coll. to the
gareson, without naming the regiment.   I would gladly
have that explain in caise the regiment or a part of it
should march out of the garisone.   So soone as he had
ended his acounts here, he desird too goe to Invernes.   I
belive he designs not to stay muth in this place, for he
never did it, tho it was represented that he was the only
persone that could doe the King good service here, in so
muth that without him it was almost imposible to live here.
This was said to my selfe, tho it is as falce as other things
that was impos'd on some at that time.   However I have
stopt his mouth of all he could desire of me, and have
ferm'd the sutlirie at a hundred and tuentie five lb. a yeare,
the halfe of which I give to my lt. coll.; so it is seen
that this is not what it was said to be, considring what
was payd for it.   What other advantages I have I shall
sho you, when I have the good fortune to see you, which
I intreate may be as soone as you come to this contrie,
for it is needfull that I speake with you.   I shall stay
as shorte time as you please, for I designe to make a
progress to kno the contrie.   I have either seen or had
letters from the most part of the gentlmen of this contrie
far and neer, and all of them profess and promice to live
peacably ;   and I belive they will doe so whilest it is their
intrest, and no longer.   You kno the comisione that is
out against Kippoch.[1]   I have made search for him, but

---

[1] *The Marchmont Papers*, vol. iii. p. 149.

to no purposs. I have offred a good summe of mony by Mcintosh desire to have him brought to me. I have some hopes, but he is ever on his keeping. He is nou gon from this part of the contrie tis thougt to Sky. He made his tenants, as I am told, take ane oath not to serve under Mcintosh, but if he comes to live on his lands, as he sayes he will, the most part of them will stay with him. I have ane order from the Councill to allow him men from this place to maintaine him in possesion of his land against Keppoch. I have a partie of theirty men in Castell Douny [1] at th Marques of Athols desire. It is belivd that Simon Fraizer is making his peace. It is given out so at least. All is quiet there as yet. I dout not by this time my tuo French captains has been with you. I kno not if they designe to sell there companies ; but if any vacancie hapen I would wish that Cap. Lieutenent Elis had the first companie falis, and the eldest lieutenont which is Nairne to be cap. lieutenont, and Ensigne Garden lieutenont in his place, and Cadet Ramsay to be the ensigne. These are the first who has their pretentions by their comisions date. The King, when he gaive me the comand of the regiment, told me he would leave the naming of officers to my selfe, and that I must be answerable for them. Now if *carte blanch* be left to some as formerly to make and unmake at their pleasure, I canot be answerable. I never in my life tooke mony on that acount, nor never shall. Your Lo⁵p is pleasd to sho me the King has trust and confidence in me. May I not outlive that day in which I deceive him. Pardon all this trouble, for I am ever in all sincerity, My Lord, Your most faithfull and most oblidged servant,

R. Maitland.

I have procurd a lettr from the Councill to the Lords Jusices of Ireland for lecence to bring 1000 boles meale and as muth malt for the uce of this garisone. If your Lo⁵p will give me a line to my Lord Galloway it would doe

---

[1] *The Scots Peerage*, vol. v. pp. 534-538 ; *Carstares State Papers and Letters*, pp. 361, 362, 431-437.

me greate service, for I am informd it will meete with opositione.

The lieut.-colonel in the letter may have been Lieut.-Colonel Forbes.[1]   In February 1698 the Scots Privy Council issued to the laird of M'Intosh letters of fire and sword against MacDonald of Keppoch.

After the peace, and before the 22nd of October 1697, the ships of the small Scots navy with their stores were laid up;[2] but the two next letters show that the arrears of pay to the seamen troubled the authorities.   On 5th August 1698 these arrears engaged the attention of Parliament, and on the 30th of the same month a poll-tax was imposed to provide a fund to clear off these arrears.[3]   So late as 7th January 1701,[4] Captain Boswell of the *Royal Mary,* and the seamen who served under Captain Burd in the *Royal William,* petitioned Parliament for payment of their arrears of pay.

MY LORD ADVOCAT AND BAILLIE CLERKS LETTER
[TO THE LORD CHANCELLOR] ANENT THE ADMIRALITY
AND THE MEDITERRANIAN PASSES.

21 *May* 1698.

MAY IT PLEASE YOUR Lo,—Baillie George Clerk and I, the only commissioners of the Admirality at present in this town, with Hugh Cuningham our clerk, have thought fitt to send to your Lo. the account of the moneys appointed by the Parliament for the use of the Admirality, as it was stated by your Lo. and the other commissioners, and whereof the principall subscribed by the commissioners is in the clerks hand.   Your Lo. may remember that this account, as the foot of it bears, was stated and recomended to your Lo. to be laid before his Matie, that his pleasure may be known therein, for payment of the sum of neir six thousand pounds starling yet resting to the captains and their men, as the accompt bears, and likewayes for direction what shall be done with the shipes, and how

---

[1] *Historical MSS. Commission, Fourteenth Report,* App., Part III., *Marchmont MSS.,* p. 146.

[2] *The Marchmont Papers,* vol. iii. pp. 141, 142.

[3] See also *Carstares State Papers and Letters,* pp. 425 and 430.

[4] *The Acts of the Parliaments of Scotland,* vol. x., App., p. 72.

they shall be preserved and imployed now in the tyme of peace. I need not putt your Lo. in mind how the Admirality ordered their equipage to be laid up at Brunt-isleand, and where the vessalls themselves should be keept, nor what were our considerations upon the whole matter. Your Lo. was at too much pains and trouble in this whole busines to need any remembrancer. But, my Lord, the shipes are now lying idle, and the equipage and stores are in hazard to perish or be imbazled, and both need some money for their preservation. The merchants also, specially the Glasgow men, would be content that the shipes were in case to cruise, were it but for decencie and to ffright away pirratts and robbers, which may take shipes when they please out of our very rodes and harbours. But the priñpll point desired is, that there may be ane instruction to the Parliament in order to this whole busines, and that the Admirality may have some ffond to pay bygane just debts owing to severall very indigent men and families, and to bear its necessary expences. Wee need not suggest to yor Lo. at this distance how these ffonds may be had, but I shall name two that shall not add a sixpence to the kingdomes charge. The one is the sixtein pence per tun on fforraign shipes, and the ffourpence per tun on our owne shipes, which hath hitherto been given to Mr. Slezer and Mr. Adair,[1] for uses in my opinion very little necessary, and whereof the kingdom hath not to this moment had the lest profite. But let the men be payed for what they have already done, and their work for hereafter discharged. And here there may be a very good and naturall ffond which will noe more be complained of. The second ffond is the imposition of six pence per pint on retailed brandie. This imposition as now laid upon retailers doth not bring to the King two hundereth pound starling, but fills the countrey with swearing and foreswearing, that at this day it is ane universall and great greivance ; whereas if it shall only be transported from the retailers to the importers, and

---

[1] *The Acts of the Parliaments of Scotland*, vol. ix. pp. 491, 492.

there laid on a much smaller deuty, halfe by way of custom
and halfe by way of excise, it will render a considerable
summ, and severall merchants declare to me that they
will not complain. My Lord, if these two ffonds be
rightly setled, and given to the mannagement of the Admirality, they will not only pay the arrears with our
necessary expences, but keep our shipes in case and
service, and it may be make our Admiralitie grow to
some better purpose. But having proposed these things
to your Lo., we shall only wish they may be considered,
and that your Lo. in these and all other his Maties or yr
own concerns may have all prosperity.—Wee are, My
Lord, Yʳ Lopˢ most humble and most obedient servitʳˢ

JA. STEUART.
GEO. CLARK.

MY LORD,—There is also herewith sent a memorial
about Mediterranean passes which I hope yʳ Lop. will
mind as much as possible. You knou hou much it is
desired by the merchtˢ, and yʳ Lo. also knoues the difficulties, so that I need add no more about it.

JA. STEUART.
GEO. CLARK.

On 1st September 1698 Parliament assigned certain tunnage
dues to maintain the Scots navy under burden of a salary £100 to
Sir Archibald Sinclair, 'Judge of Admirality,' and of payments
ordered in 1695 to Mr. John Adair, geographer, and Mr. John
Slezer, etc.

In *State Papers (Scotland) Warrant Books*, vol. xv., and at p. 225,
is given a copy of a Mediterranean pass to Thomas Gordon,
captain of the ship *Margaret of Aberdeen*, dated 8th February
1693.

MY LORD ADVOCATS LRE ANENT PEPERS AND ACCOUNTS OF
THE ADMIRALITY AND MR. BERNARD M'INZIE, was perhaps
addressed to the Earl of Tullibardine, Joint Secretary of
State for Scotland.

Edr., 21 *Maii* 1698.

MY LORD,—You have hereuith inclosed a double of our
Admirality account sent by B. Geo. Clerk and me to my

L. Chancell^r, for the end mentioned by us in our letter to his Lo. signed by us and our clerk, which we have left oppen to be perused and delivered by y^r Lo. We have also sent a double of the memorial formerly given to y^r Lo. and your collegue about passes for the Mediterranean, that my L. Chancell^r with y^r Lo. may obtain the desire thereof.   Its like some may apprehend that this is offered with a parlār vieu to the ships to be sent auay by the Affrican companie, but tho it wer it wer but just ; and nixt my L. Chancel^r and y^r Lo. knoues we ar only prose-quuting a motion that hath long depended, and is both just and nicessaire for all our merch^{ts} trading to the Mediterranean, whether for anything I knov the Affrican ships ar not bound, and therefor y^r Lo^s assistance in both these maters is verie earnestly intreated. I have nothing farder this post, but must regret to y^r Lo. the pension granted to a Mr. Bernard M'Keinzie, a light headed restless man. The Parliat. and Councel removed him from a meeting house he set up at Tranent. He hath since set up another at Kelso, where there is a placed minister, and where he officiats by himself and his viccaires to the vexation of all the well affected in the bounds ; and just nou there hath fallen out a rabling at the kirk of Neutyle in Angus, and the favourers of the rable have the confidence to desire me that Bernard M'Keinzie may be there placed albeit a man not assumed, and that ounes not the present church· constitution, and that I would moderat the moderator of that prisbytrie—(so they write in jock) ; but I hope the Counsel uill help these things, and that y^r Lo. uill also considder this insolence.—I am, My L., Y^r L. M. H. and O. S.   [JA. STEUART.]

MY LORD FFORFARS LRE

MY LORD,—Your good intentions for me in procuring an order from the Lords of the Tresurry, allowing me a preferrence, being frustrated by Jereswood, who I think is willing to pay no body, and tho I have had the same order of preferrence renewed yit have never touch't a farthing, and am told ther's none of that fond left undisposed of, which puts me under an indispensable nessessity of beseeching your Lo. to represent me favorably to the King, and let his Majesty kno that I hope I may expect so much favour as to have my pention out of the Post Office, or a locality out of the Bishops rents. That part which lyes most convenient for me is the regality and baronrie of Glasgow. I have sent up a list of a small part which is payed by my vassalls, and would make the payment easy ; so my Lord, if you 'l have the gooudnes to put the King in mind of me, and my hard circumstancess, I kno his Maͭie is too just to see me a sufferer for my early zeall to his interrest ; and if your Lo. will consider the narowness of my fortune, with the great disappointments and hardships I have met with, you 'l neither have reason to think it strange, nor I to be asham'd, when I tell you that I must be forc't to seek for shellter out of my oune country, if something of this kind that I have mention'd be not soon expediat in my favours. And as I ever have serv'd the King to my powr in my little station, so I shall ever contineu as long as my affairs will permit my stay in the kingdome. I shall end this in assuring your Lo. that nothing but meer nessessity could force me either to importune the King, or give your Lo. so much trouble, but I hope you 'l put the most favourable construction upon it as coming from, My Lord, Your Lo. ffaithffull and most humble servant,   FORFAR.

Abey, May 21, 1698.
Archibald Douglas, first Earl of Forfar, supported the revolution. He died in 1712. With the death of his son, in 1715, from wounds received while fighting on the Hanoverian side at Sheriffmuir, the peerage became extinct.

For THE EARL OF FINDLATER

Whitehall, 4th June 1698.

MY LORD,—I have receaved your Lops. in favours of fforglane. I want not aboundance of inclination to doe for him, bot at present his Maͭie will not fill any of the vacant places aither in the governement or session, and ther are above eight or ten pretendars to this vacancie of

the session. If the Parliat wer over I shall let his pretensions and what is to be sayed for him be knouen. I
ame hopefull to have the occasion of seing your Lope
verie shortly, and then yow shall knouc hou this matter
stands. I knoue not if the Parliat will sit preceisly at
the tuelt of Jully, bot if it doe your Lope and my wiffe
shall both be acquanted timeously ; and if Burdsbank be
inclyned to make any bargaine with me, I wish that he
would condescend to come to Edinburgh, ffor I being sole
Secretarie, and haveing so great concerne in the publict
affairs, I ame affraid that I shall not gett to the north
at this time. Houever if I can be use-full to my freinds,
I will come if it wer for never so short a time after the
Parliat. Your Lope will be pleased to send the tuo
inclosed to Sir James Abercrombie of Birkenbog and
Bracco, for if my countriemen will be assisting upon this
occasion I hope to be capable to doe them service, and ther
will nothing be proposed bot what our oun preservation
does absolutely require. I will forbear giveing you any
furder trouble at present.—I ame, My Lord, Your Lops.
most obedient sone and most humble servant,

JA. OGILVIE.

Two years later, in August 1700, Mr. James Steuart, Lord
Advocate, writing to Carstares about the vacancy in the Session at
that time, remarked, ' My Lord Seafield is for all of them [the
aspirants] till the Parliament sits, and then for his cousin Forglan
when its over.' Forglan was not appointed a Lord of Session
until 25th March 1706.

For THE RIGHT HONOURABLE THE EARLE OF
FINDLATER AT CULLEN HOUSE IN BANFFSHYRE

Whitehall, 7th June i698.

MY LORD,—It is my deuty to wreat to your Lope at
all times, bot I ame affraid to be troublesome to your Lope,
especially when they are hardly wourth the postage. We
are detained here long beyond expecta°ne by the Earle
of Portlands stayeing so long at Paris, ffor both the
Chancellour and Secretarie doe inclyne to sie him befor
they pairt from this. I hear he is to pairt from Paris

this day, and is expected in the end of this week. I
beleive the Parliāt may adjurne yet for eight dayes or so.
Your Lope and my Lady will be timeously advertised.
Blissed be God, my Lord keeps his health verie well, and
hes his maister's favour. He hes bein with the King today, who hes told him that he most be President of the
Parliament. Your Lope knoues this is aboundance of
honour to be sole Secretarie and President of the Parliat
at once, bot that it is no less burdine; tho I trust in God
he will discharge the trust with credit to himselfe and all
his relations, and to the satisfaction of his maister, and I
doubt not he will be acceptable to the nation. Your
Lope will be added to the Councill agt. yow come up. I
knoue not whither your pension will be then lykewayes
obtained or not, bot your being once a member of the
Councill intitles yow fairly to it, and it can not miss when
it pleases God we returne. All this is to your Lopes selfe,
if yow please, and to my Lady, ffor it is not knouen here;
and the Secretarie will acquant your Lope of it himselfe,
als soone as it is done. I most beg your Lopes pardon
to desire that you will be pleased to acquant my Lady,
that the Secretarie will not allowe me to buy the lyneing
for hir bed for reasons that he will satisfie hir Lape at
meeting. All hir other commissions for other people are
obayed, and that hir oun is not lykewayes obtempered is
not my fault. I wish your Lope and famely all prosperety
and happieness, and ame with all imaginable respect, My
Lord, Your Lops. most faithfull most obedient and humble
srt.,   JA. BAIRD.

The Dutches of Lauderdale haveing lived to a good old
age dyed on Sunday morning last at Ham House, befor it
was knouen here that she was sick. She hes bein long
infirm.

On the 24th June 1698 Sir James Ogilvie was created Viscount
Seafield.[1]

The following instructions to the Earl of Marchmont, Commis-

---

[1] *State Papers (Scotland) Warrant Books*, vol. xvii. p. 14, and *The Acts of the
Parliaments of Scotland*, vol. x. pp. 119 and 120.

sioner to the Parliament, which sat from 19th July to 1st September 1698, vary considerably from those given in the *Marchmont Papers* at pp. 160 to 164.

ADDITIONALL INSTRUCTIONS TO PATRICK, EARLE OF MARCHMONT, Comissioner for holding the Seventh Session of Parli͞at.

1. You are to pass such acts as shall be proposed in favours of the Presbiterian church government, which shall not be inconsistant with or prejudiciall to our prerogative, or the protection granted to Episcopall ministers.

2. If any of the Episcopall ministers who are at p͞ntt in there churches shall apply to the Parliament, you are allowed to pass ane act admitting them to qualifie themselves according to law, and to give them our protection.

3. If the Parliament shall give ane excyse upon all malt as an ffund, wee impower you to pass ane act discharging the three pennies upon the pint of ale, and dureing the continuance of the excyse upon malt, provyding the excyse on malt be not less then two merks on the boll,

4. If the Parliament shall think fitt to provyde for the disbanded officers untill they be payed of there arrears or otherwayes provyded for, you are to give our assent yrto, the standing forces being first supplyed.

5. You are to endeavour after the supplies for the fforces are setled to obtain ane act continuing the imposition of tunage upon ships, or to procure some other ffund for the mantaining or imploying the ffrigotts.

6. You are allowed to pass ane act allowing of a copper coynage in such termes as the Parliament shall think fitt, provyding that the benefite arising y^rfrom be left to our disposall.

7. If the Parliament shall reakon upon what is resting by the Lord Belhaven and his partners tacksmen of the inland excyse or any part yrof as an effectuall sum, in that case you are to allow the Parliat to cognosce and determine upon the grounds q^rupon they crave ane abatement.

8. You are allowed to pass ane act dispensing with

the calling out of the militia, for so long time as the Parliament shall give ffunds for mantaining the standing fforces, conforme to the present establishment except in the case of necessity, such as defending against fforreign invasions or suppressing intestine insurrections.

9. You may consent to ane act for facilitating the entries of wassalls by subaltern superiors.

10. Where the publick good of any of our burghs or seaport towns is heavily burdened with debts, or where y^r publick works require it, you are to consent to acts for such moderate excises or other impositions with themselves as shall be found necessary.

11. You are to pass ane act, after the ffunds for mantaining our fforces and other publick exigencies are given, for encouraging Mr. Adair, Captain Slezer, and Mr. Cuningham, and giveing them allowances for carrying on there serall works for the good of the publick.

12. One occasions of difficulty you are to consult with the officers of state or others of interest in the government or Parliament, or so many of them as you shall by there behaviour in Parliament judge firmly zealous for our interest.

13. If the Parliament cannot be brought to give the supplys but by passing acts contrair to yor instructions, you are in that case if no other expedient will serve, to adjourn to such a time as that you may consult us, and have our answire rather than pass such acts.

14. You are impowered to continue this session of Parliament from the time of its meetting for weeks.

You are to pass such acts as shall be proposed for incourageing of the manufacture of inland salt.

The letters of Seafield the President, and others to Carstares, printed in *State Papers and Letters*, pp. 384 to 430, the Commissioner's letters to the King, given in the *Marchmont Papers*, pp. 157-171, etc., give an account of the proceedings of Parliament, which is supplemented by the following letter to the Duke of Portland in the handwriting of James Baird. Mainly through the diplomatic management of Seafield the requisite subsidies were obtained, and the difficult questions arising out of the African company and Darien were for the time smoothed over.

Double of ane letter sent to the E. of Portl.

From LORD SEAFIELD

Edinburgh, 20*th August* 1698.

MY LORD,—I have presumed from time to time to give your Lo͠pe ane account of the way and maner of manadging his Mat͠ies affairs here ; and altho I have not hade the honour to receave his Mat͠ies commands from your Lo͠pe, yet it is a great satisfaction to me that I knowe by the other letters I have receaved, that all mine have come saife to your Lops. hands. I ame verie hopefull that matters are so ordored here that for tuo years after November his Mat͠ie will not neid to hold a Parliament, ffor the ffounds for full pay to the standing fforces are certaine for that time, and the ffounds of the civil list are lyke-wayes full ; and if his Mat͠ie doe shew his displeasur against such as have openly and undecently opposed him at this time, and give some countinance and encourage-ment to those that served him faithfully, ther will be no difficultie in getting the ffounds continoued for a longer time. I shall putt no valoue upon the service that hes bein done his Mat͠ie at present, ffor it is my deutie to doe for him what ever is in my pouer ; bot I doe beleive that my enemies most acknouleadge that we have bein success-full beyond expectation. I shall not resume what I sayed formerly the arguments that were used against us ; bot this I hope his Mat͠ie will be convinced of that we hade verie great difficultie, becaus we wer under the necessety not only of proposeing and resolveing bot of concluding what concerned his service the verie first week. The opposers did not expect that it was possible for us to doe so, and therfor they hade not in readieness the proposalls which afterwards they made ; bot we were then capable to bring them to ane good ishew. Since the granting of the founds nothing considderable hes occurred, bot what concerns the Affrican companie, of which your Lo͠pe hes a full account by the flyeing packatt. We are doeing what we can to obtaine a subsidie for arrears of the armie, bot the circumstances of the countrey renders this veric difficult, and we have not as yet thought of the ffound. Some propose the pole, and others speak of ane imposition upon peper, both which are new and uncertain founds. We are now endeavoring to bring the session to a cloase, and als soone as it is over I shall returne to London. The only newes we have here at present is that the Earle of Arran[1] is made Duke of Hamiltoun. Our opposite partie is not a litle raised by it. They say he and his freinds will nou have the manadgement. His Matie may doe in this what he pleases, bot whillest I ame imployed I shall endeavor to serve faithfullie. It is lykewayes sayed that he is to come doune to Scotland to consert measurs with his freinds, and is to returne to London about the time that his Matie comes over, that he may offer a skame of his Maties affairs. I can say this that his Maties servants have served him faithfully and effectually, and that he neids to make no alteration, for in the intervale betuixt this and the nixt session of Parliat ther remains nothing bot to manadge what is given, which can be done without any difficultie ; and his Matie hes no reason to doubt bot that, when his service requires it, we shall be able to obtaine the continuance of the subsidies or any other thing that can reasonablie be proposed, als well as any others can doe. I have presumed to wreat this only to your Lope and to non other, because you have alwayes bein pleased to countinance me in the station I nou enjoy. I doe think it for his Maties service that the vacant places be all settled at on time, and therby his Matie may have a full veue hou and in what maner he may expect to be served. I have wreatten to Mr. Carstairs fully concerning my Lord Stair. He will give your Lope full information of that matter. I beg pardon for this trouble, and I ame with all sincerity, My Lord, Your Lops most faithfull and most humble sert.

---

[1] *Carstares State Papers and Letters*, pp. 426, 430, 441.

Competition for place and position was keen, when aspirants were waiting to fill the shoes of men who were not yet dead.

For THE EARL OF FINDLATER

MY LORD,—I shal be extreamly gl[ad to hear of] your Los. weelbeing. I [shall be pleased if you] will mind my Lord Seafeild to gett that commission of Admiralitie subscrived, that it may come north with your Lo. I hope you wil also recomend to him the thing you know of. I shal be glad to hear if the person be recovering, or what circumstances he is in ; and if that fail, my Lord Seafeild may think on some other, because ther is none can know vacancies, or what may be done for a freind better then your son. I shal be glad to have the honor of a lyne from your Los. hands, to know how ye keep yor health, and leaving off further trouble, I am in all dutie, My Lord, Your Los. obedient son and most hull sert.,

GEO. ALLARDES.

Allardes, Agust 30, 98.

For THE EARL OF FINDLATER

MY LORD,—All the last week I wes attending your son the Viscount of Seafeild on his journey to London, and parted with him and his Lady and son and all the company in verie good health at Anvick upon Fryday last at twelwe aclock. I have heard that they wer well at Durham on Sabboth last, wher they dyned with the Bishop. James Baird hade a lyne from John Philp this day showeing that they wer all well at Northalartoun, but that Mr. Hay being indisposed wes left at Durham. I wish your Lop. heartilie well, and will not neglect to foreward your newes weeklie, which is the duty of, My Lord, Your Lops. most humble and most obedient servant,

J. ANDERSON.

Edr., 22 *Septer.* 1698.

In a letter to Carstares of 20th September 1698, a correspondent, who is unnamed, states that Mr. Baird was much disappointed that he was not made Keeper of the Signet, and that Seafield was not well pleased with him.

To THE EARL OF FINDLATER

MY LORD,—I cam hir on Thousday at six aclok at night. I was extremly wiered and continous so; but your granchyld keept out very weall, and is not the wores of his jurany in the lest. I shall be glad to hir of your Lo[s] saff ariffell at Cullan, for I havie not had any leater from you sinis parting. I hop your Lo. will wret frequantly, and let me have en acompt hou maters goes with you. I intret you may be carfull of your seleff; for I ashour you ther is non wishes your Lo. mor happnes and confort, or will be mor willing to contribut therto then hir who is to dath, My Lord, Your most affectionat daghter and humbell servant, ANNA SEAFIELD.

Whitehall, Sip 28, 1698.

Next letter continues the story of the settlement of Presbytery in Banffshire.

To THE RYT HON[BLE] THE EARLE OF FINDLATER
these

MY LORD,—We with all gratitude resent your Lops. constant inclinations to concurre with our Presbytrie in planting Rathven[1] now long desolate; and we are resolved whenever occasion is offered to us to make a representation of your Lops. favour and countenance to us to the several judicatories of this church. My Lord, we find the parochin of Rathven averse to receave Mr. Mortimer to be their minister, and if we can prevent it we are loath to doe what we cannot bot apprehend will be grievous both to minister and people; and therefore we have resolved to take advice of our brethren in the other presbytries of this synod, and if need be of some brethren in the south, how to proceed in this matter, before we can come to a final determination. We judge our selves bound to pay your Lop. the more deference and honour in our pro-cedure in that matter, that the gentlmen of Rathven so litle regard your Lops. advice. My Lord, we have writen a lyne to the Shireff depute of Banff, begging he will put

---

[1] Dr. Cramond's *Church and Churchyard of Rathven*, pp. 30-50.

the lawes in execution against some outed ministers for their scandalous irregularities, and particularly Mr. Arthur Strachan, late at Mortlech. If your Lop. would recommend to Castelfield to doe us justice in that matter, as it would be an acceptable service to the countrey, and might prevent sad inconveniencies which may otherwise befall families perhaps of eminent note in the nation, so it would be a new obligation upon, My Lord, Your Lops. most faithfull servants in Christ subscribing by

MR. PAT INNES, Modr. pro t̄re.

Turreff, Novr. 16, 1698.

The kirk-session records dealing with the extrusion of Mr. Arthur Strachan, incumbent in Mortlach, by the Privy Council on 7th November 1689, mentions amongst his other offences ' his conversing with rebels and pressing some of the parishioners to go into rebellion under James, Lord Dunfermline.' The Rev. Hugh Innes was ordained Presbyterian minister of Mortlach in September 1698, but as late as 1708 Mr. Strachan attempted to intrude.

Next letter from Viscount Seafield should be read along with the Earl of Argyll's letter to Carstares on 27th September 1698.

COPPY OF ANE LETTER SENT TO THE E. OF PORTLAND ANENT COLLONEL HAMILTONS REGT, ETC.

Whitehal, Septr. 30, 1698.

MY LORD,—I have dispatched for Scotland his Majesties letter to the Councel ordering subsistance to Collonel Hamiltons regement. I have sent to Mr. Pringle a skeam for altering and reforming the former establishment, that your Lo. may consider it, and therafter his Majestic may choise what is most for his service, either to reform the other regements or break Collonel Hamiltons. I belive Coll. Fergusons would have been more acceptable to the countrey. Houever I shal make the best of it in so far as I· have interest. I belive when your Lo. returns Mr. Carstairs will communicat to you what wee propose to be done, bot it is with al submission. I am veric glaid to find our proceedings in Parliamen so much noticed and aplauded by the servants and wealwishers of his Majesties goverment hier, and even Duke Hamilton and the Earle Orkney object nothing, and I think his Majestic was neaver so much master of his affairs in Scotland as he is at present. Ther is also great unanimitie amongst almost al his Majesties servants, and I pairted with them and almost with al the members of Parlament in good terms. Its my hearts satisfaction that I have been capable at this time to signifie something to my master. I long for his happy return to us, and I shal ever be sensible that it is my diutie to be, My Lord, Your Lo. . . .

ffor THE RIGHT HOLL THE EARLE OFF FFINLATER
thes

Kincorth, the 4t off October 1698.

MY LORD,—. . . I vould vishe ȳr Lo. vᵗ the first convenianse vreit seriuslie to ȳr son and to his La. to keepe him in mynde that the vaccansie in the sessione bee filled vpe bee fforgland. Yȓ hes been graitt expectatione he shuld bee the man, and sertanlie vho ever bee the pretenders ffor it, it is much ȳr sons consernment in creideit and interest he bee prefered ; q̄rffor I doubt not bot ȳr Lo. vill be everie exprese in this, and lay it on ȳr son as ȳr Lop and all his ffreinds desayr. So visheing ȳr Lo. and all ȳrs much happines, I still am, Yr Loˢ affectionat and huimble servant,   WIL DUNBAR.

Let mee heare from ȳr Lo. bee this bearrer or vᵗ ȳr first convenianse.

From Viscount Seafield's eldest son James to his grandfather the Earl of Findlater :—

Whithall, Novr. 5/ 1698.

MY LORD,—I received yoʳˢ, and I am extreamly glad to find yoʳ Lordᵖ is in good health. I thank you for yoʳ good ·advice, and I shall endeavour to make a good use of it. Altho I have the pleasant enjoyment of my parents conversation, and London affording variety of devertisments, yet I am not perfectly happy in yoʳ absence. I beg yoʳ

Lord^p sometimes to favour me with a line, wch will be a great confort to, My Lord, Yo^r Lord^{ps} affectionat grand-child,   JA. OGILVIE.

1698 was one of King William's bad years in Scotland. The letters of 9th and 15th November and 6th December all refer to the shortage of the crop that year.

For THE RIGHT HONO<del>LL</del> THE EARLE OF FINDLATER

Edinburgh, 9th Nover 1698.

MY LORD,—I came to this place upon Mundayes night, and did carefully send off your Lops. letters to my Lord Seafeild, and all the other letters I hade for him. Ther are severall letters from him or those about him in your Lops. pacquet, tho ther be non from him to your Lops. selfe. Your Lope. will sie by the inclosed list what persones are putt off the Councill, and who are ther successors. This showes my Lords pouer heir, and it will convince those with you that he hes influence with his maister. The Councill satt yisterday, and they did litle, only they have discharged exporta^{o}ne of wictuall fourth of this kingdome, and have allowed importatione; bot all other nations have discharged export als well as this. My faither and mother in law gives your Lope. ther most humble deutie, as doeth my wiffe, who admitted yor Lopes. excuise sent with me, and made me welcome. I ame in all deuty, My Lord, Your Lops. most faithfull and most humble servant,   JA. BAIRD.

The two next letters seem to refer to a marriage between Lady Marie Ogilvie and a son of Burdsbank.

ffor THE EARLE OFF FFINDLATER thes

MY LORD,—I had the honour of yours by Durn, and beggs your pardon for this second trouble, and considering some interweening accidentall contingencies connected, I wes exspecting no less from your Lop. then q̃t wes written. As I hawe heard so I am wery sensible of your faworable expressions as to me, and may say your Lop. hes no wther reason from any in q$\overline{m}$ I am concerned. And as to that profligat sone of myn (so termed by your

Lop.) as haweing dishonoured your familie, I nor any of my[n] wer not in the knowled[ge to say nay] to any such thing, and had I been spoke to or consult[ed someq]t, mil[dnes] might hawe terminat [the mat]ter for it wes needles . . . to wrestle against ane run[nin]g stream. Youthead for the [most p]airt is attended wt folye, bot [fr]eindly and forseeing men, untill weill grounded, will not allways giwe faith to wulgar reports, and will try befor they trust. As to qt your Lo^p wreits anent my interest, I sall be spairing on that by wreit, and resolwes to perform my promise both to your Lo^p. and to your sone the Wiscount off Seafeild, and q$\tilde{r}$ewer my lott sall fall and in all places qll aliwe, I sall still be to all your familye, and particularly to your Lo^p. as becometh, My Lord, Your Los. wery faithfull and most humble serwant,

GEO. LESLYE.

Burdsbank. Nov: 12 : —-98:

For THE EARL OF FINDLATER

MY LORD,—I was wery glad this day when I had your leter, but am sory that you shoud have so mortifieng a sight in the church as Burgbanks famaly. I am shour the seeing of them will be mor unesy nou, when your daghter is in shuch a famaly. I think she is as un[ha]ppy being maried to so debas [a m]an as in hir formar misfortun, save the ofens it gave to almighty God. I dou not love to wret much on this subgek, sins the thoghts of it will be unplesant to your Lo. It is most lementabell the condison of the north of Scotland as your Lo. gives acompt of it. Lord almighty help it and send relieff to the pour. My husband sayes he hath not geten a full accompt of what conserens Kampcarens affears, but will most willingly joyn with Grant and Boyn for his asistans, and if ther war clirnes wold go a gret lenth for the famaly. . . .—My Lord, Your most obedent daghter and humbell serv[an]t, ANNA SEA[FIEL]D.

Whitehall, Nov: 18, 1698.

Parliament on 30th August 1698 imposed a poll-tax to defray the arrears of pay due to the Scots army and navy. Sir William

Dunbar of Durn, who refers in next letter to the effect of that tax on himself and his family, had on 29th January that year been made a baronet, no doubt through the influence of his son-in-law.

ffor THE RIGHT HoLL THE EARLE OFF FFINLATER

thes to be comunicatt to the vither commissionars att Cullen

Durn, the 29t *off N͞ovr* 1698.

MY LORD,—Upon ȳr ffirst day apointed ffor all pollabill persons to compeere and give vp themselves to ȳr Lo. and the vither commissionars, I vas in Murray in the parischin off Dyk, q̃r I heave som interest according to my valuatione in that shyre and parishes ; and I compeered beeffoir the commissionars, and ȳr gave vpe myself ffor my interest in this shyre off Bamff and Murray in the highest capacitie anie gentįllman is pollabille, ffor an thousand p͞nds waluatione for Murray and Bamff shyres, so that I heave givein ȳr Lo. this accompt nou att ȳr second dyet, and desayres ȳr Lo. may cauis so to record it, that I may not bee rekned as thes ȳt neglects to give obedianse to the act off Parliment ; and as ffor my son James, he is so unveill off an boyll yt he is not cable to ryde or go the lenth off Cullen ffor attending ȳr meetting, tho he ver pollabille conforme to the act of Parliment as he is not ; ffor he is in no valuatione off rent, bot my self in all wee heave, and ffor an stok off ffree munnie he hes none, and onlie hes som moveabills vpon an possessione q̃ik I heave sett him, q̃rin he is not layable ffor poill ; and my son William is *in familia*, and hes no stok as yit, not heaving goit his patrimonie as yit ffrom mee. This I thought ffit to acquant ȳr Lo. and the vither commistionars off ffor ȳr infformatione and my excuise, and is all att present ffrom Ȳr Lo꜀ affectionat ffreind and servant,

WIL. DUNBAR.

For THE EARL OF FINDLATER

MY LORD,—Though my Lady hes writt to yoʳ Loᵖ this night, I hope yoʳ Lop. will pardon me to acquaint you that his Maẗy is arrived in England this day about ten acloack at Saint Margarets. He lyes at Canterburrie, and will be tomorrow's night at Kensingtone. Y^r are 60 miles betwixt this and Margarets. His presence is much wanted here, for the Parliat sitts downe on Tuesday next, and he hes very litle time to prepare things for it and secure his friends; for this is a new Parliat, and have not sitten to doe any busines as yet, but have adjourned three seᷓall times, which is as often as they can doe by law, untill they meett. The Speaker is not as yet choisen, which will be the first thing that will be done after the Kings speech. Much depends upon him, and they are endeavouring to secure one whom they find most for the Kings interest. There came no more news by the express from the King on his arrivall; but when any thing occurrs worth yor Lo^{ps} noticeing, I hope your Lo^p will allow me to acquaint you of it. I pray yor Lo^p all imaginable prosperity and happines, which you shall constantly have of, My Lord, Your Lo^{ps} most dutifull and obedt servant,

Jo. Philp.

Whitehall, 3 Decr. 1698.

The English Parliament met on 6th December, and chose Sir Thomas Littleton, who was in the King's interest, Speaker. Parliament, however, steadily refused to support the size of standing army asked by William.

ffor THE RIGHT H$\overline{\text{oll}}$ THE EARLE OFF FFINLATER
thes

Durn, the 9t off Debr. 1698.

My Lord,—Ther is an blobe grouing vpon the chyld Betties [1] eye qᷤk affrights my vyff verie much. The chyld does not compleane off anie pain bee it, bot it is grouing ffarder in vpon her eye ; ỹrffor thes serve again to acquant ỹr Lo. that you may send and see it, and also to send an horse ffor Mr. Smith att ffocobus,[2] ỹt he may give his opinion off it, qᷤk is all in heast ffrom Yr Lo^s affectionat and humble servant,   Wil Dunbar.

My vyff is restlese and much trubled; ỹrffor feall not in heast to send ffor Mr. Smith, and on heir to see it.

---

[1] Lady Elizabeth Ogilvie, afterwards Countess of Lauderdale.
[2] Fochabers.

For THE EARL OF FINDLATER

MY LORD,— . . . In caice yor Lo^{ps} letters be miscarried yor Lo^p may cause change the Banff post, and setle a carefull and diligent man, who may take care of yor Lo^{ps} letters, for I am sure they come safe enough to Abdⁿ, and the fault lyes only in the Banff post. I wrott to yor Lo^p formerly of the Kings arrivall, and the number of fforces to be keept up here and in Ireland, and since that y^r hes nothing fallen out off any news, but that my Lord Eglintone is married on a woman about 84 years of age. She hes 500 lib. st. of joynture. They are gone to the countrey to live. Her last husbands name was Kea ane English squeir. I wrott also to yor Lo^p of the death of Mrs. Craik, which very much troubled both yor sone and daūr and all the ffamily. They were att considerabl charges on her, both when she lay sick and when she was burried. I beg yor Lo^{ps} pardon for this long letter, and I ask libertie to subscrive my self in all dutie, My Lord, Your Lo^{ps} most humble most dutifull and obedient serv^t,   JOHN PHILP.

Whitehall, 22*d Decembr*. 1698.

Yo^r Lo^p hes a very good agent of my Lady for what you recommend to my Lord. I beleeve something will be done for yor Lo^p. I pray yor Lo^p a happie and good new year.

Lord Eglintoun married on 8th December 1698, as his third wife, Catherine Lady Kaye, daughter of Sir William St. Quintin of Harpham, Yorkshire. He was her fourth husband. She died on 6th August 1700.

For THE EARL OF FINDLATER

Whitehall, 27*th Decem^r* 1698.

MY LORD,—I have so much to doe, being obldiged to constant attendance, that I cannot writt so often as were necessary ; and I should not had time to have written this night had not his Ma͠tie gone to Windsor, where he is to be all this week. As yet his Ma͠tie hes had time to doe nothing save only to receave ane accott. of our pro-

ceedings in Parliat, with which he is very well satisfied.
I am in hopes by the copie of the letter yor Lo^p hes sent
me that Brecco will act as my ffriend in my absence, and
if he doe I am sure he will find his accompt in it.   I am
very desireous to have his sister's debt which doth affect
the lands off Burdsbank, which with what is owing to
myself and what is assigned me by Durne and deducing
the few dewties will arise to the true value.   But however,
if Burdsbank deal with me and dispone in corroberatione,
I would give him what pryce can reasonably be demanded.
If Brecco leave these debts in my hands, he needs be no
loser as to his security of Downe, for he may retain as
much of the pryce of Downe in his own hands, and secure
it lyable to his own warrandice.   As for Kempcairne I
shall be very ready to serve him by advanceing that money
that is desyred, but I would gladly know how it is to be
disposed off, and what security I am to have for it.   I
perceave he hes been injured by Tanachie ; [1] but if
Tanachie should be brought to take what is justly owing
him, I would gladly know if Kempcairne could preserve
his estates ; and I assure yor Lo^p nothing could perswade
me to engage in it, if it were not to doe them service.
As for the lands of Hallyairds, they ly contiguous to ffordyce, and I would be very well satisfied to have them, but
I leave it to yor Lo^p and my ffriends to make a finall
aggreement for it without giving me any further trouble.
I desyre that William Lorimer would give me accompt of
the condition of my lands and the cropt, how it proves,
and what he thinks may be payed, and whether it shall be
sold at home or att Edinburgh, and what can be gott for
it at home when sold in parcells.   Yo^r Lo^p may let Will.
Thomsone know that I have bought some seeds and
trees, which I will send home with the first oportunitie.
I desyre that the dyck in the fflower garden may be built
in the spring, and that in the most secure way can be
contrived ; and I desyre allso that Will. Thomsone may
send me a plan of the whole garden orchyaird and litle

---

[1] Patrick Steuart.

park; and though yor Lo^p will not take so much time
perhaps as to writt on all occasiones, yet Castlefield or
Will. Lorimer may writte to me every week.   This is all
I have time to writt att present.—I am, My Lord, Your
Lops. most obedient sone and most humble servant,

SEAFIELD.

Burdsbank near Cullen House was next year acquired by Seafield, and Doune (Macduff) near Banff was about the same time
acquired by Braco.   In future letters further reference is made
to the laying out and furnishing with plants from England of the
gardens of Cullen House.

The following letter may afford a clue to the discovery of the
lost poll lists of Banffshire and of other shires of Scotland.

For THE RIGHT HONOURABLE THE EARLE FFIND-
LATER AT CULLEN HOUSE IN BANFFSHYRE   ffree

Edr., 29*th Der.* 1698.

MY LORD,—My faither in law hes spoake to the Lords
of the Thearie and Sr Thomas Moncreiffe, clerk of Excheqr,
anent the pole lists, and they will be favourable till they
can be conveniently sent, bot no time would be lost.
My Lord Seafeild tooke with him, and hes gotten remitted
to him since he went to London ij000 lib. sterling; and
the laird of Grant hes gotten 500 lib. sterling by his Lops.
ordore, and he is expecting draughts from London for
more money, so that he desired me to acquant your Lop.
that he could ansře no draughts from the north without
the Secretaries speciall order upon no account qtsoever.
Ther is no newes at present.   I hade a letter yisternight
from my Lord.   I beleive I shall have some thing shortly
of importance about our alterations of state.—I ame, My
Lord, Your Lopes. most faithfull and most humble servant,

JA. BAIRD.

For THE EARL OF FINDLATER

MY LORD,—I am glad to knou that your Lop. is in
good halth, and I render you maney thanks for sending
me my letter, but our Dumbarton busines is turned to

nought ; but I would not a thought, but he might a don me kyndnes at this tym. All that I shall say, I hop to make for a lyfe. I would heaue your Lop. wreat to my brother for to get sum other pleace to me, althou that is feled; for I do not care so much for the want of the pleace as for the talk of the country. It is much talkt of, sieing that he hath but uan brother, that he negleks me and prefers others, which I ashour your Lop. I would not do so to him, if it lay in my pour to serue him. I heaue sent your Lop. the exact duble of my brothers letter, so hoping that your Lop. woll mynd my brothe, I continou, My Lord, Your Lops. affectionat son and most humble seruant,

PAT. OGILVIE,

Carenbulge, Jan. 8, 1699.

My wife giues the offer of hir humble douty to your Lop. and so doth your granchyld. I pray your Lop. send my brothers letter to him woth the furst occasion that ye wreat to him, and when the ansuer coms bak I shall pay the bearer that coms to me woth it.

Patrick Ogilvie got place on 2nd December 1701.

For THE EARL OF FINDLATER

London, Janr. i7, i69⅞.

MY DEAR LORD,—I do return yow my most hearty thanks for yoʳ keynd letter in wishing me joy in my mariage. I thank God I find my self very happie by a most kynd wife, and am placed wᵗ her in one of the pleasantest places in England ; and in makeing of it I did every thing by the advice and consent of my dear and keynd nephew yoʳ sone. Therfore ye may conclud it is good. I entreate yoʳ Lop. will continue a corespondence with me, and lett me hear some times from you, for I do assure you non wishes you and yōrs more happieness then, My dear Lord, Yoʳ most affecᵗ brother and humble servant,

EGLINTOUN.

I pray give my most humble service to my nephew, my Lord Desford, and all the rest of yoʳ childeren.

For THE EARL OF FINDLATER

Edr., 27th Jary. 1699.

MY LORD,—We are everie minutt expecting a flyeing
pacquet with the account of the disposall of the vacant
places.   My Lord Seafeild was with the King upon Satturday last, and, as John Philp in his yisterdayes letter informes me, hes procured my Lord Carmichall to be his
conjunt.   My Lord Justice Clerk[1] is Thear deputt, and Sʳ
John Maxwell[2] is Justice Clerk.   I know not as yet who
supplies the Session vacancie.   My Lord hes gott 1000 lib.
ster. to himselfe for his good services, and hes brought
all this about, and I thank God is in exterordinary favour
and esteem with his maister.   I shall give your Lope. ane
furder account pr nixt; bot this in the mean time is thought
due from, My Lord, Your Lops. most faithfull, most
humble and most obedient servant,   JA. BAIRD.

This and the four next letters on the filling up of vacant places
in the Scots government may be compared with the letters in
Carstares State Papers and Letters, pp. 457 to 464.

For THE EARL OF FINDLATER

Whitehall, 3i *Jan.* 1699.

MY LORD,—The King has given a demonstratione of
gratitude this night to those who served him faithfully
the last session of Parliat., and bestowed places pensions
and honours on them, and that by my Lords moyon and
recommendaᵒne.   He saw there behoved to be a conjunct
Secretary, so he made choise off Lord Carmichael.   He is
ane easy man, and I hope they will aggree well together.
Earle of Lautherdale is made Generall of the Mint, E.
Loudoun Extraordinary Lord of Session, Mr. ffrancis
Montgomrie Lord off Thesaurie, E. of Marr Governour off
Stirline Castle, Kellburne made a Lord, pensions given to
Annandale, to the President of the Session, and to Philip-
haugh, and 1000 lib. to my Lord himself.   The person to
be Thesaurer Depute is aggreed upon betwixt the King

---

[1] Adam Cockburn of Ormiston.
[2] The laird of Pollok.

and my Lord. His comission will be sent downe in a short time, but is not yet extended. Yo^r Lo^p will see by the persones who are setled as above, being my Lords ffriends, that it is done by his moyon and recommendatione, and it is ane evident prooff off the Kings affectione to him when he effectuates such things. It gives a great stroak to all our enemies. There came very bad news this day off the Prince off Bavaria's death. It will putt a great altera^{o}ne in fforreign affairs, which yor Lo^p understands better then I can express, and there will be great debates for the succession of Spain. My Lord and all the family are very well, blessed be God, and I earnestly pray continuance off it, and prosperity to yor Lo^p and them. There are seṽall other things done besides what I have written, but they are not worthy off yor Lop^s trouble. I am afraid I have been too tedious allreadie to yor Lo^p. I only beg leave to wish yor Lo^p all health and happines, and subscryve myself, My Lord, Your Lo^{ps} most dutifull most obedient and humble servant,

JOHN PHILP.

I had the honour off a letter from yor Lo^p, and shall not fail to obey yor commands.

For THE RIGHT HONOURABELL THE EARELL OF FFINLATUR

MY LORD,—I have bein over long of wreting to you, but I haven litell to wret med it. No dout your Lo. hath hird that my Lord Carmichall is congunk Secretary, and of all the other chayneses. I should be glead to kno hou all is talked of with you. I shall be myndfull of your Lo. pension, but your son is over modast in what conserns his oun relations much agenst my inclations. Your Lo. shall ever fynd that I am in all duty as becumeth, My Lord, Your most affectionat and obidant daghter and humbell servant, ANNA SEAFIELD.

Whithall. Feb. ij, 1699.

Forgland is mead Keepr of the Signat under my Lord, for ther culd be no other thing dun for him, but I hop ther will be in tym cuming.

Robert Watson,[1] Writer to the Signet, was at the same time conjoined as Deputy Keeper of the Signet under Lord Carmichael.

To E. FINDLATER

Whitehall, Febry. 9th, 1699.

My Lord,—I have nothing to give your Lo^{dp} an acc^t of since my last, except of what you have had from other hands, that is that my Ld Carmichael is my conjunct, which was my own desire, and all the other vaccancies are filled to our satisfaction. I long to hear what is done with Burdsbank and Hayards, and how much money is desired to be sent north against the term. I will answer Braccos letter as soon as I can. I believe that he will do me friendship, and he shall have no reason to doubt of mine. I intreat your L^{dp} will send forward the inclosed to Forglen as soon as it comes to yor hands. We are all well here, and shall be glad to hear of the continuance of yor L^{dps} health. My wife is w^t child, and so we are like to have a natural born English subject.—I am, My Lord, Your L^{dps} most obedient son and most humble servant,

SEAFIELD.

Lord Carmichael, who afterwards became Earl of Hyndford, has left a short account[2] of his associate Seafield.

For THE RIGHT HONOURABLE THE EARLE OF FFINDLATER

Edr., 15th ffebry 1699.

My Lord,—. . . . I ame glaid your Lope is bringing Burdsbank my Lords way, bot truely he payes for it by my Lord Boyns offer. Please to acquant William Thomson that his tries and other matterialls for his garden, both from London and Mr. Sutherland are shipped on board my Lord Boynes shipe for Portsoy, and I beleive she will be ther befor this come to your Lops. hands, and his box with seids goes off from this to day by land with the post to Banffe. As he ordored, I have inclosed a not

---

[1] Fountainhall's *Chronological Notes*, p. 288.
[2] *Carstares State Papers and Letters*, p. 94.

under on of the mariners of the shipes hands for the tries to the man who sent them to the Ellie to him, for he was gone ther befor we could gett them out of Lawes skiper, who brought them from London.—I ame, My Lord, Your Lops. most faithfull and most obedient humble servant,   JA. BAIRD.

Next letter to the Earl of Findlater continues the story of the planting of Rathven parish.   It came to nothing, Mr. Shanks being translated to Upper Banchory.[1]

MY LORD,—As we judge our selves obliedged upon all occasions to signify the gratefull resentments we have of your Lōps favour, in allowing us your concurrence and countenance in all the attempts we have made hitherto in the planting of Rathven, so we judge it our duety to acquaint your Lōp with all the steps of our motions in that affair.   Though our endeavours hath heretofore bein fruitlesse and ineffectual, yet we must not be discouraged, bot go on untill the Lord shall be pleased to give us succease ; and therefore we have cast our eyes upon a very reverend and worthy brother, Mr. Martine Shanks, minister at Newhills in the presbytrie of Abd., to be transported from Newhills to Rathven.   We are assured that his singulare learning and skill in controversie, the sweetnesse and obliedgingnesse of his natural temper, his industry and painfulnesse in his ministry, and many other qualifications will render him very acceptable to your Lōp and very fit for that post, if he can be obtained.   Your Lōps cordial concurrence with us in this matter will certainly facilitate our work, and have great influence both upon the presbytrie of Abd. and the minister himself to promote the transportation, whereby your Lōp will have a new occasion of testifying your zeal for Gods glory and the good of that desolate parochin, and put a new obligation upon them who by their moderator subscribe as becomes, My Lord, Your Lōps most humble and most obedient devoted servants,   WILL. JOHNSTON, modr

Turreff, Febr. 16, 1699.

---

[1] Dr. Cramond's *Church and Churchyard of Rathven*, pp. 33, 34.

To WILLIAM LORIMER, Chamberlain of Viscount Seafield

Whitehall, Febry 28, i699.

I KNOW you serve me faithfully, and therfor you shall want no encouragement. You must not think of liveing out of the house, at least for some time ; but that you may have a possession to go to, you shall have the tack of the lands of Dytach when he removes. I have ordered John Anderson to remitt money for the payment of the lands of Hawyards, and you may sett these lands to the best advantage. I do not limit nor restrict you, but I wish that the conversion may be at eight merks, since my victual of Fordice is converted at that rate. However you must do in this as my friends advise you. I know that if I get the lands of Burdsbank I must make a slump bargain, and must pay dear. However I will not grudge it, if I be well secured and have no further trouble, and in this also I must trust my friends. Money shall be ordered for R^t Ogilvie and likewise for Bailie Ogilvie. It is but reasonable that Ro^t should raise it, since it may be useful to his father. As for the price of my meal I do not limit, nor is it possible for me at this distance to sett a price. I know you will do for me as well as if I was present my self, and what ever can be got either of bear of meal out over what maintains the family largely must be sold. Continou to writ to me from time to time of every thing that occurrs in my affairs. This is all from

SEAFIELD.

I do allow of the payment of my fathers pole.

William Lorimer, cousin of John Philp, for long managed the Seafield estates in Banffshire.

Robert Ogilvie was younger son of Alexander Ogilvie of Kemp-cairn.

For THE RIGHT HONOURABELL THE EARELL OF FFINLATER

MY LORD,—I was very glad to kno by your last that your Lo^p was in no wors halth then you use to be. I dou acknolig my seleff to be in the wrong that I dou not wret

every week to you, but I have so litell to say, and am sumtyms so seek that I can not wret. I wold have bein very glad that your Lo. had bein partiklurly mynded, when the vackenses was filed ; but your son sad it was imposabell for him to dou otherwayes then he did. My Lord Carmichall is nou cum to atend as Secretary. I hop that your son and he will agric very weall. At lest both hath very firm intentions to dou so for the present. Carmichall dous owe his being Secretary in a gret degrie to your son. I resolwe to cas prepos sumthing to be got for your Lo. to my Lord Carmichall, for it is properest for him to ask it for you. Beseds your son is over modast on that poynt. But what ever the King dou, your Lo. may be still ashoured not to want any thing that is neseser, so long as your son hath any estet. And for my shear I shall still think it my gret happniss, and mack it my constante indeiver to aprove my seleff, My Lord, Your most obident daghter and humbell servant,

ANNA SEAFIELD.

Whithall, Mar. ij. 1699.

ffor THE RIGHT HONORABLE THE EARLE OF FFINDLATER　these are

MY LORD,—We have sent two notorius rogues guiltie of many crimes, who are by the court are ordained to be cerryd to Cullen, and yr to be putt to death upon Munday 17 current conform to the sentance of court sent. We know your Lōp is such a friend to justice that ye will recomend to the magistrats of the place to putt the sentance to execuᵒn, and we remain, My Lord, Your Lordships most humble servants,　　　　　　　　A. DUFF, I.P.C.

Keith, April 14, 1699.

The court referred to by Braco was the Justiciary of the Highlands, which on account of the bad times and the disbandment of the greater part of the army had to deal with many loose men. The letters of 20th and 26th April refer to similar matters.

For THE EARL OF FINDLATER

Edr., 19th Aprill 1699.

MY LORD,—I was glaid to find by a letter of [your] Lops.

to my faither in law that yow was satisfied with the accounts I hade given of the shyres affairs. The letters that came in that pacquet were cairefully sent off yisternight. My faither in law went to Glasgowe upon Munday by ordor of the Lords of Justiciarie to waite upon Sr John Maxwell, Lord Justice Clerk, ther and at Paisley to take precognition anent the witches in the west; and if ther be found cause the Lords of Justiciarie will all goe ther in May to judge them. Your Lōpe will be pleased to receave the inclosed letters from London, that came by the yisterdayes pacquet. My Lord Seafeild hes ordored me to buy tuo peices of wine for him to waite his doune comeing, in caice he be ordored to Scotland this summar as he apprehends he may; and if he doe not come he sayes that he will send for it. He wreats lykewayes that my Lady will come off befor him in the beginning of the nixt moneth. I gave your Lope ane account, that I was useing my endeavors to followe Bracco's directions in procureing ane ease to the shyre of Banff of ther proportione of the taxt roll, and I have hade so good success therin, that I have procured the on halfe cheaper then it was befor, and conforme to Bracco's oun list, as your Lōpe will perceave by the inclosed double of the dēit of proportione, which I have caused wreat out for your Lōpes and the commissioners satisfaction. This doeth stand above seven dollars besides incident chairges. I leave it to your Lōpe to make representaᵒne of it to the commissioners, and Bracco who imployed me will be assisting to your Lōpe in it. The shyre of Banff wes formerly 4 s., and now they are only 2 s. I went about amongst all the commissioners and informed them of the low circumstances the shyre of Banff was in, and they have bein als favourable as could have bein expected. I hope Thomas Gregorie will be come off befor this time. I wish him a fair wind, ffor the weather beginns to be warme. I wish your Lōpe all happieness, and ame, My Lord, Your Lops. most deutief[ull] most humble and most obedient servant, JA. BAIRD.

I have inclosed the above mentioned letters from London for your Lōpe and my Lord Boyne in the newes letters by the ordinarie post, because I thought they would be most secure that way.

For THE LAIRD OF BRACO

Abdn., 20 Apr. 1699.

SIR,—I have according as I told you sent my man south, and I am perswaded he 'l return in tyme. Since you are to be so near our meeting, I would have yow be very soon there, since we may be conserting methods before the court sit down. I have written as I told you to the comissioners. I know you have great influence upon them, and I hope you have told them of the necessity of keeping the court. There has been strong dealings here with me to alter your order as to Peter Gordown, but I know better things. I have written to the Shircf deput that I doubt not of your calling for Riach and M^{c}kphersone[1] from Bamfe. If you have not done it, pray doe it, and desire particulare care to be hade of them. I have a great many things to tell you of them, and of young Riach, but I shall forbear till meeting, which is all from, Sir, Your most humble servant,   FORBES.

James Macpherson was hanged in Banff on 17th November 1700. William, twelfth Lord Forbes, was at this time a member of a committee to consider the best means of securing the peace of the Highlands, and was active in repressing lawlessness.[2]

ffor THE RIGHT HONOURABLE THE EARLE OFF FFFINLATOR

Huntingtower, 26 *Aprile* 1699.

MY LORD,—The Commissioners of Justitiarie of the midle and south districts have laid it upon me to acquaint the Commissioners of the northern district to desyre a meeting with them att fforfar the tuentie fourth of May nixt. Your Lo. being conveener of the said district, I desyre you will be pleased to acquaint them to meet with

---

[1] *Miscellany of the Spalding Club*, vol. iii. pp. 175-191, and Dr. Cramond's *Annals of Banff*, New Spalding Club, vol. i. pp. 99-113.

[2] *Historical Papers* (1699-1750), New Spalding Club, pp. xviii, xix, and 1-3, etc.

us at that tyme and place, for the more effectuall prosecuting the designe of the commissione, which is the more
needfull att this tyme, because of the many louse men
that are presentlie in the Highlands and the great scarcitie,
soe that ther is more appearance of theveing now then
formerlie. If your Lo. can be att fforffar, I shall be glad
to waitt on you, who am, My Lord, Your affectionat
cousin and most humble servant,   TULLIBARDINE.

Both Tullibardine and Findlater were third in descent from
Sir Duncan Campbell of Glenorchy, who died in 1631.

For THE EARL OF FINDLATER

MY LORD,—I wes heartily glade to heare by yo[ur] last
leſrs that you wes in good health.   I wish your Lo. allwayes
happy.   My Lady takes journey for Scotland the 15th of
the ensueing moneth in company with the President and
Advocat,[1] who are heir about the Affrican company.   My
Lord talks of sending down his son too, tho he be not fully
resolved as yet, becaus he begins to neglect his Latine by
reason of the many divertisements he meets with heir.
Your Lo^s line to Carmichell wes very acceptable, and I
beleive the bussieness is as good as done ; for ther is ane
entire friendship betuixt him and my Lord your son, who
wes keept back hitherto from obtaineing the thing himself
meerly out of modesty.   If the K. go over to Holland
this year your Lo. will see the Secretary at Cullen—if
otherwise, not.   Tho I be not certain if your Lo. allow me
the honour to write to you, yet I have taken the boldness,
and I hope your Lo. will pardon ye presumption of, My
Lord, Your Lo. most humble and obedient sert.,

WIL. BLAKE.

Whitehall, Ap. 27, '99·
William Blake was tutor to Seafield's son James.

For THE EARL OF FINDLATER

Edr., 1*st May* 1699.

MY LORD,—The victuall is come saiff here and in

---

[1] See *Carstares State Papers and Letters,* pp. 474-477·

good condition, and is livering. I shall gett a certificat or ordor for getting up Wm Lorimers bond. Your son, my Lord Secretary, is veric well and all the familie. My Lady and the Master is expected here shortlie, and my Lord soon therefter, if the King goe over. The Earle of Portland upon some considera°ns is to retire from court, but hes the Kings favour. He wes my Lords good friend, yet I hope my Lord hes so much of his masters favour as non shall be able to skaith him. I have bein in the west countrey precognosceing witneses aḡt witches, I think to little purpose. James Baird is up at Tillibodie. Our Councill sitts on Thursday. If any thing worthie of your Lop̄s notice occurre ye shall be acquainted of it by James Baird or, My Lord, Your Lops. most humble and most obedient servant,   JO. ANDERSON.

For THE EARL OF FINDLATER

Whitehall, 2d May 1699.

MY LORD,—I am very glade to see yor Lops. affair have so good success. If yor letter had not been so late a comeing to my Lord Carmichaell, and his moneth of waiting nigh expyred, yor Lo^ps gift had passed last moneth; but the beginning of his next moneth it will undoubtedly pass, for my Lord Carmichaell is forward for it, and it will be betwixt 3 and 4000 merks. The ffamily is very well, blessed be God, and I hope my Lord will have the happines to see yor Lo^p in the north this summer, if the King goe abroad. My Lady will take journey in a fourthnight, if she come at all. Her time will not allow her La^p to staȳ longer; but it is not determined if the Mr. come w^t her La^p. There are no news here at pn̄tt. The common talk is only off our Affrican company. My Lord President and Advocat are here, who will give advice concerning it. There choise of that place is mightily commended, and if they can enjoy it peaceably it will make Scotland flourish. Pardon this trouble, my Lord, and allow me to wish yor Lo^p all prosperity, and to subscrive myself, My Lord, Your Lo^ps dutifull servant,   JOHN PHILP.

To E. FINDLATER

Whitehall, May 2d, 1699.

My Lord,—I received yor Lo^{ps} letter w^t one inclosed for my Lord Carmichael. He will use his endeavours to procure you a pension, but the truth is the funds are over burthened, yet I hope you will prevaill. I have some thoughts of being in Scotland this summer, but my wife will certainly go, if she finds her self able to travel. I am anxious to hear that that tedious affair of Burdsbank is ended. I hear Bracco has been friendly to me in it, wch I shall own as an obligation. . . . I woud gladly have my flower garden dike finished, and if this year prove plentiful I am resolved to have my house built next summer, and will take James Smiths advice about it. Give my humble service to my Ld Boyn, and I am, My Lord, Your Lo^{ps} most obedient son and most humble ser^t,

Seafield.

Next letter fixes the date of the death of Walter, Lord Deskford, which is usually given as before June 1698.

For MR. WILLIAM LORIMER, Chamberlain to the Viscount of Seafield at Cullen

Whitehall, May 11th, 1699.

The account you gave me in yor last of my brother my Lord Deskfords death did much surprise both me and my wife, we haveing heard nothing of his sickness. We were bred at schools and colleges togither, and our mother nurst us both, and therfor you may believe that I am much troubled. However it is a satisfaction to us that he was calm in his sickness, and that he had apprehensions of death. I shall be glad to hear that he has been honourably burried, and what is expended that way I do very chearfully allow.

You must be prepareing for my wifes return. She will sett out from this the next week either on Tuesday or Thursday. I wish she were well at home, for her condition at present makes her journey more dangerous then otherwise it woud be, but I have travelled already i5 miles w^t her into the country to see my Ld Eglington, and she was not the worse of her journey. It is more uncertain when I can get from this place, because tho the King be to go to Holland yet he has not appointed his time. I know you will be careful of my affairs and writ frequently.—I ame, Your assured friend,

SEAFIELD.

Next letter corrects the statement that William, son of Viscount Seafield, was born on 6th May 1699.

For THE EARL OF FINDLATER

Edr., i2th *May* i699.

MY LORD,—I hade the honoure of your Lops. yisterday, and ame sorie your Lope. is so much troubled with sore eyes. It is certainly occasioned by too much reading. I did by the last post acquant William Lorimer that my Lord Seafeild will be heir in 5 or 6 weeks at furthest. My Lady will come sooner because hir time of lyeing inn aproaches; bot my Lord most waite the Kings goeing for Holland, which will be aither in the end of this or beginning of the nixt moneth. He hes ordored his loadgings to be taken and some wine to be bought for him. He sayes he 'l not stay long heir, bot will goe north to sie in what condition his affairs are ther. I doubt not bot your Lope will give ordores for my payement of what paines and expenss I have bein at upon the shyres account, and I will alwayes be veric readie to doe the shyre all the service I can. We have no newes heir at present. We expect accounts everie minutt anent the success our President and Advocat hes at court in our Affrican affair, about which they wer called. Both they and the 2 Secretaries stand up stifely for it. I have sent to Castel feild all the printed pepers belonging or relating to that affair of the royall and unfrie burghs, which no doubt he will shew your Lope.—I ame, My Lord, Your Lops. most deutiefull humble and most obedient servant,

JA. BAIRD.

All the horses in this countrey are dyeing, and ther is a

proclamation gone through this toune today ordoring them to be buried, ther are so many of them.

Next letter gives an account of the purchase of the Earl of Airlie's estate near Banff by Braco, ancestor of the Duke of Fife, and of Braco's arrangement for Seafield's purchasing the estate of Bogmuchels in Fordyce.

For THE RIGHT HONOURABLE THE EARLE OF
FFINDLATER   these

Qhytfeild, 19*th May* 99.

MY LORD,—The reversione of the Earle of Airelays estate in this shire with the burden of the wodesetts and liferents was proferred for ane hundreth thousand merks, which without the Viscount of Seafeild his speciall command I could not hold, since for ten yeares, save the hazard of my Laidy Huntlie her death, there was nothing to make up the @ rent.   Bracco hath accepted of the proferr, haveing the advantaige of the present possession, and is willing to part with Bogemuchels as it stands himself.   But if benefitte be the rule of buyeing, I doe not see but the @ rent of the reversion of it will give the Wiscount of Seafeild many more conveniencies to his land then he can have by the buying of it, since at thirty three chalders, every thing being counted, it stands Bracco about tuo thousand four hundreth merks the chalder.   My Lord, I pray your Lo. by the bearer send me ane exact account what condition the tennents of it are in, and what the yearely walou of the moss may be, which could be hade out of the Wiscounts lands, that can be accomodate of there fire thereby.   The yearly @ rent of the reversion will be about ten or twalve hundreth merks, and I can not understand how the half of that can be made up, and the rest on the land being great, it wold be litle from buying waist land.   I shall, God willing, attend your Lo. the nixt week, and give you the particulars of my woige ; but myself and horse being tyred and my wife sick, I bege your Lo. pardon.—My Lord, Your Los. most obedient servant,

ALEXR. OGILVIE.

For THE EARL OF FINDLATER.

Edr., 28*th June* i699.

MY LORD,—I receaved the honour of your Lops. pacquet anent the shyres clearings with Sr James Oswald and James Dunlop upon Satturday last, and yisterday I receaved ane other big pacquet with my Lord Halcraigs commission to represent your toune of Cullen in the nixt Convention heir, and a report of the circumstances of the tounes harbor bridge tolbuith and the want of a schoole house, under the hands of tuo of the commissioners appoynted to visite them, and severall other letters to your Lopes. freinds who are members of the Convention. I have communicate all that was in both these pacquets to my Lord Seafeild, and his Lope. promises his assistance in them so farr as shall be found necessarie. I delyvered my Lord Halcraigs commission to him with the report, who is to conferr with the Secretarie upon the matter. All the other letters I keep them up till a day or tuo befor the Convention sitt doun, that they may have it fresh in ther heads, ffor if I should delyver them now they would forgete that ever they hade receaved them. I shall take all the caire and caution I ame capable of to make it goe on right, and shall make what freinds I can both by my selfe and others. Sr James Oswald and James Dunlop have bein both so much taken up getting the Theasurie accounts revised by the auditors, that it hes not bein possible for them to keep a meetting with me as yet, bot they will doe it aither this night or to-morrow, and the shyre will be in no hazard in the time. I ame affraid that naither Boyne nor Auchentoule will gett any allowance for the yeare 1689, because the Theasurie hes exacted it from all the others Lords that wer in place with them at that time, bot ther shall be a short bill given in and allowance craved, and if I gett a cross interloqr ther will be no help bot they must pay up the quota, and your Lope shall have ane full account of the haill matter, after I have ended with the receavers and the Theasurie. William Dumbar hes accepted the tuo

bills that were draven upon him, bot sayes he hes no
money to pay them; and Bracco and Birkenboge have
ordored the payement of the bill draven upon them and
accepted by them, bot I have not as yet receaved the
money, his sone in law being at Tulleibodie keepping
phisitians from the old man who is dyeing a veric miserable
death.   I went ther upon Satturday last, and was soric to
find him in such a lamentable condition.   His left leg is
swelled als big as a post, and it with his foote and all is
als black as pitch, and all putrified to that degrie that, if
a knife wer put in his leg from the on side to the other,
he would not at all find it naither in leg nor foote, and it
hes a veric nautious smell.   His other leg is beginning the
same way, and a few dayes will carie him off.   When I
sayed that I thought it ane odd thing that the gentleman
hade ane opulent fortune (without any debt at all) of
7000 merks a yeare, it was the straingest thing in the
world that he was allowed to dye lyke a dog, and to rott
above the ground without so much as on phistians being
called to sie him, and that I thought it would be honourable both for the dyeing man and his apparand un-
wourthie successor to call a consulta°ne of good men
togither, if they should doe no more then looke upon him
and say he was dyeing, all the ansře that I gott was that
I was impertinent, and tooke too much [on] me, and truely
we pairted at the wrong hand.   All that he takes caire
of is to sitt by him from 5 in the morning till 12 at night
to sie that non come near him, and I truely beleive, if the
old laird dye not soone, the young man will dye of melancholy.   My Lord Seafeild hes bein a litle indisposed these
eight dayes with a heate in his blood and ane outstricking
in his face and body, bot I hope he will be nothing the
worse of it.   He hes bein abroad to day.   I beg pardon
for so long a letter, and ame, My Lord, Your Lopes most
deutiefull most faithfull and most humble servant,

JA. BAIRD.

Sir John Hamilton, Lord Halcraig, was elected in 1696 commissioner for Cullen to the Scots Parliament, in room of Sir James
Ogilvie, created Secretary of State for Scotland.   In 1689 Lords

Boynd and Auchintoul[1] were extruded from the bench, and the land-tax was for that year demanded of and ultimately exacted from them. Old Tullibody, George Abercrombie of Skeith, died on the 26th of June 1699, two days before the date of the letter. Braco's son-in-law Alexander Abercrombie, second son of Sir Alex-ander Abercrombie of Birkenbog married Mary, one of his daughters. Alexander was ancestor of General Sir Ralph Abercromby and the Lords Abercromby.

For THE EARL OF FINDLATER

MY VERY NOBLE LORD,—May it please your Lop., as formerlie so now we make bold to give your Lop. the trouble of a lyne, in a matter as we judge of great importance, especially to this corner, to wit the planting of Rathven with a well qualifyed minister, who through the Lords blessing may be acceptable to your noble familie, which we reckon our duetie to have a special regard unto, and so far as is possible to the heritours and people of Rathven, and who may prove a faithful and able minister of the New Testament. We have been using our best endeavours these several years without successe, though we alwise found your Lop. most foreward to allow your co-currence; bot now we have faln upon Mr. Wm Chalmer minister at Gartlay our r. brother, whom we judge all things considered one of the fittest that we can expect to obtain; for we know him to be a person of great ingenuity of a sweet and peaceable obliedging temper, and one who hath a singular respect for your Lops noble familie, bot which is yet far more a pious and learned man, who hath a singular dexteritie of mannaging debates with popish priests and other adversaries of truth after a mild inoffensive manner. We have drawn up a Presbyterial call, being sufficiently informed that both your Lop. and my Lord Viscount of Seafield judged that the most expedit way for filling the so long desolat congregation, and withall have sent a short copie of a

---

[1] 'Banffshire in the Revolution of 1689' in the *Transactions of the Banffshire Field Club*, 1906, pp. 114, 115; and *The House of Gordon*, New Spalding Club, vol. i. pp. 134-137.

parochial call, which your Lop. with my Lord Secretary
may alter, as shall seem good in your Lops. eyes, observing
only the substance thereof, and which we humbly intreat
your Lop. may be pleased to subscribe, and endeavour
to induce the other heritours and parochiners of Rathven
to doe the like, which will exceedingly facilitat the desired
transportation. And we syncerly declare to your Lop. yt
if this project fail (especially my Lord Seafield being in
the countrey), we cannot imagine where to fix, for we
truely apprehend thàt our very r. dear brother Mr.
Chalmers is as much adapted for that post as any man
we can think upon. So begging pardon for this trouble,
we referre what we have further to say to our r. brethren
Mrs. Tait and Murray, who will show your Lop. the call
wt. the reasons for the transportation. And wishing grace
mercy and peace from the Lord to be multiplyed upon
the noble family and all its branches and descendents, we
subscribe by our moderator, Very Noble Lord, Your Lops.
truely cordial and most humble servants in Christ Jesus,

Mr. T. THOMSONE, modr.[1]

Turreff, Aug. 30, 1699.

On 24th April 1700 Mr. Chalmers[2] on his admission as minister
of Rathven was rabbled, and was prevented from preaching in the
church until August the same year. On 3rd August 1704 he was
translated to King Edward, Aberdeenshire.

To THE RIGHT HONRABLE ERALL OF FFINLATER
thes

Blairfindie, the 12*th of* 7*br.* 1699.

REIGHT HONRABLE MY LORD,—I am so very ill sir-
comstanced heere, that it obliges me to give your Lordshipe the truble to mynd yow of calling an corom of the
comisshoners, and the heritours of the heed of the shaire,
if your Lordshipe thinks it fitt, houping that your Lordshipe and the rest of the comisshoners will take care that
we be provided of beeding coll and candell and necis-
sareis for dresing our vittells in, which without these we

---

[1] Dr. Cramond, *Church and Churchyard of Rathven*, p. 31.

[2] *Ibid.*, pp. 34, 35.

cannot subsist in this cuntrie, being obliged every other day to scrche the hills and glens for robars. I had the honour to meete with Bracko after I cam from your Lordshipe, who is very willing to contribut for us. Your Lordships favorable ansur wold singlarlie oblige him who is, My Lord, Your Lordships most humble and most obedint servant,   WILL. ELLIOTT.

Blairfindie in Glenlivet was then held by John Grant in wadset from the Duke of Gordon. In October 1699 the heritors of Strathaven and Glenlivet gave bond[1] to the Commissioners of Justiciary for their tenants' peaceable behaviour.

For THE EARL OF FINDLATER

Edr., 21th Septr. 1699.

MY LORD,—My Lord Seafeild pairted from this place upon Tuisdayes morning, and I left his Lope yisterdayes morning at Cockburnspath on his road in veric good health. His Grace the Duke of Hamiltoune came with his Dutches upon Munday with a mighty great train. Some say it was no good pollacie in his Grace to have appeared so great at this time, because people thinks him a veric great man alreadie. We have hade bad newes these 2 dayes [o]f our peoples deserting ther colloney in Calledonia upon some day [i]n June; bot this dayes post does not confirme them to be true, [b]ot upon the contrary sayes that the last 2 shipes that went to [the]m are now with them, and they have abundance of provisions. . . .—I ame, My Lord, Your Lops. most deutiefull most humble and obedient servant,   JA. BAIRD.

The first colonists deserted Darien on the 18th of June 1699. The two ships referred to, the *Olive Branch* and *Hopeful Binning of Bo'ness,* sailed from Leith on 12th May, and reached Darien about the middle of August to find the settlement deserted.

ffor THE RIGHT HONOLL THE EARLE OF
FFINDLATER   thes

MY LORD,—I intreat to be excused for this trouble. I am heir as the toun of Cullen's prisoner, and sall not

---

reflect on the badd treatment I hawe mett with.   I desyre the honor to kiss your Los. hands, when and wher ye sall appoynt, and I am, My Lord, Your Los. most humble servñt.,   GEO. LESLYE.

Cullen, Sep̄r. 28: —99.

George Leslye by this time had disponed his estate of Burdsbank to Seafield.   He was in debt to the town of Cullen, and had been incarcerated on that account.   Later the same year, on 9th December, he was in prison in Banff also for debt, and was liberated that day on a letter from 'Dumwhaill to allow him libertie within the territories of the burgh, which was admitted, Dumwhaill haveing got right to the dilligence one which he is incarcerat.'   George Leslye was grandson of George, second son of Robert Leslye of Findrassie, in Moray, who acquired in 1610 Burdsbank.   His grandfather, and his father William Leslye, subsequently added to the family possessions in Banffshire.   George succeeded as third laird between 1681 and 1685.   He had previously married, *c.* 1675, Christian, daughter of Sir James Baird of Auchmedden, Sheriff-principal of Banffshire.   That same year he was appointed Sheriff-Clerk and Keeper of the Particular Register of Sasines of Banffshire.   For some years he was County Collector.   In 1723 he resigned the office of Sheriff-Clerk, and died probably in 1724.

For THE EARL OF SEAFIELD

Edr., 6th Octor. i699.

MY LORD,—This place affourds no maner of [ne]wes at present, bot I send you heir inclosed good newes from London [o]f my Lord Seafeilds safe arryvall at London, which I knowe will [be] the best newes I could send both to your Lop̄e and my Lady.   fforglen pairted from this yisterday morning and hes a good purse [wi]th him.   He will be with your Lop̄e against Wedensday.   [J]ames Dunlop, who should give me ane clear account of what is yet [re]sting by the shyre of Banff of that old rest preceeding Candle[m]ess i69i, hes bein at Glasgow with our Calledonian shipes [th]ese 8 weeks past, and tho they be now gone yet he is not returned.   So soone as he comes it shall be sent, bot in the mean time my Lords Boyne and Auchentoule should pay up what the Lords of the Theasurie refuised to allowe, and what is due over that will not be much. I shall take caire that in the mean time the shyre sustaine no damnage. . . . I ame in all deuty, My Lord, Your Lops. most deutiefu[ll] most humble and most obleid[ged] servant,   JA. BAIRD.

The third reinforcement, usually called the Second Expedition to Darien, left the Clyde on 24th September 1699, after news arrived of the desertion of the colony. The ships were the *Rising Sun*, the *Hope*, the *Duke of Hamilton*, and the *Hope of Bo'ness*.

For [THE RIGHT] HONOURABLE [THE EARL OF]
                    FINDLATOR

Edb., the *9th Nov.* 99.

MY LORD,—I gave in your Lordships letters to the first packet went of, after I came here. There was besides the adjourning of the Parliament only three papers past the Kings hand, to witt Daniel Stewarts gift for collecting the bullion, and mine as Warden, and Captain Taylours for being Commissor of Dumblen. All your Lops friends here are in good health, and I hope to hear the lyke of your Lop. Mr. Francis Montgomery inquired very kindly for you and all the family. The Council sate on Tuesday and there was an address from the Africa council and directors subscribed by Lord Basil Hamilton in very mooth terms, desyring there Lops recomendation to his Majesty for assistance in their present distress. Their Lops delayed giving an answer to it, in respect there was that morning by an flying packet an return given by his Majesty to their address sent him. The Council sate this afternoon and they sent one White of Banachy, an advocat, to the tolbooth for reflections he had put in his informations by way of answers to the Lords of Council anent my Lord Ranculer. Beazlie Edie is also put to the tolbooth, since by an letter of his written to Provest Sckeen he appeared to be a traffecting papest. I shall wish all happyness to attend your Lop, and continue to be, My Lord, Your Lordships most obedient servant,

ALEXR. OGILVIE.

The warrant for a gift of the place and office of Principal Warden of the Mint to Alexander Ogilvie of Forglen is given at p. 236 of vol. xvii. of the *Warrant Books, State Papers (Scotland).*

The excited state of feeling in Scotland over the Darien enterprise, and the resulting address of the council and directors of the African company are referred to in the *Marchmont Papers,* vol. iii. pp. 178-198, in *Carstares State Papers and Letters,* pp. 498 to 514, and in the *Fourteenth Report of the Historical MSS. Commission,* Appendix, Part III., *Marchmont MSS.,* pp. 150 to 152, etc.

To THE RIGHT HONOURABLE THE EARLE OF FFINDLATER these

Edinburgh, 22d Nov. 1699.

MY LORD,—I am wery glaid when I hear of your Lo. good health, and I hartily wish the continuance of it. Ther hath noe private papers pas'd his Maj^tles hand this moneth, only by the last p. ther came ane letter from his Matie to the Lords of Thesaurie desireing them to proceed in ther acco^ts, as also to the auditors, with ane letter to the Dutches of Hamiltone to give the Earle of Annandale the emptie roumes nearest his lodgeing. Ther was a debeat in Councell betuixt the magistrats of Edinburgh and on Moonteith the diacon conveiner of the trades, who by the Councills sentance is removed from that place. I make noe doubt but your Lordship hes heard that the laird off Inveralachie is married to Kellies sister. Ther is on Wiliam Graham of Buchwhaple putt in the toolboth for haveing bein in ffrance and supposed to be a traffecquer that way. The Earle of Panmuir and his Lady came to toune yesternight. And craveing your Lo. pardon for this trouble, I continue to be, My Lord, Yor Lo. obedientt and humble servantt, ALEXR. OGILVIE.

For THE RIGHT HONBLE THE EARLE OF FINDLATOR

Edinburgh, 28th Novr. 1699.

MY LORD,—I received your Lo. yesternight by the express Boyn sent north, and I am exceedingly glaid to hear from your Lo., and of your good-health. Ye doe me a great honour in allowing me a line from your hand. I have taken the occasion of a servant of Boyns goeing north, becaves I belive he shall be north befor the post. This morneing I received the inclosed for your Lo. It appears your neighbours are more bussie than well informed, but it evidently testifies there inclination, and I am wery confident there will be noe use for them. The account we hade on the Sabbath day that the Spanish Donn was come alongs with the Caledonia does not hold; but all the rest is true, and more and more appearing of the falshood and treacherie of Captaine Penniecook, so that it's evident there own mismanaigementt and divisions have done them the harme. However many take occasion to lay it on these most innocent, as time will make it appear.—And with my humble dutie to your Lo. is all from, My Lord, Yor. Lo. most obedient and humble servantt,

ALEXR. OGILVIE.

The 'Spanish Donn' did not come in force against the Scots settlement in Darien until February 1700.

To THE EARLE OF FINDLATER

MY LORD,—According to your Lo^p and my Lord Secretarie Seafield's desire ye prebtrie of Morayshare transported Mr. William Chalmers to Rathven. It's ye way to be truely great, and to have lasting honour, to be for ye glorie of ye highest Lord in promoting truth, religion, and righteousness. Wishing that ye Lord may preserve prosper and bless your honourable familie with all blessings spiritual and temporal, I am, My Lord, Your Lo.'s most humble servant,   A. FORBES, mod^r.

Elgin. 14th of Debr. 99.

For THE RIGHT HONBLE THE EARLE OF FFINDLATOUR AT CULL-HOUSE BY ABDN. TO BANFF

Edinburgh, 18th December 1699.

MY LORD,—I hade noe furder time then only to acquant your Lo. that this day at tuo acloack the Counsell hath published ane actt relative to his Majties letter, signifieing his displeasure with the undue maner in proceeding in the address, and bearing that these who signalise themselves carrieing on the same have given noe testimonie of ther affection to the govermentt. By the nixt post your Lo. shall have the proclamation in printt ; and with my service to your Lo. is all from, My Lord, Yor Lo. most obedient and humble sert.,   ALEXR. OGILVIE.

On the 29th of November 1699 the council of the African company resolved to send Lord Basil Hamilton,[1] brother of the Duke of Hamilton, to London to present an address to the King on behalf of Captain Pinkerton and other Darien colonists, who had been captured by the Spaniards at Carthagena and sent prisoners to Spain. A national address was also extensively signed in Scotland asking the King to recognise the right of the Scots to colonise Darien. Next two letters refer to the heat thus caused in Banffshire.

For THE EARL OF FINDLATER

Edinburgh, 5th January 1700.

MY LORD,—By the yesterdays post ther came noe pacquet, and the reason of it is conjectured to be that the K. being at Hamptoune Courtt the Secretaries have not bein returned to London when the post came of. It is reported here that since the K. will not allow Lord Basil access,[2] his Lo. hath wreat to the company for advice, whether he shall give the petition to ane other hand to deliver or how to dispos of it. I have not heard from your Lo. this great while, albeit I fail'd not to give you the accounts that were goeing here ; and since there hath bein so hott service in your countrye it was expected your Lo. wold have caused wreat the true accounts of it, and by a footman sent it to the Abdns post, so that comeing timely here it wold have prevented many reports that were runing, and hindered your Lo. name from being in the mouth almost of everie on here, some saying ye hade subscrived the address, and others not, and your friends

---

[1] *Carstares State Papers and Letters*, pp. 513, 514.
[2] *Historical MSS. Commission, Fourteenth Report*, App., Part III., *Marchmont MSS.*, p. 152.

hoped for the best ; but there being noe line out of your
family relating to what hade past either amongst yourselves
or thes about you, did fear the worst.   I shall be glaid to
know that your Lo. is well, and craveing pardon for my
freedome I continue to be, My Lord, Your Lo. most obedient
and humble servantt,   ALEX^r. OGILVIE.

For THE EARL OF FINDLATER

Edinburgh, 10th January 1700.

MY LORD,—I was wery glaid to hear of your Lo. good
health from Baillie Ogilvie, and wish ye hade honoured
me by the post with a line after Mairschall and ye parted.
The contents of your letter give great satisfaction, and I
wish that ye hade returned Mr. Patrick to Buchan for his
own reputations sake, albeit the woige I hope shall doe noe
harme where its design'd, but shew the bad temper of some
who are ungrate to a great degree.   I delivered your Lo.
letter to my Lady Lauderdale, and shee told me ye hade
wreaten wery kindly and civily to her.   I did inclose all
yours, and sent them up by the yesternights post.   Ye
have the sad news of Caledonia its being deserted the second
time by the burning of Jamieson's shipe,[1] which is said to
be occasioned by ther burning of brandie.   I never observe
extraordinary griefe for any thing, but is allwayes followed
with a greater stroke.   I wish the first pairt hade bein
more calmely taken, and submission to the will of the
Almighty used in place of blameing innocent persons.
Your Lo. will have alvayes the occasion of the post, and
I pray you be so good as to cause a servant wreat what is
goeing, for good intelligence gives ground to stope many
misreports ; for it is now the practice of these who have
nothing to support themsleves with to betake themselves
to the grossest of calumnies.   However time lets every
man appear in his own collours.   I give my humble dutie
to your Lo., and continue to be, My Lord, Yor Lo. most
obedient and humble servantt,   ALEX^r. OGILVIE.

It's reported the Duke of Gordon is gone to prosecutt

---

[1] *The Olive Branch.*

a marraige to his son, but time will make it known. I wish my Lord Seafield hade gott his affair cleared with him, certainty being always better then hope. I think Castlefield his kyndness but small, since he wold not bestow a weeks travell to seek Bracco upon a mater of such concerne.

The Marquis of Huntly married in 1707 Henrietta Mordaunt, daughter of Charles, Earl of Peterborough and Monmouth.

The following memorial, and other documents dated 30th April, 21st and 26th June, 12th, 13th, 19th and 22nd July 1700, regarding Captain Pinkerton and the other Scots prisoners in Spain, supplement the information given in Hill Burton's *Darien Papers*, pp. 102 to 110, and in *Carstares State Papers and Letters*, pp. 531 to 533, 554, 558, 559, 568, 569, 676 to 679, etc.

THE CONSUL OF CADIZ'S MEMORIAL ABOUT HIS MATY'S SUBJECTS PRISONERS THERE

MARTIN WESTCOMBE, Esqr., Consul and Agent General of his Ma^{ty} of Great Brittain in this city and those in the neighbourhood, represents that Robert Pincarton, John Malock, James Graham, and David Wilson, subjects of his Majesty of Great Brittain, sailing from Nova Caledonia the 24 of Jan^{ry} in the year last past, bound with several sorts of goods for the island of Barbadoes, being overtaken by a storm the 15th of Feb^{ry} following were shipwreckt and lost their vessell on the coast of Carthagena, and being come themselves to that city they were put in prison there, from whence they were transmitted to the Havana, where they were putt on board a ship call'd the *St. Ignatius*, admiral of the squadron, commanded by Don Martin de Savala, and being brought to this city, they were by your Hon^{rs} order putt into the King's prison, where they are at this present. And in regard the said English were not found in the exercise of any thing that was prohibited, but were only sailing to the parts of the dominion of the King of Great Brittain with marchandizes of their own manufacture, and that their approaching to Cartagena was occasioned by the violence of the weather and the shipwrack that they suffer'd, and they having served since on board the admiral with all diligence and fidelity, being the most forward on all occasions of danger that offer'd in the whole course of the voyage, and labour'd most to save the said ship from the danger she was threatned with in the running ashore upon the sands, and in regard that they have not given any new occasion for their confinement, but have deserved a quite contrary usage, after all the pains they have taken and the miserys they have suffer'd, besides those they endure in their present imprisonm^t, all which considerations, added to this that they are not guilty of any crime, render them objects worthy of your Hon^{rs} compassion, on which acc^t. the said consul does with all submission pray your Hon^r will please to give the necessary orders for the release of the said prisoners, and thereby he will receive a particular favor from your Hon^{rs} justice.

This Memorial was delivered by Consul Westcombe to the Marquis of Narres, President of the Contratation House, 16th January 1700.

Viscount Seafield was Lord High Commissioner to the General Assembly of the Church of Scotland which was about to meet.

For THE RIGHT HONBLE THE EARLE OF FFINDLATER
AT CULLEN HOUSE these
Edinburgh, 5th ffebruary 1700.

MY LORD,—Please receive inclosed my Lord Advocat his warrand for putting Baillie Ord[1] in prison. My Lord Commissioner is wery well in health, and I hope shall agree with the Assemble. They have done litle yet save appointing commitees and answering his Māties letter, wherein they give a wery ample testimony to the Commissioner. The bearer will give your Lo. ane accountt of the great burneing in this place. I shall add noe more save that I continow to be, My Lord, Yor Lo. most obedient and humble servant,	ALEX^r. OGILVIE.

Fountainhall notes that 'the fire which burnt the Parliament Close was upon the 3rd February 1700.'

---

[1] Bailie of Cullen and laird of Findochty.

For THE RIGHT HONBLE THE EARLE OF FINDLATER
BY ABERDEEN TO BANFF these

Edinburgh, 16th February 1700.

MY LORD,—I am wery glaid to know of your Lo. good health, I hade not fail'd wreating to you by Baillie Ogilvie, if he hade done me the kyndness to take leave of me. The Commissioner and his Laidy are wery well in health, and the Assembly have agreed wery well and proceeded ceriously in ther maters.   There is ane fast appointed throw the whole nation the last Thursday of March.   The Assembly will rise the begining of the nixt week, and the Commissioner will haist up.   They wrote wery favourable to the King in behalf of the Commissioner, and is all from, My Lord, Your Lo. most obedient and humble ser^t.

ALEX^r. OGILVIE.

The laird of Allardyce cam here with my Laidy, and is in good health.

For THE RIGHT HONBLE. THE EARLE OF FINDLATER
BY ABERDEEN TO BANFF these

Edinburgh, 23d Feby. 1700.

MY LORD,—Upon Tuesday last the Generall Assembly did rise with great satisfaction to all concerned, and on Wednesday my Lord Seafield went of wery honourably attended both with the nobility and gentrie.   The Earles of Marr, Loudoun, and Annandale, the Lord Mountgumrie, Major General Ramsay and many others wentt to Dunbar all neight.   I had wreat to your Lo. upon Wednesday, but goeing out of toune hade not time.   My Laidy Seafield is wery positive to take her journey from this the morrow tho the last day of the week.   I parted with the Secretarie in wery good health at Coper Smith yeasterday about twalve acloack, and with my hearty service to your Lo. is all from, My Lord, Yor Lo. most obedientt and humble servantt,   ALEX^r OGILVIE.

For THE EARLE OF FINDLATER

Morpeth, Febry. 25th, 1700.

MY LORD,—I received a letter from yor Lop. when I was

Commissioner to the Gen[ll] Assembly, wherein you did join w[t] Kempcairn, Kilminarty, and some others of the parish of Keith representing the circumstances of that parish. It has certainly been too long vaccant, and I think all concerned should concurr to have it speedily planted. I find some of the parish do object against Mr. Gillchrist, as if he did not desire to have his residence in the north; but that objection will not signify much, for he will quickly find that the ministers will not allow him to be transported to the south, and had I an interest in the parish of Kieth I would heartily concurr in setling him ther. I have heard him speak befor the Assembly, and I do think he will be found to be a young man of very good sence, and if Kemp-cairn, Kilminerty, or any of the heretors will concurr, I believe that the Commission will transport him to that parish and setle him ther. I had no letter from the laird of Bracco upon this acc[t], and nothing moves me in this matter, but that I think Mr. Gilcrist a fitt person, and that the parish will meet w[t] no difficulty in getting him. My wife will give yo[r] Lop. an acct of what occurrd whilst I was at Ed[r], and I bliss God I am this lenth in good health on my journey, w[ch] is all from, My Lord, Your Lop[s] most affect. son and most humble servant,   SEAFIELD.

The Rev. James Strachan,[1] minister of Keith, who was 'outed' in 1689, continued to intrude down to 1704. Mr. John Gilchrist was admitted to Keith in 1700, and served there until 1754.[2] Alexander Sutherland of Kilminerty or Kinminitie Keith was a cadet of the Earls of Sutherland and of the Lords Duffus.

The international trouble arising on account of Darien was forcing the question of union between England and Scotland into active politics.[3]

For THE EARL OF FINDLATER

Edinburgh, 28th Febry 1700.

MY LORD,—By the yesterdayes post the encloaseds came to my hand, and my Lord Secretary desyred I should

---

[1] Dr. Cramond's *Church of Keith*, pp. 14-29.   [2] *Ibid.*, p. 23, etc.

[3] See *The Marchmont Papers*, vol. iii. p. 178.

forward them to your Lop. I have not heard from you this good time. I shall be wery glaide to know that your Lop. is in good health. I hade a privett letter yesterday beareing that the bill for the union was read a second time, and that they leave it to the King to appoynt commissioners to treat thereon, and with my humble dutie to your Lop. is all from, My Lord, Your Lop^s obedient and humble servant,   ALEX^r OGILVIE.

For THE EARL OF FINDLATER

Edr., 5th Mairch 1700.

MY LORD,—. . . Your Lop^s newes comes to and are duely sent forward by fforglen, and that you have wanted them the 20 dayes you complean of, it hes bein occasioned by his closs waiting upon my Lord Seafeild in his station as Commissioner. I doubt not bot now he will make up that loss, and lykewayes send the *Gazet* since both should come togither, and the expense of the *Gazet* is not wourth counting in the yeare. I have letten him knowe of it. I ame hopefull my Lord Seafield is at London this night in good health after his tedious jurnay, and his faithfull service heir will render [him] veric welcome to his maister. Our Affrican adress is goeing to London upon Wedensday nixt as I ame informed, and is to be delyvered to his Mātie by the Merques of Tweeddale. Sir John Home of Bleckater, Hadden of Glenegies, etc., my Lord Duplen (who is the fourth named) is att London alreadie. Some say the Lairds of Houstoun and Livingstoune are lykewayes to goe, bot I ame informed that these commissioners are to goe upon ther own charges, and therfor I think all that I have named will not be solicitous to goe upon that head. We have surmises heir bot as yet no certain account, that we can depend upon, of the *Ryseing Sone* and those uyr shipes in his companie ther being saifely arryved at Darien, bot the account comes by the way of Spaine and wants confermation. I ame hopefull, God willing, once in Aprile to have the honour of waiting on your Lope. at Cullen, ffor I am most deutiefully, my Lord, Your Lops. most deutiefull most faithfull and most humble servant,   JA. BAIRD.

The interview of the deputation which presented the national address to the King was unsatisfactory.[1] The *Rising Sun* and her consorts arrived on 30th November 1699 to find the Darien settlements again deserted.

For THE EARL OF FINDLATER

Whitehall, March 14th, 1700.

MY LORD,—I believe the family of Kempcairn have no better friends then yo[r] Lop. and my Lord Boyn, and I am sure were they in a condition to keep the estate I should be very well satisfyed, and if on the other hand they must needs sell, it is better that it return to me then that it fall into the hands of strangers, and I believe non will deal more kindly with them than I. I wish that yor Lop. and my L[d] Boyn would bring them to some conclusion speedily, for if they and I conclude I must raise money at ye term, and if not I have enough for doing my own affairs, that is for paying Arnbath[2] at this term and Bracco at the next. I impower yor Lop. to engage in my name and to conclude, and whatever papers you engage I shall sign. I shall do it, and I shall very quickly raise what money may be needful, and I hope within a year to pay the bargain entire.

We have not yet entered upon publict bussiness since I came up, but I bliss God the King is satisfyed with the service I was capable to do him, and I am sure it is my duty to continue to serve him to the utmost of my power, and I am sure in so doing I serve my country. I cannot writ to my wife this night. Yor Lop. will let her see this. I believe I shall not be here much above 5 weeks, for the Parliament will meet at the time appointed, and I must be at Ed[r] some time befor, w[ch] is all at present from, My Lord, Your Lop[s] most affect. son and most humble sert.,

SEAFIELD.

Next letter and the letters of 25th April and 3rd May show that Seafield was preparing for the meeting of Parliament.

---

[1] *Historical MSS. Commission, Fourteenth Report*, App., Part III., *Marchmont MSS.*, pp. 152, 153.

[2] Alexander Hay of Arnbath, Fordyce, Banffshire.

For THE EARL OF FINDLATER

Invernes, 1 *of Aprile* 1700.

MY LORD,—I receaved the honour of your Lo⁸ of the 17 of March the other day from a servant of my Lord Duffuses. Ther is none wold be prouder of ane occassion of serving you then myself, as to the choosing a burgess for the toun of Dornoch. I have written to my Lord Seafield, who understands law to perfection, to know whither or not the thing can be done legaly, ther being a member existing who is choosen and hes not demitted. I don't like to expose my self or freindes by doing what is unwarantable, soe my caution in the matter is what I hope your Lo. will approve of, ther being none more then I, My Lord, Your Lo⁸ most obedient and most humble servant,

STRATHNAVER.

The Acts of the Parliaments of Scotland show that John Anderson sat for Dornoch in Parliaments during 1696 and 1698. He is not included in the roll of members for the session of Parliament in May 1700, but he appears on the roll of the adjourned session in October 1700. Strathnaver was eldest son of George, fifteenth Earl of Sutherland, and received on 1st February 1693 a commission to be colonel of a new regiment of foot.[1]

For VISCOUNT SEAFIELD

RIGHT HONOURABLE, MY LORD,—The reason of my not writing to yoʳ Lop. this while bygone was my being taken up in dispatching the ships with your victuall. . . .

Ther is gone to sea of your victuall ffive houndered and five bolls meall, and ffour houndered eightie sex bolls half boll bear, for which I have sent bills of loadning to fforgland to clear with the merchants. I could gett no more bear from the tennents this year, by reason of the scarsity in the countrey occasioned by the thinness of the last crop. . . .

I wish your Lop. a safe and prosperous journey to Scottland and good success in all your affairs; and that the Lord may preserve your Lop. and your family is the constant

---

[1] *State Papers (Scotland) Warrant Books*, vol. xv.

prayer of, My Lord, Your Lops. most humble and most obliedged servant,   WILL LORIMER.

Cullen House, Apr. 20th, 1700.

For THE EARL OF FINDLATER

Edinburgh, 22d Aprile 1700.

MY LORD,—I was troubled to hear of your Lo. indisposition, and I longed to know of your amendiment. I hope the pleasant season shall give you perfect health, whereby ye may come this lenth and see all your friends at the Parliament, and befor your returne make a fine laidy blush when cried with your Lo., lyke a maide of sixteen yeares, as was observed the other Sabbath day of my Laidy Wimes when cried with Tarbit.

It is expected that there will be a wery good agreement in the insueing Parliament. There are many prepairing to meet the Marquess of Tweddell, who is expected here this week. Mr. Middletone is safe come to Leith. I shall give your Lo. noe farder trouble, but that I continue to be, My Lord, Your Lo. most obedient servant,

ALEX^r OGILVIE.

Your Lo. letter came by the yesternights post.

DUKE GORDONS LETTER TO MY LD. [SEAFIELD]
UPON HIS LIBERATIONE

Edenbourg, 25 Aprill 1700.

MY LORD,—Sum weeks agoe I receaived the honor off a letter from your Lordship off the 6 instant. I wold imediatly haw geuen yr. Lo. my humbel thancks for itts contents, had I nott knoun that you war extraordinarly in busines wh. even hindred the delivery off the letter for my inlargment. I am extremly sensibel to y^r Lo. faver in this ocation. As to my sentiments for the great King who has had goodnes for mee, I nott only admir his heroick qualifications and ilustrius acctions, but I wishe passionatly that by on mor hee may croun all the rest, and becum by itt the most glorius and happie man in the wourld; and the greatest return I can mak to y^r Lo. frindshipp for mee is to wishe you a sharer in such dooings. I can not end this withoutt mentioning yr Lo[s] refusing yr deus for the order for my liberation. That civility most bee owing amongst many others, w[h] I haw receaivd from your Lordship, until I can mak returns worthy off them. Untill then I most bee contented with the asseurances I can giwe your Lordship that I am, My Lord, Your Lordship[s] most obediant most obliged and most humbel serwant,   GORDON.

For THE EARL OF FINDLATER

Whitehall, Aprile 25th, 1700.

MY LORD,—I am sure it is both my interest and duty to do for yo[r] Lop., but at the same time did you know the circumstances of affairs you woud not think this a fit opportunity, for it would look like bargaining for my own advantage w[t] the King. I hope his Maj[tys] affairs shall go well in Parliamt., and therafter I can be more capable to do for yo[r] Lop. and my other friends. The King has maney that he needs must gratify now, and I must press him to it, and wher I do use my influence I bliss God I do not want success in it ; but what is delayed as to yo[r] Lop. will not be a loss, and therfor I desire that you will not be discouraged, but that you may come over to Ed[r] against the sitting down of the Parliamt, w[ch] is now appointed upon the 21st of May. It would have mett upon the 14th but that the D. of Queensberrys equipage was not in a readiness. I sett of from this on Tuesday next, and will be at Ed[r] 8 dayes befor the meeting of the Parliam[t], but if yo[r] Lop. and my wife come against the down sitting of it it will be soon enough. It will be needful befor you come off that you raise some money to answer what will be needful for Kempcairns affairs. I shall have enough for Arinbath, but I cannot have likewise for Kempcairn at this term. I know not yet what vituall is delivered, and tho the half of it be payable at Whitsunday, yet I cant expect to make money of it befor Lammas. I leave that affair of Kempcairns entirely to yo[r] Lop[s] manadgement, and what bonds you give I shall ratify at my comeing to Ed^r. I cant say whither I can come to the north or not, but if I do I will transact w^t all the rest of the creditors, and clear the summ, and in order to y^e of clearing of that matter it will be fitt that I know which of the creditors I shall pay, wch is all at present from, My Lord, Yor Lop^s most obedient son and most humble sert. [SEAFIELD].

COPY OF A LETTER FROM CAPT PINCARTON, ETC., TO THE RIGHT HON^BLE LORD BASIL HAMILTON

RIGHT HONORABLE,—We have received a letter from the company signifying your being at London in order for procuring his Matie's letter for our release, but as yet we cannot learn of any to that purpose neither by the consul of Cadize nor by the consul here, for the first has received a letter from the Secretary of State, and not a word concerning us in the same. Our usage [is] still worse, for the consuls are backward in the matter, untill they should have an order from the King or Secretray. Our declarations are taken, and their determination is by some dubious, by most thought it will be hard, and we fear the event; wherefore we humbly implore and begg your Lop^s assistance and speedy care in procuring his Maties letter, or the Secretary of State's letter to the consuls of Cadize or of this place for our release, which shall for ever be an obligation on us to remain in all due respect and sincerity Your Lop^s. most dutifull and humble servants,

Sic subscribitur, ROBERT PINKARTON,
JOHN MALLOCH,
JAMES GRAHAM,
BENJ^N SPENSER alias PENSO,
DAVID WILSON.

Sevilla Prison, April 30th, 1700.

To THE RIGHT HONORABLE THE EARLE OF FINDLATER

MY LORD,—I am well satisfyed when I hear that your Lo. is well. . . . Your Lo. has your news with Drumwhenle, who did me the kindness to see me here. I'l endeavour to be busie at my book and to aprove my self, My Lord, Your Lo. most humble and obedient servant,

JA. OGILVIE.

Abdn., Ap. 1700.

Viscount Seafield's eldest son was in Aberdeen studying under his tutor Mr. Blake. Next year, as 'nobilissimus Jacobus de Deskford,' he was enrolled a student of Marischal College in the class of the regent Mr. Peacock, which ran from 1701 to 1705.[1]

For THE EARL OF FINDLATER

Newark, May 3d, 1700.

MY LORD,—I know you can't be the worse of traveling to the Parliament, and therfor I expect to see you ther. It sitts down upon the 21st, and it is better to be over a day or two sooner as to miss to be at the electing of the comittees. I wish that our Bamffshire commissioners may come up also about that time, and I hope they will not determine themselves in any thing untill they speak with me. I cannot communicate to yor Lop. what measures we have taken untill I see you, but I hope all honest men will have reason to be satisfyed. [I hope your Lop.] may bring me as clear an acc^t as is possible of the state of my affairs in the north, and particularly that which concerns Kempcairn ; and if the borrowing of money be needful on that acct. yor Lop. may do it, and I do hereby impower you to grant bond for nine or ten thousand merks, wch shall be as binding upon me as if the bond were granted by my self ; and if you find any difficulty to do this, I shall do it at Ed^r, but let it not hinder you from comeing south against the down sitting of the Parliament. I do also expect that Provost Stuart [2] will come along with yor Lop., or at least about that time, and expecting to see you so very soon I shall only add that I am, My Lord, Yor Lop^s most obedient son and most humble ser^t,

SEAFIELD.

---

[1] *Records of Marischal College and University*, New Spalding Club, vol. ii. p. 281. 'The Education of a Scots Nobleman Two Hundred Years Ago,' by the Editor, in *Transactions of the Banffshire Field Club*, 1909. ·

[2] Commissioner for Banff.

Parliament met on 21st of May 1700, and was adjourned on the 30th of the same month to the 20th of June, to prevent the passing of a 'resolve' declaring Caledonia a rightful settlement, and pledging Parliament to maintain the same. The two next letters to the Earl of Findlater and to the Duke of Queensberry show that the King would not yield. Complications with Spain, but chiefly the opposition of the English Parliament on account of trade jealousy, made it impossible for him to do so.

For THE EARL OF FINDLATER

MY LORD,—My Lord Seafield has so much to write this night that yor Lop. cannot expect to hear from him by this flying pacquet. He is in very good health, blessed be God, and had a very pleasant journey the whole way, except the first day from Belford. He posted to York, and there hyred a coach hither, which brought them four dayes from York. So they came here Saturdayes night. Since that time my Lord has been every day at Hampton Court where the King stayes, and Tuesday last the addressers at ten acloack presented the Parliaments address. They were introduced by my Lord, and when it was read the Kings answire was that he will consider it. How this will take, yor Lop. will soon learn at Edinburgh. The Parliat is adjourned from the 20th of June to the 4th July last, and the Commissioner is continued in the caracter dureing the Kings pleasure. Betwixt and that time the King will declare his thoughts as to that overture concerning Darien. The Earles of Argyle and Annandale and my Ld Seafield have importuned the King to consent, but have not yet prevailed. It is the greatest trouble can attend my Lord that he cannot bring the King to yeild speedily, though perhaps a great many will not beleeve so much. The King will very soon declare himself how he inclynes to the thing, but how and in what manner I cannot tell yor Lop.

Yor Lop. will have a coppy of the address in the flying post, so I need not trouble yor Lop. with it in writt, but shall send the news letter by this flying pacqt, because it will come sooner be two dayes then the ordinary pacquet. There are about nynty signing the address. I am afraid I have encroached too much on yor Lops patience. So begging pardon, and praying yor Lop. and the family all health and happiness, I am, My Lord, Your Lop^s most humble, most dutifull, and most obedient servant,

JOHN PHILP.

Whitehall. 13 *June* 1700.

COPPY OF THE LETTER SENT TO THE COMMISSIONER
BY THE MESSENGER

WE are well satisfied with the accounts we have had of your proceedings, and we are sensible that more could not have been done for our service then you have done. The Earls of Argyle and Anandale and my Lord Seafield have done you justice in this matter, and have acquainted us that you and all our servants doe think it needfull in the present juncture, that we should give our assent to an act of Parliament asserting and declaring the right of the colonie in Darien, and they have earnestlie desired us to do it, as what they think might divide the opposite pairtie, and satisfie all who are well affected to our goverment. We have formerlie acquainted you with our reasons why we could not yeild this point; and could we have done it at all, we would have done it at first, but the longer we think upon it we are the more convinced that we cannot doe it, and there is a necessitie for making a publick declaration thereof. Houever at present we have adjourned the Parliament for a short time, and have onlie signified our mind to you, and to our servants that are here with us; but we expect that you will call such of our servants there as you think fitt, and lett them knou this our final resolution, and lett a draught of a letter be sent to us, containing the reasons mentioned in our letter to the Parliament concerning the colonie in Darien, with there advyce as to the way and manner they think most propper for making this publick. And in this you are to use all dispatch and diligence. We doe think it necessarie for our affairs to continue you our Commissioner, and your being at Edenburgh in this juncture is indispensablie needfull. We doe repose intire trust and confidence in you, and yow may either write your mind fullie to us of all things that concerns our service, or you may send anie friend of your oun here whom you can trust. And so not doubting of your care and diligence, we bid, etc.

Given at Hⁿ Court the 13 *June* 1700.   By comand

past. SEAFIELD.

Directed to our r. b. and r.ent b. c. and c^r J. D. of Q. our Com^r to our Parl. of S^c.

To THE R^T HON^{BLE} ye E. OF JERSEY, PRINCIPAL SECRETARY OF STATE

Cadiz, the 21*st June* 1700.

RIGHT HON^{ble} S^r.,—I am obliged to trouble your Lop. with this to render a second acco^t, that in Decr last past Capt Robt Pincarton, Mr. John Mollock, James Graham, and David Wilson, Scotchmen, were brought prisoners from the Havana, and committed to the gaol of this place, where they continued for some months, and by his Catholick Ma^{ty} and Councill were order'd to that of Sevilla, where their declarations were taken and sentence of death, as I'm inform'd, was thought would pass on them, imputing them pirates, when their only crime is their having been at Darien, from whence they sailed the 25th of Jan^{ry} 169$\frac{8}{9}$ in the ship *Dolphin* with 30 odd men bound to Barbadoes to buy provisions, and were unfortunately shipwrackt the 5th of Feb^{ry} following at Cartagena by a violent storm. The rest of the men were shipt aboard the Bartavento fleet, and the above sent prisoners to the Havana. At their first coming here I represented in a memorial their case to the President of the Contractation-House, who has the whole disposition of all affairs of Spanish ships that come from the West Indies, and demanded of him their being sett at liberty as his Ma^{ty's} subjects, to which he only verbally told me, that their process was in councill, and that he could not resolve in any manner without the King's order, and that he would remitt said memorial to the council, copy whereof goes enclosed for your Lop^{'s} perusall. His Ma^{ty's} consul at Sevilla, Mr. Robt Godschall (by virtue of a power wch I gave to a proctor there), has assisted with him to make the necessary defences, but all to no purpose, since these poor men are as believed condemned by this time, of ^{wch} he will appeal to the King and council at Madrid, where in all probability their sentence will be confirmed, so I humbly request your Lop. that you will please to acquaint his Ma^{ty} with it, and procure his gracious order in their behalf.   There is also one Benjamin Spencer *alias* Penso of a Jewish extraction, but as he says is a Christian and marryed in England, who lays under the same circumstances as the others, having been an interpreter with the Scots at Darien, and was taken prisoner on the island of Cuba in going ashore for water, after their first deserting that colony.

S^r.

The 19th sailed hence 7 sail of Spanish men of war a store ship and two tenders under the command of Don Pedro Fernandez Navarrete for Cartagena, and from thence to rout the Scots from their new settlem^t. Ditto day parted Monsr Pointi towards Sally with two bomb ketches, a fire-ship, and a pink with stores, who after having joyned the rest of his squadron, which are 5 men of war that are cruising and 4 galleys wch imported here this day and 8 tartans that he has hired, designs to invest some ports of Barbary or at least to bomb them, wch being what 's worthy your Lop'^s notice, I crave leave to remain, R^t Honble S^r, Your Lop'^s most humble and most obedient serv^t,   Wm WESTCOMBE.

S^r, I humbly crave your Lop'^s answer for the satisfaction of these poor men.

TRADUCTION DE LA SENTENCE RENDUE PAR LA CHAMBRE DE LA CONTRACTATION DES INDES Á SEVILLE CONTRE LE CAPITAINE PINCARTON ET AUTRES

DANS le procés et cause criminelle entre parties, d'une part, le procureur du Roy á la Chambre de la Contractation des Indes, et de l'autre les accusés Robert Pincarton, Benjamin Spencer, Elie Penso, Jean Malach, Jaques Brayan, et David Wilson tous natifs du royaume d'Ecosse, lesquels se trouvent detenus dans les prisons de cette Chambre pour avoir passé du dit royaume d'Ecosse au pais qu'on appelle Darien avec une escadre composée de 5 vaisseaux de guerre, qui y portoit differentes marchandises, et y avoit bâti des forts et des maisons et pratiqué autres choses mentionées dans le rapport du fiscal Joseph Moreno. Apres avoir veu et examiné les actes, preuves et accusations, nous trouvons que Nous devons condamner, comme par ces presentes Nous con-damnons á mort les susdit Capitaine Robert Pincarton, Benjamin Spencer, Elie Penso, Jean Malach, et Jâques Bryan. Nous reservant leur genre de mort, aussi bien que le temps de leur execution, exceptant de la dite condamnation—David Wilson que Nous entendons sera mis hors de prison, á cause de son jeune âge, luy enjoignant neanmoins sous peine de la vie de ne plus retourner en Amerique sous quelque pretexte que ce soit : Declarant les biens des d^{ts} coupables confisqués aussi bien que le vaisseau le Dauphin arrêté par le gouverneur de Carthagéne et les marchandises dont le d^t vaisseau étoit chargé, appliquant la moitié du provenu au Tresor Royal, et l'autre moitié á la chambre de sa Majesté ; ordonnant que pour rendre efficace la dite confiscation, on remettra incessament aux gouverneur et officiers de justice de Carthagene copie de la dite sentence deuement authorisée, afin qu'ils remettent par les prochains vaisseaux de la flote, ou autres vaisseaux du Roy, le provenu des effets cy-dessus, suivant la vente qui en sera faite sur les lieux, pour en étre disposé par sa Majesté et le Conseil de Guerre des Indes, conformement á la presente disposition. Et d'autant qu'il paroit par les actes produites dans la dite procedure, que les personnes sous nommées sont aussi coupables, sçavoir le Duc d'Hamilton, le Comte de Pen-moor, le Marquis de Tweedall et autres du royaume d'Ecosse, qui quoique sujets du Roi de la Grande Bretagne formèrent sans sa permission une compagnie pour cet armement et etablissement au dit Darien, Panecop Admiral de la d^{te} escadre et autres Cap^{nes} tant de mer que de terre, plusieurs chefs et officiers aussi bien que les membres établis pour conseil de la dite compagnie embarqués sur la dite escadre, dont les noms sont mentionés et dans les actes de la dite procedure, et ceux qui sont restés dans le royaume d'Ecosse, lesquels sont tous dignes de chatiment pour un attentat si detestable.   Il a été ordonné qu'afin de pouvoir tous jours entretenir la bonne intelligence entre les deux couronnes d'Angleterre et d'Espagne, á la quelle ont contrevenus tous les accusés cy dessus, on tirera une copie authentique des actes, qui provent la verité de ces crimes, laquelle par le moyen des Seigneurs de la Jonta du Conseil, sera remise á l'ambassadeur ou ministre qui tiendra lieu d'ambassadeur en Angleterre, pour être communiqué au nom du Roy nôtre Sire au Roy de la Grande Bretagne, et le dit ministre fera des instances efficaces, á cc que sa Majesté Britannique, ordonne á ses Conseils, Parlemens oú autres Cours de Justice de punir exemplairement les dits coupables, luy representant les dommages tres considerables qu' a causé a cette couronne un pareil attentat, et les inconveniens, qui pourroient naítre de leur impunité pour toute l'Europe. Ordonnons aussi qu'on tirera des certificats de tous les bureaux dont il conviendra les tirer, de toutes les dépenses qu'on a eté obligé de faire dans cc royaume, á l'occasion de cette invasion tant pour l'armement de l'escadre qu'on envoye á Darien ct aux Isles d'Or pour les reduire que de toutes les autres depenses faites en consequence, lesquels certificats avec les susdites procedures seront representées a S. M. B. afin qu'il ordonne á Ses Conseils et Cours de Justice d'en chɛrger la dite compagnie d'Ecosse si bien qu'on en puisse reçevoir une juste et entiere satisfaction, et que le resultat des diligences que fera le dit Ministre, soit joint á ces procedures, afin que le Roy et les Seigneurs de la jointe de Guerre puissent apres resoudre sur cc qui conviendra de plus á propos pour le service de sa Majesté.

Et d'autant que le gouverneur de Carthagene devroit avoir châtié exemplairement tant les dits prisonniers, que tous les autres qui étoient sur le d^t vaisseau Dauphin sans aucune consultation, ni sans attendre nouveaux ordres, conformement aux ordonnances et aux loix ; et que non seulement il ne l'a pas fait, mais a même livré quelques uns d'eux à la flote de Borlavento, qui étoit alors dans le port de Carthagene, et que la hardiesse des étrangers s'augmente tous les jours dans les Indes, faute d'executer les peines établies, et par l'indulgence, et l'impunité, qui donnent lieu á des pareils envenemens, on supplie sa Majesté de prendre telles mesures et donner tels ordres que le d^t gouverneur et autres Ministres ne tombent plus dans pareille faute.   Tel est nôtre jugement dernier.

Signé, etc.,

Prononcé le 26 Juin.

Signifié le 26 au Procureur Fiscal et le 28 fut presentée la requête appel.

TRANSLATION OF THE SENTENCE PASSED BY THE CHAMBER FOR THE CONSERVATION OF THE INDIES AT SEVILLE ON CAPTAIN PINCARTON AND OTHERS

In the action and criminal suit brought by the King's fiscal, acting for the Chamber for the Conservation of the Indies, against the accused, Robert Pincarton, Benjamin Spencer, *alias* Penso, John Malach, James Brayan [Graham], and David Wilson, all natives of the kingdom of Scotland, who are detained in the prisons of this Chamber for having gone from the said kingdom of Scotland to the country called Darien, with a squadron of five ships of war, carrying various articles of merchandise, and for having built there forts and houses, and committed other acts mentioned in the report of the fiscal, Joseph Moreno, after having seen and examined the records, proofs, and accusations, we find that we must pronounce them guilty on these heads.   We condemn to death the aforesaid Captain Robert Pincarton, Benjamin Spenser, *alias* Penso, John Malach, and James Brayan [Graham], reserving for our decision the manner of their death, as well as the time, and excepting from the said sentence David Wilson, whom we ordain to be liberated from prison because of his youth, enjoining him never to return to America under any pretext whatsoever on pain of death.   We declare the possessions of the said culprits confiscated, as well as the ship *Dolphin* seized by the governor of Carthagena, and the merchandise with which the said vessel was laden, allocating half the proceeds to the Royal Treasury, and the other half to the Privy Purse.   To render the said confiscation effectual, we ordain that a copy of the said sentence duly authenticated be sent immediately to the governor and magistrates of Carthagena, in order that they may send by the next vessels of the fleet, or other ships of the King, the proceeds from the sale of these effects, the same to be disposed of by his Majesty and the Ministry of War for the Indies conform to this order : And whereas it appears from the records produced in the said proceedings that the persons named below are also guilty, viz., the Duke of Hamilton, Lord Panmure, the Marquis of Tweeddale, and others of the kingdom of Scotland who, although subjects of the King of Great Britain, formed without his permission a company to promote this armed settlement in Darien, Panecop [Pennicuik], commodore of the said squadron and other naval and military captains together with several other officers, as well as the members appointed as a board of the said company who embarked in the said squadron, all mentioned in the records of the said trial, and those who remained in the kingdom of Scotland, who are all worthy of punishment for so detestable an outrage, it has been ordered to the end that the good understanding between the crowns of England and Spain, which all the above accused have violated, be maintained, that there shall be drawn up a duly authenticated copy of the records proving the truth of these accusations, to be transmitted by the Lords of the Privy Council to the Spanish ambassador or the Minister holding the place of Spanish ambassador in England, to be communicated in the name of the King our Lord to the King of Great Britain, and that the said Minister make urgent appeal to his Majesty of Great Britain to order his Councils, Parliament, or other Courts of Justice to punish in an exemplary manner the said culprits, representing to him the great damage this outrage has caused the crown of Spain, and the inconvenience which will result to the whole of Europe if they are allowed to go unpunished.   We also command that an account be made out in all the departments concerned of the whole expenses we have been obliged to incur in this kingdom by reason of this invasion, for the outfit of the squadron sent to Darien and to the Golden Islands to subdue them, and all the other expenses incurred in consequence, and that these accounts with the above proceedings be presented to his Majesty of Great Britain, to the end that he may order his Councils and Courts of Justice to charge them to the said Scottish company, so that we may receive from them complete and just satisfaction, and that the result of the efforts made by our Minister together with these proceedings may enable the King and the Ministry of War hereafter to resolve what may be most fitting for the service of his Majesty.

And since the governor of Carthagena should have summarily punished in an exemplary manner the said prisoners and all the others who were on the said ship *Dolphin* without waiting for further orders according to ordinance and law, and since he not only failed to do so but delivered some of them up to the fleet of Borlavento which was then in the harbour of Carthagena, and seeing that the audacity of foreigners is increasing daily in the Indies for want of enforcing the appointed penalties, and by reason of the indulgence and impunity which occasion the same, we pray his Majesty to take such measures and to issue such orders that the said governor and other Ministers may not again fall into the same error.   This is our judgment.

Signed etc.

Pronounced on 26th June.

Presented to the Procurator Fiscal on 26th June.

The request to appeal was presented on 28th June.

An abbreviated résumé of this is given in Hill Burton's *Darien Papers,* p. 109.

The two following memorials to King William should be read along with Murray of Philiphaugh's letter of 11th July 1700 at pp. 556-558 of *Carstares State Papers and Letters.*   Parliament in May would not vote supplies until the question of Caledonia was discussed.   The King in consequence adjourned the sittings, and the government had to consider ways and means.

MEMORIALL OF LAWES TOUCHING THE MILITIA

It is declared by the 5th act Parl. j66i, intituled act asserting his Majesties royall prerogative in the militia and in making peace and war, that the power of armes and in making of peace and war or treaties and leagues with fforraign princes and states doth properly reside in the Kings Majestic and in his successors, and that yt was and is their undoubted right and theirs alone to have the power of raising in armes the subjects of this kingdom and of the comanding, ordering, and disbanding or otherwayes disposing thereof, and of all strengths, fforts, or garrisons within the same, as they shall think fitt, the subjects alwayes being free of the provisions and mentinance of these fforts and armies, unless the same be concluded in Parliament or Convention of Estates.

And by the 14th act of the same Parliament intituled act for raising the annuity of 40,000 lib. star., the Estates of Parliament make offer to his Majestic of the sum of 40,000 lib. star. yearly during all the dayes of his Maties lifetym towards the entertainment of any such fforces as his Majestic shall think fitt to raise and keep up within this kingdom, or otherwayes towards the defraying of the necessarie charge of his government according to his royall pleasure.   And this 40,000 lib. for the due and suteable support of his Majesties government, and for defraying the exigencies thereof is by act of Parliament j68i continued for the space of ffive years after K. Charles the Seconds decease.

And by the 2ᵈ act Parliament i685 the same excise is for the usefulness thereof to support the interest of the crown annexed to the same for ever.

It is true that by the act of the Convention j689 containing the claim of right it is one of the articles charged against the late K. James, his levieing or keeping on foot a standing armie in tyme of peace without consent of Parliament, which armie did exact locality free and drye quarters. And by the 18th act of the same Convention containing the grievances, the levieing or keeping on foot a standing armie in tyme of peace without consent of Parliament is declared to be a grievance. But this grievance, as severall others there sett down, is not as yet by a speciall act formally redressed; only the act j698 for granting of the supplie then given doth in the first place expressly consent to the continuance of the number of fforces upon the present establishment for two years after the first of Nomber next. But this consent is to the forces on the present establishment, and seems not to derogatt from the act j66i, specially the 14th act of that Parliament, but to leave the same in force, untill the forsd grievance be formally considered and redressed.

And therefor it is thought that his Majestic may always keep up what fforces are truely necessary for guards and garisons for the support and security of the government, providing the subjects be free of their provision and mentinance, unless the same be concluded in Parliament or Convention of Estates.

MEMORIAL TO KING WILLIAM with some PAPERS
REFERRED TO IN IT [July] 1700

In our last memorial we gave his Maᴶᵗˡᵉ an account of the present state and condition of affairs with our humble opinion and advyce, to which we add that there is herewith sent a state of the funds and how farr they will reach toward the subsistence of the forces, and what a great soume of arrears is deu.

That we conceave it absolutlie necessarie for the preservation of his Maj^ties goverment that there be a good understanding established betwixt his Maj^tie and Parliat.

That his Maj^tie comming to hold the next session of Parliat. in person is the most probable mean to make the disaffected members abate and condescend to adjust matters to his Maj^ties satisfaction.

That if his Maj^tie cannot give his own presence, there appears a necessitie that his Maj^tie agree to all demanded concerning Darien, and that the other demands in the address be referred to the Parliat., or other wayes the Parliat. must still adjourn, which continuallie makes things worse. That whither his Maj^tie resolve to come and hold the next session in person, or to hold it by his Commissioner instructed to agree to what is demanded, it is our humble opinion the Parliament should meet as soon as may be after his Maj^tys return.

That in order to the meeting of the Parliat. after his Maj^ties return, we have presumed to send the draught of a letter to be sent by his Maj^tie to his Councell, to be published with the orders for the next adjournment, with such alterations as his Maj^tie shall think fitt.

That if his Maj^tie cannot hold the next session in person, or shall not be pleased to instruct his Commissioner to agree to what is demanded, then we doe humblie crave his Maj^ties particular directions in these grouing difficulties, wherin continued adjournments doe onlie more provoke, and a Parliament seems so necessarie to support his Maj^ties goverment.

STATE OF THE FFUNDS FOR THE FORCES

10TH OF JULY 1700

Charge

	[ll.	ss.	d.]
Impr. 4 months cess whereof 2 are payable at			
Lammas and 2 at Martinmass is . 24000	0	0	

Item on quarter of the excyse payable the [ll.   ss. d.]
   1st of September, but by the tack (30
   dayes of grace being alloued) no quarter-
   ing is to be till the 1st of October. The
   tack deutie quarterlie is 10,000 ^{lb} ster.,
   but by reason of the badness of the cropts
   and low condition of the countrey no
   more can be truelie reckoned upon
   then   6500   0   0

                       Summa is 30500   0   0

                  Discharge   [ll.   ss. d.]

Impr. for subsisting the troops monthlie
   according to the present establisment
   for the months of August, Sept^r, Oct^r,
   and Nov^r, at 4900 ^{lb} monthlie is   .   19600   0   0

Item by quarterlie precepts at Lammas
   1700 including coal and candle to the
   garrisons then yearlie draun .   .   966 18   4

Item by quarterlie precepts at the 1st of
   November 1700 without coal and candle   687 18   4

Item for forrage to the troop of guards in
   attending the Commissioner conform to
   his Maj^{tys} warrand may be computed to 1000   0   0

Item by cloathing money deu to the commissaries for cloathing the troop of
   guards, which they are by his Maj^{tys}
   letter alloued to retain in ther oun
   hands, amounts to   3700   0   0

                       Summa is 25,954 16   8

Item the commissaries are to be reimbursed
   which they are in advance of   .   3066   0   0

                       In all 29,020 16   8

1700 July 10th

Accompt of the monthlie subsistence

	[ll.	ss.	d.]
Impr. to the troop of guards . . .	412	14	8
To the 1st battalion of foot guards . .	468	3	4
2d battalion thereof	352	10	3
To Maj. General Ramsey monthlie . .	50	0	0
To Fort Wm of full pay wt a 2d leut colonel	701	8	0
Edenburgh Castle	98	5	6
Stirlin Castle	77	5	7
Dunbarton Castle	42	3	6
Artillerie companie	37	5	7
Item by accompt of officers subsistence for a regiment consisting of 10 companies viz. :			
To the colonel as such and as captain .	14	00	0
To the lieut. col. as such and as captain .	10	10	0
Major as such and as captain . . .	9	02	0
Adjutant or aid major	2	16	0
7 captains	39	4	00
7 lieutenants	30	16	00
9 enseigns	18	18	0
Item 3 regiments more	375	18	0
Item 1 regiment of 8 companies . . .	104	6	0
The monthlie subsistence of the officers of a regiment of dragoons consisting of 8 companies viz. :			
Colonel as such and as captain . .	18	0	0
Leut. colonel as such and as captain .	13	6	0
Major as such and as captain . . .	11	8	0
5 captains	42	0	0
8 lewtenants	35	9	4
8 cornetts	29	17	4
1 quartermaster	2	16	0
Item a regiment of dragoons of 6 troops, viz.:			
Colonel as such and as captain . .	18	0	0
Leut. col. as such and as captain . .	13	6	0
Major as such and as captain . . .	11	8	0
3 captains	25	4	0

6 lewtenants	26 12	00
6 cornetts	22 8	00
1 quartermaster	2 16	0

In all 3117 17 5

Item the monthlie subsistence of a regiment of foot officers and souldiers consisting of 10 comp. is 335 13 0

Item the monthlie subsistence of a regiment of dragoons consisting of 8 troops, officers and souldiers 609 5 8

Item a regiment of dragoons of six troops, officers and souldiers is . . . 462 2 0

Item quarterlie precepts amounts to . . 966 18 4

5491 17 3

COPPY OF A LETTER TO HIS MATY IN FAVOUR OF
MR. PINKARTOWNE AND HIS CREW

MAY IT PLEASE Yor MAty,—I should not have presumed to have troubled yor Maty at present, nothing of consequence having occured since I wrett to yor Maty with Mr. Carstairs, but that the letters from Spain bring accot that Captain Pinkarten and those of his crew, who were taken near to Carthagena and are now prisoners in Sevilia and some other places of Old Spain, are sentenced to dye. Yor Maty may remember that you was graciously pleased to promise to the Affrican company in a letter to the Privy Council, about the time I went Commissioner to the General Assembly, that you would demand them; and some time thereafter when I was in Scotland yor Maty was pleased to allow my Ld. Carmichael to write to some of the company that you had demanded them; and after all this, if they suffer death, it will very much increase the present ferment in Scotland, and in my humble opinion it will be ane act of great injustice and cruelty in the King of Spain, and contrary both to the law of nations and yor Mats treatties with him, for the ship they were in did spring a laik and they were necessitat to run to the nearest shoar, which happened to be near to Carthagena ; and my Lord Carmichael has written with a great deal of concern of this matter, as I acquainted yor Ma^{ty} before you went, and you was pleased to allow me to speak to Mr. Secretary Wernon of this, which I have now done, and he has promised to write to Spain in there favours, and he is also to write to yor Ma^{ty} for further orders. I lykewise presume to think that if yor Ma^{ty} would be pleased to recommend this matter to the Duke of Bavaria it might perhaps be of use. My zeal for yor Ma^{ts} service and my affection for my countreymen will I hope prevail with yor Ma^{ty} to pardon my importunity in this. Many of the Parlia^t men are goeing from Ed^r to the countrey, and those of them who have signed the address are useing there outmost endeavours to procure subscriptions to it, and they make every body of whatever quality they be wellcome to signe, and so they expect to obtain a great many hands to it. This is with all submission from, May, etc., Yo^r Ma^{ts} most ffaithfull most humble and most obed^t subject and servant, *sic subs.*,

SEAFIELD.

Whitehall, Jully 12th, 1700.

The same day Seafield also wrote to Mr. Carstares[1] to intercede with the King on behalf of Captain Pinkerton and his crew.

COPPY OF A LETTER TO THE KING ABOUT CAPTAIN
PINKARTONE

MAY IT PLEASE YOUR MAJESTIE,—I have nothing to trouble your Majestic with att prasent, ther being nothing in agitation nou in Scotland bot the procuring subscriptions to the adress, in which they succeed too weal, tho a great many refuse to signe. I have sent this by the father of on John Malloch, who is condemned to die as is Captan Pinkerton and the rest of his creu al prisoners in Sevilia. I have also by this packet verie earnest letters in ther favours, intreating I may interceed for them, and by a letter direct for the councel of the African companie from them they inform that a letter from your Majestic will

---

[1] *Carstares State Papers and Letters*, pp. 558, 559.

safe ther lives ; and I doe most humblie intreat that if it is not yet done that your Majestic may be gratiuslie pleased to interpose for them and save ther livs.   I am only affraid it come to lait, and it being in favours of your Majesties subjects I have no doubt bot your Majestic will speedilie dispatch your commands to some of your Majesties servants ther.   I hope your Majestic will pardon me for trobling you so oftne for the same thing, and I am ackording to my diutie, May it pleas your Majestic, Your Majesties most humble, most faithful, and most obedient subject and servant,   SEAFIELD.

Whitehall, Julie 13, 1700.

Serenissimo ct Potentissimo Principi Dño Carolo Secundo
    Dei Gratia Hispaniarum, Utriusque Siciliæ, Jerusalem,
    Indiarum, etc., Regi, Archi-Duci Austriæ, Duci
    Burgundiae, Brabantiae, Mediolani, Comiti Abspurgii,
    Flandriae, Tyrolis, etc. : Fratri ct Consanguineo
    Nostro Charissimo.

GULIELMUS TERTIUS Dei Gratia Angliæ, Scotiæ, Franciæ, ct Hiberniæ Rex, Fidei Defensor, etc. : Serenissimo et Potentissimo Principi Domino Carolo Secundo cadem Gratia Hispaniarum, Utriusque Siciliæ, Jerusalem, Indiarum, etc.: Regi, Archi-Duci Austriæ, Duci Burgundiæ, Brabantiæ, Mediolani, Comiti Abspurgii, Flandriæ, Tyrolis, etc. : Fratri et Consanguineo Nostro Clarissimo Salutem.   Serenissime ct Potentissime Princeps, Frater et Consanguinee Charissime, quod subditis nostris Scoticis nuperrime acciderit, relictam nempe ab iis, initis cum Majestatis vestræ gubernatore Carthagenense pactis et conditionibus, regionem de Darien, rescivisse Majestatem vestram non dubitamus, quinetiam navem quandam paulo ante cursum inde suum in alias Americæ partes tenentem in vicinum litus projectam fractamque, quique in ipsa inerant dictam civitatem opem flagitaturos adeuntes comprehensos et in carcerem diductos, Hispaniam̃ postea transvectos et capite ibidem damnatos ad supremum Ma^{tls} ^{vrae} concilium Madriti provocasse : Ea vero est celeberrima ct notissima

Ma^tls v^rae in omnes clementia, ut subditos istos nostros tot ct tanta ex improbatis a Ma^te v^ra corum consiliis coeptisque jamjam perpessos eidem majorem in modum commendare non dubitemus, qua quidem indignos ipsos cognito perpensoque hominum casu Ma^tem v^ram non esse habituram arbitramur ministro itaque nostro Domino de Schonenberg in mandatis dedimus ut quod illos attinet, quoque nomine ex pœna eos eximi ct in libertatem simul restitui sperare liceat Ma^tl v^rae uberius exponi atq̃ representari curet, cujus quidem advocationi facilem fore aditum nobis persuademus, amotis jam ex regionibus istis omnibus nostris subditis, nihil de ingrato isto suscepto superesse amplius videtur, quam ut infelices isti captivi regia vestra lenitudine ct misericordia gaudeant. Opus hoc præclara ac generosa Ma^tls v^rae indole dignissimum singulare Ma^tls v^rae erga nos benevolentiæ argumentum interpretabimur, ct pari vel alio officiorum genere, quoties facultas dabitur, reciprocabimus. Adeoque Ma^tem v^ram Supremi Numinis tutelæ ex animo commendamus.

Quæ dabantur in Aula nostra apud Loo 22º die Julii anno Domini 1700. Regnique nostri duodecimo, Ma^tls v^rae frater ct consanguineus amantissimus,

GULIELMUS R.
G. BLATHWAYT.

Translation—

TO THE MOST SERENE AND POTENT PRINCE CHARLES THE SECOND, BY THE GRACE OF GOD KING OF THE SPAINS, ETC. ETC.

WILLIAM THE THIRD by the grace of God, King of England, Scotland, France, and Ireland, Defender of the Faith etc., to the most serene and potent prince Charles the Second, by the grace of God King of the Spains, the Two Sicilies, Jerusalem, the Indies etc., Archduke of Austria, Duke of Burgundy, Brabant, Milan, Count of Habspurg, Flanders, Tyrol, etc., our very dear brother and cousin, greeting.

Most serene and potent Prince, very dear brother and cousin, We doubt not that your Majesty has heard what has recently happened to our Scottish subjects, how by agreement with your Majesty's governor of Carthagena they left the country of Darien, how a short time before one of their ships sailing thence for other parts of America was cast ashore in the neighbourhood of Carthagena and was wrecked, and how those on board, when they repaired to the above-mentioned city to seek help, were seized and thrown into prison, were afterwards transported to Spain and were there condemned to death, and have now appealed to your Majesty's supreme court at Cadiz for redress. Such is your Majesty's renowned and known clemency to all men that we most heartily commend to it those our subjects who have been thus condemned for their designs and attempts against your sovereignty, and have already endured such grievous suffering. We believe that, when the condition of these men is known and considered, your Majesty will not hold them unworthy of that clemency. Therefore we have given instructions to our minister, M. Schonenberg, to explain fully to your Majesty their circumstances, and the weighty reasons why their release and restoration to liberty may be hoped for. We persuade ourselves that there will be easy access for his advocacy, and that as all our subjects are now withdrawn from those countries, nothing more remains of that unpleasant enterprise than that those unhappy prisoners may enjoy your Royal clemency and compassion. Such an act so worthy of your Majesty's noble and magnanimous disposition we will look upon as a singular proof of your Majesty's goodwill towards us, and we will make suitable return as often as opportunity may arise. Finally, we heartily commend your Majesty to the protection of Almighty God.

Given at our Court at Loo, on the 22nd day of July, in the year of Our Lord 1700, and the twelfth of Our reign.

Your Majesty's most loving brother and cousin,

WILLIAM R.
G. BLATHWAYT.

To MONSᴿ SCHONENBURG

A Loo ce $\frac{19}{30}$ Juillet 1700.

MONSIEUR,—Je vous felicite de tout mon cœur sur votre heureux retour a l'exercise de vos charges, qui vous mettent en état de rendre de services plus efficaces dans votre poste. C'est en cette consideration que sa Majesté me vient d'ordonner de vous écrire en faveur du Capitaine Pinckerton et autres Ecossois, qui sont detenus prisoniers et condamnés même, á ce que l'on mande, dans l'Andalousie. Vous sçavez comme ces affaires sont passées, et que les Ecossois ont été obligés de quitter prise a Darien, et comme il ne reste de ces dernieres expeditions, que ces pauvres prisoniers. Sa Majesté trouve bon que vous partiez et agissiez pour eux á la cour d'Espagne, representant aux ministres, qu'il sera bon de mettre fin á cette fâcheuse affaire par un renvoy de ces gens lá chez eux, ce qui pourra avoir un fort bon effet de toutes les manieres, et obligera sa Majesté á une reconnoissance pareille dans les occasions. Vous sçavez sans doute, comme l'Ecosse se prend á l'egard de cc qui est passé dans le cours d'une entreprise, qui a fait tant de bruit dans le monde, et apres la capitulation nouvellement faite avec les Espagnols, il semble qu'ils ne doivent plus garder du ressentiment envers ces malheureux. Pour qui sa Majesté vous ordonne de travailler le plus fortement que vous pourrez.

J'en écris dans les mêmes termes á nôtre consul á Cadiz, autant que cela le peut regarder, ct comme le succés que vous pourrez avoir dans cette poursuitte tournera á la satisfaction de sa Majesté, et á vôtre honneur en particulier, on ne doute pas que vous ne vous serviez des meilleurs moyens pour y parvenir.—Au reste je suis, Monsieur, vôtre tres humble ct tres obéissant serviteur, BLATHWAYT.

Translation from the French—

To M. SCHONENBURG

Loo, $\frac{19}{30}$ July 1700.

SIR,—I congratulate you heartily on your happy return to your duties, which will enable you more efficiently to discharge the same.

It is with this consideration that his Majesty has commanded me to write to you on behalf of Captain Pinckerton and other Scotsmen who lie in prison in Andalusia under sentence of death. You know how these things have come about, and how the Scots have been obliged to give up their settlement in Darien; and as these poor prisoners are the sole survivors of the last expeditions, his Majesty desires you to intercede for them at the court of Spain, representing to the ministers that it would be desirable to terminate this troublesome business by sending the prisoners home, an act which will have an excellent effect in every way and will constrain his Majesty to a like return in similar circumstances. You know, doubtless, how anxiously Scotland regards what has taken place in the course of an enterprise which has made such a stir in the world; and after the capitulation made so recently to the Spaniards, it seems that the latter ought no longer to keep up resentment against these unfortunate men, on whose behalf his Majesty commands you to make the most strenuous endeavours.

I am writing in the same terms to our Consul at Cadiz, so far as it may lie in his department; and as the success your efforts will meet with will turn to the satisfaction of his Majesty and to your own honour in especial, I do not doubt you will use the best means in your power to attain your end.—I remain, Sir, Your most humble and most obedient servt, BLATHWAYT,

To S^R MART^N WESTCOMB, Consul at Cadiz

Loo, the $\frac{19}{30}$ July 1700.

S^r,—His Ma^{ty} having sent directions to Monsr Schonenburg at Madrid to use his best endeavour with the court of Spain, for the release of Capt Pinckerton and other Scots prisoners, who are not only detained near you, but, as we are inform'd, condemn'd to die upon the acco^t of Darien, I am likewise commanded by his Majesty to signify his pleasure that you give all the assistance and succour you can to the prisoners, by furnishing them with necessarys and endeavouring their release in the best manner, and that you correspond with Monsr Schonenburg therein, and do every thing else that may conduce to the bringing this matter to a good issue.—I am, S^r, Your most humble servant,   WILLIAM BLATHWAYT.

Copie LETTER to the COUNCELL adjourning the
PARLIAMENT

WHERAS the circumstances of our affairs doe still continue such, as will not allou of the sitting of the Parliament on the 13 of August next, to which it was last adjourned, and we judging it may be necessarie we should return to Brittain before the meeting thereof, that the members may not be putt to unnecessarie trouble and charges, we doe authorise and require you to issue forth a proclamation in our name adjourning our said Parliament from the said 13 day of August to the 29th day of October next.   And we being firmlie resolved the Parliament shall then meet, you are to order all the members to attend at Edr. that day in the usual way and upon the accustomed certifications ffor doing, etc.

Parliament accordingly met on the 29th of October 1700.

MR. PRINGLE'S LETTER about the E. OF BALCARRAS
TO VISCOUNT SEAFIELD

Dieren, Aug. 6, 1700.

MY LORD,—The last post brought me your Lop^s of the 30 July, and with it we had the surprising and sad news of the Duke of Glocesters death, which your Lop. may be sure affects all here verie much, and the King hes dispatched Colonel Stanley to condole with the Princess on this sad occasion. I have not yet heard of Captain Fraser's [1] being in this countrey, but I think it veric strange it should come into his head to bring hither draughts of remissions, which your Lop. hes not seen nor approven of. I am of your Lop^s opinion, the remitting of the privat crimes would make a great clamour, and be a good handle to some to misrepresent both the King and his ministers to the people, and perhaps anie remission at this time may doe prejudice to his Maj^{tys} service. However, when the thing is laid before the King, his Majty will be able to judge what may be fitt to be done, and his orders shall be obeyed.

The Earl of Belcarras was at Loo applying for libertie to return home, and his circumstances having been laid before the King, which indeed seem to be such as plead for pity, his Maj^{ty} inclines now he should be alloued that favour, but not knouing if his servants would think it fitt in this juncture, his Maj^{ty} hes ordered me to write to your Lop. as also to the D. of Queensberrie and to my Lord Carmichael, that he may knou your Lop^s and there mind about it, how farr it may consist with his service in this juncture to grant that favour to the E. of Belcarras or not, and your Lop. may be pleased to signifie your mind either to the King himself or by Mr. Carstairs or me, as your Lop thinks fitt. I beleive indeed the Earl smarts so much for his past follie, that he thinks of nothing at present but living peaceablie.

Before my last letter went off, on Capt. Gus was come to Loo from Sr George Rook, with account of the King of Swedens landing in Zetland with 6000 men and meeting with litle or no opposition from the Danes, so it is not doubted but he will bring all that countrey under contribution, which its like will hasten a peace, a treatie being now on foot. I am, My Lord, your Lops. most humble serv^t,

RO. PRINGLE.

---

[1] *Carstares State Papers and Letters*, pp. 580-581.

Seafield in his letter to Mr. Carstares at pp. 617 and 618 of *State Papers and Letters* advised making a bargain with Balcarres before he was permitted to return to Scotland.

ffor THE RIGHT HONORABLE THE EARLE OF FFINDLATER these

MY NOBLE LORD,—The Duke of Gordon was yisternight at ffyvie, and is to be this night at Strathbogie and to keep a court there to morrow, so that he does not come this way. Your Lop. hes no questione heard of the adjorne-ment of the Parliat. to the 23d of October nixt. I shall obey my Ladie Seafeilds comandes anent Kempkairne, and gett a full account of his debtes regrat heir so soone as Thomas ffordyce, who does for the clerk, comes home, and send the same to my Ladie.—I am, My Lord, Your Lop[s] most devoted and most humble servant,

J. DONALDSONE.

Banff, 14*th of August* 1700.

John Donaldson, writer in Banff, was for some years clerk to the commissioners of supply of Banffshire, an office which he demitted in January 1706. In 1715 he acted as factor for the collector appointed by Mar to collect the county cess for the Jacobites during the rising of the 'Fifteen.[1]

MR. CARSTARES'S LETTER ABOUT THE MASTER OF WORK, ETC.

Loo., Ag. 16, 1700.

MY LORD,—No post haveing come from England since I did myselfe the honour to write my last to your Lo., I haue litle to trouble your Lo. with. My Lord Jersey is here, but I have no patron about court but the King him-selfe, nor doe I seek any. My Lord Selkirk does not speak to me, and Coll. Rosse looks not pleasantlie upon me, but I break neither my head nor heart with these things, nor have I reason to doe it. We have a new envoy from Brandenburgh, one Bondelie. There is a discourse of some changes at that court, which I hope shall be to the

---

[1] Dr. Cramond's *Annals of Banff*, vol. i. p. 116.

advantage of his Maties. affairs.   I hope Mr. Pringle shall
gett papers signed this night, for the King hath appointed
him to attend, and he hath also ordered me to doe so, and
I shall then know his mind as to the D. of Queensberries
proposalls ; but Mr. Pringle hath not a copie of a gift for
Master of Work, but I believe your Lo. hath one signed
blank, which may serve if the King grant it to Sr Francis,
but the Commissioner must take his own way to satisfie
the E. of Marr, who your Lo. knows did speak to you
about this post.   It will I humblie judge be fitt that your
Lo. writt of this to the Commissioner, that E. of Marr
may have no ground of displeasure.   I shall doe the same,
but I humblie conceive that the way of doing this must
be left to the Commissioner himselfe, because that of Sr.
Francis is a secret.   I heartilie wish your Lo. good successe
in useing the Bath.   I am faithfullie and with much respect
Your Lo.'s

It is like I may add a few words to this letter ere the
post goe.

Since writeing of what is above I had your Lo.'s of the
13th, and have since acquainted his Ma^{ty} with your Lo.'s
going to Scotland.   He askt me why you did not goe to
the Bath, for I must say he freelie allowed your Lo. to doe
it.   I answered him according to your Los. letter, and told
him it was your concern for his service that made you doe
so, seing his Matie. had formerlie insinuated that your Lo.
being there might be for his interest.   The King approves
of all that the D. of Queensberrie proposed in his letter,
and orders will be sent by the next post, so that if your
Lo. have a blanck gift for the Master of Work, then his
Matie. thinks it fitt that it should be disposed of to S^r
Francis, as the Commissioner can aggrie with him about
the terms upon which he is to have it.

Seafield's letter to Carstares of 13th and the Earl of Mar's
of 17th August 1700,[1] deal with the subject matter of this
letter.

---

[1] *Carstares State Papers and Letters*, pp. 610, 611, 618-620.

MR. KENNEIR'S LETTER ABOUT THE MEMORIALL GIVEN IN
TO THE COMMISSIONERS FOR AUDITING THE OFFICERS' ACCOTS.
AT LONDON.

Whitehall, 17 *Augt.* 1700.

MY LORD,—I waited this day on the commissioners for
examining and determining the debts due to the army, etc.,
and presented to them your Lops. memoriall, after transcrib-
ing it with a suteable title as your Lop. ordered me. They
excepted against giving in such a paper in your Lops. name,
and yet not signed, and said they could have no regaird to
it as not being signed. They also alledged that the
colonels and agents would have no regaird to such clames,
and that it must be remitted to the common law. I told
them they should have up instructions to avoutch the
justnes of the clames, but they were doubtfull they could
come in time, for they were limited by Parliament that they
could not sit a fortnight longer. We ended at this that I
should writ this night for such instructions as could prove
the severall debts, which must be the probations depositions
and the like made to the Privy Council, with their Lop[s] act,
and that a letter or memoriall signed should be laid before
them, and then they should consider what could be done in
it, if they came in time. But these being wanting they
would not take in my memoriall. They were verry cross
and obstinat, and I find they are as freindly as they can
to the officers. What is done in this must be with all
imaginable dispatch. All they would promise was, that
they would intimate these clames when instructed to the
severall colonels or their agents, to be answered by them.
It must also be remembered that the regiments be specially
designed by the colonels name, and whether horse foot
or dragoons, particularly who these called the English
dragoons belonged to at the time, about what time in
Scotland, etc. There is not yet any forreign maill, so that
we have no newes here.—I am, My Lord, Your Lop[s] most
humble, most faithful, and most obedient servant,

A. KINEIR.

Mr. Campbell was with me, and used all his endeavour
to make them inclinable.

Andrew Kineir [1] was a clerk in the office of the Secretary of State for Scotland.

For THE RIGHT HONBLE THE EARLE OF FINDLATER

Edinburgh, 2d Septr. 1700.

MY LORD,—. . . My Lord Secretarie is resolved to come of with the first of the morrows tyde, which falls about alevin or twalve acloack. He comes by the Cairne, and is to be a night with my Lord fforbes at his house, so that ffryday or Saturday I hope to have the honour to waite on your Lo. My wife and I give our humble dutie to your Lo., and wishing all hapieness to attend you I continue to be, My Lord, Your Lo. most obedient servant,

ALEX[r] OGILVIE.

While in the north Seafield was busy arranging for the success of the King's policy in Parliament.[2]

For THE RIGHT HONOURABELL THE EARELL OF FINLATUR AT EDR.

MY LORD,—I am mightly affrayed that the cold and stormy wadar, which you have had in your jurny hath doun you harem, for ther hath bein most bustring winds hear, which hath doun a gret dell of ill to the corans. I hop your Lo. will let me kno how you keep your halth at Ed[r], for I dou most sinserly wish you happness in all things, for I am, My Lord, Your most obedent daghtr and humbell servant,

ANNA SEAFIELD.

Octobr. 9, 1700.

Seafield with his father had by this time gone south to Edinburgh to prepare for the session of Parliament that met on the 29th of October.

To THE RIGHT HONORABLE THE EARLE OF FINLATOR AT HIS LUDGING AT EDINBROUGH

MY LORD,—Being come leatlie from Holand w[t] a Duch doggar with whom I brough some goods, and hes mad entrie of the same at Portsoy to John Ogilwie colector, and hes given my oblidgatione and surtie for the dewittie

---

[1] *State Papers (Scotland) Warrant Books*, vol. xxi., 3rd December 1705.
[2] *Carstares State Papers and Letters*, pp. 650, 651.

of the sd. goods, and because the goods came home on a foran bottome he hes bound us to pay double dewittie, in caise wee can not procure ane order to him from the present managers for paying onlie single dewittie, wheither ther be a law for it or not I canot tell, but this I know that evrie yeir ther comes Duch doggars both to Aberdein and Leith and to seauverll other pairts, and never payed on farthing but single dewittie, nor was it ever required of them, its hard that Coll^r Ogilwie should deal singularlie w^t me and the rest concerned in that shipp. I humblie intreat the favor of yōr Lo. that ye would be at the trouble to speak effectualie to the managers heir anent, for it will be a great lose to us if they should exact double custom. Besyds its a thing was never don in Scottland. We beggs yor Lo. will doe yōr endeavor to procur the order to the coll^r, for wee most have it to him againest the 10th December nixt. Ther is also some tuo or three pcice of muslen saised be on of the waitters belonging to me, qch the colector hes taken my lyn for to pay the wellow. In caise I procur not ane order from the managers to gett it up, most presume to recomend this to your Lo. It will be a lose to me if I pay it. Your Lo. knous my circumstances. I humblie begg pardon for my roodnes. I begg it of yor Lo. not to tak the trouble in ill pairt, and presums to giuc yor Lo. my most humble dewittie.—I am, My Lord, Your Lo^s most humble ser^t,   ALEX^r. DUNBAR.

Your Lo. commission is fullie obeyed.
Cullen, 6 Nov. 1700.

BRIGADEER MAITLAND'S LETTER ABOUT
KEPPOCHS REMISSION

ffort William, 26 Nov. 1700.

MY LORD,—The bearer is very sencible how instrumentall your Lordship was in procuring him his protection, and I most say since that time he has been very asisting to me, and very active in discouraging theift and robery, as witnes his taking Alester More. He is now to intreate that your Lo^p may be pleasd to procure him his remission, and he not only promices to serve his Majestic faithfuly the rest of his dayes, but with the help of this garison to make Lochaber free of theiving, and I truely beleive he designs to be as good as his promice. Therfor I intreat that your Lordship may make him one honest man.—I ever am, My Lord, Your Lordships most oblidged and most obedient servant   R. MAITLAND.

Earlier, on 26th April 1700, the heritors in the Presbyteries of Kincardine and Alford, Aberdeenshire, banded themselves to concert measures for the peace of their countryside, and offered five hundred merks Scots each for the apprehension of the following three dead or alive, Alester More *alias* M'Donald, John M'donald *alias* Glendey, and Angus M'donald *alias* Haked Stier, as notorious robbers and thieves.[1] There are further letters in this collection dated 8th and 10th December 1701 and 13th and 29th January 1702 about Alester More.

Next letter shows how the Kempcairn estate was coming into Seafield's possession.

For VISCOUNT SEAFIELD

RIGHT HONOURABLE, MY LORD,—All that is done in your Lōps business with Kempcairn, since you went from this place, is that the Lady Kempcairn hath renounced her liferent right of the lands you are to possess, but would not sign her husband and son's disposition in your Lops. favoures, alleadging she was under oath not to doe the same. However she hath judiciallie confirmed it, and it is now deposited in my Lord Boynds hand with the rest of the papers. . . . It is not fitt your Lop. should allow any more mōey to be payed to old Kempcairn, ffor he will be still importuning yor Lady for mōey here, and I fear the summs yor Lop. hes allready payed and is now to engage for will exceed the value of the lands you are to possess of that estate. Your valuation is now distinguished from Kempcairns, but nothing done as to the houses in Kieth. They are all waste, and none will engadge to take them, and Kempcairn will never rebuild them, so they cannot be reckoned rent to yor Lop. When I was at Kieth receiving

---

[1] *Historical Papers* (1699-1750), New Spalding Club, vol. i. p. 21 and 22.

yor Lōps rents, the tennents yr intreated your Lōp might obtain a liberty from the Parliament of other two yearly mercatts[1] in that place, the one to be on the third Tuesday of May called James fair, and the other on the last Tuesday of November called Andersmass fair. If your Lop. would obtain this priviledge they promise to tenent all yor waste lands yr, and engadge under tacks with their own. This would be very convenient for the good of the whole countrey as well as theirs, and in a short tym may add to yor Lops. rent by the customs, and it will undoubtedly contribute to the better and more tymely paȳt of your rents yr yearlie, seing both mercatts would be immediatly after the terms of Whitsunday and Mertimess. This hath made me presume to trouble yor Lōp to obtain a warrand for these mercatts, and if it be obtained your Lōp may send it north to me, and I shall cause insert it in the prognostications. They may stand on the muir where Semarivis fair stands.

It is now tym your Lōp. should think on the disposeing of yor victuall this year. I beleiv you may sell twelve houndered bolls, the one half meall and the other bear. I expect the meall rents will be ordinary well payed. The victuall is now selling here at eight merks and ane half, and in some places for five pounds p. boll, but its thought the pryces may rise towards the end of the year, yet its generallie believed it will not exceed ten m̄ks this year. There are severall of your Lōps tennents intreating me to take victuall from them this year for what they were resting the last year, and if yor Lōp can gett ten merks or more for this yeares rents it may be taken, because they have the victuall, but the countrey is drained of mōey. I have advanced two thousand merks to Robert Ogilive out off the rents, and must advance four houndered merks upon the masters going to Aberdene. . . . And that the Lord may bless and preserve your Lōp, and make you prosperous in all your affairs is the constant prayer of, My Lord, Your Lōps, most humble and most obliedged servant,

*Cullen House, De*r *2nd*, 1700   WILL. LORIMER.

---

[1] *The Acts of the Parliaments of Scotland*, vol. x. p. 332.

The right of market was then considered of value, and the acts of the Scots Parliaments show that many such rights were granted. The two markets suggested were granted by the Scots Parliament on 31st January 1701.

For THE RIGHT HONOURABELL THE EARELL OF FINLATUR

AT HIS LOUGENS AT THE BACK OF THE COURT ITS YARD, EDR.

TO THE CAER OF THE POST OF ABD.

MY LORD,—I was so huried when the horeses wint from this with sending your granchyld to Abd., that I had no tym to wret to your Lo. and to tell you that I long extremly for your north cuming. I hop the Parliment will rayse in tym, that you may coum and tak your Crismass at your own house, which will be a mighty satisfaction to me, for I am and shall ever continou, My Lord, Your Lo^s most obediant daghter and humbell servant,

Cullen Huse, Des. 20*th*, 1700.   ANNA SEAFIELD.

COPPY OF A LETTER TO MR. CARSTAIRS ANENT D. GORDON'S BUSINESS FROM LORD SEAFIELD

Ed^r., Janry. 1*st*, 1701.

SR,—We received yesterday an express signifying to us his Maj^{tys} inclinations, that the Parliamt. should be adjourned befor the end of this month, wch I am sure is the desire of all of us who have the honour to serve him, but the acts wch have been befor us have been of such importance both to his Maj^{ty} and the nation, that we could not get them despatcht sooner.

The army is now establisht again for a month, so his Maj^{ty} will have time to resolve, if the forces shall be reduced conform to his letter, or if he will make any other alteration, and his commands will accordingly be obeyed. The process [1] wch the Earl of Argile has raised against the D. of Gordon dos make a great noise. My Ld Duke dos seem to depend upon the King in this matter, and my Ld Argile is so assured of carreing it by a vote, that he is positive he will venture all befor he have it not in.

---

[1] *The Acts of the Parliaments of Scotland*, vol. x. pp. 222, 244, 252, 265, 268 ; *Hume of Crossrig's Diary*, pp. 25, 48, 57, 58, 65, 66.

My Ld Commissr. writs this night for his Maj^{tys} orders, and he will obey them what ever they be.   I have promised to writ nothing against my Ld Argile, and I cannot interpose for him, the D. of Gordons grandmother haveing been a daughter of my family, and he is my nearest neighbour in the country, and besides all this he did concurr for stoppeing of the address.   I wish that this affair could be accommodat, for it does divide his Mats. servants, and if it come to a decision bad consequences may follow upon it. However you can witnes that I have written nothing of this matter to the King.   The Earle of Argyle did shew me his memoriall.   Wee are resolved to make all the dispatch that is possible for us, but the least trifle will occasion fyve or six hours debate, and then wee are necessitat sometimes not to putt anything to the vote, because the members being wearyed goe out of the house and our opposers are sure constantly to attend.

The King has time now to sett on foott a treaty w^t the King of France for a free trade betwixt that kingdome and Scotland, for wee have only prohibite the importa^{n}ne of wine and brandy from France conditionally, and in the precise termes of the instructione to the Commissioner, that is untill our herring and other goods the product of our nation be allowed to be imported into ffrance, as they are receaved from other nationes.   I forsee that wee will have difficulties in adjusting ane address concerning Caledonia, but wee shall doe our best endeavour in that and every thing concerns his Ma^{ty}.   Our party is no weaker than it was, for wee had occasion to try them in the case of Mr. John Campbell, my cousin german, who you know compeats w^t the Laird of Bishoptowne for representing the shyre of Air in place of Rowallan.   That affair is to have its finall decision this day, and I hope wee shall carry it, and the worst that will fall out in thir case is to remitt both.   Wee are also in hopes of getting in betwixt and Saturnday a member from Galloway on our side, and ane oy^r from the shyre of Peebles.   I have not time to add any more at pñt, but I know my Lord Commissioner has written fully, so it is unnecessary for me to add any more.   You may communicate this to Mr. Pringle. I pray you give my humble duty to my Lord Portland.—I am Yo^r

M. H. S.

Marie Ogilvie, daughter of the first Lord Ogilvie of Deskford, married Sir John Grant of Freuchie, chief of the Grants, whose daughter, Marie, Marchioness of Huntly, was mother of the Duke of Gordon.

On the death of William Muir of Rowallan, commissioner for Ayrshire, a double return was made of Mr. John Campbell of Shankstoun and John Brisbain, Younger of Bishopstoun. Mr. Campbell was preferred.

MR. PRINGLE'S LETTER about DUKE GORDON and E. ARGYLES Process to VISCOUNT SEAFIELD

Whitehall, Jan. 7, 1701.

My Lord,—I did not write last post to your Lop., for I was then in expectation of orders for dispatching a flying pacquett, which, houever, I gott not till yesternight, and came hither for that end. It carries two letters from the King to the Duke of Queensberrie and my Lord Argyle, in which the King signifies his apprehension of prejudice to his service by the delay that process of the Earl of Argyles against the Duke of Gordon may bring to the conclusion of this session, which the King desires may be as soon as possiblie can be, and therfore recommends to my Lord Argyle the not insisting further in it at this time, his Maj. being resolved, as soon as the Parliament is over, to endeavour of accommodat that matter. I doubt not but my Lord Argyle will comply with this, but as I have suggested to his Lop., I beleive the King will be satisfied the stopp of this process be thought to proceed from some other cause then his interposing, which I think ought not to be known. I have just nou receaved your Lops. of the 4th, and am veric glad these neu elections hes gone so much to your Lops. mind, and I hope we may from thence presage a happie issue to this long session. The King hes signed a commission of guidon of the guards to the quartermaster,[1] and of quartermaster to Mr. Charles Campbell, which my

---

[1] Captain Archibald Douglas. In Dalton's *Army Lists* these commissions are dated 10th January.

Lord Argyle wrote for. I shall take care of what your Lop. recommends to me about the Warden of the Mints place. Having occasion to send doun for my Lady Margaret Hope a watch and some other litle things, I have taken freedom to send them with this pacquett in a cover to my brother Thomas, since it putts his Maj^{tle} to no expense.—I am, My Lord, Your Lops. most humble serv^t,

RT. PRINGLE.

MR. PRINGLE'S LETTER TO VISCOUNT SEAFIELD WITH THE KING'S LETTER DISCHARGING PERSONS TO COME TO COURT, AND ALLOWING THE COMMISSIONER TO REPAIR

Hampton Court, Jan. 25, 1701.

MY LORD,—My last to your Lop. was by a flying pacquett, signifying to my Lord Commissioner his Maj^{tles} pleasure as to the forces, and which I was obleidged to dispatch in such hast that I could not write fullie to your Lop. ; and as I doubt not but what I wrote to his Grace hes been communicat to your Lop. before this can reach you, I shall trouble your Lop. no further about it. There goes by this post two orders under his Maj^{tles} hand, on to his Grace my Lord Commissioner requiring him to repair hither as soon as the Parliament is over, and allouing him to retain the charecter of his Maj^{tles} Commissioner as long as he is within the kingdom. The other is to the Councell discharging all persons of publick trust and particularlie those of Councell and Exchequer to leave the kingdom anic time before the first of May next without his Maj^{tles} special libertie, excepting the Secretaries of State, who may repair hither when they think fitt, his Maj^{tle} apprehending much that upon the rising of the Parliament manie may think fitt to wait upon him, at a time when the surcease of justice and of the business of the Tresaurie and Exchequer, much postponed by the sitting of Parliament, seem to require there presence ; but as its probable some may take exceptions to this prohibition, so I doubt not but your Lop. will think it reasonable that his Maj^{tles} order be not known untill its presented, and for that end there is not the least notice taken of it to anic other, save my Lord

Commissioner and my Lord Carmichaell.—I am, My Lord,
Your Lops. most humble serv^t,   Ro. Pringle.

For VISCOUNT SEAFIELD

Whitehall, Jan. 30, 1701.

My Lord,—This morning by the flying pacquett I
receaved your Lops. of the 25th, which was much longed
for, having had 3 ordinarie maills without anie from your
Lōp either to Mr. Carstairs or my self.   Yours to the [K]
I delivered at his levee, and gave him account of what hes
hitherto past in reference to the armie, with which I am
confident he is veric well satisfied, and what accounts we
are further to expect shall be agreable to him.   His
Maj^{tie} came yesternight to Kensington, where its thought
he will reside during the sitting of the Parliament here,
unless it be to divert himself for on or two dayes of the
week at Hampton Court.   There is nou veric great appearance of a rupture with France, the last maills having
brought account of the King of Frances having putt
troups into Ostend and Neuport, which hes alarumed all the
trading people there, so that the actions fell yesterday
considerablie ; and its not doubted but the Dutch forces
that are in anie of the Flanders garrisons will soon be
ordered to retire, if they are not more harshlie dealt
with, some apprehending that they may be detained as
prisoners, but I am told the Elector of Bavaria hes
assured the States of Holland that they shall be honourablie
dismist.—I am, My Lord, Your Lops. most humble serv^t,

Ro. Pringle.

Written on the same sheet is

MR. PRINGLE'S LETTER showing the KING'S mind about
   the Modelling the 3000 men,[1] and that he would not
   consent to it

My Lord,—After I had writt what is above to have been
sent by the ordinarie post, his Maj^{tie} sent for me and ordered
me to dispatch in all hast a flying pacquett to acquaint my
Lord Commissioner and your Lōp with his Maj^{ties} great

---

[1] *The Acts of the Parliaments of Scotland,* vol. xi. pp. 257, 258, 268, 269,
270 ; *Hume of Crossrig's Diary,* pp. 61-68.

concern at the motion made for the Parliaments modelling the 3000 men determined to be kept up, that being such an encroachment upon his prerogative, that the Parliament here when uneasiest never pretended to, but having laid on the supplys and fixed the number, always left the modelling of these to his Maj^{tie}; and therfore I have signified to my Lord Commissioner, that in caice by anic accident the Parliament is sitting when this comes to his Graces hands, and that the Parliament hes taken upon them to modell the 3000 men and condescend upon the particular cores to be kept up, that his Grace should by no means give his assent to it, but endeavour to have it rectified and the modelling of the number determined left whollie to his Maj^{tie}; but if that hes alreadie past in Parliament, his Maj^{tie} expects that no reform nor reduction be made upon anic modell of the Parliaments, untill he be acquainted with it and his further pleasure known.

There goes with this a neu order allowing my Lord Commissioner to continue his charecter untill he see his Maj^{tie}, the last allowing it onlie untill he should be out of the kingdom.

Next day the Act for a supply of twelve months' cess to maintain the army establishment of 3000 men was touched by the sceptre, and on 1st February Parliament was adjourned.

For THE EARL OF FINDLATER from JAMES eldest son of VISCOUNT SEAFIELD

My Lord,—I am sensible of your Lo. kindness towards me, and return you hearty thanks for the watch which I have received. It will be very useful to me, and as your Lo. odered, I shal caus dress it and take care to keep it well as a token of your Lo. kindness. I had an earnest desire to shew my gratitude by some compliment, [but] after inquiry I could find nothing worth your Lo. while. [How]ever I'l endevour to ply my book, which is all your Lo. expects from, My Lord, Your Lo. most humble and obedient servant,   JAMES OGILVIE.

Abd., Mar. 1, 1701.

Next letter gives a glimpse of student life in Aberdeen.

For THE EARL OF FINDLATER

MY LORD,—I received the 22 libs. 4s. from Alex^r Elmslie and delivered him the receipt. The master continues well, blissed be God. He is very fond of the watch your Lo. has sent him, and would be glade of an opportunity to shew how much he reckons himself obleidged to your Lo. As to that rupture betuixt the colledges, it was truely very dreadfull, for gentlemens sons in both were in hazard of their lives evry hour for 8 or ten dayes together, but now, blessed be God, all differences amongst the students are composed, and they converse together in great friendship and amity. The master judged them both fools, and never thought of sydeing with either of them.

There was no paquet for your Lo. yesternight oȳrwise it had come allong with this. The letters brought nothing considerable, only great preparations for war on all hands.

The money wee had heir on bill is spent to about ten or eleven libs., so that your Lo. will neid to transmitt what may be proper with the first occasion. I give your Lo. no further trouble, but only that I am, My Lord, Your Lo^s most humble and obedient servant,   WIL. BLAKE.

Abdn., Mar. 7, 1701.

To THE RIGHT HONBLE THE EARLE OF FINDLATER
BY ABERDEIN TO BANFF

London, 20th March 1701.

MY LORD,—I hade the honour of your Lo. yesterday, and am glaid to know that ye are in perfect health and at your ease. My Lord Seafield is in as much favour with his master as your Lo. could desire. I shall be carefull of your comands, and am, My Lord, Your Lo. most obedient servant,   ALEX^r OGILVIE.

The account in next letter of the Caledonian cartoon supplements Hume of Crossrig's narrative in his *Diary,* pp. 76-79.

For THE RIGHT HONOURABLE THE EARLE OF
FINDLATER

Edr., 21st Mairch 1701.

MY LORD,—. . . I know not hou it comes that your

letter is stopt, for I have hade nothing to doe about it, since fforglen hade concerne with the Signet, and William Gairden is gone along with him to London.   It seemes it most be stopt aboue, and your Lope. most wreat to John Philp to direct it of to my caire, and it shall be carfully sent of.   We have no newes heir, only the Secret Councill have bein taken up thir 3 dayes detecting ane affront that was in agetation agt. the governement, which was this. Ther was a coperplate ingraved with Caledonia in the sheap of a fair young lady, supported by his Grace the Duke of Hamiltoune, the Merqueses of Atholl and Tweddell, and the names of all the rest who wer affectionat to hir interest in Parliat., and the names of others who would have bein so if they hade bein ther, with some proper inscriptions wreat beneth, and belowe that is the divill draiveing all the enemies of that interest befor him to hell.   It was first drawn with a pen by on Thomson a servant in the Affrican office who wreats one exterordinary fine hand, and yrafter ingraven by a young man of the name of Wood, and on Auchmoutie who is officier to the companie was taken at the press casting off the coppies.   Mr. M'Kenzie secretarie is thought to have bein in the thing.   The first tuo wer sent to the castell and the last 2 to the tolbuith, and some of them if not all are to gett ther indytments to be tryed for ther lives.   A flyeing packett was yisterday sent to the Secretaries with on of the coppies, and what is discovored in the matter.   Some coppies wer given out, particularly to the Duke of Hamiltoune and Merques of Tweddell. Both of them attended the Councill yisterday, a macer haveing bein sent to them to that purpose.   Tweddell gave in his coppie, bot the Duke sayed he hade misslayed his, and so soon as he gott it he would send it to the clerk of Councill, who hes all the rest of the doubles.   Both these persones of quality are under parroll to the Councill to appear when called for.   I was at paines in that affair agt. the Brouns, and ame sorie I hade not better success.   I did expend some money by Birkenboge and Braccos order and the Shreff depts., the account qrof I have sent to Castel-feild.   I know your Lope will sie that I be reimbursed when

the commissioners meets, ffor I was als much paines as
if the thing hade taken its designed effect. I wish your
Lope. and the famely all happieness, and ame, My Lord,
Your Lops. most deutiefull, most humble, and most
obedient srvant,   JA. BAIRD.

I ame to wreat to my Lady Seafeild nixt, and I have
bespake halfe a chist of lemons and oranges for hir, which
will be almost als cheap as the quantity she desyred from
the fruit wifes, and the merts. doe not sell under half a
chist full.

Peter and Donald Brown[1] were associates of James Macpherson,
and were probably hanged in Banff in June 1701, though an
unknown authority referred to by Sir William Fraser states that
they escaped.[2]

ffree., For THE RIGHT HONABLL THE EARLE OF
FFINDLATER AT CULLEN HOUSE IN BANFFSHYRE

Edinburgh, 8th Aprile 170i.

MY: LORD,—I hade the honour of your Lops. yisterday,
and I transmitted the tuo that wer inclosed from my Lord
Seafeild and Mr. Philp by the yisternights pacquet. . . .
We have for newes heir to day that Sr Patrick Home[3] is
off as Solicitor, and that Mr. David Dalrymple and Mr. W^m
Carmichell are named to succeed him, that Jarveswood
hes gott a bill of ease, and that Sr James Smollet and
fforglen[4] doe succeed him as Generall Receavers, and that
Mr. Robert Pringle is off from being Secretarie Dept, and
Sr Alex^r Cumming of Culter or Sr Archibald Sinclair doe
get his post. This is only talked, bot I ame affraid ther
most be something of it, for it hes bein long expected.
When I hear of any thing wourthie of your Lops. nottice
it shall be communicat to you. So wishing my Lady and
the childrine all happieness, I ame, My Lord, Your Lops.
most deutiefull, most humble, and obleidged servant,

JA. BAIRD.

---

[1] Dr. Cramond's *Annals of Banff*, vol. i. pp. 100, 103, 104, 106, 107, 110-113.

[2] *The Chiefs of Grant*, vol. i. pp. 325, 326.

[3] *Marchmont Papers*, vol. iii. pp. 220, 221.

[4] *State Papers (Scotland) Warrant Books*, vol. xvii. p. 511.

The treaty of Ryswick was followed by the two partition treaties of 1699 and 1700 regulating the Spanish succession. The latter, rendered necessary by the death of Ferdinand of Bavaria, divided the Spanish territories between the Emperor's son Charles, who was to have the crown of Spain, and the Dauphin of France. In despite the King of Spain the same year bequeathed his un-divided kingdom to Philip of Anjou, second son of the Dauphin. On the death of the King of Spain in October 1700 the Emperor and the Dutch took up arms against France to vindicate the treaty of 1700. William, handicapped by the hostile Parlia-ment in England referred to in the letter of 17th April, did not come into line with his former allies until late in 1701. Next letter, however, shows that he was at this time strengthening his position in the Low Countries.

To JAMES BAIRD

Whitehall, 10th Aprile 170i.

THIS goes by a flying packet with credit to those regiments that go for Holland, in case that they be detained by contrary winds, but I hope they are saild befor now. My Lord Strathnaver is to pay me this week nintie pound sterling here upon the account of Coll. Ferguson, for which I have given Coll. Ferguson a bill for a hundred pound sterling payable at two dayes sight by you. You may remitt the remaining twentie five pounds in guineas by the packet, and I shall take care to send you down yor. note, which I have for 125 pound, and the sooner you send it the better, which is all at present from yor assured friend,

SEAFIELD.

I will not detain the packet for writing to any other person, being resolved to writ at night by the ordinary post, but you may give my humble service to my Ld Annandale, and let him know that I will writ to him this night, and send him down the paper he desires.

For THE EARL OF FINDLATER

Whitehall, Apryle 17th, 1701.

MY LORD,—. . . The fflying post gazett and votes of Parliat̃ are duely sent your Lordship, but directed to the master att Aberdeen, and Mr. Black ordered to forward them carefully. Yor Lop. has in the votes all the proceedings

of the House of Commons, but there is one step very remarkable in the House of Lords, which I presume to trouble
yor Lop. with.   They were displeased att the Commons
address, which yor Lop. will see in the votes, against the four
impeached Lords,[1] and they aggreed yesterday to ane ante
address, I may so call it, that his Ma^{ty} would not be pleased
to inflict any punishment or shew any marks of his displeasure to the 4 impeached Lords by the House of Commons, till they have been tryed upon the impeachment.
How this will be setled I leave it to yor Lop. to judge.
Were yor Lop. here you would see hotter work then was
in our Scotts Parliament.   The Commons are lyke to
persecute the Kings old servants about the partition
treatty, but I hope they will not gett there wills, and it is
thought the House of Lords will clear them.   Will yor Lop.
be pleased to let my Lady Seafield know that my Lord is
in very good health, blessed be God ;   and I shall not
presume on yor Lop. any further, but pray all happines to
yor Lop., my Lady, and all the children, and subscryve, My
Lord, Your Lops. most obedient and dutifull humble
servant,   JOHN PHILP.

For THE EARLL OF [FINDLATER]

   MY LORD,—I wold have most willingly served fforglen in
any thing I can, but befor I heard of him I found by the
inclination of most of the town, that they resolved to have
one of ther towns men to serve in that post.   Nather have
I considerable influenc in thos matters, which hath mead me
wilyn not to meddell mor with them.   For I doe not resolve
to goe to Bamf this day, tho I hear they talk of choising
ther commissioner.   Wherein I can serve your Lo. or my
Lo. Seafield it shall be willingly performed by, My Lo.,
Your most humble servent,   PATRICK OGILVIE.

Boyn, Aprle 28, 1701.

. Alexander Leslie of Kininvie was elected commissioner for the
Burgh of Banff at this time in room of Provost Stuart deceased,
but next year Forglen was returned.[2]

---

[1] Somers, Portland, Orford, and Montague (Halifax).
[2] Dr. Cramond's *Annals of Banff*, vol. i. pp. 170, 171, etc.

For THE EARL OF FINDLATER

Holyrood house, Tuesday,
the 6th of May 170i.

MY LORD,—I got yesterday your Lops. letter of the 26th
'Aprile, and am very sensible of your Lops. zeall and concern for the government. Wee see that others wait all
occasions, and leave no ston unturned. I am sorrie for
Provost Stuarts death, but since by it there is a vacancie,
I doubt not your Lop. by your friends and interest in that
place doe all you can to make the best of it. The Councellors excepting one or two Lords of Session and the Lord
Provost are all out of town, and I am goeing this day to
the cuntrie, soe it is not like wee can have any Councill till
June. All I can advise is that if ane election happen our
friends may take care to have the law upon their side as
much as they can, and let no pains and diligence be wanting to carrie their business. If it end so as anything be
doubtfull and come to the Privie Councils determination,
it is not to be doubted but they will get right there, which
shall be carefullie looked after by, My Lord, Your Lops.
very obliedged humble servant,   MARCHMONT.

The pine woods [1] of upper Strathspey for many years supplied
much valuable timber, which was floated down the Spey. The
floaters used a round currach or wicker boat covered with leather;
hence their name 'currachers' in next letter.

For THE EARL OF FINDLATER

MY LORD,—The bearer, John Grant, deliverd your Lo.
letter to me this morneing, and since Grant was not vritn
to anent woode libertie, I cam allongs with John to inquere
annent the samen at young Grant, [2] to whom his father hath
givn the disposeing of the woods; and he sayes that he will
have three pounds Scotis mōey for ech tree, and this is
besyds the payt for cutting, leadeing to the vater, and the
currachers pains for transporting them to the bote off

---

[1] *The Transactions of the Inverness Scientific Society and Field Club,* vol. v.
pp. 186-196.
[2] Alexander Grant, afterwards Brigadier-General and laird of Grant.

Bog,[1] so yt I judge or the great trees be there they will stand your Lo. four pounds Scotis the peice. Yet if your Lo. will resolve to buy the woode, I doe think the smallest trees may be hade of the cropts of the great timber; and this is all could as yet be done in the mater untill your Lo. have your thoughts off it, and vrit to Grant if you think it convenient ; and for me there shall none be more willing according to my pouer to serve your Lo. and your familie then, My Lord, Your Lo. most obedient and verie humble serveant,   JA. GRANT.

  Castal Grant, i *of June* 1701.

ffor THE EARLE OF FFINDLATTER ATT CULLEN HOUSE
these

MY LORD,—I have now receaved from Burdsbank your daughter Lady Mary's papers anent hir bond of provisione with the bond itself ; so it will be fitt that your Lo. wreat to your advocats to stop the calling of any sumonds Lady Mary hes raised agt. Burdsbank, as likewayes to mind your sone, my Lord Seafield, to exped that commissione anent Burdsbanks sone Patrick as being conjunct Shirreff clerk with himself, for the sooner that these things be done will be the better ; and I find Burdsbank verie willing to redd all fairly and very friendlie with your Lo., which is all from, My Lord, Your most humble servant,

PATRICK OGILVIE.

  Boynd, June 4, '701·

Patrick Leslye was appointed joint Sheriff-Clerk of Banffshire on 10th September 1703.

ffor THE RIGHT HOLL THE EARLE OFF FFINLATER
these ar

Durn, the 21 *off Junn* 170i.

MY LORD,—I am so streatned att the tym ffor munnie, that I am necessitatt to request ȳr Lo. to advanse mee that 9 lb. ȳr Lo. rests on ȳr ltr and tikett. I am assheamed I shuld thus truble ȳr Lo. ffor such an small thing, vheranent I creave ȳr pardon. Send it vt anie off yr Los servants this

---

[1] The ford on the Spey at Gordon Castle.

efternoun, ffor my son George is to take jurney ffor Ed^r. Moonday tymlie ; and I say no moir, bot that I am Yr Lo^s obleidged and humble servant,   WIL. DUNBAR.

Yor Lo^s ltr ffor ye 40 libs. is in Apryll 93, vheroff I receaved in Janij 94 23 libs. 4s, and the tiket is in ye 6th of Marche 95 ffor 20 libs.

Findlater had not paid the small sum due, on 25th October following.

WILLIAM LORIMERS LETTER TO THE EARL OF SEAFIELD, WHYTHALL

RIGHT HONOURABLE, MY LORD,—Having no business of consequence to give your Lōp ane account of, I have forborn to trouble you with any line from my hand since the last concerning Kempcairns business. And yet I have nothing to write of, but that Kempcairn and his creditors have not as yet come to clear any business with your Lop., and they are now resolved to delay alltogether till your Lop. come north, which I pray God may be in safety. . . .

We have hade most pleasant weather all this spring, and now ther is ane appearance of a most plentifull cropt, if the Lord send a good harvest. The victuall is fallen extra-ordinarily, in so farr as the bear and malt sells at present for five pounds, and the meall at seven merks. There is some meall and some bear of yor Lops. unsold, but wee can gett no buyers for it. All kind of cattell sell extraordin-arily deer, and the countrey commodities are farr beyond the former pryces, but mōey is the only thing scarse. . . .

There are a great many of yor tenements in Cullen intirely waste, and no persones offering to take them. I wish yor Lop. a prosperous journey to Scotland and a safe arriveall at your own dwelling, and that the Lord may allwayes accompany yor Lop. with his blessing is the earnest prayer of, My Lord, Your Lops. most humble, most obliardged, and most dutifull servant,   WILL. LORIMER.

Cullen House, July 2d, 1701.

On 24th June 1701 Viscount Seafield was created Earl of Seafield, Viscount of Reidhaven, and Lord Ogilvie of Deskford and Cullen. His son James, in consequence of the death of his uncle, Lord

Deskford, in 1699, and of his father being an earl, now took the courtesy title of the heir to the Findlater peerage, Deskford.

THE RIGHT HON[BLE THE] EARLE OF FIN[DLATER
AT CULLEN] HOUSE IN BANFF [SHYRE]

Edinburgh, 4th Jully 1701.

MY LORD,—I hade the honour of your Lops. with Birkenbog, and sent foreward that which was inclosed to John Philp. I returne your Lop^e my heartie thanks for countenanceing my affair amongst the commissionrs of the shyre. John Donaldsone hes acquanted me that they have ordored pay^t of my account and about 40s. ster: for my paines, and he will remmitte it to me with the publict money. The King went from Hamptoun Court to Margaret upon Sundayes night last in ordor to take shipping for Holland. My Lord Seafeild wreat to me that he was to take jurnay for Scotland in 3 or ffour dayes yrafter, so I doubt not bot he is come off. He will not be heir aboue a ffourtnight, bot goes straight north. He hes gott from his Matie 500 lib. ster. for his exterordinary chairges and expenses in the last session of Parliat.[1] His collegue hes gott the lyke. Both of them are made Earles. Carmichall would neeids be a Earle, and my Lord Seafeild was forced to take on too to keep his rank with him, being alreadie a step befor him. The Earle of Argyle[2] is created a Duke, and Lothian and Annandale are Merqueses. These thrie patents are past the great seall and read in Councill. Ther are many other pepers past, bot we can say nothing about them till the Secretaries come doune. I ame, My Lord, Your Lops. most humble, most deutiefull, and obedient servant,   JA. BAIRD.

ffor THE RIGHT HONORABLE THE EARLE OF
FFINDLATER   these

MY NOBLE LORD,—I have sent your Lop^s letter and the booke to Mr. Gordon by Robert Baillie the tounes post, and agreed with him for 4s. out and 2s. home. The

---

[1] *State Papers (Scotland) Warrant Books,* vol. xviii. p. 19.
[2] *Carstares State Papers and Letters,* pp. 694-695.

Invernes post went towardes Invernes from this place this day, but had no letters for your Lop. or any of the familie, and being all of them discreit men they are loath to trouble your Lop. unles they have letters, but I have desyred them, and they promeis to call in their goeing to Aberdein, and the first I expect heir to morrow, qch I hope will begin the matter. The postage of all single letters from Cullen to any place betwixt and Kinghorne is 2s., and double letters accordingly. I shall give your Lop. no furder trouble at present, but only add that I am, My Lord, Your Lops. most faithfull and most humble servant,

JO. DONALDSONE.

Banff, 23d of July 1701.

For THE EARLL OF FFINLATER   thes

MY LORD,—I have had no letters from my son since I waited on your Lo. This day I gott the inclosed news letter by which its lyk we will have the satisfaction of seing yowr son the E. of Seafild at home werie soon.—I am, My Lord, Your most humble servant,   PATRICK OGILVIE.

Boyn, July 3i, 1701.

The Earl of Seafield had arrived in Edinburgh a few days before.[1]

ffor MASTER GEORGE GORDON,[2] PROFESSOR OF THE ORIENTALL LANGUEGES IN OLD ABD. post payed   2s.

Cullen House, the i3th *of August* i70i.

SIR,—I heave been still in expectation of Grotius booke returned from Abd. gilded, that if the price had pleased me I wold had given you further trouble that way. As for the Benachie dyamond, deliver it to the bearer that I may send it to London. I pray you doe me the favour to acquent me in what I can serve you, for I troulie am Your reall and affectionat friend,   FFINDLATER.

For THE RIGHT HONBLE THE EARLE OF FFINDLATER

MY LORD,—I am sory I could not comply with the terms of your Lo. letter exactly, but so far as was in my pouer I

---

[1] *Carstares State Papers and Letters*, p. 699.

[2] *Historical MSS. Commission, Fourteenth Report*, App. III., *Marchmont MSS.*, pp. 148-150.

have. For Dampirs voyges I have [not] them, but you may
gett them from my Lord Boyne. I have sent Thomas a
Kempis with Epictetus by Doctor Stannep also, and a new
book called Tryall of witts. So if they do not please, your
Lo. may as freely command any books I have, as him
who with all respect is, My Lord, Your Lo. most obedient
and willing humble servant,   ALEX^r ABERCROMBIE.

Glassaugh, Sptr. 2, 1701.

I shal visit of your Lo. and my Lord Seafield to morrow
precisely be eight, and if these books do not please your Lo.,
if you 'l acquaint me tonight, I' le fetch others with me
to morrow.

Alexander Abercrombie[1] of Glassaugh, Fordyce, was a cadet of
the Abercrombies of Birkenbog, being a son of Mr. John Abercrombie first of Glassaugh, second son of Alexander Abercrombie
of Birkenbog, who died *c.* 1647. On 31st January 1706 he
received a commission as lieutenant in the Earl of Mar's regiment.
On the 23rd of February following he was promoted captain. He
was member for Banffshire in the Parliament of 1716. To him
and to Alexanders Garden, elder and younger of Troup, was
remitted on 7th March 1716, by the commissioners of supply of
that county, the preparation of ' ane congratularie adress to his
Majesty King George, suitable to the present hapie juncture and
postur off affaires.' He took an active part in county government.

For THE EARLL OF FFINLATER   thes

Boyn, Septr. 20, 170i.

MY LORD,—I have sent two wolums of Dampeirs travells.
Your Lo. shall command what books I have. I wish your
Lo. wold appoynt ane court of the justic of peac how soon
its possible, for the countrie pepell clamor much for it.—I
am, My Lo., Your affectionet and most humble servant,

PATRICK OGILVIE.

I expect my daughter about the begining of the next
month.

---

[1] *State Papers* (*Scotland*) *Warrant Books,* vol. xxi. pp. 159 and 162 ; and
' Banffshire Roads,' by the Editor, in the *Transactions of the Banffshire Field
Club,* 1905, p. 89.

To THE RIGHT HONOURABLE THE EARL OF
FINDLATER at Cullen House

My Lord,—May it please your Lordship. The bearer
is sent according to your Lordships gracious commands to
receive your Lo. letter to Mr. Hugh Innes, min[r] at Mortlach,
present mod[tor] of the united Presbyteries of Alford, Turriff,
and Fordyce in my favours, wherin, if it so seem good to
your Lo., I humbly plead it be suggested as your Lo. desire,
that my answer to the charge and the particulars therein
in write from me, committed to one of their number to be
communicated to the Presbytery, may be accepted instead
of my personal compearance before their judicatory, since
I resolve to be in town that day and may be communed
with in private, in case they have not full satisfaction from
what I writ, and that my name be not blazon'd by calling
the process, I being unwilling either to offend them or
put myselfe to needles trouble by declinatures and protestations and appeals if I may avoid them.   This in all duty
is submitted to your Lo[s] wiser sentiment; and praying the
Lord to bless your Lo. more and more with a happy and
comfortable life on earth, and crown you with eternal
happines in heaven, I ever am, My Lord, your Lordships
most humble devoted   Jo. INNES.

Banff, Septr. the 26th, 1701.

Mr. John Innes,[1] minister of Gamrie, an old Episcopalian who
after the revolution qualified to government, was charged at this
time by the united Presbyteries with 'amongst other things
reviling ministers and probationers sent from the south to supply
the vacancies in the north, calling them locusts from the infernal
pit.' Hugh Innes was of the family of Lichnet Gamrie, and
Dipple, Morayshire.

ffor THE RIGHT HOLL THE EARLE OFF FFINLATER
att Cullen House   thes ar

Kincorth, the 16t *off October* 1701.

My Lord,—I long to knowe hou ȳr Lo. hes keept ȳr
healthe since the Earle off Seafeild ȳr son and his Ladie

---

[1] Dr. Cramond's *Presbytery of Fordyce*, p. 50.

vent from ȳr house. I vould gleadlie also knowe hou they and yr grandchyld La. Bettie caried out the jurney, and iff in good health since, and vhat ȳr Lo. knowes off ther taking jurney ffor London. Wee heare King James is dead, and iff ther bee anie leat letres com to yr Lo, I vishe they may bee good. I most, God villing, my Lo. jurney ffor Ed^r about ye 24^t off this munth. I am much streitned ffor munnie to make my jurney. Iff ȳr Lo. vill do mee the kyndnes to affourd mee that small soume your Lo. rests mee, it vill at the tym bee no small favor, and I assure ȳr Lo. iff it bee in my pouer I shall not bee fforgetfull to obey ȳr desayre in an greatter matter, and still bee reddic to serve ȳr Lo. as beecomethe ȳr obleidged and humble servant   WIL. DUNBAR.

In September King William joined the Grand Alliance against France. A few days later King James died at St. Germains, and his son was immediately acknowledged King of England by Louis. Faction at once ceased in England and in Scotland, loyal addresses began to flow in, and a united nation formed behind William. He returned to England on 4th, and dissolved Parliament on the 7th November. In December a Whig majority was returned ready to vote him supplies and to carry on the war against France.

To THE EARL OF FINDLATER FROM

SIR ALEXANDER OGILVIE OF FORGLEN

Edinburgh, 22nd Octr. 1701.

MY LORD,—The Earle of Marr, with three and twentie more, at a justice court in Stirling, have subscrived a wery loyall address to his Majtie. The Earle of Tillibardne, with eight or nyn of his party, did speake and votte for delaying it, and when it was carried agt. them, they went out and wold not signe. My Lord, I know the Earle of Seafield will be mos desireouse that there be ane address in lyke maner from the court at Aberdein, and therefor I earnestly becheesh your Lo. may keep the dyet, for I cannot express how it will delight your son to see your hand there, and it will incourage many in yor countrey to waite on you, and I hope this shall make amends for the discontent he hade by the last address [1] was sent out of his countrey, and the chainge on this occasion will be imputed to his presence so lately there. My Lord, I know your Los. affection to the Earle of Seafield, and your loyalty towards the King, and the mater in hand being a great test of both, I bege it of you lay all excuse asside and honour me with yor presence there. I cannot express to you how I shall be rejoyced to waite on you there. I pray your Lo. wreat effectually to all ye may prevaile with to come to Aberdein. I have not signified the designe of addressing, albeit I have wreatten to all quarters, but only in generall desir'd them to keep the dyet, and show them there was a mater of publick concerne in hand. The reason I did this was becaues your Lo. knows there are a great many ill affected who wold absent themselves, but if they be present they will more easiely be prevail'd with. I hope your Lo. will acquant your son Mr. Patrick to keep the dyet.

Earlier, in June, Forglen received his patent as a knight baronet.[2]

ffor THE RIGHT HOLL THE EARLE OFF FFINLATER
ATT HIS HOUSE OFF CULLEN   these ar

Durn, the 25t off October 170i.

MY LORD,—As I cam heir this day eight dayes, it ffell so leatt as I vas the lenth off Cullen, that I could not then see ȳr Lo. and grandchildring vt you. I am glaid to heare that, blissed bee God, yee ar all in healthe, vherin God preserve you long. I am assheamed I shuld so much truble ȳr Lo. ffor such an small thing, but heaveing an paremptor affaire att Ed^r qlk vill requeire munnie, and beeing so much disapointed vher I expected it, I am necessitatt to ask that small thing ffrom ȳr Lo.; and I assuire ȳr Lo. ȳr ffavoring off mee in this shall obleidge mee to serve ȳr Lo. in vhat may bee in my pouer. I am to send my son George

---

[1] *The Acts of the Parliaments of Scotland*, vol. x. App. pp. 79, 80.
[2] *State Papers (Scotland) Warrant Books*, vol. xvii. p. 517.

getvard[1] ffor Edr. Moondayes morning, in regaird I dar not undertake the jurney myselfe, and hes thought ffit he shuld ask ȳr Lo. iff ther bee anie thing vherin he is capabill to serve ȳr Lo. ther.   I heave sent ȳr Lo^s ltr and tikett vt him, and I say no moir bot that I am in all deutte ȳr Lo^s affectionat and humble servant,   WIL. DUNBAR.

For THE EARL OF FINDLATER

Whitehall, 30th Octr. 1701.

MY LORD,—I know my wife writs to yor Lop. frequently, and therfor it is needless that I should give you frequent trouble.   The King has been troubled with a cold, but is perfectly recovered.   He has now done all his affairs in Holland, so we expect him over very soon.

The Commiss^{rs} of the southern district have address'd his Maj^{ty} very dutyfully, and it will no doubt be very acceptable that the like be done by those of the northern districht, and in this I hope yor Lop will concurr.

Yo^r Lop. may acquaint Will Lorimer that young Grant [2] has writ to me for the money due by Kempcairn to his father, and that I am desireous it may be payed.   I have only heard once from him since I came from Cullen.   He ought to give me frequent accounts of my bussiness.

Yor Lop. will be very solitary after James goes to Aberdeen, but I think you should frequently invite Sr James Abercromby and the laird of Glassach, and yor Lop. should not have refused my picture to my Lord Boyn, for both my wife and I gave it to him, when we were at his house.   I shall take care to have another sent home for yor Lop^s use, wch is all at present from, My Lord, Yor Lops most obedient son and humble serv^t,

SEAFIELD.

Writing on 5th October from Morpeth on his way south from Edinburgh, Seafield asked his chamberlain, William Lorimer, to go to Aberdeen with his son ' about the terme and give him as much as is necessary att first, and credit for what he needs afterwards from time to time.'

---

[1] Direct.   [2] See note, p. 329.

Katherine,[1] born 1604, daughter of John Grant, fifth of Freuchie, and chief of the Grants, married Alexander Ogilvie of Kempcairn.

For THE RIGHT HONOURABEL THE EARELL OF FFINDLATUR, at Cullan Huse, Banffshayr, Scotland

MY LORD,—I have almost nothing to say sinse I wret so often. The English Parliment was desoweled yestirday, and ther is anothar sumanesed to mit in six weeks. It is the constant adreses from all the cuntary I belive hath mead the King dou it, and I belive the Kings businas will go very weall on this wintar, for it is belived that the whigs will cary the elections. The King is very weall sinse he cam to England. I will be very weell pleased that the selean be plestred under Janats chambr. Your Lo. may cas dou it, and Will Lorimar will pay for the matrels. Pray God preserve your Lo. in halth, for I am, My Lord, Your most affectionat daghtar and humbell servant,   ANNA SEAFIELD.

Whithall, Nov. 12, 1701.

For THE RIGHT HONOURABLE THE EARLE OF FFINDLATER

Edr., 19th November 1701.

MY LORD,—I acknowleadge I ame much out of my deutie to your Lope. for not giveing ansres to your tuo letters befor this time ; bot truely I have bein mor then ordinary taken up by a heaste flitting occasioned by a great ffyre, which hapened in the bounds wher I lived, which burned doune (amongst many others) the whole land wher I lived, and it tooke me some time to resetle againe. . . . Ther is litle newes heir at present. I doubt not your Lope. hes heard that the English Parliat. is dissolved, and ane new one is to meet the 30th of the nixt moneth. Its thought the English election will send ther representatives instructed to concurr with his Matie in everie thing that may tend to

---

[1] *The Chiefs of Grant*, by Sir William Fraser, vol. i. p. 196.

the security of our religeon, and the keepeing the ffrensh interest als lou as may be.—I ame, My Lord, Your Lo. most deutiefull and obedient srvant,

JA. BAIRD.

With the opening of war Patrick Ogilvie's chance of place and position came at last. His captain's commission was dated 2nd December 1701.[1]

To THE RIGHT HONOURABELL THE EARELL OF FINLATUR, BANFFSHAYR, SCOTLAND

MY LORD,—It is a long tym sinse I hird from you. Houever I hop you are not the worse of your Abd. jurny. Ther is no nous hear at this tym. I belive your son Mr. Patrick hath got a cumishon to be a capton in Inverlochy. It is well wirth two hundred and fifty pound starlen a year. I am sory Alardys is not provided for, bot I am shour my Lord will dou it the first ocation. I hop you will leet me hear frequantly from your Lo., for I am, My Lord, Your most obedent daghtr and humbell servant,

ANNA SEAFIELD.

Whithall, Dis 1*st*, 170i.

I give my blisen to Jamse and Janat.

For THE EARL OF FINDLATER

RIGHT HONOURABLE, MY LORD,—Pleas receave by the bearer your Lōps. watch. Our Justiciary court satt hear Tuisday last, to which all the Hyland clans in the north wer sumonded, but non of them came, nor the officers returned with executions, by reason as they sd when returned since was for great speatts in the burns and rivers that they wold not travell. But I judge the clans money mad the watter impassabl to the officers. So all was doon at that court, being only Bridgr. Meatland and sex or seven mor Justiciars, they mad an adreass to his Majestie to serv him with lyfes and ffortouns ageanst the pretended Prince of Walles and others conforme to the present government both in church and state as now esteablished, the which

---

[1] *State Papers (Scotland) Warrant Books*, vol. xviii. p. 52.

severalls refused to subt., because the present church government was in it. So at lenth they mad an act that the precess Colodn should signe it for all as presented. They then appnted to morrow for the clans comeing in, who ar expected, and accordingly Loachyeall is this night com. Ther was no Justiciars out of Murray but Burdgyards, nor non out of Rosse except Newmor whom Colodn called. The Brigadear hath his humble deuty given your Lop., and esteams himself mutch bound to the Earl of Seafield. I find he persuades himself his regiment will be on of those who will goe abroad in the springe, and accordingly is makeing his recroots als fast as possible. I creav your Lop[s] pardon for this long teadius letter, and I am as becometh him who is, My Lord, Your Lop[s] most humbl, most obedient, and ever obleidged servant,

JOHN OGILVIE.[1]

Inverness, Decer. 8th, 1701.

Culloden was Duncan Forbes, father of the more famous Duncan Forbes, who was President of the Court of Session during the rising of the '45. Newmore was George Munro, grandson of Sir George Munro of Newmore,[2] Ross-shire, who was Major-General of the forces in Scotland from 1674 to 1677.

To THE RIGHT HONOURABLE THE EARLE OF FINLATER

MY LORD,—The Privie Councell having remitted that famous robber Alestar More from the tolbooth of Ed[r] to be tryed at Aber. by the Comissioners of the northren district wheir he comitted the crimes, their was ane tryall of him allready the 23 of Novr. last for breaking and robbing a hous and tying man, wiffe, and famelie. The assyse found the lybell proven, but that being only on cryme, it was thought fitt to prorogat sentance agt. him, he being guiltie of a great many oyr crymes. Therfor the fiscall of court give him ane new indytment for 13 oyr robberies all heinnious, and which he is to be tryed the 16 of Decr.

---

[1] Collector, Inverness.
[2] *Old Ross-shire*, by Wm. Macgill, pp. 347, 348.

instant ; and since it is the countries interest that great villeans, such as Alestar More is, should be exemplerie punished, it is proper that the court be as full as may be. I therfor desier for the sake of comon justice ye will be pleased to attend the court at Aber. the 16 of Der. instant wheir you shall be waitted on by, My Lord, Your most humble serv^{tt},   KINTORE.

Keithall, December 8, 1701.

Alester More[1] was condemned on the second indictment, but the death sentence was commuted by the Privy Council.   He was tried a third time and condemned to death, but on 28th March 1702 Queen Anne, by letter to the Privy Council, reprieved him to 10th June, pending the Council's examination of the proceedings of the trial.

For THE RIGHT HON^{BLE} THE EARLE OF FFINLATER
these

Edinburgh, 9th December 1701.

MY LORD,—It is wery refreshing to me to know of your Lo. good health, and to be honoured with a line from you. . . . Wee have heir, praisd be God, great peace and plenty, and the ellections for the English Parliament goe wery well on, which is pleaseing to all good Protestants Desire Mr. Lorimer to wreat more frequently to the Earle of Seafield, and with my humble dutie to your Lo. is all from, My Lord, Yor most obedient servant,

ALEX^r OGILVIE.

Ladie Jean Beath bies buried this day.   I have by this bearer sent Mr. Patrick his comission to be a captain in Inverlochie.

For THE EARL OF FINDLATER

MY LORD,—I gave your Lo. the trouble of a lyne from Abd. by Durn.   It was my misfortune to fall very ill at Abd., where I was detained several days, so that I came not home till Moonday's night, and still since that time have been very ill, otherways your Lo. hade got this

---

[1] *Historical Papers* (1699-1750), New Spalding Club, vol. i. pp. 24-27 ; *State Papers* (*Scotland*) *Warrant Books*, vol. xviii. No. 136.

trouble sooner, and had a full account how all matters went at our last court. The letter from my Lord Kintore will in a manner show you. It was the surprize of all to see those having dependance on your Lo. as well as my relations and allies should have made such appearance I may say in the face of justice. They have amused the world as if the government hade a mind to mantain this famous robber and villan Alester More, and as I wrote last, sure I am it's not the Earle of Seafield's inclination that any of his friends should oppose me in the doing of justice, and farther I have a letter from Forglan of the 27 of Nover.'s date, the day before our court, giving account that the Councill hade refused a petition in favours of Alester More craving he might be alimented, be free of the irons and stocks, and allowed three procurators, all which was refused ; and I have further assurances from the Council that they will not in the least concern themselves in that affair. I shall earnestly hope and expect your Lo. will give your concurrence and assistance in this so good and necessary an affair, by, if possible, giving your presence, if not by influencing those of your dependency to stand up for just and right things. Some would perswade it was your Lo. influence which occasioned that appearance, but I shall never believe, having the honour to be come of your Lo. family, and never having been wanting in serving it, you would prefer any body to me, when to my cost I am prosecuting justice. I shall be glade to have the honour of waiting on your Lo. at Abd. the 16th instant, being that I am, My Lord, Your Lo. most affectionatt cousin and humble servant,   FORBES.

Castleforb: 10 *Decer.* 1701.

To THE EARLE OF FINDLATER
<small>TO THE CARE OF ABDS. POST MR.</small>

MY LORD,—Blessed be God, my wife is safely brought to bed of a brave livlie boy. She is now on the way of recoverie and begins to make amends for her many daughters, for she hes given me two boyes in on year, so yt if she hold on I hope she will strenthen my name, wch hath bene this

long time verie waik. My Lord, I shall be verie glaid to
hear how your Lop. keeps your health, for I am sure ther is
non on earth wishes your Lop. better. I have named my
son [1] after the Earle of Kintore and ye Master of Inverurie.
I hade a lyn from the Earle of Seafield yesterday, and he and
my Lady are verie well in health. Mr. Patrick is made
captaine in Briggadeir Metlands regment. So forbearing
further truble, I ever am, My Lord, Your Lops. most
obedient sone and devouted sert.,   GEO. ALLARDES.

All here offers ther humble dutie to your Lop.

Allardes, 15 Decr. 1701.

For THE RIGHT HONORABLE THE EARLL OF
FINDLATER   thes ar

MY LORD,—I am glad to knou that your Lop. is in good
health. I wish the continuence of it. I render your
Lop. thanks for beieing at the trouble to send doun my
letter. It was only from John Pilip. I do resolue, God
uoling, to be woth your Lop. Tusday or Wadinsday in
orders for my going for Inuerlochy. So till the[n] and euer
I continou, My Lord, Your Lops. affectionat son and most
humble seruant,   PAT. OGILVIE.

Carness, Decem. 24, 1701.

Next letter from young Grant is yet another example of
'moyen.'

E. FINDLATER

Ballnadalloch, Decr. 29, 1701.

MY LORD,—When at Aberdeen your Lo. ordered me to
acquaint you before hand of the court of Keith, that ye
might see my ffaȳr and me gett justice done us. I have
raised and execute summonds ag̃st Kincraigie, Leslie,
Inverernan,[2] and oyrs again the sixth and seventh of
Janry to compear before the court at Keith, so I hope, the
weather serveing, your Lo will be pleased to honour the
court with your presence, which will obliedge both my

---

[1] John. See *The Scots Peerage,* vol. i. p. 143 ; vol. v. pp. 240-241.
[2] John Forbes.

ffather and him who, if occasione offered, would be proud of approveing himself to be, My Lord, Your Lo^s most humble and obliedged servant,

ALLEXANDER GRANTT.

ffor THE RIGHT HONNABLE THE EARLE OFF
FFINDLATER these

MY LORD,—Your sonne the Earle of Seafeild is resteing me som mōe, and I being much straitned for mōe again Witsunday, if your Lo. will be pleased to doe me the kyndess to acquaint my Lord to remit me the mōe to Ed^r again the terme of Witsunday, wheir I have ane considderable soume to pay, itt will doe me ane singular favour. Wisheing your Lo. and your familie all health and happines, I am, My Lord, Your Lo. most obleidged and humble servant,   A. DUFF.[1]

Edinglassie, 3d *Jary.* 1702.

Nothing was scarcer in Scotland at this time than money.

For THE EARL OF FINDLATER

MY LORD,—Your Lo. has heir-with sent all the news wee had since Robert Bailie took the last away. Your Lo. shall never miss them with the first oportunity when-ever they come heir. Please accept of ten dozon of aples from my Lord Desfoord. Your Lo. might have had mor, but there was no carriadge for them.

Allaster More is to dy Friday comes eight dayes according to the sentence passed on him. The Councill was very warm about him, one half being for banishment, and the other for hangeing, and the Chancellors vote turned the ballance.

When I heard from the family at London, they were all in good health. I wish your Lo. many happy new yeirs, and continue, My Lord, Your Lo. most humble obedient servant

WIL. BLAKE.

Abd. Ja: 13, 1702.

---

[1] Laird of Braco, Commissioner for Banffshire.

For THE EARL OF FINDLATER

Abdn., Ja. 27, 1702.

MY LORD,—. . .

My Lord Deskford seeing so many addresses procured by
Carmichells influence thinks strange your Lo. will not
procure them from the town and shyre of Bamff. He
desyred me give his humble duty to your Lo. and signifie
this much. I give your Lo. no further trouble, but that
I desire to evidence my self on all occasions, My Lord,
Your Lo. hūle and faithfull servant,   WIL. BLAKE.

For THE EARL OF FINDLATER

MY LORD,—I received your Lo. yesternight, and am
glad to know that your Lo. is in good health. Long may
your Lo. be so. My Lord Deskfoord received your Lo^s with
great satisfaction. He is well, blissed be God, and had
wīn but that the post is gone this night, whereas he
expected he should have stayed till to morrow. I remember I gave your Lo. an account of Allaster Mor's reprieve. Be pleased to know that he is indited again of
two crimes mor, but its doubted if they can be proven.
Kintor was in this town this week. He saw my Lord
Deskfoord, and asked kindly for your Lo. No doubt your
Lo. has heard particularly befor this time, that Drum was
freed and Benacraige has got no redresse. Being in haste
I give your Lo. no further trouble, but that I desire to be,
My Lord, Your Lordships most humble and obedient
servant,   WIL. BLAKE.

Ja: 29, 1702.

Your Lo. has the Ed^r gazette, and Il endeavour to
provide it allwayes till the votes come.

For THE EARL OF FINDLATER

Edinburgh, 2d Febry. 1702.

MY LORD,—I hade the honour of your Lo. by the last
post, and am hartily glaid to know of your good health,
and sincerly wish the continuance of it.

By the yesternights post the Earle of Seafield desir'd me to minde your Lo. anent the sending up the address of the commissioners of your shire and the toune of Cullen, if they be not dispatcht by your last letters to him. I pray your Lo. minde it, and if ye please to let me know as it passes, I shall signe it in the up goeing.

The Earle of Seafields family are well. My Ladie is expected down in March, and the Earle when his Majty goes abroad.

Teviotts regement of dragoons, Rues and ffergusons regements of foot goe abroad, and new regments are to be levied in there place. The Collonells are not yet determined. It is fitt tyme to your Lo. to move for any friend. Acquant Glassaugh heirwith, and tell him from me he hade never a fitter opportunity of preferrment, if he inclines to chainge the plough for the sword, and I continue in all dutie, My Lord, Yor obedient and faithfull servant,

ALEX^r OGILVIE.

On 19th of March following Row's and Ferguson's regiments were on board two English frigates in the Firth of Forth on their way to Flanders.[1]

Alexander Abercrombie's letter of 28th February 1702 shows that he acted on Forglen's advice, though he was not at that time successful.

To THE RIGHT HONOURABELL THE EARELL OF FINLATUR, BANFFSHAYR, SCOTLAND

MY LORD,—Tho I have nothing to wret to you, yet I trubell you with writing, and partiklurly to ask your comands befor I leve this please, which I belive may be in the beginen of Apryll. I ashour you thy shall be obayed so far as my weak pouer can riych. Blissed to God your son is weall, and as much as any Scotsman in the Kings faver. The Parliment of England hath gon on unanimsly in the Kings affears, bot it is thoght that this day the

---

[1] *State Papers (Scotland) Warrant Books*, vol. xviii. p. 97.

impeched Lords businas will be broght in to the Huse of Commans. You shall kno nixt post what cumes of it. I shall trubell you no fardar, only add that I am, My Lord, Your most obedient daghter and humbell servant,

ANNA SEAFIELD.

Febrar 26, 1702.

For THE RIGHT HONBLE THE EARLE OF FINDLATER

MY LORD,—I have wrytten my mind as we concerted to my Lord, which please seal. I intrait, as ever I can be serviceable to your Lo. or family, that your Lo. will perswad Castlefield to goe to Abd., for he is half resolved alreaddie, and wryt to my Lord Seafield if I gett service in the dragoons, that I would wish to have Cornett Ogilvie as livetennant, who is a real servant of your Lo. family, as also anent James Ogilvie mercht in Abd. how he was at Londen last winter, and depends intirely on my Lord. I have no books but husbandry or phys, both which your Lo. may command. So I am, Your Lops most faithfull and intirely engaged humble sert,

ALEX^r ABERCROMBY.

Glassaugh, Febr. 28, 1702.

For WILLIAM LORIMER, CHAMBERLAND TO THE RIGHT HONOURABLE THE EARLE OF SEAFIELD, ETC. AT CULLEN HOUSE, BANFF

SIR,—. . . I beleive my Lady Seafeild will be heir the beginning of the nixt moneth, and the King goes over aither in the end of this or beginning of the nixt moneth, so that my Lord will be shortly after hir. The Assembly sitts doune upon ffryday, and my Lord Chancellour represents the King in the Kirk. The Marques of Annandaile went of for London this morning, being called for, some say to be Commissioner, others say to be Chancellour. I wish the Earle of Findlater all happieness, and ame, Your most affectionat cousine and humble servant,

JA. BAIRD.

Edinburgh, 3d Mairch 1702.

On the 20th of February King William broke his collar bone. On the 8th of March he died. The three next letters describe his last days and death, and the proclamation of his successor Queen Anne in London and in Edinburgh.

For THE EARL OF FINDLATER FROM THE
COUNTESS OF SEAFIELD

MY LORD,—I wret this leeter with the sadst hart I everer wrot one. This day about eght aclok in the mornen the King dayed without any disese bot perfit wekness. I dou belive his fall from his horse did dou him ill, bot the colar bon which was brok at that thym was qut holl. On Tusday last the third of March he lost his stomak, did eat no dinor, had a litell fit of the eago. On Wadsenday he had another fit, and on Thoursday a third. Thy war not violint, and that night had a litell lousness, and the nixt day vomoted whatever he eat or drunk. His wometing stayed at four aclok, and his phisions thoght that he might requer, for thay all concluded he had no fever or any disese bot weakness. At about four aclok on Seterday he turen so weak that his phisions began to loos ther hops, and he took death to him seleff, told them thy nid not trubell them selives or him with many cordiells, for he douted not bot he wold day very soon. The Bishops of Canterrebery and Sallasbeary atended him as chaplens, and prayed severall tyms to him on Saterday, and this day about four or five aclok in the mornen he took the sacrament with much confort, aftterwards spok to soom about him, recomended the cear of soom of his privat pepirs to Albemarell, and gave his hand to all his frinds about him, and bid them adeu, and imedetly closed his eys and expayred without any thrack or vielent moshon. He had all his seneses and intelectuales intir till the last minit of his liff. My Lord had a short adiens of him on Wadsenday, when he spok very kyndlie to him and of the Scots nashion and mighty fordvard for the uneion. I am shour ther is no honast or Cristien Scotsman bot will be senseabell of this ireparabell loss. God prescrive the Protastant church and the libarty of Europ.   The Parliment sat yesterday, and past the bill of abjuration and anothar.   They have sit all this day and ordared that the Prinsess be proclemed Quen, which was doun at Whithall and Cheren Cross at four aclok in the affternun.   Thy have voted an adress to hir to continou in all the aleincess and mishers which was concluded by the King, and she hath promised to dou so to the English Cunsell.

Ther sat a Scots Cunsell in this huse today about twalive aclok, and the Doukes of Quenesbery and Argyll and the two Secretarys ware sent to the Prinsess to speak to hir. She requered the corination oth of them, and tould that she wold gladly tak ther adress, and wold go in to those mishars which his formar Magasty had donn, mantin ther religon and libarty.   What is donn in Scotland your Lo. will hear from Ed^r beter then I can tell, nou when thing is only disayned.   I big pardon for this tedious and melancoly leeter, and I am yours most affectionatly.

The melancoly is very great hear, and ther is nather frind nor enemy bot outvardly apiers grived in the very looks.   Thy acknolig the loss of ther dliverer under God. Bot God is allways strong, when man is weak.

Whithall, March 8th, 1702.

Pardon this ill wret.

My Lord, if my father and brother be in the countary, pray mack exques to them for not writing to them at this tym.   I am abell to wret no mor.

For the EARL OF FINDLATER

Whithall, March 8th, 1702.

MY LORD,—This pacquet brings the most dismall and melancholy news that for a long time has happened to Brittain, I may say to all Europe.   The Lord has been pleased to remove our King.   He took a ffoott of the ague Thursday last, and wee thought he had att night growen better, but he became worse ffriday and Saturnday by vomiting and purging, and this morning about 7 acloack he dyed, as perfect a minute before he expyred as ever he was.   He took leave I may say of all the nobles who were attending him, gave Albemarle the keyes of his trunks to care for his papers, acknowledged that Monsieur Overkirk had served him honestly, and thanked him for it.   So he shutt his eyes and gave up the ghost.   The Princess was proclamed Queen att three acloack, and there are orders come downe to proclaim her in Scotland.   I need not presume to tell yor Lop what consternatione people are in att this sudden stroke.   Yo^r Lop., who knows the great things he has done and was still adoeing for Brittain, will plainly judge of it.   I forgott to tell yor Lop. that this morning about 4 acloack he very devoutly took sacrament with the Archbishop of Canterberry and Bp. of Salisberry. I will not presume to trouble yor Lop. any further, but tell your Lop. that my Lord, Lady and Lady Betty are in very good health, blessed be God, though much troubled att the death of so good a King.   I pray yor Lop a long life and good health, and I am, My Lord, your Lops. most dutifull serv^t,   JOHN PHILP.

For THE RIGHT HONOURABLE THE EARLE OF
FINDLATER, CULLENHOUSE

Edr., 16 *Mairch* 1702.

MY LORD,—I beleive this may not be the first account of the most lamentable death of our most gratious soveraigne King William.   However, this bearer comeing your way, I have thought my deuty to acquant you that it pleased the Lord to call him upon Sunday the 8 instant at 8 in the morning from his earthly croun, I hope to the enjoyment of a heavenly diadem.   He took the sacrament at 5 that morning and dyed verie well, and was distinct and perfect to the last moment, and as promised befor to those that were about him gave the signall when his royall breath was goeing out.   Great is his fall, and it will be mor senseably felt some time after this then at present.   So soone as he was at rest all those of the K.'s household waited on the Princes Anna and ouned hir as Queen, and layed doune ther pattens and offices at her feett, who tooke them up and gave them back to them desiring they might continoue to exercise as formerly.   Immediatly a proclamaᵒne was drawn, and she was proclamed Queen of Brittain at 3 aclock that afternoone with the ordinary solemnities and demonstrations of joy.   Our Scotts nobility and gentry, who wer ther and of the Councill in number i0, tendered the coronation oath of this kingdome to her, and she accepted of the administration.   Coˡˡ Rew came off express upon Munday, and brought the surpriseing newes heir upon Thursdayes afternoon, which struck terror into the hearts of his professed enemies.   The Councill was sitting at the time, and her Maties letter counter signed by the Earle of Seafeild was read giveing account of the death of her deciest royall brother, that she hade taken the oath and the administratione of the governement upon hir, and therby ordained all persones to continoue to exercise in ther stations as formerly, till she should have time to send new commissions.   And the next day being ffryday, my Lord Chancellour in persone, being attended by all the nobility, gentry, etc., upon this place, the lyon king at armes, heraulds, and pursevints and trupetts went to the cross at 4 in the afternoone, wher ther was lykewayes a theater erected, and proclamed hir Queen of this realme. I ame confident this is the most afflicting stroak ever cam upon my Lord Seafeild, ffor he hes lost a most gratious prince and a bountifull and keind maister to him, and I know it will be no small matter of murning to your Lope. The Lord make up the loss to us all.   Its sayed Portland is gone to Holland.   When the Kings body was opened his lungs was found ulcerate, bot his head most intire and no water in his belly, tho his legs, etc., have bein swelled of a long time.—I am in all deuty, My Lord, Your Lops. most deutiefull, most humble, and obleidged srᵗ,

JA. BAIRD.

CHAPTER V

LETTERS DURING THE PERIOD SEAFIELD WAS SECRETARY OF STATE AND LORD HIGH CHANCELLOR UNDER QUEEN ANNE, FROM MARCH 1702 TO THE UNION OF THE PARLIAMENTS IN MAY 1707.

To WILLIAM LORIMAR, CHAMBRLAND TO THE EARELL OF SEAFIELD, AT CULLAN, BANFFSHAYR

GRIGRY ship is cum up, and the bear is sold. Thy complened that it was not so weall dighted as the sampell was which cam hear. It is nou about the tym of taking up my custam wadars, so I hop you will be carfull in taking them up that both the oull and wadars may be good. I likways disayr that you may send up that twall or eleven pound strlen which I wrot of in Febrary last for. Forgland did advans me the muny in March, so I disayr that you may send it up with soum of thos cums to the Parliment, for Forgland disayrs it agenst the terem, eles it might cum in tym with you when my Lord sends for you, for I am affrayed that he will not cum to the north at this tym, bot of this I am not certan. I hop those which oues me any thing will pay it up nou, so you will have no defickullty in geting the muny. I disayr that the hous books may be taken up when Will Robertson cums hir, and he may bring them alongest with him, or a not of what is spent sins I left Cullan. Bot I belive this will not cum in tym, for he will be gon or nou. I can not tell my Lords dayat of being in this pleas as yet. This is all from your ashuired frind,   ANNA SEAFIELD.

Edr., May ii, 1702.

John Ogilvie hath payed in five hundred pound hear. If Bracky or Hallyeards had use for muny at this pleas, it wold be mor convenent then to transmit it north, sins he will not cary it with him. Pray mynd the muny to Forgland, for I am out of countinans that it is so long resting.

After the Queen's accession Seafield continued to act as Secretary of State for Scotland. On 12th May 1702 a new warrant[1] for a patent and commission was issued in his favour as one of the two principal Secretaries with a yearly pension of £1000 sterling. His colleague was the Duke of Queensberry, the late King's last Commissioner to Parliament.

For THE EARL OF FINDLATER

MY LORD,—I beg pardon for pairting with your Lo. so abruptly, but I was ill mounted and my horse having flung a shoe, it was not in my pouer to come up again ; besides some have a frett that the hare should be killed, so that I followed her, killed her, and gave her to the parson to eat. I presume to wish your Lo. all health hapiness and good success in al your Lo. and my Lord Seafield undertakeings dureing this session of Paliat., and if it lay in my wake pouer to contribute any thing therto, ther should none concur more francklie or forward it. I would written to my Lord Seafield, but since he has other business I shal only wish him the same favour this jorny he deservedly had in the last ; and if it falls in his Lo. way to doe me any kindness I have no doubt of his or your Lo. willingness, so that I am in all sincerity as becometh, My Lord, Your Lo. most faithful most obedient and willing hu[bl] ser[t],   ALEXR. ABERCROMBIE.

Glassaugh, May 25, 1702.

If your Lo. will favour me with a letter it would be most acceptable. Mind the adding of commrs. of supply and justices of pace, to witt Carnowcie, Munblarie, Kirkhill, young Birkenburn, Cromie, Ardmelie, and Meyen. The Lady expects your Lo. picture, since the only excuse last winter was the want of time to sitt, and its honourable your Lo. picture should be some wher. I would written a congratulatory letter to my Lady Seafield or her young son, but hopes your Lo. will give her my humble duty.

Parliament met on 9th and adjourned on 30th June 1702. On 19th June Parliament[2] added to the list of commissioners of

---

[1] *State Papers (Scotland) Warrant Books*, vol. xviii. p. 152.
Acts of the Parliaments of Scotland, vol. xi. p. 23.

supply of Banffshire George Gordon of Carnousie, Mr. Andrew Hay of Mountblaire, James Gordon of Ardmelie, John Cuthbert of Brackenhills, William Gordon of Birkenburn, younger, Alexander Abercrombie of Glassaugh, John Dunbar of Kirkhill, James [Duff] of Cromie, Alexander Wilson of Littlefield, Alexander Abercrombie of Skeith, and Major Anderson of Westertoun.

On 25th August 1702 a warrant[1] for a new gift of the sheriffship of Banff was issued in favour of Seafield.

For WILLIAM LORIMER, CHAMBERLANE TO THE EARLE OF SEAFIELD, ATT CULLEN

Whithall, Novem^r 14th, 1702.

AFFECTIONAT COMERAD,—. . . My Lord comes doun Chancellour and Tarbat succeeds him. You will be called over to Edinburgh to clear acco^{tts}.—I have no time write any more, but am, Yo^r affectionat cousin and humble servant,   JOHN PHILP.

On 21st November a warrant[2] was issued for a commission to the Earl of Seafield to be Lord High Chancellor of Scotland with a yearly pension of £1500 sterling, and an additional pension of £400 sterling for his faithful services. On the same day a further warrant[3] was issued for an approbation of his past actings and exoneration in his favour. The same day Lord Tarbat succeeded as joint Secretary of State.

For THE EARL OF FINDLATER

MY LORD,—This day about ten aclock I had a letter from Forgland with two inclosed, one for yor Lo. and another for my Lady, which he desired me to forward to your Lo. where ever you might be by an expresse, which accordingly I have done wt orders to enquire for your Lo. by the way. Wee have no news beside what your Lo. has, but that Tullibardins and Annandales comissions are come down, the first to be Privy Seall, and last to be President of the Council. Boile[4] is Treasurer Deput, and its said Prestonhall Justice Clerk. I sent my Lady

---

[1] *State Papers (Scotland) Warrant Books*, vol. xviii.
[2] *Ibid.*, vol. xviii. pp. 239-245.   [3] *Ibid.*, pp. 303-306.
[4] Afterwards Earl of Glasgow.

the proposalls made by the Scots about trade, which your Lo. may see. Wee know nothing mor as yet about the union than what I wrote to her La. My Lord Deskfoord is well, and offers his humble duty to your Lo. and my Lady, to the two young ladys and to Mr. George. I presume this expresse may be to call your Lo. south ; and I wish your Lo. fair weather and a saffe journey with all my heart, which is the pn̄t trouble from, My Lord, Your Lo. most hu[ll] and obedient serv[t],

WIL. BLAKE.

The bearer heis gott a 20s.

Abd., Decer. 28, 1702.

The question of an incorporating union bequeathed by William to the Parliaments of England and Scotland had been so far advanced that in May and June these bodies had authorised the appointment of commissioners to treat. The commissioners met in London on 10th November, but negotiations soon broke down, as England would not then accord equal trading privileges to Scotland.

The Earl of Findlater in October 1703 married Mary, third daughter of William, second Duke of Hamilton, and widow of Alexander, third Earl of Callander, and of Sir James Livingstone of West Quarter. Some of the letters of this year show the progress of the suit.

To THE RIGHT HONOURABELL THE EARELL OF FINLATOR AT HIS LOUGENS, EDR.

MY LORD,—I long very much to hear of your halth and progras in your grand affiar, if you pershew it with the wigar your inclanations lead you. I hop you may be happy in the lady, which I shall erenastly wish you to be in all condisions, and I shall allways indevar to aprou my self, My Lord, Your most obedint daghtar and humbell servant,   ANNA SEAFIELD.

Feb. 10*th* 1703.

Your grand children is all very weall. I hop nixt munth you will see them so at Ed[r], for with your sons live I resovell to bring all that is in Cullan with me to Ed[r], God willing. Bety gives your Lo. hir humbell douty.

On 5th February 1703 the Earl of Seafield, Lord High Chancellor, was appointed Commissioner to the General Assembly. Volume xviii. of the *Warrant Books, State Papers (Scotland)* contains the warrant for his commission and his instructions, as well as a letter to the Treasury ordering a payment of £500 sterling to meet his charges.

For WILLIAM LORIMER, CHAMBERLANE TO THE EARLE OF SEAFIELD, LORD HIGH CHANCELLOUR, ATT CULLEN, BANFFSHYRE

Edinburgh, March 16, 1703.

AFFECTIONAT COMERAD,—I am very glade to hear from yor self that you, my mother, and all other friends are in good health. I longed to hear from you. I have been very bussy since I came to Edinburgh, that I had not so much time as to write north. The Generall Assembly is now sitting, and wee have great deal of trouble w^t them. . . . I beleeve Durn and Glassaugh make a noise that I have gott the carrying the purse. It is now well enough knowen. Let me know what they say. My Lady I doe beleeve takes it ill that Mr. George was not prefered. I can vindicate myself so much to my Lady that I never sought it, but my Lord did me the honour before he gott his commission as Chancellour to secure me in that post. I acknowledge it is more than I deserve, and Mr. George, or Glassaugh either of them had becomed it better. Give my humble service to Castlefield and his Lady and children. I am heartely well pleased to hear that they are all well, and I long to see them. Remember me lykewise to yor wife, and I shall trouble you no further but subscryve myself, Yor most affectionat comerad and servant,

JOHN PHILP.

If you can, w^t the first bear ship that comes send some of the oats for our horses, and they will be wellcome. Let me know if John Lorimer has gott a burse att Aberdeen as was promised.

The tumult[1] referred to in next letter was occasioned by the

---

[1] *Historical MSS. Commission, Fourteenth Report*, App., Part III., *MSS. of the Countess-Dowager of Seafield*, pp. 198, 216.

Queen's letter to the Privy Council asking them to extend toleration to the Episcopal clergy.   The writer, Lord Tarbat, was
created on 1st January 1703 Earl of Cromarty—his patent passing
the Great Seal on 18th September following.[1]

LORD TARBAT'S LETTER to the EARL OF SEAFIELD

RIGHT HONORABLE,—Wee long to know whats done in
the matter of the rable.   The magistrats and regiment
seem to have failed both as to prevention and suppression.
Wee suspend our thoughts till further information, and
till wee know if the indemnity be proclaimed; for if it be,
I presume the crime pardond, and law then must be the
rule of judgment as to Sʳ Jo. Bels damnage.   If they have
therby escapt punishment, it may [be] hopt yt the clemency
will as weel cure as pardon the malice.   Mean while, it were
prudence in the Episcopall clergy to cary rather with more
rather then less moderation then formerly, and to make
no new stepp from the former practis in any place.   Wee
hope the Generall Assembly will continue in the peacable
temper which pleased her Maᵗie, and I am sure to doe
so will be at once prudence and duty.   I would have
returnd to Mr. Meldrums civill letter, but the D. of Qʸ
beeing so unweell that he could not, I referr it to the next
post ; and yt your Lop. will in this excuse my delay to
Mr. Meldrum, it will be a favour, and prevent his mis-
constructing the delay ; but the letter beeing gratiously
receaved by the Queen with expressing also herr confidence, that the rest of the Assemblies progress would be
of a peece with ther loyalty and affection exprest in ye
letter, this litle delay in return needs give no delay to the
good procedurs of ye Assembly.   For news I leave all to
ye prints, which are my best intelligence.   Its talkt heer,
how truly I know no, that the States of Holland will not
take Portmores regement from him, and so he will keep
both.   There are some promotions in England, as yʳ Lo.
have no doubt heard, and the changes also in severall
Leivtenancies.   D. Northumberlan hath gott E. Oxfords

---

[1] *The Acts of the Parliaments of Scotland*, vol. xi. p. 118.

regiment, and the Earll of Arran Kevers troop of guards. This pleases and displeases. My Lo., I flyt sometymes, but am constantly Your Lordships most humble and affectionat servant,   TARBAT.

20 *March*, 1703.

For THE EARL OF SEAFIELD

MY LORD,—I give yr. Lop. thanks for y^r concern of my health. I m pretty weall recovered, and hopes ere long to have the honour to waite one yr. Lop. I shall reccone it my hapyness to serve the Queen. Others may to more purpose, but noe body shall w^t more sincerity and inclination. If hir Maj^{tie} had named me of her Concell, I should have faithfully and impartially addvised what I judged for her treu intrest ; but I m loath for what I can doe to give her the truble to ask it, tho what ever way her Maj^{tie} pleases to imploy me I shall be very ready to doe my best. I shall so shortly waite one y^r Lop., yt I will not give you any more truble, but to assure you I am, My Lord, Yr. Lop. most affectionatt cussine and most humble servant,   MARISCHALL.

Inverugie, March 22*d*, 1703.

Inverugie is the ' bonnie ' Inverugie of Carlyle. Earl Marischal's sons were out in the 'Fifteen, and were attainted.

For THE EARL OF SEAFIELD

RIGHT HONOURABLE MY LORD,—I thought to have hade the honour of waitting on your Lop. at Edr. when my Lady now comes up, and have given you a more ample account of your affaires here than I can communicat by write, but being detained for dispatching the ships with your victuall, I have for your Lops. satisfaction sent to John Philp a double of my last yeares accounts, with ane abbreviat of what money I have given out since Mertimass last, both which your Lop. may peruse, and when you please to call me after the ships are dispatched, I shall be glade to waitt on you for clearing these accounts by instructions. Your Lady will give you a perfect account

of all your affaires here at present ; and as to the state
of your tennents (though no mōy can be hade from them)
I hope they are the most of them beginning to recover
the bad yeares, ffor I have received about five chalders
meall from them besyds this yeares dewties, and I expect
as much bear, which will clear a part of their bygon rests.
There are many of their tacks expyred, and if your Lop.
were in the countrey I believ you could sett the most of
your enterest under tacks without much loss.   Your Lady
will inform you what changes are among the tennents of
Findlater allready, and what more are designed.   There
are a great many houses in Cullen and one of the boatts
there waste, and the boatts in Sandend are litle better
than waste, ffor I can gett nothing of their dewties from
the seamen.   There are some other rooms in Kempkairn
and Bogmuchles waste, which I know could be sett if yor
Lop. were present, and there is ane absolute necessity for
your presence before right methods can be taken for
securing you anent the old rests, which are very great,
and some of the tennents turning depauperat.   I have
received no mōy for old rests this year, and was necessitat
to borrow upon some occasions this year allready, and
expect none more before summer mercats.   Gregeryes ship
sailled from Portsoye the last week with the first loadning
of your Lops. bear, for which I have sent bill of loadning
to Forglen.   I am daylie expecting another ship for bear
and two for meall.   How soon they come they shall gett
all possible dispatch.   There will be about four or five
chalders of oatts, and some superplus of meall and bear
above what is sold, and if your Lop. accept of John
Hamiltons meall, I believ there may be as much one way
or another as will frawght a small bark about twelve or
fourteen chalders, but I shall acquaint your Lop. of this
before the last ship come up with the bear.   The collector
of the vacant stipends at Abd. is allwayes calling for
money from me anent the church of Cullen, and I thought
to have sent him three hundered merks, if there hade not
been so much sent in for my Lord Deskfoord's use.   So
if he be pressing I know not what to doo, if I get no mōy.

from your Lop., but I shall keep it off as long as I can. I have allso bought timber for a rooff to the kirk of Cullen, which will coast about 400 mks, but no materialls are led to it as yet. I shall referr to my Lady what further concerns your Lops. affaires here at present. And wishing yo͏ᵣ Lop. all imaginable happiness and prosperity, I subscribe myself as becometh, My Lord, Your Lops. most humble and most obliedged servant,

WILL. LORIMER.

Cullen, Mar: 29, 1703.

For THE EARL OF FINDLATER

MY LORD,—With all the satisfaction imaginable I reseued the honour of your letter, but I was sory too fynd by it you haue bin tender. The bearer ashoured me your Lo. was prfietly recouered, and louks as will as euer he sie you, which was wery confortable nows to me. My Lord, I being at a disins makes me I cannot presoum tou ofer my adwyes, but I pray God drek you aright, and if that afear goo on, I wish it may prowe for your confort and satisfaction. I dou ashour you no chield you haue onours loues or astimes you mor, and so far as I am capable shall be mor willing to serue you then I. I am wery sory for Forglen indisposition, and my housband hiring he was so ill could not be at eas till he siee him. I am in all douty, My Lord, You most obedient daughter and duoted humble seruen,

ANNA OGILVIE.

Allardes, 5 Apryle '703·

My Lady Mary giue hir humble douty tou you.

For WILLIAM LORIMER, CHAMBERLANE TO THE EARLE OF SEAFIELD, ATT CULLEN

Edinburgh, Aprile 6th, 1703.

D. C.,—. . . . Tell Wᵐ Thomsone that I have sent his garden seeds by the post. They are directed for him, and the accoᵗᵗ of the seeds in the bag. I hope to see you very soon here to clear yor accoᵗᵗ. Skipper Gregory is come safe. My Lady appears very kind to me, and desired a sight of the purse. I doe not care for peoples displeasure so long as I serve my master ffaithfully. When Collector Ogilvie comes north you will hear him talk of me, but though he does not think it, I shall be his humble servant. Let me know if I have gotten pay^t of Baillie Sanders. Tell my mother that I shall send Elizabeth the ketle. Give my service to yor bedfellow and all friends.— I am, Your affectionat cousine and humble servant,

JOHN PHILP.

The new Parliament met on 6th May, and after a stormy session adjourned on 16th September 1703. Seafield had by this time commenced his correspondence with Lord Godolphin, Lord High Treasurer of England. Godolphin's letters to Seafield are published in the *Historical MSS. Commission, Fourteenth Report*, App., Part III., *MSS. of the Countess-Dowager of Seafield*, pp. 197-212, and extend from March 1703 to February 1712. The letters to 1707 (pp. 197-208) throw light on the important political issues then at stake, the succession to the crown and the necessity foɪ an incorporating union.

Edinburgh, May 17th, 1703.

WILLIAM,—I have seen yor letter to John Philp, and am glade that the ships with my bear are not yet sailed from Portsoy. You must take speciall care if they be there yet, that the wictuall doe not heat, and if it be necessary, you may unload a pairt or the whole to prevent it from spoyling, and they must not pairt from that till they hear that the coasts are clear. There has not these 20 dayes bypast any ships come up the ffirth, and wee haue heard of seᵣalls that have been taken, and therefor they must be as cautious as possible. Wee have written to England that there may be cruisars sent, but if it shall happen that the ships which have my bear be taken, which God forbid, I doe by this impower them to ransome them. As for the ships, that concerns the owners, and I can only be concerned in the loadning, and I am sure they can obtain that att a very small rate, if they represent that the loadning being bear would spoyle before it could reach any port in ffrance, and would be there good for nothing, and does here sell att a very small value. So recommending

to them to doe the best they can in such a caise for my
advantage is all from your assured ffriend,

SEAFIELD.

As early as 25th August 1702 the Queen had instructed[1] the
Lords Commissioners of the Treasury to fit out two of the three
Scots frigates to defend the east and west coasts of Scotland from
French privateers.   On 17th July 1703 Captain Thomas Gordon and
Captain Matthew Campbell were commissioned[2] captains respec-
tively of the *Royal Mary* and the *Dumbarton Castle,* the two ships
of the Scots navy referred to in next letter.

For WILLIAM LORIMER, CHAMBERLANE TO THE EARLE
OF SEAFIELD ATT CULLEN

Edinburgh, June 14th, 1703.

AFFEC. COUSIN,—The ketle I sent to my sister weighs
ffyfty one pound eight unces att 22s. per pound is ffyfty
six pounds Scotts, which I have paid.   You may gett me
payt. or security for the money.   Here is a note of Birken-
boges for thirty pound Scotts, which you may call for.
The government here are fitting out two men of warr to
cruise on our coast, which will be ready within twenty
dayes, and these two will be thought sufficient to beat of
the small privateers.   Besides the English have promised
to send down two men of warr from London more.   When
these come or our own ships ar ready, I shall timeously
advertise you to putt the wictuall aboard again.   My Lord
commends what you have done, and till the men of warr
be upon the coast the ships must stay, for better they
be in Portsoy than Dunkirk.   My Lord has written fully
to you, and I can say no more about what he writes.   Tell
Letterfury I shall write to him about Semples affair.   I
have serall times spoke with my Lord Eglingtone, who is
much concerned in his affairs.   He tells there are so many
preferable creditors upon Glasfoords liferent escheat, that
it will be a long time before any can come to payment.
Tell my mother that, blessed be God, I am in very good
health, and I wish you may be all so in the north.   Will

---

[1] *State Papers (Scotland) Warrant Books,* vol. xviii. p. 297.
[2] *Ibid.,* vol. xix.

Gardne sends you all the minutes of Parlia^{tt}, which will informe you of what passes.—I am, Yor. most affectionat cousin and servant,   JOHN PHILP.

For THE EARL OF FINDLATER
Westquarter, th 10 *Seper.* 1703.

MY LORD,—This night I rescued yrs by Mr. Kinkead, and am uery glad yr. Lop. is well, for all yr. close seeting in Parlement. I pray God you may find no harm by it after. I cannot the next week come in to make an end of our afare, but any time the week after, that you can get a spare day. I am sattisfied not to temp yr. pacsianc longer. I think the most privet way wode be for you to take a hakne coach, as if you ware goeing to take the eair, and let nobody know, and meet me at Mortan, and bring Mr. Meldrem along with you ; or if you cannot get him, if the Lord will, I shall meet you thar about twell or wone aclok, and bring the menester that is hear with me, but I had far rather you broght one, and it wold make les noyse and suspeesion a grat dell.   This is the quietes way I can think of, and I wode presently take with you that same night in the hakne, so that you wode not be much mised out of toune.   This is the way I incline to have it done, for I will not have it hear. Yr. Lo. may have yr. thoughts of it, and when you ples aquant her what day, how is, My Lord, Yr. Lor. humbell saruant,

M. CALANDER.

Thar is a post comes by this gate thries in the week. Dauid Broun will aquant yr. Lor. the dayes.   Pray don't tell any body what I have wret, no not yr. darlen son, nor Forglan.   If any let it be cusen Pate.

Mr. George Meldrum had on 30th March 1697 been appointed second Professor of Divinity in Edinburgh University.[1]

For JAMES WALKER, SERVANT TO THE EARLE OF FINDLATOR.   These for
Edbr., Oct. 4, 1703.

SIR,—When I was wayting on the Earle of Findlater

---

[1] *State Papers (Scotland) Warrant Books*, vol. xvi.

this forenoon, I forgott to tell his Lordship that the morrow
forenoon our election sermon is to be, so that if it can be
I would intreat my Lord would appoynt another tyme
for me to wayt on him then the forenoon.   Bot if he
cannot appoynt me another tyme I shall wayt on him.
This is from your assured friend,

MR. MELDRUM.

On 3rd October Seafield was at Belford on his way to London.
For his charges in London during the winter the Queen next year
allowed him £1000 sterling.[1]

For THE EARL OF FINDLATER

London, Novemr. 2d, 1703.

MY LORD,—My Lord Chancellour is so diverted with
company, that he has not the time to write so frequently
to yor Lop. as he designed.   He is in very good health,
blessed be God, and has frequent audiences of her Maty.
and her ministers, and is more in favour att court than
ever he was, and his ffriends needs not be afraid that it is
in the power of his enemies to shake him here.   The Duke
of Queensberry suspects that he is too much in the interest
of his opposers, but my Lord sufficiently vindicates himself, that what he proposes or designes is purely for the
Queen and countreyes service.   There is nothing yet proposed relating to the Scotts affairs, but every person who
has access giving accompt of what is past.   Forgline gives
yor. Lop. his humble service.   He designed to have
answired yor. Lop. letter, but has been so late with the
Duke of Athole that he cannot have the pacquet.   They
are making great preparationes for the expedition to
Portugall.   The new King of Spain dayly expected, and
the officers have gott orders to repair to the ships.   There
is no other news here.   The English Parliat. meetts Thursday next.   I hope your Lop. will pardon this presumption
though I have nothing worthy of yor reading.   I am, may
it please yor Lop., Your Lops. most obedient and most
dutifull servant,   JOHN PHILP.

---

[1] *State Papers (Scotland) Warrant Books,* vol. xx.

On 3rd January 1704 letters of marque were issued to Captain John Ap-Rice, commander of the *Annandale,* a ship of 220 tons and 20 guns belonging to the African company, and fitted out by them to prosecute and protect their East Indian trade.   On her maiden voyage she was captured in the Downs by the East India company, and was confiscated.   This incident, referred to in next letter, was the cause of the affair of Captain Green and his crew in 1705.

For MR. LORIMER, Chamerlaine to the EARL OF SEAFIELD att Cullen

Leith. the 14th febry. 1704.

Sir,—Mr. Stewart and I are busie just now in getting ships to come north for my Lord Chancellors bear.   Therefor make it as soon radie as ye cane.   There is noe word as yet of my Lords offcomeing for Scotland, but how soon I know of it shall acquant you.   Wee have greatt heats heir amonge our great men anent the plotte, and be all can be learned, it will end in blood.   Ane English man of warr hes run a shipe of ours on a rock, taken every thing out of her, beatt the men.   Shee was tradeing to the Indies under the companies pass.   This D. Hamilton and others concerned to that company takes wery ill, so that there is ane express goen to her Majestie thereanent from the Counsell.   My wife is safe brought to bede, blessed be God, of a daughter which frustrats my expecta°ne, for I thought to have gotten a son to your daughter.   Wee have noe other newes heir at present, only the King of Spaine is not sailed from England as yet.   My wife and I give our service to you, your bedefellow, and wish you good health and your younge daughter, and we must gett sons nixt, and wishing all hapieness to attend you all, I continue after the old maner, Your humble servant,

WILL GAIRDNE.

Draw on me for four pounds Scotts I received from skipper Balfour on your accott.   My Lord Deskford is pritty well, but Mr. Black is dyeing. . . .

Lord Deskford probably left Marischal College in June 1703.

For WILLIAM LORIMER, Chamber-lane to the
EARLE OF SEAFIELD att Cullen

London, ffebry 15*th*, 1704.

Affect. Cousin,—I am very glade to hear that all our
ffriends are well in the north, and I wish it may be long
so with them. I was very ill some time before I left
Edinburgh, but my journey did me much good, but since
I came here I have been again taken with the same dis-
temper, which was a violent colick, and it keept me three
or ffour dayes with a continuall gripping and purging, but,
blessed be God, I am now better again, and att pn̄tt in very
good health. Wee did not think of being so long here
when wee came first up, but as matters have happened
it is both good that wee came, and have continued so long.
Wee had sērall difficulties in King William's reign, but
hardly any such as has happen of late. No doubt you
have heard of Captain ffresers plott. He undertook to the
Duke of Queensberry to discover that sērall of the greatest
nobility in the kingdome were in a correspondance wt
Saint Germans, and for this end gott a protection while
he was in Scotland, and a pass yrafter to goe overseas.
He has made a very ill use of all these, and his intercepted
letters makes it appear that he was clossly carrying on the
pre[tended] Prince of Wales his interest; and lately one Mr.
Baillie has made a declaration that D. Queensbery and
Annandale would had him evidencing that there was a
correspondance betwixt Saint Germans and some of the
nobility, particularly D. Hamilton, D. of Athole, and my
Lord Seafield ; and this Baillie hes given in his declaration
to the Privy Council, but Queensberry and Annandale
denay this altogether. This bussines of the plott hes been
above two moneths work to our statesmen, and yet not
determined. All the steps in this matter are discovered,
and nothing can yet appear in it, but endeavours to putt
a task upon particular persons, that others might get there
places. In all this nothing was ever spoke of my Lord
Seafield, but this declaration of Baillies, which does him
rather good than hurt, and whatever his enemies attempt

they will not be able to doe him prejudice, though this be a very difficult time for any man to keep himself free of aspersions, when our nation stands so much divyded. This is no suiteable subject for you, and yrfor shall leave it. . . . My Lord has given orders to hyre ships to come north for the wictuall, and my Lady will write about it. When he comes to Scotland, you may expect to be called south except it be about the time you are shipping the wictuall. Give my service to yor bedfellow, and tell my mother that I long to see her, which I fear shall not be on hast. Bid her take care of herself, and it will be my greatest satisfactione to hear that she is well. Remember me to all my other ffriends, and that wee may have a merry meeting is the desire of, Yo^r affectionat cousin and humble servant, Jo. Philp.

Captain Fraser's plot was better known as the Queensberry plot. In consequence of its exposure Queensberry fell from power. The letter of 13th May 1704 refers to this.

For THE EARL OF FINDLATER

My Lord,—. . . . I have spoke twice to Glasgow who promises very fairly. I shal keep your son in mynd, and were it not that the Duke of Marleborrow goes from this Munday the 21 I should speek to him, but ther is no access to him, the throng he is in being incredible. However I shal leave no stone unturned I think can serve you, and ye may be assured yours will be payed among the very first. I shal only ad that I am in all sincerity and with the height of respect, My Lord, Your ever most faithfull and most obedient h. s., Alex^r Abercromby.[1]

London, March 19, 1704.

For THE EARL OF SEAFIELD

Edr., March 31, 1704.

My Lord,—Your Ldships. of the 25 I had yesterday, and am extremly glad that her Majesty is so ueal pleased with my conduct in this Asembly [2] hitherto. This I can say, that I have neglected nothing I was capable to doe

---

[1] Laird of Glassaugh.
[2] *Carstares State Papers and Letters*, p. 725.

for the advancment of her servic, and never shal neglect any oportunity to convinc her Majesty of my dutyfull zeal for her Majestys honor and interest. Yesterday the Asembly met fornoon, and as in other dayes wer going about ther ordinar affairs. Afternoon we met, and began about revising the Synod books, and beyond the expectation of al men they wer passed with the greatest harmony and quiet that ever was seen in ane Asembly—no motion nor insinuation about intrinsick pouer or anything of that natur, only some comon remarks about form and such like. This morning we met again at nine fornoon, and after several petitions wer heard, other affairs coming in wer al remited to the Comission. Then the moderator made the usual speech to the Asembly, then to me to assur her Majesty of ther duty. Your Ldship knous the use, so I need not writ mor of it to you, only to let you knou notwithstanding al the difficulties your Ldship knew I had, yet ther was never a hot word in all this Assembly, and such a dissolution was never in Scotland—no protest, no disent, but the greatest affection to me as her Majestys servant. Parted all with kindnes, waited all upon me to my lodgings, and have al been with me this afternoon, blesing me and praying heartely for her Majesty. I am glad I have been capabl to doe her Majesty this servic. I doubt not your Ldship. will represent it to her Majesty, and though I was oblidged in this criticall junctur to live far beyond what I expected, yet I think it ueal imployed for the honor of the Queen, who I know will not let me be a looser. I intend in a day to part from this, so shal add no mor trouble but that I am, My Lord, Your Ldships most humble and faithful servant,   Rosse.

Copie Letter to the TREASURY[1] for reducing the fforces and establishing a Third Highland Company to be comanded by Maj^r Duncan M'Kenzie

Sic Superscribitur

ANNE R

Right trusty and right welbeloved, etc.,—Wee greet

---

[1] *State Papers (Scotland) Warrant Books*, vol. xix. pp. 184-187.

you well.   Whereas wee have appointed a third Highland
company ffor the peace and security of the Highlands
benorth and bewest Lochness, to be comanded by Major
Duncan McKenzie according to the directions given by
us to our Privy Councill thereanent of the date of these
presents, the pay of which company is to be established
by reducing ten men one sergeant and one piper out of
each of the other two Highland companies, two centinells
out of each company of the Earle of Marr and Ld. Straith-
navers regiments, and one centinell out of each company
of the two regiments of dragoons: you are hereby
required to make alterations accordingly in the establishment of our fforces, and to use such diligence as the said
company may be establishd against the middle of May,
ffor which these presents shall be your warrand.   And so
wee bid you heartily farewell.

Given at our Court att St. James's the twelve day of
April 1704 and of our reign the third year.

By her Majesties command,

Sic subtr.

CROMERTIE.

For THE EARL OF SEAFIELD

MY MOST NOBELL LORD,—I am necessitat once mor to
trobubell your Lordsip, that ye vill be pleassed to confear
that honnor upon me to doe me the kendnes as to speck
to hir Majesty the Quan of Great Breatten, to proquar on
letter from hir Majesty to is Majesty the King off Suadlan
for Collenell Gordon off Achintoull and my fredom, vich
I knou, my good nobell Lord, vill cost you but on vird to
hir Majesty, God blis hir.   And is Majesty the Zar of
Muscv hes written partigular to Collenell Gordon and
others, that thau shall deu ther beast for our fredom after
vhat menner thay pleas.   So my good nobell Lord ther is
other tuo Collenells hes imploed ther frends.   The on hes
got off.   The other is just a geating of only by the moyen
of ther frends, and, my good Lord, ye knou ve hau both
good frends, and nou, my nobel good Lord, I pressum
that I hau that honner to hau the greatest poor nou in

Scotland, who is my Lord Hay Chanler, and I hope ye vill not forgeat old Dem Ogilvic grandchild Mullican longer to be in bondeg, since ye, my good nobell Lord, can reliv him out of it vhen ye plase for on vird of your mouth, and certenly, my nobell Lord, it vill be on great act of kendnes doun in this present junckter of tym. Ue are both content not to serv aganst is Majesty the King of Suadland douring this var, and be God, my nobell Lord, vith God assistans ye shall hau no dishonner by me so long as ther is on drop of bloud vithin me. I beag pardon, my nobell Lord, iff I hau fealled anny vays in giuing your Lordship all your deu tittells beloning to your Lordship, for, is I fear God, it is the first tym that ever I had ocation or the honnor to vrit to my Lord Hay Chanler of Scotland, in whom I am confident vill reliv us out of this misirabell bondeg. This all I can say, but God almighty prosper you and your nobell familly. My most nobell Lord, I am, Your most fatfull and most houmbell servant to my dath your,

JAMES GORDON.

Stockhollam, ii *Aprill* 1704.

The editor has been unable to identify James Gordon of Mullican. Colonel Alexander Gordon of Auchintoul, afterwards Major-General, the writer of next letter, was eldest son of Alexander, Lord Auchintoul, already referred to in this correspondence. His appeal to Seafield seems to have been ineffectual, for it was only in 1707 that he was released by exchange. He was second in command under Mar at Sheriffmuir. An account of him is given at pp. 137-140 of vol. i. of the *House of Gordon,* New Spalding Club, and in the editor's ' Banffshire Roads,' *Transactions of the Banffshire Field Club,* 1905, pp. 104-106.

For THE EARL OF SEAFIELD

MOST NOBLE LORD,—May it please your Lordship, I have with the utmost joy and satisfaction, in the distant and remote parts of the world fate has hurried me to, mett the most pleasing and agreeable news of the happy progress your uncommon merit and genius makes in your Princes favour ; and may your Lordship ever be gracious and acceptable with her and your felicities so increase dailly, that you may still have the opportunity of doing good to your countrey and friends, which I knowe is the cheif delight and pleasure your elevated station can yield to a temper so unbiass'd and generous as I have had the honour to remark and admire in your Lordship; nor will it, I hope, be displeasing that I take the liberty most heartily to congratulate the many distinguishing marks of esteem and eminent dignities deservedly heap'd on your Lordship, and at same time presume to offer subject for your generosity and goodness to work upon.

No doubt your Lordship can well remember the memorable passage of raising the siege of Narve in November *an.* 1700, where I had the command of a regiment of 1200 Russes. Would to God they had been of my own countrey men. Then haply our ennimies had not bought ther victory so cheap; but so it was, finding myself abandoned by them and slightly wounded, many of our generall officers shewing me the way, I submitted on tearms which I thought would have been accompanied with a totall liberty to goe of for Moscovy, or at least a treatment more becoming a cavalier, to be a prisoner att large suffered abroad on paroll; but instead of this, I have ever since been confin'd to my lodgings under a guarde, and have rarely or never leave to take the air out of doors. Yet not so much this hardship, as this tedious loss of time, my Lord, after having used all possible means and attempted often my liberty in vain, that I might not become troublesome, that now presses me to implore your Lordships assistance; and I flatter myself mainly from your condescending goodness, tho somewhat on the score of former acquaintance I had the honour of, that amidst the crowd of things that take up your great thoughts, I may be indulged the freedom of aproaching with a humble yet earnest request, for your imploying some part of the powerfull interest and credit you have with her Majesty in my behalf, with whom 'twere easie by the means of Mr. Robinson her envoy to the Sweedish court, to obtain liberty for me, on same conditions as Coll. Pendergrass, an Irishman, had his leave last harvest by her Maj^{ties} gracious recommendation not to beare arms or command aganst Sweeden during the warrs, which as I 'll readily doe, so I 'll cheerfully to the last degree be devoted to her Maj^{tles} interest, and ever be with particular gratitude and respect, My Lord, Your Lordships most oblidged and most faithfull humb. servant,

ALEXR. GORDON.

Honnest old Mullikins puts himself likways under your Lordship's protection.

Stockholm, the 12*th of April* 1704.

For THE EARL OF SEAFIELD

MY LORD,—By the Queens commands receaved from the Duke of Queensberry, I send to your Lop. a commission to ye Marquis of Tweddell to be her Matie Com^r for ye ensewing session of Par., also a letter to ye Treasury for ane allowance for his equipage being 3500^{lib}. She was pleased to aske me what ye Duke of Queensberry had, which I told her Matie was as this is. Here is also a letter to admitt his Grace into Councell, wch I thought with all submission proper to date a day sooner because of ye words in ye commission to run cousin and councellor. The letter for his dayly allowance will be sent by ye next post. I must observe to your Lop. that ye Duke of Queensberry has caryd very hansomly in all this, and others thinke soe as well as I. He reced. her Mat^s commands with all the cheirfullness and duty imaginable, and dispatched ye com^{on} and letters as soon as was possible, after receaveing the directions. He was just goeing into his coach to goe out of toun, when I came to tell him of ye Queens commands for sending this by a flying pacquett, otherways he wold have write himselfe by it. The letter to the Theasury for ye equipage and to add to ye Councell are of ye common form, soe I doe not truble your Lop. with a coppie of them. I know not, if on goe to ye strictness, whither it is very propper to stile ye Marquis Com^r yet or not, but I am sure it is full as just to doe soe, ye com^{on} being signed by her Ma^{tle}, as to call any body say only on kissing her hand, upon which I have ventured to address to his Grace as Com^r, but begg leve to put it under your Lops. covert, lest you may be of ane oyr oppinnion. I containoue with all duty, My Lord, Yo^r Lop's. most humble and obedient servant,

DAVID NAIRNE.

Whitehall, 13th May 1704.

Since writting whats above ye enclòsed came from the D. of Q.

David Nairne, Under Secretary of State for Scotland, was appointed to that office in the spring of 1703 in room of Mr. Pringle who was retired.[1] On 10th June 1704 a warrant[2] was issued to Al. Wedderburn, on the narrative that the Queen had laid aside Sir David Nairn, to officiate as Under-Secretary in the absence of the Secretary of State for Scotland.

To THE RIGHT HONERABLE THE EARELL OF SEA-FFEILD, LORD HEIGH CHANCLER OF SCOTLAND

Edr., 17th May 1704.

MY LORD,—Please pay to Balie Alexander Baird, marchand in Ed^r, the soume of sixtein hundred markes Scots, and that as ane yeares rent of yor Lordships loadgings set by me to yor Lordship, and that from Whitsonday 1703 to Whitsonday last bypast; and this with his recept shall be ane sufficient discharge ffrom, My Lord, yor Lordships most humble and most obedent servant,

THO. SMITH.

Edinburgh, May 19, 1704.—Accepts the above written precept, deducing the cess and oyr reparations paid be Mr. Stewart.   SEAFIELD.

Next three letters show that Seafield was making interest for the Queen, in view of the meeting of Parliament on 6th July 1704.

For THE EARL OF SEAFIELD

MY LORD,—Allow me to signifie to you that I have a great deal of contentment to understand, that by your Lo. conduct publick matters have a more uniform appearance than formerly. The difficulties were certainly great,

---

[1] *Historical MSS. Commission, Fourteenth Report,* App., Part III., p. 218.
[2] *State Papers (Scotland) Warrant Books,* vol. xx.

and your prudence cannot but be applauded, which hath overcome or smooth'd them. My Lord, you know I have still adhered to the interest you espoused, and am resolved to continue and will still delight to stand by you and with you, and do expect and hope your Lo. will continue your favour to and care of me, and that no scheme or model of affairs be turned to my dammage. You are too friendly and just and generous to permitt it. If my domestick affairs at this term suffered it, I would prevent the delivery of this letter, and how soon you honour me with a return I will have the satisfaction to be with you, being assured your Lo. will be carefull of all my publick concernes and of whatever relates to the safeity and interest of, My Lord, Your Lo. most obedient affectionat and faithfull servant,   FORBES.

Aberdeen, June 5, 1704.

For THE EARL OF SEAFIELD

MY LORD,—I am glade your Lop. is returned from London. I should have wret to you uhile ther, but the uncertaintie of your coming auay, uith the consideration of your being taken up with other maters hindred me from giuing your Lop. the trouble, and now, my Lord, being resolued to uait of your Lop. at Edenbrugh, hou soune the Parlement sits, q^{ch} although it be adjourned to the tuentie tuo instant, yet having advice from som freinds that is to be further adjourned, I hope your Lop. will do me the honor to let me knou the certaintie, for upon severall accompts I might plead for my absence, but upon this ocasion I deseing to attend and to be, My Lord, your Lop. most humble and most obedient servant,

ERROLL.

Slaines, 12th June 1704.

For THE EARL OF SEAFIELD

Pitsligo, June 27, 1704.

MY LORD,—I 'm very much honour'd by your Lop. in takeing nottice of a relatione that 's of so litle consequence. However since you are pleas'd to minde kindred,

I shall take care that you have ane honest man to reckon it with. I was resolvd to have prevented your Lops. desire in comeing to the Parl., but I finde myself necessarly detain'd, haveing brought a stranger here whose health is so very ill, that I cannot in decency goe so far, till I see what fate it may have. I should have offer'd no other excuse, and I hope this will be accepted. I wou'd have been very glade to have been a witness of any thing that's for the Queen's service and the cuntry's good, which are indeed inseparable, and I hope Scotland from this time shall be put in some tollerable condition, that her Majestic upon its accompt may be no longer call'd a poor Queen. I wish your Lop. all satisfaction, and am, My Lord, Your Lops. most obedient humble sert.,

PITSLIGO.

Alexander, fourth Lord Forbes of Pitsligo, did not attend the session of 1704. He was out in the 'Fifteen, and for his share in the 'Forty-five was attainted.

ffor THE RIGHT HON$\overline{LL}$ THE EARLE OF FFINDLATER
ATT HIS LODGEINGS IN EDR. thes

MY LORD,—. . . . I most allso inform your Lop. that last week Castlefeild wes desyreing from me ane discharge of any right I had or could pretend to Lady Maries papers, qch wery frankly I hawe done ; for qt I doe, I will doe it nett and cleinly, and non, God willing, sall stain me w^t any act of ungratitud or dishonestie . . . . I am much refreshat to hear off your Los. health and weill being. Wishing prosperitie to your noble familie, concludeing that as ewer I wes, so still will continow, My Lord, Your Los. wery ffaithfull and most humble sernt.,

GEORGE LESLYE.

Bannff, July : 1 : —704.

MY LORD,—I most begg pardon for my ingenuitie and freedome in this postscript. Your daughter La. Mary liwes heir wery honestlye wertewouslie and discreetlie, and since it is so it is hygh tyme shee be reponed to your owen and hir brothers fawor, and thinks truly both off you should so joyn and fall on measures to hawe hir w^t you and in

your owen companies, and thus being countenanced be
hir so high and noble freinds, who knowes qt God in his
good prowidence hes determined for hir. I sall say no
mor of this att present, beseeching your Lop. to dropp a
lyne to me w^t your first conveniencie of your sentiments
on all, for q^{ll} your Lop. and I liwes I will still relye on yow
as my wery noble and spēall good freind,

The postscript to Nicolas Dunbar's letter of 28th October 1704
continues the story of Lady Mary Ogilvie.

The Queen's instructions to Lord Chancellor Seafield for the
Parliament of 1704, at pp. 194, 195, and Godolphin's letters at
pp. 199 to 204 of the *MSS. of the Countess-Dowager of Seafield*
in the *Fourteenth Report* (Appendix, Part III.) *of the Historical
MSS. Commission* also refer to the matters mentioned in the two
next letters to the Earl of Seafield.

London, July 15th, 1704.

My Lord,—I have the honour of your Lordsp. letter
of the 8th, and would not lose the first occasion to acknowledge it, tho. the Queen being at Windsor I shall not be
able to lay it before her Majesty, so as to send you her
comands upon it till the next post.   In the meantime will
your Lordsp. have the goodness to forgive me, if upon
the honour of so small an acquaintance I presume to lay
before you with all freedome my present thoughts of
affairs in Scotland.   I find among other handles taken by
the opposers to obstruct the Queen's measures, some have
presumed to say her Majesty is not in earnest for settling
the succession.   And really, my Lord, I must be so sincere
as to own there seems but too much occasion for that to
bee said, while the D. of Atholl continues to be an officer
of state, and tho. the Queen has distinguished him very
particularlie by honours and fauours, is yet at the head
of all oppositions to what is so necessary for the peace
and quiett of her Majesty's reign, and is looked upon by
her to be so essentiall, that I question very much whether
her Majesty will think fitt to accept of any cess from those
who will obstinatly reject what her Majesty takes to be
indispensable both for her quiett and their own.   And
on the other hand, my Lord, I am very confident the

Queen will have no difficulty of taking into her consideration the loss at Darien, or doing any thing else that can
reasonably be desired for the aduantage and satisfaction
of the kingdome of Scotland, upon their agreeing to a
settlement of the Protestant succession there. I must
again beg pardon for presuming to write my thoughts to
you, before I could have an opportunity of receiving her
Majestys comands, which you shall have by the next post
from, My Lord, Your Lordsp. most humble and obedient
servant.

The claim made in next letter for the Queen to nominate commissioners to negotiate the treaty of union with England was
ultimately conceded in 1705. On the 5th August 1704 the Act
of Security was passed, which in the end helped to secure the
union on a basis of free trade.

The minutes of the Privy Council of Scotland show that in
May 1704 Captain Thomas Gordon of Her Majesty's ship *Royal
Mary* captured a French privateer, the *Marmedon*, of Dunkirk.
The prisoners from the *Marmedon* were amongst those referred to
in next letter, and were taken to Newcastle in September to be
exchanged.

For THE EARL OF SEAFIELD

Windsor, 12th Agt. 1704.

My Ld.,—I laid this day for a second time before the
Queen the account your Lop. sent of the proceedings of
Parliament upon the fift. Her Majestie again told me
she was very well satisfied with what was done, but that
this methode proposed for nameing persons to treat with
England had more of difficultie, and she would send her
mind upon it to my Ld. Comm^r; and doubtles my Ld.
Treasurer has done the like to your Lop., and theirfor I
shall say nothing of it, save that I do beleeve it is much
desired this session were at an end, for its thought whatever concessions are made new difficulties will be started,
which appears plain from the overture given in to the
Parliament in relation to the treaty, directly tending, as
is thought here, to lodge the soveraign power in the
Parliament of the two kingdomes without the Prince,
and likewise giving a plain handle to the Parliament of

England to take from the Prince here the power which was alwayes yeelded to name persons for treating on their side. I have given a memorial to Sr Charles Hedges concerning the French prisoners, and I doubt not but so soon as he is well, for he is a litle indisposed at present, they will order all the prisoners taken by our frigatts to be receiv'd at Newcastle and to be exchanged with our men as they fall in course, according to the time of their being taken. I shall take care to represent what your Lop. adds in your postscript concerning ane officer of the name of Campbel to be lieutenant to ffanabs independant company, but their are others have been before hand in asking it particularly one Mr. Stewart, recommended first by the Duke of Athol and now by the General. Ther are no particular account as yet come of the victory which I gave your Lops. account of by my last. I am with all respect, My Lord, Your Los. most humble and obedient servt.,   AL. WEDDERBURN.

Her Majesty commanded me to acquaint your Lo. that it being represented by severals that neither sallarys nor pensions are well pay'd, and that it is in some measure occasion'd by the pressing for preference, she desires that a state of the revenue be made up as soon as conveniently it can be, and likewise that a list be made of the constant and necessary payements, and than it will appear what funds their will be for pensions and gratifications, but this her Majestie desires your Lo. to move as from your selfe, and not to proceed upon a publict order for her, otherwise I would not acquainted your Lo. of it in this manner.

On 25th October 1704 Mr. Wedderburn was appointed Deputy Secretary of State for Scotland.[1]

For THE EARL OF FINDLATER

My Lord,—I have taken the boldnes to writt to my Lord Chancellour, though I am convinced itt is very unseason-

---

[1] *State Papers (Scotland) Warrant Books*, vol. xx. p. 76.

able to trouble him vith private bussines now in tym off Parliament, anent my bussines vith the ffamily off Boyne. I beleev your Lo. might hav heard how ffrankly I dealt by them in ther need. In a vord every ffarthing ves downtold money they oue me advanced in ther need, and on the ffaith of ane honest man severall tymes hav I borroued money ffrom others to supplye them, and som off itt nott yett payd. I am hopeffull they vill be just to me ; and my poore brother John his children hes betuixt ffour and ffyve thousand merks off ther stock in ther hands. And as your Lo. ves alvayes good to ffreinds and ffatherlesse children, so I hope your Lo. vill sheu the same to us on this occasione, as they I hop may ; and, God villing, I shall be on all occasiones ready to acquitt my selfe as becomethe your noble ffamilye, and, may itt please your Lo., Your Lo. most obleidged and most humble servant, ALEXR. INNES.

I presum to offer my most humble dutye to the Countesse of Findlatter.

Coxton, Agust 16, 1704.

For THE EARL OF FINDLATER

London, September 26, 1704.

MY LORD,—On Wedensday last we came to this place, together with my Lord Tweddale, whom we overtook at Borrowbridge, and my Lord Cromarty, whom we overtook at Barnet. My father is in very good health. On Friday he went to Windsor, wher the Queen is at present, and is not as yet returned. I long very much to know how your Lordship and your Lady are in health. If your Lordship would doe me the honour to write to me and give me an account how you keep your health, it would be a great satisfaction to, My Lord, Your Lordships most humble and obedient grandchild and servant, DESKFOORD.

In her endeavours to solve the difficult situation in Scotland the Queen again, on 17th October 1704, appointed Seafield Secretary of State for Scotland. His new colleague was the Earl of Roxburgh.[1]

---

[1] *State Papers (Scotland) Warrant Books,* vol. xx. pp. 40 and 48.

For THE EARL OF FINDLATER

RIGHT HONORABLE,—May it please your Lop. When I had the honor to wreat to you last, the post's importunitie to be gone made me omitt to give your Lop. ane accompt of ane setting dog, that samytyme I had on heir and wes trying him, and since that tyme I called for ane other. Both dogs are young and can doe very weill in moors, but I could not get them so tryed in dale ground for partridges. The pryce of either of them wes fourtie punds Scots, but I beleive they would have taken fiftie merks. I cannot pass my word for them. Therfor I would have your Lop. sending Donald Shaw north, that he may make a full tryall of them, and choise the best. I presume to present my most humble dutie and service to your Lop. and my Lady your noble Countess. I wish to both long lyffe and happiness. I continow to be perfectly in heart and soull, Right Honoᵇˡᵉ and my dear Lord, Your Lops. most faithfull, most humble, and most obleidged servant,   NICOLAS DUNBAR.

Castlfeild, 28th Oct. 1704.

I am sorie to tell your Lop. that Lady Marie wes maried 25 7ᵇᵉʳ to George Barkley in Bamff, sone to Alexʳ, the certainty qroff is just now come to my hands.

FFORGLINE'S LETTER TO THE EARL OF SEAFIELD
DESYRING A PENSION TO PITMEDDEN

Eder, 23rd Nov. 1704.

MY LORD,—I returne your Lo. my humble and hartie thanks for your keyndnes to my Lord Provost of Eder. Sir James Smolet and myselfe by your dayes favor and keyndnes, evidenced to them by there letter, and giving me my commission. I hope your Lo. shall feind us all true and fathfull servants qhen ye have use for us. I shall not truble your Lo. with the urgent and pressing cravings of the Lords of Thesurie for there Wittsondayes sallaries. All I shall say is that there Lo. are sore displeased with me, that I will not give them the promise of the first money cums in. They say they were never

so used. If your Lo. please to syne your name on the
inclosed letter, and returne it, I shall tacke cair of it as
mutch as if it ware my ouen. Pittmeden younger pretends a great keyndnes to your Lo., and sayes most
serieouslie to me that if your Lo. will obtain him a pension
of one houndreth pound per annum, he will be your servant
and give you a sutable returne. He would have the first
termes payment at Candlemas nixt. So this to your Lo.
consideration, and I shall containou, My Lord, Your Lo.
obedient and fathfull servant,

ALEXR. OGILVIE.

On 17th October Forglen was appointed to the office of
Receiver-General at a salary of £300 stg.[1]

On 17th November 1704 Captain Patrick Ogilvie was promoted
second lieutenant-colonel at Fort William.[2]

For THE EARL OF SEAFIELD

MY LORD,—I had the honor of your Lops. of the fift.
I render you manie thanks for the letter you tell me the
Quien hes writt to the Thesouray in my favours. I hope
hir Majestie shall never repent, nor your Lop. be ashaimd
of doeing me jusitice, for uherin I am capable of serving
the Quien, and sheuing my friendship to your Lop., I will
make it my bussiness more then ever ; but at the same
time you must excuse me never to forgett the distinguishing treatment I have mett with from our ministre, uich I
long for nothing more then ane oportunitay to repay. It
pleaseth me to think, uhen ue shall have a Parlament,
they will apier so pitifull and mien, that they will move
my compasion more then indignation. Uhat could
influence the Quien to put hir goverment in hands that ar
no maner of uay capable to serve hir is what I mightelay
uant to knou, and cannot expect, till I have the hapiness
of seeing your Lop. I had allmost forgott to intreat your
Lop. to uritt to Sir Alexander Ogilvie to take caire of my
payment. I urott tuice to him, and he returnd me

---

[1] *State Papers (Scotland) Warrant Books,* vol. xx. p. 71.
[2] *Ibid.,* pp. 106-107.

ansuers fullie as ambiguos as the Oracull of Delphos.   My young daughter is as fine ane child as can be seen.   I hope she shall live and have a husband to serve you and yours. I am, My Lord, Your Lops. most affectionat cusin and most faithfull servant,   EGLINTOUNE.[1]

Eglintoune, Dec 18, '704*

COPPY OF TWO LETTERS SENT TO THE CHANCELOR BY
FLYING PACQUET

London, Jan: 17, 1705.

THE Queen called me this morning, and told me she had good information that one Captain M'Lean has gone, or is imediately to goe for Scotland, and carries letters and commissions ffrom ffrance, and that there is also a ffrench-man sent in quality of a commissar, who has bills or money of a considerable value.   Her Ma^{ty} commanded me to speak of this to none but the Earle of Roxburgh, and to send this accompt by a flying pacquet, that all care and dilligence may be used in saising these persons and in securing there papers.   I asked if her Ma^{ty} could give me any informatione in writting, that yor Lop. and others in Scotland might know the better how to proceed.   She said that could not yet be done, but that no time ought to be lost in securing them.   Yo^r Lop. may take advyce of the President of the Council, the Advocat, the Lord Thesaurer Depute and Justice Clerk.   These her Ma^{ty} thinks the fittest persons to assist yor Lop. in this matter, but it is to be managed with all secrecy, and I have written to none but yor Lop., and her Ma^y expects you will use all dilligence in this matter.   This by her Ma^{ts} command from, My Lord, Yor Lops., etc.   SEAFIELD.

COPPY.

If the magazines are not better provyded than when I parted from Scotland, there is litle or no powder or other amunition, q^{ch} is most dangerous in the caise of ane invasion or insurrection, for I beleeve there is litle or none to be had within the kingdome for money.   If yor Lop. will after enquiry send a memoriall from the Thesaury or

---

[1] Alexander, ninth earl.

Privy Council as you think best, and with as litle noise as is possible, of what quantity of powder and oy^r amunition may be necessary, I beleeve the Earle of Roxburgh and [I] could have it att easier rates here, and have it more speedily sent than you can have it from any other place, and therfor together with the memoriall let us know at what rates you can be furnished in Scotland. The merchants that trade to Holland will satisfy yor Lop. in this. It must also be considered what moy^es can be spared from the subsistance of the troups for this use. This seems to be indispensibly necessary, ffor fforts castles and ane army without amunition signifyes nothing. This letter you may communicate to the Lords of Theasury as from yor self ; but how soon you transmitt to my Ld. Roxburgh or me a memoriall with yor opinion, wee will be able to obtain what you want. I shall write of nothing els att pntt.—
I am, My Ld., Yor   SEAFIELD.
    London, Jan: 17, 1705.

Captain M'Lean was Sir John M'Lean who figured in the Queensberry plot. With the advance of union negotiations there was a recrudescence of Jacobitism which looked to France for help.

JUSTICE CLERK'S LETTER

Edinbr., 20 *ffebry* 1705.

MY LORD,—Twas not to be doubted your Lo. approoveing of ye Councells disarming of papists. I shall say no more of it at present, but wishes the proclamation be duely execute, and I'm sure twill tend to ye security of ye governm͞t. . . . People talk every other post of new schems. This day your Lo. is Com^r and Chancellor, Annand. to preside in Parliat. and to have 500 lib st. as a Com͞issioner of ye Thēsrie. I doe beleeve 'twill pleas both my Lord Rose and the ministers that he be Com^r to ye Gen. Ass. There appears litle inclination to ane intire union. A treaty would be accepted and pass currant. But the uncertainty people are in, how the scheme will come out where your Lo. is, keeps all in suspense. I wish when it comes out it may be such as will act sincerely and vigorously for the revolution interest, and yrby they will strenthen her Maties. goverm̄t, which I pray may last long.—I am, Your Lo. m. h. s.

I am my Lord Thēsrs.[1] most ffaithfull serv^t, which your Lo. will be so good as to let his Lo. know.

LORD BELHAVEN'S LETTER TO THE EARL OF SEAFIELD

Ed^r, 24th ffeb. 1705.

MY LORD,—I protest I know not what to say to you, yet I can not bot wreit that I have nothing to wreit worth yor reading. We ar all quiet here doeing nothing. We ar full of expectations of things that the end of the Parlament and end of this month will produce ; bot what they ar I know not, nor can know unlesse yor Lop. think fitt to tell one, for I keep correspondence with non save yor self and with the honorable person to whom the inclosed is drected. I most beg the favor that yor Lop. would deliver it or cause deliver it. It is to mein him of a letter I had from his Lop. upon my being made on of the Lords of Treasury, that he had her Majesties commands to assure me that she gave me that place raither as a mark or pledge of her futur favor, than that she considered it as an adequat recompence to the zeal and forwardnes I had shown in her service. My dear Lord, I think this is the tyme that I can doe her Majestie service ; and if I had a new mark of her favor it would give me more credit both with the Dukes of H., Ath., and many others, then if I be neglected, and tho my indevors will neverthelesse be equal, the successe will not be so. I reffer my former pretentions and any thing else of this natur to yor Lops. prudent manadgment, depending intierly on yr frendship.—I remaine, *tout jours*, yer very humble server. Adieu.

Lord Belhaven was appointed a Commissioner to the Scots Treasury in August 1704. He was removed in 1705, and thereafter strenuously opposed the union.

On 10th March 1705 Seafield was again, in the ever-shifting

---

[1] Lord Godolphin.

combinations of ministers, appointed Lord High Chancellor of Scotland.[1]

E. NORTHESQUE'S EXCUSE TO THE EARL OF SEAFIELD
THAT HE COULD NOT COME TO COUNCIL ABOUT GREENS BUSSINES

MY LORD,—I hade the honour of your Lo. this night about six, and by the shortness of the time your Lo. will know its impossible for me to attend the Councell as you desire, which Im sorry for, since you say some things concerns the Queens service are to bee agitated. So I hope your Lo. will admitt the reasonable excuse of, My Lord, Your Lo. affectionate cousin and most humble servant,

NORTHESK.

Ethie, 2d Aprill 1705.

In reprisal for the seizure in England and condemnation of the *Annandale,* the officials of the African company seized in Leith roads the *Worcester,* an English ship in the East Indian trade. On the confession of two of her crew, Haynes and Linsteed, Captain Green of the *Worcester* and others of the crew were on 5th March 1705 condemned to death by the Scots Court of Admiralty on charges of piracy and of murdering Captain Drummond of the *Speedy Return,* belonging to the African company, and his crew in Madagascar waters. On 27th March the Queen wrote[2] to the Scots Privy Council ordering a reprieve until the court proceedings were looked into. Writing again[3] on 7th April, with an affidavit that Captain Drummond was alive, the Queen left the Privy Council a free hand in the matter of reprieve. Feeling was very bitter at the time against England, and Captain Green, Captain Madder, and Gunner Simpson of the crew were executed on 11th April. Several of the following letters deal with this affair. They show the reluctance of many of the Scots nobles to attend the Privy Council to support a course of clemency, and the strained relations between England and Scotland.

For THE EARL OF SEAFIELD

MY LORD,—I had not failled to write to your Lop. before now, but tho I have stayed in town I have had nothing

---

[1] *State Papers (Scotland) War rant Books,* vol. xx. p. 193 ; and *Carstares State Papers and Letters,* p. 735.

[2] *State Papers (Scotland) Warrant Books,* vol. xx. p. 211.

[3] *Ibid.,* p. 236.

of moment to write. The Tr. Deput. has noe doubt communicated to you what stuffe I did write. Some with you and others here are for absolute power and thorough changes. Schemes and measures have been written for from them and are come up. The other day nothing was practicable, and the commission was ready to be resigned. Nou they say they have made sure work, and that if the court make good their promiss the successe is infallible, and a ministry is to be setled that is to be unalterable. However none but I they say are to be out till the Duke be in Scotland. As for my own part I shall be glad matters goe well for the nation whoever have the doing of them. I am satisfied I could have done litle good had I continued in either to myself or the nation, for noe man that lives here can at present serve Scotland if he be in a post. He may possibly if he be in none. Greens business creats great uneasinesse here, and noe doubt will raise the ferment with you. The fact is so monstruous and incredible in itself and prejudice so strong, that a verry plain and clear account of that whole matter will be necessary to convince this nation. I wish your Lop. and others may keep united for the Q's service and the good of the countrey, and make all welcome that will joine with you, for those agst. you are verry united in their purpose and resentment, and if they have strenth enough will not forgive one of you, of which they make noe secret here ; but in my opinion with resolu°n and concorde you will make them low their saills. Changes in this nation are at a stand at present, and I suppose will be so till the elections be over. If any thing come to my knowledge that may be of use, your Lop. shall hear it one way or other.—I am, Your Lop. most faithfull humble servant,

J. JOHNSTOUN.

Lond., 7 Apl. '705·

James Johnstoun, who had been Secretary of State for Scotland to King William from the spring of 1692 [1] to 1696, was Lord Clerk Register from 2nd June 1704 to April 1705. Several of his letters about this time are given in the *Jerviswood Correspondence.*

---

[1] *State Papers (Scotland) Warrant Books*, vol. xv. p. 100.

THE DUKE OF ATHOLE'S LETTER TO THE EARL OF SEAFIELD ABOUT HIS COMEING TO SERVE THE QUEEN

MY LORD,—This is to congratulate yr Lps. safe arrival in Scotland. I intend, if please God, to waitte on you at the sitting of the Par^lt, where I shall endeavour to serve the Queen and our country against all theire enemies, and I doubt not we shall have yr Lps. concurrence. I desire you 'l be pleased to acquaint me if the Par^lt certainly meets the 3^d of May.—I am, My Lord, Y^r Lps. affec^tt cousine and most humble servant, ATHOLL.

Dunkeld, Ap: 8th, 1705.

Parliament met on 28th June 1705.

For THE EARL OF SEAFIELD

Yester, Aprill 8th, 1705.

MY LORD,—I had the honour of your Lo. this morning, intimating to me the gracious returne it hes pleasd her Ma^jtie to give to what the Councell at first represented to her in Capt^ne Greens affaire, and that upon it your Lo. had thought fitt to appoynt the Councell to meett on Tuesday next. I am heartily glad of it, not doubting but it will give so generall a satisfactione as will be of advantag to the Queens service in the ensuing Parliament. I should not decline to give my attendance on all occasions wherin I could testify my zeall for it, but that my privat affairs does so necessarly require my stay here for some few days longer, that I hope I may be excused at this time, especially sinc there cane be no fear of the want of a sufficient quorum without me, who am with all respect, My Lord, Your Lo. most obedient and most humble servant, TWEEDDALE.

For THE EARL OF SEAFIELD

Ormeston, 9th Ap: 1705.

MY LORD,—The end of last week my Lord Hyndfoord caried my son wast, and he took the horses wt him, which makes me in a maner a prisoner. Besides my own affairs, to wch. I have been a stranger, require my stay in this place for some dayes. This will I hope plead my excuse

wt your Lo. for this one dyet, and I 'm encouraged to
exspect it from qt your Lo. writts, that hir Maties returne
will be to the satisfaction of all. So I doe perswade my
self yr is no farther reprive to be proposed, or any thing
may occassion the least jealousy among ye people of hir
Maties proceedings, wch. I in my station shall alwayes
be ready to obviat so fare as possible it lyes in my power.
I am, wt all respect, My Lord, Your Lo. most humble
servant,   AD. COKBURNE.

For THE RIGHT HONORABLE THE EARLE OF SEAFIELD,
LORD HIGH CHANCELOR OF SCOTLAND

Beil, 9th Ap. 1705.

MY LORD,—I am verie glad to hear of her Majs. gratius
ansur, and since I find yor Lop. in no difficulty I hope ther
is no necessity of my presence, since by yors I find ther
is no nead save of a quorum to receive that which is so
acceptable to the nation. Besyds this my Lord President
and the new married folks and a great many others ar
all at my house this day, and to continue some days. I
wish yor Lop. all happines, and I hope these criminalls
shall by ther confession at death make a full disscovere of
all ther villanny, which will prove verie acceptable to the
whol nation.—My Lord, Yor Lop. most faithfull and
obedient serv^t,   BELHAVEN.

For THE EARL OF SEAFIELD

MY LORD,—If I were but able to walk down stairs, I
should certainly be in town to-night, but I have got such
a sprain, at least have made it so ill by riding and walking
and not minding it at first, that I dont know when I shall
be able to travell either in coach or a horesback. This I
am writing in the time a horse is getting ready for a
servant, and shall write on till he is ready.

I send your Lop. here inclosed a letter from my Lord
Treasurer, which I desire you would send me back by
the bearer, for its impossible for me to give a return to 't
this post, so your Lop. I hope will make my excuse and
let me know by the bearer what you write. Your Lop.

will be pleased to show the inclosed to my Lord Treasurer-Depute. It came to my hands betwixt ten and eleven, and it is now just eleven.—I am, My Lord, Your Lops. most obedient humble servant,   ROXBURGHE.

If we cannot convince them that our behaviour in this matter was both dutiful and necessary, the old partie are masters.

Floors, Aprill the 10th, 1705.

For THE EARL OF SEAFIELD

MY LORD,—Nothing has occur'd since my last in Scots affaires worth your Losps. reading, save that the Duke of Argyle parted from hence yesterday about noon. He went privatly, and some say resolves to go post part of the way. His Grace caried with him the papers past the Queens hand, wherof a list is inclosed. He left me no directions except an order to deliver to Sr David Nairn all letters and pacquets directed for him, and also to receive from Sr David whatever he shall have to dispatch for his Grace by ordinary or flying pacquets. Ther appears litle or no disposition here to give credit to the guilt prov'd against Capt. Green and confess'd by some of his men. It seems necessary for the reputation of our countrey and of the government in particular, that censure be stopt by publishing a full relation of the proceedings in this matter, and that it be clear'd upon what motives any of the accomplices have confessed, otherwise it will be spread to our dishonour that these men have either been forc'd by torture or induced by promises of life to confess any thing they perceived would be most desir'd. Such base insinuations are very uneasy to these that have a concern for the honour of their countrey and the reputation of those in the management, but I can not say all Scots men here feel it alike. The Queen and Prince went this morning for Newmarket. I went last night to receive hir Maj^{tys} commands, and gott hir hand to a letter ordering peremptorly six hundred pounds to be pay'd to my Lord Forfar of the arrears of his pension. My Lady apply'd for this hirselfe upon a letter she had receiv'd from hir

Lord, wherin he informs hir that it was your Losps. advice
to ask a letter of this sort nameing a certain sum.—I am,
with all respect, My Lord, Your Losps. most humble and
obedient serv^t,   AL. WEDDERBURN.

Lond:, 10*th Apr.* 1705.

For THE EARL OF SEAFIELD

Lond., 12*th Ap:* 1705.

MY LORD,—This is only to acknowledge the honour of
your Losps. of the 4th, and to informe you that I gave the
letter for my Ld. Treasurer to a serv^t, who promised to
send it to New Market with the first opportunity.   I return
your Losp. my most hearty thanks for the favour you have
been pleased to show in ordering money to be pay'd me,
and I think my selfe yet more obliged for the goodnes
you show in giving me your advice for my behaviour here.
It was not my fault that the opinion of the Privy Council
was not waited for, before orders were given for restoring
the Dutch prise, but that being over, the nixt thing necessary in that matter seems to be the concerting speedily
what pasports will be sufficient for securing our ships, or
reclaming them if they shal be taken into Holland.   The
clamour upon the proceedings against Green, etc., is not
like to cease.   If the last papers and advices sent in that
matter has occasion'd a new reprive, in my humble opinion
it can not give offence in Scotland to continow it in favours
of the English men, till their friends have time to represent
all can be alledged in their behalfe, provyding the sentence
be put to execution against Madder a Scotsman, own'd
by all to be noted villain.   If this fellow should confess
clamour would cease, and should he dy denying it might
afford an excuse for humouring this nation in granting a
litle delay, till all were done thats necessary or possible at
least for convincing them of the impartiality of our government, which I can not forbear saying they are too unwilling
to beleeve, though I meet with very hard censure for my
freedom on this point, and I have ground to think not
without the whispers and detracting methods of some of
my own cuntrey men.   But I shall not trouble your Losp.

with this, but conclude in assuring your Losp. that I am with all respect, My Lord, Your Losp. most humble and obedient servt., AL. WEDDERBURN.

On 7th April the Queen wrote to the Treasury ordering the ship *Katherine* of Rotterdam, captured by Captain Thomas Gordon, and condemned by the Scots Court of Admiralty as a prize, to be restored or her value paid.[1]

To THE RIGHT HONORABLE THE EARLE OF SEAFEILD, LORD HYE CHANCELLOUR

MY LORD,—It was this day ere I had the honour of your Los., soe that is not possible for me to wait on your Lordshipe in time to attend the Councill to-morrow. Ther are many more capable to serve her Majesty, but non more willing then, My Lord, Your Lordship's most humble and obedient servant, STRATHMORE.

Glamis, Ap^{rll} 12, 1705.

For THE EARL OF SEAFIELD

MY LORD,—I receiv'd your Losps. of the 6^t, and gave in the two letters inclosed with it as they were directed. Sr Charles Hedges is here, but my Lord Treasurer is still at New Market. I have nothing new to write save that just now Captain Greens brother brought to me Iserael Phippenny and Peter Freelands, the two men who made the affidavits before the Maior of Portsmouth, which I sent to your Losp. amongst the other papers with the last flying packet. Mr. Green showd me a letter from one Mr. Stewart, who he says is agent for his brother in Scotland, telling him that if these men gave their declarations before the Secretarys for Scotland of what they knew concerning Capt. Drummond, it would have more weight ; and the Secretarys being absent he came with them to me, but I having no commission to put them upon oath, and but litle time to discource with them, it being late, all I can informe your Losp. concerning them is, that

---

[1] *State Papers (Scotland) Warrant Books*, vol. xx. pp. 216-217 ; and *Historical MSS. Commission, Fourteenth Report*, App. Part III., *MSS. of the Countess-Dowager of Seafield*, p. 220.

the first says he is of New England but served his time at Glasgow with George Lockart, and went in the ship that caried Capt. M'Kay towards Darien the second time, return'd with Capt. Drummond to Scotland, and went out with him again in his last voyage, and avers that what he said relating to that voyage in the affidavit taken at Portsmouth is trew.   The other says he is a Scots man born at the Milton of Slains, and was likewise aboard of Cap. Drummonds ship till she fell in the hands of Madagascar pirats, and afterwards made his escape.   They were not very distinct in answering some of the questions I askt concerning the trafique Cap. Drummond has made, and what sort of goods he had at the time the ship was taken; but they said, being only common sailers and never having kept journals as to these, they could not cal to mind particulars on the sudden;   and indeed I can not say that I can make any probable conjecture from what past betwixt them and me either as to the truth or falshood of what they assert, and I should be in the wrong to make any insinuations either one way or other, upon such a superficial information as I have had from them.—I am with all respect, My Ld., Your Losps. most humble and obedient servant,   AL. WEDDERBURN.
   Lond:, 14th Apr: 1705.

For THE EARL OF SEAFIELD

MY LORD,—I am very sorry I cannot waite upon yor Loip. upon Tuesday nixt by reason I have created a violent cold and hoarsness, and am under a course of physick for some tyme, and untill that be discussed I am advysed by my physicians not to goe abroade.   This I hope will be to sufficient ane excuse.—I am, My Lord, Yo^r Loip̃s most humble servant,   CRAFURD.
   Struthers, 15th Ap. 1705.

ffor THE RIGHT HONORABLE THE EARLE OF SEAFEILD, LORD HIGH CHANCELOR OF SCOTLAND

Beil, 16 Ap. 1705.

MY LORD,—I am heartily sorry of what hath befallen yor Lo., yet am pleased to be informed that it was meerly accidental and no wayse designed. I most beg pardon for this once that I can not attend this diot of Councell, being following out a course of diot that I may be inabled to attend when the Parlament sitts. I hope this shall plead my excuse, and that ye^r goodnes will find it relevant, more especially since I am informed ther will be a vere full Councell Tuesday nixt.—My dear Lord, Yo^r Lo. most faithfull and obedient ser^t,   BELHAVEN.

Pardon me to tell my opinion, that I think ther should be no more executions, till God in his providence make this work of darknes more plain and evident, which I hope God in his mercy and goodnes to this poor nation will doe and that vere shortly.

For THE EARL OF SEAFIELD

Newmarket, 16th Ap. 1705.

MY LORD,—The flying pacquet with your Losp. letters to the Queen and my Lord Treasurer, giving account of the proceedings of Councill on the ij instant came to my hand yesterday about eight in the morning at London. So soon as I could gett reddy, I took post and came hither with them, and arived in time to see the Queen last night. Hir Majesty seem'd not pleas'd to find that Green and the two others that were executed deny'd the crimes for which they were condemned, and wishes no more of them may suffer till the truth of that matter be further clear'd. My Lord Treasurer was supping last night with the Duke of Devonshire, and did not see the Queen till this morning, and just now tells me that he is to write hir Maj^{tys} commands to your Losp. I wish they may arive in time, for I understand they are to be plainly signify'd that further execution be stopt, no body here, I mean amongst the English, beleeving the certanty of what has been confess'd against Green and his crew as to the murther of Drummond. Your Lordships to me mentiones plainly that the nixt day appointed for execution of these others, that are condemned, is the 19th instant, but that falling upon a Thursday, which is not an usual day for executions, makes me fear it is not right marked. If Wedensday was meant, this

can not arive in time, but if the day be right mention'd
it may.   I acquainted hir Majesty of the account your
Losp. writes of the tumultous behaviour of the people,
and that your Losp. had mett with no harm, which hir
Maj^{ty} was well satisfied to know.   The Queen is just now
gone to Cambridge upon invitation from the University,
but the Prince has excused himselfe upon the account that
he should have been obliged to walk more than would
have been convenient for him.   The Queen returns at
night.   She is to be intertaind tomorrow or nixt day at
my Lord Orfords house, passes the rest of this week here,
and returns to St. James's on Saturday.   I shall acquaint
Mr. Johnston of your Losp. compliment, and I return your
Losp. most hearty thanks for the notice you are pleased
to take of my circumstances, and I shall alwise look upon
it as an extraordinary advantage to be under your Losp.'s
protection.   I am, with all respect, My Lord, Your Losps.
most humble and most obedient serv^{t},

AL. WEDDERBURN.

I write this in hast, and therfor hopes you'l excuse the
disorder of it.

For THE EARL OF SEAFIELD

Whitehall. 17th *Apr.* 1705.

MAY IT PLEASE YOUR LOP.,—I think it my duty in Mr.
Wedderburns absence to write to you in answere to your
flying packet, which came here on Sunday morning, after
which he went post to New Market.   He did communicat
your Lops. to me before he went, and yesterday I went
to Mr. Reidpath and assisted what I could in that account
he gives of Greens execution and that tumults at Edinburgh ; and we thought it propper to back it with that
relation of the further confessions since their condemnation.   I assure your Lop. it makes as great noise as ever
any thing of that nature did here, so that Scotsmen dare
hardly goe into publick places.   I was alwayes troubled
at the method taken in ordering Green and Madder to be
executed either first or together, for it was the only way
to hinder their confessions ;   and now nothing will con-

vince these people but that they are murdered, as they boldly call it. I was in particular told from a present witnes, that the father of Haynes, who has confest, said in a coffeehouse he would much rather have seen his son hanged than that he should have saved his life by confessing a lye to the ruine of innocent persons, for now they say these confessors find it a way to save themselves. I need add no more but that I am, my Lord, Your Lops. most humble and most faithfull servant,

A. KINEIR.

For THE EARL OF SEAFIELD
Lond:, 21 Ap: 1705.

MY LORD,—All I have time to acquaint your Losp. of to night is that the Queen and Prince are arived this evening from New Market. I beleeve my Lord Treasurer will be here to morow or nixt day at furthest, and I shall take care to deliver your Losps letter. Being just come to town and very weary with my journey, I have not found it possible to inform my selfe of any thing worth your Losps. reading, therfor I shall conclude that I am as becomes me with all respect, My Lord, Your Losps. most humble and most obedient servt.,

AL. WEDDERBURN.

The execution of Green is highly resented here, and we that are upon the place will find it uneasy.

For THE EARL OF SEAFIELD
Lond., 23rd Apr. 1705.

MY LORD,—I delivered your Los[s] of the 17th to my L[d] Treasurer today, so soon as I receiv'd it, and likewise communicated to the Queen the necessary passages of that your Losp. honoured me with of the same date, togither with the journals of Council. Hir Majesty was pleas'd to find the remaining part of the *Worcesters* crew were repryved, and it seems after second thoughts, and perhaps by advice of hir Cabinet Council has sent the letter[1] whereof

---

[1] *Historical MSS. Commission, Fourteenth Report*, App. Part III., *MSS. of the Countess-Dowager of Seafield*, pp. 195-196 ; and *State Papers (Scotland) Warrant Books*, vol. xx. p. 241.

I inclose a copie, for stopping any further execution till further light be gott in this matter. The hanging of Green occasions extraordinary censure and resentment here against our nation, and the not publishing of the trial makes it hard for any to find satisfying answeres to the objections made both against the sentence and the precipitancy of the execution ; and people may flater themselves by thinking to lay the blame, if ther is any, upon a party. In that I do beleeve they may be mistaken, for if ther is ground for reproach none will escape it. Therfor in my humble opinion none should appear backward in publishing a justification of what has been done in this matter, and the sooner the better.—I am, with all respect, My Lord, Your Losps. most humble and obedient serv^t,

AL. WEDDERBURN.

I have gott so late advertisement for sending this express, that I have not time to inlarge.

For THE EARL OF SEAFIELD

MY LORD,—I acknowledge the honor of haveing your Lops. letter of ye 17th wth on to ye Duke of Queensberry which I delivered. Whatever pairt of her Matys. affairs that I shall be imployed in, I shall to ye best of my capacity most fathfully execute. That affaire of Capt. Green and his crew maks soe much noise here as is enugh to frighten Scots men in some pairts of ye city to oune themselves as such. What adds to the flame is not publishing ye tryall, and, besids ye vulgar, people of good understanding think thers some weakness in it, for wch its toe long concealed. I quetion not but your Lop. has had sufficient truble in this mater since your arivall. The insolence that was offered to your Lop. has been much talked off. I hope ere this the bottom of that affaire is discovered, and ye fomenters duly punishd.[1] The Duke of Queensberry gives his humble service to your Lop. He and his familly are in such disorder that he can not write, ye Dutchess being in labour but not bad enugh. I shall always acknowledge

---

[1] *The Jerviswood Correspondence*, pp. 75-77.

the obligations I ley under to your Lop., and containow, My Lord, Yor Lop.'s most humble and most obedient servant, DAVID NAIRNE.

24th Aprill 1705.

For THE EARL OF SEAFIELD

MY LORD,—All I have to trouble your Los^s. with to night is, that I have represented to the Queen and my Lord Treasurer the contents of the letter your Los. was pleased to honour me with by the làst post. My Lord Treasurer writes, and therfore I need not touch what hints he let fall of our affaires. The Queen directed me to put your Los. in mind to send up a state of the Bishops rents, which hir Maj^{ty} realy takes ill is not done sooner. Some here begin to abate a litle of their railling against the tryal of Green, since the last flying pacquet came out. I wish poor Mr. Ridpath may be more considered this year than he was last. This is a national service, and I hope no party will think it an injury, but we shall need stronger vindication before resentments be disownd here quite, and therfore I hope your Losp. will hasten so necessary a work.—I am with all respect, My Lord, Your Losp. most humble and obedient serv^t, AL. WEDDERBURN.

Lond., 26 *Ap:* 1705.

For THE EARL OF SEAFIELD

MY LORD,—I am extreamly obliedged to yr. Lo. kind and frank offer in medling in our affairs, and I hope ye will never repent them. I am sure yr. Lo. shall never have reason to complain of any want of duty in acknowledging them by the return of what service I am capable to render yr. Lo. or yr familie. I have seen the proposalls sent to Glassoch, and for what I can judge of them they seem verry reasonably calculate for some support to our familie, and for ane effectuall and unexpencive payment of the creditors, so far as the subject will bear. I depend entirely on yr. Lo. in the manadgement of this affair, and shall only add that I am in all duty, My Lord, Yr. Lo. most humble servant, JAMES OGILVIE.

Boyne, the 27*th of Aprill* 1705.

The Boyne estates ultimately passed fully into the hands of Seafield in 1708 after judicial sale and purchase.

For THE EARL OF SEAFIELD

MY LORD,—I wrott ane ansver of the last letter I had the honnor off from your Lo. som days sinc, which I sent to your Ladie. I am loth to trouble your Lo. with long letters, Glassow having fully given ane account of all he hath spok with of my creditors. I shall be werie willing to concur in the proposalls sent me north, and am, My Lo., Your most humble servant,

PATRICK OGILVIE.

Boyn, Aprll 28, 1705.

For THE EARL OF SEAFIELD

Kilraik, ye last of Aprile 1705.

RYT HONLL,—I head ye honour of yours, and shall as yor Lo. desyres comunicate yor advyse to ye laird of Grant. I hop to wait on yer Lo. much about ye tyme ye Parliment is to sit, so I shall forbear giving you mr truble, but subscryve myself, My Lord, Yor Lo. most affe. and most humble servant, H. ROSE.

Hugh Rose of Kilraick was one of the commissioners for Nairnshire. This and next letter show that Seafield was working up his supporters in view of the meeting of Parliament.

For THE EARL OF SEAFIELD

MY LORD,—I had the honour and the satisfaction of your Lop. letter by the sam post, and vill be alvais refreshd to hear of the veilfare of yor Lo. person, famelie, and interest ; and ver I in my vonted and leidge postour, the least signification of your pleasur should be an powerfull attraction to draw me to anie place vithin my reach, vher I could serve you. Bot the truth is I dare not ventur upon a journay albeit it be in the summer, for trulie I have not onc crossd an horse sinc ever I cam from Edb^r after the last Parliament. The swelling and reidness and hardnes of my legg continous still vith me, and it will be tyme and rest and the spairing of travel upon it, that vill bring it to the former consistancy. Nor is the habit of my bodie good othervais, that I dare sett out to a jurnay. And as I would have most villinglie answered yor Lo. cal, and obeyed your commands, so vould I vith cheirfullnes contributed my myte and mean endeavours for promoting of the Queins service and the publict interest both of church and state. My deir and nobl Lord, think not that this is anie excuse or shift in the least. All those vho may come up to the Parliat. out of the cuntrey, or from the north can bear wittness vhither it be not vith me as to my bodilie constitution as I say. And my harts desyrs shall be for the happie ishue and result of this next session of Parliat, and that God may direct and over-rule all things for the advantage off all valuabl interests of the kingdom. I vill presum to writt to your Lo. som tym heirafter by anie freind vho coms up to Parliament, and shall give yor Lo. no furder trubl att the tym, bot to add that I am still in much sinceritie, My Lord, Your Lo. most humbl and affectionat servant,	J. BRODIE.

Brodie house, Apryll 30, '705·

James Brodie of Brodie, son of Lord Brodie, was born on 15th September 1637, and succeeded in 1679. He married, on 28th July 1659, Lady Mary Kerr, sister of the first Marquis of Lothian. He represented Morayshire in the Scots Parliaments from 1689 to 1704. He was not present at the sitting of Parliament in 1705. He had nine daughters. The fifth, Emilia, married George Brodie of Asleisk, his successor. He died in March 1708.

For THE EARL OF SEAFIELD

Lond., 1st May 1705.

MY LORD,—I had the honour of two from your Los. yesterday, one of them by a flying packet directed to Sr. David Nairn and sign'd by Sr. Gilbert Elliot, which seemd extraordinary since it was my Ld. Roxburghs moneth of service as secretary. Sr. David Nairn tels me that their is a discovery that Haines and the others who have witnesed and confessed have been suborn'd. This account surprised me since your Los. takes no notice of it in your letter. If it is so, the Queen and the Treasurer may think I industri-ously conceal it, and can not but conceave an ill opinion of me, and I shall meet with abundance to improve it to my disadvantage. I had no journals of Council sent me nor any letter, save that your Los. writt, for which I return your Los. my most hearty thanks, and am with all respect, My Lord, Your Los. most humble and obedient servt.,

AL. WEDDERBURN.

For THE EARL OF SEAFIELD

MY LORD,—I have been in the country since I had the favour of yours. My being out was publick when I wrote to you, which made me not mention it. My Ld. Treasurer expresses himself in a very friendly manner to me and gives me hope that I shall be reimbursed in tyme. I am glad to hear that your Lop. and others continue in a good understanding. I shall be glad to contribute to it. I am perswaded its both your interests. I have reasons for what I say, which it is not fit to write. Greens affair has made strange discoverys here. Its strange the tryall is not published, for the first point is not whither guilty or innocent, but whether they were fairly tryed and condemned or not. The impressions taken here, which may make the unborn child cry, should not be let alone one moment, if they can be removed, and the more or lesse in such matters is a great dale. Its like with you the ferment here will scarcely be credited. I own I could not have believed it, had I not been here and seen it. It is the only thing that partyes here agree in, and its fewell for winter in the new Parlt., when they will not need it, for animosityes grow here too, and both partyes are angry to a higher degree then ever I saw them even in the exclusion tyme. As to my self I have suffered enough by my late medlings, tho I suffer not in my private circumstances ; but I shall have all the patience I can, and not be rash or undutifull in doing myself justice. However nothing shall hinder me from serving the countrey and my friends to my power.—I am, Your Lops. most faithfull humble servant,

J. JOHNSTOUN.

Lond., 1st May '705·

Ridpath by one of his papers has done the nation better service than I fear he will ever be considered for.

For THE EARL OF SEAFIELD

Lond., 5 May 1705.

MY LORD,—I am desired by Sr. Charles Hedges to acquaint your Losps. of the ministrey that Mr. Campbel of Glenderouel [1] is reddy to be sent to Scotland, and that they would be glad to know here what methode your Losps. desire may be used in doing of it, whither in custody, and at what place your Lorsps. will order him to be delivered, or whither bail may be taken for his rendering himselfe in Scotland, and for what sum it shall be accepted. I am likewise desired to know if ther is any objection against Sr John Mcclanes going into Scotland, now that he has obtain'd his pardon in both kingdomes. I delivered your Los. letter to the Treasurer, but have had no occasion of discourcing with him. Doubtles the inclosed will serve for all that I need say. I am with all respect, My Lord, Your Los. most humble and obedient servt,

AL. WEDDERBURN.

For THE EARL OF SEAFIELD

Lond., 10th May 1705.

MY LORD,—I had the honour of your Lops. of the 3d instant, and delivered that which it covered. Yesterday upon the repeated desires of several of the relations and others concern'd in the men belonging to the ship the *Worcester,* I waited on Sr David Nairn to Sr William Ashursts house, one of the present aldermen, where we heard what is contained in the inclosed paper declared by the persons therein named ; but it was not thought fitt to examine them upon oath, without there were a commission from a proper court in Scotland authorising the taking of depositions in that matter, so that the cheife design of our meeting was that Sr David and I might be informed of the grounds the persons interested have for applying to your Losps. of the government that such a commission may be given, to the end our representation may help to facilitat the granting of their sute. Sr David, whose moneth

---

[1] *The Acts of the Parliaments of Scotland,* vol. xi. pp. 235, 239.

of service it is, will doubtles transmitt a full and distinct account of particulars. All I shall add is, that many here are convinced that such light and evidences may be had in this matter, as will occasion an intire stopp of any further execution of the sentence alredy pronounced, and will prevent the giving orders for a second process against Raynolds or others that are recommitted to prison upon a new information exhibited by Capt. Drummonds relations. As to the legality or expediency of this methode proposed I need say nothing. Your Losp. can best judge of both. Yet I presume to suggest that if the men themselves were sent down they could be more fully examined, and have more apposite questions put to them than can be done here, and the satisfaction their answeres might give to the nation and government is worth the publick expense. But if this can not be done, and that your Lodp. agreed to the giving a commission to examine them here upon the interrogators to be sent, it will be fitt several persons be join'd in the commission, especially if Sr David or I be named in it, least some of us before that time be necessarily absent. I am desired by the Earle of Clarendon to put your Losp. in minde of his grandchilds claim, and intreat you would use your interest and give your advice for getting it effectually done.—I am, My Lord, Your Losps. most humble and most obedient serv^t,

AL. WEDDERBURN.

For THE EARL OF SEAFIELD

My Lord,—It is my duty to acquent your Lop. that on ye recommendation of my Ld. Com^r and ye Marquis of Annandale her Maty. has been pleased to give me a commission to act in all affairs relaiteing to Scotland in absence of ye principall Secretaries, as they could doe if present. I thinke ye place of Secretarie Deaput will not admitte of a dividend, therefor my com^{on} runs not soe, nor does it intitle me to any of the profits. I hope your Lop. will doe me ye justice to belive I shall make it my study to discharge ye trust fathfully, and most readyly observe and dispatch what instructions or commands your

Lop. charges me with.   The inclosed I recd. from my Lord
Tresr. this evening.   By this post I send under covert to
my Ld. Com^{r1} a letter from ye Queen to ye Councill for
adjurning the Parliament—the time to which is left blank
for his Grace to fill up.   I have sent to his Grace a paper
containing what I heard yeasterday severall people say
about ye two Drummonds.   There will be application
made to the Councell there for a com^{on} to examine them
upon oath, in wch caice, if granted as is supposed it will,
your Lop. will take caire ye que[s]tions be very distinct.
The not publishing the tryall maks people think it was
not faire.   Your Lop. can not imagine the noise it maks
here, and if more of ye condemned are execute, Scotsmen
here are not safe from ye mobb.   I have heard ye Duke of
Queensberry express ye great sence he has of your friendship in forwarding his papers, wch are now past.   I doubt
not but if ane opportunitye offer your Lop. will meet with
a gratefull returne from him.—I am, My Lord, Your Lop.'s
most humble and most obedient servant,

DAVID NAIRNE.

Whitehall, 10th May 1705.

Sir David Nairn was appointed Secretary-depute on 3rd May
1705.[2]

For THE EARL OF SEAFIELD

MY LORD,—I receaved the honour of y^r Losps. letter
letting me know that my signature was past, and an
account from others of yr Losps. great goodnesse and
favour in it, which I doe assure you I shall allwayes retain
a very gratefull sense off.   I have now litle to doe in this
place.   I am therfore prepareing for my retreat, as soon
as my wifes circumstances and my own helth will allow
me to undertake so great a journey.   I cannot entertain yr
Ldsp. with any thing of publick bussinesse, being as seldome at court, and as ignorant of theire measures for
Scotland as when you was here, but I shall ever wish well
to her Majestys service and the peace of that kingdome,

---

[1] The Duke of Argyll.
[2] *State Papers* (*Scotland*) *Warrant Books*, vol. xxi.

and upon all occasions shoe my selfe, My Lord, Your Ldsps. most humble and obedient servant,

QUEENSBERRY.

May, ye 10th.

For THE EARL OF SEAFIELD

MY LORD,—I am directed by my Lord Treasr. to forward the inclosed to your Lop. and one to his Grace the Com^r by a fflying packet. His Lop. told me ye import of them were to informe his Grace and your Lop. that there were accounts given this morning to ye comitte of Councell of some ships gone to Scotland as is supposed with armes. Its hoped your Lop. will take ye necessary precautions to prevent there landing, or to sease them if they doe. By last nights post I sent to my Ld. Com^r her Matie letter to ye Councell for a further adjurnment of the Parliament, and told your Lop. of ye com^{on} her Maty. has been pleased to honor me with. I shall in all capacity endeavour to make myselfe acceptable to your Lop., because I truely am, My Lord, Your Lops. most humble and most obedient servant, DAVID NAIRNE.

Whitehall, 11th May 1705.

For THE EARL OF SEAFIELD

MY LORD,—I had the honour of y^{rs} last night about five aclock, and also the Comissioners comands. I accordingly came here immediatly therafter, and have given his Grace an account of the condition of this place, wch hardly can be worse. I wish something may be ordred about it. I hope this design'd invasion shall fail. I'm sure we are ill prepaird to receave an enimie. If y^r Lop. have any further comands for me, the bearer will take cair to send them. Haveing wryten fully to the Comissioner, who I doubt not but will comuni[c]at it to y^r Lop., I will trouble you no more now, but I am, My Lord, Y^r Lops. most ffaithfull and most humble servant, MAR.

Stirling Castle,
Thursday morning, May 17th, 1705.

John, Earl of Mar, on 29th September 1705, was appointed one of the Secretaries of State for Scotland. He led the Jacobites in 1715.

For THE EARL OF SEAFIELD

MY LORD,—By this I acknowledge ye honor of your Lop.'s of ye 16th by a fflying pacquet, which came about twelve a cloak on Saturday night. It brought one from your Lop. to my Lord Tres^r which I delivered, and he desired I wold acquent your Lop., that he has noe occasion to truble you with any answer. I beg leave to tell your Lop. once more, that ye not publishing Greens tryall is a great disadvantage to all Scotsmen here, and for my own pairt I am not furnished with such a reason as satisfys myselfe for the not doeing it. What trust your Lop. puts in me shall not be abused. I am sensible of ye obligations I owe you, and shall always acknowledge them as becometh, My Lord, Yo^r Lop.'s most humble and most obedient serv^t,   DAVID NAIRNE.

22nd May 1705.

For THE EARL OF SEAFIELD

MY LORD,—By yeasterdays post I had your Lops. of ye 17th, wth one to my Ld Thes^r, wch I gave to his servant, his Lop. not being at home. As business was at a stand there, till ane answer shoud arive to what ye fflying pacquet of ye 13th brought, soe our affairs seem now to be soe here, till one answer come to one that went from hence ye 18th, for my Ld Trs^r told me two or three days agoe, that he should not till then have occasion to write to Scotland, and bid me tell your Lop. soe. I question not but, as your Lop. says, there is great need of money and of ye Parl^s sitting, but how soon affairs will be adjusted for a propper time for ye last in order to procure ye first, your Lop. will know there first, and nothing can be a greater step towards it then ye union your Lop. mentions amongst her Matys. servants, which I heartyly wish for. I am glaid ye Councell has thought fit to order a com^{on} for examineing ye people about Drummond and his crew. The people are with me about it evrie day.—I am, My Lord, Yo^r Lop.'s most humble and most obedient servant,

DAVID NAIRNE.

24th May 1705.

For THE REIGHT HONRBLE THE EARLE OF SEAFILD,
LORD HIGH CHANSLOUR OF SCOTLAND

MY LORD,—You neaded have laid noe restriction upon
me not to comunicat what you wrott to me, for I protest
I cant yett find out the secritt. You great men gett a
way of wrytting soe mistically that plain countrie gentilmen
like myself will need plainer langwag befor I can understand you. If the Comissioner has great poures allowd
him, I supos the publick will soon see itt, and when your
Lop. will be pleased to honor me with the knowledge of
any thing, I begg it may not be in soe reserved a strain.
All I desire to know is when the Parleament will sertainly
meet, which I hope will not be made a great mistery of to
your Lop. most affectionat cussine and humble servant,

HAMILTON.

Kenull, May 24, 1705.

The register of the Privy Council of Scotland records that in
June 1703 the *Dunbarton Castle* was outrigged to secure the
trade of Scotland from the insults of French privateers. On the
16th July that year a commission was issued to Matthew Campbell
to be her captain, with instructions 'to cruise from the sound of
Mulle in the Highlands to the Mulle of Galloway, and from
thence the length of Lambie island near Dubline.' On 20th
September she was ordered to be laid up for the winter in New
Port Glasgow. On 14th March 1704 she was again commissioned, and similarly on 20th February 1705. The Privy Council
records show that the French prisoners[1] referred to in next letter
were sent to Glasgow tolbooth, and were thereafter transferred
to Edinburgh. They were subsequently exchanged for Scots
prisoners in France.

MAY IT PLEASE Yor LOPS.,—Not haveing any occasione
to trouble your Lops. since your last till now, this is to
advise yor Lops. that in my statione, on the twenty fifth
of this instant of Cape Kyntyre about three in the morneing
I espyd a saile, and afr a chase from that time till nyne of
the cloack at night, I came up with her and found her a
Frensh priviteer, and after some small conflict she surrended

---

[1] *Historical MSS. Commission, Fourteenth Report*, App. III., *Seafield MSS.*
p. 221.

haveing killd his lieutennant and wounded severalls of his men. She is a priviteer of eight gunns sixty two men, nothing else on board but some few provisiones and two ransomers, one for the Dubline packet boat and the other for a Grinock barck. Haveing come in here this day with the prize and prisioners, I have sent this expresse to your Lops. to know what further is to be done with the prize and prisoners. If they are to be sent to Glasgow they can be securely sent thaire by the men I have on board, I mean the prisoners. There is a necessity for haleing my shippe ashoar to be cleand, but shall make all the dispatch I can to be reddy to waite yor Lops. orders. I am at a considerable charge in mantaining the prisoners, which I perswade my self yor Lops. will have regaurd to. I am, May it please yo Lops., Your Lops. most humble and most obedient servant, MATTHEW CAMPBELL.

Grinock Road, On board the 'Dumbartowne,'
28th May 1705.

For THE EARL OF SEAFIELD

MY LORD,—I am commanded by her Maty. to acquent your Lop., that there has been a petition presented to her by some of ye oweners of Greens ship creaveing that a commission may be granted from Scotland for examining some people concerning Cap. Drummond and his crew, from wch they hope to convince her Maty. and ye government there, that Drummond was not murdered by Green and his crew or pirated, and soe hope to lay the heat that has been against them, and preserve if possible the lives of those who have been condemned and not yet executed. I told her Maty. that your Lop. had wrote that ye Councell had already given orders for such a commission, which she was pleased with, and hope the same is already dispatched. In the mean time it is her Matys. pleasure that a further reprive be granted to those condemned then the days to which they stand reprived, and doubts not but ye Councell will readyly comply therin, and she depends much on your Lops. prudent conduct for effectuating the same. There is also ane affidavit concerning ye curing of the man said in some of ye confessions to be bled to death, wch with ye petitiones S^r Ch. Hedges was to send to me to be sent to my Ld Com^r, but its late and they are not yet come. I shall keep the post as long as I can for them.—I am, My Lord, Yor Lop.'s most humble and most obedient servant,

DAVID NAIRNE.

29th May 1705.

For THE EARL OF SEAFIELD

MY LORD,—This is cheifly for covert to ye inclosed for your Lop. from my Lord Tres^r, and to acquent your Lop. that by this fflying pacquet I have by her Matys. command sent to his Grace my Lord Com^r her Maty.'s letter to ye Councell for a further adjurnment of ye Parliament to some day of this month—the time to wch is left blank. If it is convenient I wish to know the delay of the commission your Lop. told me ye Councell had ordered for examining the people here about Drummond and his ship, and that ye tryall of Green and his crew is not yet published. Her Maty. has been pleased this afternoon to give me directions for drawing severall commissions for civill imployments according to advice from thence, which I am about and shall dispatch them as soon as I can.—I am, My Lord, Yo^r Lop.'s most humble and most obedient servant,

DAVID NAIRNE.

2nd June 1705.

For THE EARL OF SEAFIELD

MY LORD,—I must humbly beg your Lops. favour in a small affair. My brother has an affair before the Lords of the Session. It is advocated from the judge of the Admiralty to them. I am assurd it is the most just cause that can be. If it were otherwise, I would not sollicit not ev'n for a brother. Sir Alex^er Ogelvy, to whom I have taken the freedom to write tuo posts ago, can inform your Lop. if it is so or not. If your Lop. shall find that he has justice on his side, all I beg of your Lop. that you would not lett him be run doun for want of a freind in his necessity. I would not make the least oblique insinuation against the justice of so honourable a bench, but I wish it may not be too true that a man has sometimes need of freinds to obtain justice, at least in dispatch of his busines. Therfor I humbly lay the case befor your Lop., being both assurd of your Lops. justice and candour in every thing, and of your and freindship to myself in severall things ; and tho I can never pretend to requite your Lop. for any of your favours, yet if it were in my power none should be more willing than, My Lord, Your Lops. most humble servant,   JO. ARBUTHNOTT.

London, June 3d 1705.

Dr. John Arbuthnot, author and wit, son of an ' outed ' Episcopal minister, was a graduate of Marischal College, Aberdeen.   He was a friend of Pope and of Swift, and was the author of *History of John Bull*, etc.

For THE EARL OF SEAFIELD

8th June 1705.

MY LORD,—I haveing gotan a generall indulgence from yr Lo. for all bygon and future troubles of this nature, I adventure to intreat yr Lo. to let me know, if yor Lo. hes wreitin to England anent my masts.   If not, I beg yr Lo. may mynd it by the nixt post.   My Lord pray you let me know qt seyes [size] of timber yo Lo. neids, and ther dimensiones, and yr. Lo. shall comand as to the prices, My Lord, Yr. Lo. most oblidged faithfull ser^{tt}, q^{ll},

DAVID ROSS OFF BALNAGOUNE.

Balnagown's Ross-shire trees offered as masts for the English navy are again referred to in the letters of 23rd June and 7th July 1705.

For THE EARL OF SEAFIELD

MY LORD,—Your Lops. of ye 2^{d} I rec^{d} with one to my Ld. Tres^{r}, which I took ye necessary caire off.   I have not receaved any commands from ye Commissioner about the prisoners taken by Cap. Campbell.   When they come I shall observe them.   Your Lop. may remember I had the honor formerly to receave your directions in the like caice, and you was pleased to let me know they were executed to satisfaction.   When Scots men are taken prisoners, they are not distinguished from English in the exchange, unless it be very latly, and which I have not yet occasion to know, nor shall I untill I have a proper opportunity of speakeing with ye Com^{rs}, wch perhaps my Ld Com^{rs} letter next post may give me. I am very glaid of ye reprive given to Greens crew, for your Lop. can not imagine the heat that is about the tryall and execution of these who have suffered, and I can not help saying that theres too much ground given for talking, by ye not publishing of the tryall after soe long time, and ye detaining the com^{on} ordered ye 15th May by ye Councell soe long is what I am not furnished with an argument for. By this post I have sent a gift of pension or rather sallary for myselfe in ye post I have ye honor to serve in. I have too many prooffs of your Lops. kindness to doubt of your assistance in passing it—but I thought it my duty to acquent your Lop. with it as being, My Lord, Yor Lops. most humble and most obedient servant,

DAVID NAIRNE.

9th June 1705.

For THE EARL OF SEAFIELD

MY LORD,—Yeasterday I had the honor of your Lop.'s letter of ye 9th, wth one to my Ld. Tres^r which I delivered to his Lop. He told me that by it he found Sr. Alex. Ogilvie had laid aside his pretensions at this time of being made a Lord of the Session, soe that now there is noe opposition to Sr Gilbert Elliot. I wrote to your Lop. ye 29th past by ye Queens command, relaiteing to a petition then given her Maty. by some who were concerned in Greens crew. I sent ye petition to my Ld Com^{rs}. Your Lop. has not taken ye lest notice of ye recept of my letter. I am the more surprised, because I never remember that I wrote to your Lop. about any business without haveing the honor of some answer, much less when I write as that was by ye Queens command. I am told ye petitioners are goeing to Windsor to truble her Maty. again. If they doe I know not what to say. I begg also to know ye cause why the com^{on} soe long agoe ordered by ye Councell for examining people here is delayd. I am sorie I shoud be

soe often trublesome to your Lop. on these heads, but you
wold see a necessity for it, if you were here.   Therefor I
hope your Lop. will pardon, My Lord, Your Lops. most
humble and most obedient servant,

DAVID NAIRNE.

16th June 1705.

Sir Gilbert Elliot was clerk to the Scots Privy Council.

For THE EARL OF SEAFIELD, LD. CHANCELLOR

MY LORD,—I came from Windsor last night after elleven,
where I had been to get her Matys. hand to ye letter to the
Par. and instructions to ye Com^r.   They differ a litle from
what came to ye Treas^r, as I wrote to my Ld Com^r last post.
I also got ye letters signed to ye Lords of Session and
Justiciary to admitt Sr Gilbert Eliot as one of ther number.
At my comeing to toun, I found your Lops. of ye 12th with
one to my Lord Tres^r, which I sent to his Lop. this morning, because I could not goe myselfe, haveing ye above
papers and severall others to dispatch.   I shall observe
what your Lop. directs concerning the French prisoners
taken by Capt. Campbell, and by next post shall, I hope,
receave her Maty^s commands and transmitte them to your
Lop.   I containou with al duty, My Lord, Yo^r Lop^s most
humble and most obedient servant,   DAVID NAIRNE.

Your Lop. has here on from my Ld. Treas^r.

19th June 1705.

For THE EARL OF SEAFIELD, LD. CHANCELLOR

MY LORD,—I told your Lop. in my last that I shoud by
this day receave her Mat^s commands concerning ye ffrench
prisoners taken by Capt Campbell, and accordingly I went
to Windsor for that end and am just returned.   She was
pleased to ask me if any such caice had occured befor.   I
told her Maty. that there had, when I had ye honor formerly
to serve—and that then I was commanded to attend y^e
Secretarie of State here and ye Com^rs of transportation,
who tooke the same methode of exchangeing as with those
taken and brought to any remote pairt of England or in
Ireland, and thus her Maty. has ordered me to apply again,

wch I shall doe ye morrow, and I doubt not but they will doe as they did before. In ye meantime I beleive they will expect a more particular account, for your Lop. neither tells the number nor the severall station or ranks, which I remember your Lop. did formerly, and it was demanded by the Com^{rs} of transportation. As for the expense of keeping them, my Ld Tres^r was pleased to tell me that he thought those who were exchanged for them were to ballance it, but whither ye sume will be soe considerable as to oblidge any body to solicit for it I know not. Yeasterday I had ye honor of your Lop's. of the 14th, in answer to ye first pairt of wch about the laird of Balnagowens trees, Mr. Clerke not being in toune, I went to ye Princes Councill and spoak wth Mr. Churchhill, who assured me that there shoud be a letter sent from the board to ye Navy board to examine the matter, and that he wold be sure to send me an answer in three or four days at farthest, wch if he doe it shall be transmitted to your Lop. I spoak to her Maty. as your Lop. desired in the last pairt of your letter about ye Bishops precepts, which her Matie has agreed to, and commanded me to draw them, but your Lop. does not say how many of them and who they are, as I remember they were four, but if all yet liveing I must be advised by your Lop. One Mr. Reynolds brother to one of Greens crew of that name has been with me about his brother, who notwithstanding of his haveing been acquet it seems is taken up again at ye instance of Capt. Drummonds sister. I finde it is he who is most earnest for to have ye people examined here and that speedyly, for that he says his brother is to come to a new tryall, and he thinks these depositions might have weight with a jury. He is a man of a good familly, and neerly relaited to Secretarie Harly, who I finde mightyly espouses Reynolds interest. Greens tryall is reprinted here, but ye first time I heard of it was by six or seaven people, who came to me to know if it was ye true tryall as published in Scotland, which I could not tell, for noe body was soe kind as to send any, and after soe much noise as has been made of it, it wold not have been improper to have given my Ld. Tresr. and the Secretaries on each. But that I humbly conceave was yᵉ Judge Admiralls business. My Ld. Tresʳ desired I wold send your Lop. the inclosed. I have detained your Lop. too long, for which I beg pardon and am, My Lord, Yoʳ Lops. most humble and obedient servant,

DAVID NAIRNE.

Whithall, June 21, 1705.

For THE EARL OF SEAFIELD, LD. CHANCELLOR

MY LORD,—I herewith send your Lop. the coppie of a letter I recᵈ late last night from Sr. Ch. Hedges. The extract to which yᵉ first paragraph referrs I have sent to ye Earle of Loudoun. Yᵉ last pairt of ye letter I hope will excuse me to your Lop. for trubleing you on ye subject it relaits too, and lykeways convince your Lop. how necessary it is to give some answer to what I wrote ye 16th, if it were only to prevent further truble to her Maty. I had a letter this morning from ye Admiralty boord, telling me that they had wrote to ye Navy board about Balnegowens trees, and will send me there answer as soon as they have it, wᶜʰ shall be transmitted to your Lop. Sr. Charles Hedges has concerted ye exchange of ye prisoners there with the Comʳˢ here, who have agreed to receave them at New Castle as they did the former, and ye Comʳˢ want only now to adjust with the Admiralty concerning ye ships who are to receave them, and which they assure me shall be done in time for me to advise of it against next post. I have noe further to truble your Lop., soe rests, My Lord, Yor. Lops. most humble and obedient servant,

DAVID NAIRNE.

23rd June 1705.

For THE EARL OF SEAFIELD

MY LORD,—Whatever the success of this Parlament may be, I hope this somer we shall have the honor to sie your Lo. in the north countrey, which being in a perfect decay for want of trade and consequently money, is posting to a state of ruine. If the south and west parts of the kingdom be in like circumstances, divisions and privat interest a litle layd aside, this session of Parlament may take con-

clusions and make such acts, whereby neu branches of
export of naturall product may be encouraged and undertaken.   And as thereby the nation shall gain when the
first privat undertakers are lossers, so it will seeme just
and incumbent on the Parlament to give the necessary
helps thereto, and in order to this to apropriat one monthes
cess and name collectors thereof answearable to the Parlament, for the payeing of such drawbacks and out thereof,
in the termes and as the Parlament shall thinck fitt to
ordain.   And what part of this fund shall be so consumed,
by so much in a proportion will the trade of the nation be
increased, and the ballance brought on its side, the remainder being still at the Parlaments disposall.

The means of export from this countrey, and whereof
for one I resolve to be ane undertaker, are barrelled herings
such as the Dutch, barrelled cod for the east countries, dry
cod for the coasts of Portugall Spain and the Streights,
and distilled spirits of corns to Holland, where is a very
great consumption off trash Genever, farr inferior both in
taste and strength to the spirits shall be made here, so
that what drawback may be on each boll of grain exported
ought to be in proportion allowed on spirits drawne therefrom and exported, with respect had to the expense of
malting, fireing, vessells, servants dyet and wages not required in the export of the simple grain, nether can more
be proposed to be drawn from sixteen stone weight of
bear then eight scots pynts off liquor fitt for fforreigne
mercats.   And considering that we are yearly improveing
our landes to produce more and more grain, and the
number of people to consume it are still diminishing for
want of trade and profitable meanes of employement,
unless we alter our methodes, or fall on some nieu wayes of
export, our cornes will become such a drug on our handes,
that we shall neither be able to live or pay publick dues.
The countrey expects the Parliament will take into consideration the care of gardeing our coasts, so much infested
at present by privateers of such numbers and force that
Capt. Gordon allon is not able to deal with them, and as
he hath done very good service allreadie and safed much

money to the nation, so if he had the *Royall William* added (for which the Parlament should give a fund), he could act a great deal more for the honor of the nation, as well as the safety of its trade. I doubt not but that your Lo. will have proposalls of this nature from much better heads, well digested and in due forme, the good success whereof together with your Lops. wellfare and prosperity is heartiely wissed and prayed for by, My Lord, Your Los. most humble and obedient servant,

Jo. BUCHAN.

Carnebulg, 25th June 1705.

Colonel John Buchan of Cairnbulg, Aberdeenshire, was a brother of the Jacobite General who was defeated at Cromdale. Captain Thomas Gordon at this time was in command of the *Royal Mary.* On 7th November 1705 he was appointed captain of the *Royal William,* Captain James Hamilton of Orbieston succeeding him as commander of the *Royal Mary.*[1] Thereafter the east coast of Scotland was defended by two men-of-war.

The following letter shows that in the spring of 1705 the Lord Chancellor sent his son, Lord Deskford, abroad, under his old Scots tutor, Mr. William Blake, to finish his studies at Utrecht University in Holland. His career there is further referred to in the letters of 10th and 17th November 1705.

For THE EARL OF SEAFIELD

MY LORD,—The tenth of this instant my Lord Deskfoord received your Lops. first with a great deale of satisfaction ; and as he is very sensible of your Lops. fatherly kindness in giveing him an advice so good and so suitable to his pñt circumstances, he is resolved to follow the same, and to improve the time your Lop. shall be pleased to continue him here to the best advantage. As to his passeing through some of the towns of Holland, I found it his inclination, and therefore did not doubt but it was your Lops. allowance untill wee came here, and finding it had proved chargeable, as your Lop. writes, asked him if it was your Lops. orders to go by Amsterdam. He told me he understood it to be left to himself, and therefor did not

---

[1] *State Papers (Scotland) Warrant Books,* vol. xxi. p. 113.

think that it would give your Lop. any offence ; and I 'm
sure if he had in the lest suspected that it should, he had
checked his curiosity and denyed himself the satisfaction,
for never a son ever payd a greater regard to a fathers
coṁands than he does to your Lops. He is well enough
pleased with his quarters, and if he should prove uneasy
either in his lodgeing or eateing, according to paction he
may dispose of him as to either to better advantage upon
six weeks advertisement. His landlord ·is so farr from
being dissafected to the States, that in his converse and on
all occasiones he is most zealeouslie concerned for their
interest. My Lord Deskfoord lives in good friendship and
correspondance with the English and Germans here. He
walks in the fields with them, converses in coffee housses,
receives and returns their visits, but never goes allong
to the tavern, nor ever makes a pairt in their night caballs.
They doe not generally apply themselves to any study,
but for most pairt spend their time and their money in
the prosecution of their pleasures, which seemes to be their
priñll bussieness here. Your Lops. advice about readeing
the Roman history is much the same with the method he
had takn, with this difference only that in his compendize-
ing he does not take notice so much of their fights and the
accidentall pairt of the history as of the severall forms of
their government, their politicks, rites, their laws and the
occasions of them, and in my humble opinion this cannot
miss to improve his judgement, to prepare him for the
study of the law, and to ans^r evry pairt of the design your
Lo. proposes. Van Muyden is one of yor Lops. very good
friends, but neither he nor any professor will disswade
or discourage young men from entering, and he expected
he should have given up his name upon his comeing to
town, tho they had advanced very farr, and there was so
litle of the time to run. Mr. Cunninghame is here at pñt,
and haveing upon a dissobleidgment left my Lord Hart-
foord, he applys himself clossely to the compileing of that
book, which he has so long since promised the world. He
has done severall offices of kindness to my Lord Deskfoord,
and amongst the next has promised him liberty to go once

2 D

a fortnight to a privat gentlemans liberary in this town, wc̃h is reckoned the best in all this province. He offers his humble service to your Lop., and thinks it better that my Lord Deskfoord continue at history and the French this winter, provideing your Lop. allow him time enough here afterwards to study the law; but if he shall not be allowed, that then he take a colledge of the institutiones the first semestris, and the second a repetitory one of the same, that he may be master of that pairt, but not to advance any further for the first half year, which with a colledge of history and the French he thinks may sufficiently imploy all his time. But there is time enough to consider of this befor winter. As for divinity, mathematicks, and the other things your Lop. recommends, they shall be take care of, and his health shall be preferred to all. What money he has at p̄nt, if I be not mistakn, may serve to the midle of August new style, and if wee had not had such a tedious and expensive passage but come over straight in the pacquet boat, and if wee had not gone by the way of Amsterdam, considering there is no occasion for clothes and few masters to be payed, I beleive the money might have very near served another quarter after the midle of August. In the meanetime I shall endeavour to be as good a husband of your Lops. money as possible. It is very hard to loose the third pairt of the money by the way of exchange, and I cannot consider how your Lop. can save it except it should be sent in specie, which is not allowed, or goods sent over and put into a factors hand, and I can heare of non that will preserve the money entire except it be old copper, which is not worth yor Lops. while to enquire for.

It is long since it was reported here as certain that Annandale was Chancellour, and that your Lop. had retired from publick bussieness. I wish your Lop. had continued longer in the government for the good of your familie, yet perhapps it may be for your saffety and advantage to live in a privat condition in so difficult and dangerous a juncture, and I doubt not but the same kind providence that has been over you hithertoo does still attend and direct your Lop. Tho all our gısetts assure us that the French have sent a detachment to the Moselle, yet the contrary is evident by their haveing besiedged Leige. Most are of opinion that they knew Prince Lewis of Baden would not joine the Duke of Marleborrough at the time apointed, oy^rwise they had not undertaken the sd seige. In the meantime the Duke is mightyly straitned for want of provisiones. Eight thousand of the Germans have joined now, and the oyr 20,000 are expected in a litle time, but P. Lewis is retired to the bathes for his health. There is a report here that there has been an engadgment in Italy, but it is not certain, that the Grandprior is killed, Vendome wounded, and ten thousand killed on that side, that Prince Eugene is wounded and 4000 killed on his side. Your Lo. has the news much better in the prints, but when any thing remarkable occurrs yor Lo. shall be aquainted by your Lops. most humble and obedient serv^t,

WIL. BLAK.

Utr., June 19, 1705.

For THE EARL OF SEAFIELD, L ‚ CHANCELLOR

MY LORD,—I have your Lop's. of ye 23^d by a ſflying pacquet, and this comes by ane other in answer to what was ye occasion of it. It will be great happyness if what ye Queen has done as to ye changes doe compose and unite as many as will cary by a plurality, what is for the interest of ye kingdom and her Matys. service. I wish a further adjurnment of ye Par. had been practicable, for since ye alterations are made, there has not been time for people to exerce themselves, but thoughts of this kinde are out of doors before now, soe I shall only wish for good success. Befor this your Lop. will have receaved mine of ye 23^d, by wch you will see ye reason why I troubled your Lop. soe often for answers to my former about ye com^on for examin- ing people here in relation to Capt. Drummond, soe shall add noe more to that. My Ld Tres^r thinks it will make a great noise here, and may be of ill consequence ye letting these prisoners be dismised that were taken by Capt Gordon with ye Duke of Bavarias com^on. It wold have been yet better if they had been the saylors of a merchant, but a privateer is ane open offencive enimie, and to think that ye ffrench will dismiss any prisoners of ye Queens subjects, when they have not enugh to exchange for there oune is much to be doubted. I told what your Lop. said for ye doeing it, but I find it does not satisfy, and the less, that upon ye first application here caire was taken to ease ye Queen of those prisoners taken by Capt. Campbell. I wish that this methode may not make ye Com^rs here distinguish between Scots and English in ye exch^e hereafter, wch they never did hithertoo. I containou, My Lord, Yor Lop's. most humble and most obedient serv^t,

DAVID NAIRNE.

Whitehall, 28th June 1705.

The new appointments made were the Earl of Loudoun, Joint Secretary of State, and the Earl of Glasgow, Treasurer-depute. These ministers met Parliament on the same day as Sir David Nairn wrote, along with the Duke of Argyll, Commissioner, Lord Archibald Campbell, Lord High Treasurer; Seafield, Lord High Chancellor, Queensberry, Lord Keeper of the Privy Seal, the Marquess of Annandale, Joint Secretary of State, Sir James Murray of Philiphaugh, Clerk Register, and Adam Cockburn of Ormistoun, Justice-Clerk.

On 19th June 1705, on a petition from the magistrates of Aberdeen narrating that three Aberdeen ships returning from Campheir were seized by the French and Ostenders, that the detention of these crews in France depended upon the treatment given to two French or Ostend crews captured by Captains Gordon and Campbell, and praying that these two crews be liberated on their binding themselves to procure the same favour to the Scots prisoners in France, the Scots Privy Council accordingly liberated the crew of the Ostend privateer *St. Trinity,* taken by Captain Gordon.

For THE RIGHT HONOURABLE THE EARLE OF SEAFIELD, LORD HIGH CHANCELLOR, ATT HIS LOPS. LODGINGS, EDGH.

MY LORD,—This is only to acquaint your Lop. that the affair, about w̄h you were pleased to write to the north some dayes agoe, was over the day befor the post arrived there, otherwayes it scarcely could hav missed. But some friends of him who is chosen viz. P-h-ll,[1] fearing some prevention, did ensure it befor he could send any instructions from hence. However, I'm informed that, upon a view hereof, the matter your Lop. wrote of was keeped so very closs, that the post himself knowes not of it to this hour. I am as becometh, My Lord, Your Lops. most humble and obedient servant,

FRANCIS GRANTT.[2]

Colledg, 30th Jun. 1705.

For WILLIAM LORIMER, CHAMBERLANE TO THE EARL OF SEAFIELD AT CULLEN

Edin., Jully 3d, 1705.

AFFECTIONAT COUSINE, . . . Wee want the 40 bolls of oats q^{ch} you said was comeing up to my Lords coach horses. Doe not miss the first oportunity to send them. Wee have a great report of ane skirmish that was among the gentlemen in Banff shyre and that very bloody, which made us beleeve that Boynd should not have been able to have come to the Parliament, but wee see it to be otherwise. He is come up and sayes there was no such thing. If it had been, I beleeve you would have sent us ane acco^{tt}. I have litle time to write any more, for the Parlia^{tt} is now sitting and every minute diverted. Our Parlia^{tt} will be very fashious. The Queen in her letter recommends the setling of the succession, a treatty of union with England, and six moneths cess, the last of qch will please you worst, because you^{ll} bear a part of the burden. The letter and speeches are not printed, els they should have been sent you.—I am, Sir, Your most humble serv^{tt},

JOHN PHILP.

For THE EARL OF SEAFIELD, L^D CHANCELLOR

MY LORD,—I have your Lop's. of ye 30th past. I wrote to your Lop. formerly of ye inconveniency of letting those

---

[1] Probably Roderick Mackenzie of Prestonhall, Senator of the College of Justice, who had just been chosen Commissioner to represent Fortrose in Parliament.

[2] Afterwards Sir Francis Grant, Lord Cullen.

prisoners loose about ye countrie, who were taken by Capt. Gordon, and the coppie herewith sent of a letter wrote to ye com^te for exch^e of prisoners, and which they showed to me, will show your Lop. the hazards that ye poor men themselvs run. They might have been indeed sent away without formall treatys for ransome, as they doe here with the Ostenders, but to let them run loose in ye countrie may be a means to get them knockt doun by evrie countrie fellow, that has ane aversion to a ffrenchman. The best way to let your Lop. understand the answer I had from ye Admiralty abt. Balngowens trees is to send, as I doe herewith, the very papers they sent to me. What further commands your Lop. has to lay on me therin shall be observed. The petitioners about ye commission for examination abt. Greens crew doe intend again to truble ye Queen. They are constantly wth S^r Ch. Hedges and me three times a week. What maks them soe very earnest for dispatch is that two to be examined are seamen, and one is now at Gravesend goeing a voyage, and if ye com^on should not come till they are gone, it will be called a designe to conceall ye truth. I again beg pardon for trubleing your Lop. soe often on the subject and am, My Lord, Y^or Lops. most humble and most obedient sert.,

DAVID NAIRNE.

Your Lop. has here one from my Ld. Tresr.

Whithall, 7th July 1705.

On 15th September 1705, a remission was granted to the remainder of the crew of the ship *Worcester,* and the incident of Green's crew ended.[1]

For THE EARL OF SEAFIELD

MY LORD,—I have noething of business to truble your Lop. with, and shoud be now silent, but that I know good news are always acceptable to your Lop. and all such as wish well to her Maty. and kingdom. I wrote of the express from ye Duke of Malborrow to his Grace my Ld. Com^r in generall, but since sealing my letter our great guns are fired, and tho late bonfires made. The particulars

---

[1] *State Papers (Scotland) Warrant Books,* vol. xxi. pp. 85, 86.

I have not exactly, but whats brought to me are, that ye Duke of Malborrow has forced ye French lines, taken 20 pices of cannon, and three generall officers besids many other officers and souldiers, and is now encamped about Tarlemond and Luvin.   It was imposible to receave ye Queens commands to send this good news by a fflying pacquet, but I belive its true and I humblie submite to your Lop. whither upon what I write to your Lop. it is not necessary to make ye publick expressions of joy necessary on such occasions.   I think it my duty to give your Lop. account of what I know, and am, My Lord, Your Lops. most obedient humble servant,   DAVID NAIRNE.

   Whithall, 14th July 1705.

Parliament adjourned on 21st September 1705, after passing an act for a treaty of union with England.

For THE EARL OF FINDLATER

London, Octr. the 27, 1705.

   MY LORD,—I have not had the satisfaction to hear from your Lop. since I pairted from Ed^r, nor have I anie thing to trouble you with, bot that I have had a good jorney and have been weal receaved by her Majestie.   She has been pleased to express her satisfaction with what has been done in the Parlament, and in her speach this day has recommended the union.   Your Lop. will have the speach by the nixt post.   I belive it cannot be printed this night.   I have not heard from Cullen, nor doe I know if Forgland be returned, so I have nothing to wreat to him. I wish your Lop. all happiness, and I am with all respect, My Lord, Your Lops. most obedient son and humble servant,   SEAFIELD.

   I had a letter from James since I came hier.   He is verie weal.

For THE EARL OF FINDLATER

MY LORD,—My Lord Chancelor thinks very long to hear from yor Lop. of the condition of yor health.   Blessed be God he is very well himself, and is so often taken up with company that he cannot gett written to yor Lop. so frequently as he would. I shall take care to send yor Lop. the prints duely. This pacquet brings the confirmation of Barcelona's being taken and litle els materiall. They are not yet begun to doe any thing in Scotts bussiness. The Marquis of Annandale is at variance with all our states-men and visits none of them, but all his efforts att court against them will have litle effect, ffor my Lord Chancelors interest with the Queen is as great as ever, and they reakon the Duke of Argyle did good service last Parliament. My Lord had letters from my Lord Deskford lately, and tells he is in good health ; and some gentlemen just now come from Utrecht sayes he is the best scholar of what he learns in all the colledges, which will be very satisfying news to yor Lop., and I hope plead for excuse for this trouble from, My Lord, Your Lops. most obedient and most dutifull servant,   JOHN PHILP.

London, Novemr. 10th, 1705.

Annandale, who had been appointed Secretary of State on 9th March 1705, was superseded by the Earl of Mar on 29th September 1705. For a short time thereafter he was President of the Privy Council.

For E. FFINDLATER

London, Novem^r 17, 1705.

MY LORD,—I had the honour of yor Lops. letter some posts agoe, and am very glade to find that you continue in health ; and I make no doubt of what you assure me, that you are also mindfull of anything that may concern our ffamily. I hear frequently from my sone James. He keeps his health very well, and as I hear makes a very good progress both in attaining the ffrench language, and in his other studies of law and history. I would very willingly entertain any proposall yor Lop. would make for his settlement ; and in the mean time, if I can be any wayes usefull to my Lady Grenock or her daughter, I shall be very ready. As for what you write concerning my Lord Annandale, I beleeve that he will be satisfyed with his old post. However it is not fitt that we speak anything of his loadgings, unles that he were actually removed from them and had refused employment. In

that caise yor Lops. advyce to me is very good.   I have
heard nothing from the north save by one letter from Sr.
Alexander.[1]   I hope yo[r] Lop. receaves the news duely,
for I have ordered them to be sent.   Wee are doeing nothing
in our affairs, till we see if the Parliament rescind the clause.
They are to be upon this affair the next week.   This is all
att present from, My Lord, Yor Lops. most obedient sone
and humble servant,   SEAFIELD.

The clause objected to was enacted by the English Parliament
the previous year, in retaliation for the Act of Security.   It
declared Scotsmen aliens, and cut them off in England from the
privileges which had been since the union of the crowns common
to them with Englishmen.   The clause was in course repealed.

For THE EARL OF FINDLATER

MY LORD,—When any thing passes concerning the union
I shall not fail to give y[or] Lop. information.   This day the
Commons have aggreed in a committee of the whole house
to the Lords bill, and no impediment will stand now in
the way to a treatty ; but the soonest they can meett will
be the beginning of ffeb[ry], and when the Duke of Queensberry comes up they will proceed to the nomination.   My
Lord Chancelor is mightily troubled for the sad news he
has had of my Lady.   No body hath writt of it, but Lady
Betty, and she doth not give him a full acco[tt] of the
matter, which surpryses his Lop. the more ; but blessed
be God that she is recovering, and a true acco[tt] of it from
yor Lop. will ease him a great dale.   I will not presume
to trouble yor Lop. further, but beg pardon to subscryve
myself, My Lord, Your Lops. most dutifull and most
obedient servant,   JOHN PHILP.
London, Dece[r] 15, 1705.

To THE RIGHT HONOURABELL THE EARELL OF
   FINLATUR AT HIS LUGENS IN THE CHANCHLOR'S HOUS IN
   THE FIT OF THE CANIGET, EDR.

MY LORD,—I give your Lo. my harty thanks for your
conseren about me when I was seek.   I was indid very ill

---

[1] Forglen.

and for severell dayes was in gret danger, bot nou I bliss
God I am prity weall. My extrem fenting med me think
that I was to expek present dath. My stomak and saydes
was so sor for severell dayes after my womoting of blood,
that I could not sufer the woght of the clothes on them.
I wish good halth to your Lordship and a good and pro-
sprous neu year, and I allways shall continou, My Lord,
most obedent and affectionat doghtar and devoted servant,

ANNA SEAFIELD.

Your Lo. granchildren ar all weall, blissed be God, save
Janat that hath the small poox. Bracky dayed on Wadsenday last.

Ther is a sad axceedent falen out at Kindroght, when
Thomas Ogilvie was going to mary his doghtar. On the
marig day in the mornen the rueff of his hall feall, and
himseleff, his son, and brother, the bryd, and Anna Galie,
and a litell chyld in it. His brother and son was kiled
that instant, himseleff and doghter brused, and the
ministars[1] of Fordays doghter and the litl chyld saff. God
prepear us for his wieas.

Dis. 21, 1705.

The death of Alexander Duff of Braco, commissioner for
Banffshire, is thus fixed at the Wednesday before the 21st of
December 1705. On 19th January 1706 a warrant[2] of a gift of
the ward and non-entry of his estate was issued in favour of Sir
Alexander Ogilvie.

The Lords Commissioners of both nations appointed to negotiate
the treaty of union met in London from 16th April to .22nd
July 1706, and agreed on articles which were thereafter referred
to the Parliaments of England and Scotland. Lord Seafield,
as Lord Chancellor of Scotland, presided over the Scots Commissioners.

To THE RIGHT HONOURABELL THE EAROLL OF
FINLATUR AT HIS LUGENS IN THE FUT OF THE CANIGET

MY LORD,—I was very glead to kno by Martan that your
Lo. was in ordanary halth. I wish your Lo. good halth

---

[1] Mr. Gellie, Fordyce.
[2] *State Papers (Scotland) Warrant Books,* vol. xxi.

and long liff.   I fynd your son most be at Londan for soum
tym yet, which I am sory for ; bot if the unon have on
happy isiou a long tym wold be weall bestoued on it.   I
hir soum of my frinds is for my cuming south, bot that is
what I will never be persuaded to tho I war abell, which I
belive I am not, for save my Lord war ther I should have
no satisfaction, save it war in your Los. company, and your
Lo. knos I allvays lovd the contary, and I likways belive
I should loes the litell halth I have gott, if I should quet
the contary, till it war beter esteblished.   I wish your
Lo. wold think of cuming north to your ouen hous, wher
you wold be willkam to all, but in a partiklur manar to hir
who is sinserly, My Lord, Your most obedent daghtar and
humbell servant,   ANNA SEAFIELD.

   Cullan, 10   1706.

   On the 29th of June 1706 the Earl of Findlater received a
yearly pension of £200.[1]
   Next letter is written to the Town Council of Banff.   Sir
Alexander Ogilvie, who then represented Banff in the Scots
Parliament, was one of the Scots Lords Commissioners for the
union.   He was commissioner for Banff to the Convention of
Royal Burghs from 1704 to 1716.

Eder., 17th Octr. 1706.

   HONOBLL. GENTLEMEN,—By these I congratulate you
all in your new stationes, and wish you much joy and that
pace may attend you and the toun flurish in your tym.
For your diversion I have sent the minuts and artickles
of the union with the minuts of Parliament and the nues
letter.   I feind since Wm Garden went to Leith and by
my absence the sending the neus have bein altogither
neglected, but if you can name oney heere will be cairfull,
I shall give the nues to them for your use, since I have so
mutch to doe that I am affrayed my servants neglect
them.   Please receve my Lord Provosts letter, and if ye doe
judge me capable by your commission to serve you in the
Convension I shall be as cairfull of the tounes concernes
as formerlie, and save the charges of on to cum this

---

[1] *State Papers (Scotland) Warrant Books*, vol. xxii. p 58.

lenth. I would be weill pleased the honest toun ware out of debt, and shall never faill fathfullie to doe all the good I am capable to perform for it. So without aney seremoney frielie give me your commands, since I wish you all helth and good things to attend you, being sincerelie, Honobll Gentlemen, Your humble servant,

ALEXR. OGILVIE.

Edinburgh, Novemr. 27*th*, 1706.

WILLIAM,—You may compt with my tennants and allow them for what of there old rests they paid in bear and meal, ffour pound and half merk the boll of bear and fyve merks for the boll of meal, qc̄h is fully as much as I gott for the last years wictuall deduceing ffraught and other charges ; and for the rests of cropt 1705 I leave it to my wife to determine as she shall think best for getting my rents duely paid hereafter, qc̄h may be higher than what I allow them for there former rests.

You may give Thomas Murray ffour bolls of meal out of this cropt, and I shall hereafter determine what yearly allowance I 'll give him for being clerk to my regality court and barronrie . . .

You may transact with Hary Cathell about the vacant stipends as conveniently as you can, and send me south what bond is to be signed to him, for I beleeve his right will be sustained, and I would have it setled without any debate, for I doe not desyre to be heard with the Church. You should write frequently to me of what occurs in the north, and send me ane abbreviat of last years accompts.— I am, Your assured ffriend, SEAFIELD.

Seafield's regality court was that of Ogilvie in Banffshire. An account of that court is given by Dr. Cramond in the *Transactions of the Banffshire Field Club* of 18th March 1886.

The Scots Parliament met on 3rd October 1706, and the Act ratifying the treaty of union was passed on 16th January 1707.

For WILLIAM LORIMER, CHAMBERLANE TO THE
EARLE OF SEAFIELD ATT CULLEN

Edinburgh, Janry. 22, 1707.

D. C.,—. . . The treattie is ended and sent to London

four dayes agoe. By all the accompts wee have from thence, it 's generally beleeved it will not meett with great difficulty in passing in the English Parliat. I fear my Lord Chancelor will be oblidged to goe to London when the Parliament rises   He cannot gett any bargain for his wictuall this year, but has fraughted two ships to bring some of it about, and they sail next week. Mr. Stewart will write you accompt of there chartour parties. You have not yet sent me yor opinion of Burdsbanks acco^t with my Lord. He is requiring his pay^t, and considering his circumstances my Lord will clear him. . . . Give my humble duty to yor bedfellow and my mother and all friends.—I am, D. C., Your affectionat cousine and humble servant,   JOHN PHILP.

To WILLIAM LORIMER, CHAMBERLANE TO THE
    EARLE OF SEAFIELD ATT CULLEN
                                        Edinburgh, ffebry. 6, 1707.
    D. C.,—. . . I wrote formerly to you about the purchass of yor uncles houses. Am satisfied with the disposition, if it contains the warrandice, but by Mrs. Lorimers letter she seems to scruple it. You 'll need to advyse her, and if she pleases I 'll pay her interest for her money till Whytsunday next, though it will be above a years @rent loss upon any money that people may have in there hands att that, if the union succeed, for no species y^{r}after will pass but att the English rates of ffyve shillings the crown, and so proportionally. The Parliat. inclynes to make up the loss of the money out of the equivalent, but that 's uncertain and will take a time to be good. For guineas they 'll pass att no more than 21^s and 6^d ster. and no repara-tion for the loss.[1] I send you accompt of the proceedings of Parlia^t by these minutes. They 'll best informe you. Scotland is exempted from the malt tax dureing the warr, and in time of peace its never imposed. For what all the nobility and gentry brews they are to pay no excyse. Ale sold above two shilling the pint payes 4^s and 9^d sterline of excyse for 10 gallons.[2] This will very litle affect the

---

[1] Article XVI. of the union.   [2] Article VII. of the union.

north. When my Lords wictuall comes up send me two
bolls of best meal and I 'll pay you. Perhaps William
Strachan may give it in pairt of his rent for the lands he
has in Bruntowne. If he doe, let it be good, and if wee be
gone to London advyse Mr. Stewart or Will. Gardne to
send it to my wife. . . . I am, D. C., Your most affectionat
cousine and servant,   JOHN PHILP.

LETTER FROM LD CROMERTIE TO THE EARL OF SEAFIELD,
    RECOMMENDING ONE WHO HAS A PROSPECT OF DISCOVERING
    THE LONGITUDE

MY LORD,—Barring our yesterdays discord, allow me
this day to favour yr Lp. wt ane opportunity to serve one
who, beeing of the family of Kilraok and so descended of
yours, hath in Dr. Gregory's, Dr. Pitcairns, and my little
apprehension made at least as great, and in our opinion
a more demonstrative progress towards severall of the
most knotty and usefull theorems of mechanick philosophy,
and particularly towards the finding a fixt rule of computation of longitudes, and in order to that of the uninterrupted mobile, and that with more probable success then
any preceeding attempter. The theory convinces us. The
practise is above his stock, but it were a great pity that
it should be abortive. If it hold, Scotland, for so it is as
yett, may be vaine of it, and Holland will help ye reward,
by what their publick faith is ingadged. If he faile, *magnis
tamen excedit ansis, et cum maximis erravit.* What wee
can do is to give drink money to ye midwife of a desirable
birth, and a litle now, and a just recomendation to those
who can doe more is what 's suitable ; and yr Lps. interest
in ye nation, yr zeall for glory, yr relation to the person
and the honor of our phœnix Caledonia, will be such illus-
trious motives for yr Lp., that I fear to low them by
further recomendations from so litle a thing as your Lps.
most humble servant,   CROMERTIE.
    12th Mʳ 1707.

For WILLIAM LORIMER

Edinburgh, March 12th, 1707.

D. COUSINE,—My Lord is desyreous that you accept to

be factor upon the estate of Boynd. You should not decline to accept of it, because you will gett considerable allowance for it, and after tryall if it be uneasy you may quitt it. The roup will soon come on, for the most of the rights are produced, and Lord Minto is the ordinary for the ranking. . . . Mind to send me up two bolls of good meal with my Lords first wictuall ships that comes to Leith. Mr. Stewart tells me he sent you doubles of the chartour parties of two ships thats come for bear, and I told you by my last letters that Major Gen¹¹ Maitland had bought 600 bolls of meal, and to receave it att Portsoy. The delivery of this will be work for you this moneth, and there shall be more ships sent the next moneth. Wee expect my Lord Deskfoord here next week, and I beleeve he will be marryed before wee goe to London with Major Gen¹¹ Ramsayes daughter. The bearer John Dunbar tells me he comes back here speedily. I beleeve it 's to be his servant. I did not ask him since my Lady has been the doer of it. You need not speak of my Lord Deskfoords marriage, because it will be uncertain till he come here himself. I shall write more fully by Glassaugh.—I am, D. C., Yours, · JOHN PHILP.

Deskford's proposed marriage did not take place.

The Scots Parliament adjourned on 25th March 1707.

To WILLIAM LORIMER, CHAMBERLANE TO THE RIGHT HONLL THE EARLE OF SEAFEILD, LORD HIGH CHANCELLOR OF SCOTLAND

Edr., 22nd Apryll 1707.

SIR,—I have sent you ane double of Skipper Mouse charter partie, with ane note of my instructions relating to you on the foott yrof. His last loadning amounted to three hundreth bolls. He sailed yesterday and will be very soon at Portsoy. I shall dispatch Wm. Grigory the end of this week, soe I hope you will be pleased to give me account with this bearer what victuall may be left behinde, and I shall obey your instructiones. What bills you draw upon my Lord or me shall be answered. Receive lykewayes ane letter from my Lord, qch I gott by ane flyeing packet yesterday. I have noe news to send you, but that my Lord was most graciously received by her Maťie, and was mett ten miles from London with fyve hundreth horse and fourty coatches, and gott hosas from the entry of the city to his own lodgeing. Soe much for foraign news. Yesterday the G. Assembly raise, and upon Thursdays night I am to committ matriomony with one Janet Blackwood. Soe if I have forgott anything, I hope you will excuse, Sir, Your most humble servant,

Jo. STEWART.

I have sold my Lords victuall as yet at 4 lib. half a merk.

CHAPTER VI

LETTERS FROM THE UNION IN MAY 1707 TO THE END OF THE FRENCH INVASION OF SCOTLAND IN MAY 1708.

Alexander Abercrombie of Glassaugh, writer of next letter, succeeded Alexander Duff of Braco as one of the commissioners for Banffshire to the Scots Parliament.[1] He sat through its last session, 1706-7, and voted for the union.

For THE EARL OF FINDLATER

MY LORD,—Seing I presume the account on the other syde in relation to Spain may perhaps be fuller then the prints, I give your Lo. the truble therof, as also to satisfy you that did this place afoord any other thing worth writing, I would not neglect, if I did but know, so that I hope your Lo. will doe me the justice to belive it is not for want of all due respect you doe not hear oftner from me, seing I shal never neglect ane oportunity to testify how much I am in all sincerity as becometh, My Lord, Your Lo. most faithful and obedient humble servant,

ALEXR. ABERCROMBIE.

London, May 29, 1707.

Scots affairs in every thing are as I wrote David Ogilvie last post, and desyred him to communicat them to your Lo.

A list of the E. of Gallaways forces made prisoners, as contained in a letter from ane English officer who was prisoner att Albacet some days before the battle. He was informed of the following particulars by the English who

---

[1] *The Acts of the Parliaments of Scotland*, vol. xi. p. 306.

passed thorow prisoners :—Colls. 7, liv^t colls. 7, majors 7, capts. 68, livts. 100, ensigns 54, sergants 264, drums 97, private men, corporals included, 2815. All the rest of the foot killed.

A list of pairt of the slain the said prisoners saw :— Colls. Roper, Dormer, Lawrence, Woolet, Withers, Lecet, Ramsay, Arsken, Wade, Horindige and Clyton, Major Goring, two captains of Carpenters regt., Coll. Ostten and Stenhope of the guards, Maj. Dalouch of Peterbourrows dragoons, Capt. Dutanges, Coll. M^{k}neal of Suthrige regt.

All Stewarts regt. officers and centinels with the French refugies.

List of the prisoners that passed thorow Albacet :— Count Donar, Maj. Generall Shrimpton, Brigadier M^{k}ertny, Brigadeer Bretton, Livt. Coll. Hamilton of Montjoys, Coll. Hill, Coll. Alnut, Coll. Swan, Coll. Talbot, Livt. Coll. Cooper. The reason of this unhappie defeate is said to be the E. of Gallaways being necessitate to fight or starve for want of provisions, and the D. of Orleans horse joining the D. of Berwick the night before unknown to the E. of Gallaway made the French 33,000 in the line of battle, whereof there was 9000 horse, whereas Gallaway had only 17,000. The French had the town of Almanza in their centre, which gave them liberty to surround our foot with their horse, and to charge them in flank and rear, whilst they too briskly pursued the French foot to the town and took severall prisoners. In the mean tyme the Portuguese horse and an Irish regiment of foot, which some tyme before they had mounted on horseback, gave way. Most of the horse escaped with the E. of Gallaway, but it's thought the foot have fallen in the enemies hands, the towns refusing to receive horse or foott. Wee expect clearer and more certain accoumpts dayly.

The London Gazettes of May and June 1707 give detailed accounts of the defeat of Almanza. On 1st June 1707, Colonel Wade arrived in London with the official despatches.

Next two letters deal with the seizure by English customs' officers of Scots vessels laden with goods of foreign origin which arrived in London after 1st May 1707, from Scotland, into which they had been previously imported on payment of smaller duties than those prevailing in England.[1]

For THE EARL OF SEAFIELD, LORD CHANCELOR

My Lord,—I had the honour of yrs of the 6th some posts ago, but delay'd answering it til I shou'd speak w^t the Treasurer, who 's at Windsore. The Duke of Queensberry, my Lord Loudoun, and I went there a purpose to speak of what y^r Lop. wrote me and of the goods that are now come from Scotland. Loudoun and I are but this minut returned. My Lord Treasurer keept Naughtie's papers, and has given orders to inquire into it, and will then give me an answer to wryt to y^r Lop. He told us that he had alreddy given orders to the people belonging to the custome house to show all the favour to our marchants that posiblie they could consistant to law, but that he was to be in toun on Thursday and wou'd then speak to them again. I am indeed affraid that the goods will be seased, but I belive they will be made very easie as to their bail, and I hope the affair will be so manadged that they will not have much cause of complaint. We did all we cou'd, and I hope not without effect, but we will not give it over as long as our speaking can do any good. I did not at all doubt of y^r Lops. being receaved w^t satisfaction in the judicatures. I hope you will preceed long in them, wch I 'm sure will be to most people's likeing. T'other day when I had occation of speaking to the Queen, she told me that she had spoke to y^r Lop. and expected that you wou'd bring up w^t you a compleat account of the civill list and of the pensions she had given, and ordred me to put yr Lop. in mind of it, wch I told I shou'd do, but that I knew you did not want to be put in mind of any thing her Majestie recomended to you. My Lord Treasurer has been a little indispoased w^t a coald, so wryting is uneasie to him, but he desired me to give his service to yr Lop. My Lord Loudoun read yo Lops. letter to him, but I know he wryts to you, so I will not trouble you w^t any thing of that.

---

[1] *Historical MSS. Commission, Fourteenth Report*, App., Part iii., *Seafield MSS.*, pp. 221, 222,

We will long to hear from y^r Lop. after you receave ours concerning the equivalent. I wrote to you some dayes ago w^t the four English gentelmen of the equivalent, wch they are to deliver themselves. 'Tis only recomending them to your favour. This place is so dull and so little passing, that I will have but seldome occation of wryting to y^r Lop.; but when anything happens worth yr while, y^r Lop. may be sure I will not neglect giveing you an account of it. I am w^t all respect, My Lord, Yr Lps. most obedient and most humble servant,   MAR.

Whythall, Julie 15th, 1707.

Ten at night.

My brother wryts me of that affair w^t my Lord Glasgow being ended.

On the 20th June 1707 Seafield received a new warrant[1] for a commission as Lord High Chancellor of Scotland. Next year, on 13th May, he received a warrant[2] for a commission as Chief Baron of Exchequer.

For THE EARL OF SEAFIELD

MY LORD,—This afternoon I have ye honor to receave your Lop's. of ye 17th with ye memorall. I immedeatly got a meeting of ye Duke of Queensbery and ye Lords Secretaries. They had all taken leive of Windsor and designd to set out ye morrow for ye Bath, I mean ye Secretaries, for ye Duke is somwhat indisposed and can not travell for a day or two. Yet his Grace and ye Earle of Loudoun designe on the subject of ye memorall to goe back to Windsor the morrow, whither I shall have ye honor to attend them, that I may be ye better able to write what is to be said on it, for there Lops. can not well staye longer from ye Bath. I shall by this beg leive to give some answer to one point of ye memoriall, viz., ye provideing the necessarys for conage. I had a letter from Doctor Gregorie two posts agoe with a notte of ye severall things wanting, which I caryd immediatly to Sr Isack Newton and convinced him of ye necessity of a speedy dispatch,

---

[1] *State Papers (Scotland) Warrant Books,* vol. xxv. p. 21.

[2] *Ibid.,* p. 143.

soe much that I perswaded him to give ye necessary orders for preparing them without ye formes used in such cases, viz. of presenting a memorall to ye Treasury and then geting a referance and on that a report, soe that at this time people are at worke about them. Last night I met with ye merchants and ye solicetors of ye customes and adjusted ye paper ye merchants were to signe, and this day Mr. Wm. Graham signd. I have given ye Earle of Loudoun a coppy of ye paper which he transmitts to your Lop. By this post I send bills too for about 1500 ᶫᶦᵇ towards paying ye forces there. If I come from Windsor ye morrow, I hope to send ye rest next or ye following post. I am sorie ye business of ye merchants oaths will be determined befor your Lop. can receave my Lord Tres^{rs} letter on that subject. Whatever hapens in absence of ye Secretaries shall be communicat to your Lop. by, My Lord, Your Lop's. most humble and most obedient servt.,

DAVID NAIRNE.

Whithall, 21 *August* 1707.

Sir Isaac Newton was Master of the Mint of England. His letter, of 12th August 1707, to the Earl of Seafield, given at pp. 223, 224 *of the Seafield MSS. in the Historical MSS. Commission Fourteenth Report*, App., Part III., also refers to the conduct of the Scots mint.

For THE EARL OF SEAFIELD

MY LORD,—You know I am no statesman nor a medler in state effeyres, bot hearing the Parliament was like to abolish theCouncell in Scotland or North Brittayn, I judged it duty to give your Lordship notice, that it is thought it may occasion both confusion and discontent for the Churches by intrusiones, and such like other disorders may increase, if there be not some provision of some other judicatory to whom application may be made for redresse in such cases. Your Lordship knoweth there are too many discontents in this country already. I wish no occasion be given for more. . . . I pray God may preserve and blesse your Lordship, for the comfort of your noble relationes, and for the service of God, and your countryes good, and that God may guyde you and others

who are members of that high and honorable court. I
shall adde no more, bot that I am, My Lord, Your Lordships humble servant,   MR. G. MELDRUM.

Edr., Decr. 15, 1707.

The Scots Privy Council was abolished in 1708.

To THE RIGHT HONOURABLE MY LORD DESFURD
AT LONDAN.

DEAR JAMES,— . . . You will let me kno what truth
is in the matar as to what you wret about your marage.
I am litell capabell to give advies, tho a good wieff te
you be what a gret dell of my hapness depends on as
weall as yours. I wish that God may derect you and
your fathar in it, and it is from his over ruling goodness
that I expek a good event in it. For my advies in
generall, which is all I can give till I hir the partiklur
disayn, it is that you wold choys the doghter of a good
famaly—I min a sober senesabell pipell. And I can not
denay bot I wold wish you to mary in a famaly of
qualaty. I dou not min by quality only the nobility. I
wold not have hir much above your ouen eag, bot above
all sobirly and religuisely edecat, and I wold have you
inforem your seleff of hir parsonall qualatiys both as to
wit and inclanations. But all thos precousions ar mir
uncertantys, and tho you did as much as man could dou
yet you may be disapynted. Ther-for my first and last
advies and prayer is, that you may ernastly big Gods
directions, and that he may derect you in the matar. If
your fathar layes tw or thri befor you let mi kno what
they are. I wish your fathar nor you may not engag
rashly in anything. Remember the last. I wish you
halth and to hier frequantly from you. I am, your most
affectionat mothar,   ANNA SEAFIELD.

Cullan Dis, 1707

For THE RIGHT HONORABLE THE EARL OF
FINDLATR AT EBR.

Loundon, Decm. 27, 1707.

MY LORD,—I am glad to knou by Johnstun his later that

your Lop. is in good halth. I wish the continunce of it, and I must say that I am oblidged to your Lop. for the care ye heau of me in my abesence conserning Relogys affare. I do think that I am in no fear about him. I knou he is an man of an good forton and a considrable stock, houeuer I heau wreat to Jeames Bard about the busines conserns me. I woud not fear his warindes for much mor muney then I heau giuen him. Al the nous that we heau hear is only that we ar laying on gret soums of money to carie on the wars, and that we ar trubled woth the Squadrony, that is douing al that thy can for tacking auay the Counsel. Euerything is extrordnarly dear hear saue ladys, and thos that tack most of them hath the worst peneworthes. So wishing your Lop. an good nou yeir I continou, My Lord, Your Lops. affectionat son and most humble seruant,   PAT. OGILVIE.

MY LORD REGISTER'S LETTER about the calling in of
    Scots Coin, and about the New English Standards of
    Weights and Measures.

Edinburgh, Jan. 10*th*, 1708.

MY LORD,—This afternoon a committee of the Privie Council met, to consider off calling in the Scots coyne, and the giveing out the Inglish standarts of weights and measurs. There wes at the committee E. of Northesk, Lord President of the Session, Lord Advocat, Minto, Provest of Edinbrugh, and your humble servant. Some of the committee inclined to have all the Scots coyne call'd in at once, at least befor the 15th of March conform to a resolve of the Privie Council, when they made the setlement with the bank for receiveing in the forreign coyn, but several directors of the bank were at the committee, and asserted positively they would not be able to ansuear the demands might be upon them in that case, and if that method wes taken the countrey would be disapointed of a sufficient stock of current money, and their credite would be in danger. So the committee came to this resolution, that a proclamation should be issued on Munday pro-hibiteing the currency of the follouing species of Scots coyne, viz. old and new croun pieces, the fourty shilling, tuenty shilling, and ten shilling pieces, after the tenth of February nixt, but that the bank should receive these species at full valeu, untill the 25th off ffebruary. It wes thought fit to apoint the last day of its being received by the bank in ffebruary, because when the bank knous the amount of these species, and what forreign coyne is recoyned in the interim, they will be able to inform the Council hou soon they can take in the rest of the other species of the Scots coyne ; and it wes resolved, that it wes necessary befor the Session rose, the last touch should be given to the calling in of all other species of Scots coyne. As to the weights and measurs : Resolved that the standarts of the several weights and measures should be ordered to be given to the brughs that keeped the respective old standarts, but it wes thought no ways adviseable to isseu any proclamation, ordaineing all the weights and measurs to be reneued according to these standarts, for certainly that would bring a heavy charge upon the countrey, and might be the foundation of vexatious persuits against many poor people, and all that our neighbours of Ingland can be concerned in the matter is only with relation to the inland excyse, and export and import ; and as to the first there is an adjustment betuixt the justices of peace and commissioners of excyse, which will be a rule over the whole countrey. As to import and export, the standarts being given out, the commissioners of the customs can have from the several burrous the weights and measurs they need conform to the Inglish standart, and can soon adjust the proportion betuixt our old weights and measurs and the new ones, for the committee thought it wes necessary to be alse easy to the people as possible, without prejudice to the customs and excyse. I knou nothing else worth your Lop. while, but we long what to hear what becomes of the resolves of the house of Commons about our affairs, and of the new model of our Exchequer,—I am, My Lord,

Y. L. M. H. S.

MY LD ADVOCATS LETTER about Contributions for
Charitable uses and the Commissaryes

Ednr., 20*th Jan.* 1708.

MAY IT PLEASE YOr LP.—I am loath to give yor Lp.
any unnecessary trouble or diversion, but there are two
things at present occurs.   Yor Lop. hath been acquainted
with a design of a contribution for charity schools, and
for propagating Christian knowledge particularly in our
Highlands and Isles, and the project of it, which yor Lop.
both approved and encouraged, is generally well liked, only
the countenance of her Mats authority is thought wanting,
for which the draught of the proclamation inclosed is put
in my hand to be transmitted to yor Lp.   The draught tho
not so formal yet is sutable enough to the matter, and yor
Lp. upon revising may help what is amiss, but being told
that you would willingly give your best concurrence I
adventured to transmit it.   The other particular is concerning the commissaries for the pay and provision of the
fforces.   Their contract is now ended, and John Campbel,
who was the most active and serviceable among them, tells
me of a proposal made for a commissary to serve for a
sellary and to provid forrage at a certain rate but without
the poundage, which because of the uncertainty of prices
cannot be accepted.   But, my Lord, some course must be
taken in this affair before the first of ffebruary, otherways
the troups in the country may fall in some disordor.
And yor Lp. knows that John Campbel hath had the greatest
experience in this matter, and is most capable to provid
with the countrys ease and to the satisfaction of the
officers ;   and therfore he suggests to me that, if he be
ordored, he will continue to forrage the troups and refer
the sallary for his pains to be considered ;   but must also
be entrusted with the setting of the prices, which he doubts
not but the officers will be content with, and if he exceed
he may be also controuled by the fiers, but this trust may,
and it seems must be given for a year at least, untill some
other course be setled.   This he desired me to write to yor
Lp., and with all that an answer is necessary again the

beginning of ffebruary, for then he must pay his sub
commissaries, otherways they will give over providing the
troups, and therfore he will expect ordors from above.—
I am, My Lord, Yr Lops. most humble and most obed^t
servit^r,   JA. STEUART.

SᴿWILL: BAIRD'S LETTER to the EARL OF SEAFIELD
ABOUT THE ELECTION OF A COMMONER FOR LOTHIAN

MY LORD,—Ther are a greatt deall of pains ta5keing hear,
for secureing the ensueing elections thowrow the shyres
of North Brittain, and I thowght it my dewtie to lett yowr
Lo. know that I have designed to stand for the electione
heer in MidLothian, and for that end I begg yowr Lo^s
protectione and approba°n, and I can assur yowr Lo. that
I stand addictted to no partie, but shall be verie readie to
goe in to yowr Lo^s measures. Ther are severalls in the
shyre who will deferr verie much to your Lo^s approbatione
as Mr. Baird, who is a new purchasser heer, and severall
uthers, therfor your Lo^s declaring in my favors will confirm them in ther inclination of bestoweing ther votes one
me, and your Lo. may always make compt upon me as,—
My Lord, Your Lo^s most humble and most obedient
servant,   WM. BAIRD.

Edr., ye 19 *feb*: 1708.

Sir William Baird of Newbyth, eldest son of Sir John Baird.
Lord Newbyth was made a baronet in his own right during his
father's lifetime. He succeeded in 1698, and died in 1737. He
was a far-off relative of Mr. James Baird of Chesterhall, the writer
of next letter.

For the EARL OF SEAFIELD

MY LORD,—After no small trouble, Captain Charters hes,
for ane overvaloue payed him, yeilded his interest of
Cranstoune in Mid Lothian to me. This, if I wer infeft,
capacitats me to vote in the enshewing ellection of a
member to represent the shyre in the enshewing Breitish
Parliat. Adresses mor then on hes bein already made to
me on this account, amongst whom Sir William Baird is
on, and appears to be well staited in this juncture with the
gentrie of the shyre. I told him, as the treuth is, that

under God I owed my ryse and being to your Lop., and what ever should be your inclinations in that matter, if signefied to me, the same would infallably determine me, bot nothing els should alienate me from his interest. And besydes I told him I knew his relation to the famely of Tueddell, who was of the Squadrona, naither did I know hou your Lop. and they stood assorted to ūyrs, qrupon he made solemne protestàtions and asseverations, that he was in no pairtie nor under ingadgement to non, that he hade vast honour and esteem for your Lop., ffound you alwayes upon the right and saife syde, and declaired that if he should be the man, he would take your Lops. advice and goe into your measurs, and promised to give it under his hand to your Lop., which I heirwith transmitt. If your Lop. countinance him in this matter with me, he will get I suppose ūyr tuo, viz., Graycrook and Mr. Patrick ffalconer of Murtoun ; bot if uyrwayes he will get naither of us, ffor I doe assure your Lop. no interest shall ever alter me from depending upon your Lop., and contributing my weak interest and endeavors to support yours, and I ame in all deuty, My Lord, Your Lops. most obedient and obleidged humble servant, JA. BAIRD.

Edinburgh, 2*ith ffebry*. i708.

On 29th June 1706 Mr. James Baird, Writer to the Signet, and Depute Clerk of Justiciary, who had been appointed to that office in room of his late father-in-law, Mr. John Anderson, was allowed by royal warrant a salary of £40 in place of the old salary of £10.[1]

The treaty of union carried against the Jacobites, who, in view of its political advantages to the exiled Stuarts, were keen for the independence of Scotland, against those of the type of Fletcher of Saltoun, who advocated a federal union, against the weight of the Presbyterian Church establishment and other interests, had few whole-hearted supporters in Scotland. These did not arise in popular numbers until, after the risings of the 'Fifteen and 'Forty-five, the long-delayed advantages of free trade with England outweighed the more immediate exasperations and defects of the Anglified rule of Scotland that immediately ensued. That rule had at once introduced into Scotland unpopular English methods

---

[1] *State Papers (Scotland) Warrant Books*, vol. xxii. pp. 62-64.

of collecting revenue, had instituted alien Commissions of the Peace and a Court of Exchequer in the English style, and was engaged in abolishing the old Privy Council of Scotland, and in extending further toleration to Episcopacy. The memoirs of Colonel Hooke, a Jacobite emissary from Louis xiv. to Scotland, the writings of Lockhart of Carnwath, a disappointed placeman, and Defoe's political works, give us glimpses of a political intrigue in which the old Chevalier's adherents sought to take advantage of the unpopularity of the union, by combining such extremes as the Cavalier and Catholic Jacobite with the westland Cameronian Whig. The old active supporters and mainstay of the revolution of 1689, the westland Covenanting Whigs of Galloway, Lanark, and Ayr, discontented with the union, were sulkily, through some of their agents, flirting with Jacobitism. The unsettled state of Scotland, and the fairly concrete promises of support carried from that country to the court of Louis by Colonel Hook, the young laird of Boyne, and others, made a French and Jacobite invasion of Scotland in the interests of the Chevalier a feasible counter-stroke, for the Duke of Marlborough with Queen Anne's troops and the allied Dutch were pressing hard on the French in Flanders, in the campaign of 1707. The victory of Almanza in Spain, gained by the Duke of Berwick, gave Louis additional encouragement, and the French invasion of Scotland was planned. However much the ostensible cause was Jacobite, Louis's predominant motive was to seek relief from the pressure of Marlborough in Flanders, and to that extent alone it temporarily succeeded. In the remaining letters here published is given a wonderfully complete, original, and contemporary account of this invasion, which amplifies and corrects in many points the brief accounts of our historians, based on the writings of Hooke, Lockhart, and Defoe. An interesting reprint of a journal by an officer of the Dunkirk squadron, in their intended invasion against Scotland, printed in Maidment's *Analecta Scotica* (first series), p. 190, gives an account of the episode from the Jacobite point of view. Next year the Naval Records Society may publish an account of this French invasion, drawn from the Admiralty Records of Great Britain and edited by the writer.

To WILLIAM LORIMER, Chamberlane TO THE EARLE OF SEAFIELD at Cullen

London, Febry. 25, 1708.

D. Cousine,—My Lord has write you fully about his private bussines, and I am to tell you that wee are allarmed with a ffrench invasion from Dunkirk. There are great preparations makeing there. They say about 12000 men are to be embarqued and twice as many stands of arms with 2000 horse. We have no particular information where they designe, but I hope there project will be disappointed, for the Queen and Dutch will have a ffleett of fyfty men of warr in few dayes to block them up in there harbours, and if this be at sea before they gett out they dare not attempt it. I shall give you further information as wee learn it, and advyse you to take care of my Lord's papers and other things if it be found necessary. Maldavat[1] owes me three hundred and twenty pound Scotts with two years @rent preceeding Candlemas last. Give my humble service to my mother and all ffriends. Blessed be God I am much better than I was. My Lord Deskfoord has keept his health very ill this winter. The phisicians have advysed him to drink asses milk and Bath water, and finds himself better with it. I pray God preserve him, and am, yours,   John Philp.

For THE EARL OF SEAFIELD

Edr., 2d March 1708.

May it please yr Lp.—. . . Her Mat[s] letter to the Privy Council, intimating the informations you have of a threatned invasion, came by a flying paquet to my hand Sunday about ten at night. The nixt morning I caused the clerk intimat to the Privy Councilors in town to meet at nyne acloak, and y[r] Lp. will see by the minuts that we met a full quorum and read her Mat[s] letter, and what ensued upon it. My Lord, the Major General [2] hath been carefull that the troups wherever they are should be ready to march upon a call. He also gave an account of the

---

[1] Hay of Muldavit, Banffshire.   [2] The Earl of Leven.

fforts and garrisons, that generally they were ill provided of amunition, but that he had writ about this formerly and expected a good supply from England. In discoursing of the state of the country severals thought it intollerable that meeting houses should be suffered and specially in Edin^r, where the preachers are not qualified in law nor do pray for Queen Ann by name, but in effect under the notion of our soveraign or some such terme, wherin they certainly includ the Prince of Wales or King James the eight, which is too visible an encouragment to that disaffected party and a manifest weakening of the hands of her Mats. good subjects, and therfore did occasion the ordors given in the minuts. The Highlands were also spoke of, and the clerk ordored to produce the last lists of the chiftains and their cautionries, which is to be laid before the Council tomorrow. Dispatches are sent to call in the rest of the Councilours, but farder intelligence is expected every day from above, and in the meantyme nothing I hope will be wanting that is in the Councils power. But the truth is that generally the country is ill provided in arms, and as yor Lp. knows not very well satisfied with the union, and yet I do not apprehend that many will be found so desperat as to joyn with the French. And their number of 6000 men, with the quantity of arms 12000 firelocks and six thousand case of pistols, appears to many to be rather a design for amusement and diversion than for a solid invasion, so that I hope the divine providence our great protection, with her Mats. care and prudence, shall quickly dissipat our present feares. But certainly all honest men and true countrymen cannot but abhor even the design of this invasion, as that which threatens all confusion and ruin. My Lord, I am an old and dying man, but shall not be wanting to my outmost both to her Matie and my country, only I wish that I could serve better, and that it might please the Lords of her Mats Privy Council to lay no more upon me than I am able to bear.—I am, My Lord, Y^r Lops. most humble and most faithfull servit^r,   JA. STEUART.[1]

---

[1] The Lord Advocate.

MY LORD JUSTICE-CLERK, CONCERNING THE THREATENED INVA-
SION, MR. INGLIS'S AFFAIR, AND MY LORD WHYTLAW'S PENSION.

For THE EARL OF SEAFIELD

Edinbr., 2d Merch 1708.

MY LORD,—What comes from your Lo. is alwayes
acceptable to me   Twas what I could not exspect your Lo.
should give your self the trouble to writt accŧs of ye
proceedings in Parliat.   I have had occassion to see the
prints, and further I have not enquired.   I am as much
now out of the road of publick bussines, as ever any
thought me unfitt for it.   The Advocat yesterday morning
called the Councell, when hir Maties letter was read.
Twas very satisfying to know the precautions the Queen has
taken to prevent the designs of the enemye, and thou 'tis
not to be doubted they are encouraged from this, and yt by
more y^n ordinarye assurances, yet I still hope as yr designes
have hitherto proven abortive they will no less at this time.
I have formerly used the freedome w^t your Lo. as to discourse you upon the discouragemts were justly taken to
medle in makeing discoveries of bade practises agst. ye
government, and while the knowen unfriends have such
influence, and friends endeavours slighted, I shall think no
wonder enemyes take y^r advantage and improve oppor-
tunities.   Your Lo. pardon this freedome.   It's more then
perhaps I ought to have adventured upon.   I beleeve by this
post Sir John Inglis gives your Lo. the trouble of a letter.
He was concerned he had not the honour to kiss your
Lo. hands while he was at London.   His time was but
short, being under necessity to hast home, the Ld. President
pressing hard upon him in his absence, in relation to his
claim upon North Berwick ; and scarse is he at home when
he is required by E. Roseberrie to answer to ane appeal his
Lo. has moved in the Hous of Lords.   This appeal or protest
for remeed of law was taken in ye year 1695, and never
moved in since.   'Tis about ye fishing the water of Cramond.
I need not enlarge to your Lo.   You know more yn I doe
in ye matter, for I see your Lo. was yn for Sir John.   We
are altogether strangers as to ye forms of proceeding in

such things. I should wish the Lords would lay doun rules wch we in ye north may be apprysed of, for it may appear hard for a young gentleman to be forc't to leave his studies abroad to attend a considerable action before our sessions, and at ye same time, or sooner after yn 'tis possible for him, to attend ye Hous of Lords. Your Lo. kindnes to your country and to this gentleman in parlar would appear in preventing any procedour in our appeals this session of Parliat., and yt some course may be laid doun how we may know ye method either in prosecuting or defending.—I am w^t. all respect, My Lord, Your Lo. most humble and obedient servant,   AD. COKBURNE.

I returne your Lo. thanks for your good opinion of my wife's cause before the session. Your Lo. elbou made me all the opposition could be. 'Tis not quit ended, but I putt on patience, for yt will even overcome what delays humour has occassioned me. The Lords of Session have been putt in hopes of some addition to yr sallaries. I shall make it welcome q^n it comes, but must be allowed to say I might have exspected some more care of my concerns upon ye civill list, especially in relation to qt was due to Lord Whitlaw. Your Lo. well knows 'twas not in ye nature of a ordinarie pension, and if neither his services nor mine cane procure to have justice done me, yet it will not be denyed me I have served faithfully. When I hade ye honour to wait last summer on my Lord Thesr., I did plead his favour in it. I did since writt to his Lo., but it were too great presumpton in me to exspect my concerns should take up one minut of his thoughts. My Lord, 'twas reading over ye last words in you Lo. gave me a rise for this too long p.s.

Lord Rosebery's appeal to the House of Lords seems to have been one of the earliest from Scotland after the union. It had been taken in 1695 to the Scots Parliament.

For THE EARL OF SEAFIELD

MY LORD,—I was to wait on your Lordship when at London, but had not the good fortune to find you at home, and my affaires hasting me sooner home than I expected obleiged me to fail in my duty of asking your Lordships commands hither. My Lord the Earle of Rosberry has wakened his appeal of an decreet of the Lords of Session concerning the fishing of Cramond water, which decreet having been obtained by your asistance I now beg your Lordships concurrence to mantain it in the House of Lords, and to divert its being determined this session of Parliament, and begs your Lordship may pardon this trouble from, My Lord, your Lordships most humble and obleiged servant, Jo. INGLIS.

Edinburgh, March 2d, 1708.

For THE EARL OF SEAFIELD

Ednr., 6 *March* 1708.

MAY IT PLEASE YOR LP.,—In yours to me about this threatened invasion, you appear'd sollicitous that the Presbyterians specially their ministers should shew their zeal against it ; and I must confess that tho many of them be but ill affected toward the union, yet I never apprehended that any of them would be so desperat as to joyn with a French popish party to the overthrow of religion and liberties and all dear to men. I have heard that there is a manifesto come home promising the fairest things on the p. Prince of Wales part, but I can neither get a sight of it nor the knowledge of particulars ; and there are also whisperings that the French have a correspondence here more than is imagined, but yet by all the inquiry I can make I cannot give any farder information. However the Commission of the last Gen[ll] Assembly met here Wednsday last. I was not in caice to attend them, but I heard that on Thursday some motion'd that this threatened invasion did call for a solemn fast, but then they fell into their ordinary scruples about the power of inditing fasts, which considering the late fast we have had I thought very unseasonable. However on Friday some of the bretheren came to me and spoke of the motion had been made for a fast. I told them that their zeal against the invasion was very just, and would be acceptable, but that the questions

moved about the power of indicting fasts were very unseasonable, and therfore I wish'd that some of the graver
men of the Commission might be appointed to confer
with such of the government as are also of the Commission,
to know their mind and to signify to them that this emergent did greatly call for fasting and humiliation, if the
government would go in to the motion, but if not that the
Commission would at least signify to all ministers and
Presbytries to stir up the people to fervent prayer and
supplications for to avert this invasion, and I added, that
this way might be readier and more expedit than a general
national fast.   And so we parted, but when the Commission met, bretheren were forward for a solemn national
fast, and some of them so forward as to ordain it, albeit the
civil sanction would not be obtained.   And thus an act was
brought in for a general national fast to be keept the first
Thursday of Aprile, albeit many thought that before that
tyme the hazard might rather be over, or the fast too late ;
and the motion of recommending it to ministers and
Presbitrys was laid aside.   I must also regret to yor Lp.,
for no doubt you will hear it, that severals stuck not to
say that this manner of appointment was better and
would be more satisfieing than the appointment of the last
fast from England, and that also they would have the
day the first Thursday of Aprile insert in the act, tho the
day uses to be left blank, that the fast might proceed tho
the civil sanction should not be obtained.   My Lord I can
only regret that so good and solemn a work should be thus
manadged.   The act indeed is fairly drawn, both as to
the causes and with all respect to the revolution and her
Ma^{ts} person and government, and against a popish successor and the threatened invasion, and they have also
appointed some of their number to attend the Council
Tusday nixt for the civil sanction, but many have their
feares how the Council may understand this, albeit I see all
good men tender above all things that there be no breach.
My Lord, these things I write to you plainly, both to
prevent misinformation and other ill consequences.   I
hope God shall avert our danger and our fears, and lykways

give us all a better mind on all such occasions.—I am, My Lord, Y^r Lps. most humble and most obed^t servit^r,

J. St.[1]

For THE EARL OF SEAFIELD

MY LORD,—I had the honor of your Lop's.   I was very sensible of your concern to preserve a court judged necessary for the peace of the countrey and welfare of the church.   By a letter from Elgin at this time we are informed that the dissaffected boast already that there will be no Council[2] to complain to.   I shall heartily wish what is substituted may ansuer the design.   We have done but little in the Commission at this time.   Mr. Black is continued at Perth, but it is humbly expected yor Lop. w^t others or freinds will concur for obtaining a presentation to a minister well qualified for that post.   At the close of our meeting there was a motion made for a fast through this whole church.   The certain prospect we had of its being urged at the Assembly with greater inconveniencies, and the hopes of doing some service to the Queen at this juncture by it among the people, after we understood most of the Councellors upon the place were for it, prevailed w^t us to goe in to the overture.   The draught is herewith sent, and the Privy Council is to be addressed Tuesday nixt about it.   My Lord, it is earnestly intreated yor Lop. would be pleased to mind the proclamation against profaness, and I doe also presume to beg on the university's behalf you wou'd be pleased to mind the gift, which was promised to be dispatched when I left London, the granting wherof wou'd be of good use at this time.—I am, My Lord, Yor Lop's. most humble most obliged and most obedient servant,   Jo. STIRLING.[3]

Edr., 6th March 1708.

---

[1] The Lord Advocate.   [2] The Scots Privy Council.
[3] Principal of Glasgow University.

For MR. WILLIAM LORIMER, Chamberlane to MY LORD SEAFIELD, at Cullen, Banffshyre

London, March 8th, 1708.

Dear Cousine,—Wee have now certain information that the ffrench designe ane invasion upon Scotland. They have brought eleven men of warr from Brest to joyn those at Dunkirk, and the pretended Prince of Wales is there to come with them with 10000 men and a considerable quantities of amunition and arms. The ffrench ffleett will be near 32 men of warr besides transports and priva-teers, but I hope in God the English and Dutch ffleet, qch are above 40 men of warr, will stop there project, and if they cannot block them up in there harbours will beat them off the seas ; and if the wind shall favour them to gett landed, the Queen is to bring from fflanders 20,000 men, qch cannot miss effectually to defeat there projects. It's reported they designe to land in fforth or at Aberdeen, but whatever happen you may have my Lord Seafields papers in such a readines that they may be secured in some safe place, if there be any hazard in that part of the countrey, for where they land first they will doe damnage to the countrey and lands of those who are not affected to there interest before any releef come up. Our officers are ordered to there severall posts. The Parliat. and City of London have addressed the Queen, that they will stand by her with there lives and ffortunes against the common enemy, and it's certain, though these preparations may amuse us a litle, the bad consequences will be soon remedied and the danger easily prevented. Give my humble duty to Castlefield, and tell him what's above, and that his sone getts his commission in my [Lord] Strathnavers regiment, and will come to Scotland very soon. My Lord Deskfoord, blessed be God, is much better. We will be all at Edin^r about the end of next moneth. Give my humble duty to my mother and sisters to yor wife and children. Give the enclosed to my mother, qch comes from my wife.—I am, D. C., your most affectionat cousine and humble servant,

JOHN PHILIP.

Next letter,[1] from the Earl of Sunderland, one of Queen Anne's Secretaries of State, to the Earl of Leven, conveyed the latest official information regarding the invasion. The action of the Privy Council of Great Britain, while the Scots Privy Council was in existence, in issuing warrants for the arrest of suspected rebels in Scotland is interesting.

For THE EARL OF LEVEN

Whitehall, March 9th, 170$\frac{7}{8}$.

MY LORD,—Yor Lordp. will receive by this express the warrants of the Council of Great Britain for the seizing 31 persons of those her Maj[ty] has most reason to suspect. They are addressed to your Lodp. not only as commander in chief in that part of Britain, but as one in whom her Maj[ty] has a particular confidence, and who she is satisfy'd will execute them with the greatest zeal and diligence. As for the particular maner of doing it, you will be so fully instructed by the Queens order, that I will not trouble you with anything of that, but begg leave to refer you to the orders and instructions you will receive from him.[2] The letters that are come in since you left London confirm the arrival of the pretended Prince at Dunkirk with some 12 or 15 battallons of French and Irish ; and yesterday we had an account of 5 men of war and 6 privateers being got into Graveling from Brest and St. Malo's. However we have so great a strength at sea, and Major General Cadogan has got our troops in such a readyness for embarking that I hope the enemies will not venture out, but we must not rely upon that, but take the best precautions we can to secure ourselves and disarm our enemies at home. I have nothing more to trouble yor Lordp. with, but to wish you good success in all you shall undertake.—I am with great respect, My L[d]., Yo[r] Lodp[s] most obedient serv[t],

SUNDERLAND.

In the memoirs of Colonel Hooke one figure seen ˙flitting through the maze of Jacobite intrigue is James Ogilvie, younger of Boyne, at this time a broken and a landless man, with his expectant estate falling into the hands of his relative the Earl of Seafield. With no hope of preferment except through revolution,

---

[1] *State Papers Scotland*, Ser. 2, 1707-10.   [2] Probably the Earl of Seafield.

he dipped deeply in Jacobite intrigue, and as doer for the Duke of Athole we find him passing between Scotland and France, and flitting about Scotland arranging for a French descent and a Jacobite rising in Scotland. The two next letters deal with his landing in Scotland in February 1708.

For THE RIGHT HONOURABL THE EARELL OF SEA-FIELD, Lord High Chanchlar of Scotland, Londan.

March 9, 1708.

DEAREST HEART,—Tho I have nothing to say, yet I dou wret all-most every week, and I fear my leetres is rather trubelsum then aceptabell. We are migitly aleremed hier with the invation from France. I send you a leter to Castilfild. I shall say nothing of the matar. It is sead the leard of Boyn is a colnall. I wish you wold yet midell no mor in his affears, bot I kno this is impartanat, siens you have so farr gon in that matar alredy. God of his infinit maresy direct you and preserive you and pour James, who I hier hath bein very ill this wintar. I should think his oun contary aer should be good for him, bot that I dou not disayr him hier whin thir is such comosions in the contary. I most agen pray God to preserive you, and only add that I am most intirly yours

[ANNA SEAFIELD.]

You have on ship loded with bear. I hir my Lord is at his mothares, bot hi hath nathar sent nor bein hiar.

To NICHOLAS DUMBAR of Castellfeld, Shirreff dpt. of Bamf

SIR,—I forgot to writ concerning that matr, but this present commossion which is suddenly in all apearanc to fall in by a Frenc descent maks peopl they know not how to order ther busenes. No doubt ye hav heard of the gentl-man hes set a shor heer from Franc and who is gon to Boynd and thenc to the Hichlands and thorrow ye kingdom. If ye hav not heard it, then I can assur you the truth of it. He wes all night the 29 Feby in William Hards at Nether-miln, and went away the first of March befor the sun tuo hours ; he landed about 6 hours at even. He passed for a Edr. merchant. The ship wes about 16 or 20 guns 70 to 90 men. Giv not me for your author. Giv my servic to the Countess. I pray God preserv her and all her femily.—I am your most affectionat frend and humble svt.,

ALEX^r GAIRDNE.[1]

For THE EARL OF SEAFIELD

Edinr., March 11, 1708.

MY LORD,—The Councill mett again yesterday, and the journalls are inclosed. I was so ill upon Tuesday last, that I could neither attend the Councill nor writt your Lop. We now begin to belive ane invasion is designed, and upon my word the enemy could not have hade a fitter oppor- tunity since the revolu°ne, for their is nothing heir to with- stand a very small force, and perhaps now experience will show what will be the fatall consequences of the want of our Councill, for I am apt to belive their orders will not be obeyed, knowing they can doe nothing after the last of Apryll, so that they only have to keip out of the way till that tyme. I wish I may be disappointed but am afraid of the contrair, and I am not singular in my opinion. I am in all duty, My Lord, Your Lo. most oblidged and most humble servt,   Ro^t FFORBES.

Sir Robert Forbes was clerk to the Scots Privy Council which was about to cease.

The allegiance of the Whigs of the west country was somewhat suspected. The following letter and that of 19th March from the magistrates of Glasgow to Seafield set out their views during the crisis, when in spite of the anticipations of Hooke and Lockhart they rallied to the revolution settlement and Queen Anne.

MY LORD,—Your Lordship having on all occasions appear'd for the interest of the toun of Glasgow, is the reason why we give your Lop. the trouble of a coppie of ane address from this city, which we sent to the Secretary that attends to be by him presented to her Majesty. We pray your Lop. to second our address with your Lops. countenance, and recomend us as hearty in our affection to her Majesties person and government, ffor we assure your

---

[1] The laird of Troup.

Lop. we shall demonstrat, so farr as we have access, our zeall to serve her Majesties interest, and how much we are, My Lord, Your Lops. most humble and most obedient ser^{tts},

ROB. RODGER.
JOHN BOWMAN.
THOMAS SMITH.
J° BROWN.

Glasgow, 12th March 1708.

For THE EARL OF SEAFIELD

Eder., 13th *Mertch* 1708.

MY LORD,—After staying four nights with my mother and feinding hir in the way of recoverie, in three dayes I com back to this place yesternight, qhere I shall with all caire attend. The road was werie deip with snou and froast in the night. Yesterday of Montroas cuming from the north appeared fortie ships, and about the sam tym of Berrick tuentie eight, the first having a flag. Qtt they are is not knouen. This toun is werie faire, but much of the north ill affected by a mistacke of the excyse. I shall be cairefull of your Lo. concernes as of my lyfe. So frie to command, My Lord, Your Lo. fathfull humble servant,

ALEX^r OGILVIE.

For THE EARL OF SEAFIELD

Ed., 13th *Mertch*, 8 *at night*, 1708.

MY LORD,—Since the last express sent of at three ackloack, the accompts beare that from Dunbar ane hundreth saile of ships have bein sein passing to the north, and just nou there is one express from Eylle beares that they uare sein pass by this eivening. I hope advyse uill be sent hou to behave on so sad ane emergent, qhich in all licklehood uill rouin this nation before reliefe can be sent, for the feu forces heere will be necessetat to save themselves by flight, and maney of the cuntrie uill doe aney thing to save themselves and there effects. As for my selfe I intend thoro the help of the Allmightie to be fathefull to hir Majestie, and in hir service for the defence of religion to wenture my selfe and all I have. God mack all ueill.

Mr. David com just now, butt no lyn from your Lo., which is not right, for on so speciall ane occasion ye should have wreaten and given advyce to, My Lord, Your Lo. fathfull servant, ALEX^r OGILVIE.

The British fleet under Sir John Byng had been for some time blockading the French fleet in Dunkirk. The French, however, eluded the blockade on 6th March, and with two days' start sailed northward. They overshot their objective, the Firth of Forth, and by the time they doubled south the British fleet had arrived off the Forth. The issue was really being tried while Lord Forglen was writing his letters of Saturday the 13th March. His estimate of the numbers of ships was much exaggerated. The 'ane hundreth saile' is superinduced in the letter on the word 'twentie.'

To THE RIGHT HONOURABLE THE EARLE OF SEAFIELD, LONDON

Edinburgh, ye 14th March 1708.

MY LORD,—I had this day your Lops. letter of the 9th by the first express. The second is not yett arryved, but is nou of noe consequence. This comes by a flying packquett to give ane accompt that Sir George Bings with 30 men of war under his comand came up with and actackqued the French squadron off of Montross yesterday the 13th instant betwixt the hours of 4 or 5 in the evening, but the French retired so fast that the best halfe of Sir George squadron could not come up with them. The engagement continoued till it wes dark, and I hope they would mett againe nixt morning, ane accompt qrof I expect with great impatince, and am hopefull to have it some tyme too morrow. As soon as I receave any such accompt I will be sure to transmitt it by a flying pacquett. I am nou setting about the obeying of the orders I received this day by the express, which your Lop. may expect ane accompt of within a few dayes. I shall give your Lop. noe furder trouble nou, but assuring you that I am, My Lord, Your Lop. most humble and most obedient servant,

LEVEN.

The orders referred to were evidently those contained in Lord Sunderland's letter of 9th March to arrest suspected rebels in Scotland.

For THE RIGHT HONOURABLE MY LORD FORGLEN
AT EDR.   these heast

ffeteressie March 14*th*, 1708.

MY LORD,—Since that from Montross I gave your Lo.
som small accoumpt of a fleet of great ships seen of this
cost on ˙Saturday last, I'l give you the trouble of
reading what farder accoumpts I have heard and seen of
ym. As they cam by Montross, that toun, I told your Lo.,
was in great dread of ym̄, and I stayd yr till they were
past the toun and horsed ȳn, qch gave me occation to see
the whole ingagement as I went on the rod, qch is heer
affter related. I shall not trouble you wᵗ my owen, perhaps
not so perfite accoump of the matter, but heir give your Lo.
the double of a letter wryten by a gentilman of undoubted
creadet, who hes inquered about the storie. The letter is
as followes dericke for the E. Marischall, who is heir just
now :—

MY LORD,—The news your Lo. gott does not seem
groundless. Caterlaine[1] is positive ther was a skirmish att
sea yesterday, qc̄h began of Bervy about 3 aclok, and he
saw two destinck fleets, on consisting of about 26 saill the
oȳr about 30, and 4 ships at a distance from either. Affter
some scattering single shots he saw 5 of the last fleet of
great bigness and forse attack tuo of the first fleet about
yr̄ owen size, qch tuo mentainained a runing fight from
betwixt 4 and 5 to eight, yt they gott out of his sight.
He saw sevurall broadsides given on both sides and the
watter visubly rise wᵗ the ball. He thought the tuo shot
much sharper then the 5, who wer much blounter. He saw
no boarding nor disableing. The tuo had the advantag
of the wind, and during the time they wer in exercise the
fleet to qc̄h the 5 belonged mad the best of ther way off.
The Montross seamen are landed and tell strange stories.
They say they were French who took them abourd, and
that they were brawlie intertained the first night, to witt
Friday, but that when this oȳr fleet cam up upon them
they were in a great confusion. The ship they wer in

---

[1] A Kincardineshire laird.

was not ingaged but had 500 men in hir.   She and ane oȳr
who hes as many lost the fleet, and are yett on the coast.
They sounke ther boat and hes sent 8 of them ashor, and
keepts tuo to pillut them where they are bound, qch they
say was to have been in the Firth yisterday, if the fleet had
not ingaged them.   They tell that K. J. was irt the fleet,
but they know nothing of the sucsess of the ingagment,
haveing been separat.   The fleet we see to the north-east
is certainly the fleet qc̄h attacked, qc̄h we take to be the
English and Dutch.   This is all I can learen.   A short
tyme will give us the certaintie.   I wish your Lo. all
hapienes, adeu.   This of the 13 deat.

.   Thus your Lo. hes that letter transcrived.   I am told
som of the abov mentioned fleets touk tuo uȳr boats w^t
six men in each, qc̄h are not as yett returnd; and I am told
that great shooting hes been heard this night by a fleet that
is farr off att sea.   What accoumpts may be fourder had
of these fleets tym will produce.   It is werie probable the
English and ffrench have mett.   It was on of the most
deverting shows I ever see to behold ther firing and ingaging
on Saturday as I did, qc̄h I have given your Lo. ane
attested accoumpt of.   I see the ball as rebuted raise the
watter strongly, qc̄h I till now thought to be the sourage
on the watter, for we could hardly know if it was a reaill
ingagment, since I see non of the ships disabled.   I am
sheur they fired sevurall thousand shot.   I hop your Lo.
will pardon the trouble of this long letter and belive me to
bee, My Lord, your Lo. most obedient and most humble
serv^t,   [*signature torn off*]

The fleets wer only about tuo or three miles or yrby
of land, and when they cam up to Bervie they wer not ovor
halfe a mile from our vew, at which tym they begun to fire
fastest, and I thought ther wold have been neer tuintie
saill ingaged.   At Bervie they mad out to the sea, and the
smoke of ther gouns eclipsed seavrals of these lay furdest
of.   Neer Montross I see on ship turn from the front and
fall in to the shor.   I conclouded hir disyn was to sound.
Your Lo. freinds att Alardess are in good health.   My Lady
Anna is werie feard lest the French land neer hir.

For THE EARL OF SEAFIELD

Edr., 15*th March* 1708.

MY LORD,—I had wrytten to your Lop. by the last flying packett, but being in bed and sound sleeping when Mr. Watson called, my servants neglecghted to waken me, which did very much trouble me. This afternoon the English fleet came in to the road of Leith the wind being easterly, and on Saturndays night the French haveing outsailled save one ship, whereof your Lop. hes the enclosed account. All dew care shall be had of your concerns. It is confidently reported young Boynd landed in Angus.— I continue, My Lord, your ffaithfull hum^le serv^t,

ALEX^r OGILVIE.

To THE RIGHT HONORABLE THE EARLE OF SEAFEILD, LORD CHANCELLOR OF SCOTLAND, LONDON

MY LORD,—The journalls of this days sederunt of Counsell are inclosed. Your Lop. will hear from oyr hands, yt the ffrench fleet supposed to be at Aberdeen upon Sunday last appears now to have been Sr George Bings squadron, which putts this place in some further quyet. The ffrench shipe taken is said to be valueable both in persons and in money. It is to be wished yt any resolves of the House of Comons in relation to this invasion wer sent down and dispersed heir among the people, which I am perswaded will produce good effects. The Chiftans of clanns are imediatly to be called in, but I cane scarce understand what good yt cane produce, when the endureance of Counsell is so short, and which they but too weell know, and will doubtless lay hold on.—I am, My Lord, Your Lops. most obedient and humble servant,

RO^t FFORBES.

Edr., 16*th March* 1708.

For THE EARL OF SEAFIELD

Ed:, 16 *Mertch* 1708, 8 *at night.*

MY LORD,—This morning there com ane express from Aberdein with a letter from the Baylives and Provest, bearing that on Saboth last the French ware before there toun. It made a great stirr heere, Sir George Bing being in this harbor. By the computation of tym and other sircumstances it appeares to have bein Sir George. Liven and a feu of the Councell met with S. G. at Leith this afternoon, and it eases the mynds of maney. There are a good deall of wailouable goods in the *Salseburrie*, such as pleat and gold. We long to heare of Cadogan, and pray your Lo. favor me with a lyn to keep my countenance with these ask qhen I heard from you. Trulie I doe not mynd, but still am, My Lord, your Lo. fathfull, humble servant,

ALEX^r OGILVIE.

The *Salisbury* was the sole trophy of the sea fight. She was captured from the French off Montrose by Captain Thomas Gordon, who sometime commanded the *Royal William* in the Scots navy, and who was then in command of the *Leopard*. Major-General Cadogan had by this time sailed from Flanders for Newcastle with troops to reinforce the army in Scotland, and Louis's design of weakening the forces pressing him in Flanders was so far attained.

For THE EARL OF SEAFIELD

Edinbr, 16th March 1708.

MY LORD,—The frequent accts. the Earle of Leven gives of q̄t occurrs here will be very satisfying, that at last our warme alarums have all evanished in nothing. Indeed had not Sir Geo Bing come up Saturday morning this place had been in unspeakable confusion. But hir Maties care of us and the ready assistance of the fleet is q̄t honest people ought never to forget. We had acct. this day from Aberdeen of a fleet being seen near ỹt place Sunday last, but after enquirie we find 'twas Sir Geo Bing. We doe not yet hear of any persons stirring. Severals are of opinion the enemy will yet attempt to land. I shall not contradict it, but I'm sure yr measurs have failed ym for once, and for all yr exspectations of multitudes to join ym, honest men keeps as yet ye croun of ye casaway.

Your Lo. allow my friend Mr. Colline M'Kenzie who has bought Sir James M'Kenzies place of clerk to ye Exq̄r, a share of your Lo. favour, ỹt he be not neglected qn ye

Exqr is establisht. Tis w^t a reluctancy I give your Lo. trouble of this kind, for I must judge it's so ỹ your Lo. takes no notice either of Wm Cokburne meerchant, Sir John Inglis, or my own concerne of wch I gave your Lo. a p.s. However I am wt. great respect, My Lord, Your Lo. most humble and most obedient serv^t,   AD. COKBURNE.

For THE EARL OF SEAFIELD

Edn^r, 16th March 1708.

MAY IT PLEASE YO^r LP.,—I have this day two of yours, one of the 12th, the other without a date. Yo^r Lop. gives a very good account of her Mats. preparations against this invasion and for our safety, and I firmly beleive this hazard will evanish, tho, if a descent should happen, it will occasion confusion. Yo^r Lp. needs not doubt either the concern or zeal of all good men agt. this invasion. There are only a foolish people that follow M'Millan in Dumfreisshyre and other parts therabout that speak lightly of this invasion, and that it is not so bad as the union. But generally all good men are otherways minded, and if God should permit the ffrench to be our scourge, they would soon correct the worst of us. Yo^r Lp. will no doubt have a particular account from the Earl of Leven of Sir George Bings happy arrival to prevent the French entring into our ffirth, and of his chasing them northward. But how he came to give over his chase and to return again to the ffirth is dissatisfying to many, for his ffleet is certainly of double strength to the ffrench, tho the ffrench be cleaner and sail better. And tho Sir George thinks that he has cleared our coast, yet most men are of another opinion, but that he ought to have chased, cruised, and watched untill he had broke the enemies design. We should have had a Council this afternoon upon report of what past betwixt the Earl of Leven and Sir George Bings at Leith, but it hath not held, only I beleive my Lord Leven by a fflying paquet will supply all and prevent this my post letter. And therfore I will not detain yor Lp. longer on things that may be stale before this come to yor hand, tho I thought it my duty not to omit the ordinary post.—I am, My Lord, Y^r Lps. most humble and most obed^t servit^r,   JA. STEUART.

Lord Forglen, in next letter to Seafield, with its numerous postscripts, continues the chronicle of events in Scotland.

Ed., 17th Mertch 1708.

MY LORD,—This flying packet brings ane dutiefull letter to hir Majestie from the Councell syned by such as are in toun. Yesterday we ware in sore paine by a letter from Aberdein bearing the French to be lying before there toun. We nou think it was the English in there returne. Qhither the French will land or not is uncertain. Sum think they will, others they will not, but the putting them by this harbor was a peice of good service to this nation. All is in quyet. Barks cum from Murray did not sie aney appearence of the French. The prisoners of the ship[1] are sillie lyck men and ill clothed. This day one horse of Seafords and one of Hopetounes run for the cup. The last gained it by as far as from the Luckenbooths to the Netherbou. The fliet contanioues in the harbor. Captan Gordon will mack three thousand guineis by the ship[1] he did tack. There is fyveteen hundreth pound of pleat in hir, qhich he hath got. We have frost and snow. It is yet a cold seasone. The report contanioues of Boynes landing. I have not heard of him from your cuntrie. I wish your Lo. all happienes, and am, My Lord, your fathfull humble servant,   ALEX^r OGILVIE.

Gordon says there are four score oficers in the ship he did tack. By the post cum in this day from London I have no lyn from your Lo. family. Tho I had bein north your Lo. could not think me lost, since qhere ever I be I am your Lo, fathfull servant, and I hope ye shall never be ashamed of me.

12 *ackloack of the day.*

There com just nou ane express from Aberdein bearing on Mundayes forenoon the French ware sein before them, and that it was the easterlie wind did hinder there landing.

---

[1] The *Salisbury.*

We still think it hath bein the English.   The publick neues by this day ware werie refreshing, and the Comons address I had pleased our Lords of Councell so weill they desyred instantlie to print it.   My publict letter is in great reputation amongst them.   The D. of Gordon, Seafort, Kilsyth, Sincklar and others are on there paroll of honor confyned to there chambers.

For THE EARL OF SEAFIELD

MY LORD,—We thought it our duty at this juncture to inform your Lop. of the state of this west countrey, and particularly of this city, that thereby might appear to your Lop. our zeall and asertion to her Majesties government, and how groundless the expectations, and false the assertions of some have bein, who gave it out that the toun of Glasgow and all the west would joyn the pretendit Prince of Wales.   The true state of the matter is as followes. The prejudices of a few at the union had made them so unwary as to say, they'd rather joyn with the Pretender, then that the union should not be broke.   The disafection of others to the government made them industrious on this occasion to impose on these unthinking people by lessening the dangers of a bred papist's sitting upon the throne, assuring them that he would establish their religion, break the union, and become everything they could desyre him to be.   But, God be thanked, these prejudices and crafty insinuations have not prevaill'd upon the better and more judicious sort of people in this place, or any where in the west that we know ; but on the contrairy, since the dangers of this invasion seem'd to be imminent, there appears a resolution in all true Presbiterians to oppose the Pretender and the threatned invasion to the outmost of their power.   And here, my Lord, we cannot but take notice of the unanimity and zeall of all our ministers, who upon all occasions from the pulpit lay open the danger of the invasion and a popish pretender, and have publickly disown'd all persons to be of their persuasion, who will not appear against him.   We have taken all the care we can in our stations to animat our people against

this mischievous attempt, and have given orders for apprehending severall persons, who we are informed have bein active in perverting and seducing ignorant people; and are resolved to imploy the power given to us by our Privy Councill for the restraining and curbing malignity and disafection to her Majestys government in whatever person it shall appear. The government not allowing a publick rendevouz, we are falling upon the toun of Edr^s method by subscription for encouraging of the poorer sort, and have in the meantyme given warning to all well afected persons to have their arms in a readiness, and have sent the same notices to the principall places in the west countrey with whom we keep a constant correspondence. Upon the first allarm of the French fleet being in our coasts, we secured all the ammunition in this place, doubled our guards, and sufered no stranger to pass without being examined. We have committed one, who having suspected papers about him says he was lately a servant to the Dutchess of Gordon, and the papers we have sent to the Advocat. It gives no small vigour to our resolutions that both Houses are so unanimous and zeallous against this undertaking. The Jacobites gave it out here that some of the greatest men at court were concerned in it, but we have been too often amused wt. their lyes to give any credit to what they say, and we assure your Lop. we shall advyse you of every thing materiall, which may occurr here, and however our enemys the Jacobites may represent us we shall not be neutrall in so good a cause.—We are, My Lord, Your Lops. most humble and most obliged servants,   ROB. RODGERS.
                                        JOHN BOWMAN.
                                        THOMAS SMITH.
                                        J^o BROWN.

Glasgow, 19 *March* 1708.

For THE EARL OF SEAFIELD

Edinb^r, 20*th March* 1708.

MY LORD,—We are all in perfeit peace here, and by the latest accounts easterday from Inverlochy there is nothing stirring neither there, nor between and that. Soe we have ground to beleive the ffrench have not touched on this coast, since there is noe accounts of their being seen on it, since the chase this day and the morrow seven night. The regular fforces are in very good condition, and I beleive tho the ffrenches were landed, and the assistance from England not come our lenth, yett with what help Edinbr., Glasgow, and others would give, they would stop them passing Stirling bridge. Bellhaven came in Thursdays night, and easterday desired to appear before the Councill, but there Lops. refused to allow him, only desired he might give his parole of honour to appear when called and keep his chamber in the mean tyme. This day the Presidents lady being dead, he desired freedome to attend her funerall, and to goe to the countrey and be confined at his house. The first was yeilded to be granted him upon his application to my Lord Leven for it. I only add I continue, My Lord, Your ffaithfull humbl servant,

ALEX^r OGILVIE.

For THE EARL OF SEAFIELD

Edinb^r, 20 *March* 1708.

MY LORD,—After wryteing to your Lop. by this nights packett, I was betwixt 10 and ii honoured with your Lops. of the 16th, which was most acceptable to me, since for many dayes and weeks I had not heard from you. We are, blessed be the God of heaven, in perfeit quiet and peace, and if any confusion had happened, I hope all your Lop^s effects here should have bein secured to your satisfaction, without sending any of them from this place. We know not what is become of the ffrench. Only one of three must be their fate, aither they are gone backe, at sea, or landed in the north, and in aither of these cases miserable. We have noe fear of them, ffor by the blessing of the Almighty and her Maties care, we reckon the worst to be over, since they were by the fleet disappointed of landing here. The fleet continues in Leith road. The Aberdeens reports of the ffrench fleet seemed to be the English, and we have noe accounts of the ffrench being seen on this coast since the chase. My Lord, I shall take all dew care of what is yours, as if it were my own heart.—I am, My Lord, Your ffaithfull humble sert., ALEX^r OGILVIE.

Glassaugh came easternight with Roseberry, who wes so tyred that his Lop. caused yoke ane cart and lay ane feather bed on it, and so drive him for 2 stages. This maner of travelling and the fancy of seeing his Lop. I hope will make you laugh now, after in all probability our fears are over. I shall not part from this while the worst be over. I pray your Lop. cause send what is done in Parliat, since it revives and refreshes the spirits of ffaithfull subjects to know that care is taken of them. We think the ffrench have shoun a great dale of inclination with much weaknes, since they were not able to hold their face to so great a designe, but run like theives.

For THE EARL OF SEAFIELD

MY LORD,—Your Lop. has been so fully informed of what has hapned here, that I have nothing to add, since my Lord Forglain informs me he is to send you a list of the prisoners, so that I shal truble your Lo. with nothing on that subject. Grants [1] regt. marched from this today, as doeth ours [2] to-morrow for Stirleing, and I goe allong. I shal leave the keys of your cabinet and my tresure here with my Lord Forglain, tho I am fully satisfyed ther will be no occasion for removeing any thing, nor can I as yett understand the least inclination of any Scots man to support the pretended prince, so that I belive ther has been very few let into the secret, but if I can learn any thing you shold be advysed therof by Your Lo. most faithfull and obedient humble servant, ALEX^r ABERCROMBY.[3]

Edr., March 20, 1708.

To THE RIGHT HONOURABLE THE EARLE OF SEAFEILD, LONDON

Edinb., ye 21st March 1708.

MY DEAR LORD,—I receaved your Lop^s of the 16th

---

[1] Afterwards Brigadier-General.   [2] Lord Strathnaver's.
[3] The laird of Glassaugh.

instant, and returnes a thousand thanks for your good wishes, and for the expressions of your kyndnes to me. I have bein very bussie since I came here, and am still doeing what I can to putt ourselves in the best poistour of defence. I have given orders for provyding of the castles, and hes sent the two regiments of Grant and Strathnavers to keep gaurd at Stirling. I can give your Lop. noe accompt of the French fleet, but I persuade my selfe, that if they are to make any furder attempt upon Scotland, which is but still too probable, that they are landed by this tyme, wherof I cannot faill to have ane accompt of it in a very feu dayes. I had ane accompt from Angus last night, that there were twenty bigg shipps seen to the northward of Montross upon Thursday morning standing to the north-ward, but what fleet this hes bein I cannot imagine, if it is not the Breist squadron, which our London letters this day advyses sailled about the 13th or 14th instant. Sr George Bing is still here, and I beleive waites for the returns of his letters which were dispatched from this the 16th. I have brought in the following persons in pursuance of warrants directed to me by the Councill of Great Brittain : the Duke of Gordoun, the Earles of Murray, Seafoorth, and Traquair, the Viscount of Kilsyth, Lord Sinclair, and Bal-heaven, and Collonell Balfour of ffearnie, and Sir William Bruce is to be heir too morrow, and I expect the Earle of Aberdein heir in a day or tuo. When any thing els occurres worthie of yor Lop{s} knowing, you shall be informed by, My Lord, Your Lop{s} most humble and most obedient servant,   LEVEN.

This designe of the French invasione hes given ane opertunity to the Presbiterians in the west countrey both ministers and others to justifie themselves from the false aspertions of being favourers of the Prince of Wales, for now they loudly declaire themselves, and are ready to take armes when called in defence of her Maties title and goverment.

The Countess of Seafield in next letter tells of the landing of a part of the French fleet at Garmouth, near Gordon Castle an interesting episode of this invasion not touched on in any accounts the editor has hitherto seen.

To THE RIGHT HONOURABELL THE EARELL OF FINLATUR at his lugenes in the fut of the Caniget, Edr., to the car of the post master of Abd. hest and cear.

My Lord,—No dout you have hird of thrie French shipes being at Spaymouth and Buky of gret foras, and on litell on, which had about 24 gouns, which cam and wint to them as apired with inteligans. They wint of the 20 in the mornen, bot war seen afar of today agenest the Carnose.[1] It is sead ther was twall mor seen of Spaymouth as it war from Cromarty. I wondar your Lo. is so creuell that you dou not wret fuly to me both your advies and all the neues that pases. It is hard to think that all the frindes of the famaly shall forget me at such a tym, bot God is all sufisent, and I bliss God I am in no kynd of teror or fright, tho I think this silense unkynd in my frinds. I hird inded from your son to day which was confortabell to me. Your Lo. may be ashoured that nothing shall alter me from being in all sinserity and douty, My Lord, Your Lo. most affectionat daghtar obedent servant,   Anna Seafield.
    March 21, 1807.

From LORD FORGLEN to THE EARL OF SEAFIELD
                              Edinb^r, 23rd March 1708.

My Lord,—I did give your Lops. service this morning to the Earle of Leven, Justice Clark and Advocate. They all expressed themselves very kindly of you, and gave their services heartily to you. The accounts of the landing of the forces from Ostend, and the march of the English towards this place putts us out of all fear even the ffrench were landed. But at present we have noe account of them. They were not at Cromertiee Wedensday last. The ships that went to scout the lenth of Aberdeen have noe account of them, and these went to Cromertiee are expected this night. We continue in perfeit peace longing to know where the ffrench can be found. Sir George Bing

---

[1] Scarnose, near Cullen.

is to saill with the first fair wind in search after them. It is most like the being putt by their landing at this place hath blasted their whole designe, and in place of being terrible, they now appear weak and foolish. Yesterday in Councill there were produced ane packett of letters taken at the Quensfferry upon a servant of the Duke of Atholes direct to Patrick Scott wryter to the signett, soe far as I mind to this purpose, showing Mr. Scott that he had sent Robisone of Straloch with letters to Edinbr., but that he had heard something of him, which give him ground to beleive he was not woorthie of the trust he putt in him, and desired Mr. Scott instantly to delyver the letters sent with that bearer and to ask Straloch if he had delyvered his letters, and if any of them were not delyvered to take them and burn them before Straloch. There was a letter directed to the Duke of Gordon, the Bishop of Glasgow, Ballmerino, and Mr. Dougall Steuart all of one strain, shewing that he had write to them by Straloch, and haveing ground to beleive he was not to be trusted, desired they should be cautious of what they spoke to Straloch. When Straloch was examined before the Councill he deneyed the whole, and confidently said, he neither received letters nor any commission to any of these persones, albeit the Duke of Atholes letters with his signed hand to the former purpose were read and shoun to him, with ane letter directed by the Duke of Athole to Straloch quarrelling him that he had not returned sooner, and requireing and commanding him upon sight to return to him, and bring him what newes he heard, and upon the other side of the same letter desired him, if any of the letters he sent with him were yet unde-lyvered, instantly to burn them. He is putt closs prisoner in the toolbuith of Edinb^r. The Justice Clark searched for Straloch Sabbath night, and found him in his bed. He is a chamberlain of the Duke of Atholes, and hath ane hundered pound of heritadge. Mr. Scott was called but knew nothing, as he said, and was desired to attend the Councill when called. There is noe return from Marishall or Erroll, who were written to by the Councill to have appeared this day. Mr. Campbell of Carmichaels dragoons, who was sent to desire the Duke of Athole to come here, went to the gate of the Blair, but got noe access to the Duke, only was told by a servant, his Grace knew nothing he had to doe neither with generall nor souldiers. His letter to Mr. Scott had the same accompt with this further addition, that he desired to know from the Register and Advocate how he could give baill for his appearance, since he was willing to give baill. Soe wishing your Lop. all happines, I remaine,

Major-General Cadogan had arrived at Tynemouth with reinforcements from Flanders under the convoy of Rear-Admiral Baker. Meantime the Duke of Marlborough was rapidly concentrating the army in England on the Scottish border.

To THE RIGHT HONOBLL THE EARLE OF SEAFIELD,
LORD CHANCELLOR OF SCOTLAND

Ed., 24th Mer., 8 at night.

MY LORD,—By ane express from Glasco they report the French are at Mull. Friday last sum of them landed at Garmoch, did no harm, dyned, payed weill, and weint aboord. The nyn persones presented themselves are putt in the castle this day. The Councell are werie uneanymus. I hope and wish the worst may be over. Those wreat to by the Councell and calld for by the Generall, who have not cum, are to be sited to appeare in six dayes under paine of treason.—I am faithfullle your Lo., A. O.

In the following letter Glassaugh refers to the only approach there was to a Jacobite rising in Scotland. It took place in the neighbourhood of Stirling, whence Stirling of Keir, Seatoun of Touch, Stirling of Carden, and Lord Nairn with some mounted followers commenced to march on Edinburgh. His suggestion regarding the representation of Banffshire in Parliament in course bore fruit.

For THE EARL OF SEAFIELD

MY LORD,—Your Lo. will have every thing that passes in Scotland so tymely from Ed^r, that any information I can send you from this would rather be a truble then anything else. Strathnavers and Grants regts. mount 70 men and all the officers are present, so that I reckon this pass is in a pretty good posture. I understand James Seten of Touch and most of all the gentlemen of note hereabouts are absent with ther horses from ther houses, and a considerable number of them were with my Lord Nairn some myles from this. If your Lo. inclyns I serve in Parlat. nixt year, your Lo. will writ to my Lord Forglaen, for I hear it sur-mysed that Grant of Carron has been makeing interest. How soon our fears are over, which every body expects will be very soon, the officers will be sent arecruiting ; so if your Lo. has any commands for the north they shall be punctually cared for by, Your Lo. most faithfull and obedient humble servant,   ALEX[r] ABERCROMBIE.

Stirleing, March 24, **1708.**

For THE EARL OF SEAFIELD

Edinbr., 26th March **1708.**

MY LORD,—There were about thertein interrogators prepared for the prisoners putt in the castle yesterday relative to the invasion. The first being, when and from whom they heard of it, all their answers were, by the publict newes. As to the rest of the interrogators, they aither said, they were criminall, and so were not holden to answer, or that they knew nothing anent them. We have noe certaine account of the ffrench from the north, further then that they were seen about Speymouth, and that some of them landed, diverted themselves, drunk with severall people thereabout, told them King James was at sea, had beat the English fleet, and would shortly land. The Councill appointed the Provost of Edinb[r] to search the town about one of the clock, which is accordingly done. The enclosed came to my hand easternight. Soe wishing your Lop. all trew happines I continue, My Lord, Your ffaithfull humble serv[t],   ALEX[r] OGILVIE.

The Earles of Erroll and Marishall have wrytten they will appear against the twentie nynth courant.

For THE EARL OF SEAFIELD

Edinbr., 27th March **1708.**

MY LORD,—After searching easterday, Sir George

Maxwell of Orchyeardtoun and Mr. Abercrombie of Auchorseik were seized. The first bailled by Baillie Cockburn and the other by Sir ffrances Grant. The wind is easterly. Sir George Bing is not yet out of sight, being now about ten of the clock forenoon. We have noe further [news] from the north. Collonel Ogilvie and Allerdyce are well after their journey. The Collonel goes this day to see his meistres, and Allerdyce on Munday to his lady. The Councell met at eliven. My Lord Provost gave accompt of the seartch. All tacken ware bealled, save two putt in the tolbooth, on a deserter from the fliet, and the other a brocken mertchant whom they will give for a recruit. Lord James Murrey and old Buchan ar cum to toun and on beall each for three thousand merks containoued to Teusday. Drummond, Erroll, and Marischall are expected at furthest begining of the nixt weick. Atholl wreat to the Justice Clerk and Advocat that he was indisposed in his helth, would give beall, and desyred to be excused from coming, and assoored he would never joyn with papists nor a French pouer. The Councell did not tacke notice of them, but both told they would wreat to him without his ouen presence there could be no excuse. Roseberrie and Durrie on the streit talking anent the appeall, as I heare Durie said Rose: had spock of him q^{tt} was not true, qhereupon Rose: gave him a box on the eare, and Durie gave him tuo. Both are confyned to there chambers. After ten at night I hear Marishchall and Erroll are cum to toun, and that Patrick Scot is gon to the Duck of Atholl to persuade him to cum in. The uind containoues esterlie and holds Bing in sight. I wish your Lo. all happienes, and am, My Lord, your fathfull humble servant,   ALEX^{r} OGILVIE.

Next two letters[1] from the chief English officer of excise in Edinburgh to an official in the Treasury, London, along with the letters of 5th and 27th April and 8th May, give an account of the questionable removal of the Jacobite prisoners to England under

---

[1] *State Papers* (*Scotland*), Series ii. (1708-10).

warrant of the Privy Council of Great Britain. In the end they were returned to Scotland, where they were tried and acquitted.

To GEORGE TILSON, Esq., in the Secretary's Office, Whitehall, London

S^r,—On Wensday last Sr George Bing with the fleet sailed to the mouth of the Forth, and continued cruising there till Sunday morning, and then returned into Leith road again, where he now lies at anchor. About the same time that he sailed, the several persons whose names are subscribed were secured in our castle :—Duke of Gordon, Earls of Murray, Seaforth, Traquair; Lds. Belhaven, Kilsyth, Sinclair; Sr Willlam Bruce, Coll^{ll} John Balfour, and since that the Earls of Aberdeen, Marshall and Erroll.

The Marquiss of Huntly and Ld Drummond are sent for. The former is coming to town, but the latter has not answered. Tis said the Duke of Athol will not come till forced by law. His chamberlain is close prisoner in the tolbooth. We have no manner of account what's become of the French fleet. I am yor most humble serv^t,

RICH. DOWDESWELL.

Excise Office, Edenburgh, 30 Mar. 1708.

All's quiet here. .

S^r,—This comes to acquaint you that Sr George Bing with the fleet is now in Leith road waiting for a fair wind to sail to convey the troops back to Ostend. Yesterday Admiral Baker with nine men of war came and joined Sr George, the sea being too rough to continue off Tinmouth. Alls quiet here.—I am, Your hum^{ble} serv^t,

RICH. DOWDESWELL.

Excise Office, Edenburgh, 3d Ap. 1708.

To Mr. WILLIAM LORIMER, Chamberlaine to THE EARLE OF SEAFIELD, from Aberdeen to Bamff

Leith, ye 5th Apryll 1708.

Sir,—. . . The Parliat. of Brittain is to raise this week, and his Lop. designes to take journey very shortly, and I hope to see him the begining of May. I expect the two barks I have sent north up before that tyme in better condition then you have sent this. I have fraughted Mr. Morison again for halfe bear halfe meall. I hope he will be ready to saill the end of this week. The fear of ane invasion is over. There are a great many gentlemen taken up and committed to prison. One Mr. Scott writter to ye signet, and lately servitor to ye Duke of Atholl, and Robieson of Straloch his Graces chamberlaine are to be put aboard Sir George Bing this day to be try'd at London. The fleet are ordered to saill with the first fair wind. Give my humble duty to the Countess of Seafield, and let her see the letter, and tell her Lap. that I shall doe my outmost endeavor to get ye victuall put off to ye best advantadge. Tell Sir James Dunbar of Durn that I shall writt to him by ye nixt post, and doe him all ye service that lyes in my power. This with my service to yourself is the present trouble from, Sir, your affectionat commerad and servant,   Jo. STEWART.

To GEORGE TILSON, Esq., in the Secretary's Office,
Whitehall, London

Sr,—This acquaints you that the Marqs of Huntly, Earls of Erroll, Marshall, Seaforth, and Nithsdale, Ld Drummond, Viscounts Stormonth and Kilsyth, Lds. Nairn and James Murray (brother to the Duke of Athole), Sr Geo. Maxwell, Sterling of Keir, Murray of Pomeas, Seaton of Touch, and Stirling of Carden are all to be at Berwick the 1st of May under a guard of Scotts dragoons in their way for London. The remove of these people makes many here very uneasy,   RICH. DOWDESWELL.
Excise Office, Edinburgh, 27th April 1708.

To GEORGE TILSON, Esq.

Sr,—. . . The prisoners following set out for London, viz., on Fryday, 30th April : —
Marq. Huntly, Earl Seaforth, Visct. Killsyth, E. Nithsdale, Ld Drummond, Ld Nairn, Murray of Pomeas, Sr Donald M'Donald, Visct. Stormont, Sr Geo. Maxwell, Stirling of Kier, Stirling of Cardan.

Yesterday :—D. of Gordon, Vis. Kenmure, Ld James Murray, Fortheringham of Pourie, Lyon of Auchterhouse, Robertson of Strowin, Gordon of Gollachie, Seton of Touch, Stewart of Tannachie, Ross of Kippendavie, Newton of Edmestoun, Mackdonald of Keppoch.

The D. of Gordon would not provide himself with coach or horse for his journey, so that one of the troopers was forced to be dismounted, and he exalted on the outside of the uncouth beast. The D^s friends do not admire his fancy. The carrying up of those gentlemen occasions too much uneasieness here.—I am, Yo^r most obedient and humble serv^t,   RICH. DOWDESWELL.

Excise Office, Edenburgh, 8 Maij 1708.

The French landing at Garmouth had rendered many in the county of Banff suspect, and Colonel Grant had been sent north, and had arrested some who who were said to have consorted with the French. These, the Countess intreated her son to interest his father, her husband, in. Gordon of Gollachie, Rathven, and Steuart of Tannachie, Rathven, Banffshire, are both mentioned in Mr. Dowdeswell's letter of 8th May as Jacobite prisoners.

To LORD DESKFORD

DEAR JAMES,—I wonder that you never write to me nor causes any other do it, which you might do and sign it, if it were uneasy for you to write. I 'me truely impatient to know what is come of my Lady Peterburgh's letters from her daughter,[1] which came under your ffathers cover and yours. Pray let me have some satisfying answer concerning them. I believe this shall find you on the road, if not at Edinburgh, where I intreat you make no long stay, for I am sure it would be for your health to have your own country air. If you be curious to wait there to see the election of the nobility, you may easily return to Edinburgh again from this. I send you inclosed some letters to that Mrs. Lindsay I wrote of last to you. They are open and you may read them, and if your father will not hear of her, you may send back the letters, but I hope

---

[1] The Marchioness of Huntly.

he will not hinder it, since her father's dead, and his
daughters for aught I think must want a woman, since I
know of none other, and she is recommended to me as a
modest, grave, and discreet woman.   You'll have no
further trouble with the letters than to seal them and
recomend them att London to Alex^r Campbell's care to
deliver them out of his own hand, for he knows the people
very well.   I beg it of you take care of and dispatch them
quickly.   If my Lord will not allow of it send back the
letters, and let me know of it as soon as can be.   When
you come to Edinburgh, as long as you stay in toun I
would have you take my apartments in your fathers
lodgings.   I intreat if it be in your power to serve any of
the prisoners that have gone from this country to do it,
and to speak your father that he may use his interest that
there be no more trouble given to the people of our nigh-
bourhead, for wee hear Grant has a commission to take
a wast many gentlemen, and amongst the rest poor
Findochty[1] and his two son's.   He is your father's vassal,
ane old man, I 'me sure in no plot, and was never near the
French ships.   Our nighbour Milldavid[2] has heard to be
among the same number.   I 'me sure they have no reason
to suspect him of any practise agst. the government, so I
do again earnestly recommend to you, that you may do
all you can to serve this country, particularly these two.
I cannot write to your father this night, because I am not
able to write with my own hand.   My cough is increas'd to
a great degree, and I truely have no good health.   God
Allmighty send me the comfortable accounts of your perfect recovery, for I am your most affectionate mother,

                                        ANNA SEAFIELD.

*Cullen House, May ij*th, 1708.

You may tell your ffather that Ardoch came back and
sought the address to sign.   The town of Banff, Cullen and
the Presbytrye's addresses were sent off with the Mundayes
post for him.   The Shires will be ready in a week.   No
more, but God bless you.   Adue.

---

[1] William Ord.   [2] See note on p. 444.

For THE RIGHT HONOURABLE THE EARLE OFF
FINDLATER, Edinburgh

MY LORD,—I have nothing to say, yet I cannot let such
ane occasion as this go, without assuring your Lop. of my
constant good wishes and affection to you. I must likewise recommend unto you the laird of Buckie,[1] your
relation, that whereever your Lop. finds his business or
person is concern'd or in hazard, you may give him your
ffriendly assistance, and likewise speak to your son in his
behalf. I pray you do it as from your self, and not from
me alltogether. I doubt not your Lop[s] good wishes
towards him. There may come a time after this, which is
all I shall say. This is with Katharine Dunbar, which I
have sent up to have the charge which she had when I was
in the ffamily. I hope her modest and discreet carrage
will engage your Lop. to be unto her, what you was
formerly, very civil and discreet, which will be ane obligation on, My Lord, Your most obedient daughter and
humble servant,   ANNA SEAFIELD.
Cullen House, May 24, 1708.

For LORD DESKFORD

DEAR JAMES,—I really am not able to write with my
own hand, which makes me use a borrowed hand. I hope
this shall find you taking journey north, if not on it. I
would have sent the horses I have here south for you,
but they have all taken the epidemical disease, which is a
cough and some other ill thinge I cannot tell you of, so
that they are not able to travell above two miles. I
believe they 'll all die. If you be at Edinburgh, when this
comes to your hands, I must recommend the laird of
Buckie[1] to you that you may serve him, when you hear of
his business, and speak to your ffather in his behalf, as if
it were from your self, that he may have liberty to live
peaceably at home, for it may be it will be of more influence
than from me, because I have written of many others.
You know there may come a time after this. I shall

---

[1] George Gordon.

write more fully of him afterwards. This is with Katharine Dunbar, whom I have sent up to have the charge of your fathers house, which she had when I was there, which I hope she shall performe descreetly enough. I shall write no more just now, but add that I am your most affectionate mother, ANNA SEAFIELD.

Cullen House, May 24*th*, 1708.

I received your letter with Doctor Kieths adwice, which I heartily thank you for. Pray give me ane answer as soon as possible anent Mrs. Lindsay.

Lady Seafield did not survive long. She died on 14th August 1708, probably of consumption, to judge from the symptoms of her illness.

With this letter ends the account in the Seafield Correspondence of the French invasion of Scotland in 1708, an attempt which, viewed as an invasion, failed from lack of nerve, but was otherwise successful as a *ruse de guerre*. The state of feeling in Scotland was sufficiently inflamed against the union to render a landing in force dangerous to the government, considering the handful of troops they had in the country. During the crisis the feeling and excitement were therefore intense, but when the French fleet vanished into the North Sea in flight, the feeling of danger and uncertainty gave place to contempt. Lord Forglen, in his letters exhibiting these successive phases, exemplified the prevailing feelings, which in the end found expression in the many addresses presented to the Queen and medals struck to commemorate the victory and the defeat. One interesting medal struck in London in 1708, shows on its obverse the image of Queen Anne with the motto ' *Fugere non fallere triumphus,*' a variant on the line which Horace put into the mouth of Hannibal on his brother's death—' *Fallere et effugere est triumphus.*' After recounting in Latin phrase on its reverse how the great Queen by her vigilance frustrated the French in their attempted invasion of Scotland, it bears in relief on the rim the sarcastic words—' *Sic pueri nasum rhinocerotis habent,*' expressive at once of a coarse wit and of the great rebound in feeling in London, when the danger of invasion had passed away.

INDEX

Printed by T. and A. CONSTABLE, Printers to His Majesty
at the Edinburgh University Press

ERRATA.

Page 36, line 17, *for* We *read* He.

,, 456, ,, 5, *for* Sir John Byng *read* Sir George Byng.

𝔖cottish 𝔥istory 𝔖ociety.

THE EXECUTIVE.

1910-1911.

RULES

1. THE object of the Society is the discovery and printing, under selected editorship, of unpublished documents illustrative of the civil, religious, and social history of Scotland. The Society will also undertake, in exceptional cases, to issue translations of printed works of a similar nature, which have not hitherto been accessible in English.

2. The number of Members of the Society shall be limited to 400.

3. The affairs of the Society shall be managed by a Council, consisting of a Chairman, Treasurer, Secretary, and twelve elected Members, five to make a quorum. Three of the twelve elected Members shall retire annually by ballot, but they shall be eligible for re-election.

4. The Annual Subscription to the Society shall be One Guinea. The publications of the Society shall not be delivered to any Member whose Subscription is in arrear, and no Member shall be permitted to receive more than one copy of the Society's publications.

5. The Society will undertake the issue of its own publications, *i.e.* without the intervention of a publisher or any other paid agent.

6. The Society will issue yearly two octavo volumes of about 320 pages each.

7. An Annual General Meeting of the Society shall be held at the end of October, or at an approximate date to be determined by the Council.

8. Two stated Meetings of the Council shall be held each year, one on the last Tuesday of May, the other on the Tuesday preceding the day upon which the Annual General Meeting shall be held. The Secretary, on the request of three Members of the Council, shall call a special meeting of the Council.

9. Editors shall receive 20 copies of each volume they edit for the Society.

10. The owners of Manuscripts published by the Society will also be presented with a certain number of copies.

11. The Annual Balance-Sheet, Rules, and List of Members shall be printed.

12. No alteration shall be made in these Rules except at a General Meeting of the Society. A fortnight's notice of any alteration to be proposed shall be given to the Members of the Council.

PUBLICATIONS

OF THE

SCOTTISH HISTORY SOCIETY

For the year 1890-1891.

11. THE RECORDS OF THE COMMISSIONS OF THE GENERAL ASSEMBLIES, 1646-47. Edited by the Rev. Professor MITCHELL, D.D., and the Rev. JAMES CHRISTIE, D.D.

12. COURT-BOOK OF THE BARONY OF URIE, 1604-1747. Edited by the Rev. D. G. BARRON.

For the year 1891-1892.

13. MEMOIRS OF SIR JOHN CLERK OF PENICUIK, Baronet. Extracted by himself from his own Journals, 1676-1755. Edited by JOHN M. GRAY.

14. DIARY OF COL. THE HON. JOHN ERSKINE OF CARNOCK, 1683-1687. Edited by the Rev. WALTER MACLEOD.

For the year 1892-1893.

15. MISCELLANY OF THE SCOTTISH HISTORY SOCIETY, First Volume—THE LIBRARY OF JAMES VI., 1573-83. Edited by G. F. Warner.—DOCUMENTS ILLUSTRATING CATHOLIC POLICY, 1596-98. T. G. Law.—LETTERS OF SIR THOMAS HOPE, 1627-46. Rev. R. Paul.—CIVIL WAR PAPERS, 1643-50. H. F. Morland Simpson.—LAUDERDALE CORRESPONDENCE, 1660-77. Right Rev. John Dowden, D.D.—TURNBULL'S DIARY, 1657-1704. Rev. R. Paul.—MASTERTON PAPERS, 1660-1719. V. A. Noël Paton.—ACCOMPT OF EXPENSES IN EDINBURGH, 1715. A. H. Millar.—REBELLION PAPERS, 1715 and 1745. H. Paton.

16. ACCOUNT BOOK OF SIR JOHN FOULIS OF RAVELSTON (1671-1707). Edited by the Rev. A. W. CORNELIUS HALLEN.

For the year 1893-1894.

17. LETTERS AND PAPERS ILLUSTRATING THE RELATIONS BETWEEN CHARLES II. AND SCOTLAND IN 1650. Edited by SAMUEL RAWSON GARDINER, D.C.L., etc.

18. SCOTLAND AND THE COMMONWEALTH. LETTERS AND PAPERS RELATING TO THE MILITARY GOVERNMENT OF SCOTLAND, Aug. 1651-Dec. 1653. Edited by C. H. FIRTH, M.A.

For the year 1894-1895.

19. THE JACOBITE ATTEMPT OF 1719. LETTERS OF JAMES, SECOND DUKE OF ORMONDE. Edited by W. K. DICKSON.

20, 21. THE LYON IN MOURNING, OR A COLLECTION OF SPEECHES, LETTERS, JOURNALS, ETC., RELATIVE TO THE AFFAIRS OF PRINCE CHARLES EDWARD STUART, by BISHOP FORBES. 1746-1775. Edited by HENRY PATON. Vols. I. and II.

For the year 1895-1896.

22. THE LYON IN MOURNING. Vol. III.

23. ITINERARY OF PRINCE CHARLES EDWARD (Supplement to the Lyon in Mourning). Compiled by W. B. BLAIKIE.

24. EXTRACTS FROM THE PRESBYTERY RECORDS OF INVERNESS AND DINGWALL FROM 1638 TO 1688. Edited by WILLIAM MACKAY.

25. RECORDS OF THE COMMISSIONS OF THE GENERAL ASSEMBLIES (*continued*) for the years 1648 and 1649. Edited by the Rev. Professor MITCHELL, D.D., and Rev. JAMES CHRISTIE, D.D.

For the year 1896-1897.

26. WARISTON'S DIARY AND OTHER PAPERS—
JOHNSTON OF WARISTON'S DIARY, 1639. Edited by G. M. Paul.—THE HONOURS OF SCOTLAND, 1651-52. C. R. A. Howden.—THE EARL OF MAR'S LEGACIES, 1722, 1726. Hon. S. Erskine.—LETTERS BY MRS. GRANT OF LAGGAN. J. R. N. Macphail.
Presented to the Society by Messrs. T. and A. Constable.

27. MEMORIALS OF JOHN MURRAY OF BROUGHTON, 1740-1747. Edited by R. FITZROY BELL.

28. THE COMPT BUIK OF DAVID WEDDERBURNE, MERCHANT OF DUNDEE, 1587-1630. Edited by A. H. MILLAR.

For the year 1897-1898.

29, 30. THE CORRESPONDENCE OF DE MONTEREUL AND THE BROTHERS DE BELLIÈVRE, FRENCH AMBASSADORS IN ENGLAND AND SCOTLAND, 1645-1648. Edited, with Translation, by J. G. FOTHERINGHAM. 2 vols.

For the year 1898-1899.

31. SCOTLAND AND THE PROTECTORATE. LETTERS AND PAPERS RELATING TO THE MILITARY GOVERNMENT OF SCOTLAND, FROM JANUARY 1654 TO JUNE 1659. Edited by C. H. FIRTH, M.A.

32. PAPERS ILLUSTRATING THE HISTORY OF THE SCOTS BRIGADE IN THE SERVICE OF THE UNITED NETHERLANDS, 1572-1782. Edited by JAMES FERGUSON. Vol. I. 1572-1697.

33, 34. MACFARLANE'S GENEALOGICAL COLLECTIONS CONCERNING FAMILIES IN SCOTLAND; Manuscripts in the Advocates' Library. 2 vols. Edited by J. T. CLARK, Keeper of the Library.

Presented to the Society by the Trustees of the late Sir William Fraser, K.C.B.

For the year 1899-1900.

35. PAPERS ON THE SCOTS BRIGADE IN HOLLAND, 1572-1782. Edited by JAMES FERGUSON. Vol. II. 1698-1782.

36. JOURNAL OF A FOREIGN TOUR IN 1665 AND 1666, ETC., BY SIR JOHN LAUDER, LORD FOUNTAINHALL. Edited by DONALD CRAWFORD.

37. PAPAL NEGOTIATIONS WITH MARY QUEEN OF SCOTS DURING HER REIGN IN SCOTLAND. Chiefly from the Vatican Archives. Edited by the Rev. J. HUNGERFORD POLLEN, S.J.

For the year 1900-1901.

38. PAPERS ON THE SCOTS BRIGADE IN HOLLAND, 1572-1782. Edited by JAMES FERGUSON. Vol. III.

39. THE DIARY OF ANDREW HAY OF CRAIGNETHAN, 1659-60. Edited by A. G. REID, F.S.A.Scot.

For the year 1901-1902.

40. NEGOTIATIONS FOR THE UNION OF ENGLAND AND SCOTLAND IN 1651-53. Edited by C. SANFORD TERRY.

41. THE LOYALL DISSUASIVE. Written in 1703 by Sir ÆNEAS MACPHERSON. Edited by the Rev. A. D. MURDOCH.

For the year 1902-1903.

42. THE CHARTULARY OF LINDORES, 1195-1479. Edited by the Right Rev. JOHN DOWDEN, D.D., Bishop of Edinburgh.

43. A LETTER FROM MARY QUEEN OF SCOTS TO THE DUKE OF GUISE, Jan. 1562. Reproduced in Facsimile. Edited by the Rev. J. HUNGERFORD POLLEN, S.J.

Presented to the Society by the family of the late Mr. Scott, of Halkshill.

44. MISCELLANY OF THE SCOTTISH HISTORY SOCIETY, Second Volume— THE SCOTTISH KING'S HOUSEHOLD, 14th Century. Edited by Mary Bateson.—THE SCOTTISH NATION IN THE UNIVERSITY OF ORLEANS, 1336-1538. John Kirkpatrick, LL.D.—THE FRENCH GARRISON AT DUNBAR, 1563. Robert S. Rait.—DE ANTIQUITATE RELIGIONIS APUD SCOTOS, 1594. Henry D. G. Law.—APOLOGY FOR WILLIAM MAITLAND OF LETHINGTON, 1610. Andrew Lang.—LETTERS OF BISHOP GEORGE GRÆME, 1602-38. L. G. Græme.—A SCOTTISH JOURNIE, 1641. C. H. Firth.—NARRATIVES ILLUSTRATING THE DUKE OF HAMILTON'S EXPEDITION TO ENGLAND, 1648. C. H. Firth.— BURNET-LEIGHTON PAPERS, 1648-168-. H. C. Foxcroft.—PAPERS OF ROBERT ERSKINE, Physician to Peter the Great, 1677-1720. Rev. Robert Paul.—WILL OF THE DUCHESS OF ALBANY, 1789. A. Francis Steuart.

45. LETTERS OF JOHN COCKBURN OF ORMISTOUN TO HIS GARDENER, 1727-1743. Edited by JAMES COLVILLE, D.Sc.

For the year 1903-1904.

46. MINUTE BOOK OF THE MANAGERS OF THE NEW MILLS CLOTH MANUFACTORY, 1681-1690. Edited by W. R. SCOTT.

47. CHRONICLES OF THE FRASERS; being the Wardlaw Manuscript entitled ' Polichronicon seu Policratica Temporum, or, the true Genealogy of the Frasers.' By Master JAMES FRASER. Edited by WILLIAM MACKAY.

48. THE RECORDS OF THE PROCEEDINGS OF THE JUSTICIARY COURT FROM 1661 TO 1678. Vol. I. 1661-1669. Edited by Sheriff SCOTT-MONCRIEFF.

For the year 1904-1905.

49. THE RECORDS OF THE PROCEEDINGS OF THE JUSTICIARY COURT FROM 1661 TO 1678. Vol. II. 1669-1678. Edited by Sheriff SCOTT-MONCRIEFF. (Oct. 1905.)

50. RECORDS OF THE BARON COURT OF STITCHILL, 1655-1807. Edited by CLEMENT B. GUNN, M.D., Peebles. (Oct. 1905.)

51. MACFARLANE'S GEOGRAPHICAL COLLECTIONS. Vol. I. Edited by Sir ARTHUR MITCHELL, K.C.B. (April 1906.)

For the year 1905-1906.

52, 53. MACFARLANE'S GEOGRAPHICAL COLLECTIONS. Vols. II. and III. Edited by Sir ARTHUR MITCHELL, K.C.B.
(May 1907 ; March 1908.)

54. STATUTA ECCLESIÆ SCOTICANÆ, 1225-1559. Translated and edited by DAVID PATRICK, LL.D. (Oct. 1907.)

For the year 1906-1907.

55. THE HOUSE BOOKE OF ACCOMPS, OCHTERTYRE, 1737-39. Edited by JAMES COLVILLE, D.Sc. (Oct. 1907.)

56. THE CHARTERS OF THE ABBEY OF INCHAFFRAY. Edited by W. A. LINDSAY, K.C., the Right Rev. Bishop DOWDEN, D.D., and J. MAITLAND THOMSON, LL.D. (Feb. 1908.)

57. A SELECTION OF THE FORFEITED ESTATES PAPERS PRESERVED IN H.M. GENERAL REGISTER HOUSE AND ELSEWHERE. Edited by A. H. MILLAR, LL.D. (Oct. 1909.)

For the year 1907-1908.

58. RECORDS OF THE COMMISSIONS OF THE GENERAL ASSEMBLIES (*continued*), for the years 1650-52. Edited by the Rev. JAMES CHRISTIE, D.D. (Feb. 1909.)

59. PAPERS RELATING TO THE SCOTS IN POLAND. Edited by Miss BEATRICE BASKERVILLE. (*Publication delayed.*)

For the year 1908-1909.

60. SIR THOMAS CRAIG'S DE UNIONE REGNORUM BRITANNIÆ TRAC-
TATUS. Edited, with an English Translation, by C. SANFORD
TERRY. (Nov. 1909.)

61. JOHNSTON OF WARISTON'S MEMENTO QUAMDIU VIVAS, AND DIARY
FROM 1637 to 1639. Edited by G. M. PAUL, LL.D., D.K.S.
(May 1911.)

SECOND SERIES.

For the year 1909-1910.

1. THE HOUSEHOLD BOOK OF LADY GRISELL BAILLIE, 1692-1733.
Edited by R. SCOTT-MONCRIEFF, W.S. (Oct. 1911.)

2. MISCELLANEOUS NARRATIVES RELATING TO THE '45. Edited by
W. B. BLAIKIE.

3. CORRESPONDENCE OF JAMES, FOURTH EARL OF FINDLATER AND
FIRST EARL OF SEAFIELD, LORD CHANCELLOR OF SCOTLAND.
Edited by JAMES GRANT, M.A., LL.B. (March 1912.)

For the year 1910-1911.

4. ACCOUNTS OF THE CHAMBERLAINS AND GRANITARS OF CARDINAL
DAVID BEATON, 1539-1546. Edited by R. K. HANNAY.

5. SELECTIONS FROM THE LETTER BOOKS OF JOHN STUART, BAILIE
OF INVERNESS. Edited by WILLIAM MACKAY.

In preparation.

REGISTER OF THE CONSULTATIONS OF THE MINISTERS OF EDINBURGH,
AND SOME OTHER BRETHREN OF THE MINISTRY SINCE THE
INTERRUPTION OF THE ASSEMBLY 1653, WITH OTHER PAPERS OF
PUBLIC CONCERNMENT, 1653-1660. Edited by the Rev. JAMES
CHRISTIE, D.D.

A TRANSLATION OF THE HISTORIA ABBATUM DE KYNLOS OF
FERRERIUS. By ARCHIBALD CONSTABLE, LL.D.

MISCELLANY OF THE SCOTTISH HISTORY SOCIETY. Third Volume.

ANALYTICAL CATALOGUE OF THE WODROW COLLECTION OF MANU-
SCRIPTS IN THE ADVOCATES' LIBRARY. Edited by J. T. CLARK.

CHARTERS AND DOCUMENTS RELATING TO THE GREY FRIARS AND THE
CISTERCIAN NUNNERY OF HADDINGTON.—REGISTER OF INCH-
COLM MONASTERY. Edited by J. G. WALLACE-JAMES, M.B.

RECORDS RELATING TO THE SCOTTISH ARMIES FROM 1638 TO 1650.
Edited by C. SANFORD TERRY.

PAPERS RELATING TO THE REBELLIONS OF 1715 AND 1745, with other
documents from the Municipal Archives of the City of Perth.

THE BALCARRES PAPERS. Edited by J. R. MELVILLE.